# THE DEFENDER

# THE DEFENDER

## HOW THE LEGENDARY
## BLACK NEWSPAPER CHANGED AMERICA

*From the Age of the Pullman Porters
to the Age of Obama*

## Ethan Michaeli

*Houghton Mifflin Harcourt*
BOSTON · NEW YORK
2016

*Library of Congress Cataloging-in-Publication Data*
Michaeli, Ethan.
The defender : how the legendary black newspaper changed America
: from the age of the Pullman porters to the age of Obama / Ethan
Michaeli.
pages cm
ISBN 978-0-547-56069-4 (hardback) — ISBN 978-0-547-56087-8 (ebook)
1. Chicago defender — History. 2. African
Americans — Illinois — Chicago—Newspapers. 3. African American
newspapers — Illinois — Chicago — History. 4. African American
press — Illinois — Chicago — History. I. Title.
PN4899.C395D55 2016
071.73'11 — dc23
2015017437

Book design by Chrissy Kurpeski
Typeset in Warnock Pro

Printed in the United States of America
DOC 10 9 8 7 6 5 4 3 2 1

For my beloved parents, Chana and Avri, who taught me with their words and deeds that all women and men are equal in talent and ability, and that there should be no borders between us.

# Contents

# Preface: Delphi on the Prairie

T HE SKIES WERE clear over the North American prairie on Saturday, August 14, 2004. A summer sun rose across the blue expanse of Lake Michigan and crept along the city's sandy beaches until it hit the glittering ridge of skyscrapers downtown and then filtered into the neighborhoods beyond.

Very early that morning, a stream of people began to converge on the city's South Side, on a tree-lined boulevard that had gone by several names in its long history but was now Martin Luther King Drive. Some walked, but mostly they came in cars, buses, and on the city's El trains. They came from all across the metropolitan area and well beyond, from the luxury high-rises dominating Chicago's coast and the Bungalow Belt neighborhoods on the South and West Sides, from stately homes in the suburbs, and from the housing projects nearby. A fair number arrived after long journeys from other states, from the South and the West Coast as well as New York and other points east.

By 10:00 a.m., more than a million people had gathered, nearly all of them African American. They filled the fairways, side lanes, lawns, and balconies of King Drive, setting up tents and grills on spots that many families had claimed every year for decades. It was the seventy-fifth year Chicago's black community had gathered for the Bud Billiken Parade, and everyone knew that this was a day set aside for wholesome fun and remembrance.

The Bud Billiken Parade was the brainchild of Robert Sengstacke Abbott, founder of *The Chicago Defender*, the newspaper that had chronicled and catalyzed this community's greatest accomplishments for nearly a century. At the height of the newspaper's circulation and influence, Abbott had devised the parade to give African

American children a sense of pride and dignity, and even three-quar-
ters of a century later, there were still a few old-timers in the crowd
who remembered him in his later years when, ravaged by illness but
still impeccably dressed, he waved to the crowds from the balcony of
his home, a brick-and-stone mansion that still stands on the parade
route just south of Forty-Seventh Street.

For decades, the Billiken Parade, named for a long-forgotten figurine plucked at random from an editor's desk, had attracted black
America's greatest celebrities and athletes, from Duke Ellington to
James Brown, from Joe Louis to Muhammad Ali. But along with the
food, socializing, and entertainment, the Billiken was also a day for
politics. Elected officials and those seeking office from across the nation, white and black, Democrats and Republicans, knew that the parade was a necessary campaign stop, a singular opportunity to make
a pitch for Chicago's all-important black vote, and they lobbied the
organizers intensely to secure their place among the marching bands,
military units, corporate floats, and neighborhood dance troupes.
Black Chicago's electorate, politicians knew, was unified, organized,
and savvy, fully informed by *The Defender*.[1] Historically, the community had played a decisive role both as kingmaker and spoiler in innumerable campaigns for mayor, governor, senator, and even president.

It was a political tradition that went back to the days when African Americans voted Republican in honor of Abraham Lincoln, and
continued through their conversion into New Deal Democrats. Even
in the decades when the African American vote was suppressed in
the rest of the country, Chicago's Bronzeville had elected their own
sons and daughters as county officials, state legislators, aldermen,
and congressmen. In more recent years, they had elected the city's
first black mayor, Harold Washington, and Carol Moseley Braun, the
nation's first black woman U.S. senator. On this particular parade day,
however, the community would get the chance to inspect a rising star
unlike any they had propelled before: Barack Obama, a little-known
state legislator and first-time candidate for the U.S. Senate, then just
forty-three years old.

Three weeks earlier, Obama had delivered an electrifying keynote
speech at the Democratic National Convention in Boston, and even
though he had yet to win the upcoming race for the Senate, some
were already urging him to seek the presidency. But victory in No-

vember would be determined by whether Chicago's black community would come out en masse to the polls, a reality that made this
Billiken Parade nothing less than a crucial test of Obama's support.

Barack Obama and his wife, Michelle, cruised up Martin Luther King
Drive on a float surrounded by a phalanx of hundreds of supporters in matching blue-and-white T-shirts, carrying signs emblazoned
with OBAMA FOR SENATE. All along the parade route, the crowds
roared as the candidate passed. At every point where he stopped to
shake hands, the people erupted in chants of "O-Ba-Ma," flashing
homemade banners as well as official campaign signs.

Struck by the crowd's enthusiasm, a television reporter, a veteran
of many Billiken parades, asked the candidate when he disembarked
for an interview, "Where in the world did all these Obama signs come
from?"

"We did pretty good on signage today," Obama answered, smiling
cheekily. "We've just had wonderful support. This is obviously my
home area here." Then he added, "It's nice to come back to the South
Side."[2]

Obama's eventual Republican opponent in the 2004 campaign, the
former diplomat Alan Keyes, was also participating in the Billiken,
though with decidedly different results. Not from Illinois and seriously underfunded, Keyes had been recruited by desperate Republicans after their first candidate's implosion following a sex scandal.
To the Billiken crowd, Keyes, who was African American, seemed a
cynical choice to run against Obama, with many clearly suspecting
that his ethnicity was the operative, if not only, qualification for his
selection. If there was one thing this crowd did not like, it was being
pandered to. For much of the parade, Keyes remained inside his car,
subjected to frequent booing and heckling. On one of the rare moments Keyes did emerge, a woman confronted him and waved a placard in his face, shouting at the top of her lungs, "Obama for *President.*
Obama for *President.*"[3]

By 2004, the Billiken Parade was the most enduring part of Robert
Abbott's legacy, though once upon a time he had built his newspaper's circulation into the hundreds of thousands, with fiery editorials
under giant red headlines that chastised southern whites for lynching

and other atrocities. In the 1920s and '30s he was even dubbed the Moses of Black America for the role *The Defender* played in motivating the multitudes to leave Dixie for the Promised Land of America's northern cities. Some sixty thousand came to Chicago during World War I alone, doubling the city's black population and ensuring that *The Defender*'s hometown would become the nation's center of African American politics, culture, and commerce. Ultimately, what Abbott referred to as the "Great Northern Drive" would live on in the nation's consciousness as the Great Migration.

The early twentieth century was an era even more color-conscious than our own, and Abbott's dark complexion caused not only whites but many blacks to underestimate him. He met such racist assumptions head-on, with a keen intellect he had sharpened at Hampton College, the alma mater of Booker T. Washington, where he became a "race man," part of a generation of activists who infused unwavering patriotism into their struggle for civil rights. Abbott preached and exemplified the American values of self-reliance and capitalist success, along with the constitutional gospel of freedom of speech and legal equality. Ignoring death threats and circumventing southern authorities who tried to ban his young newspaper, he drafted Pullman porters, the famed valets of the interstate train system, to smuggle bundles across the Mason-Dixon Line and sell subscriptions.

Abbott died in 1940 and was succeeded by his nephew John H. Sengstacke, who took *The Defender* to even greater heights during his five decades in command. During World War II, Sengstacke staffed the newspaper with an international, interracial roster of writers that included poet Langston Hughes and public intellectual W. E. B. Du Bois, turning it into a journalistic champion of universal human rights. In 1956 Sengstacke made *The Defender* a daily, competing with white-owned newspapers and broadcast media for coverage of the "race beat," just as Martin Luther King Jr. was shifting the civil rights movement into high gear.

In 1960 Sengstacke dispatched his protégé Louis Martin to the campaign of John F. Kennedy and then worked closely with Martin and the black press to energize the African American electorate around the country. It was Martin who suggested that JFK call Coretta Scott King during one of Dr. King's incarcerations, a gesture of support that swayed the black vote in the days leading up to the election and proved decisive to the victory over Richard M. Nixon.

In the '70s, *The Defender* lost circulation and influence, pinched on one side by a black power movement that saw the newspaper as too accommodating to the white establishment, and on the other by the large daily newspapers and television stations suddenly embracing integration, which to them meant siphoning off black journalists as well as black readers. Sengstacke maintained the symbolic power of *The Defender* as long as he lived, but after his death in 1997 the paper's influence ebbed, a process that accelerated after it was sold in 2002.

By 2004, the year Obama ran for the U.S. Senate, many of those who had played key roles at *The Defender* for decades had moved their focus to the Billiken Parade. Eugene Scott, a distant relative of the Abbott-Sengstacke clan who had served as publisher of *The Defender* until the sale, had become president of the Chicago Defender Charities, with overall responsibility for organizing the parade. Called "Colonel" by most of the parade staff, Scott had served two tours in Vietnam and was a U.S. Army base commander before he came to *The Defender*. He was the calm center in the chaotic storm of the day's events.

From his command post in the reviewing stand at the entrance of Washington Park, the Colonel could see much of the parade route down the slight incline on King Drive, and he could not help but notice the wave of enthusiasm as Obama's float approached. He knew the Billiken crowd was not supporting Obama simply because he was black; after all, in the 1950s and '60s, they cheered for Mayor Richard J. Daley, just as they now cheered for his son, Mayor Richard M. Daley. Billiken crowds would even cheer for a Republican, if he or she made sincere outreach efforts to the black community, while those who had not done so could expect to be booed or heckled.

Having seen many politicians come and go, the Colonel was reserved in his expectations where Obama was concerned. Still, he could not help being proud of the role he and *The Defender* had played in the candidate's ascent. During his tenure at the "Oracle of the Black Community," as he called the newspaper, he had seen to it that Obama's activities were thoroughly covered by reporters, while the editorial page provided forceful endorsements as well as critical assessments at key junctures.

Watching the enthusiastic reception this young candidate was receiving, the Colonel thought back to their initial meeting on February 11, 2000, when Obama came to the historic *Defender* building at Twenty-Fourth Street and Michigan Avenue to seek the newspaper's endorsement for his first, ultimately unsuccessful, bid for the U.S. Congress. Scott greeted Obama in the broad, dark lobby, next to a glass cabinet that contained several of the paper's seminal issues, and they shook hands under the watchful gaze of Robert Abbott, whose black-and-white portrait hung over the receptionist's desk.

After escorting Obama into the building's tiny, squeaky elevator, the Colonel conducted the candidate up to the newspaper's third-floor boardroom, a wood-paneled treasure trove of artifacts accumulated over the past century. Obama presented the editorial board with a placard picturing himself, Michelle, and their daughter Malia (Sasha had not yet been born) as well as a few other souvenirs from his campaign, before sitting down at one of the well-worn leather chairs around the room's large wooden table. Facing a veteran U.S. representative in the upcoming Democratic primary in this overwhelmingly African American, Democratic district, Obama listed his modest legislative successes in the state capital at Springfield up to that point, underscoring his support for early-childhood education, the creation of affordable housing through public and private partnerships, and a "stronger and better coordinated job training effort"—all uncontroversial, even conservative, positions. He touted his strength at fundraising as well, noting that he had already taken in more than $300,000 by that point in the race.[4]

The Colonel was impressed with Obama's resumé and his presentation at the editorial board meeting, though admittedly less so by the candidate's threadbare suit and scuffed, thin-soled shoes. In a community where most professional black men dressed accordingly, with tailored clothes and handkerchiefs that matched their ties, Obama lacked the uniform of a serious politician. Scott wondered, too, whether Obama, as a recent arrival to the city, without roots in the community, was tough enough for the rough-and-tumble of Chicago's politics.[5]

But Obama had his supporters, too. Beverly Reed, a reporter and columnist who commanded great respect from the city's tight-knit set of black nationalists and grassroots activists, had vouched for Obama before the meeting and remained undeterred by his performance. A deeply spiritual person, Reed had first encountered Obama as a student in a class he taught at a local community center and immediately experienced a premonition about his destiny. "He's the one," she thought, listening to Obama explain the principles of organizing.[6]

Nevertheless, at least in the short run, Colonel Scott's reservations were born out. For one thing, Obama had rather badly misjudged the strength of his opponent, U.S. representative Bobby Rush. A former Black Panther and Chicago alderman, Rush came back hard against his inexperienced challenger. Claiming credit for tens of millions of dollars in federal grants to save hospitals, wire schools for Internet access, and create a military-themed high school, Rush argued persuasively that Obama would be unable to deliver for the South Side. As for Obama's experience at Harvard Law School and as a law professor at the University of Chicago, surely, Rush averred, that made him too soft to fight for the black community's immediate needs.

"If you can't run with the big dogs," he told *The Defender*'s editorial board during his own visit, "then you need to stay on the porch."[7]

When *The Defender* finally issued its endorsements, in the weekend edition before the primary, the nod went to Rush, but the paper included some oracular advice for Obama: "Experience, education, longevity, dedication, qualifications and seniority do count in the real world of politics," the editorial read. Obama was "highly qualified for the job, but still ha[d] much to do in the General Assembly. A U.S. congressional run might be better advised for another time in the future."[8]

*The Defender*'s assessment proved, if anything, somewhat understated. On March 21, 2000, Rush beat Obama with nearly two-thirds of the vote, a devastating loss that also made it abundantly clear how much Obama still had to learn about Black Chicago. But in the days that followed, *The Defender*'s redoubtable political reporter, Chinta Strausberg, would document his climb back from the brink of obscurity. A tiny woman with a high, soft voice, Strausberg was indefatigable, cranking out half a dozen stories every day about every level of black political personage, from neighborhood activists to the community's powerful aldermen, state legislators, and members of Congress. In politics-obsessed Chicago, her columns offered vital clues to the mood and agenda of a massive electorate that could make or break a candidate.

The weekend after his bruising defeat in the Democratic primary, Strausberg covered Obama's appearance with Congressman Rush at a "healing" event at the South Side headquarters of Jesse Jackson's Operation PUSH. Though not typically thought of as a Chicago-based leader, Jackson had been headquartered in the Windy City since 1966, when he arrived at the behest of Martin Luther King. Then a lean twenty-five-year-old sporting dashikis and an enormous afro, Jackson burrowed into the city and by the '70s had become the community's preeminent spokesman. By the turn of the twenty-first century, as he presided over the meeting at a section of the Operation PUSH complex called Dr. King's Workshop, Jackson was a corpulent, well-trimmed elder statesman. Stepping up to the microphone, he directed his sermon at Obama.

"In this struggle for public policy/public service leadership, you can't plant a seed tonight and expect to get a crop in the morning. You've got to plant a seed, cultivate it, water it, cut away weeds until your season comes.

"It's easy to say 'I'm qualified, vote for me, trust me.' Sometimes, it takes time to build trust . . .

"Those who fight the battle gain the respect of the people and, Obama, you've gained the respect of many people."[9]

Strausberg's article signaled to readers that Obama still had a future in black politics. Even though he had not yet found his way, he'd been accepted by the community. Sure enough, as the months ticked by, *The Defender* covered Obama's legislative initiatives in the state senate — initiatives in which he often stood right next to former rivals — and touted his grants to local schools.

The comeback took three years, but Obama was every bit as methodical as he was disciplined, and Strausberg was there for the big moment: on January 21, 2003, the day after Martin Luther King Day, Obama announced at a downtown hotel across the street from the Chicago City Hall that he was running for the U.S. Senate. In her coverage, Strausberg listed among those standing behind Obama some of the state's highest-ranking black Democrats, including many of the very figures who had actively opposed his congressional run against Rush.

This time, Obama displayed the charisma for which he would soon be known, incorporating themes that in the months to come would be reiterated and refined.

"We need politics of hope in this country," Obama said. "We don't need politics of division. We don't need small politics in this country."[10]

The African American leaders behind Obama were there for their own, highly rationalized, reasons, and they had little to lose in supporting him, since there was little chance he would actually win. Obama would be facing a tough Democratic field for the nomination, and then, in the unlikely event he made it to the general election, he would have to take on a wealthy Republican incumbent who had self-financed his first campaign with $11 million. They knew the math, having elected several black candidates to statewide office previously. Black votes in Illinois could be decisive in a Democratic primary, but to win a general election a black candidate needed to attract so-called swing voters — white suburbanites who responded mainly to television advertising, which was expensive.

But as the primary approached in March 2004, all of Obama's opponents either vanished from the field or destroyed each other: the wealthy Republican incumbent announced he would neither seek reelection nor back a successor, while both the Democratic and Republican front-runners found themselves embroiled in sex scandals. Obama began to surge in the polls and, sensing that victory was within its grasp, Chicago's black establishment rushed to his side.

Now Jesse Jackson became an Obama field marshal, urging African American voters to "take their souls to the polls," hosting a get-out-the-vote rally at Dr. King's Workshop, and calling for blacks to rally around *their* candidate. Jackson told Strausberg that he was on the lookout for operatives who were working for other candidates.

"We have to know who is on our freedom train," Jackson said, urging voters to report any campaign workers who claimed to be for Obama but were actually shilling for others.[11]

With 54 percent of the statewide Democratic vote, Obama demolished his opponents in the primary; the second-place finisher got just 23 percent. Turnout was especially heavy in the majority-black sec-

tions of the state, netting Obama as much as 90 percent of the ballots cast in some precincts. Also notable was Obama's fundraising
total — $5.5 million, from eight thousand separate donors.[12]

Then, in the general election, Obama thrashed last-minute Republican nominee Alan Keyes, becoming overnight not only the junior
U.S. senator from Illinois but, as predicted, an increasingly viable
presidential candidate. *The Defender* had been there at every step,
sometimes encouraging him, often prodding, and always serving as
a vital conduit to his base constituency. In 2005, during an interview
for *Paper Trail,* a PBS film about *The Defender's* centennial by acclaimed documentarian Barbara Allen, Obama acknowledged his
debt to the newspaper.

"Is *The Defender* story more an American story than an African
American story?" Allen asked him at the beginning of her interview.

"Absolutely," replied Obama. "*The Defender* chronicles the passage
of the African American community from the South to the North.
And in that sense it captures the immigrant's story of America. I
mean that that was an immigrant process that was taking place. And
the need to assimilate to the big city. And to find jobs and to have
bigger dreams for the next generation. And *The Defender* was part of
that process the whole way.

"*The Defender* recorded our expansion of democracy — the degree
to which African Americans were locked out of the process. *The Defender* recorded the injustice and then became part of the process of
opening up opportunity and making people more aware of the civil
rights issues that were at stake. Both in the South and in the North.

"And so in that sense *The Defender* represents the best of American journalism, which has always had a function not just of reporting, but also of advocacy and having a point of view."

Detailing the role *The Defender* had played in his own political
rise, Obama tellingly skipped over the 2000 contest against Congressman Bobby Rush.

"*The Defender* has historically been supportive of my state senate
races. And then in this U.S. Senate race, I think *The Defender,* as one
of the major mouthpieces of the African American community, provided tremendous symbolic boost to my candidacy. You know, but
I would go beyond that and say that the most important thing *The*

*Defender* did for my candidacy was to report on the work that I was doing down in Springfield in ways that a lot of the mainstream, larger newspapers were not reporting on.

"When I passed videotaping of interrogations and confessions in capital cases or I passed racial profiling legislation or I worked with other legislators to create laws that would help ex-offenders, you know, those kinds of legislative initiatives that oftentimes are beneath the radar screen were reported actively sometimes on the cover of *The Defender.*

"And that gave me exposure within the African American community that was vital to my ultimate election."[13]

In the spring of 2006, as anticipation built over Obama's impending presidential campaign, Beverly Reed, now working for the Billiken as well, suggested to Colonel Scott that Obama be made grand marshal of the parade that year. The Colonel immediately telephoned Obama, who readily accepted. The senator's staff then engaged in lengthy discussions over logistics: because of the crowds, U.S. Secret Service agents refused to let Obama march in the parade, agreeing only to let him ride in a convertible driven by one agent and flanked by other agents on foot.

Still, the people roared as the car carrying Obama cruised along King Drive, jostling for position in the hopes of getting a glimpse of the senator in his sports shirt and sunglasses. This time, at the end of the parade route, instead of mingling with the crowd, Obama was quickly escorted to an armored black van with tinted windows waiting on the grass below the reviewing stand. Once the senator was safely inside, the vehicle sped off through Washington Park. Obama was headed to the airport to catch a flight to New Orleans, where he would speak at graduation ceremonies for Xavier University on the one-year anniversary of Hurricane Katrina. After that, he was scheduled to travel to Kenya to promote AIDS awareness.

Colonel Scott and Reed lingered after Obama's departure, proud of their role in his rise yet fully aware that behind his remarkable ascent was more than a century of hard work from an entire community, led and guided by *The Defender.* Indeed, Scott remarked to Reed that Obama's van was passing very near the spot where it had all begun, in the so-called White City of the World's Columbian Exposition. The World's Fair of 1893 was, after all, where Robert Abbott had his first taste of Chicago's enormous potential and where he met the great Frederick Douglass, from whom he received the source code to create a newspaper that would carry the cause of liberation all the way through the twentieth century.[14]

# THE DEFENDER

# 1

## A Defender of His Race

O N AUGUST 25, 1893, Frederick Douglass spoke to a crowd gathered for Colored American Day at the World's Columbian Exposition. At 3:00 p.m., the twenty-five hundred people filling Festival Hall — two-thirds black and one-third white, in the estimation of the *Chicago Tribune* — greeted Douglass with applause as he stepped onto the stage. In the three decades since the end of the Civil War, this escaped slave and former leader of the abolitionist movement had become a diplomat and elder statesman, the principal spokesperson for his people. Seventy-five years old, his long hair and beard now white, his six-foot frame lean and erect, the Sage of Anacostia smiled and waved to the crowd.[1]

In the years immediately following the Civil War, the ex-slaves of the South were making rapid progress economically as well as politically, exercising their newly won right to vote and electing their own to local and state governments as well as the U.S. Congress. But even before federal troops withdrew from the old Confederacy in 1877, southern whites used extreme violence to block African Americans from the ballot box and otherwise restore the antebellum racial hierarchy. More than one hundred black men had been murdered by white mobs across the South in the first six months of 1893 alone; three were burned alive. At the same time, millions of black men and women found themselves in conditions no better than slavery, as sharecroppers or as convict laborers under a system known as peonage, whereby they were charged with petty crimes and sentenced to long terms working on farms or in mines or factories — without pay, of course.[2]

The national government, in response to these troubling developments, did little more than shrug its shoulders. Both the executive and legislative branches of the federal government were dominated at this time by the Republicans, yet the party of Abraham Lincoln was backing away from its commitment to African Americans, lest it alienate southern white voters and their representatives in Congress. Such acquiescence to white supremacists extended to the U.S. Supreme Court itself, which increasingly applied the protections of the Fourteenth and Fifteenth Amendments to corporations, rather than African Americans, ultimately leading to the justices' shameful sanction of legal segregation in the South and beyond under the "separate but equal" doctrine enshrined in *Plessy v. Ferguson*.[3]

So on that hot August day in 1893, Frederick Douglass did his best to stem the tide, striding onto the stage with an individual who represented the best of the nation's past, Isabella Beecher Hooker, sister of Harriet Beecher Stowe, whose *Uncle Tom's Cabin* had been a fulcrum of the abolitionist movement. The program itself, meanwhile, showcased the talents of a new, freeborn generation of African Americans that included Paul Laurence Dunbar, a tall, cerebral twenty-one-year-old who would come to be seen as black America's first nationally known poet, as well as Will Marion Cook, an up-and-coming black composer who was then studying under the great Antonín Dvořák. Cook had arranged the event's program of classical pieces, which featured a number of beautifully sung arias as well as a violin performance by Joseph Douglass, grandson of the Sage.

Following all of these heartening appearances, the room was filled with anticipation as Douglass stepped back up to the podium to deliver the closing speech. But as he began to read from his papers, the great man's voice failed him, either because of the heat or exhaustion, and a group of white men in the gallery began to shout slurs and insults.

Unable to make himself heard, Douglass paused, then slammed his printed speech onto the podium. He yanked the glasses from his temples and began speaking extemporaneously, his voice steadily rising in volume and depth until it succeeded in drowning out his hecklers.[4]

We hear nowadays of a frightful problem called a Negro problem. What is this problem? As usual, the North is humbugged. The Negro problem is a Southern device to mislead and deceive. There is, in fact, no such problem. The real problem has been given a false name. It is called Negro for a purpose. It has substituted Negro for Nation, because the one is hated and despised, and the other is loved and honored. The true problem is a national problem.

There is no Negro problem. The problem is whether the American people have honesty enough, loyalty enough, honor enough, patriotism enough to live up to their own Constitution.[5]

The applause shook the building at the end of Douglass's speech, ringing out into the White City and over the blue waters of Lake Michigan beyond. Douglass's decision to speak at this event had been controversial among many African American activists, who feared that a Colored American Day would simply be used to perpetuate the worst sorts of stereotypes and ridicule, if not provide a tacit recognition, even acceptance, of segregation. But Douglass felt that the fair was a singular opportunity to focus the world's attention, if only for one moment, on black achievement, and he succeeded, as the *Chicago Tribune* indicated in its coverage of the event.

"There was classical music rendered by black men in a way that would grace the grand opera stage," the *Tribune* reported, "and there was an oration, which, with its vivid eloquence, burned itself into the memory of those who listened."[6]

Among those listening was the future founder of *The Chicago Defender*, who would remember every word. Then in his early twenties and a student at the Hampton Institute in Virginia, Robert Abbott had come to the World's Fair to sing tenor with the Hampton Quartet. Already absorbed by "the plight of my people," he was both radicalized and urbanized by his experience. What he saw in Chicago that summer convinced him that this city was the perfect place to realize his dreams.

"Tell father if he will back me," he wrote to his family enthusiastically, "I will stay out here in the West and try and make a fortune. Let me know his intentions before I begin to make up my mind as to what steps to take."[7]

Robert Abbott was born in November 1869 in a cabin on St. Simons Island, an island just off Georgia's Atlantic coast.[8] More than in most places, St. Simons's black inhabitants maintained a strong connection to the African continent by speaking Gullah, a language incorporating vocabulary and grammar from several West African languages as well as English. His parents' home was near Ibo Landing, a place that figures in a legend about a shipload of new slaves who jumped into the water wearing their chains, drowning themselves to escape further abuse onshore. Today their ghosts are said to be visible in the ocean's turbulent waves, their songs heard in the breeze blowing through the trees.[9]

Robert's biological father, Thomas, born around 1847, was a native of the island and lived most of his life as a house slave to one Captain Charles Stevens, who held a plantation there. After the Civil War, each member of the Abbott clan was awarded a plot of land on the island, but Thomas sought out instead the excitement and opportunity of nearby Savannah. There he met Robert's mother, Flora Butler, an intelligent, determined woman with a defiant streak, whose parents were slaves brought as teenagers from the Portuguese-held territories in West Africa. In an unpublished, unfinished autobiography included in Robert Abbott's files, Flora describes how she taught herself to read and write in secret, using tissue paper to trace the names of area families engraved on metal plates affixed to their homes.[10]

When she was eighteen, Flora encountered invading Union troops who informed her that she was emancipated. In an experience replicated many times over by newly freed slaves, she found herself suddenly on her own. "A soldier met me and told me that I was free, and I must ask the people where I was staying to pay me for my work," she recalled, "but I was afraid to ask for money so I decided to look for work." She found a job with the editor of *The Georgia Gazette,* the oldest newspaper in the state, carrying copy to the printer and bringing proofs back for correction.[11]

Marrying in 1867, Flora and Thomas Abbott set up their household on St. Simons. Their home was roughly built, essentially just a shack with a dirt floor, and as Thomas was often in Savannah for long periods of time, Flora was left in the company of the extended Abbott clan, who did not entirely embrace her. The couple's first child, a girl named Harriet, died in 1868 when she was less than a year old. A year after that, when Robert was born, Flora was entirely on her own through labor and childbirth, unassisted by the Abbotts or her husband. Thomas, indeed, may never have even seen his son; he died of "sudden consumption" in Savannah in 1869 when Robert was just an infant.[12]

By the time Robert was four months old, Flora had moved back to her mother's apartment in Savannah, where she soon developed a friendship with her new landlord, John Hermann Henry Sengstacke. Johnny Harmon, as he was known by his neighbors, had been raised in Germany and had a fair complexion, brown eyes, straight, black hair, and a short, trimmed mustache; most people assumed he was white.[13] His father, Hermann Henry Sengstacke, was born in a town near Bremen, in what was then the Kingdom of Hanover. Arriving in Savannah as a sailor, Hermann Henry settled there in the 1840s and opened a general store. He bought a young, newly arrived African woman named Tama from the city's slave market, married her, and established their household above the general store, a living arrangement not uncommon at the time. Tama gave birth to John in 1848; a second child, Mary, was born the following year, but Tama died shortly thereafter, presenting Hermann Henry with a dilemma. Because he had not emancipated Tama before her death, under the twisted antebellum racial code, John and Mary were technically born as slaves; even if they were freed themselves, then, they would be vulnerable to myriad oppressions and could easily be impressed back into slavery. Hermann Henry did not object to the institution of slavery; in his will, he bequeathed to his children two slaves, "Rose and Ansel, with the future increase of the said Rose." He did not want to see his own offspring in bondage, however, and so he sent John and Mary to his sister's home in a village near Bremen. Hermann Henry never followed his children back to Europe, staying in the South even as the Civil War cut off regular overseas communications, and died in 1862.

Reared in a caring home, John and Mary were educated in German schools, but when John turned twenty-one, he decided to return to America to investigate what had become of his father's property in the years after the Civil War. He arrived in Savannah in 1869 to discover that the war had dissolved most of his inheritance, while his father's executors had apparently taken a share as well. He attempted to make a career for himself as a translator and teacher, but found that whites refused to hire him once they learned of his African heritage, and no African Americans could afford his services. He might have moved back to Germany, where no one cared about his mother's origins, but Johnny decided instead to stay in Savannah, feeling a strong sense of identification with, and even duty toward, the former slaves around him.

Or perhaps it was love. Flora later recalled that Johnny worked with his students "day and night," and she soon began assisting him. "He found out that I could read and write," she wrote in her remembrances, "and got me to help at night with his pupils. We became fond of each other and decided to marry."[14]

In 1876, when Robert was seven years old, Sengstacke, who had legally adopted Robert, was ordained a minister in the Congregational church, a Protestant sect based in New England and Great Britain that had long supported the abolitionist cause. Sengstacke received a grant to start a church and school in a small farming community on the outskirts of Savannah called Woodville. The community's four hundred inhabitants were former slaves and their descendants from two now-abandoned plantations, who raised peas, strawberries, cucumbers, and other crops. This was rough country, especially in summer, when malaria was a problem, and the Sengstackes returned to their "city home" in the Yamacraw section of Savannah for a few months every year.[15]

Robert described his childhood as happy, if limited. John and Flora had eight more children together, making for a bustling home life. Blacks could not attend the schools in the area, which were reserved for whites and were scarce in any case, but the Sengstacke children attended the school their father founded, connected to the church he had built, which was in session five months a year. Outside of church, the main social activity was the occasional "shout" on special occasions such as birthdays or weddings. Furniture would be cleared from a family's parlor or other communal space, and neighbors and friends would gather together, moving in a circle, clapping their hands and stamping their feet to keep the beat, while individuals stepped forward to sing various registers and parts, first bass, then baritone, tenor, contralto, and finally soprano voices taking their turns. Shouts were a traditional pastime imported from West Africa, but for Robert, these informal celebrations provided training in vocal performance that would prove essential to his college education, and would ultimately bring him to Chicago.[16]

In addition to music, Robert developed a passion for military service that he carried with him throughout his life and transmitted to future generations, although he never served in the armed forces himself. He was awestruck by the Georgia Cadets, a paramilitary unit of African American teenage boys who would parade on the streets of Savannah, exhibiting their skills — until they were banned, along with other black paramilitary units, as legal segregation was installed in Georgia. That, too, made an impression on young Robert, as did the subsequent departure of many cadets for the North.[17]

By far the greatest influence on Robert, however, was his beloved stepfather. As the eldest child in a rapidly growing band of siblings, Robert accompanied his stepfather as he traveled around the area, lecturing to the poor farmers about hygiene, science, and culture, and to the county court, where the Reverend John Sengstacke often acted as informal counsel for African Americans facing charges. A dedicated Republican who paid his poll taxes without protest, Sengstacke was quiet, frugal, and abstemious, while in the pulpit he was a "book preacher," who, in a community where many were illiterate, often read to the congregation from the newspaper.

"He endeavored to lift the minds of the people above the soil," Robert wrote as an adult, "and prayer meetings became a forum at which world events were discussed."

Eschewing the more demonstrative style of the Baptist churches, Sengstacke sacrificed popularity as a result. Nevertheless, to his adopted son, Sengstacke was a transformational figure: "It was his teachings that gave me a lust for travel. He fed my cultural nature while my mother, endowed with practical common sense, kept my feet on the ground."[18]

Sengstacke also sidestepped the conventions of the times to build young Robert's self-esteem when it came to the young man's dark complexion. In an era when blacks, no less than whites, tended to equate a lighter complexion with intelligence and competency, the dark-complexioned Robert was frequently teased, bullied, and discriminated against. (Even after reaching the pinnacle of his fame and influence, he would be derided as "Black Abbott," albeit behind his back at that point.) But thanks in large part to the influence of his

stepfather, he refused to let others' reactions to his complexion ham-
per his own expectations. Sengstacke was militant on this issue, even
participating in an intrachurch battle over complexion before the
move to Woodville. When his church broke into two factions, one
open to all complexions and the other reserving special privileges for
"lighter" members, Sengstacke sided with the open faction. His stepfather's colorblindness built a reserve of self-confidence in Robert on
which he could draw in the coming years, as indeed he would have to
do.[19]

Robert attended boarding schools in the area as well as his stepfather's classroom, and as he grew older he was eager to pursue higher
education and develop a broader worldview. In June 1888, at the age
of eighteen, he pleaded his case in a short note to General Samuel
Chapman Armstrong, founder of the Hampton Normal and Agricultural Institute. Demonstrating exemplary penmanship, the note reveals the run-on syntax and tendency toward earnestness that would
come to characterize Abbott's writing.

"I wrote you last year to find out if I could get in school," he began,
"but you was crowded can I get in this year and can I work my way
through school please let me know if I can get through school in this
way and can I get work out here in the summers so I could help me
the next year. Please try and let me enter here. I want to work through
school if possible."[20]

It took Sengstacke two years to assemble the necessary sum, much
of which came from a lady in New England he'd contacted through
the church, but Abbott finally began his tenure at Hampton in 1890.
His first night on campus, singing in the chapel with a group of boys
from Savannah, Abbott's operatic tenor — trained through the communal shouts of his youth — rang out through the building and attracted the attention of General Armstrong himself, who promptly
recruited him for the Hampton Quartet, the school's nationally renowned singing group.

Born in Hawaii, where his parents were missionaries, Armstrong
had led black troops as a Union officer in the Civil War. He founded
Hampton in the shadow of Fort Monroe, where many escaped slaves
found a haven during the conflict. The core of his mission was to help
his students develop practical skills that would allow them to be self-

sufficient, and no one better exemplified this academic philosophy than Booker T. Washington, star of the class of 1875. Armstrong had personally dispatched Washington to Tuskegee, Alabama, to start his own institution based on the Hampton model, and it, too, was now thriving.[21]

Abbott would spend the next six years at Hampton, gathering with the other students under the Emancipation Oak, a symbol of the school's unique history, and building his academic skills. His practical education included studying the fine points of printing, a profession that was rapidly evolving from an art form that required the manual setting of type to a highly mechanized process with the introduction of the Linotype machine. Robert's Hampton years also gave him the opportunity to travel the nation for the first time, as a member of the Hampton Quartet, which frequently went on tour as a fundraising vehicle for the school. In 1892 the quartet sang in New York City before Walter Damrosch, the German-born composer and conductor, who had married into a prominent Republican political dynasty. Damrosch took a particular interest in Abbott and invited the quartet to perform at his home in Bar Harbor, Maine. There, Damrosch described Robert as having "one of the most promising tenor voices of that day," and offered him a scholarship to complete his musical training. Abbott was tempted, but Hampton's vice president, Hollis Frissell, who was traveling with the quartet, advised against the move out of worry that Robert would face discrimination in pursuing a music career and wind up destitute, without any marketable skills by which to support himself in the long term.[22]

In the summer of 1893, the Hampton Quartet, by now one of the most prestigious black singing groups in the nation, traveled to Chicago to perform at the World's Columbian Exposition. To an America still largely rural and agricultural, dark and quiet at night, the World's Fair and its central exhibition area, the so-called White City, was an explosion of light, sound, and ideas that left no one untouched.[23]

Visitors were amazed by the smooth-running electric boats and elevated trains, the telephones and loudspeakers, the massive industrial machines and scientific displays. Nineteen nations had erected pavilions, from Ceylon to Canada, Norway to Siam, each using their space to replicate the cultural trademarks of their respective homelands. Brazilian bands played Afro-Portuguese music in their pavilion, while the Empire of Japan erected a Shinto shrine on an island in one of the fairground's many lagoons.[24]

The White City, however, represented only a part of the World's Fair. Across a bridge to the west was a rectangular stretch of land known as the Midway Plaisance. In contrast with the high cultural theme of the White City, the Midway offered fairgoers entertainments that were of a more sensory, even prurient, nature. More than a million people took a ride on the Ferris wheel, a marvel of engineering that was Chicago's answer to the Eiffel Tower, the technological wonder of the Paris World's Fair of 1889, while hundreds of thousands of attendees took a ride on a camel or marveled at the feats of the escape artist Harry Houdini. The sinuous movements of the exotic belly dancers in the "Street in Cairo" exhibition both entranced and scandalized viewers, while the country's by-now massive population of immigrants got a taste of the lands they left behind in reconstructed German and Irish hamlets that served the food and drinks of home.

The Midway also housed what were originally intended to be serious anthropological exhibits, but which were inevitably tinged by the crass commercialism and racism of the day. Visitors gawked and scoffed at the simulacrum "villages" of "Eskimeaux" and "Dahomeyans," as the group of Inuit recruited from the Arctic and the clan of Fon who came from West Africa were called, respectively. Just off the fairgrounds, they flocked to Buffalo Bill Cody's Wild West Show to see a reenactment of the Sioux defeating General George Armstrong Custer at Little Bighorn in 1876, and likewise gathered to see re-created battles between hundreds of Zulu warriors from South Africa with their assegai stabbing spears, their charges met by a hail of imaginary bullets from actors portraying British Army soldiers.[25]

As one of the leading African American academic institutions, Hampton had an impressive exhibit of student-built items in the fair's Manufactures and Liberal Arts Building, as well as the honor of its quartet singing in the White City, where organizers generally restricted performance to classical music and patriotic marches like those by John Philip Sousa. The Hampton Quartet's religious folk songs, so-called Negro spirituals, with titles like "Were You There When They Crucified My Lord?" were popular among Americans of all races and often elicited tears from their audiences. Among those particularly moved was the bearded Bohemian composer Antonín Dvořák, who had recently taken the helm at the National Conservatory of Music in New York City. "I am now satisfied that the future music of the country must be founded on what are called Negro melodies," Dvořák stated at one of the conclaves exploring African American cultural contributions.[26]

Abbott's Hampton affiliation also facilitated his introduction to prominent members of Chicago's black community, not the least of whom was John R. Marshall, grandson of the fourth chief justice of the U.S. Supreme Court. Marshall had been born a slave in 1859 in Virginia to the chief justice's son and his "unmarried wife." Though not officially acknowledged by the family, the Marshalls had arranged for John R. Marshall to receive a military scholarship to attend Hampton, where he excelled, before moving to Illinois in the 1880s.

Marshall, fair enough to be mistaken for white, sometimes had passed for white to secure masonry jobs during his early years in Chicago, but he soon prospered and established himself among the city's few dozen African American doctors, lawyers, journalists, and businessmen. Chicago's black community was just fifteen thousand in a city of more than one million, but it had a proud legacy owing to Chicago's origins as a station on the Underground Railroad, conveying escaped slaves to Canada so effectively that it was derided by one pro-slavery newspaper editor as a "sink hole of abolition." After the war, the city's African American community had been joined by freedmen as well as black veterans of the Union army, a nucleus that survived the Great Fire of 1871. By the time of the 1893 World's Fair, most of the city's black men worked in hotels and restaurants, foundries and docks, or as Pullman porters and domestic servants.[27]

Concentrated in a corridor on the South Side, the community had several large churches and thriving businesses, as well as Provident Hospital, a small medical facility that was staffed by blacks and whites and had been founded by the pioneering black heart surgeon Daniel Hale Williams two years before the World's Fair. Marshall had secured a commission as a lieutenant in the all-black Ninth Battalion of the Illinois National Guard and was a member of the city's active contingent of black Republicans, who had already succeeded in electing several of their number to state and county offices. Denied the vote in the South, blacks in Chicago voted enthusiastically and were leveraging their numbers to pass civil rights laws blocking the kind of legal segregation being installed throughout the South.[28]

Marshall and others introduced Abbott to a city where African Americans enjoyed relative freedom in the public way. Blacks rode shoulder to shoulder with whites on streetcars; nor did they have to worry about stepping off sidewalks to let whites pass, or otherwise showing deference to whites at the risk of assault or murder. In Chicago, the police stopped lynchings rather than abetting them as was often the case in the South. On one occasion in April 1893, a fight between a black worker and a white worker on the fair's construction crew turned into a near-lynching when a crowd of white men attempted to hang the African American. A police officer intervened and held off the crowd until he was reinforced by a fellow officer. Their revolvers drawn, the officers dragged the wounded black man into a nearby store and barricaded themselves inside until several whole squads of police arrived, swinging their clubs to get through and arresting especially aggressive members of the mob. The fact that these officers risked their own lives to protect a black man stood in stark contrast to how most southern police forces handled similar incidents.[29]

Frederick Douglass was indefatigable during the World's Fair, speaking at events both on and off the fairgrounds, both scheduled and impromptu. Within days of the opening, he spoke at the World's Congress of Representative Women, in which he praised the event's organizers for including black women in the program. Underscoring the crucial linkage between the movements to secure full rights for African Americans and for women, Douglass proclaimed that "a new heaven is dawning upon us, and a new Earth is ours, in which the discrimination against men and women on account of color and sex is passing away."[30]

In June, Douglass was a main speaker at the Congress on the Negro, which was organized by two African American politicians based in Chicago, Edward Morris and Edward Wright. Morris and Wright assembled three hundred men and women representing all forty-four states to hear speakers denounce segregation in the South and argue over emigration to Africa, with several respectable figures advocating resettlement in Liberia and Sierra Leone, a proposal that

Douglass strongly opposed. In the final weeks of the fair, Douglass participated in the Congress on Africa, which assembled the nation's black leaders along with delegates from the few remaining independent African nations as well as European colonies for a week of lectures and discussions, a rare conclave on Africa that included the opinions and perspectives of Africans themselves.[31]

Another African American leader whom Abbott met at the Chicago fair was Ida B. Wells, a fearless, confrontational investigator and journalist who, though just a few years older than Abbott, had already established herself as a leading spokesperson against lynching and segregation.

Wells had developed her seemingly limitless resources of self-reliance and stubborn defiance early on. Born in Mississippi in 1862, just months before President Lincoln issued the Emancipation Proclamation, she took charge of her younger siblings as a teenager after her parents died, keeping the family together by posing as a trained teacher some years older than she actually was. The defining moment in her life and career came in 1892, when she was living in Memphis, Tennessee, and a mob of seventy-five masked white men lynched three of her friends. Wells's writings about the incident infuriated Memphis's white leaders — particularly her avowal that the most common accusation used to justify lynching, the rape of white women, was almost always a provocative excuse to cover up for what were, in fact, consensual relations between blacks and whites. In response to her articles about this topic, a short time later, while she was traveling in Philadelphia, another mob destroyed the offices of her Memphis newspaper, *Free Speech*.[32]

Wells understood her life was under threat in the South, and she remained in the North, where she began writing for black newspapers, including *The New York Age*, as well as white-owned publications such as *Chicago Inter Ocean*. She sought out Frederick Douglass, who advised her to take the antilynching cause overseas, as he had done with abolition in the years before the Civil War. After touring Great Britain for several months, Wells returned to the United States in June 1893, after the World's Fair had opened, to join a circle of intellectuals, artists, and activists gathered around Douglass at the Haitian Pavilion, a specially built structure filled with historical artifacts, which served as his office and receiving room. A former American ambassador to Haiti, Douglass had been named commissioner of the island nation for the duration of the fair.[33]

Douglass gave Wells a desk at the Haitian Pavilion, from which she distributed *The Reason Why the Colored American Is Not in the World's Columbian Exposition,* a booklet she had conceived the previous fall, piqued by fair organizers' failure to include African Americans in the planning for the event. Douglass himself was a coauthor, along with the historian I. Garland Penn, and Ferdinand L. Barnett, publisher of *The Conservator,* Chicago's most significant black newspaper. It had taken all summer to find the funds to print just twenty thousand copies of *The Reason Why,* by which point the title of the sixty-page booklet hardly seemed accurate, given Douglass's ubiquity at the fair as well as the myriad ways in which the African American presence had been felt during the event.

Nevertheless, the pamphlet was a defiant statement against lynching and segregation as well as a first-rate work of investigative journalism — a spiritual template of sorts for *The Defender.* In his introduction, Douglass described the fair as a "whited sepulcher," a sanitized presentation of American culture, and stated that the booklet's publication was necessitated by the failure of the nation to tell the whole truth about its past and present. Wells then included three chapters on lynching, peonage, and the disenfranchisement of African Americans in the South, citing academic research, reports from white-owned newspapers, and her own investigations.

To underscore her point that the South was abusing the legal system to oppress African Americans, Wells wrote about the state-sanctioned executions of children: South Carolina's hanging of a thirteen-year-old girl accused of poisoning a white infant to whom she was a nurse, and Alabama's hanging of a ten-year-old boy, both in the previous year. She traced the origin of lynching as a tool of frontier justice and documented its increasing use in the South to deny blacks their political rights, including vivid firsthand descriptions of gruesome mob hangings, shootings, burnings, and tortures of men as well as women, a catalog of brutality that continued unabated even as the World's Fair was underway. Just as she was finishing the booklet, on July 22, Wells received a taunting telegram signed by the editor of one of Memphis's white-owned newspapers inviting her to cover a lynching in the city — ten hours before it occurred: "Lee Walker, colored man, accused of raping white women, in jail here, will be taken out and burned by whites tonight. Can you send Miss Ida Wells to write it up?"

Wells's response was to include the telegram in *The Reason Why* as evidence that white men in positions of authority were orchestrating the campaign of terror in the South for their own political and economic advantage.[34]

Ida Wells stayed in Chicago after the World's Fair, having begun a romantic relationship with Ferdinand Barnett, the widowed lawyer and publisher who had collaborated with her on *The Reason Why*. But despite his desire to remain in "the West," Robert Abbott left Chicago for home, his stepfather unable to fund an extended sojourn in the city. Abbott returned to Hampton University in the fall, where he would remain for another three years.[35]

Meanwhile, the leadership of black America changed hands. Frederick Douglass died suddenly on February 20, 1895, having remained active as a protester and organizer until the end.[36] Filling the void he'd left as the paramount spokesperson for black America was Robert Abbott's predecessor at Hampton, Booker T. Washington. The Wizard of Tuskegee, as Washington was rapidly becoming known, departed sharply from Douglass in his approach to racial equality. In September 1895 he argued, during a speech at the Cotton States and International Exposition in Atlanta, Georgia, that instead of struggle and protest, African Americans should take a passive approach to gaining their civil rights.

"Cast down your bucket where you are," Washington said. "Cast it down in making friends in every manly way of the people of all races by whom we are surrounded. The wisest among my race understand that the agitation of questions of social equality is the extremist folly.

"In all things that are purely social we can be as separate as the fingers, yet one as the hand in all things essential to mutual progress."[37]

Washington's conciliatory language, interpreted widely as an accommodation of segregation, is difficult to reconcile with today's values, but his message of self-reliance struck a positive chord with many African Americans of his day and was particularly successful at attracting the material support of influential whites, which Washington used, in turn, to create and strengthen black institutions like Tuskegee. In the face of the South's ferocious racism, the North's ambivalence, and the fact that most African Americans continued to live in severe poverty, dependent on whites for their immediate survival, his "cast down your buckets" philosophy, as it came to be known, made a provisional sort of sense.

Ida Wells and Ferdinand Barnett married that same year in Chicago, their wedding an important social and political event drawing hundreds of friends, white as well as black, and announced in both *The New York Times* and the *Chicago Tribune*. Afterward, Barnett received an appointment in the county prosecutor's office, while Wells took over *The Conservator,* suspending her work only temporarily to rear the couple's six children, including two sons from Barnett's marriage to his first wife, who had died of illness. Like many of the "New Negroes," as Washington had dubbed this new generation of militant African Americans, Wells was prospering in a safe northern city, though she never stopped fighting the murderous segregationists of her home region.[38]

After graduating from Hampton, Robert Abbott returned home with plans to use his newly minted printing skills to help his stepfather publish the *Woodville Times,* a four-page, four-column broadsheet the Reverend John Sengstacke had launched several years earlier. The newspaper provided its local readers with information on science and culture — one front-page article, for instance, featured the latest inventions of Thomas Edison — while also inveighing against the Baptist Church.[39]

Chicago beckoned, however, as it did for so many others who had been to the World's Fair. In the fall of 1897, a year after his graduation, Abbott returned to the city to attend the Kent College of Law. He rented a room on Twenty-Seventh Street in the heart of the black community, from which he could walk to class every day, paying his landlady twenty-five cents a day in exchange for breakfast and dinner. To support himself, he hoped to find work as a printer, but encountered fierce discrimination within the printers union. Time and again, white men, even newly arrived immigrants, were given jobs ahead of him. Protest as he might, explaining to union officials that he was "not looking for a colored man's job, but a printing job," he continued to be rejected. Robert would later recall this period as particularly penurious: "I would go hungry and probably would have starved to death but for the generosity of some folk who would lend me a dime now and then."[40]

One of those who interceded on Abbott's behalf was his close friend Louis B. Anderson, an assistant county prosecutor and fellow World's Fair veteran, who threatened one printer that he would lose city contracts if Abbott didn't get some work. A southerner by birth, Anderson had traveled to the fair as an assistant to Moses P. Handy, its director of publicity, and when the White City shut down, he accepted an offer to work as secretary to Buffalo Bill Cody. Anderson followed the Wild West Show to Cody's ranch in North Platte, Nebraska, but finding prairie life too rugged, he soon returned to Chicago. Anderson preceded Abbott at the Kent College of Law and, like John Marshall, Ferdinand Barnett, and other prominent blacks, served as a loyal and assiduous activist for the city's Republican political apparatus.[41]

Marshall was just then nearing the pinnacle of his public influence, having become a national figure during the Spanish-American War as the highest-ranking black officer in the history of the American military. Having risen to the rank of colonel in the city's all-black National Guard unit, he was in command when the war broke out, and the unit was commissioned as the Eighth Illinois Regiment of the U.S. Army. The prospect of a black officer in the field — potentially giving orders to white troops — stirred strong opposition in the ranks, all the way up to President William McKinley, but in the end Marshall and his men were permitted to go, overseeing an occupation force in Cuba for eight months before returning home to a hero's welcome led by then-mayor Carter Harrison II.[42]

Ida Wells-Barnett, Louis Anderson, and John Marshall were just a few of the success stories in an African American community whose size, by the turn of the century, had doubled to thirty thousand. Chicago's Dearborn Street corridor, as it was now called, was convenient for those employed as servants in the mansions of the wealthy along Grand Boulevard to the east as well as for the Pullman porters who worked in the rail yards just northwest, and for those employed in Little Cheyenne, the black section of the Levee vice district, directly north. The corridor was by no means an exclusively black neighborhood, perhaps even one-half white on many blocks. Still, its first black-owned businesses — barbershops, tailors, and restaurants — were thriving.[43]

Abbott's early efforts to join the community's upper echelon were consistently thwarted owing to his dark complexion and Georgia accent. Although he had graduated from law school in 1900 as the only African American in his class, attorney and politician Edward Morris advised Abbott that he was "a little too dark to make an impression on the Illinois courts." Though light-complexioned himself, Morris was a militant on race issues and had not meant to insult Abbott; he was simply doing his best to convey that the color line, though less pronounced than in the South, still existed in Chicago, particularly when it came to elite groups such as attorneys. Complexion proved a social obstacle for Abbott within the black community as well; Sixth Grace Presbyterian Church refused to let him join the choir despite the quality of his voice.[44]

None of these rejections dispelled Abbott's ambition, however, or his enthusiasm for the city. Shortly after graduation from law school, he began subletting a small bedroom in a gaslit, second-floor apartment at 3159 South State Street, just steps away from the main intersection of "the Stroll," the stretch of State Street that served as the black community's main commercial zone. For Abbott, being on Thirty-First and State meant that he could spend his time "along the curbstone in the enjoyment of the 'after-dinner' cigar," chatting with passersby and taking the pulse of the entire African American world, as Chicago was rapidly becoming a crossroads for black America. It was a place where a man "can meet all of his friends and here he can talk 'shop' to his 'heart's content' and learn in an hour everything of interest that has occurred during the last day, week or year," Abbott would later write. This particular corner was home to two hotels whose bars "are establishments of the highest class . . . The best of decorum always prevails and women are ABSOLUTELY barred."[45]

In his black derby hat, white shirt, white tie, and blue suit, Abbott cut a respectable, if threadbare, figure, his thin overcoat stuffed with newspaper in winter, the holes in his shoes patched with cardboard. He spoke with everyone and anyone about the "race question," in and out of the neighborhood's various cafés and bars, though he never drank, and only smoked cigarettes in private, regarding it as a personal vice that ought to be concealed. Whenever he got the chance, he volunteered at *The Conservator,* whose print shop was now run by a former instructor at Hampton.[46]

Despite his straitened financial circumstances, Abbott felt that the city had "golden opportunities for anyone with energy and determination," as he described it in his memoirs years later. He marveled at the signs of technological progress all around him, the streetcars plying the city's broad avenues, the steam trains rolling along elevated tracks. Just as he was settling into Chicago, officials built a new railway encircling the city's downtown, which came to be called the Loop, replacing the elevated steam engines with electric trains. For the rest of his life, Abbott lived within a block of the El, the rumble and squeak of the cars audible to him as they cruised along the tracks, sounds at once comforting and exciting.[47]

In the years after his graduation from law school, Abbott had tried and failed to establish himself as an attorney and printer, but he succeeded in finding a circle of friends, young, ambitious intellectuals and activists like himself, including Archibald Carey, an up-and-coming leader of the black church, and Oscar De Priest, who, though he was working full-time as a house painter, had a thriving real estate business on the side. Gathering with this group on many Sunday mornings in 1904, Abbott expressed his belief that what African American people needed was a newspaper that would "wake them up," expose the atrocities of the southern system, and make demands for justice. But his friends scoffed when Abbott announced that *he* would be the publisher of this newspaper. Abbott was broke, they pointed out, and no African American newspaper had been a profitable venture. Previous publications had been heavily subsidized by their publishers or by philanthropists, usually white do-gooders. Even *The Conservator* was profitable only because it used its press during its off-hours to print handbills and other items. Abbott's friends counseled him instead to get a job as a Pullman porter or redcap, or advised that he return to the South, where his law degree and printing skills would make him highly employable.[48]

To be sure, Abbott had his supporters, not least his landlady, Henrietta P. Lee. A churchgoing widow active in the women's Elks Lodge, Lee acted as his surrogate mother, supporting him when he was broke and even nursing him back to health when he contracted pneumonia. But his early efforts were not promising — he ran out of funds to print the first publication he attempted after just a few issues — and after the sudden death of his stepfather, on June 23, 1904, he almost gave up on Chicago and journalism altogether. John Sengstacke had died of nephritis, a kidney ailment, at the age of fifty-six. Later that summer, Abbott wrote to Hollis Frissell, who had taken over as president of Hampton Institute after General Armstrong's death, indicating that he was planning a permanent return to Georgia to help run his stepfather's school.

Requesting a letter of support and help in contacting "influential friends," Abbott wrote, "I have accomplished my work here in this city at law and have now decided to return back to the South and enter into my life's work doing what I can to help my people both from an educational standpoint and in the way of giving them legal advice."[49]

But in the end, Abbott stayed in Chicago, determined to publish his newspaper. In the late spring of 1905, he cajoled a printer in the community to provide him with credit and convinced a black real estate broker to rent him just enough office space for a card table, a borrowed kitchen chair, and a used typewriter. He spent his last twenty-five cents on pencils and notebooks, and without any capital to hire a staff, resolved to be his own reporter, editor, and circulation crew as well as publisher. Just one question remained — what to name this publication. A friend from his Sunday-morning strategy sessions finally came up with it, inspired by Abbott's vow to make his newspaper a "defender of his race."[50]

The first issue of *The Chicago Defender* appeared on May 5, 1905. Three hundred copies were printed, a six-column four-pager the size of a handbill that resembled the *Woodville Times* in layout, with a banner that read, "The Only Two-Cent Weekly in the City." None of the copies of that first printing survive; the earliest *Defender* seen by historians and biographers dates from September 1905. Even this later issue, however, reflects the many influences that had shaped Robert Abbott — his youth in post-slavery Georgia, his education at the pragmatic Hampton Institute, his radicalization at the 1893 World's Fair, and, of course, the formidable black leaders he had met, Frederick Douglass and Ida Wells in particular.

The front-page story of that earliest extant issue is entitled "Chicago's Progressive Men," and quotes a speech by Booker T. Washington's representative in the city, Dr. George Cleveland Hall, a physician at Provident Hospital. The other major front-page article is headlined "Africa, the Land of Milk and Honey," featuring an interview with a Liberian visitor to Chicago, a generally positive portrait of Africa at a time when the white press ignored the existence of Africans altogether.

The bill for the first edition's printing was $13.75, a sum Abbott raised through the pennies collected from the sales of individual copies as well as from advertising. Page 4 of the September 1905 issue is taken up by thirty-seven ads of varying sizes, from a butcher, a lawyer, a doctor, an undertaker, two tailors, and a moving man, as well as hotels, barbershops, nightclubs, and a candy store. One ad for "Ford's Original Ozonized Ox Marrow," complete with before and after pictures, claimed the product would straighten kinky hair, while several other notices describe various sizes of rooms and apartments for rent. Abbott sold these ads at rates that were highly negotiable—"as much or as little as an advertiser wanted, at his own price," he recalled years later.

Just a few weeks into publishing *The Defender*, Abbott realized that he would not be able to afford even the simple desk space he had rented at the real estate office, but Mrs. Lee solved that problem by offering to let him use her dining room as a newsroom. He took her up on this offer readily. Without his own resources to subsidize *The Defender*, Abbott had to depend entirely on the community's support. His strongest income stream came from subscribers, who paid a dollar per year. It was a business model created out of necessity rather than design, but it ensured the newspaper was beholden to the whole community, rather than one family, business concern, political party, or interest group, and created a bond with readers that would propel the newspaper through its precarious early years.[51]

## 2

------

# If You See It in *The Defender,* It's So

IN SEPTEMBER 1906, after Atlanta's most popular newspapers published unsubstantiated stories of black men committing sexual assaults against white women, a mob of ten thousand whites rampaged through the heart of that city's black neighborhood for three days. Hundreds of black men, women, and even children were assaulted; some were pulled off streetcars and beaten to death, their bodies hung from lampposts. Atlanta's police did nothing to stop the mayhem, while the rioting resulted in the deaths of at least twenty-four blacks and two whites, destroying dozens of businesses and homes in the process. Finally, state militia took control of the city, although unsurprisingly, the state's legislature, already dominated by segregationists, responded to the violence by passing laws further restricting blacks' voting rights.[1]

The Atlanta riots, taking place in his home state just one year after he began publishing *The Defender,* was a formative moment for Robert Abbott, deepening his resolve to make his newspaper a force to combat the pervasive racism of the era. Abbott's close friend and biographer, Dr. Metz T. P. Lochard, wrote that Atlanta "twisted Abbott's heart. Watching these riots as the vile manifestations of everyday discrimination and hate against Negroes, he developed a theory and a plan for solution which called for fearless militancy in protesting against wrongs, so that, with a sensitized mass population of Negroes, America would eventually be unable to avoid granting equal rights and opportunities."[2]

*The Defender*'s militancy, in turn, attracted an ever-greater number of supporters and volunteers to Mrs. Lee's kitchen table, where they wrote out their copy longhand until the Thursday-night deadline, when the paper was taken to the printer for typesetting. Like many of those who joined the newspaper in its early days, Frank "Fay" Young had no experience or education as a journalist. What he did have was a position as a dining-car waiter on the night shift of the Chicago and North Western Railway, a job that enabled him to collect the newspapers that were left behind by his passengers. Beginning in 1908, Young brought these publications to *The Defender*'s "office," where he and Abbott would scan them each morning for items they could rewrite from an African American angle, or simply copy wholesale. Young learned on the job, covering political stories, sports games, and social events at his own expense. He even bought his own typewriter on an installment plan.

The atmosphere in *The Defender*'s makeshift office was convivial to the point of being familial, with Mrs. Lee as a nurturing presence for the entire newspaper: "We swiped her cookies, used her kitchen, used her gas, cooked lunch on her stove with her utensils. Time and again some hungry soul got a free cup of java and a roll and went back to scribbling out his copy. We looked upon her as our MOTHER, and of course, felt that her home was ours."[3]

Mrs. Lee's generosity and Fay Young's free labor notwithstanding, *The Defender* in its first few years was sustained by Abbott's nearly superhuman ability to stretch a dollar. Publishing the newspaper had actually worsened Abbott's financial status at first, effectively giving him another mouth to feed when he could barely feed himself. He went without new shoes or clothes for years to ensure that *The Defender* had ink and newsprint, and often skipped meals. He limited the pennies he spent on public transportation, as well, walking where he needed to go every day but Friday, when the new issue came out.

"I used the street car but once a week," he recalled some years later, "and that was when I came from the [printing company] with my fifteen hundred or two thousand copies. Many have been the times that the 'old-timers' standing at the corner of 31st and State St., or along the route that I would travel going to 3159 S. State St., would stop and call me across the street and buy a paper from me. They would have a good laugh on me, saying 'I've got to buy a paper from this man. He's only kidding himself.'"[4]

Abbott withstood such mockery with equanimity and a reserve

of confidence in his mission. Along with the headlines on broad national topics, he filled the pages of his newspaper with information
and gossip that he collected about every church group, fraternal organization, and business, referencing as many individuals as possible
in keeping with the newspaperman's maxim "Names Make News." He
solicited subscriptions from his church choir and at city pool halls,
barbershops, bars, cabarets, restaurants, and residences, even going
door to door in the black neighborhood. If he was unable to inveigle
the adults, Abbott would entice the children with his youth column,
an innovation at a time when other black newspapers were just beginning to experiment with departmentalization. Nevertheless, his
competitors — there were already three other weekly black newspapers in Chicago when Abbott launched *The Defender* — ridiculed his
tactics, which they saw as cheap ploys to get readers.[5]

Amid the sniping from his journalistic peers, Abbott had to rely on
his influential friends, including Colonel John Marshall, who placed
notices in the paper publicizing his effort to build an armory for the
Eighth Regiment, which would also serve as a community center. As
the 1908 presidential elections approached, Marshall introduced Abbott to prominent figures within the campaign of Republican Party
nominee William Howard Taft, ensuring *The Defender* got a share of
the presidential advertising going to the city's black newspapers. *The
Defender*, in turn, covered Marshall's activities extensively, providing
a useful counterpoint to the frequently stereotypical articles about
the colonel in the white-owned press.[6]

Whether the Republicans advertised or not, *The Defender* steered
a decidedly independent line when it came to national politics, urging blacks to withhold their votes or even consider voting Democratic if the GOP did not deliver, a heretical proposition for most
African Americans at the time. But on the local level, Abbott's vision
for his newspaper aligned closely with the ambitions of Ed Wright,
the attorney who had organized the Congress on the Negro at the
1893 World's Fair. Brilliant and charismatic, with large, almond-
shaped eyes and a prodigious mustache, Wright had his sights set on
becoming the city's first black alderman on the City Council. Nearly
omnipotent in their wards, Chicago's seventy aldermen exercised
significant control over the city budget and staffing at various city

departments, appointing their supporters to jobs as policemen, fire-fighters, and the like. Wright had come to understand that the growing concentration of the black electorate in Chicago's Second Ward, where African Americans had become a quarter of the population, made the City Council an attainable goal.

Abbott was a reliable ally in Wright's effort, printing editorials in *The Defender* that cast the election of an African American alderman as a mark of empowerment. "We must have a colored alderman," read one editorial, "not because others are not friendly, but because we should be represented just the same as the Irish, Jews and Italians."[7]

Although many of Abbott's key supporters were, like him, young, ambitious militants, *The Defender* also won the backing of one of the community's most successful underworld figures. This came about on one particularly lean week in 1908, when Abbott was so desperate to raise the twenty-five dollars he needed to pay his printer for the latest edition, he even attempted to get money for his personal possessions: "I went to several places and tried to pawn my overcoat but found out that it would only bring me 30 cents," Abbott recalled. "I had no jewelry, not even a watch I could pawn to give me the necessary funds to pay for the expenses of my paper."[8]

All of Wednesday and Thursday, Abbott roamed the community, rebuffed by every businessman and banker along the way, until finally, at 3:00 a.m. Friday morning, just hours before he was due at the printers, he turned up at the Lakeside Club. Modeled on an Old West saloon, the Lakeside was equipped with a fine kitchen, expensive billiard tables, and a stage for performances, but its real business was gambling. The billiard tables were actually used for dice games; a lookout on the building's roof kept watch for police, using a buzzer to signal the gamblers to hide their cash and replace the dice on the tables with pool balls and cue sticks.

Having already heard that Abbott was in a quest for cash, the Lakeside's owner, Henry "Teenan" Jones, raised his hands above his head in a mock gesture when he saw the publisher push through the folding doors. "Here's the hold-up man," Jones quipped. But then he loaned Abbott fifty dollars, double the needed amount, explaining to the publisher later that he had admired his professionalism and dedication.[9]

Dapper and well-spoken, a derby typically perched on his head and a Havana cigar tucked in his mouth, Teenan Jones had been born into slavery in Alabama in 1861 but was liberated by Union troops along with his family and brought to rural Illinois by abolitionist missionaries. He came to Chicago as a restless teenager and spent the 1880s as an underground boxing promoter, gambler, and gunslinger in the district of bordellos, bars, and drug shops just north of the Dearborn corridor known as the Levee. Having earned his place as one of the vice district's bosses, Jones concentrated on opening clubs and cabarets that offered dazzling stage shows and, in the back rooms, a variety of other activities.[10]

Jones thrived in Chicago, where segregation did nothing to proscribe his activities and the police were thoroughly corrupt. He took care to establish amiable relationships with all of the city's political players and made himself an active presence at the community's major events, from the 1893 World's Fair on. Jones had more at stake in the struggle for civil rights than most, since his cabarets were among the few places where blacks and whites mixed socially and were thus targeted frequently, by both segregationists and self-declared moral reformers who saw something fundamentally indecent in interracial fraternization. Fortunately for Jones, both the police and the elected officials who controlled them were reliably bribable.

The relationship between the silk-smooth Jones and the upright Abbott grew closer after reformers shut down the Lakeside Club and Jones bought an ownership stake in another club, the Elite, which was across the street from Mrs. Lee's apartment. Now that they were neighbors, Abbott began to use Jones as an informal bank. The gambling lord, meanwhile, often insisted the publisher stay and enjoy a meal on the house when he came by on a fundraising visit. Abbott wrote frequently in *The Defender* of his appreciation for Jones's support, and handled him gently in print, quoting him as a spokesperson for the "sporting crowd."[11]

But just as the support of prominent Republicans had not stopped Abbott from keeping *The Defender* politically independent, Jones's patronage and friendship didn't stop Abbott from demanding in various editorials the closure of the Levee and the prohibition of alcohol. Abbott, concerned about the encroachment of the vice district into the black neighborhood, fulminated against the employment of young black men and women as "maids and piano players" in the corrupting Levee.[12]

In 1909, four years after the founding of *The Defender*, Mrs. Lee's teenage daughter Genevieve began handling clerical duties for the newspaper, while Phil Jones, another teen, came in after school to manage circulation, quickly displaying an innate talent for organization. The young man proved particularly adept at getting the paper to newsstands, recruiting newsboys, and sending out mailings, all of which resulted in an exponential growth in the number of issues sold. Soon, Abbott was boasting on *The Defender*'s banner a readership of twenty-five thousand, a figure he had calculated by multiplying the actual number of papers sold, between four thousand and six thousand, with the number of times he expected the paper was passed from person to person. It was a modest readership compared with the white-owned dailies, but already larger than all of the city's other black papers combined, reaching one out of ten African Americans in Chicago.[13]

Abbott raised his prices now, with a single copy costing five cents at the newsstand, and a yearly subscription a dollar fifty. On the strength of these increases, he hired J. Hockley Smiley, a talented journalist with skills as a reporter and editor as well as a designer. Until Smiley's arrival, *The Defender* resembled the other weeklies of the day, with a seven-column broadsheet layout in which articles on varying topics were arranged in a steady stream on a page, all of the headlines in identical sizes. Smiley quickly began using modern design concepts borrowed from the Hearst- and Pulitzer-owned dailies, separating the news and sports sections and spreading out headlines, with giant red letters across multiple columns to grab readers' attention. As with any other newspaper in the country, there were plenty of crime stories laced with salacious details, but the articles that really built circulation were those focusing on the atrocities committed in the South. Week after week, droves of new readers were drawn in by headlines like "100 Negroes Murdered Weekly by White Americans," "Texas Has Bloody Spree," and "Fifty Years of Frenzied Hatred."[14]

Some of the incidents hit closer to home. In the winter of 1909–10, *The Defender* covered Ida B. Wells-Barnett's investigation of the lynching of Will "Frog" James in Cairo, Illinois, a town just across the

Mississippi River from Missouri and Kentucky. James had been accused of murdering a white shop girl, but before he could be brought to trial, a mob numbering as many as ten thousand people dragged him from his cell, hanged him in the town square, and subjected him to gunfire until the rope around his neck snapped. The lynchers then dragged the body to the site where James had allegedly killed the young white woman and burned his mutilated corpse.

Wells-Barnett took on the white sheriff of the town who had allowed the lynching to take place and pressured the governor of Illinois to replace him, a campaign *The Defender* wholeheartedly endorsed. "If we only had a few men with the backbone of Mrs. Barnett," the newspaper editorialized, "lynching would soon come to a halt in America."

Stirring outrage was but one-half of Abbott and Smiley's formula to bring in more readers. Inspired by Frederick Douglass's words at the Chicago World's Fair, Abbott instructed *The Defender*'s staff to employ the word "Race" to denote African Americans, as in "The Race needs justice." Where dailies including the *Chicago Tribune* placed "colored" in parentheses after the names of African Americans, as in "Frederick Douglass (colored)," *The Defender* used the parentheses only to indicate that someone happened to be *white*, as in "Judge Richard Stone (white)."

The clear message to its readers was that *The Defender* was *their* publication, where they would find news about every aspect of their community that was ignored by the white-owned daily press.[15]

*The Defender* found its biggest story yet at the beginning of 1910 with the rise of another southern migrant who epitomized the spirit of defiance then emerging from the new generation of African Americans. Six feet tall, 220 pounds, with a shaven head and a dark complexion, John Arthur "Jack" Johnson was a Texas native who became the first black heavyweight boxing champion of the world in 1908 after defeating Canadian Tommy Burns in Australia. Johnson then moved to Chicago's black neighborhood, purchasing a house just off the Stroll at 3344 South Wabash Avenue and then moving his mother to the city from Texas; she stayed at home while he traveled frequently on theatrical tours that included boxing exhibitions.[16]

Johnson's 1908 win was internationally certified, but the sports columnists of America's daily newspapers, nearly unanimous in their indignation that a black man had won the heavyweight title, demanded a new match with a suitable white challenger. Johnson was willing, but no one could find a plausible "Great White Hope," as several columnists described this prospective contender, until finally, in early 1910, former champion Jim Jeffries agreed to come out of retirement. Jeffries, who had refused to fight African Americans during his tenure, now challenged Johnson to "regain the pugilistic crown for the white race," as the *Chicago Tribune* phrased it.[17]

*The Defender*, of course, was in Johnson's corner from the beginning, bringing all its journalistic tools to bear on behalf of the champion. The newspaper did not yet have a formal editorial page, but Abbott expressed his opinions in front-page commentaries as well as through the work of his editorial cartoonist, L. N. Hoggatt. A native of Mississippi and a graduate of the Art Institute of Chicago, Hoggatt gave a visual dimension to the newspaper's positions on myriad issues, from discrimination in the workplace to the federal government's purported predilection for sending aid to foreign governments over helping African American communities here at home. When the Johnson-Jeffries fight was announced, Abbott understood that the contest would have repercussions far beyond the athletic sphere, and directed his cartoonist to craft an appropriate image.

Hoggatt's cartoon depicted a smooth, serene, and smiling Johnson in the face of a brutish Jeffries, flanked by a trio of menacing wraiths labeled "negro persecution," "race hatred," and "prejudice," while an impish, rather sinister-looking Uncle Sam, labeled "public sentiment" and smoking a cigarette, cheers Jeffries on. In the stands surrounding the ring, Hoggatt placed throngs of angry birds in top hats and coats; these were, of course, the "Jim Crow delegates," booing Johnson in favor of their chosen champion, Jeffries. "He Will Have Them All to Beat," Hoggatt wrote over the drawing, with an equally portentous caption underneath: "The Future Welfare of His People Forms a Part of the Stake."[18]

Johnson, for his part, was a canny public relations operator who understood the newspaper's value in communicating with his core fans in the community. And so the athlete cultivated a relationship with the newspaper as he did with various other community institutions, visiting Abbott at Mrs. Lee's one day in early 1910 and purchasing a one-year subscription. "He stated that *The Defender* was the paper that the people needed," read the account of Johnson's visit, "and that he was proud to see a public organ so qualified to give real good and new advice and ever ready to defend those oppressed."[19]

In the run-up to the big fight, the difference in coverage of Johnson between the white-owned press and *The Defender* could not have been starker. The *Tribune* was typical of the dailies in that it occasionally interviewed Johnson but more often printed noxious content characterized by bias and stereotype. When Johnson spoke at a political rally supporting Ed Wright's efforts to become Chicago's first black alderman, the *Tribune's* reporter, after acknowledging that Johnson was articulate and clever, wasted ink by focusing on the boxer's gold-capped teeth and diamond tie pin. A bizarre poem about the upcoming fight published on another day included the author's desire to castrate Johnson and "hide him in a deep dense woods with barbed wire fence around."[20]

As he traveled around the country in towns that had never seen a black celebrity, Johnson was frequently arrested on charges that ranged from speeding to allowing his dog to bite a pedestrian — all cases that were eventually dismissed outright or in which Johnson was found not guilty. The dailies wrote about these incidents as if Johnson was an inveterate troublemaker, while *The Defender* treated them as obvious cases of harassment of a high-profile African American man.

That same spring, *The Defender* published a story entitled "Rich Pullman Car Clerk Stuns Judge," relating the case of a porter from New York who was indicted for speeding down Broadway at the rate of thirty miles per hour. At the hearing, the judge was astonished to learn that the porter was not a chauffer but had been driving his own car, all the more so when the porter explained he was speeding because he was on his way to close an important real estate deal. The judge set bond at a relatively high figure, $100, but the porter promptly paid and went on his way.

"This is nothing new in New York for a porter or a sleeping clerk to own a car, for it seems that there is an entirely new class of men getting into the service," *The Defender* wrote. "The twentieth century clerk [is] a real man and not the grinning monkey who cuts up didoes to get a tip."[21]

To the white public, the porters were a closing echo of the nation's antebellum past — the first porters had, in fact, been handpicked by the industrialist George Pullman, founder of the "Palace Car" company that bore his name, for their experience as house slaves — but their portrait in the pages of *The Defender* reflected the true respect they inspired within the African American community. Resplendent in their immaculate uniforms and caps, the porters were worldly and well informed from their travels across North America and their conversations with the nation's power brokers and business leaders. And in Chicago, they were a particularly visible presence. A majority of the nation's sixty-five hundred porters lived in the city, the nexus of rail lines from throughout North America and the headquarters for the Pullman Company, and they were active in politics, business, churches, and social clubs.[22]

*The Defender* celebrated the porters' entrepreneurial accomplishments and advocated for those who refused to tolerate racist behavior from passengers, even endorsing their carrying handguns when they traveled. The porters, in turn, reciprocated Abbott's support, stopping in *The Defender*'s office when they returned from their travels to bring news from far-flung places. Soon porters became not just subjects of articles in the paper but authors as well. The summer of 1910 saw the debut of "In the Railroad Center," a column written by a porter and featuring a combination of gossip, news, and business propositions. Read one typical item: "C. P. Marvin, onetime dining car conductor, at other times journalist, advertising man and raconteur, has a new system of reserving seats in the dining car, all his old friends wish him success."[23]

At the same time, the porters were becoming an integral part of *The Defender*'s circulation side. With the overwhelming majority of black people continuing to live in the South, Abbott knew that to make his newspaper gain enough subscribers to be self-sustaining he would have to reach people around the country. The porters, in regular contact with the black communities dispersed across the South and beyond, were perfect emissaries for *The Defender*; they knew every newsstand, barbershop, and other potential distribution point, from the largest cities to the tiniest rural settlements.

Through Fay Young, who worked the rails himself, Abbott offered the porters commissions to take bundles of the latest edition on their routes and sell subscriptions as they traveled. Many took him up on this, both because they supported the paper and because it provided them with additional income. It was not without its dangers, distributing the newspaper; authorities in some southern towns occasionally tried to seize what they regarded as a "radical" publication. The porters had many places on the trains where they could hide their copies, however, and it was not long before *The Defender* had begun to penetrate the entire Southland.[24]

"The railroad men circle the globe, and *The Chicago Defender* goes with them," enthused an early article thanking the porters for their efforts.[25]

As the July 4 Johnson-Jeffries championship approached, newspaper coverage grew more intense on both sides of the color line. Much was at stake, money as well as racial pride. Beyond the tens of thousands of dollars promised to the boxers and their promoters, there was private gambling, illegal but ubiquitous; the dailies all reported on the odds of the fight, which bet-makers set at 10–6 in favor of Jeffries. Ignoring the boxers' career records, whites mainly put their money on Jeffries while blacks backed Johnson.

With just days to go before the fight, the *Tribune* ran a column by one of Jeffries's coaches, another former champion, James "Gentleman Jim" Corbett, who summed up the sentiments of many American whites while inadvertently revealing their anxieties. "Will Johnson be able to check and master the overwhelming fear of a powerful white man," Corbett asked, ignoring the reality that Johnson already had beaten many white opponents, "a fear of centuries of growth that will undoubtedly well up in him when he sees the great adversary approaching with the light of grim battle in his eyes?"[26]

After legal wrangling prevented the fight from being held in California, it was set for Reno, Nevada. *The Defender* didn't have the funds to send a reporter out West, and besides, as July 4 that year fell on a Monday and the paper was printed on Friday, any coverage of the bout would have been days old in any event. On the night of the fight, then, Smiley, the managing editor, joined thousands of others at the Chicago Coliseum, an arena just north of the black neighborhood that usually held hockey games and political conventions. The crowd at the coliseum was both white and black, and Smiley reported that all were "agog" as "illuminated electrical figures nine feet high" acted out each move as relayed through telegraph reports, on a massive electrical board erected inside the arena.

Interest in the fight was unprecedented all over the country. Large crowds gathered outside the offices of daily newspapers in many cities, including the *Chicago Tribune* and *The Atlanta Georgian and News*, where large placards relayed blow-by-blow accounts of the fight as received over the wires.[27]

In Reno, a town of just a few thousand people, the event's organizers had created an open-air arena to hold twenty thousand spectators. Sheriff's deputies searched every man entering, all of them white, for weapons, while the five hundred white women who attended were seated in a special, cordoned-off area. Before this crowd, Johnson sized up Jeffries for the first three rounds under the blazing desert sun, striking small blows and then quickly retreating. Realizing how badly out of shape Jeffries was, however, Johnson began taunting his opponent, landing increasingly harder blows. By the eleventh round, Jeffries was bleeding profusely, unable even to gauge the distance of his punches, though still standing. In the fifteenth round, Johnson launched a right from his hip to Jeffries's jaw that sent him staggering. Jeffries dropped down to one knee, unable to get back up, and the fight was called.

"The fight of the century is over," wrote John L. Sullivan, a former heavyweight champion of the late nineteenth century, "and a black man is the undisputed champion of the world."

Sullivan, too, had refused to battle African American boxers during his tenure as champion, but Johnson had won him over with his skill and sportsmanship. Even Gentleman Jim Corbett, who had predicted that Johnson would crumble in racial fear, admitted that his man had been totally "outboxed."[28]

Angered by both the racial humiliation and losses from gambling on Jeffries, whites across the country attacked African Americans in the immediate aftermath of Johnson's victory, from the rural areas of the South to cities like Los Angeles, Cincinnati, and New York. The

*Tribune* summarized the incidents with a front-page report that began with a scorecard of the number of African Americans dead and injured. In Georgia and rural Tennessee, white gangs engaged groups of African Americans in gun battles, while in Houston, "Charles Williams, a negro [*sic*], was a little too vociferous in announcing the outcome on a trolley, and a white man slashed his throat."

The situation was even worse in Shreveport, Louisiana, where the *Tribune's* correspondent reported that law and order had broken down completely: "John Anderson, a negro [*sic*], is dead. His son, Henry Anderson, is dead; An unknown negro woman is dying, shot through the head. One or two negroes are injured and a race riot is imminent. The authorities seem to have no control over the situation in Madison and East Carroll parishes, and posses are scouring the whole country tonight."[29]

The violence waned after a couple of days, and then began the effort to erase the prize fight from the public consciousness. When a group of fledgling motion picture studios, which had pooled their resources to pay Johnson $50,000 and Jeffries $66,000 to film the event, tried to distribute their movie, it was banned in Washington, D.C., Atlanta, and Boston, as well as in Johannesburg, South Africa. Christian ministers and police commissioners led the crusade to stop the screenings, stating that the film would "corrupt public order." Chicago, where Republican mayor Fred A. Busse told the *Tribune* that he would not censor the film "simply because it showed a white man being knocked out by a negro [*sic*]," was an exception.[30]

If *The Defender's* columnists were appalled by the violence that erupted following the boxing match, they couldn't help but be thrilled by the fight's outcome. Johnson's victory had dealt a body blow to the *idea* of white supremacy even while obviating the use of a Johnson loss by propagandists. "We knew that editors in every state had already composed and pigeon holed their editorials of mockery and spite — and we shall not conceal the fact of our satisfaction at having these homilies and editorials all knocked into the wastebasket by the big fist of Jack Johnson," wrote Talladega College professor W. M. Pickens, in an article that was printed jointly by *The Defender* and *The Alabamian,* an African American paper in that southern state. "But sincerely now, it was a good deal better for Johnson to win and a few Negroes to be killed in body for it, than for Johnson to have lost and all Negroes to be killed in spirit for the pronouncements of inferiority from the whole white press."[31]

When Johnson returned home several days later, Chicago's black community came out in force, assembling a caravan of automobiles outside the Northwestern railroad station to escort the champion home. But the black welcome wagon was dwarfed by thousands of white men who swarmed the station as well, so many that the police were unable to hold them back, despite "free use of clubs and fists," according to the *Tribune*. Johnson emerged from his private railcar with a look of apprehension as the throng surrounded him, but the men were friendly; many had defied the odds and bet on Johnson, winning significant sums of money. The celebration continued all along Johnson's route home, and this time, police stopped him only to get his autograph.

The *Tribune* reporter described Johnson as a "simple, good-natured giant," and remarked on the public display of equanimity. "There was racial feeling in enormous quantities, for the colored people of the city were delirious with joy, but even when they were vastly in the majority there seemed to be no disposition to be obnoxious to the whites.

"On the other hand, any number of white men generously cheered their fellow American, fellow Chicagoan, in recognition of skill and physical prowess, and in disregard to the Provenance in wrapping it up in a black package."[32]

In the wake of Jack Johnson's victory, Chicago's African American community began to flex its own muscles, politically and legally. In late August, *The Defender* reported extensively on Ida B. Wells-Barnett and Ed Wright's efforts to stop the extradition of an African American man to his home state of Arkansas. Steven Green was accused of killing his landlord in a shootout that had left him severely injured. Having fled to Chicago, Green recovered from his injuries only to be arrested by city police and held for the arrival of an Arkansas sheriff.

Wells-Barnett and Wright led a team of civil rights activists who challenged the extradition in court, obtaining a writ of habeas corpus from a Cook County judge, but the police ignored the court order and turned Green over to the Arkansas sheriff. The sheriff escorted the accused onto a southbound train, taunting him that there was a "reception committee of a thousand waiting for [Green] with a lighted fire in Arkansas."

Wright kept up his efforts to halt the extradition, sending telegraphs to every station along the train's route, and at 4:30 p.m. he received a phone call from Sheriff Fred Nellis of Cairo, Illinois, the last stop before the train crossed into Missouri. Nellis, who had been appointed to replace Cairo's previous sheriff after a protest by Wells-Barnett a year earlier, agreed to intercept the Arkansas lawman and his prisoner at the city's depot, where they would have to get off the train in order to board the ferry across the Mississippi. Taking Green into his own custody, Nellis escorted him back to Chicago.

Before a packed courtroom several days later, Wright pointed out various anomalies in the extradition order and argued that Green would not get a fair trial in Arkansas. Green testified on his own behalf, admitting to the shooting but claiming that it was in self-defense, and said he feared being extradited because of the realities of the southern justice system.

The judge invalidated the extradition order, effectively freeing Green, and *The Defender* heaped praise on Wells-Barnett and Wright, pronouncing the legal victory as reminiscent "of the many miraculous escapes of our forefathers during slavery times."[33]

*The Defender* was taking shape as the first modern African American newspaper, with an attractive front page centered on a lead story and accompanying photo, and interior pages that contained a growing number of regular columns and feature articles geared to different sections of the readership. Abbott made a point of recruiting writers who appealed to church members, women, and theatergoers, as well as residents in outlying neighborhoods and suburbs.[34]

Abbott expanded the paper's appeal further when he convinced Julius Avendorph to become his society columnist. Like Fay Young and the porters who played a crucial role in *The Defender*'s distribution, Avendorph worked for the Pullman Company. But Avendorph was a messenger in the president's office, a well-positioned job that, combined with his impeccable personal style, allowed him to command great respect from the community's elite, a tiny number of families with hereditary wealth, as well as with the much larger group who aspired to such status. Avendorph's first contact with *The Defender* occurred when he wrote a scathing letter to the editor to deny comments attributed to him by "The Rambler," a gossip column. In response, Abbott persuaded him to improve the newspaper's coverage by writing his own column, and Avendorph was soon lecturing the parvenu on proper dress and manners, while admonishing his own set for failing to live up to his exacting standards. "Diamonds are beautiful to wear and valuable to have," Avendorph scoffed on a typical week, "but they have no place at all when it comes to evening dress, and gold is only to be used when a dinner coat is to be worn."[35]

The same winter of 1910 that Avendorph began his column, Abbott launched a campaign to win better wages and working conditions for Pullman Company porters. Articles in *The Defender* pointed out that the porters were expected to respond to any request from a passenger at any hour while the trains were moving, and that they had nowhere to sleep except for the cars used for dining and smoking. Many passengers thoughtlessly called the porters "George," the name of the company's owner, or used outright racist epithets, insults the porters rarely protested, a reticence Abbott attributed to a dependence on tips. Most galling was that there was no chance for advancement: blacks could not become conductors or hold other positions on the railways.

"They spend many days from home and often in places where they are obliged to go hungry," Abbott wrote in one editorial. "The travelling public must know that these men work 24 hours a day and a rich railroad company should no longer try to elect their services for practically nothing."[36]

Abbott's genius was to create a newspaper that could simultaneously offer news for the Pullman porter as well as the social climber, the "Race Man," and the businessman. *The Defender*'s independence had been hard-fought, a consequence of its editor's stubbornness as well as his principles, but by the beginning of 1911, enough revenue was trickling in that Abbott could ask Fay Young to leave his railroad job and work full-time for the newspaper. Abbott could only offer a salary comparable with a position at the Post Office, less than what he made as a dining-car waiter. Young knew that the newspaper's finances were still precarious, however, and, anxious to do what he could to help the Race, accepted the job readily.

Young did ask Abbott to assume responsibility for the installment payments on his typewriter. A one-hundred-dollar Oliver, it became the newsroom's first real machine, placed reverently on an upturned egg crate. In addition to writing and editing, Young's duties now included distribution and serving as the newsroom's cook. On those nights when the staff stayed late, each of them contributed ten cents for meat and vegetables, which Young cut up, placed in a pot, and stirred until it was stew.[37]

In March 1911, *The Defender* launched an all-out effort to block a theatrical production in Chicago called *The Clansman*. Based on a best-selling novel of the same name written by Thomas Dixon, a white southern minister and author, *The Clansman* was part of a widespread effort in universities and popular publications to rewrite the period of American history just after the Civil War. Dixon and his ilk, including a childhood friend, Princeton University professor Woodrow Wilson, wrote scholarly essays as well as outright fiction that ennobled the ex-Confederates who violently resisted efforts to emancipate the former slaves. Dixon himself boasted that his book was a propaganda piece that would help white southern oligarchs justify segregation in their states.

Labeling Dixon a "Negro-Hater Playwright," *The Defender* enlisted editorial cartoonist L. N. Hoggatt, who drew Dixon's head on a snake's body, wriggling through the Mason-Dixon Line to terrify a young girl wearing a sash that reads "The Northern Public." A subsequent editorial urged its readers to use any and all means to block the production: "Friends, brothers, countrymen, don't lend me your ears, but use your common sense, the almighty dollar, the shot-gun or anything that will stop this Virginia Dog from staging this infamous lie in our city."[38]

It was the beginning of an all-out propaganda war with the South, a contest in which the tiny *Defender*, an eight-page broadsheet with a circulation approaching ten thousand, held together by the willpower of its editor and the commitment of Chicago's nascent African American community, would take on the most powerful media entities of the day. It would be a high-stakes campaign that saw the white South strike at Abbott directly, but one that ultimately positioned the newspaper for its greatest accomplishment yet.

# 3

## Getting the South Told

THE FRONT PAGE of *The Defender*'s November 4, 1911, issue was dominated by an article headlined "Southern White Gentleman Rapes Colored Lady; Is Killed by Husband." Written by an anonymous correspondent in the town of Washington in Wilkes County, Georgia, the article recounted a series of events that began when an African American woman, Mrs. A. B. Walker, was assaulted by a white planter named C. S. Hollenshead, whose family owned the land on which Walker and a number of other black families lived and worked. Describing Hollenshead as a "blood sucking vampire," the correspondent said the planter attacked Mrs. Walker when she visited his store, leaving "her clothes in shreds, her body lacerated."

When Mrs. Walker's husband learned of the assault, he got his shotgun and, seeking out the planter, "went to the store of the beast," the correspondent explained, "and shot him down like the dog he was."

Perfectly aware of his likely fate, the husband, A. B. Walker, turned himself in to the local sheriff, W. O. Bobo. Sheriff Bobo bound Walker and put him on a horse-drawn car under cover of night, ostensibly to transfer him to the Washington town jail. But as they reached the town's outskirts, they were intercepted by a mob of fifty armed men, who overpowered the sheriff and took Walker off to be murdered. The would-be lynchers were thoroughly drunk, however, and Walker was able to slip away unnoticed.

Walker was still at large when *The Defender* went to press, though the correspondent wrote that whites in the area were determined to exact their vengeance, citing their outrage over Walker's allegation that Hollenshead had assaulted his wife. The anonymous correspondent scoffed at such professed pique.

"It is a well-known fact," the correspondent wrote, "that the majority of the white males of the south revel in the intimacy of our women and think, like the small, narrow-minded dogs that they are, that all our women are susceptible to the allurements of their arts and persuasions."[1]

The Walker case was big news in Georgia, with reports in both *The Atlanta Constitution* and *The Atlanta Georgian and News* offering nearly identical facts to those in *The Defender,* right down to the drunkenness of the would-be lynch mob. But while those other papers admitted that there had been some sort of confrontation with Mrs. Walker, they denied the charge of rape and presented A. B. Walker instead as an "assassin" of an innocent Hollenshead. Instead of anger over the sexual assault of his wife as Walker's motive for the slaying, these papers argued, improbably, that Walker was the ring leader of a group of Hollenshead employees who had conspired to murder the planter and thereby hide their debts. In its coverage of Walker's escape, *The Constitution* betrayed its bias in the subhead: "After Taking Walker from the Sheriff, Mob Bungles the Job," stating in the text of the article that Walker had escaped en route to a "suitable lynching place."[2]

*The Defender's* article was reprinted in a black-owned publication based in Atlanta called the *Georgia Broad Axe.* Although the *Broad Axe* misattributed the article to a nonexistent newspaper, the "Chicago Chronicle," the real source was soon discovered, and *The Constitution* reported that white people in Wilkes County organized a mass meeting at which they decided to hire detectives from the Pinkerton Agency to travel to Chicago and investigate *The Defender's* charges. The allegation of rape, concurred the Wilkes County residents according to *The Constitution,* was "a reflection against every white citizen of the South."[3]

In late November 1911, two white Pinkerton agents did indeed travel to Chicago, where they entered Mrs. Lee's second-floor apartment at 3159 South State Street, confronted Robert Abbott in the kitchen, and threatened to haul the editor back to Georgia if he didn't reveal the identity of the correspondent who wrote the initial article about the Walker case. Abbott stalled the Pinkertons while a messenger ran through the neighborhood alerting the community's leaders; fortuitously, his plea was answered by Ed Wright and George Cleveland Hall, a physician at Provident Hospital, who also happened to be the personal representative of Booker T. Washington.

Years later, Abbott recounted what happened when Wright and Hall arrived: "The papers of Atlanta all published big stories speaking of the fact the editor of *The Defender* was to be brought back there on a certain morning on the 9:40 train. Ed Wright and Dr. Hall came into the fight with these two men. They ran the Georgia 'gentlemen' out of *The Defender* office and finally out of Chicago, and the men went back without 'his honor,' the editor."[4]

Abbott did not record the precise strategy his friends used against the detectives, but the Pinkertons' case against him was flimsy, of course, as he had not committed any crime in Georgia, and there was little legal precedent to prosecute a publisher of a newspaper in another state, let alone extradite him. One thing is clear: whatever combination of arguments and threats Hall and Wright employed, the tables had been turned. The Pinkertons not only let Abbott alone, they were sufficiently intimidated to offer Wright a consulting contract after the encounter, keeping him on the payroll for years to come.[5]

On the other side of the Mason-Dixon Line, there was neither justice nor free speech, however. After Walker got away from the lynch mob the first time, a Washington town policeman traveled to Atlanta and took Julian St. George White, the editor of the *Georgia Broad Axe,* into custody on a charge of criminal libel, and then brought him back to the town. *The Atlanta Georgian and News* frankly predicted "rough treatment" for White, but members of Georgia's black community interceded, issuing a public apology and demanding that *The Defender* retract its article. *The Constitution* quoted a letter from a black leader in Atlanta named H. L. Johnson, who implored, "In God's name, can't you good white people there forgive this crime after White has begged pardon, made public retraction in the newspapers, and have *The Defender* to do like?"

Three days later, *The Constitution* reported that a Washington judge, conceding that the editor indeed faced a strong chance of being lynched, had ordered a transfer of the accused to a jail in Augusta. White arrived in the new town unmolested and was allowed to post bond and return to Atlanta.[6]

As for Walker, however, the white authorities employed a variety of tactics to capture him, including taking hostages. After his initial escape, *The Georgian* reported that four other African Americans from the Hollenshead plantation were jailed in Washington town, allegedly as members of the conspiracy dreamed up against the planter, but more likely to pressure Walker into surrendering; one of the "suspects" was released when it was determined he was a child. Walker was indeed captured a few days later, put through a hasty trial, and sentenced to death, but on November 26, he escaped Sheriff Bobo a second time, bolting as the sheriff prepared to transfer him to another town, again for the official reason of his safety. One hundred and fifty men assisted by bloodhounds were "now scouring the woods in search of the negro [*sic*]," *The Constitution* noted. "A lynching seems inevitable if he is recaptured."[7]

Sheriff Bobo spent his Thanksgiving holiday looking for the escapee, and finally, on Saturday, December 2, after an all-night chase by dozens of men from three nearby counties, Walker was captured a third time. Defying *The Constitution*'s prediction, Walker was not immediately lynched, perhaps because several businessmen and politicians had placed an $800 bounty on his capture and several factions were claiming the money.[8]

Three days later, just before his trial in Washington began, Walker gave an interview to a reporter from *The Georgian* in which he confessed to the murder of the planter but said he acted alone and had planned the killing for more than two weeks, a point he presumably underscored to dispel the conspiracy theory and keep others from suffering his fate. Immediately after the interview, Walker was brought into the courtroom for resentencing, but as the judge read out the order of execution, T. B. Hollenshead, the dead planter's brother, who had been observing the proceedings in the courtroom, produced a pistol and fired it straight at the accused. The bullet tore through Walker's right cheek and left jaw, but that didn't stop the execution — Hollenshead was restrained, the wound was bandaged, and Sheriff Bobo escorted him to the gallows. There would be no third escape: Walker died when the rope snapped his neck. His body was turned over to the state medical college.

There was a minor brouhaha over the shooting of Walker during the resentencing, however. *The Constitution* noted that while there had been "great sympathy" for the murdered planter's family, "the dignity of the court had been grossly outraged" by the shooting. Nevertheless, no charges were ever filed.[9]

By the beginning of the new year, the Walker case and *The Defender's* role in it had attracted the attention of the new national civil rights organization founded by W. E. B. Du Bois and others, the National Association for the Advancement of Colored People. The January 1912 issue of *The Crisis,* the NAACP magazine edited by Du Bois, called Walker's story "a most extraordinary case of lynching," noting that editor White himself was still facing a legal penalty and *The Defender* had been "persecuted" by the Pinkertons, even as Hollenshead's brother was undisturbed after firing a handgun and injuring an accused man during a public court proceeding. "Georgia law declares that the truth is libel if it incites to violence," *The Crisis* wrote.[10]

*The Defender* took issue with *The Crisis* only in its implication that the Pinkertons had been a serious threat to the newspaper, maintaining instead that the Pinkertons' visit was aimed at terrorizing blacks in the South by demonstrating that authorities in Georgia could reach all the way up into the North. "We would like our race in Georgia to know," the newspaper proclaimed, "that so long as a God liveth and as news comes to us in the regular course, *The Defender* will print, print, print."[11]

In March, editor White of the *Broad Axe,* pleading guilty to a charge of libel, paid a $400 fine and was sentenced to a year on a chain gang. *The Constitution* was pleased with the outcome, though it had to explain that White had not actually pleaded guilty to libeling Hollenshead. In fact, the charge was related to his admission, under questioning, of purposely misattributing *The Defender's* article to the entirely fictitious "Chicago Chronicle." In other words, White pleaded guilty to libeling *The Defender,* almost surely a legal concoction that resulted from the Georgia court's need to find him guilty of *something.*[12]

For a few years, Smiley and Abbott had printed a tag line on *The Defender*'s masthead, "If You See it in *The Defender*, It's So." That summer, they added new tag lines. "A Fearless, Honest Champion for the People" and "World's Greatest Weekly Newspaper" appeared in boxes flanking the paper's name, now printed out in a neat Gothic type. No mistake that the masthead now closely resembled the *Tribune*'s, which had declared itself the "World's Greatest Newspaper" some years earlier.[13]

In July 1912 *The Defender*'s J. Hockley Smiley attended the grand opening of Jack Johnson's Café de Champion, just off the Stroll's main intersection. It was a haphazard affair; Smiley waited outside the club with a large crowd all day, while inside, a legion of workers scrambled to get the establishment ready. Johnson finally arrived at 9:00 p.m. in one of his racecars, accompanied by his mother, and the doors opened to the public a short time later. Upon admittance, Smiley was dazzled by the club's hand-painted ceilings, glittering chandeliers, well-stocked bar, and magnificent furnishings, all decorated in red with touches of gold. Smiley noticed, however, that Johnson remained mysteriously silent throughout the festivities, brooding in the corner of the room when he should have been enjoying the high point of his popularity within the community.[14]

It soon became obvious that all was not well in the Johnson household. One evening that fall, while patrons danced below and the band played, Johnson's wife, Etta, a thirty-one-year-old former New York socialite, shot herself in the head in their third-floor apartment above the café. Johnson returned home to find her gravely injured and brought her to the hospital, where she died after several efforts to revive her.[15]

*The Defender* covered the event sympathetically, noting that the champion was "agonized" by the incident. But in the white press, Johnson came under immediate suspicion. The *Tribune*, for instance, ran a story under the headline "Johnson Denies Beating Up Wife." Without quoting any sources by name, the story claimed that Etta, who was white, had been ostracized by many of her former friends in New York's social scene after her marriage to Johnson, while Johnson's black friends, stung by the champ's decision to marry outside the community, had shunned her.[16]

When, just two months later, Johnson began a relationship with another white woman, Lucille Cameron, a nineteen-year-old former prostitute, the *Tribune* went from suspicious to apoplectic. Cameron's mother, the newspaper dutifully reported, was so outraged by her daughter's dating a black man that she traveled to Chicago to try to end the union. Curiously, she hadn't protested Lucille's previous career as a prostitute. Interracial relationships might have been legal in Illinois, but they were still anathema to most whites in America. During a public protest, a mob hung Johnson in effigy from a downtown lamppost, and the Chicago City Council considered revoking the license of the Café de Champion. The *Tribune* also quoted Booker T. Washington at length, the first time that a black leader had received such respectful treatment, denouncing Johnson for "doing a grave injustice to his race." Ultimately, federal prosecutors announced they would charge Johnson for violating the Mann Act, which had been passed by Congress in 1910 to stop human trafficking of women.[17]

Within the black community, feelings over Johnson's behavior were decidedly mixed. Interracial relationships were nothing new; a club for biracial couples called the Manasseh Society had been active in the city for decades. But these couples were still rare, and each high-profile relationship was carefully scrutinized. Consorting with prostitutes, on the other hand, clearly crossed a line for the community's upright leadership. The elders of the Appomattox Club, a political fraternity founded by Ed Wright, demanded that the boxer come before them, and enlisted Teenan Jones, who knew Johnson from the days when boxing was still an underground sport, to escort him in. Ever the intermediary between the world of vice and the elites, Jones characterized the meeting in a column for *The Defender* some years later as an inquisition. Community elders got up one after another to criticize Johnson's character and express their disapproval for intermarriage generally, but the champ flatly told them he would do what he wanted when it came to matters of love. "I do want to say," Jones recalled Johnson saying, "that I am not a slave and that I have the right to choose who my mate will be without dictation from any man."[18]

In November 1912, Woodrow Wilson was elected president of the United States, the first Democrat to fill the White House in a generation. Well aware of his past pronouncements on race and wary of the influence of southern segregationists on the Democratic Party generally, *The Defender,* nevertheless, covered Wilson's campaign extensively and openmindedly. As a professor at Princeton, Wilson, a Virginia native whose father had been a chaplain for the Confederacy, had been part of the group of revisionist historians who twisted the conventional narrative of the Civil War and its aftermath to justify segregation in the modern day. Writing about the Reconstruction era in the January 1901 issue of *The Atlantic Monthly,* for example, Wilson had characterized the newly emancipated slaves as "a host of dusky children untimely put out of school," not ready to assume the responsibilities of voting and holding elective office.

In this election, however, the Republican vote had been split by incumbent William H. Taft and ex-president Theodore Roosevelt, who was running as an independent under the Progressive, or "Bull Moose," Party. Neither Taft nor T.R. had an especially close relationship with African Americans, whereas Wilson had made a concerted personal effort to court black votes, recruiting black representatives and meeting with black leaders like W. E. B. Du Bois. One minister who met Wilson wrote in *The Defender* that the candidate promised to veto any legislation "inimical to colored people," denied that he would repeal the Fourteenth and Fifteenth Amendments to the Constitution, and generally came across as "conscientious and sincere."

With the Republican vote split, Wilson won the general election through a plurality, rather than an outright majority, capturing a number of states in New England and other regions that were normally out of reach for Democrats. Although exact figures of the black vote were hard to come by, *The Defender* determined that a "substantial" number of blacks supported him. Nevertheless, the question remained as to whether Wilson would revert back to type once he was installed as president.[19]

In May 1913 Jack Johnson was convicted under the Mann Act for having taken a white former girlfriend from Pittsburgh to Chicago and "establishing her in an immoral flat," providing her with the resources to open her own bordello on the South Side. One month later, a judge sentenced the champ to one year and a day in the Joliet penitentiary, noting that Johnson had not fulfilled his duty as a role model. "The defendant is one of the best-known men of his race," the judge said, "and his example is far-reaching."[20]

Johnson was granted two weeks in which to file an appeal, however, and a few days later, he turned up in Montreal, Canada, with Lucille and a small entourage by his side, preparing to board a steamship for France. If the *Tribune* editorial page was infuriated, *The Defender* was delighted, publishing a front-page article under the headline "Famous Fistic Gladiator Sails for France After Being Persecuted in the United States." The columnist noted that the Mann Act was, in fact, intended to stop the trafficking of women, which could not possibly be said to apply to Johnson; moreover, there were actually women being held in virtual slavery at that moment, many of them in brothels regularly patronized by white men in positions of power. "Jack married one or two white women," the columnist wrote. "He did not dishonor them. How many congressmen, governors, judges and clergymen of the white race have consorted with colored women?"[21]

When Johnson arrived in the French port of Le Havre on July 7, a *Defender* correspondent was there waiting. Though he promised to return to the United States in time for a trial on additional Mann Act charges in October, Johnson gave other indications that he might be planning an extended exile, announcing, for instance, his plans to open a Café de Champion in France. Abbott, in turn, promised to publish regular reports on the champ's activities in a new column called "Jack Johnson's Doings Abroad."[22]

By the first summer after his inauguration, President Wilson had greatly disappointed black leaders, not only reneging on his promises, but also segregating federal departments, including Treasury and the Post Office, which had long had integrated workforces. In August 1913 *The Defender* printed a petition from the Boston-based publisher Monroe Trotter, who, having actively supported Wilson during the campaign, felt betrayed by the segregation of the federal government. One month later, an editorial lambasted Wilson for ignoring the NAACP and kowtowing to southern white Democratic congressmen, characterizing him as a "figurehead in the president's chair who will jump at the beck and call of such wreckers of the Constitution."[23]

The protests continued into the new year. In February 1914, *The*

*Defender* tallied all of the African American federal officials in the Justice Department, foreign service, and postal service who had been replaced by white southerners. Meanwhile, Democrats in the U.S. Congress had introduced bills to repeal the Fifteenth Amendment to the Constitution and, among other such measures, segregate street-cars in the District of Columbia, prompting *The Defender* to editorialize that Wilson's first twelve months in office had been "politically the most disastrous year since Reconstruction."[24]

Smiley continued to fine-tune the newspaper's design, plucking ideas from the mainstream press and adapting them to *The Defender's* purposes. In March 1914 he had one of the cartoonists draw a new masthead that closely resembled the shield-and-eagle design of the Hearst-owned *Chicago American,* albeit with an owl in place of the eagle, and that fall, he added an eighth column to the layout, such that *The Defender's* front page now blended in very easily with other publications on the newsstand.[25]

The updated look was accompanied by a more confident editorial posture. In the summer of 1914, *The Defender* stepped up its campaign to support the Pullman porters, covering a series of meetings with company officials at the newly opened Black Belt YMCA, a recreation and housing facility at the corner of Thirty-Eighth Street and Wabash Avenue where many of the porters lived. The porters demanded relatively minor improvements in their conditions, such as better sleeping quarters on the rails and guaranteed meals when they arrived in segregated southern towns, but Pullman Company officials responded obdurately, suggesting that better treatment of passengers would bring in larger tips. "We are after helping the porter to discard that grouch he wears and put on a smile that won't come off," said the company's chief service inspector during an interview with *The Defender.*[26]

Undaunted, the porters spoke out during the meetings and then flooded *The Defender* with letters expressing their frustrations: "After having your rest broken day and night," wrote one porter, "and after travelling from two to six thousand miles per week, waiting on all sorts of people who don't give you a penny, why would you smile?"[27]

• • •

When World War I erupted in Europe that summer, a cartoon appeared on *The Defender*'s new, dedicated editorial page showing a skeleton on a throne wearing the military uniform and spiked helmet of the German Kaiser under the headline "Ruler Pro-Tem," with an extended caption that began, "We should be thankful we are not subjects of Europe."[28]

Black America was in accord with the large national majority who demanded, for the moment, that the country stay out of the conflict in Europe and supportive of President Wilson's declaration that the United States would remain strictly neutral. But in every other area, *The Defender* chronicled a rapidly deteriorating relationship with the president. That fall, Boston publisher Monroe Trotter led a delegation to the White House and objected in strong terms to the segregation of federal agencies. As recounted in *The Defender,* Wilson told the black delegation that he had investigated their complaints and concluded they were unfounded. "Segregation had been inaugurated to avoid friction between the races," the president lectured.

Trotter wasn't having it, challenging the president directly: "Only two years ago you were heralded perhaps as the second Lincoln, and now the Afro-American leaders who supported you are being hounded as false leaders and traitors to their race." These words led Wilson to charge that the publisher "sassed" him, a description *The Defender* mocked in an editorial that accompanied the news article describing the meeting: "The President was angry — we are glad. We hope he was angry twice, first because he forgot the high office he was holding and second we hope he was angry with Woodrow Wilson for breaking faith with the high ideals he has professed to represent."[29]

"It has been the custom of the Black press to teach conservative means to stop this outrageous treatment of this defenseless group of people and let law take its course," began a January 1915 front-page editorial on a recent spate of lynchings in the South, "but such counsel has been so much wasted breath." The editorial recounted an incident that occurred the prior week in Monticello, Georgia, where a man accused of illegally selling liquor was beaten by a mob, then hanged along with his son and two daughters. In providing the horrifying details of the incident, *The Defender* applauded the daughters for displaying a courageous defiance even as they were about to be killed, noting that "while these two defenseless women stood with the hemp ropes around their necks, and while the fiends taunted them in unspeakable language, they courageously told them of their faults and had their teeth knocked down their throats for it."[30]

*The Defender* was filled with reports of such incidents during these months, leading the editorial page to call more and more regularly for a militant response to southern cruelty. A series of news stories and editorials that winter focused on the case of Green Gibson in the unfortunately named town of Fairplay, North Carolina. Gibson and his son were driving a horse-drawn buggy through the countryside when a confrontation with a group of white men turned violent. Green's son was pulled from the buggy and beaten to death, but Green was able to grab his rifle and take cover behind a nearby bridge. Before it was over, he had killed eight white men and wounded four others before he was killed himself. The high death toll shocked the whites in the area, *The Defender* reported, and prompted them to bury the men shot by Gibson in secret. "Those eight silent funerals after dark have brought peace and quiet in and around the town of Fairplay, N.C.," stated an editorial, "and they taught the race a wholesome lesson: If you must die, die fighting."[31]

*The Defender* never went so far as to call for armed insurrection, only armed self-defense, but this militant language attracted droves of new readers, even as it provoked more southern law enforcement to try to seize the newspaper. Nearing the end of his first decade at the helm of his newspaper, Robert Abbott was still living at Mrs. Lee's and still struggling frequently to make payroll, but he could see great progress. Circulation had tripled in the past five months, and the newspaper was on sale throughout the country as well as abroad, in London, Monrovia, Liberia, and the Philippines. The porters had extended not only *The Defender*'s subscription base, but its news network, across the continent. The paper now included news from California to Minnesota and Kansas as well as from all points south and east. For deliveries within Chicago, Abbott now had two trucks and twenty-five paperboys, boasting that it took four men eight hours to supply the newsstands for the newspaper's forty-two thousand readers.

And Abbott was only getting started. He called on the porters as well as dining-car waiters and touring actors and musicians to sell ever more subscriptions. His readers' dollars were directly helping the newspaper advance the cause of the Race, and the more they contributed, Abbott pledged, the faster things would change. "*The Defender* is in the fight hot and heavy," read another missive from that time. "Its generals are massing their army. It has the men ready to fight; it needs only the ammunition. That ammunition is your subscription."[32]

For the February 1915 primary elections, Chicago's black vote was being heavily courted by one candidate for mayor, Republican William Hale Thompson, known as Big Bill. Tall and wide as his moniker suggested, Thompson, scion of one of the city's wealthiest families, had worked briefly on western ranches in his youth, where he had acquired a penchant for speaking bluntly and wearing cowboy hats. Big Bill had forged his alliance with the black community at the turn of the century, when he had served a term as alderman of the Second Ward and the community was just a fraction of its current size. Now the black population held a clear majority in the Second Ward and probably the Third as well, a base sizable enough to sway the Republican primary one way or the other.

Big Bill paid special attention to Ida B. Wells, who played an important role in the woman suffrage movement and was thought to be influential with these new voters—the 1915 elections, after all, would be the first in which the women of Illinois were able to cast ballots. Making a special appearance at Wells's political organization, the Alpha Suffrage Club, which she had formed to train and organize women to vote, he pledged to distribute city jobs to African Americans, according to the group's regular column in *The Defender*.[33]

Big Bill's efforts notwithstanding, the newspaper was focused on a more local contest: Ed Wright was on the move, coordinating with *The Defender* in an all-out effort to finally get the first black alderman elected. Having been unsuccessful in his own bid, Wright decided to become kingmaker to his protégé, Louis B. Anderson, Robert Abbott's close friend from the days of the 1893 World's Fair. Wright had built up a formidable political organization by this time and was well prepared for the Republican primary; still, Anderson was an insurgent challenging the white men who ran the Second Ward, who were well aware of their fiefdom's shifting demographics and had put forward their own African American candidate, Oscar De Priest.

Six feet tall, with an athletic build and a pompadour of curly hair, De Priest was fair enough to be mistaken for white, but he was no puppet of the ward bosses. In fact, he was another veteran of the 1893 World's Fair, one of those who gathered in the cafés on the Stroll along with Abbott and his cohort. As well as amassing a small fortune from his real estate business, De Priest had learned, like Wright, how party operatives got out the vote through networks of precinct workers directed by a hierarchy of captains and committeemen: he had assembled his own support base among waiters and barbers unions, Baptist and Methodist ministers, physicians and pharmacists.[34]

*The Defender* supported Anderson over De Priest and six other candidates, but in the end, De Priest won the primary decisively, with 3,194 votes to Anderson's 2,632, and the newspaper devoted the entire front page to his victory. Anderson wholeheartedly endorsed De Priest, who also issued a conciliatory message to his rival, and for its part, the newspaper announced that it too would devote its efforts to ensuring a black candidate would be elected alderman. "From this issue we will as vigorously and as persistently advocate the election of Mr. De Priest as we did the nomination of Mr. Anderson," stated an editorial in that issue.[35]

*The Defender* didn't mention the results of the party primaries for mayor, but Big Bill Thompson had also won that night, securing the Republican nomination by just over 2,000 votes, with heavy turnout from the black community having been the decisive factor in his victory. Nevertheless, the Democrats had outpolled Republicans in the primary by more than 100,000 votes, suggesting that Thompson would be the underdog in the upcoming general election, so he enlisted Wright and Anderson as well as De Priest directly into his operation to ensure a massive black turnout.

Thompson was direct in his promises: "I'll give your people jobs," he said at one rally. "And if any of you want to shoot craps go ahead and do it. When I'm mayor the police will have something better to do than break up a little friendly crap game." The latter words were surely calculated to attract the support of underworld figures like Teenan Jones, who continued to wield great clout even after reformers had officially shut down the Levee district several months earlier.

In practice, the vice dens had done little more than change the signs out front.[36]

At the end of March, with the election less than two weeks away, Thompson gave an extended interview to *The Defender,* a notable move at a time when most white politicians simply ignored black newspapers. But what Thompson said was even more interesting to *The Defender*'s readers, especially when he answered directly a question about whether schools in the black neighborhood would be segregated. "There will be no discrimination in my administration," he declared.

He said little else, but that had been more than enough. A portrait photograph of the candidate accompanied the article, with a caption endorsing him as "the choice of the Afro-American voters."[37]

While Chicago was absorbed by its own politics, activists in other parts of the country were fighting to stop the silent film *Birth of a Nation* from being shown. Ostensibly the story of two white families, one from the North and the other from the South, during the years before, during, and immediately after the Civil War, *Birth of a Nation* won audiences over with epic battle scenes using thousands of actors, horses, and set pieces. The film's director, D. W. Griffith, son of a Confederate officer, had adapted the script from Thomas Dixon's *The Clansman,* and it contained many plot elements calculated to inflame white resentment, especially incidents of sexual trespass committed by black men against white women. The film concludes with the Klan's triumphant ride to block African Americans from reaching the polls on Election Day, hammering home the theme that blacks could not be trusted — not with white women and not with the ballot box.[38]

Dixon used some of Woodrow Wilson's historical writings in *Birth of a Nation*'s intertitles and convinced the president to screen it in the White House in February 1915, just ten days after the film's opening in Los Angeles. Griffith subsequently showed the film to the chief justice of the U.S. Supreme Court and a select group of congressional representatives and senators before taking the film on the road.[39]

Nevertheless, when *Birth of a Nation* arrived in New York City in March, *The Defender* reported that the Board of Censors blocked it from being shown. In an interview, the board chairman zeroed in on one scene in which a black man chases a young white girl with the intent of raping her. "My objection was personal," the chairman told *The Defender*'s reporter. "It is because the story was bound to arouse race hatred."[40]

When *Birth of a Nation* opened in Boston the following month, *The Defender* gave front-page treatment to a mass protest of thousands of blacks and whites who gathered outside the theater. Led by Monroe Trotter, the protesters at first tried to buy tickets to see the film. But when the black members of the group were refused, they tried to force their way in; it took two hundred club-wielding policemen to drive them back. Trotter was among those arrested that day, and the article compared the event to the antislavery gatherings in Boston during the 1850s, noting that one of the last living abolitionists was involved in the protest. Trotter and his colleagues took their case to Massachusetts's governor, but the film continued to play to large crowds while they waited for the state legislature to block further screenings.

"Meanwhile," *The Defender* lamented, "this photo-play continues to bring in revenue for the promoters at the expense of the Afro-American race everywhere."[41]

Still in exile, Jack Johnson agreed to fight Jess Willard for the world heavyweight boxing championship in Havana, Cuba, on April 5, 1915. Interviewing Johnson in the days before the contest, *The Defender*'s columnists found him as confident as ever. Lurking in the text of their articles, however, were details that suggested doubt: Johnson was thirty-seven, overweight, and worn out from his involuntary sojourn, whereas his opponent, Willard, a former cowboy who had quickly risen to the top of the boxing world, was only twenty-eight and in the best shape of his life.[42]

*The Defender* edition covering the fight has not survived, but the *Tribune*'s coverage depicts a scene of unbridled hostility directed at Johnson from the men in the Havana arena. Chanting "Viva la Blanco!" many in the crowd of twenty thousand people taunted Johnson with racist epithets as well. The fight itself, meanwhile, was a rout: Johnson tried to knock Willard out several times in the first twelve rounds, but failed to penetrate the challenger's defenses. Johnson held out for twenty-six rounds, weakening to the point where he could barely stand, before Willard finally delivered a body blow and then a straight right to Johnson's jaw that knocked him on his back. After the fight was called, a squad of soldiers and policemen hoisted Willard on their shoulders and carried the new champion amid drawn swords and waving rifles.[43]

*The Defender* mourned the fate of its fallen hero. In one of the surviving issues from the weeks after the fight, a reporter interviewed several people who saw Johnson that night at a gathering in which the citizens of Havana gave him a watch and Willard gave him a trophy cup as a tribute to their contest. "Jack felt the loss severely," the reporter wrote. "His smile was there, but the lump came down in his throat and he would cast his head downward and say, 'I'm just plain Johnson now.'"[44]

Still unable to return to the United States because of the threat of federal prosecution, Johnson headed to Spain to perform exhibition matches and avoid the war. *The Defender*'s editorial page, meanwhile, called for an all-out ban on interracial boxing, having concluded that such matches only served to inflame racial passions. "The public peace and welfare and the interest of both races demand that such spectacles be banned in the future," the editorial lamented. "We are as a nation not fully civilized and cannot stand sports as this as foreign nations."[45]

Johnson's loss did effect one positive change at *The Defender.* The issue covering the outcome of the fight had been the largest-selling issue ever — with newsboys selling an additional five thousand copies — and that provided Fay Young with the data he needed to convince Abbott to dedicate an entire page to sports. Young would soon become the newspaper's first sports editor, indeed the first sports editor in the black press. He covered the Negro League baseball teams, the Chicago Giants, in particular, as well as other African American athletes, traveling the country to record the games of college leagues as well as professionals.

Young used the sports page to advocate for the integration of professional athletics, both with direct advocacy and simply by broadcasting the accomplishments of black athletes. Once Abbott saw how the new section boosted sales, he gave it his full support, advancing the cause of equality in athletics as a key component of *The Defender*'s broader push for racial equity.[46]

Thanks to overwhelming support from black voters, Big Bill Thompson and Oscar De Priest both won big in the general election of April 1915. Thompson defeated his Democratic opponent by nearly 140,000 votes, the largest margin ever in a mayoral contest, with the Second Ward and the Southeast Side's "dinner pail wards" near the steel mills getting the lion's share of the credit from the *Tribune*. So impressed was the newspaper that it speculated as to whether Big Bill might run for president in 1916.[47]

Inauguration Day dominated the front page of *The Defender*'s May 1 edition. The new mayor led a "Prosperity Parade" of fifty thousand from Grant Park through the Loop, where a crowd of one-half million people lined the streets. "All nations were there with their multitongues, colors and costumes," *The Defender* reported. "Never before in the history of any city has such a multitude gathered to do homage to any one man."[48]

The black community was prominent in the parade, with its own floats, cars, and marchers. Louis Anderson led a procession of twenty cars to represent the now-unified political forces of the Second Ward, followed by African American Boy Scout troops and all of the various men's lodges in their particular uniforms — Elks, Pythians, Masons, Odd Fellows, and Patriarchs. Ed Wright, riding in a car alongside one of the community's most powerful ministers, passed by black policemen on duty for the first time in the Loop. That evening, Oscar De Priest, described as a "cynosure for all eyes during the inauguration ceremonies," took his place among the other aldermen at the first meeting of the new City Council, and received assignments to the committees on schools, fire, police, and health.[49]

Amid all these positive signs, Mayor Thompson soon proved himself further, reversing the decision of the previous administration to allow *Birth of a Nation* to be shown in the city. "Whatever power there is in the mayor's office will be used to stop this film or any other films that reflect on any race or nationality," he told the press. "We want nothing of this sort in Chicago."

*The Defender* celebrated Thompson's ban with a front-page headline and a satisfied editorial entitled "Killing a Film." There was also an article about the state's two African American state representatives, who introduced a bill in the state legislature making it a misdemeanor to show "any lithograph, drawing, picture, play, drama, or sketch that tends to incite race riot, or race hatred." The bill passed the Illinois House 111 to 2, yet more evidence of the community's rapidly growing political sophistication.[50]

Thompson was doing far more than just coordinating with black state legislators, however. Soon after he took office, he made good on his promises and appointed Ed Wright and Louis Anderson, among others, as assistant corporation counsels at a relatively generous salary of $5,000 per year. Like many of Thompson's other decisions, *The Defender* editorial page noted these appointments as symbols of a new attitude from City Hall.[51]

That spring, the porters brought their fight against the Pullman Company before the new Industrial Trade Commission in Washington, D.C. They testified about their poor working conditions and low salaries and especially about the reliance on tips, which they found demeaning as well as penurious. The porters also compelled the testimony of the Pullman Company's chairman, Robert Todd Lincoln, President Abraham Lincoln's son.

The Pullman Company had a long association with the Lincolns — it had transported the funeral party of President Lincoln back to Springfield after the 1865 assassination and had long involved Robert Todd at the top echelons — but this latter-day President Lincoln denied imposing any inhumane conditions on the porters and asserted that the Pullman Company, in fact, had done a great service to African Americans by opening these positions to them in the first place. If the porters were in a dire predicament, he told the commission, it was their own fault in that African Americans had "not made the progress [they] should have made."

Expressing its dismay, *The Defender* editorial page contrasted the behavior of father and son: "Compare the statesman-like edict upon the battlefield of Gettysburg, where breathes the spirit of love, truth and liberty, the soul of mankind moved by the highest sense of divine justice so commonplace in that great man, to the sorrowful, appalling mockery of truth uttered by his son."[52]

• • •

The show of clout by Chicago's black community to block the screening of *Birth of a Nation* had been impressive, but ultimately it was not enough. Director D. W. Griffith won an injunction in state court against Mayor Thompson's ban, and his film had its debut on June 5 at the Illinois Theater.

*The Defender* did not cover the opening, but the *Chicago Tribune*'s theater critic Kitty Kelly did, from a decidedly sympathetic angle. Kelly reported that the theater was packed with an enthusiastic crowd conducted to their seats by ushers dressed fancifully in both Union and Confederate uniforms. Griffith himself came to the opening, and made a speech in which he regurgitated the revisionist history underpinning his production. "We cannot portray the great heart of Abraham Lincoln unless we show the wrong of other hearts," he told the crowd. "As I have said before, we must have villains of some sort, and if every nationality becomes so sensitive, soon we will have none but American villains."[53]

The film continued to be shown in Chicago for months, and the black community seethed. On September 11, *The Defender* printed a review of the movie from Mrs. K. J. Bills, a frequent correspondent who was also a member of Ida B. Wells's Alpha Suffrage Club. Bills, who had lived in the South as a child during Reconstruction, compared the film with her own experience. She actually enjoyed the first half of the movie, which focused on the re-created Civil War battles, but took issue with the heroic portrait of the Klan in the second half. Recalling the night the Klan came to her home and demanded that her father turn over his rifle, she wrote that the reality differed sharply from the movie. "There was no noise, no fast horseback riding, no clash between them and the Negroes," she explained. "It is true [Klan members] went around on horseback, but very quietly, like thieves."

More offensive yet to Mrs. Bills was the image of the former slave threatening to assault the young white girl. She pointed out that during the Civil War many black men were left alone with the white families who owned them while the white men of the household went off to war, and yet there were few reports of assaults. "They protected them as no other person would have done," she recalled.[54]

The myth of the predatory black man, however, was a key component of the white South's propaganda campaign to impose and maintain segregation. Writing in the same issue, Zachary Withers pointed out that whereas the accusation of a sexual crime had been used to justify individual lynchings of black men for generations, now, in *Birth of a Nation,* it was being employed for a broader political purpose with consequences for the entire nation. To Withers, a former Pullman porter and author of two analytical books about race in America, *Birth of a Nation* was simply a new weapon in the white South's continuing insurgency to reverse the gains of the Civil War. "There was no way to overthrow the new political order except through public sentiment," he wrote. "The foulest deed in the annals of crime was ascribed to him — that of rape. For that accusation he was lynched without trial, murdered in his home and upon the public highways. His voice was silenced. His ballot was stolen."[55]

The effects of *Birth of a Nation* were further reaching than anyone at *The Defender* could have imagined. In the outskirts of Atlanta, a small group of men reconstituted the Knights of the Ku Klux Klan and turned to the film to re-create the group's rituals and policies. The Klan, after all, had disappeared two generations earlier, outlawed during the years Union troops occupied the South; but now, *Birth of a Nation* provided a ready set of symbols and rituals, not least the burning cross, which, invented for the film by Griffith and Dixon, became the new Klan's signature act of terror. The film's imagery facilitated the Klan's spread throughout the country among those who had seen it, reaching even into northern cities, including Chicago, and states where the Klan had a footprint.[56]

J. Hockley Smiley, the managing editor who had done so much to update *The Defender*'s content and design, died at the beginning of October 1915, after a three-month illness. An alcoholic bachelor with little formal journalism education, Smiley had transformed *The Defender* from a run-of-the-mill black weekly into the "National Journal of the Race." His photo was printed on the front page along with tributes from *Defender* colleagues and from other black newspapers around the country. An editorial cartoon pictured his empty desk with a wreath on it, while a personal message from Robert Abbott published in the newspaper credited him with being "the greatest newspaper man of the race and day."[57]

Smiley had been a propaganda warrior of unquestioned bravery, taking on white-owned daily newspapers in the South and in Chicago without hesitation. He had covered Jack Johnson from the time of his greatest victory to his ignominious defeat, steered the newspaper through its disappointment with President Wilson and its battles to block *Birth of a Nation,* and chronicled the rise of Black Chicago's political power. His efforts were only beginning to pay off when he died — a receipt from *The Defender*'s printer shows that the print run was fourteen thousand copies weekly at the end of the summer — but the newspaper was growing fast. Just before his illness, Smiley had expanded the paper to twelve pages to accommodate the flood of contributions from around the country. And while he would not live to see the paper in its full glory, Smiley would be remembered by his boss and his friends alike as the man who did much to make it all possible.[58]

# 4

---

# The Great Northern Drive

ARLY IN THE morning of Sunday, November 14, 1915, Robert
Abbott was awakened by the sound of a motorcycle sputtering
down his street. He went to the window to see a messenger dismount
from the vehicle, dash up the front steps, and ring his bell. The messenger had a telegram for the publisher: Booker T. Washington had
died a few hours earlier at his home in Tuskegee, Alabama. Though
stunned, Abbott quickly composed himself and assembled his news
team. Within two hours a special edition of *The Defender* had rolled
off the press for distribution. "World Weeps for Washington," read
the massive headline on the cover of that weekend's final edition.[1]

Until his death, Washington was revered by the black public and
showered with accolades as well as donations from white philanthropists, but his premature death at age fifty-nine ended an internecine
fight among African American leaders. For some years, militants like
Ida Wells-Barnett, W. E. B. Du Bois, and Monroe Trotter had been
challenging the Wizard of Tuskegee and demanding a more active
response to southern oppression. Washington had always dismissed
his critics outright, but lately, as both the frequency and audacity of
southern atrocities had increased, a *Defender* columnist found that
the militants were finally gaining some traction. There was a time
when "Dr. Washington's partisans could, without fear, pooh pooh the
laughingly small Du Bois coterie," the columnist wrote. "That day has
passed, however."[2]

Abbott and *The Defender* remained neutral in the squabble over
Washington's tactics. Though he personally admired Washington, a
legend at Hampton, and was trusted by the Wizard's emissaries in
Chicago, he made a point of not taking financial support from Tuske-

gee, as so many other black newspapers did, and *The Defender*'s editorial page consistently called for unity among the various factions.[3]

Indeed, where Washington had argued for building on the foundation already established in the South and Du Bois advocated for stepped-up protest and federal intervention, *The Defender* called for both, using language even more militant than Du Bois's when it came to resistance to brutality, yet focusing, as Washington did, on improving immediate conditions in the South. An editorial from July 1915 entitled "Southland, Farmers," for instance, advocated a diversification of crops in the traditional cotton-growing region to meet the increased need of war-torn Europe, noting that African Americans owned about 15 percent of the farmland in the South.[4]

Migration was not yet an option for most African Americans, since there were few jobs available to blacks in the North. In Chicago as in other cities, the unions for stockyard and factory workers were obdurate in refusing to admit African Americans. Most union workers were immigrants or their immediate descendants, whose experience of African Americans was limited to strikebreakers brought in during union walkouts, and their resentment against "scabs" mixed all too easily with the racism so prevalent among native whites.[5]

Despite this historic enmity and Abbott's own experience at being stymied by the printers union, *The Defender* was not opposed to the concept of organized labor. But so long as unions drew a color line, the newspaper had no objection with African Americans crossing picket lines. Excluding African Americans, *The Defender* argued, was a self-defeating tactic for the unions.

"It seems strange that unions do not realize they will always have the black man as a competitor if he is shut out of their organizations," stated an October 1915 editorial. "As things stand, labor unions are his worst enemies for they deny him the opportunity to earn an honest living."

The unions' opposition was decisive for Abbott, who knew firsthand just how cruel the North could be, having endured years of penury himself despite his advanced education and relative worldliness, and the editorial concluded that it was "best for ninety and nine of our people to remain in the southland and work out their own salvation."[6]

All through 1915, even as conditions in the white South grew ever more intolerable for blacks, *Defender* editorials had discouraged migration. Following the flood in Galveston, Texas, that fall, *The Defender* reported that thousands of African Americans were left homeless and denied access to food aid and other basic assistance that was distributed to whites, while armed, mounted men took captive two hundred black men, including the president of a local black college, impressing them into what the newspaper described as a "regular peonage slave camp" where they were forced to dig levees, fill sandbags, and perform flood relief in white areas. The black community, meanwhile, was left to its own devices.[7]

Even under these extreme circumstances, *The Defender* did not recommend blacks flee the South, demanding instead that the federal government intervene and urging its readers to respond with donations of clothing and other charitable items. At the beginning of 1916, however, things went from bad to worse in the South even as opportunities suddenly opened up in the North. To start with, a boll weevil infestation had begun devouring much of the cotton in its path as the voracious species of beetle, arriving in the United States from Mexico, spread from west to east. The livelihoods of many farmers and sharecroppers alike were wiped out; many plantation owners simply told their sharecropping families to find new places to live, effectively evicting thousands from land they had farmed for generations with little more than the clothes on their back. Even on plantations that had managed to escape the boll weevil scourge, owners colluded with speculators to squeeze the farmers. "Cotton growing is so unprofitable under current conditions," warned one *Defender* correspondent from Mississippi, "that those who stick to it do so under starvation conditions."[8]

At the same time, the effects of the ongoing world war across the ocean were beginning to be felt in American cities like Chicago. A January 1916 *Defender* editorial described the war in Europe as "an ill wind that blows no one good," but noted that as a result of the fighting, the economic prospects for African Americans were changing dramatically. As European governments drained the labor pool further by recalling many of their citizens for military service, the flow of immigrants fell from more than 1.2 million in 1914 to just over 300,000 in 1915. Facing a shortage of employees, stockyard owners sent agents to the South to recruit African Americans, while labor unions quickly changed their policies, recognizing that keeping blacks out at this point would only guarantee the establishment of a large, nonunionized force in their midst. Steel mills, factories, and other industries suddenly opened their doors as well. "The European war, as bloody, tragic and deplorable as it is . . . has meant that the thousands who a year ago were dependent on charity are today employed and making a comfortable living for themselves and their families," a *Defender* editorial observed. "Whatever the reason to be, now is our opportunity."[9]

Soon reports began trickling in to the paper of southern blacks heading north to capitalize on these new opportunities, and southern whites beginning to panic. On February 5, 1916, *The Defender* printed a dispatch from Selma, Alabama: "The white people of the extreme South are becoming alarmed over the steady moving of race families out of the mineral belt. Hundreds of families have left during the past few months and the stream is continuing. Every effort is being made to have them stay, but the discrimination and the race prejudice continues as strong as ever."[10]

The spring of 1916 saw the beginning of the presidential campaign, one that would not be easy for the incumbent president, Woodrow Wilson, who was facing a reunified Republican Party and an electorate skeptical of his pledge to keep the United States out of World War I. All too happy to heap on the criticism, *The Defender* declared Wilson a "colossal failure" and challenged his foreign policy over the invasion of Haiti the previous year, as well as for sending troops into Mexico to pursue the revolutionary leader Pancho Villa. "If President Woodrow Wilson is so anxious to teach the world good morals," carped one editorial on the subject, "let him begin by placing the U.S. Army in the South; institute a chase of the lynchers as earnestly as the one he is now carrying on in Mexico."[11]

By most measures, the total number of lynchings was, in fact, down; it was the severity of the incidents that had increased. In May, *The Defender* printed a letter from a white resident of Waco, Texas, a witness to the horrific murder of seventeen-year-old Jesse Washington. The letter writer was outraged by what he had seen, a mob of "fifteen to twenty-thousand men and women intermingled with children and babies in their arms" gathered to torture Washington and then burn him at the stake. Accused of the murder of a white woman several miles from his home, Washington was convicted by a jury despite scant evidence, and then, as happened all too often, dragged from the courtroom and hung from a tree, then burned on a funeral pyre. "The crowd was made up of some of the supposed best citizens of the South," the letter writer noted. "Doctors, lawyers, business men and Christians (posing as such, however). After the fire subsided, the mob was not satisfied: they hacked with pen knives the fingers, the toes, and pieces of flesh from the body, carrying them as souvenirs to their automobiles." The correspondent went on to conclude that it was absurd to send troops to Mexico "when the troops are needed right here in the South."[12]

For the moment, *The Defender* continued its reflexive call for federal intervention as the only meaningful solution to the brutality of southern whites. But as hundreds of blacks arrived in Chicago's train stations every week throughout the summer, *The Defender*'s position on the migration evolved. In August, under the headline "Southerners Plan to Stop Exodus," the newspaper reported that recruiters for one of the Pennsylvania-based railroad lines convinced all of the workers on one steamship line in Jacksonville, Florida, to quit and move to the North en masse, leaving the steamship owners suddenly without a crew. The Jacksonville City Council responded by passing a law requiring labor agents from northern companies to pay $1,000 for a license.[13]

Incidents like this one convinced Robert Abbott that migration was at once an effective tactic for hurting the white South and a real opportunity for African Americans to live in freedom. "The bars are being let down in the industrial world like never before in this country," observed an editorial in the same issue as the coverage of the Jacksonville departure. "Unless we spread out to the four corners of the earth and accept every chance for advancement, we will continue to vegetate, as many drones in the southland are now doing."[14]

The movement picked up steam quite literally in the fall of 1916, as tens of thousands in Georgia, Mississippi, Louisiana, and other states boarded northbound trains. The front-page photograph of *The Defender* on September 2, 1916, shows a crowd of neatly dressed black men and women waiting for a train in Savannah, under the headline

"The Exodus." The migrants were leaving, according to the caption, because they were "tired of being kicked and cursed," and their departure was causing great consternation to the overlords of the South.[15]

An editorial cartoon in that same issue, under the headline "Desertion," shows a black man with a broken ankle chain, the word "labor" on his back, running toward a car labeled "northern industries," whose driver is a smiling white man, his hand stretched out in welcome. Chasing the black man, meanwhile, is another white man, dressed in a hat and cloak and gripping a shotgun, accompanied by hounds labeled "lynchers," with the soil underneath their feet labeled "The South."[16]

Observing how the flight of African Americans from the South was damaging its economy, and persuaded that there were actually jobs for the new migrants, Abbott finally embraced the movement as a "Second Emancipation." In October, a *Defender* editorial entitled "Farewell Dixie-Land" posited migration as a militant, manly act of defiance against the South's propaganda. "Every black man for the sake of his wife and daughters especially should leave even at financial sacrifice," the editorial urged. "We know full well that would mean a depopulation of that section and if it were possible we would glory in its accomplishment."[17]

Faced with this dangerous drain on its human resources, the white South reflexively resorted to brute force. In November, police in Savannah arrested 125 people among the hundreds waiting on the train platform, including many who were not migrating, such as a Pullman porter on his way to work, as well as two editors from *The Savannah Tribune,* an African American newspaper, who had come to the scene to investigate the commotion. That same month, in Hattiesburg, Mississippi, police officers spent days searching for an agent representing one of Chicago's packinghouses who had recruited 200 men and women. When the officers couldn't find him, they blocked access to the train ticket booth on the scheduled day of departure. But the migrants boarded the train anyway and were met by the agent, who emerged from a hiding place once they were underway and handed out the tickets.[18]

In November, as Woodrow Wilson won a narrow reelection victory, the editorial page published "Bound for the Promised Land," by M. Ward, a heretofore unknown poet, whose portrait photo shows a young man, nattily dressed with a satin bow tie, recounting the experiences of those who had already gone North, found jobs, and sent for their wives, as well as the efforts from the South to ban the work of labor agents:

> From Florida's stormy banks I'll go, I'll bid the South goodbye;
> No longer will they treat me so, And knock me in the eye,
> Hasten on my dark brother, Duck the Jim Crow law.
> No Crackers North to slap your mother, or knock you on the jaw.
> No Cracker there to seduce your sister, nor to hang you to a limb.
> And you're not obliged to call 'em "Mister," nor skin 'em back at him.[19]

So popular was the poem that the issue sold out, prompting *The Defender* to reprint it a few months later. "This poem caused more men to leave the Southland than any other effort," the newspaper proudly noted.

On the letters page, readers praised *The Defender*'s role in the exodus. "We have one or two little papers here but they dare not say what you say," read a typical letter from Atlanta, enclosed along with clippings of antimigration articles from southern newspapers. "They are trying to say everything they can to change the Race man's mind so he will not leave Georgia, but they are leaving Atlanta every day, and I am proud to see it, for I am expecting to do the same thing in short."[20]

*The Defender* estimated that 250,000 black people had left the South by the beginning of that winter, and noted that a shift was taking place in white public opinion. In white-owned southern newspapers that, just a few months earlier, had been enthusiastic about lynching or had advocated expulsion of African Americans to Africa or Mexico, editorials and letters to the editor began to reconsider the Jim Crow system. *The Defender* reprinted these anxious columns with relish, including a letter originally published in *The New Orleans Times-Picayune*, which *The Defender* ran under the headline "Getting the South Told." The letter acknowledged the harassment of African Americans by police, the denigration of their labor and pride, and the reality of sexual interaction between the races: "Dogs, horses, monkeys, pets of all kinds," the author lamented, "receive more thoughtful consideration at the hands of indulgent masters than does this product of God's handiwork no less a degree cast in the image of his Maker than his lighter-hued brother — and in many cases a kinsman."[21]

A *Defender* columnist who went under the byline "The Scrutinizer" quoted an editorial from Georgia's *Macon Telegraph* in which that newspaper described farmers who awoke to find "every male negro [sic] over 21 on his place gone — to Cleveland, to Pittsburgh, to Chicago, to Indianapolis. Better jobs, better treatment, higher pay."

Labor agents, *The Telegraph* editorial asserted, were "stealing" blacks from the South; the paper warned that the migrants would freeze to death in the North. Forced, however, to admit that the southern economy needed cheap African American labor, the newspaper demanded that state authorities use every method at their disposal to keep blacks from leaving. "We must have the Negro in the South," the editorial insisted. "He has been with us so long that our whole industrial, commercial and agricultural structure has been built on a black foundation. It is the only labor we have — if we lose it, we go bankrupt."

The Scrutinizer scoffed at the idea that blacks were climatically unsuited for the North, writing that he had checked in *The Defender*'s "statistics department" and found no recorded deaths of African Americans in the region. And as for work, he wrote that there were 1.5 million open jobs, a virtually unlimited demand for labor. "Better a thousand times, even if it was true, to run chances of being nipped by the fingers of Jack Frost," he wrote, "than to shake off this mortal coil at the end of the lynchers' rope, or to the crackling of the lynchers' fire brand."[22]

And so the migrants kept coming, even as temperatures continued to drop. *The Defender,* having predicted that the arrival of migrants would slow down during Chicago's frigid winter, was surprised when groups of men turned up in the middle of January 1917. A front-page report under the headline "Northern Invasion Starts" provided details of thirty-one men from Hattiesburg, Mississippi, who had come into the city the week before, properly prepared for winter with overcoats and rubber overshoes. Thirty-five men from Mobile, Alabama, arrived several days after the Mississippians, and immediately came to visit *The Defender*'s office. Both groups had found jobs by the time the newspaper went to press, some in the slaughterhouses, while others were hired by manufacturing plants in Detroit. Those who stayed in the city found places to live at the Wabash Avenue YMCA and other apartment buildings that specialized in rooms for single working men.[23]

The newspaper subsequently ran articles of African Americans dying of cold in the *South,* accompanied by hard-hitting editorials that asked rhetorically, "If you can freeze to death in the North and be free, why freeze to death in the South and be a slave? *The Defender* says come."[24]

The very migration *The Defender* had helped to encourage, in turn, served to expand its circulation along with its influence, allowing Robert Abbott to hire more staff, starting with Lucius Clinton Harper, who had met the publisher at a neighborhood delicatessen four years earlier and had volunteered at the newspaper ever since. Tall and fair-complexioned, Harper, twenty-two, worked as a bellboy at the all-white Chicago Press Club, where he collected publications from around the world and added them to the newspapers and magazines brought in to the *The Defender*'s office by the train porters. He learned journalism the same way Fay Young had some years earlier, scanning these publications for stories that could be rewritten or revised to suit *The Defender*'s readers.[25]

When Harper finally gave up his job at the press club, he joined seven other staff members — four men and three women — in addition to Abbott. The newspaper by now had taken over a bedroom adjacent to the kitchen that had become vacant when one of Mrs. Lee's children moved out. Still, the office continued to be a cramped, domestic arrangement. "Every morning that we arrived — eight thirty — Mr. Abbott was in bathrobe and slippers, in the office, greeting us and opening the mail," Harper would write some years later. "And Mrs. Lee — God bless her — was in the kitchen cooking, usually fried rice, biscuits, sausages and coffee. Those of us who had skipped breakfast — and that was no miracle in those days — inhaled those combinations of odors as a sort of tantalizer."

Julius Avendorph and many of the other *Defender* columnists preferred to compose their articles elsewhere, bringing in their copy to be laid out for typesetting. The newspaper's theater and movie critic,

Tony Langston, for instance, had a desk at a nearby music store, while political writer W. Allison Sweeney wrote his trenchant pieces in a basement office some blocks away. Harper was initially assigned to a section of one of the desks at Mrs. Lee's, but Abbott soon reclaimed that space to consult with advertising clients. "I took my typewriter to an old, weather-beaten desk that had been discarded on the back porch, which was concrete and roofless," Harper recalled.

Still watchful over every penny, Abbott was always willing to take on even the most mundane tasks if other staff members were otherwise engaged. Harper recalled that, when needed, the boss would bundle copy and board the trolley himself to take it to the printer's, as he had done in the paper's earliest days. If a potential advertiser called, Abbott would immediately head out on foot, walking long distances to avoid paying for public transportation. "Many times these ventures netted only thirty or forty cents a trip," Harper explained, "but he never tired."[26]

In the spring of 1917, *The Defender* announced May 15 as the day of the Great Northern Drive, encouraging a million people to leave the South in a show of solidarity. The newspaper made no provisions for those who undertook to make the journey or to accommodate the migrants once they arrived; indeed, hundreds of African Americans responded to the paper's challenge in advance of that deadline. But *The Defender* saw the Great Northern Drive as a way to underscore the political reasons behind the migration, declaring that "the maltreatment of the whites toward members of the Race is the sole cause of the exodus."[27]

In the run-up to the Great Northern Drive, *The Defender*'s circulation soared to eighty-two thousand, and the newspaper stepped up its pro-migration campaign by publishing positive portraits of life in Chicago. One photo-essay featured a shot of Chicago's Lindblom High School, a modern structure "where no color line is drawn," beside an image of a shack, identified as the Freetown School, which served as both the elementary and high school for African Americans in Abbeville, Louisiana.

The article exaggerated somewhat in its portrayal of public education in Chicago: despite Illinois law proscribing racial discrimination, *The Defender* and other community leaders had to constantly battle "reformers," including the editorial board of the *Chicago Tribune,* whose members saw the segregation of public schools as a solution to various perceived problems with educating African Americans and whites together. Regular readers would have known that Ida B. Wells-Barnett had objected to the segregation of social events at the integrated high school her own children attended, Wendell Phillips, before several school administrators were ultimately replaced. Nevertheless, it was clear enough to southern readers of *The Defender* that Chicago offered their children a chance for a comprehensive education, the kind they would never have at home.[28]

The migration accelerated throughout the spring, as evinced in *The Defender*'s national section, which included state-by-state reports from black communities across North America and beyond. Departures for the North were interspersed with compilations of personal updates, achievements, gossip, and rumor, alongside notices of garden parties, club meetings, illnesses, and employment situations. Typical is the "Down in Georgia" column from the first week of April, which includes the goings-on in the town of Rome: "The Twentieth Century Club entertained their wives * John Goodson has gone to Detroit * Albert Walker has gone to Ashburn, Ga. * Zell Nealy, who was shot in the mouth by a white man, is improving * Miss Wilson Durham and Miss Ellen Humphries have gone to New York City * Mrs. Sarah Byrd has gone to Chicago * Will Stuart, Harry McAffee, Ed Malone, Joe Howard, Maurice Hall, Chas Jackson, Albert Love, T. E. Monroe, Art Hatcher and Louis Johnson have all gone to Detroit."[29]

On April 6, 1917, the United States declared war on Germany and the Central Powers, putting a new urgency on the ongoing mobilization of the armed forces and bringing to the forefront the continuing question of African Americans in the military. As in the Spanish-American War, Chicago's Eighth Regiment and its black officers were an issue for southern segregationists inside and out of the U.S. Army and Navy. Robert Abbott's mentor John Marshall had retired as commander of the Eighth, replaced by Franklin A. Denison, another fair-complexioned man with a disciplinarian style. Denison had led the Eighth during the U.S. Army's failed mission to the Texas border to capture Pancho Villa the previous summer, when the unit's command, now subjected to the rules of the segregated South, was ignored by white officers and enlisted men.[30]

During the Mexican campaign, *The Defender* had assigned a reporter to document the indignities suffered by Colonel Denison and his men. Now that the war in Europe was officially on, black manpower would be crucial to enhancing America's underpowered military. Finally, the editorial page felt, black America had serious leverage on the federal government. The newspaper's first demand was for full integration in a military ostensibly fighting for freedom and democracy overseas. An editorial entitled "Jim Crow Training Camps—No!" challenged the idea, held by W. E. B. Du Bois and other leading figures in the NAACP, that segregated facilities to train black officers were a necessary evil, without which there would be no new black officers. Any endorsement of segregation, no matter how tacit, *The Defender* maintained, was unacceptable. "We have put up with the crumbs that have fallen from the white man's table as our portion for so long," the editorial analogized.[31]

Amid this debate over the black role in the war, the Chicago office of the Bureau of Investigation, a precursor to the FBI, assigned African American agent J. E. Hawkins to investigate *The Defender.* Hawkins was detailed to check out conspiracy theories—launched, unsurprisingly, in the South—that Mexican agents of the German government were attempting to recruit allies among African Americans. His surveillance turned up no evidence of international intrigue, however. Short on anything more damning, Hawkins reported to his superiors a mistaken belief that *The Defender* was secretly owned by media baron William Randolph Hearst, and went on to observe that Abbott was "a coal black negro [*sic*]" and "somewhat of an egotist." Hawkins also concluded that the newspaper was "not in good standing" with the "better sort" of African Americans.

Abbott was ordered to report for an interview in Hawkins's headquarters just a few days after the declaration of war. Unflappable, the editor shot down Hawkins's assertion that *The Defender* was owned by Hearst and recounted the tale of how he had begun the newspaper on his landlady's kitchen table with only a quarter. To underscore his patriotism, Abbott said he had supported the war effort through the provision of free ad space for recruitment and editorial support of the military. Another agent who summarized the meeting wrote that, while Abbott "may have overstepped the bounds of propriety," there was no proof of sedition.[32]

The same month he was called into the Bureau of Investigation, Abbott was interviewed by the *Daily News.* "Unknown to persons who look at the influx of colored people entering Chicago alone at the rate of 100 a day as the inexplicable, spontaneous movement from the south," wrote the *Daily News*'s reporter, "the movement is the result of consistent propaganda by northern colored newspapers and the migrants are being systematically handled after they arrive here." The reporter, crediting Abbott with having "done as much as any one person to start the movement northward," asked for his opinion.

"It is merely one group of American citizens moving in their own home country to try to better their conditions," Abbott responded, a bit defensively. "They are coming north where they can get a man's wage and feel that their wives and children are safe from mob violence."

Abbott went on to compare the loyalty of immigrants with that of African Americans: "The negro [*sic*] is a good class of emigrant for he either spends or invests his savings where he lives and does not send them to some European country to buy bombs or build submarines to kill Americans." It was a forceful, if somewhat awkward and nationalistic, plunge into the "mainstream" media.[33]

Its front page is gone and only a few interior pages remain, but a portion of the issue of *The Defender* from the week of the Great Northern Drive has survived, and among the legible articles are dispatches from places in the South that show just how damaging to the southern agricultural economy the migration really was. A report from Hopkinsville, Kentucky, for instance, found that so many black workers had left the region that berry growers had to recruit "white women and girls" to harvest the perishable crop in time. Another report from Greenwood, South Carolina, stated that a white man had been arrested for facilitating the migration by loaning money to black people who wanted to leave. "In a number of instances," this report concluded, "the farms are without help to plant crops."

Much of the editorial page from the Great Northern Drive issue is readable as well, and it shows how the newspaper, along with the rest of the nation, was shifting its gears to a wartime footing. Advocating full inclusion of black troops in the U.S. military, it also stepped up its calls for African Americans to leave the South. For now, the migration could be framed as a patriotic movement, an effort to fill the very factories that supplied the troops and their allies, while the white South's efforts to douse the migration could be reasonably cast as anti-American. *The Defender* continued to devote considerable effort to counteracting the idea that African Americans were especially susceptible to the cold weather in the North and would perish if they abandoned the South. Such stories, according to the last lines of a partially torn editorial, were having a decreasing effect on the pace of departures. "It is about time," concludes the editorial, "the south stopped playing to the gallery."[34]

Their propaganda rendered useless, the white South now ratcheted up the level of resistance to black flight, using the police to block train stations in Savannah and Jackson on days that were scheduled for mass departures of African Americans. But there was no border between the South and the North, and the would-be migrants simply took streetcars or walked to other stations or bought tickets to nearby towns, and from there to other nearby towns, and so on, until they managed to cross the Mason-Dixon Line. Indeed, the migrants' resolve only strengthened as the white South persisted in oppressing African Americans with absolute impunity.[35]

By now, the migration — and *The Defender*'s essential role in it — had captured the attention of the Wilson administration, which appointed Emmett J. Scott to produce an extensive report on its causes and predict its effects on the entire nation. Scott, chief aide to Booker T. Washington until the latter's death, was now named a special advisor to Secretary of War Newton Baker, making him the highest-ranking African American in the federal government at the time. He used this clout to secure funds from the Carnegie Endowment for International Peace and assemble a research team that went into key states north and south, as well as into the archives of the federal government, the Tuskegee Institute, and a Washington, D.C.–based research center run by Carter G. Woodson, among other institutions.[36] *The Defender* was both a key resource and subject of Scott's study. Scouring every issue from 1916 and 1917 for migration-related articles, the research team made extensive use of the newspaper's files, and paid special attention to the thousands of letters sent to the newspaper from southern readers, which Scott later published in two additional volumes. He tracked the newspaper's booming circulation and found that throughout the state of Mississippi, the paper sold out on the day it arrived. Copies were passed around until they disintegrated. In one town reached by Scott's researchers, they reported that reading *The Defender* conferred the impression of being "intelligent"; in another place, even old men who were illiterate made a point of carrying a copy under their arms.

Citing letters from migrants as well as other data gathered by his team, Scott concluded that the Great Northern Drive had been a highly effective tactic in *The Defender*'s campaign to use the migration against the South. By positioning positive stories about life in Chicago against accounts of the horrific treatment of blacks in the South, the newspaper proved "successful in inciting thousands of restless negroes [*sic*] to venture north, where they were assured of its protection and the championship of their cause. There are in Chicago migrants who attribute their presence in the North to its encouraging pictures of relief from conditions at home with which they became more and more dissatisfied, as they read."[37]

In addition to the articles in *The Defender*, letters from friends and relatives who had settled in the North generated enthusiasm bordering on mania in many southern communities. In barbershops and grocery stores as well as in churches and other family gathering spots, migration became an obsessive topic of conversation. Scott described locals in Hattiesburg, Mississippi, eagerly questioning Pullman porters about conditions in the North, the weather in particular. "You could not rest in your bed at night for Chicago," he quoted one of the migrants as recalling. People sometimes left in a hurry. "Drivers and teamsters left their wagons standing in the street," Scott found. "Workers, returning home, scrambled aboard the trains for the North without notifying their employers or their families."[38]

The migration swept up the laborers of the South as well as the black professionals who had catered to the African American community under the Jim Crow system. After their clients, customers, and congregations vanished, lawyers, doctors, teachers, funeral directors, pharmacists, and ministers made the migration as well. In Jackson, Mississippi, Scott found that 25 percent of the businessmen

and one-third of the professional men, as well as the pastors of two of
the town's largest churches, joined hundreds of their parishioners in
traveling to the North.[39]

Like many at the time, Scott used the word "movement" to describe
the migration, sparking an association of this term with the struggle
for civil rights that would hold for generations. But he documented,
too, the deep spiritual feeling many experienced when they left the
South, the echoes of the biblical Exodus for these men, women, and
children no more than one or two generations removed from slavery,
now escaping a land of subjugation and entering into a new world,
where the milk and honey were, if not freely distributed, at least attainable. Scott found these feelings widespread, as in the group from
Hattiesburg who, crossing the Ohio River, began to cry and sing of
deliverance, "I done come out of the Land of Egypt with the good
news."[40]

For the most part, the migrants traveled to those cities along the
train line directly north, such that African Americans from Florida,
South Carolina, Virginia, and Georgia tended to settle in New York,
New Jersey, and New England, while those from Mississippi, Alabama, Arkansas, and Louisiana made new homes in Indiana, Illinois,
and Michigan. As a railway hub, Chicago became the jumping-off
point for African American settlements throughout the Midwest,
especially in the industrial boomtowns dotting the Great Lakes. In
Gary, Indiana; Milwaukee, Wisconsin; and dozens of other towns,
African American communities sprang up in a matter of a few weeks.
Between 1916 and 1917, the African American population in Rock-
ford, Illinois, a town of 55,000, jumped from 500 to 1,500. Detroit had
just 5,741 African Americans in 1910; by 1919, there would be 35,000.
Altogether, Scott estimated some 400,000 African Americans left
the South during the war years.[41]

Scott was less sanguine than Abbott about the long-term effects of
the migration, however, noting that African Americans had accumulated a great deal of property in the South *despite* segregation, and
that much of it, in the rush to get north, was abandoned or sold for a
fraction of its worth. He found, too, that wages rose as a result of the
migration, while upgrades were made in the farm credit system and
to the public infrastructure in black neighborhoods. He documented
places where southern authorities installed streetlights, paved roads,

and built playgrounds as well as new sewage, water, and electricity facilities. But the migration was not driven by economics, and Scott confirmed *The Defender*'s assertion that the major cause was lynching, a finding he underscored by quoting dozens of remorseful editorials from white southern newspapers that took up fully twenty pages of his two-hundred-page report. "If Georgia is injured, agriculturally and industrially, the white people here have no one to blame but themselves," declared one particularly handwringing column from *The Atlanta Constitution*, itself reprinted from *The Tifton Gazette*. "They have allowed negroes [*sic*] to be lynched, five at a time, on nothing stronger than suspicion. When the negro is gone, his loss will be felt in every large agricultural section and every industrial economy of the South."[42]

But if the success of the Great Northern Drive caused some whites in the South to feel regret, to self-evaluate or even change course, others were provoked to shoot the messenger. In Savannah, just after the date of the Great Northern Drive, police arrested five young men for reading the poem "Bound for the Promised Land." Officially charged with inciting a riot, one man received a lesser sentence for possessing a copy of the poem, while two of the men — described by the judge as the "instigators"— were sentenced to thirty days in a penal facility called the Brown Farm, which *The Defender,* in an article protesting the men's arrests, described as "not fit for human beings."[43]

Meanwhile, Mississippi's legislature passed a law making it a misdemeanor to distribute publications advocating "equality or marriage between the white and the Negro race." More than a dozen vendors and subscription agents of the newspaper were harassed and threatened with death throughout the South, and not a few were so frightened they fled north themselves. In Meridian, Mississippi, a town particularly depleted of its African American population, the chief of police ordered the confiscation of *The Defender*. None of these efforts to censor or ban the newspaper were at all effective; southern authorities respected, at least, the integrity of the U.S. mail; if *The Defender* was simply inserted into a plain brown envelope, it generally arrived at its subscriber's home intact.[44]

Tensions rose in the South as the migration picked up steam. Just ten days after the date of the Great Northern Drive, *The Defender* reported on the lynching of Eli Persons in Tennessee, a crime that involved thousands of people and was organized with particular brazenness by some of the area's most prominent elected officials and business leaders. Arrested for the brutal rape and ax murder of a white schoolgirl, Persons, a woodworker, initially came under suspicion simply because he was black and owned an ax. Officers tortured him for twenty-four hours, and by the end of the interrogation he had confessed to the crime.

After his arrest, Persons was held in Nashville, in proximity to the governor's mansion and a National Guard unit, allegedly for his protection. But, as so often happened in the South, just as he was being placed on a train to be taken to Memphis for trial, Persons was seized, then dragged to a crossroads a few miles from town. There, a mob of three thousand had been assembled around a pit filled with gasoline and a stacked pile of wood. Members of the crowd, led by a policeman, cut off his ears and toes and then placed him on the pyre, where, in front of the giddy whites as well as a few terrified black adults and children who had been forced out of nearby homes to watch, he was burned alive. Persons's burned corpse was then dismembered. After driving back to Memphis, his murderers threw his arm and head into the crowd on Beale Street, the prosperous main thoroughfare in the city's black community.[45]

*The Defender*'s coverage of Persons's murder focused on the involvement of high-level officials and the complicity of the area's leadership, providing details of the semipublic meetings between members of the "ruling class, sheriffs, judges, editors, lawyers, priests, preachers, philanthropists, millionaires and merchant princes," who had raised money, hired spies, and planned the entire gruesome event. The area's white newspapers played their part by publishing manufactured evidence against Persons as well as salacious details of the crime sure to inflame the passions of whites. Some local newspapers, it turned out, had announced the lynching the day before, far enough in advance that several carloads of people from Mississippi drove all night to reach the lynching site by 9:30 a.m. None of the participants feared prosecution from local or federal officials; even the clergy in the area, the newspaper noted, were intimidated into silence.

"Do you wonder at the thousands leaving the land where every foot of ground marks a tragedy?" asked *The Defender.* "Leaving the grace of their fathers and all they hold dear to seek their fortunes in the North. And you who say their going is to seek better wages are insulting truth, dethroning reason, and consoling yourself with a groundless allegation."[46]

Nevertheless, white newspapers continued to resist the connection between lynching and migration. The *Tribune* editorial about Persons's murder, entitled "Black Man, Stay South!" warned that northerners resented blacks as well, even if they were better at concealing it, and called the movement thus far a "huge mistake." African Americans should be satisfied with a few simple modifications to southern practices, the editorial argued, rather than a complete reformation of the established segregation system. "Our observation goes to show that the Negro is happiest when the white race asserts its superiority," the *Tribune* editorial maintained, "provided that sympathy and understanding accompany that assertion."[47]

*The Defender* did not let this latest salvo from the *Tribune* go unanswered. "It is not enough for this great metropolitan daily to continuously remind Chicago's generous commonwealth of its growing hatred for the colored man," wrote a *Defender* columnist about the editorial, "but to apparently condone a crime in the public, lawless burning of a human being, the chief charge against whom is that being black, is commensurate in character with the unconscionable criminals who participated in the mob."[48]

# 5

The Greatest Disturbing Element

O N JULY 1, 1917, the city of East St. Louis, Illinois, erupted into an orgy of murder, arson, and looting that left as many as two hundred African Americans dead and the black section of town in ruins. *The Defender*'s front page included a large photograph of burning wreckage in "Black Valley," the African American enclave in this industrial outpost of seventy thousand people situated across the Mississippi River from St. Louis, Missouri.

For two full days, blacks were beaten, gunned down, and hanged from lampposts. Particularly vulnerable were those who were riding in streetcars, such as one woman with her husband, teenage son, and thirteen-year-old daughter who were visiting from St. Louis for the day. A mob detached the streetcar from its power line, dragged the family off, and attacked them with bricks. Knocked unconscious, the woman awoke in an ambulance next to her dead husband and son; only later did she discover that her daughter had been rescued by a white store owner who hid the girl until the violence subsided.

National Guard soldiers had been stationed in East St. Louis to guard the bridges to St. Louis as well as the city's factories and meatpacking plants against the unlikely event of an act of sabotage by German agents. But many of these troops were locally drawn, ill prepared, and badly led, so that rather than stopping the rioters, *The Defender* reported, they had mostly looked on while atrocities were committed. Some troops even arrested blacks who tried to defend themselves, and a few soldiers gave over their rifles to the members of the mob. In one case, a soldier aiming at a group of fleeing black men shot the arm off of a young girl.

After two days of mayhem, the National Guard units in place began acting to stop the violence. These troops were reinforced on July 3 by hundreds more guardsmen from units in Chicago with experienced officers, who placed contingents of soldiers at hot spots around town with orders to use whatever force necessary to stop the rioting. The official death toll was thirty-nine African American men, women, and children, as well as at least nine whites, including policemen killed by blacks' gunfire and at least one store owner killed by other whites who robbed him of guns and valuables. Not included in that final count were those who were incinerated in their homes and businesses as a result of arson, or those who were thrown into the swift waters of the Mississippi, such as one man decapitated by a laughing, knife-wielding killer who tossed his victim's head off one side of a bridge and his body off the other.[1]

*The Defender*'s correspondent in East St. Louis was soon joined by Ida B. Wells-Barnett, who, arriving while Black Valley was still smoldering, interviewed survivors, soldiers, and the city's political leaders for a pamphlet she would publish, *The East St. Louis Massacre: Outrage of the Century.* W. E. B. Du Bois, who would write about the events in East St. Louis for months in *The Crisis,* followed a few days later.[2]

East St. Louis became the focus of the daily newspapers as well, with white leaders of all stripes condemning the violence, even southern whites, albeit for their own reasons. The *Chicago Tribune,* seeing the riots as a dangerous distraction from the war effort, castigated local, state, and federal government officials as well as the police and the National Guard for failing to avert or stop the destruction.[3]

Not that the *Tribune*'s sympathy prompted any reexamination of its previous stance against the migration, however. Just a few pages removed from the chagrined editorial about the riot, regular columnist Henry M. Hyde described the migration with this scurrilous headline: "Half a Million Darkies from Dixie Swarm the North to Better Themselves." Warning of the negative consequences of this great population transfer, Hyde did concede that the brutality of the South, taken alongside the economic opportunities in the North — as well as the influence of newspapers like *The Defender* — made it certain that African Americans would keep coming. "One result of the great war is that the Negro problem has moved north with a vengeance," Hyde wrote, "and the North does not yet begin to realize it — even with the outrage at East St. Louis still sounding its terrible warning."[4]

In the South, meanwhile, the East St. Louis riots gave the white supremacists the rare opportunity to chastise the North and denounce the migration. "Others may disconcert the negro [*sic*] by painting before his eyes a roseate picture of broadened rights and racial equality to be enjoyed in the North," wrote *The Atlanta Constitution,* conveniently forgetting its own city's riots a decade earlier, "but in the South a negro never yet was killed simply because he wanted to work and earn a living for himself and family by honest labor!"[5]

*The Defender*'s editorial page rejected the blithe contention that foreign agents or labor unions were somehow responsible for the violence, placing the blame squarely on the racism emanating from the South. In the first week of August, the newspaper featured coverage of the "Silent March," an assembly of more than ten thousand people who marched down New York's Fifth Avenue in silence, carrying signs that made the unmistakable connections between the rioting in East St. Louis and the lynching of Eli Persons in Tennessee and of Jesse Washington in Waco. The front-page photograph pictures hundreds of women and girls dressed entirely in white, walking hand in hand in neat rows.[6]

The Silent March had been organized by James Weldon Johnson, one of those who had gathered around Frederick Douglass in the Haitian Pavilion during the 1893 World's Fair, now the field secretary for the NAACP, and he wasted no time building on its success. Just a few days later, Johnson led a delegation to the White House that included the entrepreneur known as Madam C. J. Walker, a hair products magnate who was the nation's wealthiest African American woman and a major advertiser in *The Defender*. Told when they arrived that President Wilson was busy, Johnson met instead with Wilson's private secretary, Joseph Tumulty, then took full advantage of the time in the capital to meet with a number of congressmen. *The Defender,* impressed with what had been accomplished through this new form of public protest, called for more silent marches to take place around the country. "Whether an immediate remedy against these wrongs will be accomplished remains to be seen," stated one editorial, "but one thing the whites did understand, and that was the Race is waking up, are together as a unit, and are doing things."[7]

"Read This, Then Laugh," stated a headline in *The Defender*'s September 15, 1917, issue accompanying a short article reprinted from the white-owned *Athens Daily Banner* in Georgia:

> Investigation by state and federal officials into the Negro exodus situation has brought to the conclusion that the greatest disturbing element which has yet entered Georgia is the circulation of the Negro newspaper known as *The Chicago Defender* which has agitated the Negroes to leave the south on the word picture of equality with the whites, the freedom of hotels, theaters and other places of public amusement on an equal basis with the white people and "equality in citizenship" in the north and east.[8]

*The Defender* delighted in its new notoriety. In less than a decade since its confrontation with the Georgian press over A. J. Walker's shooting of the planter C. S. Hollenshead, the newspaper had evolved, in the eyes of the region's white newspapers, from a libelous scandal sheet to a threat to the very stability of the South. *The Defender*'s strategy was working — the migration *was* hurting the southern economy by siphoning off its best workers. It *was* forcing whites to reevaluate their treatment of their African American neighbors.

As African Americans kept coming from the South, *The Defender* and other black advocates began focusing on how the migrants were settling into their new urban environment. In his report, Emmett Scott found that the first waves of migrants to Chicago moved into the old Dearborn corridor, which had been abandoned both because of the decline in quality of the housing and because of the lingering presence of brothels, bars, and gambling dens associated with the old Levee vice district. But by the summer of 1917, with migrants continuing to arrive in large numbers, Scott found that the new families were finding space in neighborhoods to the west in buildings and apartments formerly occupied by whites. More often than not, the whites left blocks that had been mixed. Still, the housing market was extremely tight, Scott noted; the transfer from white to black tenants was accompanied by an increase in rent of between 5 and 50 percent, and many families made do with a single room.[9]

*The Defender* took a paternalistic approach to the migrants, assuming responsibility for educating them as well as for marshaling resources on their behalf. But in the absence of formal social services like the settlement houses set up for foreign immigrants by wealthy philanthropists, not infrequently with government support, the African American arrivals could rely only on those who had come before them, and when the first waves of newcomers reached Chicago, the editorial page praised those "earnest men and women" who worked with them. For a time, while jobs and housing were plentiful, these resources were sufficient. "Clean, sanitary, homes were found, work secured and friendly talks given on the don'ts of the big city," observed *The Defender.*

But by the fall of 1917, the community had already doubled in size and was continuing to grow at an exponential rate, leading the newspaper that had done so much to catalyze the movement to become increasingly alarmed. Editorials chastised newcomers for holding "high carnival"— wild parties — in their apartments, and admonished stockyard workers to refrain from riding the streetcars in their bloody work clothes. In the past, *The Defender* had censured such behavior as part of its program to shed the images of servitude, but now the newspaper was concerned as well that northern whites might put a stop to the migration. "A fierce agitation is being waged by certain classes of citizens against immigration of Southern people to northern cities," explained an editorial from the fall of 1917, before introducing a number of rules that sought to "disarm those who are trying to discredit our Race," including "Don't use liberty as a license to do as you please"; "Don't allow yourself to get drawn into street brawls"; "Don't be made tool or strikebreaker for any corporation or firm"; "Don't leave your job when you have a few dollars in your pocket"; and "Don't be a beer can rusher or permit children to perform such service." These guidelines were intended as much to help the migrants as to make a political statement to the white majority in the city. For just under the surface, *The Defender* understood, the tension was building.[10]

Thousands came out on the morning of Friday, October 12, 1917, to see the Eighth Regiment head off for war. People waited patiently outside the Eighth Infantry Armory built by Colonel Marshall on

Forest Avenue, lining Thirty-Fifth Street all the way to State Street and then onward to the railway station. Finally, the troops emerged from the armory, led by Colonel Franklin Denison on horseback and in full dress uniform, followed by his top officers, the unit's band, and the seven companies of enlisted men, each led by their own captains, with the machine gunners and the hospital corps bringing up the rear, some two thousand men altogether, resplendent in their crisp khaki "doughboy" uniforms and signature high-peaked, wide-brimmed hats.

It was a remarkable sight — the only all-black regiment in the United States — and a point of pride for the entire city. Marching under colors purchased for them with a $1,000 donation from *The Chicago Daily News,* the soldiers were followed by one hundred black policemen led by a black lieutenant, the only black ranking officer on a major metropolitan police force in the nation. Chicago's African American community was making a statement about its accomplishments and acceptance, defying those who would impugn their competence, patriotism, or manliness. Among the soldiers marching that day was Lieutenant Ferdinand Barnett Jr., Ida B. Wells-Barnett's stepson, and Sergeant Benote Lee, son of *The Defender*'s landlady Mrs. Henrietta Lee. Former *Defender* managing editor Zachary Withers, now the editor of *The Pullman Porters' Review,* noted that the troops were drawn from every class in the community, including "draftsmen, map-makers, painters, designers, chemists, lawyers, physicians, clerks, accountants, horseshoers, black-smiths, strategists, statisticians, machinists, chauffeurs, mechanics; in fact, this regiment is a military organization of brains, a military unit of rare qualities, for this we are most proud."[11]

*The Defender* covered the Eighth's departure with an entire page of photographs, including images of a mother embracing her uniformed son, an enlisted soldier leaning out of a train car window to kiss a young woman held aloft by a helpful police officer, and an aged African American veteran of Gettysburg, sporting a white goatee and wearing a top coat against the cold. "We taught the rebels how to behave," the Civil War vet told the young troopers before him. "Now you teach the Kaiser."[12]

While the Wilson administration had not agreed to the demands of black activists to fully integrate the military, a manpower shortage had necessitated the inclusion of a handful of experienced home-grown units such as the Eighth and also the training of new black troops, including fresh cadres of African American officers. *The Defender's* editorial page knew that all these soldiers' conduct and performance, good or bad, would serve as fodder for those who were continuing to fight a propaganda war over segregation at home. In the same issue featuring coverage of the Eighth's departure, the newspaper quoted Emmett Scott's speech to the first class of graduates from the African American officers training program in Des Moines, Iowa. "You will remember, I am sure, that you are on trial," Scott told the cadets. "It will be for you to prove that men of your race when led by competent, efficient and fearless men of the same race, are not afraid to do, to dare and to die."[13]

The following March, *The Defender* ran a photo on its women's page of Flora Abbott Sengstacke, Robert Abbott's mother, who had traveled to Chicago from Savannah, posing in front of the printing press running the one hundred thousandth copy of that week's issue, a high point in the newspaper's circulation. A short, stout woman whom Robert resembled, she appears in a dark, satiny, lace-trimmed dress covering ankle to wrist, a fine, feathery hat gracing her head, her eyes gleaming, lips betraying just the hint of a proud smile.

Impressive as the press run was, though, Robert Abbott had greater ambitions. For one thing, the printing press in front of which Flora Sengstacke posed did not belong to him; *The Defender* was printed by *The Drover's Journal,* a publishing company based in the Chicago stockyards from which Abbott purchased press time every week. He was taking steps toward the day he had his own plant. Just a few weeks earlier, he had raised the price of a yearly subscription to two dollars, and now he added four pages to his newspaper for a total of sixteen, the additional space intended to meet the demand for more news from hometowns across the USA. In addition to being a mouthpiece for the African American community, *The Defender* had become a national communications vehicle, allowing far-flung families to reconnect and helping migrants keep in touch with those they left behind.[14]

With his bankroll finally accumulating, Abbott took care of a few long-overdue matters. He presented his landlady Mrs. Lee with the deed to an eight-room brick home two blocks from the State Street building, a gift for all her help supporting the newspaper over the years. As soon as she moved out, *The Defender* expanded throughout the residence, taking over all of what had been her apartment as well as the building's second and third floors. It was still a quirky office space, but Abbott liked that 3159 South State Street was so close to the old Stroll as well as the up-and-coming areas of the community along Thirty-Fifth Street and Grand Boulevard. One biographer even described Abbott as "superstitious" about the address, although its proximity to the community's post office, which, with its African American staff, could be relied upon to send *The Defender* out, was reason enough to stay put.

As for his own quarters, Abbott moved temporarily into Mrs. Lee's new home as a boarder, but in a few months, he would announce that he was making big changes in his personal life as well.[15]

Until March 1918, the masthead's shield-and-owl logo closely resembled the shield and eagle on the masthead of Chicago's two Hearst-owned newspapers, the *Examiner* and the *American,* to the extent that customers at newsstands sometimes picked up *The Defender* by accident, or at least that is what Hearst's attorneys charged in a lawsuit they threatened to file. Whether or not the allegation had any truth to it, Abbott chose to avoid legal entanglements by changing the masthead. He asked one of his cartoonists to come up with an alternative, and just a few days later, *The Defender* debuted an image of the sphinx in place of the owl.

It was the perfect symbol to represent Abbott's great ambition for *The Defender,* Egypt's mythological half man, half lion drawing on the heritage of the grandest African civilization to claim an equal level with the *Tribune*s and *Herald*s of the world.[16]

Certainly the community was making progress at a pace no one had foreseen before the war. An editorial from that same month, "Readjustment of Labor," celebrated the fact that the walls to union membership had come down: the stockyards that in 1910 had employed fewer than two hundred black workers now employed "many thousands of our people."[17]

For years, *The Defender* had argued that the unions' segregation policies were self-defeating, allowing employers to use African

Americans as strikebreakers who undermined the unions' own ability to halt production. For African Americans, the absence of union protection left them working longer hours for less pay with no job security. Nor had the labor movement's abrupt change of policy dispelled the negative feelings that many African Americans still harbored about the unions. Nevertheless, the editorial strongly advocated accepting union membership, concluding that it would be an "unpardonable blunder" if African Americans did not join now that they had the chance.[18]

In early May, before an overflow crowd in the massive auditorium at South Park Methodist Episcopal Church, Robert Abbott opened a "Big Patriotic Meeting" featuring a keynote address from the increasingly prominent Emmett J. Scott, who spoke on the theme of national unity. Enthusiastic participation in the war effort would yield great benefits for the community, Scott said, boasting that there were already more than a thousand black officers in the military. Scott was followed by Dr. George Cleveland Hall, who had become president of the Chicago chapter of the Urban League, a new organization that was busy helping migrants get jobs, find housing, and otherwise adapt to city life. Dr. Hall also argued that African Americans' goals for World War I went well beyond victory in Europe.

"We want to make the world safe for democracy and we want to make democracy safe for the world," Dr. Hall said, echoing President Wilson's pledge, "but we also want to make the South safe for the Negro." These comments brought the strongest round of applause of the night, according to the newspaper's account.[19]

It was a moment of triumph for Robert Abbott, sharing the stage with national black leaders like Emmett Scott as well as onetime mentors like Dr. Hall. His ascent, however, would not proceed unchecked. Also in Chicago at that time was Major Walter H. Loving, the sole African American working for the Military Intelligence Bureau, a dangerous careerist who was on a secret mission in Chicago to intimidate Robert Abbott into moderating *The Defender.*

During a long tenure in the American occupation of the Philippines, Loving had become well known for directing popular military bands with Filipino performers. Under his "Loving Touch," the bands performed their martial marches and classical pieces at the 1904

World's Fair in St. Louis and to great acclaim at President Taft's inauguration. Shortly after the United States officially entered World War I, Loving, by now in his midforties, retired, and living in California, got himself hired as an employee at the Military Intelligence Branch with a wide mandate to investigate reports of German influence in African American communities around the nation.[20]

Loving took it as part of his mission to monitor black newspapers for editorials he deemed unfriendly to the war effort, even as other government agencies were pursuing the black press. The Justice Department was just then prosecuting A. Philip Randolph, the editor of *The Messenger*, an antiwar, socialist publication, for his allegedly seditious opposition to American involvement in the war. Justice Department agents had also met with members of the NAACP board to demand that W. E. B. Du Bois dial down his tone in *The Crisis*. When it came to *The Defender*, however, the Justice Department had done its own exhaustive investigation by the end of 1917 and concluded that it was "loyal to the core. There is nowhere connected with it the slightest evidence of German influence."[21]

This assessment was not good enough for the head of the Military Intelligence Bureau, who regarded *The Defender* as "the most dangerous of all Negro Journals" and ordered Loving to confront Abbott, regardless of whether the military had any actual power to contain or punish a civilian newspaper. During their meeting, Loving produced a letter with allegations against Abbott's loyalty and told the editor "that the eye of the government is centered upon his paper, and caution should be his guide."[22]

Abbott wrote his response to Loving in a formal letter, denying that *The Defender* had ever "spoken disloyal," and listing all of his patriotic gestures, including his personal purchase of $12,000 in liberty bonds and the printing of messages on *The Defender*'s masthead urging readers to buy bonds themselves. He blamed segregationists for casting aspersions upon his newspaper, noting that his distributors in several locations had been threatened and forced to flee. Abbott himself regularly received death threats, he complained to Loving, and yet, all during the wartime period, *The Defender* had been a steadfast supporter of federal authority, glossing over prior critiques of the Wilson administration. But if Abbott was unwilling to roll over under baseless charges, he also understood he had a "hand in the lion's mouth," and assured Loving that he would continue to restrain his staff from printing anything that was incendiary or might "inculcate in the heart of any member of my race the spirit of revolt against the laws of the national or state governments."[23]

Abbott's letter satisfied the Military Intelligence Bureau, though Loving pledged to continue his monitoring, and *The Defender* continued to blast away at segregation without interruption. "Southern Stunts Surpass Huns," read a front-page headline on June 8, 1918, depicting an incident in Jonesboro, Arkansas, in which a drunken mob of white men seized a black man named William McKenzie and brought him to a railroad crossing, where they tied his hands and feet and then strapped his neck across the rail as the mail train approached. McKenzie was decapitated, and his mangled body was deposited at a local funeral home with a cryptically worded note: "a drunken darkie had been killed by the Frisco train."[24]

One white postmaster in Denison, Texas, incensed by *The Defender*'s coverage of McKenzie's murder, not only withheld delivery of that edition to his town, but wrote to his superiors that the article — rather than the murder — was an act of "rank race hatred which shows signs of German conspiracy . . . that stirs in the negro's [*sic*] revolutionary mind not only the seditious thought but the seditious act."

A postal service lawyer agreed with the postmaster, writing an internal memo analyzing *The Defender*'s coverage of lynching incidents. "In the narratives the publications rarely, if ever, mention the provications [*sic*] furnished by the victims," the lawyer whined, "and if such provications are mentioned they are usually discredited. Such articles can have but one effect on the negro [*sic*] and that is to cause him to hate the whites and the white man's government."

A few days after that memo was written, Robert Abbott received a letter from the U.S. Post Office Department warning him that the "Southern Stunts Surpass Huns" story may have violated the freshly signed Espionage Act. The letter warned that publishing anything "that tends to create in the minds of members of your race the idea that they have no part in the struggle against the Imperial German government and that they are being just as badly treated by the whites of America as they would be by the whites of Germany tends to interfere in the cause of the United States and should have no place in a loyal newspaper."[25]

Beyond these vaguely menacing words, however, the postal service lawyer's letter admitted that the article did not warrant suppression of the newspaper. Shrugging off this warning, Abbott continued to compare segregation and violence against African Americans with the atrocities committed by the Germans. Later that summer, an editorial signed by Abbott called out a Chicago school board member who advocated segregation, stating that he "could do no more to support the Kaiser among our people by raising the issue of separate schools while we are engaged in a war to convince the Hun that class and race distinctions must forever be banished."[26]

A torrent of complaints about *The Defender* from politicians and minor officials, almost all of them white southerners, continued to pour in to the Bureau of Investigation, whose chief called for one last review in June 1918 to determine if there were any links to German conspiracies. Agents went through the motions again, finding only that *The Defender*'s circulation had risen to 120,000 per week since they had last checked several months earlier.[27]

Even as the Post Office Department was harassing *The Defender*, the Wilson administration was changing tack when it came to the black press. Emmett Scott was planning a conference in Washington, D.C., with all the major black publishers in the country, an unprecedented meeting at which Robert Abbott would play a major role. In mid-June, the week before the conference, Abbott boarded a train in order to make several stops along the way, disembarking first in Rochester, New York. Intending only to meet with his circulation agent there, Abbott was soon recognized by an old friend, a prominent local pastor who "knew the Editor in his early days of struggle" and quickly assembled a dinner of prominent citizens to celebrate the visit from "king of the weeklies."

After the meal, Abbott gave an impromptu lecture to a packed church auditorium just over the basement print shop where Frederick Douglass had produced *The North Star* and other publications. Never an especially elegant public speaker, Abbott found his voice when he spoke about Douglass's legacy. "As I stand here on the very spot where Douglass published his anti-slavery newspaper," said Abbott, "I feel like pulling off my shoes and must admit that I feel the spirit of greatness and honor emanating from the soul of that grand old man, hovering over us all at this hour."[28]

In New York, Abbott stopped at *The Defender*'s newly opened Harlem office on 135th Street before being treated to a theater show and a banquet dinner by his staff there. Managed by one of his cousins, the New York operation included a general manager and a business manager who were husband and wife, as well as a staff correspondent and a stenographer. This tiny crew assembled an entire page of news from the disparate black neighborhoods in the city and beyond, selling thirty-one thousand copies weekly—thirteen thousand in Manhattan, five thousand in Brooklyn, and the balance distributed by agents throughout the region.[29]

Abbott finally arrived in Washington and on Wednesday, June 19, Emmett Scott opened the three-day conference in the Interior Department's new headquarters on Eighteenth and F Streets, with forty editors representing black newspapers from across the South, East, and Midwest, as well as prominent African American ministers, government officials, and academics. The attendees included W. E. B. Du Bois, along with the editors of *The Richmond Times* and the *Baltimore Afro-American*—all of whom had been subject to various levels of government investigation and harassment—as well as such august figures as P. B. S. Pinchback, who had served as governor of Louisiana during the Reconstruction era and was now living in the capital. The government side was led by Secretary of War Newton D. Baker and George Creel, the chairman of the Committee on Public Information, but also included a long list of junior officials, including Franklin Delano Roosevelt, then the assistant secretary of the Navy. Two French officers were on hand to discuss the treatment of black colonial troops, a topic *The Defender* had covered for some months, noting with admiration that in the French military, Africans fought side by side with white soldiers in the trenches.[30]

*The Defender* was the giant in the room in terms of circulation and national reach, selling as many copies every week as all of the ten other black newspapers combined, but Robert Abbott kept a modest profile in favor of letting his peers speak. A freewheeling conversation remarkable for its "utmost freedom and frankness" ensued among the participants, according to *The Defender*'s account of the gathering. The newspaper quoted Robert R. Moton, who had succeeded Booker T. Washington at the helm of the Tuskegee Institute, arguing that any unrest among African Americans was the product of "apparently increasing frequency of lynchings of brutal and barbarous character." This earned the applause and agreement of everyone in the room.[31]

Du Bois took the lead drafting a statement that affirmed the black editors' commitment to the war effort while also underscoring just how much influence they had over the twelve million Americans comprising their readership, a crucial component of the workforce and the military. African Americans, taken together, were loyal but restive, he observed, noting that the black press could help bolster morale only if there were real changes to trumpet. The editors' presence alone in Washington, they calculated, was proof that they had the attention of the nation's powerbrokers, and they attached fourteen demands to match President Wilson's famous Fourteen Points, number one being the enactment of federal laws to stamp out lynching. They called as well for the admittance of African American women to the Red Cross, African American men into the U.S. Navy, and an end to the segregation holding back black officers. "German propaganda among us is powerless," the statement concluded, "but the apparent indifference of their own government may be dangerous."[32]

In the face of this advocacy, Secretary of War Baker began to lobby President Wilson to make a personal statement against lynching, but in the interim, the editors came under criticism for appearing to capitulate to the Wilson administration just as the community finally was gaining power. Boston's Monroe Trotter, for instance, refused to make an appearance at the Washington conference, opting instead to attend a "Liberty Congress" that called out the editors for being "wined and dined at the government's expense for the sole purpose of muzzling them."[33]

Two weeks later, Du Bois became a target of particular scorn when he published "Close Ranks," a short editorial in *The Crisis* in which he called for a suspension of African American protests against discrimination in order to fully support the war effort. "Let us, while this war lasts," read the editorial's most notorious sentence, "forget our special grievances and close our ranks shoulder to shoulder with our own white fellow citizens and the allied nations that are fighting for democracy."

A remarkable departure from the nuanced militancy of the editors' statement, this provoked a firestorm. "The learned Dr. Du Bois has seldom packed more error into a single sentence," wrote *The Pittsburgh Courier*, whose editor, Robert Vann, was one of the attendees at the Washington conference. The editor of the *New York News*, another conference member, accused Du Bois of "crass moral cowardice."[34]

The backlash grew particularly vehement within the NAACP after the revelation that Du Bois had been seeking an appointment as a captain in the military, the implication being that he had written "Close Ranks" in no small part to strengthen his chances. The front page of the July 20, 1918, issue of *The Defender* reported that the Washington, D.C., chapter of the NAACP — with a membership of seven thousand — was upset by the editorial as well as by the prospect of its chief spokesperson donning a military uniform. "The entire NAACP organization is greatly stirred over what many members claim was an abandoning of the Race by Dr. Du Bois," *The Defender* summarized.[35]

In the end, Major Walter Loving used the controversy to torpedo Du Bois's bid for a military commission. In an official letter to his superiors, Loving cited the "storm of protest" that had erupted after the publication of "Close Ranks," adding that "Dr. Du Bois has been bitterly assailed and called a traitor, while the Government has come in for its share of criticism for having brought about this condition by influencing Dr. Du Bois to abandon his former principles."[36]

For most of July, Abbott and the other editors who had attended Scott's conference found themselves on the defensive. Then, a most unexpected thing happened — Woodrow Wilson spoke out against lynching.

"We are at this very moment fighting lawless passion," began a statement issued from the White House on July 26. "Germany has outlawed herself among the nations because she has disregarded the sacred obligations of law and has made lynchers of her armies. Lynchers emulate her disgraceful example.

"I say plainly that every American who takes part in the action of a mob or gives any sort of countenance is no true son of this great Democracy but its betrayer, and does more to discredit her by that single disloyalty to her standards of law and of right than the words of her statesmen or the sacrifices of her heroic boys in the trenches can do to make suffering peoples believe her to be their savior.

"They can at least say that such things cannot happen in Germany except in times of revolution, when law is swept away."[37]

*The New York Times* and the *Chicago Tribune* tried to link Wilson's statement to the lynching of a white German immigrant in Illinois some months earlier, and it was true that Wilson never mentioned African Americans directly, stating only that lynching took place in "many and wildly separated parts of the country." But the language in the statement was nearly identical to many similarly inclined editorials in the black press, and *The Defender* claimed full credit for Wilson's dramatic change of heart. "Editors' Conference Yields Big Results," read the front-page headline celebrating the "frank, positive and unequivocal declaration of the President of the United States against mob spirit," adding that it would lead to a "keener impulse to assist" in the war effort.[38]

The article listed other gains achieved by the conference as well, including the acceptance of black women into the Red Cross as nurses and hostesses for black troops based in the United States. True, Wilson had not outlawed lynching, and such atrocities continued to occur in the South on a daily basis, including, for instance, the killing of a young woman seven months pregnant whose child was cut out of her. Still, the statement on lynching was significant, and *The Defender* asserted that this once-reviled president now deserved African Americans' support. An editorial in the same issue, entitled "Our President Has Spoken," characterized Wilson as having been "too weak" to face down southern white Democrats in the past, but praised him nonetheless for being the first president since Lincoln who "had the backbone to publicly denounce this evil."[39]

In August, President Wilson went even further, intervening in two Democratic primaries for the U.S. Senate, coming out against the re-election bid of one incumbent, James Vardaman of Mississippi, as well as against the candidacy of Coleman Blease, who was seeking to enter the Senate from South Carolina. Both Blease and Vardaman were notorious for their overt support of lynching, and Wilson wrote a supporter that he would consider a victory for Vardaman a "condemnation of his administration," while labeling Blease, in a separate statement, an "undesirable." When both Vardaman and Blease were defeated, *The Defender* gave Wilson full credit, observing that "the words from the mouth of the chief executive of the nation came like a hammer blow to the Vardaman supporters."[40]

Between the Great Migration and the development of wartime industry, the demographics of the cities of the North had changed irrevocably, as had the dynamic between labor and landowner in the South. And now the ground was shifting in the national political landscape as well.

# 6

# The Bonds of Affections

B Y THE END of July 1918, all of Black Chicago was on edge, waiting for news from the community's men in uniform. Many relatives of the soldiers hoping for word came to *The Defender's* office or called in on a daily basis, but military censors were enforcing an information blackout. The newspaper had been able to confirm only that the old Eighth Infantry, recast as the 370th Infantry Regiment in the American Expeditionary Forces, had been deployed under French command in a division with other mostly black former National Guard units. By regularly scanning announced troop movements, the newspaper's staff guessed the men were involved in heavy combat, but in terms of specific information, they could but wait alongside everyone else.[1]

Letters that had been written in early July finally began arriving in early August, after they were cleared by censors on both sides of the Atlantic, and *The Defender* printed correspondence that was written directly to the newspaper as well as messages shared by their recipients. These first letters detailed the troops' progress from their landing in France in April, when they had slept in barracks built for Napoleon's Grande Armée, through their training in a village with breathtaking views of the Swiss Alps. Their first assignment was in a relatively quiet district near the Swiss border, overlooking the French town of Saint-Mihiel, which was occupied by the Germans. They suffered few casualties there, with just one killed, although one soldier wrote that volleys of artillery fire from the French and German side "rock us to sleep at night and awaken us in the morning, and then the machine guns chime in the chorus."

Already the war had provided these men, for the first time in their lives, the experience of a racially tolerant environment. Their letters are filled with descriptions of the international array of fighting men that had gathered as part of their coalition, the "jaunty and debonair" French and English officers, along with the Italians, Japanese, Russians, and even Chinese troops. They were amazed, most of all, by the French, who welcomed them into their military as well as their bars, restaurants, and nightclubs, and even their homes. The black troops were stunned to find themselves billeted in French houses — with enlisted men assigned to haylofts and officers given spare bedrooms. It was the sort of openness that most American whites, North or South, would never have countenanced.

Instead of pariahs, the black troops were often treated like celebrities. Where white American officers turned their backs or worse when Colonel Denison passed, French officers — even those at the top ranks — often invited him to meals, a courtesy extended down the line as well. Not that the black troops could escape Jim Crow entirely in Europe: whenever they appeared on the streets with their French girlfriends, black troops had to watch out for American military police, many of whom were white southerners who would assault them on sight.

In the next round of letters, written in the middle of July and printed in *The Defender* a month later, was a missive from Colonel Denison to a friend who worked in the Chicago office of the public prosecutor. Though indicating that he was limited, like the other soldiers, by what the censors would allow him to write, Denison expressed great satisfaction at having completed the training of his men and "made a first-rate fighting force out of indifferent material."[2]

Like his predecessor Colonel Marshall, Denison was the highest-ranking black officer in the American military; all of the other African American National Guard units incorporated into the AEF had white officers beyond the rank of captain. And there were many who hoped he would fail. To obviate the prospect that Denison or the other black officers might command white *Americans,* the American high command had placed these African American troops in their own division under French command. For the black troops themselves, this meant that they had French commanders with whom they could not easily communicate, not to mention foreign equipment with which they had not trained. Worst of all were the French rations, which were smaller than the Americans' and barely edible.[3]

Soon after Denison led his troops to the Argonne Forest region, a white colonel, Thomas A. Roberts, appeared at camp and began telling the black officers that Denison was "a very sick man," too ill to command the unit. Immediately suspecting that Roberts had been sent to supplant Denison, the 370th's officers began to grumble. On July 12, Denison was, in fact, recalled to headquarters and Roberts became their commanding officer. There was no time to protest, however, as two days later, the black troops had to defend their positions against a massive German onslaught, a desperate summer drive toward Paris.[4]

*The Defender* got final confirmation of Colonel Denison's removal in the last days of August from a letter by Benote Lee, the son of the paper's longtime landlady, recently promoted to lieutenant. Writing to his mother from a newly created shell crater, with ordnance whizzing over his head in every direction, Lee mentioned the change in command only in passing, focusing instead on the "Hun Plane" that stalked him one evening while he and another officer were inspecting a frontline communications trench on horseback. "Just as we spied him," he recounted, "he dove into some clouds but the hum of his motor was very distinct. Presently, he opened up with his machine gun." Lee and the major were pinned down until French antiaircraft fire drove the plane away.[5]

Deep in *The Defender*'s September 21 edition, on page 11, in the "All Around the Town" section, appeared a small notice sandwiched between items covering a matron's return from her sojourn to the Northwest and an upcoming guest speaker at a local church. Under the subhead "Editor Abbott Becomes Benedict," the blurb announced the forty-eight-year-old publisher's marriage to Helen Thornton Morrison, from his home state of Georgia. "The bride comes of one of the leading families of Athens and represents the highest point of Southern culture."[6]

The wedding had taken place ten days earlier in the home of a minister, the notice indicated, and the couple would be residing at 4847 South Champlain Avenue. Finally moving out of Mrs. Lee's domicile, Abbott set up his new household in a five-room bungalow on the edge of the community, where the city's wealthiest African Americans lived. The wedding had caught many completely off-guard, since until that point, Abbott had been extremely low key about his personal life — even longtime employees could recall only one relationship of a possibly romantic nature, an "actress friend" of Abbott's who lived near *The Defender*'s office, whom he visited under the pretext of using her phone.[7]

As was customary at the time, the bride's age was not announced, though Helen was said to be in her twenties. It was not the difference in their years, however, that caught most people's attention. Tall and thin, with blue eyes, hair described as "titian," and a complexion so light she was often mistaken for white, the new Mrs. Abbott's appearance inspired cocked eyebrows among many and prompted some — even among Robert's own family — to deride him as "color struck." Certainly the story of a wealthy, older, dark-complexioned man marrying a lighter, younger woman to upgrade his social status was a familiar one. But Helen was so light that the sight of the editor and his bride was positively provocative to a good many. Anecdotes of the time indicate that Abbott enjoyed the resulting confusion and excitement the union stirred up both within the community and whenever they made an appearance at a public event. Indeed, the editor saw his marriage as one more way to show the whole world, blacks *and* whites, that a black man could do anything a white man could, even marry a white(ish) woman.

For her part, the new Mrs. Abbott came into the marriage seeking a fresh start, having fled to Chicago after her first husband, back in Athens, committed suicide. When he met her, Helen was working as a clerk at the Carson Pirie Scott department store in Chicago's Loop, a job she'd obtained by passing as white, but she quickly adapted to the role of wife of the nation's foremost African American journalist, becoming an enthusiastic society hostess and participating in charity activities. Formal in demeanor, she could come across to her contemporaries as aloof. In public, she maintained a reserved veneer, addressing her husband as "Mr. Abbott," while in her diary, she relaxed into the more familiar "Mr. A."[8]

• • •

From the moment its reporter confirmed the news that Colonel Denison had been replaced, *The Defender* had been skeptical of the military's official reason — that Denison had had an attack of "acute rheumatism"— and at the end of September, Abbott got the chance to investigate the matter himself. Tipped off that the colonel was back in the United States and would be stopping in Chicago for a few hours between trains on his way to a military hospital in Des Moines, Iowa, Abbott accompanied Mrs. Denison and Teenan Jones, a mutual friend, to Union Station.

Caught off-guard when he saw Abbott, the colonel quipped, "Everywhere I go I see *The Defender.*"

Though Denison was coy about the reason for his dismissal, Abbott, having observed the colonel sprinting upstairs to catch his connecting train, suspected that ill health had nothing to do with it. As a military officer, Denison was not inclined to make his protest public, but the newspaper had confirmed its suspicions that the real reason for Denison's removal had been his race, not his health.[9]

For the men of the 370th, meanwhile, the final weeks of the war proved the meanest. In the middle of September, they were deployed opposite the section of the German Hindenburg Line near the Allette Canal, where, amid a landscape of destruction, they slept in caves. On October 12 and 13, after a series of courageous attacks on fortified machine-gun nests, the 370th took possession of a number of enemy trenches before liberating the town of Laon, losing forty men in the process. At the beginning of November, thirty-five more men were killed and fifty wounded when an artillery shell hit a mess tent. But by then, the Germans were being routed all along the front, and the 370th joined in the pursuit, even after the cease-fire was officially declared. On November 11, the date of the armistice, Lieutenant Colonel Otis Duncan, the highest-ranking African American in the active U.S. Army after Colonel Denison's removal, led a charge on the town of Gue D'Hossus, Belgium, just a few moments before the armistice was signed.[10]

Deeply moved by the bravery and dedication of these African Americans from Chicago, the French awarded sixty-eight members of the 370th the Croix de Guerre. Another twenty-one soldiers received the American Distinguished Service Cross, and one soldier was awarded a Distinguished Service Medal, making it, by some measures, the most decorated unit in the AEF. The toll, however, had been extremely high: ninety-five men killed and more than five hundred wounded, a casualty rate of 20 percent.

"We have hardly had the time to appreciate you and already you depart," wrote the French general commanding the 370th, in his final orders. "The blood of your comrades who fell on the soil of France, mixed with the blood of our soldiers, renders indissoluble the bonds of affections that unite us."[11]

In mid-December, immediately after the 370th was officially transferred out of French command, Colonel Roberts further antagonized the men by demoting several black officers, reassigning several others, and then bringing in white replacements. Nevertheless, the men of the 370th stayed in France without serious incident until the end of January, then sailed for the United States, arriving in New York on February 9. At some point during this demobilization period, the troops' French equipment, helmets, and other items were replaced with standard American items.[12]

As part of a small group of black leaders working with city officials, Abbott made plans for a parade and other public gatherings to celebrate the return of the 370th. But because the "Black Devils," as the daily newspapers preferred to call them, were the first contingent of the city's men to return home from the war, an enormous crowd of whites *and* blacks were waiting for them when they disembarked from their train early in the morning. The men marched from the La-Salle Street train station to the Chicago Coliseum to find more than sixty thousand family, friends, and supporters gathered, and the official agenda quickly gave way to joyous scenes of reunion mixed with somber requiems to the fallen. The crowd went wild when Franklin Denison arrived; he had been promoted to brigadier general upon his retirement, the highest rank ever achieved by an African American. Mayor Big Bill Thompson, who was running for reelection, made an unscheduled appearance in the coliseum, but even his booming voice couldn't overcome the din when he tried to speak.

"My son," exclaimed Lieutenant Colonel Duncan's mother, who joined him onstage after not seeing him for two years, "you are so good." Duncan sat down and held his sobbing mother's hands.

After the event at the coliseum, the troops were to march down Michigan Avenue to Grand Central Station in full combat gear, including their newly issued American steel trench helmets and rifles. As soon as they assembled, however, the crowds streamed off the sidewalks and mixed among the soldiers, waving French and American flags in celebration of the victorious end to the conflict. From a reviewing stand between the stone lions on the steps of the Art Institute, Robert Abbott and his wife, Helen, along with Ed Wright and Mayor Thompson and their spouses, looked on — whether with amusement or consternation is not recorded — while the orderly proceeding they had planned dissolved into a mass of people flowing very slowly toward the station. "Again and again, the line of march was not distinguishable," wrote *The Defender*, in language very similar to the description in the *Tribune*, "with girls carrying rifles and men carrying soldiers."[13]

Both *The Defender* and the *Tribune* devoted extensive coverage to the return of the troops, but as usual, their angles differed significantly. *The Defender* filled its front page with photos of the 370th and added four pages to the edition to recount the exploits of the unit as well as the history of the "Old Eighth" going back to Colonel Marshall's day. Already, the newspaper was thinking about the contributions these troops would make now that they were home. "We who remained at home expect much of you," asserted an editorial in the same issue. "The same fighting spirit which you displayed on the battlefields of Europe is needed in the titanic struggle for survival we are passing in this country today. If you have been fighting for democracy, let it be a real democracy, a democracy in which the blacks can have equal hopes, equal opportunities and equal rewards with the whites."[14]

For the *Tribune*, the return of the city's "dusky heroes" was yet another remarkable moment of racial solidarity, one in which the streets were filled with a "checkerboard of faces" and "whites waived the color line and sent up cheer after cheer." But though the newspaper devoted all of page 3 to the unit's return, it couldn't restrain itself from characterizing the black soldiers as "bucks," and quoting the men using dialect, including one soldier anxious to return to civilian life reported as saying, "What ah want is mah discharge."[15]

• • •

With an all-out effort from Ed Wright's political operation in the black community, Mayor Big Bill Thompson won reelection that spring in the April 1 General Election. The Second Ward, which now held a black population of 70 percent, delivered 11,000 votes for Thompson all on its own, allowing the mayor to squeak by several opponents with a plurality of 17,600 votes. Had black voters turned toward another candidate, divided their votes evenly among the candidates, or simply stayed home that day, Thompson would have lost.[16]

The mayoral victory was a triumph for *The Defender* as well, as the newspaper had been alone in dismissing charges of corruption in Thompson's City Hall, while the *Tribune, The Daily News,* and the Municipal Voters League endorsed one of his opponents. After the election, the staunchly Republican *Tribune* joined with Democratic Party leaders in blaming Thompson's victory on the black vote, which was interpreted as further evidence of Big Bill's perfidy. But for *The Defender,* even these hostile reports were further evidence of the growing political sophistication of the black community as well as the newspaper's influence. "Modesty prevents us from claiming that the 'World's Greatest Weekly' wields more political influence than all of the Chicago dailies combined," the newspaper wrote on its front page, "but results are what count."[17]

As the unending flow of people from the South to Chicago's South Side continued to erase the city's racial borders, tensions continued to build among those whites who objected to the influx. While some were happy to sell to African Americans, others tried to devise mortgage and lease provisions that would prevent blacks from moving in. Some even resorted to violence.

In May 1919 *The Defender* covered a series of bomb attacks on the home of Gertrude and Richard Harrison, on Grand Boulevard just south of Forty-Eighth Street. The first time the house was attacked, a man arrived in a taxicab at 11:00 p.m., deposited the explosive on the Harrisons' porch, and then returned to the waiting cab before the bomb detonated, shattering several windows on the front of the building. Neither Gertrude nor Richard, a famed actor who traveled the country performing the works of Shakespeare and Paul Laurence Dunbar, was home at the time; they returned a half hour after the explosion to find their neighbors inspecting the damage, which was minimal, probably because the bomber didn't want to damage neighboring properties.[18]

The Harrisons had only moved into the home on the first of the month and knew that they were taking a risk, Forty-Eighth Street marking the latest racial dividing line. They had received warnings, which they had dutifully passed on to the captain of that police district. The police did nothing, however, and predictably, the Harrisons' home was bombed a second time less than two weeks later. This time, the incendiary device was thrown from the fire escape of the next building through a skylight into the house's interior, although it damaged the house no more seriously than the first had done. The Harrisons' white neighbors must have had foreknowledge of this bombing as well, for they were gathered outside the home even before it occurred. Again the police investigation was cursory; a lieutenant arrived, asked a few questions of the Harrisons, and left without interviewing any of the neighbors.[19]

*The Defender*'s editorial page accused the police in the precinct surrounding the Harrisons' of collusion with the bombers, and named the Kenwood Improvement Association, a civic group closely associated with Realtors in the neighborhood east of the black community, of instigating the violence to manipulate the property market in the area. But the police continued to ignore the issue, and the bombers attacked next the Harrisons' landlord, a white attorney named William B. Austin. An explosive placed underneath Austin's house on tony North Lake Shore Drive destroyed his basement but failed to injure him or his family, and he gave a defiant interview to *The Defender*'s editorial page columnist in which he supported the expansion of African Americans' reach in the city as a necessary consequence of the migration. "The Colored people of Chicago form a very important and extensive part of our population. 100,000 of them cannot live where 10,000 of them once lived," Austin said. "They will live forever on the South Side."

The Harrisons themselves, discouraged by the lack of police protection and the continued hostility from their neighbors, moved out before the end of June. But the realities in each community remained constant — blacks, on one side, needed more space, while a hardcore group of whites, on the other, were determined to keep them out.[20]

The community's western border was patrolled by a white gang called Ragan's Colts, which, like the Kenwood Improvement Association, escalated its attacks against blacks that summer. In late June, *The Defender* reported that on a particular night, one group of Colts shot to death a forty-seven-year-old married father of six in front of a candy store, while another group beat a twenty-seven-year-old veteran, leaving him unconscious but alive. The newspaper reported that large bands of Colts had previously destroyed the few streetlights in the area and performed other acts of vandalism, but police were lenient with them because many members of the gang were related to officers.[21]

Indeed, Ragan's Colts and other "social clubs" were composed of more than mere thugs: based in pool halls and saloons of the working-class, mostly Irish neighborhoods between the African American community and the malodorous stockyards, they were part of the city's political structure, adjuncts to the Democratic Party who served as registrars and hypervigilant poll workers, ever ready to use their fists to persuade a wavering voter. Their ranks also included ambitious up-and-comers like Richard J. Daley, the future mayor, who was just then graduating from a nearby Catholic high school and was a member of the Hamburgers, a club from the next neighborhood north, known as Bridgeport.[22]

The main battleground for the Colts that summer was Washington Park, a modest green space that was one of the few parks accessible to African Americans. Progressing to ever-more violent tactics, the Colts moved from fists to knives as they attacked groups of young blacks in Washington Park, and then, amid continued inaction from the police, to blackjacks and brass knuckles and finally to firearms.[23]

Beyond the housing shortage and the street gangs, the racial tension in Chicago was exacerbated by frequent labor strikes that drove up prices on basic commodities. But there was one other factor that made the whole social mixture especially combustible — the criminalization of alcohol. At the beginning of July, Chicago was declared a dry town as Illinois politicians elected to enforce the Wartime Prohibition Act in advance of the new constitutional amendment installing prohibition as national law. *The Defender,* having campaigned in favor of prohibition for years, was thrilled.[24]

Soon enough, the bars, nightclubs, and gambling dens would reopen, as law enforcement looked the other way in exchange for a few dollars. And while reformers reveled in what they hoped would be the dawn of a new era of sobriety, the wealthy continued to access alcohol in their private clubs, if they did not have ample supplies in their cellars. But for working men, black and white, the sudden withdrawal of cold beer during an especially fetid summer was a blow.[25]

To cool off, many were drawn to the coast of Lake Michigan. Though theoretically open to all, these public spaces were, in practice, segregated. The unofficially designated black beach at Twenty-Sixth Street had its own lifeguard and bathhouse facilities. *The Defender*, sensing that the beaches would be the focal point for all the pent-up frustration in the city, urged caution during the Fourth of July holiday. "The parks and the bathing beaches are more inviting these warm days than State Street," an editorial stated. "A word to the wise should be sufficient."[26]

Shortly after the July 5 edition of *The Defender* hit the streets of Longview, Texas, a group of white men ambushed the newspaper's correspondent, Samuel L. Jones, and interrogated him about an unsigned report that appeared in the issue, an article describing a recent lynching in Longview, the victim of which was "shot to pieces" after "a prominent white woman declared she loved him, and if she were in the North would obtain a divorce and marry him."

Though Jones had indeed written the article, he was able to convince his assailants, the brothers of the lynching victim's girlfriend among them, otherwise. Jones then hid at the office of a friend, Dr. Calvin P. Davis, before gathering twenty-five black armed men to fend off the inevitable white mob that assembled to find them. Jones, Davis, and their defenders were able to fend off the whites' initial assault after an exchange of gunfire that left several of the attackers wounded. But soon, there were thousands of armed whites searching for Jones and Davis, and they were forced to run for their lives, using circuitous routes and disguises as they made their way to Chicago. The white mob, meanwhile, rampaged through the town they fled, burning black homes and businesses and beating men as well as women.[27]

On the front page of the following week's edition was news of another race riot, this time in Bisbee, Arizona, where black soldiers from the Tenth Cavalry, one of the famed "Buffalo Soldier" regiments, clashed with military policemen and townspeople in a wild shootout that left ten people wounded. Like some sort of contagion, armed clashes between the races were spreading across the country, throughout the South and as far west as Omaha and San Francisco, and even along the East Coast, in Connecticut and Delaware.[28]

*The Defender*'s editorial page asked if Chicago was next, citing the bombings of the Harrisons' home as well as the Colts' attacks in Washington Park to argue that the reluctance of police, prosecutors, and judges to act on these cases only made the situation worse. "If the existing force is inadequate," one editorial on the topic concluded, "then provisions should be made for more policemen."[29]

In June 1919, Carl Sandburg spent ten days in the black community to research a special series for *The Chicago Daily News*, where he was the editorial page columnist. Sandburg, forty-one, was by then a writer of some renown — his book of poems depicting Chicago as the "City of the Big Shoulders" had been published three years earlier — and he surveyed churches, community organizations, factories, union halls, gambling dens, and slums as well as "newspaper row" on South State Street, where *The Defender* was the flagship of an armada of black weeklies.[30]

Sandburg shadowed a *Defender* reporter and sifted through the piles of letters arriving at the newspaper's offices daily from southerners hungry for information about opportunities in the North. Seeing that the newspaper was ubiquitous, he determined that each issue, when one counted how many times copies were passed from hand to hand or read aloud, must have been read by more than a million people. Both the newspaper and the migration, Sandburg concluded, were components of a mass campaign of resistance to southern segregation. "Not only is Chicago a receiving station and port of refuge for colored people who are anxious to be free from the jurisdiction of lynch law," he wrote, "but there has been built here a publicity or propaganda machine that directs its appeals or carries on an agitation that each week reaches hundreds of thousands of the colored race in the southern states."[31]

By now, Chicago's black population had surpassed 125,000, and the city was a hub for tens of thousands more passing through on their way to other spots in the Midwest. In this teeming commercial

and cultural environment, Sandburg detected a new militant attitude, especially from the black veterans of World War I, who proudly
displayed the relics and souvenirs of their time in France and spoke
of the principles for which they had sacrificed.[32]

Black Chicago was prosperous enough to support a thriving business sector that included five banks, four of which had opened just
in the past three years, and spiritual enough to fill Olivet Baptist
Church, with a membership that, in the same time period, had doubled to eighty-five hundred members, making it the largest Protestant
church in North America. Recognizing the essential role the political
organization built by Ed Wright had played in Mayor Thompson's
reelection a few weeks earlier, Sandburg rated it as "the strongest effective unit of political power, good or bad, in America."[33]

A strong supporter of labor rights as well as racial equality, Sandburg was thrilled to discover that unions which had previously drawn
the color line were now actively recruiting African Americans. Union
leaders seemed to have come to understand that one way or another,
the empty spots in factories and along the cutting lines would be
filled with African Americans. By mid-1919, Sandburg estimated that
there were fifteen thousand blacks working in the stockyards, including two thousand at Armour and Co., the second-largest group there
after Poles. Black men could also now get hired as molders, shipping
clerks, construction workers, and auto mechanics, and at tanneries,
mattress factories, foundries, and steel mills, while black women,
previously restricted to domestic work, could now find jobs at garment factories as well as hotels, restaurants, and laundries.[34]

Sanguine as he was, however, about the new world that the migrants had built for themselves in Chicago, Sandburg also saw the raw
hatred that bubbled up whenever African Americans tried to settle
in a previously all-white area. He investigated a number of bomb attacks, including those directed at the Harrisons, as well as the allegations against the Kenwood Improvement Association, finding substantial evidence that it was, in fact, involved. Sandburg interviewed
L. M. Smith, the head of the association, who, though denying that
his organization had sponsored the bombers, vowed openly to prevent African Americans from moving into white areas. "They injure
our investments. They hurt our values," Smith alleged. "I couldn't say
how many have moved in, but there's at least a hundred blocks that

are tainted. We are not making any threats, but we do say that something must be done."[35]

Sandburg investigated Smith's assertion that the presence of African Americans diminished home prices but found this accusation to be false, citing the case of a wealthy woman who was induced to sell her home at a loss by an agent who warned that "colored people were coming into the neighborhood and the property surely was going to take a slump." Sandburg found a nearly identical building that had already been turned over to black tenants, and the rent in its apartments had jumped from $35 to $50 per month, contradicting the claim that African Americans somehow lowered property values. Like *The Defender*, he came to the conclusion that real estate interests were using the fear of African Americans to skew property prices in their favor. "The fact is that it wasn't an open market," Sandburg concluded. "It was a panicky market."[36]

As Sandburg was aware even while he was documenting the realities in his city, bloody battles between the races continued to erupt throughout the country. In Washington, D.C., beginning on the night of July 20, mobs of white men, including off-duty soldiers, sailors, and Marines in uniform, attacked blacks on the streetcars and in other public places, shooting, robbing, and beating more than one hundred and, over three days of bloodshed, murdered at least four. Carter G. Woodson, dean of Howard University and a contributor to *The Defender*, narrowly escaped a large group of white men by hiding in a basement, from where he witnessed the mob catch another black man, hoist him above the street, and shoot him to death. Several black men were beaten in front of the gate to the White House, and in at least one instance, white men in uniform forced their way into an upscale restaurant searching for black wait staff to assault.[37]

As with many previous riots in the South, the violence in the capital was spurred by the white-owned media. The day before the riots broke out, *The Washington Post*, then at a low point in terms of both circulation and ethics, ran a story under the headline "Negroes Attack Girl," which depicted a fictional assault by two black men. It was the kind of story that consistently generated violence in the South. *The Post* even continued in this vein *during* the riot, printing a story two days into the violence that called for a mass gathering of armed white men whose "purpose is a 'clean-up' that will cause the events

of the last two evenings to pale into insignificance." As instructed by
*The Post,* some four hundred men showed up at the Knights of Co-
lumbus building on Pennsylvania Avenue and roamed the downtown
area, looking for blacks to attack.[38]

Blacks fought back, setting up barricades around Howard University and other locations, pulling white soldiers off of streetcars that
passed through *their* neighborhoods and stationing snipers — many
of them black veterans of World War I — on rooftops. Both sides
drove "terror cars" bristling with armed men into each other's neighborhoods to shoot at pedestrians. The violence was stopped only
when President Wilson finally authorized the secretary of war to
deploy two thousand battle-hardened troops into the streets, commanded by a no-nonsense veteran. With bayonets on their rifles,
these soldiers quickly dispersed the crowds of combatants, their efforts aided by a drenching rain that began that evening.[39]

In his articles, Sandburg wondered whether the violence would
hit Chicago next, interviewing a hopeful police official who argued
against its likelihood, noting that Chicago's police force was more
integrated and its institutions stronger in general. But two weeks into
Sandburg's series, just as he was about to propose a set of solutions
to the issues he had identified, an incident catalyzed the city's most
volatile elements into a racial conflagration on a scale never seen before in the North or the South.[40]

As *The Defender* had rightly feared, the unrest began on the beach.
On Sunday, July 27, blacks arriving at a "white section" of the shore
at Twenty-Ninth Street were pelted with rocks by a white crowd.
The blacks responded in kind, prompting a melee between the two
groups. One of the white skirmishers began targeting a group of five
black boys who were swimming offshore attached to a raft and were
oblivious to the fighting. One of the boys, fourteen-year-old Eugene
Williams, was struck on the forehead and sank beneath the surface.

By the time Williams's drowned body was recovered a short time
later, large crowds of blacks and whites had already formed, and a
white policeman inflamed passions further by refusing to arrest the
man, still on the scene, who had thrown the rocks, instead arresting
a black man as demanded by a white member of the crowd. A black
man in the crowd then produced a handgun and opened fire on a
group of police officers. Soon, people were firing in every direction,

while fistfights between whites and blacks radiated out from this epi-center for the rest of the afternoon.[41]

In the *Tribune* the next day, the riot on the beach got the second-deck headline across the front page, "Report Two Killed, Fifty Hurt, in Race Riot," while the top headline went to a local murder case. The newspaper detailed the events on the beach that morning — albeit with a number of significant errors — and listed many of those who were killed and wounded, indicating after each name whether they were "white" or "colored." Along Cottage Grove Avenue, the commu-nity's eastern border, "outbreaks were conspicuous at every corner," while along the western rim, white men "were armed with clubs, and every Negro who appeared was pummeled."[42]

A frantic *Tribune* editorial placed blame for the violence chiefly on the Industrial Workers of the World, the leftist union that was also, perhaps not coincidentally, the target of a secret Justice Depart-ment smear campaign. At the same time, the editorial conceded that housing segregation was a problem and that it was the responsibil-ity of whites to ensure that there were sufficient opportunities for African American families. "The colored family must live and live well, in good surroundings," the newspaper concluded, "if we expect its members to grow up with respect for institutions and a desire to serve the nation."[43]

The next morning, Lucius Harper, now *The Defender*'s city editor, put on a new straw hat and went out into the community to gauge the mood. Thousands of African American men were gathered along South State Street all the way from Twenty-Seventh to Thirty-Ninth Streets, talking about the drowning of Eugene Williams and the street battles that had raged into the previous night. The crowd was "inflamed by rumors of brutal attacks on men, women and children," Harper wrote, "some voicing sinister sentiments, others on their way home to grease up the old family revolver."[44]

Harper pushed his way to the center of a group at Thirty-Sixth Street that had gathered around a man whose face was encased in medical plaster. The man explained that he had been set upon by whites west of the black neighborhood, and warned that mobs were on their way "with guns and torches." Several men from this crowd, Harper observed, became so enraged by the man's speech that they attacked the first white man they saw, a Greek street merchant who had the tragic misfortune of passing by with his pushcart at precisely that moment. "It was men from this crowd who stole silently away and knifed the peddler to death," Harper wrote. "But hell was yet to break loose, and by fate I was destined to be present."

Harper stayed in the vicinity all day and into the evening. One block away, at Wabash Avenue, he came upon a large group of men who were stopping passing streetcars by disconnecting their power lines, then smashing the windows with bricks and bats to terrorize the whites inside. On the same corner was an apartment building known as the Angelus, which housed primarily white, single men. When a rumor spread that someone inside had thrown "tin cans and other missiles" at the blacks below, the mob surged toward the structure. They were met by a squad of fifty police officers, both on foot and horseback, determined by any and all means to block them from entering the building.

At precisely 8:10 p.m., Harper recalled, the police drew their revolvers and began firing into the crowd. Blazing away at anyone who moved, the officers hit at least three men and one woman. Harper, dropping to the ground along with many others, lost his straw hat and had his back covered with broken glass from the shattered windows of the nearby storefronts. But he didn't flinch, even when a man above him tried to run and was hit in the back of the neck, such that "heated corpuscles bathed my left cheek." The bullets continued flying for what felt to Harper like an eternity; he felt the heat of one round as it flew past his collar and over his back. Finally the police stopped shooting, and one officer yelled at everyone lying on the ground to get up. "He said it in the 200-point type we use on the front page of extras," Harper recalled. "His command was obeyed."[45]

The wounded were taken by ambulance to nearby hospitals, while Harper brushed himself off and returned to *The Defender*'s office at Thirty-First and State, just five blocks north. He was already back at the newsroom when a woman called the office and asked if the newspaper had been informed of the recent shootout. "Yes madam," the paper's managing editor said drolly, glancing at Harper, "a *Defender* reporter was passing."[46]

But if the violence Harper witnessed was within the community, for the most part, it was all of Black Chicago that was under siege. In the white neighborhoods on the South Side, African American postal workers were dragged out of their vehicles and beaten, as were black passengers on the streetcars. At Forty-Seventh Street and Grand Boulevard, a large group of white men targeting blacks was disbursed by police several times only to re-form a block or two away. In the Loop, a large band led by five sailors hunted the black employees of the district's hotels and restaurants, robbing, beating, and murdering any they found.[47]

At the Wabash Avenue YMCA, students, black war veterans, and other residents took to the building's fire escapes and the roof, using rifles, bricks, and even rocks in an effort to fend off the "terror cars" loaded with white gunmen speeding past. Inside Provident Hospital, the city's sole interracial medical facility, harried doctors and nurses treated more than a hundred blacks and whites, and sometimes had to worry about being victims themselves when mobs of angry men invaded the medical facility looking for other combatants.[48]

The *Tribune* edition that came out Tuesday morning counted 20 people killed in the previous twenty-four hours, 13 whites and 7 blacks, and more than 150 injured of all races. In their narrative, the mayhem at the edges of the African American community was caused by confrontations between armed black men and police, but still, the race riot did not merit the top headline; that honor fell to the beginning of a strike by drivers of the elevated trains and street-cars.[49]

For many African Americans who worked in the stockyards, the streetcar strike was the final seal on their isolation. Now, even if they were willing to risk appearing in the slaughterhouses surrounded by angry white men armed with knives and saws, they would have to walk through hostile areas controlled by Ragan's Colts and their ilk just to get there. Most stayed home; of the nearly two thousand blacks employed at Armour and Co., only nineteen reported for work that day.[50]

Indeed, many residents of the South Side stayed indoors despite the stifling heat, and the only fatality that day was a young black man on the West Side caught riding his bicycle through an Italian neighborhood. Incensed by a false rumor of a black man having committed a sexual assault on an Italian girl, a crowd there stabbed, shot, doused in gasoline, and then set aflame the eighteen-year-old in what the

*Tribune* described as "the most atrocious lynching of the whole series of murders that came with the sudden gust of hate at the bathing
beaches Sunday."[51]

In the late afternoon, small groups of uniformed black men, veterans of World War I mostly, patrolled the edges of the community
armed with service revolvers. Barricades went up on the streets at
key junctures and streetlights were shot out in preparation for the
approaching combat. The South Side had become nothing less than
a war zone.[52]

It was in this context that Robert Abbott used his clout to appeal
to the community. That night, *Defender* newsboys darted through
the streets, handing out thirty thousand handbills emblazoned with
the newspaper's masthead and the word "EXTRA" in large bold type,
followed by a message signed by the editor. Calling on his readers to
stay indoors and obey police orders, Abbott urged them to "do your
part to restore quiet and order." Despite substantial evidence that police had themselves targeted blacks or at least failed to interfere in
the work of white mobs, Abbott pleaded with the community to allow police to handle "rowdies," adding that "this is no time to solve
the race question. "Never mind who started it," he wrote. "Let proper
authorities finish it. We must have order at once for our own good
and the good of Chicago."[53]

Sure enough, the number of black mobs dwindled that night, although white mobs still mobilized and the situation remained tense.
Those who tried to invade the black neighborhood found the roads
blocked, dark, and eerily quiet, with snipers taking aim from the
shadows. "White men passing through the darkened streets were
picked off, one by one," the *Tribune* recounted.

Blocked from entering the black neighborhood, the white thugs
instead targeted the homes of blacks living outside the community,
setting eleven fires that night. On several occasions, police and firefighters who responded to these blazes were met by rock-throwing
neighbors intent on seeing the structures thoroughly destroyed. So
determined were these white mobs that the black families not return,
they made a point of destroying even valuable items such as Victrola
phonographs. But few individuals were actually hurt in these attacks,
since many of the black homeowners and renters had already fled.[54]

Finally, on the front page of the Wednesday-morning edition, the riot got top billing. The *Tribune* counted a total of twenty-six dead, eleven whites and fifteen blacks, with as many as three hundred injured on all sides since the riot had begun. For three full days, black men and women had been unable to go to work, stores had been unable to stock their shelves, and garbage rotted in huge piles on the streets, baking under the brutal sun, leaving the community in a dire situation indeed. In the afternoon, a delegation led by Ferdinand Barnett and Franklin Denison met with Mayor Thompson and demanded he deploy the National Guard.[55]

That evening, arsonists set more than forty fires along the edge of the black community, torching not only single-family homes but larger structures as well. Firefighters who arrived at one two-story brick building "found a howling mob outside and two old Negro men, two colored women and a white girl cowering under a large table on the second floor."[56]

A little later that evening, two hundred members of Ragan's Colts assembled outside a nearby apartment building where nine black families lived and used guns, rocks, and bricks to chase them out before thoroughly destroying the structure.[57]

At 9:00 p.m., Mayor Thompson requested that Governor Frank Lowden order the National Guardsmen into the field. By that point, there were more than sixty-five hundred soldiers assembled, mostly white men from the suburbs led by a veteran commander, and a plan was quickly drawn up to deploy one-half of the troops, keeping the remainder in reserve. The men of one regiment boarded trucks and rolled out of their armory with bayonets fixed to their rifles, while another regiment based on the North Side took a fleet of a hundred taxicabs to the South Side. By midnight, the soldiers had taken up position all around the black community's perimeter, prepared for vigorous resistance. "No white persons were allowed to pass east of this deadline, no blacks west of it," the soldiers said of Wentworth Avenue, a north–south artery just west of State Street. At midnight, rain began to fall, which helped to cool the city's tempers even further.[58]

The Thursday-morning edition of the *Tribune* came out with the banner headline "Troops Act; Halt Rioting," while an editorial described the mayor's decision to call in the troops both "wise" and "overdue," before lamenting the damage already done to the city's image. "Chicago has an emergent task," the *Tribune* opined. "Its reputation is at its lowest point. It has had the worst race riots in American history."[59]

That editorial page also included a letter from *The Defender*'s managing editor lauding the *Tribune*'s coverage during the first day of the race riot. Although by modern standards, the *Tribune*'s tone and skew were unacceptable, *The Defender*'s editor was likely comparing its downtown colleague to the incendiary language found in newspapers such as *The Washington Post* when he wrote, "Your treatment of the race riot in your edition of today was marked by fairness to our people and showed a lack of coloring so often found in articles dealing with such situations and will undoubtedly act as a sedative," the letter began. "Our paper for years has worked assiduously to bring about a better understanding between our white and colored citizens, and we are glad to have your assistance in the work."[60]

*The Defender* had often lambasted the *Tribune* in the past but in this case, the daily's coverage had dispelled the rumors of a takeover of the Eighth Infantry Armory and helped spread the message in Robert Abbott's antiviolence handbill as well. The *Tribune*'s editorial page, moreover, had advocated housing reforms that would go a long way to prevent a recurrence of violence.[61]

The soldiers' presence during the day allowed the black community to replenish their supplies as food trucks rolled in under military guard and employers distributed badly needed payrolls. It still wasn't safe to return to work in the stockyards, however, as a small group of desperate men discovered when they tried to go back to work and their white coworkers became menacing; the guardsmen had to be called in to escort them out.[62]

As darkness descended, soldiers who had expected to be fighting insurrectionist blacks found themselves instead confronting whites attempting to murder blacks and burn their homes. At several locations, the soldiers aimed machine guns at large groups of unruly whites to persuade them to disburse. At Sixty-Third and Campbell, the soldiers stopped one throng just as they were about to hang a black man from a telegraph pole. At Fifty-Fourth Street and South

LaSalle Avenue, they stopped another from burning down a house and then formed a square around the black family who lived there, projecting their rifles and bayonets toward the crowd. "The mob, numbering several thousand, hooted and jeered," the *Tribune* reported, "but they didn't dare pass that wall of steel."[63]

# 7

# Reaping the Whirlwind

A S THE TRUCE began to take hold, Robert Abbott and his staff faced a seemingly insurmountable obstacle to getting the weekly edition of *The Defender* printed. Usually, the production process began on Wednesday evening, at which point the staff delivered the mockup to *The Drover's Journal;* copies would then be printed late on Thursday so that they could be dropped into the mail and delivered around the country by Saturday, the date actually printed on the masthead. But *The Drover's Journal* presses were located in the stockyard district, and in the aftermath of the race riot, the white pressmen feared they would be targeted for printing a black newspaper. Abbott was able to persuade the workers only to set his type and create his page templates.

All day Thursday and into the evening, Abbott and his staff racked their brains to come up with an alternative printer. Finally, cartoonist Leslie Rogers thought of the *Gary Tribune,* the main newspaper in his hometown of Gary, Indiana, a burgeoning industrial outpost on the coast of Lake Michigan, twenty miles south of Chicago. The new edition finally began rolling off the presses Friday evening, but to get the printed bundles back to Chicago, Abbott had to make multiple trips, with his own Apperson Jack Rabbit automobile serving as an additional, makeshift delivery truck. Even after this supreme effort, it was too late for the mail trains and for the first time since its founding, *The Defender* reached its subscribers around the country a few days late.[1]

The August 2, 1919, edition of *The Defender* reflected the chaotic circumstances in which it was created. The boxes to the left and right of the masthead, usually filled with self-promotional phrases about the newspaper, urged readers to "Stay Off the Streets. Let the Law Settle It," and "Foolish Talk Is No Good Now. Stop It." The front page included lists of those killed and injured as well as Lucius Harper's narrative and other accounts of riot-related incidents that varied greatly in their accuracy. One account, almost certainly apocryphal, described an "unidentified woman and her three-months old baby" who were trying to board a streetcar when "the mob seized her, beat her, slashed her body into ribbons and bashed her baby's brains out against a telegraph pole." Curiously, this report was unattributed, with neither the woman nor her child appearing on *The Defender*'s own list of casualties.[2]

Beyond outrage, however, a thread of triumph ran through the edition. The dominant narrative emerging in national public opinion was that throughout the tumult of the "Red Summer," Chicago's African Americans had fought back, earning the respect of a nation. "The Black worm has turned," read *The Defender*'s main editorial, "Reaping the Whirlwind," frankly reveling in the community's new-found reputation for strength. "A Race that has furnished hundreds of thousands of the best soldiers that the world has ever seen is no longer content to turn the left cheek when it is smitten on the right."[3]

There were other racially charged incidents in the days that followed, but by the middle of the week, the National Guard and the police had established a protected cordon around the streetcars and elevated train line so that the men of the Black Belt could return to their posts in the stockyards. By the end of the week, tensions had dissipated to the extent that the troops were allowed to disband and go home, leaving the final death toll at 38 men and boys, 23 of whom were black, and at least 537 people injured, 342 of whom were black.[4]

For the moment, the riot had emboldened those who wished for segregation in the city, especially those aldermen with wards adjoining the black neighborhood that were home to gangs like the Colts and the Hamburgers. Meanwhile, the Cook County state's attorney, Maclay Hoyne, a political enemy of Mayor Thompson and his Second Ward allies, brought twenty-six blacks, but not a single white, before a grand jury investigating the riots, prompting the jurors to resign in protest and the judge overseeing the case to rebuke the prosecutor as he dismissed the charges. "Colored people couldn't have been rioting with themselves," said the judge from the bench. "Bring me in some white prisoners."[5]

Worried that a biased prosecution would reignite the violence, Robert Abbott held an emergency meeting with Ida B. Wells-Barnett and other leaders and then emerged to challenge Hoyne's tactics head-on. "We are not rioters," Abbott told *The Chicago Daily News.* "We did not start this trouble and Mr. Hoyne is merely shielding the guilty ones."[6]

In the South, meanwhile, Chicago's race riot caught the attention of the enemies of migration, such as a planter in the Mississippi Delta who offered to pay the train fares south for up to two thousand blacks willing to take jobs on his plantation. On the other side of the Mason-Dixon Line, the *Rochester* (N.Y.) *Democrat and Chronicle* printed a false report that railway authorities were prohibiting blacks in the South from buying northbound train tickets, helping to spread panic in the wake of the riots that the federal government was putting brakes on the exodus. Dismissing these rumors, *The Defender*'s editorial page expressed absolute confidence that the departures from Dixie would continue at full steam.[7]

The newspaper was now back in production at *The Drover's Journal.* A brief notice on the front page signed by circulation manager Phil Jones apologized for the singular disruption of the newspaper's delivery, stating that "a condition brought about by circumstances over which the management had no control prevented us from maintaining our usual punctuality in the delivery of papers to our agents and subscribers."[8]

Nevertheless, the lesson of the riots had been fully absorbed: so long as it did not own its own presses, *The Defender* would be vulnerable. Robert Abbott had been saving for his own plant for some years, but now he stepped up the effort, motivated by the certainty that a future conflagration like the one the community had just endured could derail his whole operation. In the meantime, Illinois's governor, Frank Lowden, appointed Abbott to the twelve-member board of a special commission to investigate the violence, a rare entity for the times in that it boasted equal numbers of blacks and whites, including Abbott's friends Dr. George Cleveland Hall and attorney Edward

Morris, as well as the white businessman Julius Rosenwald, principal at Sears, Roebuck and Company, and *The Chicago Daily News* owner Victor Lawson.

"The two races are here and will remain here," Lowden said in chartering the commission. "The great majority of each realizes the necessity of living on terms of cordial good will and respect . . . That condition must be brought about. To say it cannot is to confess the failure of self-government."[9]

Though the accounts of the violence were read around the country, there was no noticeable effect on the migration to Chicago. In Birmingham, Alabama, Timuel Black Sr. and Mattie McConner Black were among those who were undeterred. Former sharecroppers who had left the plantation for better financial opportunities in Birmingham, the Blacks realized that they were still vulnerable to southern oppression after a family friend was lynched, accused of the rape of a white woman, a crime he almost certainly did not commit. It was just the sort of random violence carried out to keep African Americans terrorized. Timuel Sr. was outspoken and proud, and the Blacks knew that he was a likely target for any future attack. Even if Chicago had the kind of racial violence that required the National Guard to descend on the city, that news, ironically, still made the North seem better than the South; in the South, after all, the Guard never would have intervened.

To this family, among many others, *The Defender* was more than just a periodical. "The newspaper carried with it messages, dreams, and hopes and plans," Timuel Black explained in an interview nearly nine decades later. "They weren't just selling a newspaper. They were informing the people of a better world."

And so the Black family — Timuel Sr., Mattie, and their three children, ten-year-old Charlotte, four-year-old Walter, and the infant Timuel Jr. — left Alabama clean and pressed, only to arrive the next day at the Twelfth Street train station, worn out from the long trip and covered in coal dust. They were greeted by an extended family already settled in Chicago who put them up until they got situated. Soon Timuel Sr. found work in the stockyards and moved his family into their own apartment at the edge of the Black Belt, amid immigrants from Estonia and Bohemia and their descendants. The whites

soon moved out, however, driven by fear, racism, and their own ethnic solidarity.[10]

Despite this sort of hostility, the Black children did not grow up
feeling constricted in their new urban home. To the contrary, the
black South Side was expanding in those years, getting visibly more
prosperous and politically ascendant. All around them were offices of
black professionals — doctors, lawyers, dentists, and others — as well
as businesses ranging from mom-and-pop stores to insurance companies and banks. There was the Eighth Infantry Armory at Thirty-
Fifth and Forestville and the Wabash Avenue YMCA at Thirty-Fourth
and Wabash. Movie theaters screened African American–produced
films alongside major Hollywood studio productions while the cabarets and bars served as incubators for jazz and blues.

Provident Hospital was particularly important to the new arrivals,
who had no access to modern medical facilities back in the South,
and that was just one of the institutions that distinguished Chicago
from other black urban centers, even Harlem in New York. Blacks
ran the show at every level in Chicago, from the street hustler to the
doctor, the activist on the street corner to the alderman. It was nobody's idea of paradise, but it did offer freedoms unavailable elsewhere, freedoms every child knew had been secured with blood in
the streets.[11]

In the fall of 1919, Marcus Garvey came to Chicago to promote his
dream of a black Utopia on the continent of Africa, and galvanized
the community with his message of racial independence.[12]

A native of Jamaica, Garvey had spent several years in London,
where he mingled with scholars and revolutionaries from colonial
societies throughout the British Empire, studying African and Asian
history as well as Booker T. Washington's autobiography, *Up from
Slavery*, from which he absorbed a strong self-help philosophy. Back
in Jamaica in 1914, Garvey fused all of these ideas into a new organization he called the Universal Negro Improvement Association
(UNIA), the mission of which was to "take Africa, organize it, develop it, arm it, and make it the defender of the Negroes the world
over."

Garvey originally came to New York City in 1916 to raise money
for a school in Jamaica that would be modeled on Washington's

Tuskegee Institute. Immediately attracted to the thriving community of West Indian expatriates living in Harlem, however, he decided to base UNIA in this community. He quickly launched a series of businesses, including a clothes-cleaning service and several restaurants; but the most successful enterprise was a monthly newspaper, *The Negro World*, which, within a few months, achieved a circulation in the tens of thousands. All of Garvey's businesses, including *The Negro World*, depended on irregular infusions of cash from UNIA members to stay afloat, but it didn't matter — he had tapped into a deep well of sentiment within the African American community, which appeared willing to subsidize any and all of his efforts.[13]

In late 1918, Garvey invited Ida B. Wells-Barnett to New York to attend a rally of more than three thousand people at his Harlem headquarters. Wells-Barnett was impressed with Garvey's ability to draw and energize a crowd with provocative statements about oppression in the American South, though after hearing him move beyond the language of militant self-defense and into violent retaliation for white abuses, she also came away with doubts. "For every black lynched in the South," Garvey had roared during a particularly emotional moment, "a white should be lynched in the North." This was going too far for Wells-Barnett, as well as for many others.[14]

*The Defender* began covering Garvey in earnest during the summer of 1919 with the debut of his most ambitious venture yet, a shipping fleet that would carry both goods and passengers between the African continent and the African diaspora in the Americas. Garvey envisaged dozens of ships staffed by all-black crews hauling Africa's rich natural resources to the West and returning with African American settlers as well as machinery and other technological items. Dubbed the Black Star Line, to contrast with an existing White Star Line of commercial ships, it was to be financed by the sales of $5 shares of stock in the company, just one of the features of the scheme that brought the Black Star Line to the attention of state authorities.[15]

At the end of August, Garvey held a UNIA rally at Carnegie Hall to announce a departure date for the first ship in the Black Star fleet. To many, it seemed as if his vision was being realized. *The Defender*, however, remained decidedly skeptical. In its issue of September 6, 1919, a large section of the New York page was dedicated to ridiculing Garvey as an alien and a charlatan, noting that state authorities were investigating the Black Star Line's finances as well as charges of libel against him from several former UNIA associates. *The Defender's* correspondent blasted him as well for making incendiary comments against the white race, arguing that his proclamations would alienate those whites who were sympathetic to the black cause. "Our people will not be frightened into giving up their fight for equality," the correspondent opined, "but we can well dispense with the help of a man like Garvey."[16]

Garvey responded with visceral anger. He dedicated one-half of an entire edition of *The Negro World* to attacking Abbott, distributed twenty thousand copies in Chicago, and scheduled a trip to the city, renting space in the Eighth Infantry Armory to sell shares of stock in the Black Star Line and, presumably, to denounce Robert Abbott further just a few blocks from *The Defender's* headquarters. On Tuesday, September 30, Garvey showed up at the armory in evening dress and sat on the stage while several local leaders addressed the 150 people gathered to hear him speak. A Chicago minister, before introducing Garvey, spoke of enormous quantities of rubber, gold, ivory, diamonds, and rubies in the nation of Liberia that could be exploited through the Black Star Line.[17]

Then, just as Garvey prepared to take the podium, a white plain-clothes detective appeared from the crowd and walked to the side of the stage, deftly escorting Garvey out of the hall and into a waiting police car. Garvey was gone before anyone in the armory knew what had happened, arrested on charges of violating Illinois's blue-sky law, which regulated the sale of stocks and bonds, based on a warrant issued by the Illinois attorney general, which was, in turn, based on evidence — two shares of stock in the Black Star Line — purchased by a black private investigator in Abbott's employ. Abbott also filed a libel lawsuit against Garvey demanding $100,000 in damages before delivering the coup de grâce — an article on the front page of *The Defender.* "Instead of sailing on the Atlantic Ocean en route to some foreign port," *The Defender's* reporter wrote rather gleefully, "the compass of the Black Star Line, Admiral Marcus Garvey, anchored at the Harrison Street police station Wednesday morning."[18]

Bailed out of jail by his supporters, Garvey left Chicago never to return, but once he was safely out of the city, he responded to attacks on his character and his enterprise in kind, accusing Abbott of lacking sufficient pride in his African heritage and pandering to similar weaknesses within the black American population. "Abbott has always through rivalry and jealousy been opposed to me," he said, attributing the editor's enmity to "my not being born in America and my criticism of his dangerous newspaper policy of advising the Race to lighten its skin and straighten out its hair which was kinky."[19]

The feud continued into the fall, with Garvey filing his own libel suits against Abbott and *The Defender,* one demanding $200,000 on behalf of the Black Star Line, and another, for an additional $100,000, claiming Garvey's personal reputation had been maligned. Abbott responded with an editorial entitled "Self Appointed Spokesmen," which insulted Garvey without mentioning him by name. "We have on our streets a poor, half-witted fellow making a precarious living by amusing passersby with his antics," the editorial stated, adding that Garvey's "mouthings give food to a depraved set and feed the columns of yellow journalism."[20]

Behind the scenes, Abbott went even further, his private investigator sharing information on Garvey with the Bureau of Investigation. The bureau's young, ambitious new director, J. Edgar Hoover, whose previous job had been to gather evidence on radical groups for the Justice Department, had long desired an excuse to deport Garvey. Previously skeptical of the entire black press, Hoover had singled out *The Defender* as a "radical publication," but now agents in the Chicago office wrote to the director that Abbott "has been ever ready to cooperate with this office on all investigations pertaining to Negro radical activities."[21]

Both Abbott and Garvey were committed Race Men who had come from impoverished backgrounds and made something of themselves by virtue of their personal discipline. Both were trained printers who knew how to use publications to move the masses, and both had advocated a renewed pride in their people's African heritage. But their differences were deeply rooted as well: Abbott was a clumsy speaker, personally modest and deeply loyal to his staff, whereas Garvey was bombastic, imperious, and capricious, frequently turning on his immediate associates and calling them out for public repudiation whenever he imagined they might be plotting against him. Abbott was a penny pincher, closely monitoring his expenses and making sure his subscribers received every issue of his newspaper, every week. Garvey was a prophet, issuing visions as they came to him and demanding financial tribute from his followers.

Most importantly, Garvey was an advocate of black independence, while Abbott was a steadfast believer in integration. Abbott's own family was, after all, mixed race, and he couldn't help seeing Garvey's dream of a separate nation for African people as a utopian fantasy that would only distract from the cause just as it was gaining momentum. In explaining his staunch opposition, Abbott told one of his close friends that Garvey's movement was "unmistakably a symptom of despair" resulting from the "sting of segregation," and that the black nationalist was using the wrong strategy. "The walls of discrimination," Abbott critiqued, "can only be scaled with determination to fight the enemy on his own ground."

Several of Garvey's supporters in Chicago tried to broker a truce between the two leaders, but Abbott rebuffed them and began preparing himself instead for protracted warfare, having determined that there could be no accommodation with this existential threat.[22]

In early February 1920, Robert Abbott received a telegram from Savannah informing him that his forty-three-year-old half sister Mary had died suddenly, leaving his mother overcome with grief. For what may have been the first time since he launched *The Defender*, he boarded a train for the Deep South to attend his sister's funeral. From Chicago to Cincinnati, he rode in a private compartment in a Pullman car, as other businessmen of his status would have done. "I paid my way, tipped the porter, smiled at the conductor, ate in the dining car," he recounted later in an article describing his journey for *The Defender*. "That is, I acted like a human all the way through, and, along with others riding with me, I had a boiled shirt and a stiff collar."[23]

But when he told the ticket agent in Cincinnati that he was headed into states where segregation laws were in effect, the agent refused to sell him a berth, and from that point on, Abbott endured the same humiliations that were a regular feature of life for African Americans traveling in the South. The trip required multiple stops and train changes, beginning with the Harriman Junction in the Tennessee foothills in the middle of the night, where, out of pure malice, the ticket agent kept black passengers waiting until the very last moment, causing those unlucky enough to be last in line to have to run and jump onboard the moving train. The Jim Crow car was itself a study in discomfort; closest to the front of the train and the locomotive, with its noisy, smoky, sooty steam engine, its location alone ensured that even the most fastidious passengers would arrive at their location filthy and exhausted. And black passengers had to share even this space with the conductor, the porters, and other train personnel, cramming into the few empty seats that were available even when the white sections of the train remained half empty. Abbott was particularly offended that black men and women had to use the same bathroom, while in the white section of the train, men and women had separate facilities. Worst of all were the white men who used the Jim Crow car as a lounge where they "smoked cigarettes and eyed our men and women as if they were 'strangers in a strange land'— the women as if they were prey for the lustful sons of a lustful land."[24]

More than fifty years old now and used to creature comforts, Abbott sat on the hard cane bench stoically throughout the entire ride over the Smoky Mountains into Asheville, North Carolina, and then toward the coast via Columbia, South Carolina. Each time he changed trains, he encountered the dirty, dilapidated "Colored Waiting Areas," deliberately maintained to reinforce a sense of second-class citizenship. Here were specially designated bathrooms for men and women, at least, but they were built too close together to allow for much privacy. "'Equal but separate accommodations' is the word used in the telling of separate cars in the South," Abbott observed. "That is lying sweetly."[25]

After two full days and nights of travel, Abbott arrived at the family compound in Woodville in time for the funeral. He found his mother distraught but still vital, well looked after by her children and a rapidly growing number of grandchildren. His younger half brother, Alexander, ordained as a Congregationalist minister, was running the school and church their father had founded, as well as the newspaper, now renamed the *West-End Post*, with the close assistance of their eldest surviving sister, Rebecca. Alexander and his wife, Rosa, had six children, the third of which was their first boy, named John Herman Henry Sengstacke in honor of the patriarch whose presence still loomed over them all. Like the community around them, the family was poor, though they were decidedly better off than their neighbors, especially now that Abbott was successful enough to subsidize their finances.[26]

Abbott did not stay with his family for long, as both local and national politics were calling upon him. With President Wilson's health and popularity failing, the resurgent Republican Party hoped to take back the White House as well as the U.S. Congress in the November 1920 general election. The African American electorate could very well play a decisive role in such a scenario, particularly in the upcoming Republican primaries, and Abbott found himself the spokesperson for millions of African Americans, not least the two million or so who, having moved to northern cities, comprised an important swing vote. His role would be only further magnified by the fact that the Republican National Convention was being held in Chicago that year. His journey back North, equal in length and discomfort to his descent into the South, gave Abbott many hours to meditate on party politics, review the civil rights records of various aspirants for the Republican nomination, and plot out precisely how best to leverage his power for the benefit of his people.[27]

Abbott's article about his journey, "Riding the Hog Train," was printed alongside copies of letters he wrote to Black Chicago's congressional representatives demanding desegregation of the railway system, which had been brought under federal control during the war. An editorial in the same issue, meanwhile, reminded any would-be Republican president that, after eight years of disappointments under Woodrow Wilson, African Americans expected the next administration to do better.

"The Republican Party must not fail to understand that to get our support the platform should be emphatic and outspoken on these wrongs," stated the editorial, "and the public record and the utterances of the presidential candidate should be such as to justify the expectation that, if elected, these declarations will be carried into effect."[28]

Just a few days after returning from his trip to Georgia, Robert Abbott was off again, this time to California with Mrs. Abbott, presumably traveling in his own Pullman Palace car this time, arriving in Los Angeles on March 12 to a reception committee of fellow black journalists. They stayed with well-to-do friends for several weeks as

Robert spoke with local black leaders about the upcoming election and gathered information about one of California's up-and-coming candidates, Herbert Hoover.[29]

Leaving L.A., the Abbotts continued up the coast to Oakland and Portland, Oregon, staying with well-established African American families at every stop, and then boarded a ship for Honolulu. Hawaii was a pure vacation, Robert's first ever, where they stayed with yet more friends — obviating the need to find a hotel at a time that many public institutions discriminated against blacks — and met with several of Abbott's former Hampton classmates. As the days unfolded into weeks, they ate well and relaxed, though Abbott couldn't help but make sure *The Defender* was available wherever there was any African American community to speak of.[30]

Three months after their original departure, the Abbotts returned in late May looking refreshed. The whole staff lined up to give the editor a hearty handshake when he walked into the office. "The trip has broadened and helped me in every way," he told his troops. "Boys, I am glad to see you one and all and to know that you published such a splendid paper during my absence."[31]

In mid-June, *The Defender* was found guilty of libeling the Black Star Line, but the court awarded Garvey and his team just six cents, a verdict the newspaper was happy to broadcast on its front page. Nevertheless, Garvey expanded his movement greatly that summer, launching his first ship, the *Frederick Douglass,* and making a successful run to Jamaica with a cargo of whiskey, a voyage that was celebrated by UNIA cells and their supporters around the globe. On August 1, Garvey led his African Legion through Harlem, hundreds of men in elaborate blue military uniforms complete with swords, followed by two hundred nurses from the Black Cross (modeled after the Red Cross) in all-white outfits. This was the dramatic opening to the International Convention of the Negro Peoples of the World, at which twenty-five thousand people, including delegates from some twenty-five nations, acclaimed Garvey the provisional president of Africa.[32]

Branches of UNIA sprang up all over the globe while circulation of *The Negro World* surged to as much as one hundred thousand; Chicago alone claimed some seventy-five hundred members. Garvey took to riding around New York in an open-top car, wearing an elaborate uniform with a massive red-and-blue plumed hat he felt befitted his new rank. He appointed his own ambassadors, generals, and cabinet ministers, bestowing titles on his followers such as "Supreme Potentate" or "Lady Commander of the Order of the Nile." Many of his American followers, though they had no intention of ever leaving the country, seized on the chance to transform themselves, even for just one day, by exchanging their workaday clothes for uniforms and marching proudly through the heart of their city.[33]

"The Solid South is much stirred up over the possibility of our vote changing the complexion of things political in their section," began *The Defender*'s lead editorial on the eve of the 1920 presidential election. "Their fears are well grounded for with the women's vote we will in many cases hold the balance of power and that power will be thrown to the Republican Party."[34]

The Republican nominee, U.S. Senator Warren G. Harding of Ohio, had reached out to the African American electorate, praising the conduct of black soldiers in World War I, promising to desegregate the federal government, and hiring *Defender* society editor Julius Avendorph to organize train workers on behalf of the ticket. The Republican Party had a long history of disappointing its African American supporters, however, and support for Harding in black communities around the nation was but lukewarm. In this election, the newspaper actually called for its readers only to rally against the Democrats, who continued to make segregation in the South the centerpiece of their agenda, "not because we feel the word Republican is synonymous with the word friend, but because we have gumption enough to choose, of the two evils, the lesser."[35]

Still, the newspaper could not have been happier with the results of Election Day, nationally or locally. On November 2, Harding won thirty-three of forty-eight states, capturing the entire Northeast, Midwest, and the West, as well as Tennessee, leaving his Democratic opponent with only a stubborn redoubt in the old Confederacy. Republicans secured comfortable majorities in both houses of the U.S. Congress as well, while African American candidates themselves captured state offices in Ohio and downstate Illinois, in a few cases beating white opponents, and made credible runs for the U.S. House of Representatives in districts of Maryland, Missouri, and Virginia. "Everywhere indications point to an awakening in politics among our people," wrote *The Defender*'s political reporter.

The results within Illinois, thanks to another extraordinary turn-out from Ed Wright's political organization, were even more satisfying. Wright's Second Ward helped place a Republican in the governor's mansion, while in Cook County, the judge who had rejected the charges brought against black rioters, Robert E. Crowe, was elected state's attorney. All through the campaign, Crowe's Democratic rival had ridiculed the judge for his open affiliation with African Americans, but Wright's forces produced a landslide. Referred to now as the "Iron Master," Wright had recently been elected the Republican committeeman of the Second Ward, a partisan post that assured him access to the cigar-smoke-filled rooms where political leaders assigned patronage jobs and otherwise divided up the spoils.[36]

Tempering any excitement over the political victory, however, *The Defender*'s front page the next week contained a story under the headline "Lynched Man Who Wanted to Vote," reporting the murder of James Perry in Ocoee, Florida. When he appeared at the polls on Election Day, Perry, who intended to cast his ballot for Harding, was confronted by armed white men and told to go away. Perry produced his own firearm, and a shootout ensued in which he killed two of the white poll officials before being knocked down, dragged to a nearby churchyard, hanged, and then shot. His corpse was placed near the polling place with a sign hung around his neck reading, "This is what we do to niggers that vote." Photographs of the grisly scene were sold at a nearby drugstore for a quarter.[37]

One day in early 1921, a little boy entered *The Defender*'s newsroom and approached Lucius Harper, now the managing editor, and asked him to publish a poem he'd written. "Papa says if I get in *The Chicago Defender* he'll buy me a quart of ice cream," the boy explained, handing the poem to Harper, who promised to print it.

The boy left happy, but now Harper was faced with a dilemma, for *The Defender* had not had a column for youth since its earliest years. Indeed, there was "nothing to interest a person between the ages of eight to fifteen," as Harper recalled a few years later. Harper tucked the poem in his pocket with a plan to "slip it in somewhere, and suffer the consequences from the editor-in-chief, Mr. Abbott."[38]

The more he thought about it, however, the more a youth section seemed like a good idea. Wandering through the building's various chambers, Harper spotted a papier-mâché Billiken doll, a figurine resembling a Buddha, sitting on an employee's desk. The Billiken was something of a fad at the time, thought to bring good luck, and Harper sat there brainstorming and holding the figurine. Then and there, he conceived of a character he named Bud Billiken ("Bud" had been an early nickname of his), a role that could be filled by a young person from the community who would be specially recruited to "edit" the youth section. It was a concept that had never been tried in the black press before, but Harper now presented the idea with sufficient passion that Abbott was convinced to let him give it a go.

To find the first "Bud Billiken," Harper scanned the ranks of the newsboys who came in to get their daily allocation of newspapers; preteens from a wide variety of backgrounds, they were, in general, "a rude and rowdy bunch," but Harper spotted one who was a little different, "a quiet, sad-eyed, soft-spoken and well-mannered little fellow about ten years old," Harper noted. This one "didn't scramble like the other boys to get his wares."[39]

Harper's newest editor was surely his youngest, but Robert Watkins got his mother's permission to take the job and was assigned a desk in the corner of one of the rooms at 3159 South State Street, with regular hours after school to write his columns and answer letters from other young people. Nestled into a corner of the Woman's Page, the debut edition of the "Chicago Defender Jr." had its own mini masthead, which proclaimed it was the "Children's Greatest Newspaper."

"Now I am just breaking into this newspaper game and you will have to help me out," wrote Watkins in his first column, under a headshot in which he wore a green eyeshade and had a pencil stuck behind his ear. "I am not like the other folks on this newspaper who think they know everything." Watkins called for contributions from young people, including the announcements of parties and other events, and underneath his column was the poem written by the boy who had originally approached Harper, a sanguine ditty called "Little Ugly Deeds."[40]

The following edition of the "Defender Jr." contained a clip-out membership form for the Bud Billiken Club, which was open to boys and girls and free to join. Within a few days, piles of filled-out applications began arriving at the newspaper office from towns all over the United States and points around the globe, including Africa.

"Bud, I live in the country but I would like to live in your city," wrote one ten-year-old girl from Georgetown, Texas. "I hear so much about it; papa says some day we will be there."[41]

On the front page of the April 30, 1921, edition, a notice invited the public to the grand opening of *The Defender*'s new headquarters, to be held the following Friday afternoon. In the months after the riot, Abbott had combed the neighborhood for what would become the newspaper's production facility, finally settling on a three-story, red-and-yellow-brick structure at 3435 South Indiana Avenue. Built at the turn of the century as the Anshe Doron —"Men of the South"— synagogue, the building had been sold to a storage company when the neighborhood became mostly African American, and months of costly renovations had been required to transform the interior into proper business offices.

Once the building was ready, Abbott ran the notice in the newspaper urging the entire community to come and see the new *Defender*, sending out hand-signed invitations to many of the city's notables as well, for good measure. By noon on the day itself, throngs of people were lined up outside the building's entrance. Guides welcomed visitors as they streamed into the high-ceilinged reception room, decorated with two murals by the French-trained African American artist William Edouard Scott. The first depicted "a Daughter of Ethiopia holding in one hand *The Defender*, or Light, and in the other the balance scales of the rights and wrongs of men before the oppressed of all lands and climes," according to the newspaper's description. The second mural pictured an idealized image of the publication "chronicling the achievements of mankind and how it stands as a champion of progress."[42]

Beginning with a glimpse into the offices of the publisher and at the circulation department, the guides escorted the visitors through the building before whisking them upstairs onto the first floor. Here they entered a large, high-ceilinged chamber bathed in multicolored light pouring through stained glass windows. This room, originally built as the synagogue's sanctuary, the sacred space where observant men had formerly gathered before the holy scrolls in their ark to pray and kibitz, had now been transformed into a modern newsroom. Dozens of reporters, columnists, editors, and artists sat at desks that represented the full breadth of African American life, from art to women's news, sports to politics.

At the back of the editorial department, a glass wall separated the newsroom from the composing room one floor below. Copy was lowered in a basket to four Linotype machine operators, who transcribed every handwritten word into molded shapes on metal "slugs"—a metal strip produced by the Linotype machines—and each visitor was given his own name in reverse type on a slug as a keepsake. The visitors invariably gawked at the typesetters, not because of their technological skills, but because these men were white.

Another marvel awaited in the next chamber, a slightly used, double-deck Goss Straight-Line Sextuple printing press, nearly as long as the entire building and standing two stories high in a specially constructed bay where the building's basement had been. And this was but the auxiliary press: just next door, a brand-new Goss press took up the entire building. Altogether, it was a printing operation capable of folding and counting thirty-five thousand copies of the newspaper every hour. All the stereotypists and pressmen were white as well and, in a gratifying irony, members of the Chicago Typographical Union, the very group that had discriminated against Abbott when he first came to the city. Abbott really had no alternative, however, since there were just a handful of African Americans printers throughout the country, and in the end, he was proud of this experiment in biracial staffing.

By 10:00 p.m., when the doors closed for the night, more than five thousand people had come through the building and some were still waiting for their chance to tour the new space. Abbott had been there the entire time, graciously greeting the guests and personally accepting the many flowers, cards, gifts, and telegrams that poured in. Seeing that people still wanted to see the newspaper, he announced that the newspaper's plant would be open to the public every day.[43]

A brochure distributed to visitors in subsequent days boasted that the building, its reconstruction, and the Goss presses had cost

$375,000 in total, all of which Abbott had paid in full. The previous summer, in the run-up to the purchase and renovation of the new facility, Abbott had raised the newsstand price of the paper to ten cents a copy, causing circulation to dip for several months, but by the time of the grand opening, it had surged back to 283,571 copies weekly. It had been a worthwhile investment. With the new presses, he steadily added colors as well as photographs, began publishing a local and a national edition, and increased the size of the paper to twenty-two pages. *The Defender* staff numbered sixty-eight people in the newspaper's home office, boasted a brochure distributed to visitors, as well as five hundred newsboys within the city and twenty-three hundred newsstand agents around the country. Altogether, no fewer than thirty-four hundred people derived their income from the newspaper.[44]

For Abbott, the printing press was the centerpiece of the whole enterprise. Sometimes, late at night after a social outing, he would stop at *The Defender* building just to gaze at the somnolent machinery glistening in the dark. "We often went to the theater in the Loop," recalled one of Abbott's friends to his biographer, "but before Mr. Abbott would go home nights, he always passed by the plant and looked at it admiringly, as if he was surprised it was still there."[45]

# 8

# Bombing Binga

SOMETIME PAST MIDNIGHT on September 1, 1921, someone hurled an incendiary device at the home of Jesse Binga on the southwestern edge of Washington Park. It was the seventh time Binga's home had been bombed since 1919, when he and his wife had become the first African Americans to move into an area designated by the Kenwood Improvement Association for whites only. As with all of the other attacks, the explosive had not been powerful enough to seriously damage the house, lest a conflagration at the Bingas' ignite one of their white neighbors' properties. Only the front porch was destroyed, and the windows, both at the Bingas' and in a wide radius around the house, were shattered.

The Bingas were at their vacation home in Idlewild, Michigan, when this latest bombing occurred, and a security guard had to draw his revolver to hold off neighbors who tried to loot the home in their absence. Police who arrived disarmed the guard and tried to invade the home themselves, but now the maid locked herself inside, following Binga's strict orders, and refused to allow the officers in. Jesse Binga, hurrying back to the city, was met at the train station by a *Defender* reporter who asked if, after this latest attack, he would leave. "I will defend my home and my property to the extent of my life," Binga replied, before adding with sardonic wit, "I will let my home stand as a monument to Chicago law and disorder."[1]

A brash, self-aggrandizing former railroad porter who had come to the city for the 1893 World's Fair and made a fortune in real estate, Binga was a ubiquitous figure in Black Chicago. His Binga Bank had become a state institution that year and his parties were must-go social events for the elite. But Binga also had a reputation as a landlord who raised the rent and cut services whenever he bought buildings in white areas and began renting to black tenants.[2]

Nevertheless, Binga's resolve and courage in the face of this continued campaign of terrorism earned him great public support. An editorial, "Bombing Binga," chastised the bombers and the real estate interests behind them as well the police for failing to catch those responsible for the attacks on Binga's home.[3]

Under the headline "Chicago Girl Is a Full-Fledged Aviatrix Now," the front page of the October 1, 1921, edition featured an interview with Bessie Coleman, the first black woman to earn an international pilot's license. Beautiful and visionary, Coleman, thirty, had just returned from France, where she became the first African American to be accepted as a member of the Aero Club of Paris, and she gave an extensive interview to *The Defender* in which she detailed her ambition to inculcate a love for flying among African Americans. "I thought it my duty," she declared, "to risk my life to learn aviating and to encourage flying among men and women of the Race who are so far behind the white man in this special line."[4]

Born in Texas, Coleman had come to Chicago several years earlier and found work as a manicurist in a barbershop that catered to prominent African American men like Robert Abbott and Jesse Binga, both of whom she counted among her clientele. Her fascination with flying originated with stories of air combat she heard from the soldiers returned from France. None of the flight schools in the United States, however, would accept her, partly because she was a woman and partly because she was black. Advising her to travel overseas to find an institution that would not discriminate, Robert Abbott even gave her some funds for the journey.[5]

After she arrived in France, Coleman continued to face difficulties finding a flight school; the first two where she applied turned her down because two women had recently died during training, leading these schools' administrators to conclude that women simply were not suited for flight. Finally, she found a school that would accept her in a rural town where, fittingly, Joan of Arc had been imprisoned by the English centuries earlier, and over a period of weeks, she learned to handle the biplane at altitudes as high as five thousand feet. From there she went on to Paris, where she took additional lessons from a former World War I flying ace who taught her advanced techniques such as tailspins, banking, and looping the loop.

Determined to be the African American apostle of flying, Coleman dreamed of opening her own chain of schools that would admit men as well as women, whites as well as blacks. But to that end, she needed her own plane, and for that, she needed more funds. She stayed in Chicago for just a few busy weeks upon her return, just long enough to convince Robert Abbott to give her an even larger grant before she headed back to Europe.

She gave another interview to *The Defender* before she left, telling the reporter, "Do you know you have never lived until you have flown?"[6]

At the beginning of 1922, *The Defender* reported with glee that federal agents had arrested Marcus Garvey at his Harlem home on charges of mail fraud related to the Black Star Line, amid increasing evidence the enterprise was a shambles. One of its two ships was restricted to sailing the Hudson River, while the other was in the custody of the American consul in Cuba, held by court order for past debts. Garvey blamed the NAACP's executive secretary, James Weldon Johnson, for instigating his arrest, prompting a vehement denial from Johnson, but Garvey's flock remained loyal, showing up en masse at his court hearings and contributing generously to his defense fund.[7]

All through that spring and summer, *The Defender* did its best to amplify the voices of Garvey's critics and dissenters with a steady stream of reports and opinion pieces, even as Garvey often inflicted wounds on his own reputation. His plan for racial separation sometimes veered into strange territory, as when he spoke sympathetically of southern segregation during a speech in New Orleans. "This is a white man's country," he told his audience. "He found it, he conquered it, and we can't blame him if he wants to keep it."[8]

Then, on the heels of these bizarre comments, an even more troubling revelation came to the fore — that Garvey had held a secret meeting in Atlanta several weeks earlier with Edward Clarke, the imperial kleagle of the Ku Klux Klan. *The Defender* pounced on this news, printing denunciations of Garvey by a broad spectrum that included elected officials, leftist activists, conservative commentators, and erstwhile supporters. "It is not known that the Ku Klux leaders have at any other time felt impelled to discuss the problem of race relations with other Race leaders," the newspaper wrote acidly. "The only point of similarity between Mr. Garvey's group and that being led by Clarke is 'superiority,' Garvey flaunting the black flag and Clarke a white one."[9]

*The Defender* had tracked the Klan's rise ever since it burst out of the South earlier that year, presenting itself as a modern and responsible fraternal organization for white, American-born Protestant men, with an agenda that was anti-Catholic, anti-Jewish, and anti–labor union, as well as favorable to Prohibition. In order to show that this new organization had moved away from the violence of the past, the Klan's hierarchy in Atlanta even ordered its members to stop wearing robes, hoods, and masks in public. Klan affiliates sprang up in Westchester and Duchess Counties, outside New York City, and tried to incorporate in Colorado, while in California, sixty members of the Los Angeles Police Department formed the "Knight Buzzards Brigade," a Klan auxiliary.[10]

Garvey believed that his goals were complementary to the Klan's in that a mass exodus back to Africa would also give the Klan what it wanted — an America inhabited exclusively by white people. But he had seriously underestimated the visceral revulsion the meeting would inspire among the vast majority of African Americans, who simply could not countenance any black leader consorting with an organization that, regardless of the current effort to sanitize the Klan's image, embodied the use of murder, rape, and terror as tools of oppression. Garvey's meeting with the kleagle became exhibit A for those who argued that he was ill equipped to lead African-descended people in the United States, and turned off many potential supporters.[11]

Garvey lashed out at his critics with a combination of threats and counteraccusations, naming his opponents in an issue of *The Negro World* under the headline "A Warning to the Enemy": "We do not want a fight among Negro organizations, because it does not help the Race," the editorial raged, "but it will appear that some people desire a fight. If you want a fight you are going to have it."[12]

The anti-Garvey forces were coalescing, however, their ranks swelled by disaffected UNIA members and onetime supporters. During the world war, the socialists Chandler Owen and A. Philip Randolph, coeditors of *The Messenger,* had strongly opposed American involvement, putting them on the side opposite Robert Abbott and the other principals in the black press. But when it came to Garvey, they agreed to pool their efforts. *The Defender* gave prominent coverage to Owen and Randolph's efforts to forcibly deport the UNIA leader Garvey, while articles in *The Messenger* described Abbott as "modest, unassuming, yet courageous" and a "man of vision and character."[13]

"We do not believe we are of the same political, fraternal or religious faith," wrote Owen about Abbott in *The Messenger*'s July issue. Nevertheless, "On some things we are in complete harmony. Chief among which is Robert Abbott's belief in and advocacy of social equality."[14]

The Ku Klux Klan arrived in Chicago that summer, beginning its local recruitment drive with a mass meeting in June, and establishing chapters in Englewood, Woodlawn, and Kenwood, South Side neighborhoods facing an influx of African American residents. Other Klan chapters were established on the North and West Sides in places that abutted the teeming Jewish area of Maxwell Street and the Catholic immigrant neighborhoods near the stockyards.[15]

If *The Defender* was alarmed by the Klan's rapid infiltration, it was, for once, not alone. This was Chicago, after all, a city with over 1 million Catholics and 125,000 Jews, in addition to its African American population. Indeed, the Klan's potential membership of North American–born, white, Protestant men was just 15 percent of the city's population. The City Council unanimously pledged to expel the Klan, while the chief of police banned any Klan parades in which hoods were worn, and Illinois's governor formed an anti-Klan organization that was joined by a thousand members of the Ragan's Colts street gang.[16]

In August, a multiracial, ecumenical coalition of clergy and businesspeople formed the American Unity League, its mandate to uproot the Klan. The AUL's executive director, a white Catholic criminal lawyer named Patrick O'Donnell, noted that the local Klan had twenty-seven thousand members, large enough to be a decisive force in some races in the upcoming 1923 city elections, and cited the Klan's recent role in electing a United States senator from Texas.

"We had hoped that this un-American organization would succumb to the exposés which have showed its true character," O'Donnell told *The Defender*, "but the fact is that its membership is increasing rapidly and its power is becoming stronger and more dangerous."[17]

The *Chicago Tribune*, in contrast, had described the Klan's goals as "commendable" in an editorial some months back, and was open-minded when the group established itself in the city. This new, media-savvy variant of the Klan, in turn, allowed a *Tribune* reporter privileged access when it staged a macabre ritual in a field on the city's southern outskirts. On Saturday, August 19, the *Tribune's* reporter arrived in the early afternoon and looked on as Klansmen drove in from all of the chapters in Cook County and parked their cars in a semicircle around a twenty-foot-tall wooden cross wrapped in white cotton.

At dusk, leaders gave a signal and the Klansmen donned their robes and hoods, lit torches, and turned on their automobiles' headlights to illuminate the great cross. Then, at midnight, a representative from the Atlanta headquarters and the Illinois "grand dragon" led a silent procession into the center of the semicircle, assembling around the cross while 4,650 men in regular clothes, applicants for membership, were marched before the ring of robed Klansmen for a final review.

"Searching eyes inspected them," wrote the *Tribune's* reporter, "to make certain at the last minute none should enter who were 'not fit' for the ritual of the Klan."

Finally, the cross was set ablaze, the initiates repeated a pledge of allegiance to the Klan, and the entire gathering, some 25,000 men, sang "Onward, Christian Soldiers" before dispersing silently into the night.[18]

Even at this event, however, anti-Klan forces were at work. One week after the mass initiation rally, *The Defender* announced that among the new recruits were some fifty African Americans with complexions light enough to pass as white. These infiltrators had collected Klan documents, robes, passwords, secret signs, and, most significantly, the names, addresses, and businesses of many other members.[19]

At the beginning of September, Robert Abbott printed a signed front-page editorial cautiously welcoming the newly formed AUL. Certainly African Americans would participate in this effort, but he was skeptical that whites would do what was necessary to defeat the Klan. Liberal white leaders had consistently failed to confront segregation in the South, Abbott noted, and stopping the Klan now that it metastasized to the North would require sustained, determined action. "Will Jew and Catholic, Hebrew and Irish continue to join in the villainy of hypocritical Protestantism in hatred, persecution and scorn of darker people, or will true brotherhood be the watchword? If the Ku Klux Klan is ever routed, it will yield to men, to men only; yield to no cry but this — To Hell With The Ku Klux Klan."[20]

Nevertheless, Abbott was soon impressed by the craftiness displayed by his white allies. In early September, the AUL began publishing a weekly magazine, *Tolerance,* that featured lists of Klan members' names, addresses, and business affiliations, which the group had obtained. "We feel that the publication of the names of those who belong to the Klan will be a blow that the masked organization cannot survive," O'Donnell told the media. "Many Klansmen are in business or the professions and are dependent largely upon patronage of those groups they classify as alien."

The first issue of *Tolerance,* containing the names of 150 Klansmen, sold out its entire run of 1,700 copies at newsstands, bus stops, and Catholic churches. Within a few weeks, *Tolerance*'s press run was up to 150,000, and the AUL compiled its Klan lists in a twenty-five-cent pamphlet entitled "Is Your Neighbor a Kluxer?" Salesmen, grocery store owners, and milkmen reported losing business from their African American, Catholic, and Jewish customers. When the president of the Washington Park Bank was exposed as a Klansman, its Jewish and Irish depositors began withdrawing their accounts, forcing the board of directors to fire the president despite his protestations that he hadn't known what the group stood for.

Now many of those who had donned their white robes and hoods and pledged their undying loyalty to the Invisible Empire trekked into *Tolerance*'s office and begged the newspaper not to publish their names. The Klan itself also began to panic, filing a lawsuit against the AUL to stop the publication of its members' names.[21]

*The Defender* was delighted, referring to the AUL in an editorial as "that splendid and magnificent organization," and urging its readers to become members. "We hope our readers throughout the country will carefully scan these lists," urged the editorial, "for we must not fail to throw the weight of our influence along all lines in favor of those who are friendly and against those who are unfriendly to our group, the same as is being done by other groups who are proscribed as we are."[22]

Bessie Coleman arrived by ship in New York City at the end of August with what *The Defender* described as a "giant aeroplane" she had purchased in Holland, a Fokker C-2. She had spent the past months in France, Holland, Germany, and Switzerland, practicing in different planes and learning advanced techniques, hosted wherever she went by flying societies and aviation enthusiasts.

With *The Defender* as her primary sponsor, Coleman held an exhibition flight on Long Island, her first in the United States, before some two thousand people on Sunday, September 3. After a first run with a copilot, she took off alone while the renowned band from the Fifteenth New York National Guard Infantry Regiment, the "Harlem Hellfighters," played "The Star-Spangled Banner." "With bared heads, the people stood until the last strains of our national anthem died away," *The Defender*'s correspondent wrote, "marking the first public flight of a Race woman in this country."[23]

By the end of the month, Coleman was back in Chicago planning another performance. Meanwhile, *The Defender* bolstered her public image by producing a film of her flights entitled *World's Greatest Race Aviatrix,* which was screened in one of the neighborhood theaters. On Sunday, October 15, some two thousand people, most of them African Americans from the South Side, gathered in Checkerboard Field, a small airfield on the southwest side of the city, where they saw Coleman perform a series of heart-stopping aerial stunts and maneuvers.

When she executed a figure eight, "it looked as if she had lost control of her great plane and that it was turning and twisting, pilotless, back to earth," *The Defender*'s reporter narrated breathlessly. "But thousands of hearts sighed with great relief when the machine was seen to right itself and soar straightaway through the air."[24]

After the performance, Coleman took willing crowd members up on short flights in her own plane as well as five other aircraft that had been made available to her for the event, to give the maximum number of Chicago's African Americans their own first journey through the skies. People continued to queue up until dark.[25]

Robert Watkins, *The Defender*'s first Bud Billiken, left the paper when he matriculated into high school, but at the beginning of 1923, Harper found the perfect replacement, a bookish ten-year-old named Willard Motley, who had already published a multipart short story in the newspaper. Entitled "Brother and Sister," it was a Dickensian tale about two orphans on the road, enduring cruel treatment as they make their way to Chicago, where they find fortune as well as a stable home with a new family. Hailing from an artistic family — his uncle Archibald Motley Jr. was already making a name for himself as a painter — Motley proudly assumed the mantle of Bud Billiken, writing how much he enjoyed reading other young people's missives as well as composing his own pieces. "I like to write letters, stories and everything," Motley declared. "Before I came here I used to come home in the afternoon and write. Now I come down to *The Defender* office and see how many of you have written to me."[26]

Like his predecessor, Motley spent most of his time going through the huge volume of mail that came in from young readers around the world. He also processed hundreds of new applications for the Billiken Club every week, with every applicant receiving a personalized membership card and identification button. New recruits saw their names printed in the "Defender Jr.," while regular members saw their birthdays announced.[27]

In addition to polishing submissions and corresponding with readers, Motley wrote many articles himself, gathering stories and developing a writing style that he would later exploit as a best-selling novelist. That fall, he interviewed a French-speaking African American man who had been born a slave in 1844 on a plantation in Assumption Parish, Louisiana. As a teenager, this man, known as Captain Zeno, had escaped when the Union army invaded Louisiana, managing to persuade a passing officer to make him a company bugler. He stayed with the army through the end of the war, blowing his horn in grief on April 15, 1865, when Zeno's commanders received word that President Lincoln had been assassinated.

Zeno had come to Chicago only a few years before Motley's interview, when he was already over eighty years old, after learning about an older brother he had never known who was still alive and residing in the city. The long-lost siblings wrote to each other for several years before Zeno decided to travel to Chicago, meeting his brother for the first time in a tearful scene at the Dearborn Street train station just a few days before the interview. Passersby had been stunned to see the two old men embracing each other and crying tears of joy.

"As I held Captain Zeno's hand when he completed his story," Motley wrote, "I felt a potent sorrow at having to part with such a man, perhaps never to meet again, nor another like him. Thinking of this, I held his hand a little longer than necessary and tried as best I could to smile when I replied to his cheerful, 'Au revoir.'"[28]

As Bessie Coleman toured the country, her zeal for flying sometimes put her in harm's way. Flying from San Diego to Long Beach late one afternoon, Coleman's plane was unexpectedly diverted by weather along with five others and forced to fly at eight thousand feet, over mountains and ocean, as the sun set. After a terrifying journey over the as-yet-unelectrified landscape, the lost flyers noticed large spotlights pointed into the sky from Long Beach and flew toward them. One by one, the flight crew in Long Beach used these beams to guide the planes in — all except Coleman, who overshot the Long Beach airfield and landed uneventfully in an open patch of land.

"The crowd which was awaiting the fliers below thought she had been killed," wrote *The Defender*'s Los Angeles correspondent, "until she walked onto the airfield unscathed some minutes later."[29]

In February, Coleman was flying in Santa Cruz when her plane struck an air pocket at two hundred feet, stalled, and then crashed. She suffered a broken leg and other injuries but remained undaunted by this mishap as well. "You tell the world I am coming back," she told a *Defender* reporter from her hospital bed. She maintained that the fact that she had survived proved that "flying in the air is no more dangerous than riding an automobile on the surface."[30]

*The Defender* and its allies continued their crusade against the Ku Klux Klan into 1923, even as the city approached municipal elections in which the Klan was threatening to play a decisive role. At the normally fractious Chicago City Council, a five-member committee with aldermen from the Irish, Norwegian, Polish, Jewish, and African American enclaves promised to bring down the "Iron Hand of Justice" on the Klan and root out any members who held city jobs, especially in the fire and police departments, where there was said to be substantial infiltration. In January, the committee announced the forced retirement of a fireman who was also a kleagle, a midlevel executive in the Klan hierarchy, and the transfer of four others, including a captain, from a fire station on the West Side.

"So long as the Ku Klux Klan confined its efforts to crushing Negroes, [the American people] were passive," Alderman Louis Anderson told the newspaper, "but when they took to practicing the same methods on the whites, it was a horse of another color, hence the local, state and national attempt to crush this iniquitous and bloodthirsty organization."[31]

But the Klan was just one of the wild cards threatening to unravel the political gains made by Black Chicago since the start of the Great Migration. Mayor Big Bill Thompson had shocked the political establishment a few weeks earlier when he unexpectedly announced that he would not run for another term, having been hounded into temporary retirement by allegations of corruption from the *Chicago Tribune* and his rivals in the Republican Party. In addition to the unexpected departure of their most powerful ally, Ed Wright and his political organization were scrambling to adapt to boundaries that had been redrawn to create fifty wards with just one alderman each, meaning that a fair number of elected officials would be unemployed after the next ballot.

Committeeman Wright at this point had two aldermen in his operation, Abbott's old friend Louis Anderson in the Second Ward and Robert "Fighting Bob" Jackson in the Third, but the new Second Ward had many white ethnic neighborhoods. Moreover, election rules had been changed so that the first round of voting at the end of February was nonpartisan, meaning that a Republican candidate would not have any automatic advantage. And with the community so full of fresh migrants, black leaders were understandably concerned over what would actually happen when they went into the voting booth.

"Newcomers," urged *Defender* columnist Roscoe Simmons, a Republican Party loyalist, "don't forget that Mr. Anderson belongs to the crowd that kept Chicago free until you could get here."[32]

With *The Defender*'s reporters chronicling every move, Wright and his precinct workers spent the frantic weeks before Election Day trying to extend their apparatus to the new, non–African American sections of the Second Ward, plying the streets right up to the moment that the polls closed on Election Day, February 27. That night, the whole organization gathered nervously at the Pekin Theater, usually a lively cabaret, until a relieved Ed Wright emerged and announced that Anderson had been reelected by a wide margin of close to four thousand votes, more than enough to avoid a runoff. *The Defender*'s ecstatic coverage of the event revealed just how effective Wright's outreach had been in pulling together a multiethnic coalition. "Jew, Greek, Italian, German, Anglo-Saxon and the sons of freed sons and daughters from the South's oppression, a composite American group, acclaimed in frenzied outbursts precinct returns that indicated Anderson's swelling majority."[33]

Wright's organization was not just intact, but stronger for having faced down threats and obstacles and establishing itself outside of Big Bill's patronage. Still, voters tossed out many Thompson allies, and the Republican faction led by the *Chicago Tribune* secured the party nomination for its candidate, Arthur Lueder, a reticent Lutheran who served as the city's postmaster. There was distinct evidence of Klan influence in certain races, too, as two of Anderson's colleagues on the anti-Klan committee, Aldermen Stanley Walkowiak and Robert Mulcahy, were defeated.

Wright faced a dilemma, then, in the second round of balloting in April. Ordinarily, the African American electorate would have been expected to vote en masse for the Republican Party, for whom many had a visceral attachment equivalent to the revulsion they felt for the Democrats. But the whispers of Klan involvement within the victorious Republican faction, as well as its open hostility to their beloved mayor Thompson, drove many African Americans toward the Democrats. "There was a time when a Republican nomination, even for a local office, was all that was necessary to command our solid support," explicated a *Defender* editorial, "but 'them days are gone forever.' The word 'Republican' is no longer an attraction and the word 'Democrat' is no longer a scarecrow."[34]

Ed Wright played a double game in this election, publicly supporting the Republicans but privately directing his lieutenants, Alderman

Anderson and former alderman Oscar De Priest, to lead a mass defection from Lueder in favor of the Democratic candidate for mayor, William Dever, a judge and former member of the City Council. De Priest issued a circular that urged African Americans not to vote for the Republican Lueder, citing rumors of a secret agreement to appoint a Klan member as chief of police.

*The Defender* editorial page was open about its support for the Democrat in this election, playing up Lueder's support from the *Tribune*, which was almost as unpopular as the Klan, with one columnist writing that Lueder was "tarred with the brush of that conscienceless and implacable enemy of the Race, the *Chicago Tribune*."[35]

But Lueder himself emphatically denied any affiliation with the Klan and took his case to the Appomattox Club and other community institutions, specifically refuting the notion that he would appoint a Klan member to head the police force.[36]

With just two weeks to go before the election, Lueder's denials swayed the majority of the community in his direction, according to *The Defender*. But the issue of Klan infiltration into city government burst into the news once again in mid-March when two of the firemen accused of pledging loyalty to the Invisible Empire contested their firing before the city civil service commission. In a theatrical two-hour hearing, the AUL's Patrick O'Donnell and Ed Wright, in his capacity as a private attorney, acted as the prosecution while the firemen were defended by an attorney paid by Klan headquarters in Atlanta who argued that their membership should not be a bar to employment.[37]

On Election Day, Wright's strategizing and *The Defender's* information campaign won out over an emotional attachment to the Republicans, contributing heavily to Dever's landslide victory with a margin of over one hundred thousand votes. "The Second and Third Ward turnover for Dever was the most remarkable of a series of shifts made by the Race in the North in the last few years," *The Defender* declared in a postelection article on the front page.[38]

In the end, the Klan's involvement, the newspaper argued, had provoked a backlash against the Republican candidate from Chicago's diverse electorate. However respectable Lueder himself might have been, the taint of Klan involvement in his campaign had united the city's various ethnic factions against him. The Klan's candidates for alderman all lost their bids as well, many by thousands of votes, data that was proudly discussed in *The Defender* as well as in immigrant newspapers around the city.

Robert Abbott was in South America for all of the election excitement, his first-ever journey outside the United States. He had long nurtured what he described as a "golden dream" of traveling to the region because of its parallel history with the United States, its legacy as part of the African slave trade, and its experience postemancipation. With this quasi-academic purpose in mind, he had planned to travel as any other successful businessman might have, only to discover even before his departure that his own nation's bizarre racial policies applied internationally as well.

In the winter, Abbott entered the Chicago office of one of the international steamship companies with the intent of purchasing a first-class cabin, but was told that they were all booked. Suspicious that he was being discriminated against, Abbott sent in his wife, who almost always passed for white, and she was immediately offered a first-class ticket. He received the same service at all of the other steamship lines, with several of them actually explicit about refusing to sell tickets to African Americans. It took Abbott weeks of constant effort and a letter of protest to the headquarters of one steamship company before he finally obtained a booking.

But this was only the first obstacle: the Brazilian consul in Chicago flatly refused to issue the Abbotts a visa, prompting Robert to contact the congressman who represented the South Side. When that, too, proved unsuccessful, he turned to U.S. Senator Medill McCormick, who dutifully intervened with both the Brazilians and the U.S. State Department.

Finally, on February 3, 1923, after a series of farewell dinners and parties in both Chicago and New York City, the Abbotts boarded the steamship *Pan American* and headed out into the Atlantic Ocean. As they entered Rio de Janeiro's legendary Guanabara Bay twelve days later, Abbott was overwhelmed by the beauty of the city, its "rich golden sunlight, the riot and abundance of infinite life and color," as he described it in his memoir of the trip published in *The Defender.* Bursting with energy and curiosity as they drove from the harbor along the spectacular Avenida Central, he noted the tropical jungle encroaching all around the city's edges. But when they tried to check into the American-owned Hotel Glória, which had been recommended to them by other first-class passengers on their voyage, they were refused. "Even in the fair land of Brazil," Abbott wrote, "the slimy thing of American color phobia would presume to assert itself."[39]

They went next to the Hotel Victoria, a first-class Brazilian establishment, where they were welcomed by the owner and treated as distinguished guests. The owner introduced them to Alfredo Clenendon, a seventy-year-old African American dentist who, having emigrated from the United States forty years earlier, had served on the staff of Brazil's last emperor. Through Dr. Clenendon, the Abbotts met native Brazilian politicians and physicians, lawyers, police, and military officers, all of whom expressed pride in their African heritage. Abbott photographed the dark-complexioned police chief of Rio as well as police officers and electrical engineers, noting with envy that African Americans at home were still largely restricted from such professions. The Brazilian Press Association gave Abbott a formal reception, according him full honors, and asked him to give a speech. When he left, the Brazilian journalists gave him a card of farewell that read, "The voice of truth. The soul is without color."

Abbott was deeply struck by the Brazilians' welcome and the contrast he saw with race relations at home. "There is no kind of race problem in Brazil," he declared, carried away by the difference between this system and his own.[40]

On their way by train to São Paulo, the Abbotts crossed into Mato Grosso state, the country's cotton-growing region, a full-day's journey to the Amazonian interior that took them through lush jungle and coffee fields. Like the United States, Brazil was in the midst of an industrial transformation, and Abbott saw that fortunes were being made from railroads and factories, steamships and mines. Brazil was likewise a nation of immigrants; he was struck by the intermingling of Germans, Italians, Russians, and Japanese among the native people. Only, unlike in the United States, African-descended people had the benefit of full participation in the nation's riches. Even miscegenation, the most taboo subject of all in the United States, did not register among the Brazilians. "Negroes and whites intermarry without provoking the slightest social criticism," Abbott noted with surprised satisfaction.[41]

From Brazil, the Abbotts stopped briefly in Montevideo, Uruguay, and then went on to Buenos Aires. Argentina had a small African-descended population compared with Brazil's, but Robert Abbott detected no race prejudice. From Buenos Aires, they took a trans-continental train six hundred miles to the foothills of the Andes, and from there, a narrow-gauge train over the mountains, rising from the steaming jungle to the cool highlands and down into the arid plains of Chile, a three-day journey overall until they arrived in the city of Valparaiso on the Pacific coast.[42]

Once again they encountered the hostility of white Americans in their hotel, only racial discrimination was against the law in Chile, and Abbott complained to the American consul general. When the consul refused to help, Abbott turned to his Chilean contacts, who escorted him inside the hotel, fully prepared to make a stand on principle. The staff greeted them professionally, however, having decided to ignore the complaints of white Americans who did not want to share the hotel with *Negroes*.[43]

From Chile, the Abbotts traveled by steamship north to Peru, touring the colonial buildings of Lima and examining the relics of the Inca Empire and other civilizations, before continuing through Ecuador and into the Panama Canal Zone, which was then under American control. Abbott discovered that blacks were barred from all of the first-class hotels and restaurants as well as the public parks in the American Zone, while in Panama proper, there was no discrimination.[44]

From Panama, the Abbotts began the final leg of their journey, a four-day trip across the Caribbean Sea to Havana. There they met former heavyweight champion Jack Johnson, who, after making amends with the U.S. criminal justice system and spending nearly a year in a federal penitentiary, had settled temporarily in Cuba to take part in exhibition fights. Abbott and Johnson had formed a friend-ship fifteen years earlier, when the boxer won the world heavyweight championship, and Johnson lent the Abbotts his automobile during their stay.

Though enjoying the sights as well as Cuba's famous cigars, Abbott noted that the conditions for African-descended people in the island nation were marred by the United States' projection of a racist agenda. Race consciousness had been introduced under the American occupation following the Spanish-American War, and had been subsequently maintained through the influence of American corporations.

"There has been much American capital invested in Cuba," Abbott observed, "and with it has come the assertion of racial prerogation."[45]

While the Abbotts were traveling, *The Defender*'s society editor, Julius Avendorph, the African American community's ultimate arbiter of taste, died suddenly after a short illness. He was buried by the Knights of Pythias, one of the many fraternal organizations to which he belonged, as his wife and two teenage sons looked on. The Episcopal church where services were held was filled to capacity, and hundreds more were turned away. "No gathering in the last quarter of a century was complete without him," read the newspaper's emotional obituary, "and on most occasions, debuts and coming out parties were lacking if he was not there as master of ceremonies."[46]

His continual popularity notwithstanding, Avendorph's death coincided with the end of the Edwardian world and its associated customs and manners. He was the same age as Abbott, fifty-four, and like Abbott, he was a child of slaves who had come to Chicago from the South — in his case, Alabama. But Avendorph represented an era that was already being washed away by the tides of migrants who had filled the old Dearborn corridor and transformed it. Even now, they were pushing the community's borders into new territory, geographically and culturally as well as economically and politically. Avendorph had never been entirely comfortable with the new elite that had formed as a result of this demographic shift, least of all with the wealthy class of businesspeople who had amassed huge fortunes in its wake, supplanting the genteel professionals whom Avendorph so admired.

For him, the period from 1887 to 1910 remained a halcyon time when the city's "first families" had entertained others of their set at exclusive events in which the conduct and conversation were exemplary. As the parvenus invaded the homes of the old elites and inevitably hosted their own, to his eye, invariably gauche events,

Avendorph filled his column in *The Defender* with a litany of perceived style errors, such as men wearing gold buttons on their jackets, or white socks, or diamond pins, or other items "that have no place with evening clothes."

Finally, exasperated by the breaches in etiquette he observed, he called on the community's social clubs to put their collective foot down, purge their membership rolls, and otherwise reaffirm the standards of the glorious past. "Here is the solution for cleansing Chicago society," he wrote. "Those who stand for high class, clean, intelligent association should ignore all persons whose character is in the slightest way questionable."

It was too late, of course, for any such correction. But Avendorph continued to hold himself and his circle to the highest standard, even when it came to his employment at the Pullman Company. Despite a quarter century of dedicated service that had included various sensitive responsibilities, he had never risen above the rank of clerk, and even this title was bestowed belatedly; Avendorph had been a mere "messenger" for most of his tenure at Pullman. But he never complained, never noted the irony that a company whose reputation depended on its legion of impeccable African American porters had no black executives.[47]

The Abbotts returned to Chicago after their three-month sojourn just a few days after Julius Avendorph's funeral. Waiting for them in the drizzle outside the train station were twenty-five cars loaded with *Defender* staffers and community leaders, including millionaire Jesse Binga, city editor Lucius Harper, and former alderman Oscar De Priest. Proceeding to the corner of Thirty-Ninth Street and Grand Boulevard on the South Side, the convoy was met by the forty-piece band and ROTC unit from Wendell Phillips High School, who led the caravan of cars in a parade all around the perimeter of the neighborhood. The streets were lined with people waving their hats and cheering Mr. and Mrs. Abbott, while many businesses were draped with banners reading WELCOME HOME, R. S. ABBOTT.[48]

The Abbotts were treated to a reception in the newspaper's lobby officiated by William Braddan, former Eighth Infantry chaplain, who told the editor that he had returned just in time. Buoyed by the results of the last election, the minister predicted that the Black Belt would soon have the opportunity to send one of its own to the U.S. Congress, an effort that would require Abbott's contribution.[49]

For his part, Abbott was gracious, confessing to the crowd that he was nearly overcome with emotion when the convoy turned onto the old Stroll. "My heart swelled because I knew I was going to have my chance to see the center of my life, my old haunts, that have crowded my dreams at night and day while I have been away, State Street, where I began my life's work."

Depicting the racial harmony he had experienced in Brazil, he vowed to redouble his efforts to improve conditions for African Americans: "I have come back to you to work. I know nothing but work. I love to work. I have come back more determined than ever to make our country like Brazil, like the Argentine, lands of true democracy, rather than a country of mock democracy."[50]

# 9

# Chicago Vindicated

T HE FEDERAL TRIAL of Marcus Garvey on charges of mail fraud began in New York on May 25, 1923, with the selection of an all-white jury in a courtroom packed with UNIA supporters. Garvey was charged with improperly handling more than $1 million, and prosecutors began their case the next day by explaining that the government was "not concerned in whether Garvey's scheme was a dream or not."[1]

When his turn came, Garvey announced that he would be questioning witnesses himself, with his lawyer functioning only in an advisory capacity. Garvey had not informed his attorney of this decision prior to addressing the judge, and the stunned lawyer argued with his client for several minutes before finally resigning from the case in exasperation. Garvey was now on his own legally, as the government prosecutors called a series of witnesses, starting with the former secretary general for UNIA, who testified that collection of money for the Black Star Line had begun before it was incorporated and, further, that Garvey had only formalized the company after he was forced to by state authorities. Another witness testified that Garvey had paid six times the value for his first ship, the SS *Frederick Douglass,* which had been purchased for nearly $165,000 as a result of a swindle involving the ship's captain.

Without any legal training or background, Garvey attempted to cross-examine these witnesses only to be censured by the judge repeatedly for overstepping courtroom protocols. After a week of proceedings, the case was interrupted when two of the witnesses, former UNIA members who were preparing to testify for the prosecution, approached the judge and pointed out a large man in the courtroom who they said had threatened to kill them if they testified against Garvey. The judge immediately stopped the trial, ordered the jury out, and directed bailiffs to seize the man, who turned out to be a subway porter and member of UNIA's African Legion, and sentenced him to two months in a federal penitentiary for contempt of court. After this incident, extra security personnel were assigned to the courtroom, including an escort of four federal agents for the judge.

"Garvey's Stock Drops Lower Than the German Mark," read that week's headline on the front page of *The Defender.*[2]

As the trial stretched on, prosecutors continued to put a series of former UNIA officials and business partners on the stand, demonstrating the human cost of the alleged malfeasance by including a dock worker who paid $500 for passage to Liberia for himself and his family. "He is still waiting," *The Defender*'s correspondent opined, "a sadder and much poorer man."[3]

Finally, after twenty-seven days, the case went to the jury. When the predictable verdict of "guilty" came in eight hours later, Garvey's supporters sat in the courtroom, displaying a mix of emotions; some wept, others expressed anger and defiance. Government agents circulated in the crowd in an effort to keep things calm, while Garvey himself let loose one brief stream of invective against the prosecuting attorney before catching himself and sitting back down in a gesture of resignation. A few days later, Garvey was sentenced to five years in federal prison and fined $1,000. He spent his thirty-sixth birthday in the Tombs, but was freed at the beginning of September on $25,000 bond, pending his appeal.[4]

As Garvey's legal troubles played out, Robert Abbott confronted a scandal in his own house. Shortly after he returned from South America, Genevieve Lee Wimp, the daughter of his former landlady, Mrs. Lee, who worked as the newspaper's assistant treasurer, revealed to Abbott her suspicions that several employees were not only pilfering cash but also charging the newspaper for deliveries of coal and other household goods to their homes. Worse yet, the trail led back to business manager Phil Jones, who had been Abbott's first newsboy, starting with the newspaper as a child after school and growing up alongside the newspaper.

To investigate Wimp's charges, Abbott engaged an auditor, who determined that the allegations were true and that in addition to Jones, several other senior employees were involved in the thefts: Tony Langston, the theater critic; Alf Anderson, an administrator at Provident Hospital, who was one of Abbott's oldest friends; and Roscoe Conkling Simmons, a well-known orator and political operative who had facilitated many contacts for Abbott in the newspaper's early years. Abbott was devastated. He had regarded Jones as a surrogate son, to the extent that he had granted him full access to the newspaper's funds and even given him a share of the Robert S. Abbott Publishing Company, the corporate entity he had created to house *The Defender* and any other ventures he might try.

Ever since the opening of the new plant, the flow of money into the newspaper had become a torrent. Fully one cent of every ten-cent copy of the paper sold was pure profit before even factoring in advertising revenue, all of which enabled Abbott to draw a salary of $2,000 per week, a figure that placed him among the very wealthiest African Americans of his time. Jones and the other staffers partook in these profits, too, earning far more than their colleagues at any other African American publication.

All through 1924, Abbott's health declined. He had endured worsening bouts of weakness for several years, a condition that was diagnosed as Bright's disease, a chronic liver ailment that was now incapacitating him for weeks and even months at a time. As a result, Abbott sat on the results of the audit for months, taking no action.[5]

On January 18, 1925, *The Defender* covered Marcus Garvey's inspection of the SS *Booker T. Washington,* the latest vessel he had acquired to facilitate trade with the African continent. Undeterred by the prospect that continuing his activities while he was free on bail might annoy the federal court considering his appeals, Garvey had organized a new company, the Black Cross Line, and purchased the ship with $160,000 in stock sales shares to 3,600 UNIA members and others, launching it for Central America from 125th Street that evening amid great fanfare.

But just a few weeks later, on February 5, Garvey exhausted his last appeal when a federal judge decided that he would be required to serve out the five-year sentence as well as pay the $1,000 fine. Garvey failed to show up in court for this hearing, and the judge issued a bench warrant for his arrest. A *Defender* reporter accompanied deputy marshals and Bureau of Investigation agents as they searched the city, finally finding Garvey at the 125th Street train station, relaxing with his wife in a Pullman car having just arrived from Detroit. Garvey was promptly handcuffed and escorted back to the Tombs.[6]

Appearing before the appellate court shortly thereafter, Garvey requested three more days of liberty in order to settle his affairs and then asked to make a final speech. The judge unhesitatingly denied both requests and ordered Garvey transported to the federal penitentiary in Atlanta, Georgia. Meanwhile, the SS *Booker T. Washington* was stopped in midcourse, seized by Cuban authorities who impounded it as collateral for Garvey's previous debts.[7]

Just a few days after he became prisoner 19,359, *The Negro World* published Garvey's letter "If I Should Die in Atlanta," which sounded themes of divine retribution were he to be executed, rather than incarcerated for a few years as stipulated by his sentence: "Look for me in the whirlwind or the song of the storm, look for me all around you, for with God's grace I shall come and bring with me the countless millions of black slaves who have died in America and the West Indies and the millions in Africa to aid you in the fight for liberty, freedom and life."[8]

Robert Abbott was still processing the revelations of embezzlement at *The Defender* in early March 1925, when he rose to deliver the keynote address at a "Father and Son" banquet at a church in nearby Joliet. "Help your boys to prepare themselves to be the best possible, whether they choose to be a lawyer or a mechanic," Abbott told the fathers, knowing full well that the young man whom he had seen as his own son had been anything but. "Young men, when you face prejudice, fight it and fight it hard."[9]

Ultimately, Abbott couldn't bear the thought of Jones's betrayal, and on April 10 issued him a letter of dismissal; Langston, Simmons, Anderson, and other employees were also purged from the publication. Jones protested, denying that he had done anything wrong, but Abbott took pains to avoid the young man, refusing to answer notes and failing to appear at appointments, even going so far as to step off a streetcar when he saw Jones get onboard.

Yet as deeply stung as he was by his former employees' treachery,

Abbott never pursued legal action against Jones or any of the others, even when Langston sued him for back commissions. He kept the incident quiet, referring in the newspaper only to the "reorganization of *The Chicago Defender*'s business office."[10]

Nevertheless, news of the scandal soon reached *The Chicago Whip*, an upstart local weekly published by two Yale University Law School graduates. Reveling in schadenfreude, *The Whip*'s editors dubbed Jones, Simmons, Langston, and Bell "The Four Horsemen," making the allegations of theft a matter of street gossip.

Into the breach stepped Nathan McGill, an attorney who was married to Helen Abbott's sister Idalee. Enticing McGill to relocate with his wife and two young children from Florida to Chicago, Abbott installed him as the newspaper's general counsel, and sweetened the deal by convincing the Cook County state's attorney to give McGill an appointment as well. But even if McGill was, as an article about him in *The Defender* insisted, "a man of exceptional ability and rare legal talent," he was not a newspaper man, nor did he have Abbott's understanding of the political and business networks that underpinned Chicago's African American community. These were deficits that would leave him short at crucial moments in the newspaper's future.[11]

In the summer of 1925, a small group of Pullman porters formed a nascent labor union called the Brotherhood of Sleeping Car Porters and hired as its executive director A. Philip Randolph, the fiery editor of *The Messenger*. Randolph was at a low point in his work — his partner Chandler Owen had left the movement and the magazine's circulation had fallen to unsustainable levels — but he jumped into the porters' cause with all of the passion and vitriol he had previously channeled toward the effort to exile Garvey.[12]

That August, Randolph held five consecutive meetings in Harlem to rally support and membership for the Brotherhood, bringing onto the stage a multiracial roster of civil rights activists and labor leaders, including James Weldon Johnson from the NAACP, Abraham Baroff of the International Ladies Garment Workers Union, and William Green, a white former coal miner who had become the president of the fast-growing American Federation of Labor. The success of these gatherings emboldened Randolph to schedule further rallies in cities in the Northeast and Midwest and even in one location in the South, New Orleans.[13]

Just as Randolph was holding these meetings, the porters' working conditions were improved, if only slightly. In Pennsylvania, railroad officials announced that the names of dining-car waiters would now be printed on menu cards. This was to discourage passengers from referring to the porters as "George," a demeaning practice just one step removed from the southern habit of calling an African American man "boy," or worse. *The Defender* celebrated this long-overdue change in an editorial, entitled "Good-By, 'George,'" that characterized the practice as a holdover from eighteenth-century attitudes toward servants. Today, "we are all servants in one sense or another," the editorial maintained, "and the waiter is as much to be considered in his class as a city mayor is in his."[14]

Having spent the winter months of 1925–26 in Florida, aviatrix Bessie Coleman settled herself in Jacksonville in the last week of April to prepare for an upcoming exhibition flight. In the days before the performance, she spent her off-time encouraging African American schoolchildren to pursue the aviation field and, as usual, searching for sponsors who could replace the aircraft she destroyed in rapid succession. This time, she persuaded Edwin Beeman, heir to a chewing gum fortune, to put up $500 so that her mechanic and business partner William Wills could bring her latest aircraft to Florida from its hangar in Dallas, Texas, where she had been based previously.

Wills, a white man of twenty-four and a pilot himself, flew the plane, an older, military-style model without many of the refinements and safety features of newer planes, to Jacksonville before the scheduled exhibition on May 1, having to land twice along the way to deal with engine trouble. Wills made the necessary repairs when he arrived, however, and Coleman completed a few practice flights without incident, even feeling comfortable enough to take up several passengers for their first journeys into the sky. One of those was John H. Sengstacke III, Robert Abbott's teenage nephew, who happened to be in Florida at that moment. Sengstacke's short flight left him with a lasting impression of the experience of flying with Coleman: "terrifying."[15]

On Friday, April 30, the day before the exhibition, Coleman was driven to the airfield by a young protégé, a recent graduate of Howard University, whom she promised to take up later that day, after she made an initial training run. Before taking off with Wills in the driver seat, she knelt before the plane for a brief prayer. They climbed for about twelve minutes until they had reached an altitude of three thousand feet, at which time something went terribly wrong. The plane suddenly flipped over, and Coleman, who was not wearing her harness, was thrown out of the cockpit and sent plummeting to the ground. The impact left her body "crushed and mangled," according to *The Defender*'s correspondent, who witnessed the accident. The plane went into a steep dive, flipping end over end until it crashed through the branches of a pine tree and into the ground near the edge of the airfield. Wills, strapped into the plane, had surely been killed by the impact, but before emergency crews could pull his body from the fuselage, someone at the scene carelessly dropped a lit cigarette, setting the whole pile of oil-soaked wreckage ablaze.[16]

The city's Negro Welfare League, which had sponsored Coleman's trip to Jacksonville, took charge of her remains and brought them to a local funeral home, where, the day after the accident, streams of people, men, women, and children, black and white, came to pay their respects. Her funeral the next day attracted thousands to the local Baptist church. "Millionaires and sons of millionaires, along with sportsmen of high and low degree rubbed elbows in the little church to pause for a second before the open casket that held the shattered body of 'Brave Bess,'" wrote *The Defender*'s correspondent.[17]

Coleman's body arrived in Chicago five days after her death, and thousands came to see her while she lay in state at a location on the South Side. When it was time for her third and final funeral, a lieutenant led six sergeants from the Eighth Regiment who served as pallbearers, bringing her flag-draped casket up the steps of Pilgrim Baptist Church, one of the city's largest, past thousands who lined the steps and packed the pews. Ida B. Wells-Barnett was the master of ceremonies, recounting for the crowd how she had met Coleman shortly after her first return from Europe.

The number of well-wishers had dwindled by the time the burial party got to the gravesite in Lincoln Cemetery on the far South Side, and her casket was silently lowered while the soldiers stood at attention and Coleman's mother waved farewell. Finally, Bessie's youngest sister, Georgia, summarized the sentiments of many. "Oh Bessie," she sobbed, "you tried so hard."[18]

On a spring day in 1926, Robert Abbott asked his driver to take him to the Rolls-Royce dealership in the Loop. Entering the showroom, he perused the various models, finally deciding on one with an exterior billed as "sea fog grey." But when Abbott attempted to buy the car, the salesperson informed him that it was not for sale and that he was unable to order it. Flummoxed, Abbott left the dealership. Over the next several weeks, repeatedly rebuffed in his efforts to buy the Rolls, Abbott concluded that the company had a policy, written or unstated, of not selling to African Americans, presumably to avoid what it considered would be damage to the brand.

Determined to acquire the vehicle, however, Abbott persuaded a white friend to buy the car in his stead and then transfer title to him. From that moment on, Abbott's Rolls-Royce represented defiance as well as success, evidence that an African American man with means could live in any manner he pleased, despite social convention. The Rolls appeared in a photograph on page 8 in the July 31, 1926, edition of *The Defender,* parked in the driveway of Abbott's new mansion under the headline *"Defender* Editor's New Home," with no mention of the struggle to purchase it.

The house, with three stories, fourteen rooms, and a red-brick exterior trimmed with limestone, made its own statement. Located just south of Forty-Seventh Street on South Parkway, in an area that just a few years earlier had been off-limits to blacks, Abbott's home was surrounded by theaters, stores, and restaurants that catered to African Americans. Abbott was proud to note that all of the bathrooms in his new home were built with appliances from an African American manufacturer in Florida.[19]

His new status as a member of the upper class was not always an easy fit for the workaholic publisher, but keenly aware of his responsibilities as a role model, he did his level best to maintain an active presence in society, even when that meant pushing the boundaries with whites. He purchased life memberships at the Natural History Museum and the Art Institute, and attended the opera as well as other theatrical performances, even though he was the only African American at many of these events, made all the more conspicuous by having his light-complexioned wife by his side. Extremely uncomfortable in these situations, Abbott sometimes nervously pretended to be an African potentate, a routine that greatly embarrassed his wife. But he was more relaxed during their frequent dinner parties at home with a mostly African American guest list, sometimes exercising his still-gorgeous tenor with an impromptu song. Even in these friendly social scenarios, however, Abbott's mind remained fixed on the cause, and he took every opportunity, whether in the midst of a bridge game or a silly story, to steer the conversation back to the "Race Question."[20]

While Abbott was increasingly preoccupied with activities outside the newspaper, he entrusted his brother-in-law Nathan McGill with ever-greater levels of responsibility at *The Defender*, with results that infuriated longtime allies, the Pullman porters in particular. In the summer of 1926, an unsigned commentary printed on the same page as the photograph of Abbott's new mansion commended the Pullman Company as well as longtime board member Robert Todd Lincoln, the son of President Abraham Lincoln, in what seemed like a reversal of the newspaper's long-running critique of Pullman's management. Most suspiciously, the commentary endorsed the system of tipping, which Abbott abhorred, arguing that "good porters regard [tips] not as degradation but as recognition of friendly, personal service."[21]

A. Philip Randolph, the hotheaded chief of the Brotherhood of Sleeping Car Porters, responded to this turnabout immediately. In *The Messenger* and in public speeches, he derided *The Defender* as "The Surrender" and the "World's Greatest Weakly," alleging that the newspaper had given in to "gold and power."[22]

More damaging yet, Randolph called for the porters to boycott the newspaper. Train workers were no longer the key component of the paper's distribution and marketing efforts as they had been in the early years; still, they remained influential within the community, and their disapproval could only be seen as a blow to *The Defender*'s credibility. The rift with the porters opened an opportunity for a rival African American newspaper to seize the national primacy that *The Defender* had long enjoyed. In no time at all, *The Pittsburgh Courier* and its charismatic editor Robert Vann took up the porters' cause.[23]

• • •

That same year, in a segregated elementary school in Gibson County, Tennessee, first grader Vernon Jarrett was assigned to memorize one of Robert Abbott's speeches and write a short essay about *The Defender*. Several hundred miles away, in Arkansas City, Arkansas, Johnny Johnson grew up loving the feel of newsprint and tracing the newspaper's red headlines with his finger, getting an "intellectual and a physical thrill" from reading the reports of the big city and its liberated ways, as he recalled many years later in his memoir.[24]

Inspired by *The Defender*, both of these young men were already embarking on courses that would make them nationally renowned journalists, John H. Johnson as the publisher of *Ebony* magazine and Vernon Jarrett as the first syndicated African American columnist for a white-owned daily publication. But other young people were benefiting in even more direct ways from the institution Robert Abbott had built. Now six years old, Timuel Black Jr. saw Abbott at the newspaper's headquarters when he accompanied his older brother Walt, a *Defender* paperboy, to the newspaper's headquarters at 3435 South Indiana Avenue to get his allotment of papers for the week. There were more than five hundred paperboys by then, but the system was the same as when there had been just a handful — the boys got their newspapers in advance just by writing down their names and addresses, with a pledge to return a couple of days later with the money. Out of the ten-cent cover price, the paperboys got a four-cent commission on every issue sold, a sum that was maximized because the boys almost always sold out all of their copies. "They gave out the papers first, on credit, and then collected money later," Dr. Black recalled. "This was one of the few institutions that trusted blacks in this way. It made enough to pay for recreation and maybe have a little left over to help mom and dad."

On one of the Black brothers' trips to the newspaper, Robert Abbott came out to speak with his paperboys. Abbott's words were not especially eloquent — he never shook the Georgia accent from his nasal voice and he used clunky phrasing to urge the boys to pursue their education, stay out of trouble, and try to earn some money. Still, the boys were suitably impressed. How often did they meet a modern Moses who led the people out of the South? How often had they heard about his mansion and his chauffeur-driven limousine? They noticed his impeccable style, his fine suit and hat, perfect shoes, and weather-appropriate coats. This man had started with nothing, the boys knew, and he had become one of the first African American millionaires through pure determination. That he was short, portly, and dark-complexioned only underscored his success, and consequently, what was possible for African Americans in this new world. But what really impressed them was that Abbott had remained with the people, taking a few moments to speak to his paperboys when he might have been luxuriating on some tropical beach. "There was a class difference," Dr. Black admitted, "but people like Abbott bridged that." The Black brothers knew that it had not always been this way — Abbott had been threatened, harassed, and vilified, and yet he had never wavered. Abbott was a role model for remaining in the struggle.

Whether they were city kids or living in small southern towns, a new generation was growing up with fresh expectations about their right to speak freely and about the power of their words to change the country.[25]

"We're for Thompson," declared *The Defender* in early 1927, announcing the editorial page's endorsement for Big Bill's return to City Hall. Four years earlier, the African American electorate had shifted its support to Democratic mayor William Dever, but even then, many had hoped for Thompson's return. Now *The Defender* urged its readers to support Thompson, both because of his past support for the community and to stop current efforts to segregate the city's schools. The fire department had been segregated in recent years as well as public cemeteries, and only Thompson, the newspaper maintained, was committed to stopping the tide.[26]

This time, however, Big Bill would lack the vital support of Ed Wright, who, after feuding briefly with the former mayor, abruptly resigned his post as committeeman, releasing all of his precinct captains and aldermen, effectively abandoning a political machine he had assembled over a lifetime just as it was poised for its greatest victory. *The Defender*'s political reporter reconstructed the words Wright uttered to his crew informing them of his decision: "I have chosen my own course," he told them. "I am not asking any of you to quit your jobs, but I can take care of myself. I was not born a slave and refuse to become one at this late day at the command of Thompson and his friends."[27]

Wright's replacement as ward committeeman was Dan Jackson, a college graduate, professional undertaker, and an acquaintance of Thompson's since childhood. But readers of *The Defender*'s political coverage also knew that Jackson, like Teenan Jones before him, was a powerful intermediary between the world of vice and the police force. Jackson collected protection money from the thriving clubs where Louis Armstrong and Cab Calloway entertained the "black-and-tan" crowds, as well as from the brothels, the gambling operations, and the speakeasies.[28]

Big Bill partnered with gangsters in the white sectors of the city as well, not least Al Capone, who by 1925 had emerged as the leader of the white crime syndicate on the South Side. Though he oversaw a prosperous empire of vice and booze that was several times larger than Jackson's, Capone had been unable to penetrate the Dever administration, and so was determined to install a friendly face as mayor. From his headquarters in the Metropole Hotel on South Michigan Avenue on the city's tony Automobile Row, he directed his men to collect money for Big Bill and to harass his rivals' campaign workers.[29]

Thompson's increasingly overt partnership with the underworld inspired reform-minded elements within the Republican Party to mount a spirited effort to stop this restoration in the primary phase, but to no avail. Thompson won the primary with more than 340,000 votes and received overwhelming support from the black community, which, despite Ed Wright's absence, now held the majority in three city wards. Thrilled with the primary results, *The Defender* predicted that Thompson would win the general election by a wide margin.[30]

Big Bill opened the campaign at the Eighth Regiment Armory, where his enthusiastic supporters began queuing up outside the building hours before the official start time of 7:00 p.m. By the time he actually took the stage at 9:45 p.m., at least ten thousand of his supporters had gathered, cheering, stomping, and applauding. Removing his trademark cigar from his mouth, Thompson labeled Mayor Dever a "Cossack" who had instituted a "reign of terror on the

South Side," adding that he would put an end to the police raids many felt were being unfairly meted out on the black community at a time that every neighborhood was positively awash with gambling clubs and speakeasies.[31]

Democratic Party bosses tried to capitalize on Thompson's outreach to black voters by distributing racist fliers in white neighborhoods. One had a drawing of a rail car in Georgia loaded with African American migrants over a caption that read, "This train will start for Chicago April 6, if Thompson is elected." In some neighborhoods, the Dever campaign paid for trucks with mounted calliopes to drive through playing "Bye Bye Blackbird," while in the North Side's Lincoln Park neighborhood, signs appeared that read, "Do you want Negroes or White Men to run Chicago? Ask Thompson."[32]

On Election Day, Thompson waited nervously in his suite at the Sherman Hotel across from City Hall, downing highballs as exit polls showed him losing to Dever. But as the evening wore on, the tally turned decisively in Big Bill's favor. Crowds outside the hotel began to cheer his name until finally he appeared in the hotel's Louis XVI ballroom, which was packed with election workers, and confirmed what everyone already knew — in a landslide, Thompson had won a third term. Receiving a total of 512,000 votes, he had won by a margin of more than 83,000 votes, a total that had depended heavily, of course, on a massive turnout from the three African American wards, which delivered 71,424 votes for Big Bill all on their own. The *Tribune* gave credit to the African American electoral machine as well as to the unpopularity of Prohibition, which cost Dever a slice of the support of traditional Democratic bastions in the Polish, German, Scandinavian, Bohemian, and Italian communities.

The night saw parades of Thompson supporters marching through the Loop carrying brooms bought just for the occasion — the better to "sweep out" the previous administration — while back at the Sherman Hotel, well-wishers and sycophants crammed the hallway outside the mayor-elect's rooms trying to cajole their way in. Among those privileged enough to be welcomed inside that cigar-smoke-filled chamber was Oscar De Priest, who had played a major public role in the campaign.[33]

At *The Defender*, the predominant reaction was relief. "Chicago Vindicated," declared the newspaper, interpreting Big Bill's success as a repudiation of the racist tactics from the Dever camp. Certainly Thompson's return to office meant hundreds of jobs to the community and new restraints on the police department, but even more meaningful than those steps, in the newspaper's eyes, was this: *white* voters had not responded to the fliers and the constant slurs. "The election of Thompson is a direct slap in the Democrats' face for attempting to raise the color question," the newspaper editorialized. "His election as mayor of Chicago is a lesson to the entire country and particularly to the South."[34]

On August 20, 1927, *The Defender* editorialized that it was time for A. Philip Randolph and his Brotherhood of Sleeping Car Workers to give up their two-year struggle against the Pullman Company, arguing that the company's in-house union was doing an adequate job of representing the train workers. "The fight between the Pullman Company and its employees, if a fight actually existed, has come to an end," the newspaper proclaimed. "The affair is now ended. Let it be forgotten. Let the Pullman Company and the porters proceed as though nothing had happened to mar their relationship."[35]

It was a continuation of the editorial line that had emerged when Nathan McGill took over as the newspaper's general counsel, a distinct tilt away from the porters and their struggle and toward the owners of the Pullman Company and other railway corporations. In place of incisive critiques and biting cartoons, *The Defender* lauded the company for including porters in its disciplinary process and suggested, gently, that it open to blacks all of the professions on the trains. "*The Chicago Defender* is now, and always has been for justice in American industries," the editorial concluded. "It does not, however, feel that the points desired can be gained through antagonistic methods."[36]

The confirmation of this turnabout in editorial policy prompted Randolph and others to accuse McGill of accepting a bribe from the Pullman Company, a charge McGill never answered. Meanwhile, the ambitious owner of *The Pittsburgh Courier*, Robert Vann, continued to take advantage of *The Defender*'s feud with the porters by running a regular column about the Brotherhood activities and proclaiming Randolph "the Most Outstanding Orator of the Present Day on the World of Black and White Workers," among other plaudits. Vann

saw the benefits of this strategy in his circulation when the porters
became the marketing arm for *The Courier*, selling subscriptions all
over the country along their train routes, just as they had in the early
days of *The Defender*.[37]

Finally, that fall, Abbott stepped in to countermand McGill's position, asking Randolph to come in for a meeting, and using his stature as an elder statesman to mollify the union leader. Then he ordered McGill to reverse the newspaper's policy once again, a move
announced in a subsequent editorial: "There has been considerable
criticism pro and con the so-called attitude of *The Defender* on the
movement to organize the Pullman porters and maids," explained the
newspaper in mid-November. "After a careful survey and review of
the determined and lawful struggle of the Pullman porters, led by the
fearless and brilliant A. Philip Randolph over a period of two years,
*The Defender* herewith announces its determination to fight with the
porters, arm in arm, shoulder to shoulder, for a living wage and better
working conditions."[38]

Randolph authored his own article accompanying this editorial
detailing his efforts to win recognition for the union and assailing his
critics. "Some prominent men of color hired their souls for Pullman
gold to lie and deceive," he wrote. "In pulpit and press, like mad der-
vishes howling for the blood of their victims, they hunted, hounded
and harassed, libeled and slandered those militant men who stood
their ground for the right of porters to organize and be men."[39]

Having uncovered evidence that the Pullman Company's attorney
had purchased a majority share in *The Chicago Whip*, Randolph believed that *The Defender*, too, must have received money from the
company. Still, Randolph accepted Abbott's word and cut short his
criticism as soon as the newspaper resumed its prior support for the
Brotherhood. In fact, Randolph needed all the help he could get; his
union had not received federal recognition and the Pullman Company was firing any porter they suspected of involvement in the
Brotherhood.

After the rapprochement with *The Defender*, Randolph began
sending information to that newspaper as well as *The Courier*, greatly
irritating Vann, who, after months of printing every press release the
Brotherhood sent, suddenly described one missive to be "useless propaganda" and refused to run it. Now it was Vann's editorial page that

was attacking Randolph, calling on him to resign from the Brotherhood's leadership and allow the reconciliation with the corporation. "The Pullman Company will not divide the waters so long as you stand as the Moses," Vann wrote in a letter to Randolph, using language similar to that which he used in editorials in *The Courier* shortly thereafter.[40]

In late 1927, Robert Abbott changed course completely when it came to Marcus Garvey. "Marcus Garvey has been in prison long enough," opined a *Defender* editorial. "Whatever he, in his far-fetched dreaming, did to incur the wrath of the government, he has now expiated through his years in Atlanta."

Other public figures had been caught in far worse violations of the law with far less consequence, the newspaper argued, and Garvey had already served two years of his five-year sentence. *The Defender* praised Garvey, moreover, as a "good organizer" who "is too valuable a person to be lost to the Race through persecution."[41]

Abbott now invested as much energy in liberating Garvey as he had in incarcerating him, following up on the editorial by sending a representative to meet with President Calvin Coolidge and plead for his release. Such was *The Defender*'s influence that the federal government reacted almost immediately, with the president commuting Garvey's sentence just two weeks later. "Free at Last," read the headline over a photo of Garvey in his plumed hat and uniform.

"What if his efforts to build the Black Star Steamship Line was a failure?" asked the editorial. "What if the provisional government of Africa was the wildest dream imaginable? Do these facts remove the very glaring one that Marcus Garvey stirred his people as they have never been stirred before?"[42]

Garvey's release was bittersweet, however, in that he was still slated for deportation, and the following week's front page carried news of him in the port of New Orleans about to depart for Kingston, Jamaica. Despite a driving rainstorm, five hundred men, women, and children gathered to see Garvey off, waiting in single file to shake their leader's hand and hear a few final words of wisdom. A delegation of UNIA chapters from around the country presented him with $10,000 before escorting him, under cover of an umbrella, along the wharf and onto the ship. Nattily dressed in a brown checked suit and carrying a silver-headed cane made with malacca wood, Garvey couldn't resist the opportunity to deliver one last speech.

"Good-by America. Farewell my people," he said from the ship's upper deck. "I leave America fully as happy as when I came, in that my relationship with my people was most pleasant and inspiring, and I shall work forever in their behalf. The program of nationalism is as important now as it ever was."

*The Defender* reported rumors that Garvey was planning to recruit thousands of black professionals and then establish himself in West Africa. But in the short run, Garvey simply returned to Jamaica and tried to reorient himself to the land he had left behind before he began his roller-coaster ride through North America.[43]

"All America Mourns for Martin Madden," read the headline on *The Defender*'s front page at the beginning of May 1928. Madden had represented Illinois's First Congressional District, including a large section of the South Side, since 1905, and the British-born politician had become a beloved figure to his African American constituents. When he died suddenly at the age of seventy-three on April 27, 1928, in the offices of the appropriations committee, where he was then the chairman, Madden was lauded for his efforts to pass antilynching legislation, his interventions on behalf of black-owned institutions including *The Defender*, and for securing jobs for thousands of individuals at the Chicago branch of the U.S. Post Office Department.

"All the twits about catering to 'Negroes' hurled at him by Southern representatives failed to daunt him," *The Defender*'s obituary for Madden read. "He fought for every measure that meant added protection and security for the Race, and fought desperately against whatever he found to be detrimental."[44]

While he lived, Madden's popularity obviated support for any black challenger who might have wanted his congressional seat, even though the majority of the First District's population had become African American. But now that he was gone, *The Defender*'s political reporters wrote that Oscar De Priest had already secured Mayor Thompson's backing as well as the unanimous support of the city's Republican bosses, an overwhelming advantage in this district. If De Priest did win, he would become the first African American member of the U.S. Congress in more than a quarter century and the first ever from the North.[45]

In honor of this historic event, *The Defender* printed the final speech of the last African American congressman, George White from North Carolina, who departed in 1901, just as segregationists were installing Jim Crow throughout the region. Even under these dire circumstances, Representative White had predicted confidently that this would not be the end of African American participation in American democracy. "This, Mr. Chairman, is perhaps the Negroes' temporary farewell to the American Congress," White said on the floor of the House, "but let me say, Phoenix-like, he will rise up some day and come again."

Now it seemed to *The Defender*'s editorial page, and many others, that White's prophesy was finally to be fulfilled.[46]

Frederick Douglass had been gone more than three decades by 1928, but his voice still resounded clearly on *The Defender*'s editorial page. That summer, the newspaper began printing a "Platform for America" underneath the masthead, a new mission statement that laid out an ambitious agenda for all of those struggling against segregation. Robert Abbott told friends the Platform's first precept paraphrased Douglass's speech on Colored American Day during the 1893 World's Fair: "American Race Prejudice Must Be Destroyed."

Six other demands filled out the Platform: the opening of all labor unions to African Americans; the appointment of an African American to the presidential cabinet; the inclusion of blacks in all police forces in the country; the opening of jobs as engineers and firemen on the railways, steamships, and "government controlled industries"; the opening of schools "to all Americans in preference to foreigners"; and employment of blacks in streetcars, buses, and other public transportation agencies. A few months later, two additional points called for the enactment of a federal antilynching law and for "the full enfranchisement of all American citizens."[47]

If the Platform was a statement from a confident, prosperous community, it revealed as well just how much was left to do before real equality could be achieved. In the same issue of *The Defender*, an editorial entitled "Who Won the Rebel War?" reflecting on the decades that had passed since the end of the Civil War, found little good news.

"Today the South reigns supreme in its own code of injustice. Actual slavery has given way to peonage: prison camps and mine prisons still prevail. Disenfranchisement still plays its part. Segregation, discrimination on the basis of color, still plays its flagrant role in the workings of our government.

"Sixty-five years after the war of rebellion, 30 years after the Spanish American War and 10 years after the war for the sublime doctrine of world equality, and the rebel flag still waves over America, still waves its dirty bars over the Stars and Stripes, which symbolize the independence of man!"[48]

## 10

---

# The Burdens of the Future

I N  T H E  F I N A L  weeks of the 1928 general election, *The Defender* printed a series of articles and editorials that listed postwar grievances with the Republican Party. In Washington, D.C., where the federal government was in direct authority, Republican presidents Harding and Coolidge, as well as Republican majorities in the U.S. Congress, had not only acquiesced to the segregation of public transit, but failed to stop or even criticize parades by thousands of Ku Klux Klansmen before the White House. The newspaper was particularly dissatisfied with the current Republican nominee for president, Herbert Hoover, who had spoken favorably of making the party "lily white" and excluded African Americans from their traditional role in that year's Republican National Convention. Most troubling of all was the candidate's covert backing from the Ku Klux Klan, whose members despised the Democratic nominee, New York governor Al Smith, because he was Catholic.

Finally, in an October 20, 1928, editorial entitled "What We Want," *The Defender* made a dramatic announcement: "We want justice in America and we mean to get it. If 50 years of support to the Republican Party doesn't get us justice, then we must of necessity shift our allegiance to new quarters."[1]

It was the first time *The Defender* had failed to endorse the Republican presidential candidate since 1912, but this Democratic nominee was different: born in New York City's Lower East Side, a product of German, Irish, and Italian immigrants, Al Smith represented the growing influence of the northern, urban branch of the Democratic Party, which until now had been subordinate to the party's base in the old South. The Democratic Party was still mostly hostile to blacks; African Americans, admitted to the Democratic National Convention that year only as observers, were kept in a cagelike enclosure made with chicken wire. But where both major candidates had gone to the South to court votes, *The Defender* noted Smith made a point of praising Lincoln and blasting the Ku Klux Klan during his tour while Hoover had shunned African Americans and openly courted the support of segregationist politicians.[2]

Nevertheless, *The Defender* soft-pedaled its endorsement for Smith, focused as it was on electing Oscar De Priest to the U.S. Congress as a Republican and worried that an all-out effort for the Democrats at the top of the ticket might inadvertently lead to voters choosing Democrats lower down the ballot as well. In the end, Hoover trounced Smith, winning many southern states that had previously gone Democratic; even De Priest initially appeared headed for defeat. As *The Defender* went to press that week, De Priest was behind by four thousand votes, although he refused to concede. "It looks bad for the Republican candidate," the newspaper assessed.[3]

Only after all the votes were counted and recounted days later was the actual result announced — De Priest had, in fact, eked out a victory by several thousand votes, bringing the long-cherished goal of an African American in the U.S. Congress close to fruition (there were still worries that southern whites would somehow block De Priest from being admitted to the House). In an interview with *The Defender*, De Priest said that once his victory was announced, he had received thousands of letters and telegrams from around the nation, all of which underscored his sense that he would be representing not just a single district on the South Side of Chicago, but all fifteen million African Americans. "I consider my election a real victory for the Race," he told one *Defender* reporter, "rather than a personal one."[4]

It was another victory for the generation of train workers, lawyers, activists, students, gamblers, intellectuals, musicians, and poets who first came together in Frederick Douglass's Haitian Pavilion at the 1893 World's Fair and chose to make Chicago their base of operations. They had frequently pooled their efforts, sometimes maneuvered against each other, but always kept their focus on the liberation of black America in the South as well as the North. Now the concepts they had honed in the cafés and on the corners of the Stroll would become part of the conversation on Capitol Hill.[5]

In the summer of 1929, the Abbotts traveled overseas again, this time to western Europe, which Robert regarded as the fountainhead of "white civilization." In Paris, he made an effort to enjoy Notre Dame, the Louvre, the Latin Quarter, the Champs Élysées, and the Arc de Triomphe as well as the palace at Versailles outside the city. But what impressed him most was the ease with which they and other dark-complexioned people could move about, finding "not the slightest restrictions anywhere," he wrote after his return in a series of articles detailing his journey.[6]

Black Frenchmen, both those from African colonies as well as others with multiracial lineage, served as members of parliament and as high-ranking military officers, scholars, novelists, and influential civil servants. Abbott saw black men and women living among whites as well as whites and blacks dancing together at clubs. He met fellow African Americans who had established themselves as musicians and club owners, and confirmed in conversation with them that France was far more racially tolerant than their own country. To Abbott's surprise and satisfaction, the French accorded him full honors as an important African American leader, inviting him to place a wreath on the Tomb of the Unknown Soldier. "France has taught America and the Anglo Saxon race," he wrote, "that black and white human beings can get along as peaceably and civilized as black and white cows, dogs, or any of the so-called lower animals."[7]

Even here, however, the Abbotts were vulnerable to the racist hostility of their own countrymen. One night, Robert and Helen returned to their hotel to find a note from the owner politely asking them to leave the establishment for other accommodations. Abbott immediately called on a prominent Afro-Frenchman he had met in Chicago some years earlier and brought him back to the hotel, where together they confronted the owner and threatened him with prosecution under French antidiscrimination laws. The owner backed down after confessing that he had been pressured by white American guests, and the Abbotts remained in the hotel for the remainder of their time in Paris as a matter of principle.[8]

But from native Europeans, they encountered no difficulties. After France, they traveled on to the North Sea resort of Ostend in Belgium, where Abbott was surprised at the ease with which he checked in to one of the finest ocean-view rooms in one of the best hotels along the shore. He was able to walk down to the beach and enter the water alongside everybody else, again without incident. "In Atlantic City and Asbury Park, they do not want us even on the water front," he wrote with bemusement. "Here at Ostend all that one needs to do regardless of color is to go down to the waterfront, hire a bathing machine — a portable bathhouse — and go into any part of God's ocean that he cares to."[9]

In a suburb of Brussels, they visited the Congo Museum, a large, elegant building set amid lush gardens and artificial lakes dedicated to Belgium's rule over the enormous colony in the center of the African continent. Inside, Abbott was impressed by the museum's presentation of the enormous natural wealth of the colony, represented in agricultural products from palm oil to pineapples to cotton, as well as raw material hauled and dug out of the jungle, from lumber to precious metals including gold, silver, and radium. One whole room was dedicated to rubber, Congo's most important source of revenue, which was produced by workers hacking vines out of the canopy under brutal conditions, while another chamber honored the ivory trade with a display of tusks taller than a man.

Abbott was deeply moved by those sections of the museum focused on the Congolese themselves, beginning with a display of locally manufactured beds, clocks, and other items. He lingered over the vast array of Congolese musical instruments, strings as well as woodwinds, trumpets of carved elephant tusk, and an assortment of metal cymbals, bells, and gongs. Rather than emerging with an appreciation of the benefits of colonial rule, Abbott marveled instead at "how excellently well these black people got along by themselves before the coming of the white man."

"Really, after all of this," he wrote, "it will be more amusing than ever to hear the story about the degraded state of the native African, for Europe has nothing of greater artistic sincerity to offer than have these Congolese."[10]

· · ·

The Abbotts drove through Holland to Bremen, Germany, where they visited the relatives of Robert's stepfather. John Sengstacke's sister Elizabeth was gone, but her children and grandchildren now numbered some twenty people in all across four separate households. Welcoming their American relatives with open arms, family members took the couple to local pubs where live music was played every night, leaving Robert with the impression of the Germans as a "merry people." Only a few of the offspring in this generation had features attributable to Elizabeth's African mother, kinky hair or a slightly copper complexion. Robert truly stood out, and the couple were frequently met with open astonishment, although he felt no hostility, describing the locals' interest simply as a "friendly gaze full of curiosity."[11]

From Bremen, the Abbotts continued on to Hamburg, where they stopped in the Hagenbeck Zoo and were horrified to see crowds gawking at a simulacrum "village" housing fifty black people from East Africa, a permanent exhibit. Robert spoke at length with the village's residents, who were surprised to learn that there were African-descended people in North America and expressed a longing for their homes. The German attitude was far different, however, at their next stop, Berlin, where Robert was slated to attend the International Publishers Conference, representing not only *The Defender* but the entire black press in America. As in so many other cities, when the Abbotts tried to check in to their hotel in the Charlottenburg neighborhood, white American tourists approached the management to complain. But in Berlin, unlike any other place they'd traveled, the hotel management grew angry at the white Americans and told them that if they didn't want to stay in the same hotel as the Abbotts, then it was *they* who should leave.[12]

But if Berlin had been surprisingly accommodating, the Abbotts' next stop, London, proved surprisingly hostile. When the Abbotts showed up at the hotel where they had reservations, they were refused, and told flatly that the hotel did not accept blacks. They found a room at another hotel, only to be told the following morning that they had to leave. At the next hotel, Robert sent Helen in first and she was immediately given a room, but when Abbott appeared, the management stopped him and asked them both to leave. They were likewise refused at several other places before finally giving up and accepting an offer to stay at the home of an Afro-British acquaintance.

Robert would not let this outrage go unanswered, however, protesting through every official channel and holding a formal press conference covered by several British newspapers. "If I tried to enter a hotel in New Orleans, they would lynch me," Abbott told one of the British reporters. "But in England, which has millions of Colored People under the flag, I expected different treatment."

The *Daily Express* ran an article about the Abbotts's treatment under a three-deck headline, "LONDON HOTELS COLOUR BAR/ Ordeal of Negro Millionaire/30 Refusals." A torrent of letters, telegrams, and telephone calls from throughout the British Empire followed, prompting a member of Parliament to meet with Abbott and promise to take up the issue with the prime minister. The hotels were obdurate, however, a sign for Robert that Great Britain was not nearly as free as it presented itself.[13]

The final leg of their trip was in Italy, where Robert was fascinated by the confluence of ancient ruins and medieval and Renaissance buildings alongside modern factories and farms. In Rome, the Abbotts did not experience any of the discrimination they had suffered in other countries, and in Venice, they checked into one of the city's most luxurious hotels without issue; if any American guests complained, they were simply ignored by the Italian staff. That evening, Robert stood on the balcony, watching the gondolas ply the canal and listening to Venetians sing to each other.[14]

Hundreds of other hotel guests came out to the balcony, attracted as well by the music, and Robert's thoughts inevitably drifted back home. "I looked sideways at my fellow guests, most of whom were Americans," he wrote in *The Defender*, "and wondered what they thought of a black man in their midst who could enjoy the same things they enjoy and who did not mar the serenity of the occasion by his presence."[15]

It had been a journey of highs as well as lows, but Robert came away from his European tour more optimistic than when he'd departed. Despite the occasional challenges he met as one of the few African American travelers at his station, he had interacted freely with white Europeans and been welcomed into the homes of his German relatives, among others. Whatever barriers existed between blacks and whites in America, Robert now had firsthand evidence that they could be removed.

"All my life, even from my earliest childhood, I have felt in the depths of my being that the theory that color makes the man was one of the greatest lies ever told," Robert wrote. "Now, after months of daily contact with the white man on his native soil, I am more firmly convinced than ever before that I am right."[16]

In December 1929, Abbott received a letter from the assistant commandant of the Hampton Institute regarding his nephew John Sengstacke, who was a seventeen-year-old student there at the time. The commandant wrote that though Hampton's instructors had initially hoped that this promising student would be ready for college-level work, he was failing two of his subjects and his teachers now thought it would be best to place him in a remedial program on campus.

The young man, however, was not so ready to let himself off the hook. "In talking with him today," the commandant wrote, "[John] said that he did not feel that his failure was due to his unpreparedness but because he had not worked hard enough." John pledged to redouble his efforts, and both Abbott and the school's administrators agreed to allow him to continue on the current track. Over the subsequent months, John Sengstacke proved himself: while he never became an exemplary scholar, his determination and discipline ensured that his grades stayed well above passing.[17]

This was an early indication of the character of the young man destined to be his uncle's successor at the helm of *The Defender.* Lithe, compact, neat, and copper-complexioned, John possessed few of his uncle's editorial gifts, but he was a keen negotiator and a natural leader who displayed a preternatural confidence that wherever he might fall short, he could compensate by working harder than everyone else.

Reared in Woodville as the third-oldest and first boy of seven children, John first attended the Sengstacke Academy attached to the church in Woodville that his father, Alexander, and Aunt Rebecca ran. There he got practical training as a printer's devil, helping his father publish and distribute the *Woodville Times.* John's mother died when he was eleven, and his aunts played a key role in his development while Abbott paid for his education, as he did for all of the young people in the family. But well aware that his uncle Robert was grooming him to take over *The Defender* one day, John made every effort to prepare himself.[18]

On Saturday, February 15, 1930, the temperature in Chicago sank to a frigid zero degrees Fahrenheit, weather distinctly inopportune for a parade. Nevertheless, a few dozen boys and girls clambered into the trailer of waiting trucks while others got into their parents' cars as a caravan assembled at *The Defender*'s headquarters. Cold or not, this was the second annual parade to honor the children who delivered the newspaper as well as the members of the Bud Billiken Club, and everyone was determined that it go ahead.

Rolling through the neighborhood's frosty streets, the convoy was escorted by Chicago Police officers on motorcycles with Robert Abbott in his flag-draped Rolls-Royce limousine in the lead, followed by cars carrying Nathan McGill and the Illinois attorney general, floats from local companies, including the Wet Wash Laundry, and finally, the trucks holding the most redoubtable newsboys and girls in the USA. A few onlookers braved the cold to stand on the sidewalk, but many opted to view the parade from behind the windows of their warm houses, apartment buildings, and offices.

Finally, the procession came to a halt at the back of the Regal Theater, just across the street from the Abbotts' mansion on South Parkway, where the newspaper had promised a day of free candy, entertainment, and contests. Anticipating a huge crowd, *The Defender*'s staff had booked the Regal precisely because it was one of the larger venues in the community, but even with the frigid weather keeping some away, it took an excruciating three hours for managers to get all of the forty-five hundred people who had queued up inside, a task they accomplished only by asking the smallest children to share seats with their peers.[19]

This celebration was the culmination of a ten-week subscription drive, with the top two sellers, both of them boys, crowned "kings" for the day while the top five — three boys and two girls — received awards as well as new bicycles before the ecstatic applause of their peers. Robert Abbott praised the winners for their capitalistic acumen. "You are indeed commended not just for outstripping your fellow newsboys for winning this award," the publisher told the eager young people, "but because you have shown yourselves skillful young business folks and energetic, hustling competitors."

The day's festivities included the work of a professional clown who organized a number of onstage activities, such as a greasy-pole climbing contest and a shoe-lacing competition, as well as a feature film with white actors, *Navy Blues*. But the main event was a concert from the great Louis Armstrong, who blew his famed coronet, accompanied by the house band, and "played tunes that made little feet shake," according to an account of the day's events in the newspaper. An honorary member of the Bud Billiken Club, Armstrong "stands ready to help Bud and his Billikens at all times," *The Defender* proclaimed.[20]

Youth editor Willard Motley, like his predecessor, had moved on when he entered high school, with the job of managing the Billiken department falling now to an adult, David Kellum. Dapper, energetic, and audacious, Kellum had bounced around *The Defender* for several years serving in multiple positions, including sportswriter and, for a short time, as a driver for Mrs. Abbott, until the minor crash he got into while taking her to a card game. Running the Billiken initiative, though, proved his real forte, and he soon displayed a unique promotional genius that by the end of his first year raised the club's membership to sixty-five thousand.

The success of the event at the Regal had only whetted Kellum's appetite for even grander events, though he decided that future parades would be held in Chicago's warmer seasons.[21]

The effects of the stock market collapse in the fall of 1929 rippled through Chicago's African American community in the months that followed. Tracking the growing ranks of the unemployed through regular check-ins with the Urban League, *The Defender*'s editorial page was sufficiently alarmed to recommend a temporary halt to the migration from the South. "Those who are contemplating moving from one city to another — coming from small towns into the cities of the North — are advised that it is a poor time to make a change," the editorial urged. "The only way to stabilize industrial conditions is for each of us to anchor ourselves where we are."[22]

The prospects for economic advancement, however, were dry-ing up everywhere. In March 1930 the Urban League reported that there were at least 330,000 blacks unemployed throughout the nation, confirming that black America was bearing the brunt of the economic crisis that would come to be known as the Great Depression. Scanning both North and South, the Urban League found disturbing statistics everywhere: a 70 percent disparity between the numbers of blacks and whites unemployed in Buffalo, New York; one-half of South Carolina's common laborers, most of them black, unemployed, as jobs previously available to them went instead to out-of-work whites; the few charitable organizations serving African Americans in Cincinnati overwhelmed with requests for temporary housing from homeless single men as well as whole families. After running through the Urban League's data, *The Defender* concluded that the sagging fortunes of the nation's major financial institutions were holding down the economy and, even more worryingly, that even when conditions improved, African Americans would lag well behind. "It is well known that whenever a wave of unemployment strikes the country," an editorial surmised, "Race workers are the first and hardest affected."[23]

*The Defender* had only to look at its own circulation numbers to confirm that something was wrong. From a high of more than a quarter-million copies weekly in the years after World War I, the newspaper was by 1930 selling only about 110,000 copies of each edition. Figures were headed down among all the members of the black press, with both the venerable *New York Age* and *The Pittsburgh Courier* falling below 50,000 a week. Many less stable newspapers folded altogether, such that the overall number of black publications dropped from approximately 200 in 1925 to just 150 five years later. Where white-owned dailies earned about two-thirds of their revenue from advertising, black newspapers like *The Defender,* heavily dependent on subscriptions and newsstand sales, were therefore especially sensitive to fluctuations in the economy that took the change out of their readers' pockets.[24]

Bad as the economic circumstances were in the North, they remained better than in the South, and *The Defender*'s call to slow the migration was ignored. Chicago's African American community continued to grow at a rate that outpaced the city's own expansion, pushing the racial boundaries ever outward: a total of 231,000 now lived in an area on the South Side that stretched even farther south than Sixty-Third Street in some spots, four blocks beyond Jesse Binga's once-controversial address on South Parkway, and extended to Lake Michigan from Thirty-First Street all the way to Forty-Seventh Street. There were new pockets of African American settlement as well on the West Side and even in a few locations of the North Side. Overall, blacks were nearly 7 percent of a city in which people identified closely with their ethnic backgrounds, whether they were actual immigrants or the descendants of immigrants. Poles were the second-largest group, with 4.4 percent of the population, and the Germans were third, with just over 3 percent.

In the decade since the end of World War I, another 1 million blacks had left the South; more than one-quarter of African Americans now lived in the North. But it was the jobs in the factories, slaughterhouses, and foundries of the northern cities, *The Defender* knew, that made the migration possible in the first place, and its staff worried what would happen in these cold, crowded enclaves now that the work was gone.[25]

On Thursday, July 31, at 1:37 p.m., a state auditor placed a sign on the doors of the Binga Bank building at Thirty-Fifth and State Streets that read "Closed for Examination and Adjustment." Word spread rapidly throughout the neighborhood, and crowds formed outside the bank. For years, visitors had been taken to see the magnificent granite edifice of the Binga Bank building as evidence of Black Chicago's prosperity. But now *The Defender* described a scene of men, women, and children gathered around the building in a despondent mood. "There was a death-like pall that hung over those who had entrusted their life savings to Binga," read *The Defender*'s coverage, "not so much that they had any love for the head of the bank, but it was pride — that pride of seeing one of their Race behind the cages that led them to 35th and State streets to do their banking."[26]

Uncharacteristically silent, Jesse Binga remained in seclusion. At the onset of the Depression, he had boasted that his bank had $1.2 million in deposits but in the wake of its closure, *The Defender* discovered that the institution had been teetering for some time: once the first signs of the national economic catastrophe had become evident, a number of board members began to question Binga's real estate purchases, ultimately demanding that he resign. When Binga refused, the board members themselves stepped down. Binga then wrangled with state officials for some time before they finally moved in and closed the bank, which had just $156,600 in cash on hand.[27]

The Binga Bank's collapse precipitated still more economic turmoil on the South Side. Thousands of panicked depositors showed up at all of the other banks in the area, seeking to withdraw their accounts before most of these institutions suffered a similar fate. By the following Tuesday, state regulators were forced to shut down two more banks, white-owned in these cases. The city's only other black-owned bank, directed by cosmetics magnate Anthony Overton, survived for the moment but only through a cash infusion from larger institutions downtown. Totaling the losses from all of the banks combined, some $2 million of accounts representing tens of thousands of African American depositors had been wiped out; the Binga Bank alone had 16,274 depositors whose accounts, when it failed, had less than $100 in them. Its two largest stockholders were Robert Abbott and Oscar De Priest, with $5,000 and $6,500 invested, respectively.[28]

In the weeks following his bank's closure, *The Defender*'s editorial page defended Jesse Binga as a victim of the discriminatory real estate practices of major financial institutions, which refused to provide mortgages in designated "black belts," effectively devaluing the assets of community banks like Binga's. The newspaper railed against this practice, which was becoming normative in Chicago, as elsewhere, for perpetuating segregation while also denying African Americans the right to gain wealth by participating fairly in the real estate market. But by this point, Binga's reputation was in tatters, his fortune was rapidly dwindling, and criminal action seemed inevitable.[29]

Finally, on the afternoon of Thursday, March 5, 1931, two white sheriff's deputies in suits and hats appeared at Binga's South Parkway house to arrest him on charges of embezzlement, which had been approved by a grand jury earlier that day. *The Defender*, tipped off to the deputies' arrival, had a photographer and a reporter waiting, but no one answered when the deputies knocked on the front and back doors, although the reporter noticed someone peeking from under the curtain in one of the windows on the second floor. The deputies left for a few hours but returned after nightfall and then hid nearby for several more hours until they saw the family doctor arrive.

When the door was opened for the doctor, the deputies barged in and took Binga into custody, despite declarations that he was ill. Binga was then transported to the Cook County Jail. Unable to post bail of $55,000, he was housed in the jail's hospital.

Five others were indicted along with Binga, ranging from his personal secretary to the individual in charge of the bank's vault, all of whom, according to prosecutors, were involved in a scheme to create phony mortgages, which he cashed. Altogether, it was alleged that Binga pilfered $180,000 from his many small and large depositors and used the funds to develop the Binga Arcade, a five-story combination residential and entertainment complex adjacent to the Binga Bank.[30]

As he entered the election season in early 1931 to seek a fourth term as mayor, Big Bill Thompson had to contend with the widespread perception that he was allied with gangster Al Capone, who for the past four years had waged open warfare with his rivals in the city's streets. No less scandalous had been Thompson's governance over fiscal matters: the previous year, he discovered the city was short $23 million and in jeopardy of not being able to make payroll for one hundred thousand policemen, firefighters, garbage men, and other municipal employees. The business community ponied up an emergency fund to cover the shortfall but took control over government expenditures out of Thompson's hands.[31]

During the Republican primary at the end of February 1931, Big Bill still won his usual lopsided victory in the African American strongholds of the Second, Third, and Fourth Wards. To many in Black Chicago, he remained the "Second Lincoln," and in the weeks before the April mayoral election, he courted the black vote through various public appearances, making a particular effort to be seen with U.S. Representative Oscar De Priest. *The Defender* reported with glee about a luncheon Thompson had arranged in Washington, D.C., shortly after the primary win, making sure to invite his numerous white friends from the South, as well as De Priest. When news of the luncheon leaked, *The Times-Picayune* lambasted New Orleans Mayor T. Semmes Walmsley for sitting across the table from De Priest, who was regarded by the southern white press as a radical. Mayor Walmsley, in turn, was forced to concede that he and other segregationists in the room had seen De Priest, of course, but did want to insult Thompson, a key ally in accessing federal funds, by abandoning his banquet. "As I am just as passionate an adherent to the cause of white supremacy that it is possible for any human being to be, I hasten to give the true facts to my people," said Walmsley, quoted by *The Defender*. "After a hurried consultation, we all decided to sacrifice our personal feelings and remain."[32]

Big Bill's final campaign stop was at the old Eighth Regiment Armory, where he spoke to a crowd as enthusiastic as ever. But this time, there was no percentage of the African American electorate that could compensate for the wholesale defection of disgusted white voters from the Republican camp. Though the black wards delivered a combined total of 57,000 votes for Thompson, a record even for this vaunted political machine, he lost nonetheless by more than 190,000 votes citywide, itself a record. Forty-five of the fifty wards went against the incumbent mayor, including many that had been staunch Thompson supporters four years earlier.

Nor would there be an easy comeback this time, as the victor, Democrat Anton Cermak, was a machine builder himself. Derided by Thompson during the campaign as "pushcart Tony" for his humble origins, Cermak was indeed a tough Bohemian immigrant who had clawed his way out of poverty, but he served as an alderman and president of the Cook County Board, and assembled a formidable coalition that included every community in the city. Describing Cermak's "vigorous campaign on the South Side," *The Defender* noted that he made his final stop at the mostly African American Wendell Phillips High School, just three blocks from where Big Bill was speaking at the armory. Cermak's efforts had earned him 15,000 votes from the three predominantly black wards, an impressive showing for a Democrat.[33]

As for Big Bill, even *The Defender* could generate but a modicum of sympathy for the mayor, recognizing that he had outlasted his legend. "Thompson Defeated Himself," read the headline of that week's lead editorial, which blamed the loss on his association with gangsters and frankly admitted that the reputation of Black Chicago had been tarnished by remaining with the mayor through this disastrous last stand. "Our regret," the editorial concluded, "is that so great a heart, a mind once so noble as William Hale Thompson, whose record for equality no man can ever change, took up with a political banditry whose advice undid him and turned the greatest Republican city over to the party of bigotry, intolerance and oppression."³⁴

*The Defender's* words proved prophetic: the Republican Party would never resurrect itself in the city, having been overtaken by a new Democratic Party that was shifting away from the South and toward the big cities of the North. For the moment, Black Chicago was caught on the wrong side of this seismic upheaval in the American political system but within days of Cermak's election, those most in need of accommodation with City Hall had already begun making their political conversions. One by one, the various gambling-parlor operators and cabaret owners whose empires were growing amid the worsening economic conditions were the first to make the conversion to Democrat.³⁵

Over the years since he had bought *The Defender's* headquarters on Indiana Avenue, Robert Abbott had established a busy routine that centered on the newspaper's production cycle. On Friday mornings, he received several copies of the first run that rolled off the presses and scanned them carefully, writing his notes in the margins as he looked for errors in editorial and composition as well as any article that might be a "hustle," published in exchange for cash to the writer. A proponent of the "big headline — short story," he was remembered by his secretary, Agaliece Westbrook Miller, for constant arguments with his editors. "He would fuss and fume and pace up and down the office complaining that he couldn't get anyone to do what he wanted," the secretary told Abbott's biographer. "Everyone thought they knew more about the paper than he — he who had founded it."

On the other hand, the secretary also recalled that Abbott loved to speak with visitors to the plant, especially the high school and university students, both black and white. Standing at the receptionist's desk in the lobby, the same spot where he welcomed guests on the plant's grand opening a decade earlier, he regaled these groups with stories of his trips to South America and Europe before advising the black youths to pursue a wide variety of professions to ensure African Americans had a diverse workforce. To the white students, however, he spoke about the "race issue," sometimes to the chagrin of *Defender* staffers who thought he was berating their white guests.

"But then, he was a man who lived a purpose, who had an all-consuming desire to be free and to gain freedom for his people," Miller explained. "He never missed an opportunity to drive home that point to any white person in his presence.[36]

Abbott could be challenging, asking Miller to take dictation of his rapid-fire, stream-of-consciousness communications far beyond her ability to transcribe. But he was also generous, paying for her tuition at Northwestern University and modifying his own work schedule to allow her to attend classes.

By this time, despite his determination to keep working, Abbott's routine was frequently interrupted by bouts of illness. Miller recalled that the editor received a painful weekly injection of insulin to treat his Bright's disease, and that in 1931 he also developed a debilitating cough that may have been a symptom of tuberculosis. Often, his staff tried to limit his visitors, as he would often engage guests in enthusiastic conversation until he was past the point of exhaustion. Abbott would speak until "he was gasping for breath," Miller recalled, "coughing between every sentence — but it seemingly just had to be said."

On Saturday, August 15, 1931, Dave Kellum held the first summertime Billiken Parade, a mass event that involved nearly the entire community, above all the children, who gorged themselves on free ice cream, candy, red lemonade, and Cracker Jack under the hot sun. As with the previous parades, the convoy assembled at *The Defender*'s headquarters and became a long, slow-moving line along Thirty-Fifth Street and down South Parkway. A troop of Boy Scouts and a drum and bugle corps led the procession, followed by a fancy new Lincoln carrying Kellum and a Pierce-Arrow bearing jazz great Duke Ellington. After the flotilla of convertibles came a row of trucks provided by a local furniture company carrying some ten thousand cheering Billikens from the South Side as well as sizable contingents from the West and North Sides, along with the private cars of club members' parents and other supporters.

Robert Abbott was too ill to attend but just past Forty-Seventh Street, the parade paused in front of his house, where the editor stepped out onto his front porch with his wife, Helen, perfectly dressed in a suit and tie as always, and addressed the cheering youths.

"I am happy to see you youthful and happy children who are to take on the burdens of the future," he told them. "You must learn early to understand what your rights are and fight for them. Fight with your pen, fight with your speech, fight with your conduct and fight with your prayers." He stayed on the porch for more than an hour as the passing youths saluted him and cheered before he went back inside to rest.

When the marchers reached the grandstand at Washington Park five blocks farther on, there were two more celebrities waiting for them — Freeman Gosden and Charles Correll, white actors who played the African American characters Amos and Andy on the radio. Immensely popular with both whites and blacks, *The Amos 'n' Andy Show* depicted the travails of two migrants who journey from Georgia to Chicago. The show's fifteen-minute daily episodes followed a serial format. Gosden and Correll had developed *Amos 'n' Andy* after spending years performing minstrel theater wearing blackface, and their show was rife with racial stereotypes, attracting significant controversy. *The Defender's* chief rival, *The Pittsburgh Courier,* had called for one million signatures on a petition to the Federal Radio Commission demanding that "the comedians so exploiting our group be driven from the air as a menace to our self-respect, our professional, fraternal and economic progress."

But as far as *The Defender* could see, the Amos and Andy characters were relatively upright, decent, and sympathetic, if ultimately foolish, and the show lacked the sort of white supremacist agenda that marked D. W. Griffith's poisonous *Birth of a Nation*. Gosden and Correll, moreover, made frequent appearances with African Americans, and even made donations to civil rights causes. They had also eschewed appearing in blackface since launching the show, and the large black audiences voted with their ears, as it were, to express their support.

The radio stars arrived at the parade dressed in suits and hats, and were able to reach the grandstand without attracting much attention, but just before they spoke, Kellum cued the band to play "The Perfect Song," the theme for *The Amos 'n' Andy Show,* which the crowd immediately recognized. Now the throngs began to gather around the stage, exclaiming their enthusiasm at such high volume that they drowned out Gosden and Correll's amplified comments.

"Amos 'n' Andy mounted chairs with megaphones but you couldn't hear your ears," wrote *Defender* reporter Nahum Daniel Brascher. "The radio guys waved greetings, smiled, laughed and tried to talk, but in vain. It couldn't be done." Gosden and Correll spent hours shaking hands and speaking with their fans. When they finally decided to depart, hundreds of youths and adults followed them to their car, waving enthusiastically until they were out of sight.[37]

This first-ever summertime Billiken Parade had been a tremendous success, but *The Courier*'s owner Robert Vann editorialized against Gosden and Correll's appearance under the front-page headline "Has *The Defender* Turned Amos and Andy?" Vann was incensed by the show's use of "The Perfect Song," noting that this music had originally been used to score *Birth of a Nation*. By the end of September, Vann boasted that he had already collected 515,000 signatures for his petition. "If I allow myself to become the 'national joke' for men, women and children of my community, state and nation," Vann wrote in a signed front-page editorial in October, "then I have absolutely NO SELF RESPECT."[38]

But *The Courier*'s petition campaign topped out as supporters of *Amos 'n' Andy* also began registering their support. The Chicago Urban League conducted a survey that found widespread approval for the show, and up-and-coming NAACP leader Roy Wilkins wrote an editorial defending it as "clean fun from beginning to end." Even *The Courier*'s own letters pages were filled with messages from fans. Perhaps the oddest measure of their popularity was that Gosden and Correll were preferred to Flournoy Miller and Aubrey Lyles, two African Americans who had a show on a rival network that was also based on their years in the blackface minstrel theater.[39]

*The Defender*'s longtime entertainment columnist Salem Tutt Whitney dismissed *The Courier*'s petition campaign as a publicity stunt, arguing that whites as well as blacks could distinguish between the buffoons presented in a radio show and African Americans in real life. "It is hardly fair to persecute Amos and Andy and ignore Miller and Lyles just because they are race artists," Whitney concluded, "when their show is of the same style as that of Amos and Andy, or vice versa."[40]

• • •

One evening in October 1931, a seriously ill Robert Abbott sat up in his bed and wrote to his nephew John Sengstacke at Hampton. "Push yourself to the front," he urged him in shaky handwriting nearly devoid of punctuation, a single, run-on sentence that stretches on for several pages. "Always remember that you are a 'front' man," he wrote, "and not a man to be in the back ranks." Abbott encouraged his nephew to study hard and to acquire foreign languages, German, in particular, so that he could communicate with his relatives, and to remember him to the instructors and staff at Hampton: "You must take up where I left off and make a name for the family and for me. Please hold up my honor and let those fools see that the Sengstackes and Abbotts are go-getters. Now let's go — I want you to make your own fortune like I did and have a lovely family home like I have, even better. I have lots of money in the bank. Don't buy so much property. Just have plenty of ready cash at all times — don't be a director in a bank or nothing — don't loan out your money and clothes to anyone . . ." Abbott concluded by calling his nephew "old boy" and urging him to build a memorial to the family patriarch, Rev. Sengstacke. "Be a good fellow now," he signed off, "and remember that I have chosen you to head up the family."[41]

A subsequent letter from John back to his uncle in early 1932, just after he returned to Woodville for the holidays, is written in careful pen with proper grammar, revealing an ambitious young man anxious to get involved in his uncle's newspaper and already planning to make his way in the big city. "I like going back home to spend a few weeks but to stay I could not stand it," he confessed. "Uncle, please see what you can do to get me a job next summer if you are not planning for me to go to summer school. I really want to work and make some money this summer, as I said before that is if you haven't other plans."

He remained frank and self-critical, especially about his academic prowess. "I did not 'flunk' in anything before Christmas and am trying hard not to 'flunk' these two more," John wrote. "Anyway, I am an average student, I know."[42]

Three months later, John asked, "How are you getting along now? Are you at your office each day now? I really hope that you are." Robert had indeed rallied slightly, at least enough to make an occasional presence in the office, and promised his nephew that he would find a job for him either at the newspaper or in another business.

"All right, Big Boy," he closed, in a letter typed by his secretary, "bring me some marks of promotion this Spring. I am not going to take any excuse about it, just bring me some good marks, and if you can't bring me good marks, just bring me promotion.

"Best wishes to you.

"Your loving uncle."[43]

# 11

# We'll Take the Sea

A N ARTICLE ON the front page of the June 4, 1932, edition informed readers that Robert and Helen Abbott were divorcing. Under the headline "Wife Sues R. S. Abbott, Seeks Share in Huge Estate She Says Husband Built," the article provided extensive details about its editor's home life and finances, quoting Helen's court filing that she was asking for a divorce because he had abruptly stopped living at his home several weeks earlier. She wanted the court to order Robert to support her at a level similar to her current lifestyle, citing his annual income of over $100,000 as well as assets of over $1 million, including real estate and stocks, the house on South Parkway, the Rolls-Royce, and a Pierce-Arrow convertible.

Although surprisingly objective, the article also quotes unnamed sources who alleged that Helen focused on attending social functions and neglected Robert during his intermittent illnesses, driving away a succession of nurses and also preventing his friends from visiting. At the end, the article mentions that Helen's first husband had committed suicide after an argument.[1]

Thus did a once-happy marriage dissolve publicly and acrimoniously. Another front-page article later that summer printed Helen's charges in court that Robert had a violent temper and that he had slapped and shoved her on several occasions. In his own court filing, Robert denied that he had struck her and rejected her assessments of his wealth, claiming that he had not received a salary in two years and had only drawn cash to pay for expenses; *The Defender* had lost $40,000 in 1931 and would go even further into the red before the end of the current year. Nevertheless, the court ordered that Robert provide Helen with $300 weekly, use of the house and their Pierce-

Arrow convertible, as well as a chauffeur and a maid until a final settlement was reached.[2]

For generations, a popular adage in the African American community had been "The Republican Party is the ship, all else is the sea,"
reflecting both the loyalty felt by many as well as the sense that there
was no other political option, the Democrats being explicitly positioned as the party of southern whites and thus segregation. But by
the summer of 1932, with the general election approaching, all sectors of the public were registering dissatisfaction with President Herbert Hoover's handling of the economy, with African Americans feeling especially slighted. Blacks were even barred from working on the
Hoover Dam, one of the few public works projects initiated by the
administration.

An editorial cartoon pictured an African American diving out of
a boat that contained an elephant as well as several men in top hats,
bound for open water whose waves were labeled "Constitutional
Rights" and "Principles of Government." The caption made it clear
that whatever sentimental attachment the Republicans had been able
to generate in the past was all but gone.

"If this is the 'Ship,'" quipped the caption, "we'll take the sea."

The Republican National Convention was held in Chicago that
summer, which, to those at *The Defender,* made the near-absence of
African Americans all the more galling. So consistently had Hoover
pursued his policy of making the party "lily white," that the newspaper had to fight even to get African American delegates seated. *The
Defender* frankly lamented that Hoover would be renominated, as-
sessing his first term as a time when the GOP was dominated by special interests and party bosses "in secret alliance with crooked and
powerful corporations," according to an editorial that June.[3]

Just one month later, the Democratic National Convention, too,
was held in Chicago, and, in contrast with the Republicans, made
what appeared to be a sincere effort to open themselves to African
Americans in general and *The Defender* in particular. Gone were the
cages for African Americans in the convention hall, and black delegates were able to speak at several public events including the resolutions committee, where Nathan McGill and other representatives of
the newspaper argued for inclusion of a specific pledge to uphold the

Fourteenth and Fifteenth Amendments to the Constitution as well as a declaration backing "Equal Rights to All, Special Privileges to None." The newspaper praised the Democrats when they included the latter phrase in their final platform statement, even if the committee eschewed the reference to the amendments.[4]

*The Defender* was even granted an exclusive interview with the new Democratic nominee for president, New York Governor Franklin Delano Roosevelt. A meeting was arranged by a leading African American Democratic activist, and the reporter was ushered into the Roosevelts' suite in the Congress Hotel on Michigan Avenue, whereupon FDR immediately brought up *The Defender's* role in the platform statement.

"Your effective presentation to the resolutions committee won many friends for the colored people," FDR told the reporter, "and you can tell *The Chicago Defender* that I stand 100 percent for the whole Democratic platform." Roosevelt added that he would do "everything in my power to secure justice for all our citizens regardless of race or creed."[5]

Asked about whether he would appoint an African American to the cabinet, one of the points in *The Defender's* platform, Roosevelt answered vaguely, "I will speak openly and frankly on every subject during the course of the campaign." But when the reporter pressed him, FDR smiled broadly and responded with a question: "What do the Colored people think of Colonel Roosevelt's ideas on the subject as well as his record of performance?" He was referring to his distant relative, former president Theodore Roosevelt, whose White House dinner with Booker T. Washington was still fondly remembered among African Americans. FDR employed his trademark mix of personal warmth and verbal opacity to suggest that he was aware of the need for progress on racial equity but cautious about the political impediments.

At just this moment, Franklin's wife, Eleanor, cut the interview short to announce that she would distribute sandwiches "to our fine policemen out in the hall, I know they must be hungry." *The Defender* also read into this gesture the Roosevelts' positive attitude toward African Americans, noting that one of the officers on guard duty that day was an African American sergeant.[6]

An editorial in that same issue made it clear how impressed *The*

*Defender* was by this new breed of Democrat. The newspaper praised the convention for being inclusive and for explicitly coming out to overturn Prohibition, and it also liked FDR's pedigree, which went some way to counterbalance the party's history and suggested a progressive agenda. "Mr. Roosevelt comes from that preferred class of America's body politic," the editorial stated. "Will he be able to sense the social and economic needs of the man furthest down?"[7]

*The Pittsburgh Courier* jumped on the Democratic bandwagon in September, with Robert Vann predicting that African Americans would defect from the Republican Party and vote for Roosevelt. But *The Defender* was hesitant, noting that FDR's vice presidential nominee, U.S. House Speaker John Nance Garner from Texas, came from the all-white town of Uvalde, where a sign warned, "Nigger, don't let the sun go down on you here." There were reasons to distrust Roosevelt as well, dating from his term as assistant secretary of the Navy in the Wilson administration, when he played a key role in the American occupation of Haiti, in which native institutions were suppressed, natural resources seized by American business interests, and thousands of protesters killed by U.S. troops.[8]

Moreover, the Republican Party still had a formidable champion in Chicago, in U.S. Representative Oscar De Priest, who went on the offensive to block the Democratic Party from wresting control of the city's African American electorate and his own congressional seat, which also happened to be on the line that fall. At a time when Roosevelt's disability was considered off-limits for public discussion, De Priest came perilously close to disclosing the matter when he worried aloud that if FDR was elected, he would soon die in office and leave Garner in the White House.[9]

In late September, the Hoover campaign cannily dispatched De Priest to cities on the West Coast and in the Midwest, from San Diego to Seattle to Minneapolis. In early October, with the election just weeks away, President Hoover invited three hundred black leaders to the White House for a tour and meeting, an event covered by *The Defender*. "You may be assured," Hoover told the gathering, "that our party will not abandon or depart from its traditional duty toward the American Negro." Hoover still refused to be photographed with the group, however, maintaining his policy of not appearing in print with African Americans.[10]

At the end of October, an editorial in *The Defender* suggested that, like much of the African American community, it was not quite ready to jump ship. Asking, "Hoover or Roosevelt Which?" the newspaper answered that regardless of who the front man was, the people running each political party were still essentially the same as in the past, and in the end, it was not worth the risk to vote for Roosevelt and put his party in charge of the machinery of government.[11]

FDR, of course, won in a landslide nevertheless. "Republican Party Swamped by Anti-Hoover Vote," read *The Defender*'s postelection headline, blaming Hoover's defeat on obdurate policies that had failed to alleviate the Depression, reverse Prohibition, or make progress on racial justice. Roosevelt won every state but Kansas, Vermont, New Hampshire, and Pennsylvania, and Democrats also won sizable majorities in both houses of the U.S. Congress, a decisive victory that left *The Defender*'s editorial page nervous as well as optimistic. "The hope of the American people," the editorial explained, "is that [FDR] will be guided by the high principles of fair dealing to all American citizens."[12]

Oscar De Priest won reelection handily, but Chicago's African American community was one of the few bright spots for the Republicans in the entire country. Even in Harlem, where the Republicans had a comfortable majority in the last presidential election, Democrats captured a majority of the African American vote. Already the lone African American presence in the House, De Priest would now be even more isolated as part of a shrinking caucus from a party that had lost its way and its influence with the American people.[13]

At the end of January 1933, the Robert S. Abbott Publishing Company held its annual meeting, where it detailed the newspaper's grim financial situation as well as its editor's ongoing health issues. Abbott owned almost all of the company, 2,498 shares, but both Nathan McGill, who served as the board secretary, and Benote H. Lee, son of *The Defender*'s former landlady, each had a single share as well. The meeting's minutes reveal that the newspaper lost $66,383.14 in 1932, forcing Abbott to forgo his own salary and transfer $261,751.45 from his personal account to keep *The Defender* afloat. The minutes also recorded that Abbott had been ill for the past twenty months.[14]

Even as *The Defender* was losing money, Abbott continued to generously sponsor his family. That same year, he paid for two of his nieces, Flaurience Sengstacke, the eldest child of his brother Alexander, and Roberta Thomas, his sister's oldest daughter, to take a sixteen-month sojourn through Europe as a reward for graduating from Fisk University. Elegant and insouciant, Flaurience and Roberta joined a number of friends from Hampton College for a trip that began in Italy and continued into Switzerland and Germany, travels they detailed in articles for *The Defender.* Only once did this group encounter the kind of racial hostility that had dogged Robert and Helen, when they were confronted by a group of white students from Texas, but local authorities intervened before the incident could get out of control.[15]

In general, the Europeans were delighted to engage with this group of young, wealthy African Americans; at worst, they were regarded as a curiosity. In the German city of Heidelberg, a perfectly preserved medieval cityscape with a world-famous university, local students invited Flaurience and Roberta and their friends to dinners, dances, and happy evenings at the ubiquitous beer halls. But they also got a glimpse of the storm that was coming when they stumbled onto a Nazi rally in the city's thirteenth-century castle. "From a distance, one would think the city was burning," the young women wrote in one of their *Defender* articles, "but it was only a celebration in which the bridge and castle appeared to be burning. Everything was in an uproar as the famous Hitlerites staged a political scene." Not that they knew to be exceptionally concerned; the "Hitlerites" seemed just one of many political parties vying to win elections in the republic.[16]

Most of the Hampton group returned home after Heidelberg, while Flaurience and Roberta continued on their own to Bremen, where one of their cousins met them at the train station. The young women were warmly welcomed into the homes of their extended family in town as well as in the countryside, and they spent nearly a year learning the German language as well as the customs of the people. Treated as minor celebrities by their neighbors and strangers alike, they were invited to many parties and affairs. "Everyone wanted to dance with us and did their best to make things pleasant for us," they wrote in *The Defender.*

Flaurience and Roberta found the Germans both well informed and appalled by the treatment African Americans received in their home country. The young women noted that they were often invited to come to Germany as refugees. "We were asked many times about the Race problem," they wrote. "One fellow wanted to know why Negroes stayed in America and did not go to countries where they treat people like they are human beings."[17]

The Defender issue for the week of April 24, 1933, featured several items about Nathan McGill's increasing prosperity and status at a time when the newspaper and its owner were both hemorrhaging cash. An article on the front page announced that McGill had been nominated as a Republican candidate for Cook County Circuit Court judge, a move that was arranged by Robert Abbott as yet another effort to smooth his protégé's path to success. For his part, McGill gave all the credit for his ascent to his mentor. "As great as the honor might be," he told The Defender's political reporter regarding his candidacy for the judiciary, "I know of none superior to the honor I have in my feeble effort to carry out the ideas and the ideals for which The Chicago Defender stands and as promulgated by its illustrious owner."[18]

A second article deeper in the newspaper announced McGill's divorce from his wife, Idalee, Helen Abbott's sister. The separation was described as amicable, and McGill agreed to provide Idalee and their two sons, ages eight and fourteen, with a comfortable lifestyle: Idalee received new furniture and a car as well as the family home in a fashionable part of the neighborhood, while the two boys each received their own six-flat building to guarantee their future.[19]

McGill's sudden prosperity, his tight hold over Robert Abbott and The Defender, as well as his divorce from Idalee, all became issues in the final stage of the editor's own divorce case, which reached its final stage just two months later. Nearly a year had passed since Helen initially filed with the court and there had been little legal activity in that time, but after the McGills divorced, she amended her initial complaint to demand that The Defender be placed in a receivership and that Nathan be removed from his job, claiming that he had interfered both with the newspaper and their marriage. Most scandalously, she also alleged in this new filing that she had caught Robert in bed with his nurse several years earlier.

As front-page news for The Defender's rivals within the black press, the Abbotts' breakup even became a kind of celebrity story in the white-owned media. Time magazine characterized Robert and

Helen Abbott as the African American version of Edward and Evalyn McLean, who owned *The Washington Post* and were just then undergoing their own public separation battle. Like Edward McLean, Robert had been accused of "peccadilloes," although *Time* also pointed out that *The Defender*'s estimated value at that time was $1 million as compared with *The Post*'s sale price of $850,000.[20]

*The Pittsburgh Courier* covered the Abbotts' divorce with a decidedly sardonic glee in front-page headlines like "Society Wife Files New Charges: Nurse Named as Abbott's 'Friend.'" But when the newspaper tried to interview her, Helen demurred, citing Robert's public status. "I should hate to have reports of our affairs circulated," she told *The Courier*, "which would embarrass him or me or injure his influence with the public."[21]

Stung by the national coverage of its publisher's personal life, *The Defender* insisted that Helen had actually sought reconciliation with Robert, as long as Nathan McGill was removed from the newspaper. But unwilling to accept any criticism of his protégé, Abbott told the court that he had given up on reconciling with his wife. "In view of the false charges she has made against me and Mr. McGill and her efforts to damage my business," Abbott proclaimed to the judge overseeing his case, "I do not care to live with her again. I cannot trust her. I want an absolute divorce."[22]

By the end of June, the Abbotts finalized their divorce, with Robert agreeing to pay Helen a onetime $50,000 settlement and her lawyer's fees as well as provide her with the Pierce-Arrow convertible coupe and personal property including her bedroom suite, clothing, Chinese rugs, silverware, cocktail set, four paintings, and bed linens. Robert retained ownership of the house on South Parkway and the Rolls-Royce.[23]

Under the terms of the divorce, Robert insisted that Helen sign a statement retracting her allegations "concerning the conduct and character of Nathan K. McGill and concerning the management and conduct of the Robert S. Abbott Publishing Company management by said Nathan K. McGill and concerning the interferences between my husband and myself in our relations by said Nathan K. McGill." The renunciation of the charges against McGill were reprinted on that week's front page.[24]

• • •

That fall, Abbott wrote to John Sengstacke, then beginning his senior year at Hampton, with an eye toward preparing his nephew to join him at *The Defender* after graduation. Commenting on the newspaper's deteriorating financial status, he was frustrated by his slow recovery from his latest bout of illness. "While I cannot walk any distance yet," Abbott wrote to John, "I think in a few months I will be able to get around but it is so hard for me to work as I am working, seeing things going to the devil, and unable to go into it for fear of injuring my health again . . . I am hitting the ground in spots as my dirigible is trying to rise."

Abbott praised his nephew for taking courses in typesetting, though he warned him not to let this technical training supersede his academic subjects, and instructed him to be cautious with his spending. "I am depending on you, Old Man," he wrote. "Don't let me down. It doesn't mean much to prepare yourself to carry on this great load, and I need you. Study hard to finish this year so that together we can fight this thing to a finish."

Financial conditions at *The Defender* continued to worsen that winter and in February, Abbott informed his nephew that he had laid off Genevieve Lee Wimp, Mrs. Lee's daughter. "She has the privilege of coming back should the work warrant it," he penned in firm, fluid handwriting, "now that the business is about on the rocks we just had to trim everything. I have not had a salary for 3½ years. Neither has Mr. McGill for two years."[25]

John remained positive in the face of this bad financial news, using every opportunity during his last few months at Hampton to prepare himself for his future at *The Defender.* He stayed up late in the school's typewriter lab to master that machine and used the school's resources to study the challenges of selling advertising in the black press.

When graduation was finally near, Abbott wrote to his nephew with fond reminiscences about his own time at Hampton but apologized for not being well enough to attend the commencement ceremony. "I am anxiously looking over the Alleghenies to see you when you hit the road coming West. Foggy days, I wonder whether or not you have started, and on clear days, I go up in my balloon and look for you."[26]

John did graduate that May and, after making a brief stop to see his family members in Woodville, came to Chicago as planned. Living in his uncle's home on South Parkway, he went to work at *The Defender* for $15 per week, in the bookkeeping department to start with. Even in this fledgling position, he quickly discovered disturbing information about the newspaper's finances: $350,000 that Abbott had moved from his private accounts in the Continental Bank to *The Defender* was gone and several factors pointed to Nathan McGill as the culprit. First of all, Abbott had transferred the funds at the suggestion of McGill. John traced some expenses drawn from those accounts to promotions for the 1933 World's Fair, but the lion's share of the money had gone directly into accounts controlled by McGill.

John spent weeks painstakingly compiling evidence of McGill's financial misdeeds. Most damning, he uncovered a series of checks that had been signed exclusively by McGill, despite an earlier policy stipulating that Abbott sign off on all spending.

"Now I was doing all of this on the Q.T.," Sengstacke recalled to an interviewer years later, "and when I had gathered my facts, I told my uncle about the situation. Being a kid of twenty-one, I still had to prove to him that I knew what I was doing. So I documented all of this for him, showing where he wasn't signing the checks, and where there was a separate account at the bank where money was being placed."

John implored his uncle to fire McGill and several others, but Abbott decided to defer making any major moves in the short run, claiming that he would not be able to step in and take over at that moment because of his health. John insisted, arguing that the newspaper itself was in jeopardy, but his uncle responded with a mixed metaphor: "When you've got your head in the lion's mouth, you got to ease it out. What we'll do is cut the branches off the tree, then cut down the tree."[27]

As it happened, Abbott was distracted by a major change in his personal life that summer. In late August, he married Edna Denison, the widow of his friend Franklin Denison, who had died two years earlier. An article in *The Defender* explained that the two had reconnected that spring in the resort town of Benton Harbor, Michigan, in the home of attorney Edward Morris. The new Mrs. Abbott moved into the South Parkway mansion immediately after the wedding.[28]

Though pale and enervated from his illnesses, Abbott attended that summer's Bud Billiken Parade alongside his new wife and both Nathan McGill and John Sengstacke. But just a few weeks later, he roused himself, summoned the Rolls-Royce, and came into the office to issue a fateful decree: Nathan McGill had been fired. Though Abbott himself ostensibly took the helm of the paper, he was too frail to command the day-to-day operations and so, on the first of October, he issued a memorandum effectively placing the reins of the organization in the hands of his twenty-one-year-old nephew:

TO DEPARTMENT HEADS

I have selected my nephew, John H. Sengstacke as Office Manager, his service in that capacity to begin immediately.

He understands my wishes, my desires, and my impulses. You can help me carry this load with more ease if you will cooperate with him. Take many of the little problems that under ordinary circumstances you would bring to me, to him. I know that you will find him willing at all times to do anything that will help lighten my burden. He and Mr. Simpson are working jointly in the same office. It is also my desire that employees do not hold anything from either of us which you feel will benefit the company. We must let down the bucket where we are for a bigger and better *Chicago Defender*.[29]

The pressure on John Sengstacke was immense; few knew just how precarious *The Defender*'s finances were, or how sick Robert Abbott was. To add to the young man's concerns, no sooner was he named office manager than his father, the Rev. Herman Alexander Sengstacke, died in Savannah after a short illness at the age of sixty-one. Three of John's siblings were still in high school, with the newspaper supporting an extended clan that even included some of their German relatives, to whom Robert Abbott had been sending regular checks since his visit to Europe in 1929.[30]

Sengstacke wasted no time in taking dramatic action to boost *The Defender*'s public stature as well as its bottom line, beginning with the replacement of the newspaper's white typesetters, composers, and pressmen with African Americans. At a time that circulation had fallen below one hundred thousand, these thirty-five white printers, he saw, had become a liability in the newspaper's ongoing competition with its peers. Both the ascendant *Pittsburgh Courier* and Baltimore's staid *Afro-American* were criticizing *The Defender* for keeping whites on their payroll while a disproportionate number of blacks in Chicago were unemployed. A local rival, *The Chicago Whip*, also lambasted *The Defender* through its popular campaign entitled "Don't Buy Where You Can't Work," which urged a boycott of businesses not employing African Americans. While the "Don't Buy Where You Can't Work" campaign was directed against the many white-owned stores in the black neighborhood with discriminatory practices, it positioned *The Whip* as the more radical choice of newspaper, boosting its circulation to approximately sixty-five thousand weekly, within striking distance of *The Defender.*

"We were losing sales because at that time, during the Depression, Negroes were out of work, in the soup line," Sengstacke explained to a biographer some years later, "and *The Defender* was catching hell because we were paying white employees top dollar to print our paper."[31]

But if the decision was clearly the right one, implementing it would prove a significant challenge. As the various printers unions had never eased their discrimination against African Americans, there were very few qualified black printers in the city. And so Sengstacke spent months surreptitiously assembling a black crew before making any announcement, recruiting his former Linotype instructor from Hampton to scan the entire globe even as he quietly brought some of his former classmates to Chicago. Throughout the summer of 1934, *The Defender* lured employees away from other black newspapers around the country as well as several from other professions; one had been an attorney while another had been working with the Australian touring company of *Show Boat.*[32]

Finally, in early October, just after his promotion to office manager, Sengstacke made his move, locking out the white workers and bringing in his new team in one fell swoop. The white printers took their case to the Chicago branch of the newly created National Labor Relations Board, but *The Defender*'s lawyers agreed to pay its new black workers according to the union scale while pressing the issue of discrimination against black printers, citing *The Whip*'s "Don't Buy Where You Can't Work" as evidence that the union's policy hurt *The Defender.* Robert Abbott testified at the labor board's hearing that he might be forced to close his plant unless he was allowed to reduce payroll by hiring black printers with less experience. The board decided in *The Defender's* favor.

With little practical experience actually running a plant, the African American printers at first struggled to make their deadlines but they worked hard, collectively, to build their skills and within a few months, the new typesetters were surpassing the union per-word requirements and the press functioned smoothly.[33]

On one Saturday night that same month, *The Defender* sponsored an event at the Eighth Regiment Armory at which a crowd of several thousand people acclaimed a local tavern owner the "Mayor of Bronzeville" and named a recent graduate from Englewood High School as "Miss Bronze America." An editor at the *Chicago Bee*, a weekly with an intellectual readership, had dreamed up the mock mayoralty several years earlier and brought it with him when he moved to *The Defender*. At first, it had been just another contest to boost circulation, but somehow, "the mayor" had become an important figure, recognized both by his own putative constituents as he walked through the streets and called to weigh in on actual political events. In the future, these mock elections became a far sight more serious, with candidates campaigning in earnest for the job and balloting conducted in barbershops, pool halls, clubs, and restaurants throughout the community.[34]

Even bigger than the mayoralty, however, was the word "Bronzeville"—a new name for a new feeling in the neighborhood, a sense of independence and self-sufficiency in what had become by now a permanent home. No longer was the community just another black belt; with a population surging past a quarter million, now double the number of Poles in the city, Bronzeville surpassed even the glory of the Harlem Renaissance, which, in the new decade, had already begun to fade, along with the dwindling white patronage of its artistic endeavors. Even in the depths of the depression, Bronzeville's tycoons, politicians, and gangsters prospered alongside painters, novelists, poets, and legions of blues and jazz musicians. It was true that blacks were increasingly barred from downtown and other parts of the city, but they had everything they needed right within Bronzeville, from the basic necessities to the finest luxuries.

The old Stroll along South State Street was still a major artery, though the center of Bronzeville had moved south and east along with the mass of the population, to the intersection of Forty-Seventh Street and South Parkway, the "urban equivalent of the village square," as it was described by St. Clair Drake and Horace Cayton, two African American sociologists who were both participants and chroniclers of Bronzeville's vibrant intellectual scene: "There is continuous and colorful movement here," they wrote in their landmark study, *Black Metropolis,* which relied extensively on *The Defender's* archives and staff.

"Shoppers streaming in and out of stores; insurance agents turning in their collections at a funeral parlor; club reporters rushing into a newspaper office with their social notes; irate tenants filing complaints with the Office of Price Administration. Today a picket line may be calling attention to 'unfair labor practices.' Tomorrow a girl may be selling tags on the corner for a hospital or community house. The next day you will find a group of boys soliciting signatures to place a Negro on the All-star football team. And always a beggar or two will be in the background — a blind man, cup in hand, tapping his way along, or a legless veteran propping up against the side of a building."[35]

Everywhere one looked was evidence of Bronzeville's industry and clout: at the newly built public library, named for Dr. George Cleveland Hall, Abbott's physician and sometime bodyguard; at the monument to black soldiers who fought in the world war; and at Provident Hospital, with its staff of black doctors and nurses. Money flowed through the neighborhood, via both the offices of businesspeople and professionals and the "sporting crowd," the lords of gambling and vice. For all those who doubted whether African Americans could really manage their own affairs, Bronzeville demonstrated just how much the community could accomplish when left to its own devices.

Despite U.S. Representative Oscar De Priest's attempt to act as a one-man dam against the electoral tide, Bronzeville was fast becoming a Democratic district. *The Defender* covered De Priest as he protested the Democrats' continued support for segregation on the floor of the House and traveled around the country to rail against the "socialism and radicalism" of the Roosevelt administration's New Deal programs, which he also accused of excluding African Americans.

"The door of opportunity and hope is closing against the Negro in America," De Priest warned in one speech to Congress.[36]

But as the congressional elections approached in 1934, the newspaper reported that De Priest was having trouble keeping the rivalries within his own organization in check even as President Roosevelt's popularity grew nationally and the Democrats used their monopoly on patronage locally against him. Chicago Mayor Ed Kelly, who had succeeded to the helm of City Hall after Anton Cermak's assassination the previous year, used the jobs available through New Deal programs to woo De Priest's campaign workers as well as his constituents while also reaching accommodations with the underworld figures who still played an important role in De Priest's political organization.

That summer, Kelly found an impressive African American candidate to carry the Democratic Party banner in the election against De Priest: Arthur Mitchell, a graduate of Tuskegee, Harvard, and Columbia with experience as an attorney, college professor, and spokesperson for the New Deal. On November 6, Election Day, Kelly's forces carried the erudite Mitchell along as part of a massive Democratic wave all over the country. De Priest was replaced as the sole African American in the U.S. House of Representatives, with Mitchell one-upping his predecessor by becoming the first African American ever elected to the Congress as a Democrat. But in fact, African Americans had supported the Democratic ticket all across the board, leaving just a handful of Republican officials in place.[37]

"It appears from the records disclosed that in the various Race Republican districts that thousands of the brothers have bid farewell to the Republican Party and wiped their weeping eyes," wrote *The Defender*'s political reporter Archie Fields. "From all indications not only in Illinois but all over the country black voters across the nation have taken President Franklin Delano Roosevelt at his word, that the New Deal is not to be circumscribed by races, colors or deeds."[38]

In early 1935, John Sengstacke hired Enoch Waters, a classmate of his from Hampton, as a reporter at *The Defender*. Waters had worked at the Virginia-based *Norfolk Journal and Guide* for nearly two years after graduation, but after tangling with the family who owned the newspaper, he'd quit in a huff. Stuck in Virginia, with his money dwindling, Waters had telegrammed Sengstacke, who, fortunately enough, had an opening on *The Defender*'s staff and even offered to pay Waters's train fare to Chicago.

Arriving in the city, Waters proceeded immediately to *The Defender*'s office on South Indiana Avenue, where Sengstacke met him at the door and gave him a guided tour through the building. Waters was impressed with the staff and the facility, so much larger and more professional than any of the other African American newspapers he had seen. Given a desk space next to another young reporter, Albert Barnett, Ida B. Wells-Barnett's stepson, Waters was assigned the fledgling's duties of copyediting in-house pieces, rewriting stories from other publications, and covering the occasional gruesome crime scene.[39]

The unrivaled boss of the newsroom was Lucius Harper, who had become both thicker around the waist and more confident over the years, having traded in his straw boater for a Borsalino hat and preferring now to drive through Bronzeville in one of his expansive cars. Harper spent his days surrounded by an entourage of fellow writers and raconteurs, some of whom did not even work for *The Defender*, retelling old tales and sifting an unending stream of gossip for fullfledged news items. In this way he was effortlessly able to keep the paper going, directing the staff and instructing newbies like Waters on how to develop their own sources and put together their articles. It was Harper who wrote most of the newspaper's editorials and decided on the composition of the front page, with its large photographs and red banner headlines.

Another of Waters's mentors was foreign editor Metz Tulius Paul Lochard, nicknamed Doc. Diminutive and brilliant, with an erect bearing and impeccable sense of style, Doc Lochard was born in Haiti in 1896 and had acquired degrees at the Sorbonne and Oxford before coming to the United States as an official translator for Field Marshal Ferdinand Foch in 1918. With the war continuing to devastate Europe, Lochard stayed on after Foch's trip and began teaching French, first at Howard University and then at Fisk College. He met Abbott at a card game in 1932, impressing the publisher immediately with his linguistic ability, his erudition, and his intellect. Abbott brought Lochard to Chicago in early 1934 to work at the newspaper and live at the South Parkway mansion as a personal secretary and tutor. Lochard rarely came into the office, writing his own column on foreign affairs and composing editorials at home in the name of "the Chief," as the staff increasingly referred to Abbott. He sent copy to the newsroom via the Chief's chauffeur.[40]

Waters was eventually dispatched to the mansion himself, where he sat at Abbott's bedside for months, recording the publisher's instructions for articles that he wanted published. Waters found Abbott feeble and depleted, but still "mentally alert, militant, knowledgeable and determined." Waters also discovered that Abbott, weak as he was, could still become angry when his abilities were questioned. In a memoir published decades after the editor's death, Waters's fear is still palpable as he recalled piquing Abbott's temper during one of their sessions.

"Because I was fully committed to his positions on civil rights and had heard him express them so often, I interrupted him one day while he was making a point," Waters wrote. "I thought I knew what he was going to say and interrupted to save time and show him how familiar I was with the subject. He fell silent, raised himself from his pillow and lashed out at me. 'Don't ever try to anticipate me again,' he warned. 'Nobody can tell what I want to say because nobody thinks like I do.'"

Waters got the point—Abbott had indeed built *The Defender* when others said it was impossible and had made it a profitable business when no other black newspaper had been able to do the same. But Waters came to appreciate, too, the publisher's fundamental kindness and humanism; he was a radical proponent of interracialism and committed to the eradication of the laws and customs of discrimination as embodied in the first plank of *The Defender*'s Platform for America: "American Race Prejudice Must Be Destroyed." It was a creed that stood in opposition to the kind of racial separatism and black nationalism espoused by Marcus Garvey, one that was as pragmatic as it was forgiving. Despite the discrimination Abbott had faced early on from whites as well as lighter-complexioned blacks, Waters detected no lasting bitterness or enmity from the publisher toward either group.[41]

Though Waters had grown up in Philadelphia's relatively liberated, integrated African American community, he was amazed by his first Bud Billiken Parade that summer. Unlike any other holiday he had experienced, Billiken Day was an ecumenical African American event that saw nearly the entire population of Bronzeville crowd onto the fairways, front yards, and balconies of the grand façades along South Parkway. He had been on the job for just a few months, but Waters swelled with pride on Billiken Day, especially when *The Defender* newsboy band and basketball team passed by.[42]

Renting a room at the Wabash Avenue YMCA, Waters explored all that Bronzeville had to offer, including the neighborhood's world-famous clubs, which featured live jazz every night of the year. This was the center of the African American universe at its moment of greatest glory. Waters greatly respected the Harlem Renaissance's output of literature, poetry, and theater, but it felt remote to him, as he recalled in his memoir.

"Harlem's cultural outburst was a heyday for artists, writers, performers and intellectuals, but it meant very little to the masses. The Chicago boom, on the other hand, was shared economically and spiritually by the man on the street. He got a piece of the gambling revenues and gloried in the successes of black businesses and the victories of Joe Louis. It was a time of pride and prosperity for every Southsider."[43]

On New Year's Day 1936, a young graduate student at the University of Michigan named Louis Martin Jr. wrangled an invitation to a dinner party at Robert Abbott's South Parkway mansion and approached the publisher with copies of several articles he'd written in the *Savannah Journal,* an African American–owned weekly newspaper in their mutual hometown. A tall, handsome intellectual whose father was the Sengstacke family's doctor in Georgia, Martin explained to Abbott that he wanted to work at *The Defender,* to which the editor replied that he was ailing and did not make hiring decisions anymore, referring Martin to his nephew.

Sengstacke agreed to give Martin a position when the semester ended later that winter, impressed by his academic background as well as his confidence. Martin had inherited a worldly, defiant outlook from his father, Louis Martin Sr., who, born in Cuba to a well-off family, had traveled around the globe as a merchant marine before deciding to become a doctor. Louis Jr. adopted a militant ideology after studying the ideas of W. E. B. Du Bois and the poetry of Langston Hughes in high school before entering the University of Michigan as one of only five black undergraduates. In his years on campus, Martin earned a reputation for representing the civil rights cause at social gatherings and public debates where African Americans had never before been a presence.[44]

Martin started at *The Defender* in February 1936 and received an exciting first assignment — covering the National Negro Congress, a mass gathering of civil rights organizations and black colleges at the Eighth Regiment Armory. Led by A. Philip Randolph's Brotherhood of Sleeping Car Workers, more than eight thousand activists from hundreds of organizations and schools across the country came to hear speakers on a wide range of topics, from the segregation of the South to the question of whether to join integrated labor unions. It was a raucous event in which the crowd interacted freely with those on the dais, shouting down the advocates of unpopular causes or perspectives.

Martin met luminaries like Langston Hughes and former U.S. Representative Oscar De Priest, still a force in city politics, but was moved most by the interviews he conducted with students who had spent their scant funds and even pawned their personal belongings in order to attend the congress and make themselves heard. Noting that these students were themselves inspired by other young people in Europe and Africa who were pressing for *their* rights, Martin wrote that the conclave resolved to press for equal accommodations in public and freedom to travel both within the country and internationally.

"The National Negro Congress has blazed the trail," Martin wrote, "and the torch to guide the way through the wilderness of despair to the great day now hangs in the sky like the star of Bethlehem. Members of the Race everywhere are aroused! A new day has dawned. Black America must be heard!"[45]

Confined to his bed for months at a time, Robert Abbott's mind turned to thoughts of a better future, and a world purged of racism. In February 1936, he wrote an enthusiastic review in *The Defender* of a new seven-hundred-page book detailing the history and beliefs of the Baha'i faith, which he had personally adopted for its message of interracial unity and egalitarianism. "They fear not to break bread with the members of the darker races," Abbott wrote, "for the cardinal theme of their spiritual postulate is the oneness of all mankind."

Abbott had first encountered the Baha'i in the White City at the 1893 World's Fair, when the group's leaders made their first official journey outside of the Middle East. In 1910, he met with Baha'i leader Abdul-Baha, who told the publisher that he would perform "a service for the benefit of humanity."[46]

In 1934, Abbott visited a massive domed temple the group was building in Wilmette, a northern lakefront suburb of Chicago, and publicly declared his belief in the tenets of the Baha'i faith. Although he had been reared by a Christian minister, Abbott had been disillusioned by the segregation of the church as well as its reticence when it came to social justice. "While the wise and unwise alike are presenting gold, frankincense and myrrh at the altar upon which lies the unreconstructed cradle of the son of man," Abbott wrote in another article praising the Baha'i, "the Christian soldiers are marching onward with spears, shotguns and ropes to slay and hang innocent black men upon the altar of prejudice and ignorance.

"No religion can bring peace which sanctions prejudice and discrimination at its very door."[47]

In early 1936, Sengstacke brought his two youngest siblings, brothers Whittier, nineteen, and Frederick Douglass, seventeen, to Chicago from Woodville now that their parents were gone. The trip north was the young men's first experience with segregated trains, and they were shocked at the conditions of the Jim Crow car and at the stations below the Mason-Dixon Line, where they were prohibited from buying food or drink. Fortunately, the trip was otherwise uneventful and the brothers arrived in Chicago hungry and exhausted but otherwise safe and sound.

Whittier and Frederick were assigned rooms on the third floor of the South Parkway mansion, where the maid made up their room every day and they could summon the butler with a push of a button. Although they were in the epicenter of Bronzeville, Uncle Robert enforced a high standard of behavior, and life at the mansion was formal and regimented, culminating every evening in a white-glove dinner served promptly at 6:00 p.m.; anyone late or not properly dressed would go hungry that evening.[48]

With just a few months of class work left before he could graduate from high school, Frederick transferred into DuSable High School, a modern institution in the heart of Bronzeville with a mostly black student population. Assiduous and reserved by nature, Frederick understood that, precisely because he was a relative of *The Defender*'s illustrious owner, he had to be even more circumspect than the average student. His uncle's influence, after all, extended to the very name of the school he attended: earlier that year, Abbott and the newspaper had played a key role in getting the school renamed in honor of Jean Baptiste Pointe DuSable, the African-descended trader who founded Chicago early in the nineteenth century. Until that time, all children in Chicago's public school system were taught that the city's first resident was a white fur trader named John Kinzie. Beyond the symbolic significance of being among the first classes to study under the DuSable name, however, Frederick knew that the school's principal was a close friend of his uncle's, while the assistant principal lived just next door. Even the slightest transgression would surely be reported instantly, and Fred had no intention of testing the rules.[49]

In June, *The Defender* announced proudly that 206 students would graduate from DuSable and that the senior class president, John H. Johnson, would speak at the ceremonies on the topic of "Builders of a New World." This John H. Johnson was, in fact, the same young man who several years earlier had been living in Arkansas reading *The Defender* and dreaming of the big city, and he burst with pride seeing his name printed in the newspaper.

Johnson's parents had struggled to find work in Chicago, and the family relied on federal food assistance programs, but their son's academic success gave them all hope for the future. Johnson had not wasted any time launching his journalism career, either, securing a part-time position at the National Youth Administration, where he organized events for other young people and began publishing a mimeographed magazine, *Afri-American Youth*, an early progenitor of the magazine that would make him a legend, *Ebony*.[50]

· · ·

Having proved himself in his first few months at *The Defender,* Louis Martin was dispatched to Detroit in June to take over as editor and publisher of *The Michigan Chronicle,* a new weekly publication that would be written, sold, and distributed in that city as part of a new strategy that Sengstacke was implementing. With Detroit's black population surging past 130,000, Sengstacke had determined that this market was not being fully served either by the Detroit news sections in *The Defender* or by his competitors, which included the national edition of *The Pittsburgh Courier* as well as two local black weeklies. He had founded *The Louisville Defender* some months earlier to compete in that market and had succeeded spectacularly; the new publication was appealing to both local readers and national advertisers. Moreover, by printing *The Louisville Defender* and *The Michigan Chronicle* on the days when the presses on South Indiana Avenue would have otherwise been idle, Sengstacke was finally utilizing the Goss presses to their full capacity.

Sengstacke agreed to pay Martin $20 per week for the first six months, after which he would have to generate his own salary, although *The Chronicle*'s printing costs would continue to be covered by *The Defender.* Soon thereafter, Martin traveled to Detroit to meet up with Lucius Harper, who had spent several months getting *The Chronicle* up and running. Harper gave Martin some basic instructions, underscoring the fact that he had to sell copies rather than give them away, and advised him to take public criticism in stride as long as sales were increasing; indeed, controversy would only attract readers. Harper then handed Martin the keys to the one-room office and the roll-top desk as well as the newspaper's total assets, a little over $17 in a cloth bag, and wished his young colleague luck. "From now on, it's your baby," Harper said on his way out the door.[51]

Martin was a one-man operation, reporting, editing, and designing his eight-page newspaper, then sending it by train to *The Defender*'s Chicago plant before his Tuesday deadline, returning to the station the next day to pick up the bundles of the new issue and distribute them in his own car. At first, he placed crime stories on the front page and filled the interior with sports articles, local news, and stories of "advancement"— African Americans who had achieved some new rank or mark previously denied.

After nine weeks, circulation was still at just a thousand papers per week. Without any funds to pay staff, Martin recruited anyone who would write for free and then boosted circulation by contracting with "street speakers," men who would stand on busy street corners and hawk publications. *The Chronicle's* chief speaker, a Harlem native named Arthur Caruso, combined the talents of a town crier with comedic skills. Standing on a ladder, he would read out headlines and then point at passersby, saying, "You didn't know that, did you?" In exchange for an allotment of newspapers to sell for his own profit, Caruso drove up sales with his engaging style, and after several months of these concerted efforts, Martin had raised *The Chronicle's* circulation to four thousand copies per week, enough to satisfy Sengstacke that the experiment was working.[52]

It was welcome news, since Sengstacke was still struggling to get *The Defender's* finances in order. At one point that year, there was no money for payroll. Going to every bank in the city to try to secure a business loan, he was consistently denied. Finally, in desperation, Sengstacke turned to Teenan Jones, seventy-five years old and largely retired but still possessing substantial clout and wealth. He also turned to the Jones brothers, a trio of well-educated younger men, unrelated to Teenan, who were that era's most substantial "policy kings," bosses of a homemade, underground lottery that employed some five thousand people, had an annual gross turnover of $18 million, and subsidized hundreds of legitimate businesses, such as laundries or groceries, which sold tickets known as "policy slips." These gambling lords prevailed on a small South Side bank to allow Sengstacke to place his stock in the newspaper as collateral for a $6,000 line of credit, enough to pay the staff and start returning *The Defender* to profitability. The situation was still dire — circulation was hovering at just 73,000 weekly, while *The Pittsburgh Courier* was selling more than 145,000 copies of all its regional editions — but for the moment, the policy kings' loan had stanched the bleeding.[53]

# 12

# Farewell Chief

I T WAS THE fall of 1936 and FDR's reelection campaign was in high gear, but Robert Abbott remained loyal to the Republican Party, authoring a series in *The Defender* that enumerated the president's misdeeds when it came to African Americans. Abbott railed against discrimination in New Deal programs and the exclusion of skilled black workers from the administration's large public works projects. The Social Security program specifically left out domestic workers and farmers, reportedly at the request of southern white congressmen, while the southern administrators of farm programs had deliberately worsened already desperate conditions for millions of sharecroppers. Abbott also took on the administration's failure to advance antilynching legislation, describing Roosevelt as "silent as a sphinx" on the matter.

Perhaps the Republicans had failed as well, Abbott conceded, but Roosevelt had not fulfilled his vaunted promise to lead the Democrats in a new direction. "I have not in this article portrayed the Republican Party as a patron saint," he wrote in the concluding article. "It has made its mistakes. Its punishment was defeat. What I maintain is that the present Democratic regime with the greatest opportunity to do good and with more power than any other administration has failed to meet the issues fairly and squarely and should be relegated to the scrap-heap just like the Old Guard in the Republican Party."[1]

Abbott's passionate advocacy notwithstanding, FDR won reelection by a landslide, carrying Democratic candidates with him at the federal, state, and local level, all the way from Illinois's governor's mansion to the First Congressional District, where the incumbent

U.S. Representative Arthur Mitchell won a rematch with Oscar De Priest by a margin even wider than in their previous contest. Mitchell had wisely hitched his campaign to the New Deal, while De Priest, for his part, announced that he had expected defeat and complained that his old cronies in the Second Ward refused to support him this time around. "I'm a good loser," he told *The Defender*.[2]

At the end of November 1936, Flaurience Sengstacke Collins, John Sengstacke's oldest sister, returned from another trip overseas with disturbing news about how the family's branch in Germany was faring under the ascendant Nazi regime. Flaurience had stopped briefly in Bremen during the first leg of a four-month round-the-world voyage. Five years had passed since she was last in Germany, and the atmosphere had changed from one of warmth and openness to oppression and paranoia. The oldest of these cousins was just one-quarter African, but under the Nuremberg Laws of racial purity passed the previous year, even that ancestry had become a dangerous liability. All of the Sengstackes' relatives had been labeled "non-Aryans," a status under which government officials removed the younger family members from school, fired the adults from their jobs, cut their food rations, and even blocked them from mundane activities like wearing a brown shirt, part of the uniform of the Nazi paramilitary units.

The family members explained to Flaurience that they had not written to "Uncle Robert" previously about their situation because they feared the Gestapo was reading their mail and would have punished them for relating any information portraying the Third Reich in a negative light. Their worries were only magnified when one great-grandson of the first John H. H. Sengstacke and Tama, a young man named Heinz Boedeker, somehow circumvented the Nazis' strict rules for "racial purity" and joined the party himself.

Each night during Flaurience's visit, the family nervously locked their doors and drew their curtains. Inside the homes, she noticed that a photograph of Robert Abbott that had hung proudly in their parlor during her last visit had been put away, as well as all the photos of their maternal ancestor, Elizabeth Sengstacke Boedeker, because of her distinctly African complexion. Finally, they asked Flaurience before she left to bring a message back to Chicago to please stop sending them copies of *The Defender,* "because the Germans don't like unfavorable comments about their people."[3]

Pessimistic as Robert Abbott was in his assessment of President Roosevelt's first term, there was one member of the administration with whom he maintained a warm personal and professional friendship, the incomparable Mary McLeod Bethune, who, as FDR entered his second term at the beginning of 1937, became the most powerful African American in the federal government. Bethune was sixty-two that year and served as director of the Negro Affairs Division of the National Youth Administration, a job with a sizable budget and payroll, but her real strength was in the personal relationships she enjoyed with President Roosevelt and the two most important women in his life, his wife, Eleanor, and his mother, Sara.[4]

Tall and heavy, with a dark complexion, the daughter of sharecroppers in Florida, Bethune was the only one of her siblings to receive an advanced education, a degree from the Moody Bible College in Chicago, before she went on to found a school for the vocational training of black girls in her native Daytona in 1904. Even creating a school of this type was considered a radical act in those days in the South, and Bethune had to endure harassment from the local branch of the Ku Klux Klan. Nevertheless, through relentless fundraising and promotion, she grew her school into a full-fledged coeducational academic institution called Bethune-Cookman College and, in the process, caught the attention of Sara and Eleanor Roosevelt, who frequently invited her to their home in New York.[5]

Bethune, who had supported FDR enthusiastically in his first run for president, had been appointed to the board of the NYA early in the term. But even she found herself often frustrated in trying to make the New Deal programs serve African Americans. In July 1935, Bethune visited Chicago, where she stayed with Robert and Edna Abbott in the South Parkway mansion, toured *The Defender*'s plant on South Indiana Avenue, and gave an interview to the newspaper's women's page editor. "Work in the South moves under handicaps," she admitted frankly. "Only courage, faith and fight keep us going."[6]

She was no less blunt when she met with FDR in April 1936, departing from her prepared report to demand that the administration do more for the enormous number of black families in need. "We have been eating the feet and the head of the chicken long enough," she told the president. "The time has come when we want some white meat."

Instead of taking Bethune's challenge as an insult, the way President Wilson had taken Monroe Trotter's comments, FDR was moved by her words and shortly thereafter appointed her director for the newly created Negro Affairs Department in the NYA. Bethune "has her feet on the ground," FDR told an aide when he made the appointment, "not only on the ground, but deep down in the ploughed soil."[7]

Bethune was able to get several additional private meetings with FDR, at which she was equally passionate and direct. For his part, FDR met all of Bethune's requests, demands, and observations with his characteristic equanimity, often saving or restoring funds for programs she indicated were essential, while demurring on those items, such as antilynching legislation, that he deemed politically unfeasible. At least as important as Bethune's irregular conversations with the president, however, was her constant communication with Eleanor, who included Bethune's agenda items on her own "to-do" list for her husband, and appeared at many events of importance to Bethune.

Bethune's influence extended into the various agencies of the federal government through the "black cabinet," an unofficial group of ranking African Americans at work in various federal agencies in the nation's capital. Composed of young men like the Harvard-educated Dr. Robert Weaver, an advisor to Interior Secretary Harold Ickes, the black cabinet was an elite group that held regular meetings and informal gatherings and card games, often coordinating their efforts across the various federal agencies in which they were ensconced, as well as with outside entities, including the black press. Bethune was their benevolent dictator, calling them to assemble and organize around her agenda whenever she needed them, wielding her singular access to the White House as a scepter to command or club, as need be.[8]

In the days before the second inauguration, Bethune brought many of the members of the black cabinet together with prominent clergy and advocates for a national conference addressing "The Problems of the Negro and the Negro Youth." FDR sent a message to be read aloud, and Eleanor attended as the keynote speaker, calling for an expansion of federal housing programs and better education for young mothers.[9]

The First Lady's appearance at the conference confirmed Bethune's indispensability and prompted the attendees to shower her with praise. A *Defender* editorial entitled "Dr. Bethune Leads On" added to the accolades:

"Thirty years ago, if one of our men — or women — within the space of a few weeks had been heralded throughout the nation in honored and dignified pictures with the mother of a president of the United States, wife of a president, likewise members of the president's cabinet and other dignitaries, it would have been a national news sensation — an eternal inspiration in American ideals.

"Today, such is accepted with trite comment — all a part of a day's work — and the world moves on."[10]

On the evening of Tuesday, June 22, 1937, millions of people around the world focused their attention on Chicago's Comiskey Park, where Joe Louis, the "Brown Bomber," was trying to wrest the heavyweight championship of the world from James J. Braddock, known as "Cinderella Man." It was the first time an African American boxer had vied for the title since Jack Johnson more than a quarter century earlier, and the fight was being held amid continuing repression in the South as well as a rising tide of Nazism, fascism, and other forms of white supremacy in Europe. Just as Johnson had been a symbol of defiance in his time, Louis was a hero to all of those who hoped to prove that a black man was as good as any "Aryan."

*The Defender* sent a team of reporters and photographers into Comiskey, which was conveniently located at the western end of Bronzeville just a few blocks along Thirty-Fifth Street from the newspaper's headquarters. Billiken editor Dave Kellum and sports editor Al Monroe sat ringside in the official press box among some four hundred other journalists from newspapers, wire services, and radio networks across the globe, while additional *Defender* scribes and photographers roamed among the fifty thousand spectators who filled the stadium. The ringside seats not reserved for journalists were filled with a multiracial A list of wealthy individuals and celebrities, including Hollywood stars Clark Gable, Kay Francis, and Bill "Bojangles" Robinson. But the seats in the grandstands were affordable — even if they required opera glasses to see the action — and thousands of African American fans came into the city from locations around the country, including many women and children.

There was definite racial tension both in the area around Comiskey, which abutted the white working-class Bridgeport neighborhood, and in the stands, where there were sizable contingents of men looking for trouble. But order was maintained by thousands of Chicago policemen marching in and around the stadium brandishing their "polished night sticks, head crackers or 'persuaders,'" as they were described by one *Defender* columnist grateful for their presence.[11]

*The Defender* had covered Louis extensively since he emerged from Detroit to win the Golden Gloves amateur competition in 1934 at the age of nineteen, noting his unique style of maintaining a "poker face" while he delivered devastating blows with his right. The sports reporters had tracked Louis as he racked up victory after victory, often by knockout, shrugging off all challengers who crossed his path. Many qualified black fighters had simply been ignored during the decades since Jack Johnson's downfall, but Louis's African American managers carefully nurtured his image as a pugilistic wunderkind, a clean-living professional athlete on a meteoric rise. Where Johnson had secured the public's attention by being as provocative as possible, Louis, reflecting the mores of this new era of heightened expectations and opportunities, wouldn't even allow himself to be photographed with any woman other than his wife.[12]

Louis maintained a disciplined routine in the days leading up to the fight, sleeping at his country villa in Kenosha, Wisconsin, the night before, eating a modest breakfast, and then boarding a special train to Chicago with a smoke-free car. At just a few minutes past 8:00 p.m., Louis's convoy of cars arrived at Comiskey Park led by two police motorcycles; Braddock arrived ten minutes later.

As soon as the fight got underway, it became clear that both combatants were ready and motivated. In the first round, Braddock hit Louis with his right and knocked the challenger off his feet momentarily, while in the third and sixth rounds, it seemed that Braddock had Louis on the defense. But by the eighth round, with both men battered and bleeding, Louis continued to hammer away until finally he landed a decisive blow on Braddock's jaw, causing the champion's knees to soften and his body to sink onto the canvas. Braddock lay there unconscious well past the ten-second count while the crowd in the stands roared, sending an audible wave of enthusiasm through the park and out into Bronzeville beyond, where hundreds of thousands of radios were tuned in to the live broadcast of the fight.[13]

Unlike Jack Johnson's victory over Jim Jeffries in 1910, Louis's win did not provoke violence from whites around the country. Even in his hometown deep in the South, Lafayette, Alabama, the Associated Press reported, the one thousand African Americans who staged a public party were not met with a lynch mob.[14]

As for Louis himself, the new champion took no part in any festivities, giving a short interview to reporters in which he praised Braddock as "tougher than iron or steel or hickory or whatever else there is that's tough" before changing into a gray suit and leaving for the countryside to get a good night's sleep.[15]

Louis already had his next fight on his mind — a rematch with Max Schmeling, a German-born boxer who had knocked out Louis the previous year, the only time he had ever lost a fight due to a knockout. Louis repeatedly told the public that he would not consider himself the true champion until he had beaten Schmeling, but because of the highly charged political context, what would have been a mere grudge fight had assumed epic proportions. Although Schmeling did not support the Nazis, his German nationality made him their standard-bearer, while Louis was automatically the representative of multicultural democracy, regardless of the failings of American society itself toward black people.

"Bring on Schmeling," Louis said that night as he left for his rural refuge.[16]

"It is time to call attention to this menace in a voice that can be heard," *The Defender* editorialized in the summer of 1937. "This message should reach both our own people and those of the other race who yet desire that America should remain the land of the free."[17]

The newspaper was sounding the alarm against restrictive covenants, a legal clause included in many mortgages and leases that specified homes and apartments could not be sold or rented to African Americans. Used since the 1920s, restrictive covenants had been upheld by the U.S. Supreme Court in 1929, but their effect had been limited by the economics of neighborhood change; since African Americans were generally willing to pay higher rents for smaller spaces and would buy homes at a premium as well, white owners had ample incentive to violate any such covenants. Thus, while restrictive covenants covered nearly every home in some areas, the territory available to African Americans had nevertheless steadily increased throughout the years of the Great Migration.

There was one part of the South Side, however, where the covenants held, a one-mile-square of homes on the south end of Washington Park that, even as the neighborhoods south and west became all black, had remained all-white. In the summer of 1937, several well-off African Americans led by businessman Carl Hansberry convinced several white owners to sell their homes, even though over 95 percent of the properties in the "little island of whites," as it was called by *The Defender,* were covered by the covenants. After moving into their home, Hansberry and his family were immediately subjected to violent attacks as well as legal assaults seeking to remove them. Were the covenants upheld by the courts, *The Defender* feared, African Americans would be forced into tiny ghettos all over the country. "If one covenant in any city is legal," the editorial continued, "every covenant may become legal and a whole city, a whole county, or even a whole state may become so restricted that our Race may be forbidden to live anywhere within its borders."[18]

*The Defender* added special appeals to the Jews as well as the Poles who lived in the "island," noting that the covenants were similar to legal mechanisms just then being used by the Nazis to oppress races they saw as inferior. But the editorial page was especially disappointed in the University of Chicago, which dominated the Hyde Park neighborhood just east of Washington Park and was acting behind the scenes to maintain it as a hedge against an influx of African Americans. The newspaper traced the activities of neighborhood organizations like the Woodlawn Property Owners League, which were defending the covenants in court, back to the university's business manager, who was not only funding these groups but also coordinating their legal activities. *The Defender* had frequently praised the university's liberal policies on admitting black students, as well as its prominent role as an advocate for civil rights, the editorial page argued, but these public efforts were inconsistent with a sub-rosa campaign to stop African Americans from becoming neighbors to professors, staff members, and students.

"What is new, and shockingly new to us," the editorial explained, "is the bizarre spectacle of an academic institution going out of its way to deny our people certain fundamental rights."[19]

Hansberry pressed his case with the backing of lawyers from the NAACP, as well as a wide array of community leaders, who met with elected officials, including Illinois's newly elected governor. By the end of October, the NAACP had won an initial legal round allowing the Hansberrys to remain in their home while the case proceeded up the hierarchy of appeals. It was prepared to take the case all the way to the U.S. Supreme Court.

*The Defender* celebrated these tentative victories in its coverage of the legal proceedings, excited by the prospect of the justices striking down these covenants. But the editorial page knew that it was entirely possible the Supreme Court might affirm this kind of discrimination again and that the consequences of that ruling would be made painfully real in the streets of Bronzeville. "If the Hansberrys lose," concluded an article about the case, "the boundary line of the so-called 'Black Belt' will become tighter and rents will begin to increase because of a lack of space to accommodate the growing Race population."[20]

On December 30, 1937, Marjorie Stewart Joyner, businesswoman, beautician, political activist, and columnist for *The Defender,* bought a ticket for a private compartment aboard the Texas Rocket train from Houston, where she was attending the national "boule" of her sorority, Zeta Phi Beta, to Tulsa, Oklahoma, where she was slated to speak to yet another group of cosmetology students. As the vice president of the C. J. Walker Company, Joyner was a perpetual traveler, overseeing a chain of schools of "beauty culture" and establishing supply lines of cosmetics and other products all around the country. As such, she was accustomed to decent treatment on the trains, even in the South. On this fateful trip, however, the train's staff escorted her not to a private compartment but to the luggage car, where they pointed to a corner designated as her space.

Joyner, understandably upset, said she preferred to get off, but as the train was already in motion, her protests were met only with verbal abuse from the conductor. With no other choice, she did her best to endure the trip, settling in among the bags as best as possible, but the task was made all the more difficult when the train stopped and a casket was loaded into the baggage car; Joyner found herself for a time riding next to a corpse.[21]

Personally trained by Madam C. J. Walker herself, Joyner became one of the principals in the company after Walker died in 1919, carrying on her mentor's legacy by recruiting and managing fifteen thousand "Walker Agents" who sold hair straighteners and other cosmetics. Joyner never accumulated Walker's wealth, but with a network of thousands of influential women across the country, she was able to organize beauticians into a powerful political force, forging strong relationships with Mary McLeod Bethune, Chicago's Mayor Ed Kelly, and other political leaders.

When the federal government began a consideration of licensing for beauticians, Joyner went to Washington, D.C., to meet with the appropriate officials at the U.S. Department of Labor and convince them to consider the particular issues of black women in the industry. On a lobbying mission to the state capital in downstate Springfield, Joyner led one hundred perfectly coiffed cosmetologists and testified before state legislators that white cosmetologists had excluded their black counterparts from the crafting of the proposed new rules.

For *The Defender*, Joyner's column, "Irresistible Charm," covered topics ranging from the use of shampoo to the proper treatment of scars, but she was also heavily involved in the newspaper's charitable activities. She had worked closely with Robert Abbott on the first Billiken parades, personally doing the hair and makeup for dozens of girls involved in the event, and in the summer of 1937, when floods struck towns all along the Mississippi River, Joyner led *The Defender's* relief committee efforts and wrote regular reports to the newspaper. She also served in the cabinet of the mayor of Bronzeville, handling the Children's Welfare portfolio in this mock government that was taking on ever-more tangible responsibilities.

Having spent decades working to build up the African American beauty industry and organize the legion of women entrepreneurs who made up its workforce, Joyner was not one to easily accept the indignities she suffered aboard the Texas Rocket. And so, back in

Chicago, she secured an attorney and filed suit against the railroad company. African Americans were enduring humiliations aboard the segregated trains daily, of course, but Joyner's stature and reputation were such that the company offered her a substantial settlement, *The Defender* reported.[22]

At the end of June 1938, Joe Louis finally got his rematch with Max Schmeling at Yankee Stadium in New York City. For *The Defender* and many others, Louis represented "Modesty, Confidence, Clean Living, Reverence and Balanced Intelligence," whereas Schmeling, regardless of his own anti-Nazi stance, was being used by Hitler's propagandists to carry the banner of German superiority. This would be more than a boxing match — it was a crucible of ideologies.

"Let us hope and pray that Joe Louis gives a good beating to Mr. Schmeling," wrote an "American citizen of German-Irish descent" in a letter to the editor in *The Defender,* "not because he is a white man, no, because he belongs to the nation that preaches race and religious hatred."[23]

On the day of the fight, Wednesday, June 22, there were intermittent showers in New York City as the print journalists and radio crews gathered at Madison Square Garden for the weighing-in ceremony. Schmeling was on time but Louis was uncharacteristically late, too late, in fact, for the scheduled broadcasts. "Unlike in previous years," observed *The Defender*'s Al Monroe, "Louis was not cool, calm and collected. He showed signs of extreme nervousness while Schmeling was every bit smiles."[24]

That afternoon, despite the rain, thousands of people arrived at Yankee Stadium hours early and patiently took their seats, wearing raincoats and carrying umbrellas. But the showers subsided toward evening, as the stadium filled to capacity with more than eighty-three thousand boxing fans from across the city's diverse communities. The *Tribune*'s chief sportswriter, Arch Ward, found the crowd tense with expectation, counting at least a thousand fans from Germany who had come to cheer on Schmeling. An extra three thousand New York City policemen had stationed themselves between Harlem and the stadium to keep order.

The fight began with Louis charging out of his corner, throwing blows from multiple angles, feinting, jabbing, hooking, and punching, landing his powerful right on Schmeling's jaw multiple times in the first seconds of the first round. Schmeling succeeded in grazing Louis's jaw but once, which only provoked the most furious response yet from Louis, who now left Schmeling hanging onto the ropes. When Schmeling disentangled himself, Louis pounced with a left and a right to the head that sent him to the mat for the first time. Schmeling got up after four seconds only to be knocked down again by Louis shortly after; he got up a second time, but Louis immediately launched his hard right fist into Schmeling's chin with a loud crack, knocking him over. This time, when the count reached four, Schmeling's team threw a towel into the ring. The whole battle had taken exactly two minutes and four seconds.[25]

Throughout the brief fight, the streets of Bronzeville, Harlem, and every other African American community were silent save for the crackling of the national radio broadcasts. But after Louis's victory, spontaneous celebrations erupted everywhere. "Chicago's South Side resembled New Year's Eve," The Defender wrote. "Along forty-seventh, fifty-first, forty-third, fifty-fifth, fifty-eighth and thirty-fifth, there was snake dancing. There was a happy crowd that stopped, shook hands and exchanged greetings with each other. On the lips of all these persons was 'I knew he could do it.'"[26]

Dave Kellum had hoped to convince Louis to appear at the 1938 Bud Billiken Parade just a few months after his victory over Max Schmeling. But Louis retreated from public view after the fight, canceling an upcoming bout with another challenger and spending most of his time at his manager's home in rural Michigan with only occasional trips to Detroit, where he was supervising the construction of a new house for his mother.[27]

It took Kellum an entire year of lobbying but finally Louis agreed to come to the Billiken Parade scheduled for August 1939. He arrived dressed in a green summer tweed suit and sat on the folded top of a sleek black Lincoln convertible touring car, waving to the multitudes and stopping frequently to pose for photographs and shake hands with those who slipped through the barricades and swarmed around his car the whole way.

"Saturday, Joe belonged to the people," The Defender's reporter wrote of this largest-ever Billiken Parade. "Not all his own people — but the people — because there were all races, creeds and colors in that colorful crowd of 250,000. Women screamed, men waved and yelled as Louis' car passed slowly behind the massed flags of the boy scouts. People were on the porches and on the tops of houses, perched in windows — all to get a glimpse of the hero who rode nonchalantly, smiling, bowing, turning and waving."

For once, the calculating, aloof champ interacted freely with his fans, seeming even to enjoy the journey along South Parkway. Larger crowds yet were waiting in Washington Park, so many that even a phalanx of police officers was unable to hold them back. "Where did you get all these people?" Louis exclaimed to *The Defender*'s reporter, adding that he "didn't know there were so many children of my own race in Chicago."[28]

It was the largest single gathering ever on the South Side, a showcase for the cultural and economic power of Bronzeville, with dozens of marching bands as well as floats from local businesses, labor unions, and the policy kings. Robert Abbott was not at the parade — his health had deteriorated to the point that he was unable even to make an appearance on his balcony — but his presence was nonetheless tangible. Among other measures, he had overruled the vociferous objections of both Dave Kellum and John Sengstacke in allowing the Young Communist League to march in the parade. Abbott was a patriotic capitalist in ideology but he had noticed that the Communist Party not only spoke out against racism but fully included African American members in their organization. "If there's a Bud Billiken parade," he told Kellum and Sengstacke, "these young people will march."[29]

Abbott's failing health put the future of *The Defender* foremost on his mind, and that same year, he took steps he thought would both ensure the newspaper's future and provide for all his loved ones, creating a trust that named John Sengstacke, his second wife, Edna, and a prominent African American attorney named James B. Cashin as the executors of his estate. Legally, Sengstacke held almost all of the shares of stock in the Robert S. Abbott Publishing Company, but the trust would contain all of Abbott's assets, including the newspaper, until 1956. The agreement was structured to make sure that Edna would have support for her and her children while Sengstacke continued to control the newspaper, relying on Cashin to act as the guarantor of the arrangement. A former captain in the Eighth Regiment who had fought in France during World War I, Cashin had established himself as one of Bronzeville's most prominent attorneys and seemed an honorable, upright character who had the competence to manage this complex arrangement.[30]

Certainly John Sengstacke had demonstrated that he was committed to meeting the challenge. Reporter Enoch Waters recalled that by 1939, the staff looked to Sengstacke, rather than Abbott, and understood that he was trying to modernize the newspaper. As his friend, however, Waters was also privy to how John's new role affected his personal life, especially with his new wife, Myrtle Elizabeth Picou, a beautiful socialite who had been born in New Orleans and reared in Los Angeles. "So thoroughly had Abbott instilled in Sengstacke's mind that he was to dedicate himself to *The Defender*," Waters recalled in his memoir, "that he told his bride Myrtle, in my presence, that she would always have to play a secondary role to the paper."[31]

Nevertheless, running *The Defender* was a nearly impossible job and Sengstacke was just twenty-seven, so Abbott still harbored doubts, which he voiced in early 1940 during one of his last conversations with Mary McLeod Bethune.

"John is my nephew. I am depending on him, Mamie," Abbott said frankly during this final bedside chat. "I am committing my unfinished task to him. Mamie, do you think he can do it?"

Bethune patted him on the shoulder and reassured him. "Rest Abbott, my big brother, he can do it. He will do it. He will carry on."[32]

John Sengstacke spent the first weeks of 1940 trying to organize a conference of African American publishers in Chicago. It was a difficult task, since *The Defender, The Pittsburgh Courier,* the *Afro-American* chain of newspapers, and the various smaller members of the black press were direct competitors whose owners had long histories of insults both perceived and actual. Nevertheless, Sengstacke pressed on in trying to realize what had long been a dream of Robert Abbott's, assembling all of the nation's great African American journalists in one place. Flattering and pleading with his competitors, he assured them the conference would be geared toward "harmonizing our energies in a common purpose for the benefit of Negro journalism," exploring common solutions to their shared problems, especially when it came to advertising.

On the morning of February 29, 1940, after weeks of such diplomacy, Sengstacke proudly opened the first conference of the Negro Newspaper Publishers Association. Held at the Wabash Avenue YMCA, the conference hosted a group of twenty-six men and two women representing twenty-one different black newspapers from cities and towns "from New York to Nebraska," as *The Defender* trumpeted in its coverage of the gathering. Sengstacke had not been able to completely smooth over the discord between owners; Robert Vann of *The Pittsburgh Courier* had refused to attend, sending only a reporter to cover the meeting. Still, this was a real start and Sengstacke, for one, was in excellent spirits.

No sooner had he finished his welcoming remarks, however, than the assembly received word that Robert Abbott had died in his sleep that morning. The publishers, editors, advertising managers, and other journalists there — many of whom had known Abbott well — decided to adjourn for several hours. When they reconvened that afternoon, D. Arnett Murphy, son of the founder of the *Baltimore Afro-American,* paid warm tribute to Abbott and wished Sengstacke success while a committee was formed to write the proper condolences for the "Dean of Negro Journalism."

They got back to work now, these putative adversaries, with a new solidarity that would have thrilled Abbott, moving with a sense that the black press was well positioned to take advantage of its unique access to its readers, a fast-growing market of fifteen million people who turned over $2 billion annually. The publishers agreed to collaborate on surveys of their readers and other projects, and by the end of the three-day agenda, the whole group had adopted an organization plan declaring that they represented "independent, secular newspapers sold to the general reading public," and agreed to meet again in Chicago the following year. Sengstacke was acclaimed as president of the NNPA with Murphy as eastern vice president.[33]

The NNPA conference ended on Saturday, by which time Abbott's body was already lying in state at the South Parkway mansion. Letters and telegrams poured in from all over the world, from top-ranking Republicans as well as Democrats, from judges, lawyers, teachers, and musicians, from Pullman porters and chauffeurs, from the Urban League and the YMCA, from the president of Abbott's beloved alma mater, Hampton, and the leaders of Fisk and Tuskegee, from clergy of all denominations and from dozens of fraternal organizations and lodges. Colonel Robert McCormick, the irascible owner of the *Chicago Tribune,* registered his grief, as did the performer Josephine Baker. Walter White of the NAACP sent a message, as did blues musician W. C. Handy. Tributes were published in countless newspaper articles, and the black vocal group the Southernaires broadcast a musical paean on their hit radio show over the National Broadcasting Service.[34]

Many of those who felt compelled to send a message of condolence knew Abbott personally, but many others were simply inspired by him: Boy Scout Troop No. 32 from the backwoods town of Potts Camp, Mississippi, for instance. Organized in 1927 with donations from Estelle Williams, a Chicago social worker, who sent copies of *The Defender* along with her financial contributions through the years, the African American troop named their unit in honor of the publisher, and they were grief-stricken when they found out about Abbott's death. "We have never met Mr. Abbott but Mrs. Williams kept us informed of his activities," they wrote. "Even when the paper was forbidden to be sold here, Mrs. Williams forwarded our copy. We deeply feel the loss of Mr. Abbott."[35]

On Monday morning, *The Defender* building at Thirty-Fifth Street and Indiana Avenue was draped in black and the flags at City Hall and other municipal buildings flown at half-staff while the body was taken down the street to Metropolitan Community Church for Abbott's funeral. Placed in an open casket surrounded by flowers, Abbott was viewed by "a sea of human faces ranging from the purest black to the purest white," as *The Defender* described it, while outside the church thousands of others gathered to listen to the proceedings inside over loudspeakers that had been set up. Just after 11:00 a.m., a fifty-person choir dressed in white robes sang "Lead, Kindly Light," followed by a series of tributes from notables including Mayor Ed Kelly before a eulogy from the Rev. Archibald J. Carey, the son of one of those young activists who had planned resistance to the South in the cafés of Chicago in the years just after the 1893 World's Fair.

As the funeral cortege left the church, it was led by a police mo-

torcycle escort and a formation of dozens of African American firemen and police officers in dress uniform who marched along for four
blocks and then formed an honor guard to salute Abbott's body as
it passed by. The caravan to the funeral now drove south along the
street that had become the route of the parade Abbott loved so well.
"Along South Parkway," *The Defender*'s reporter recounted, "thousands who had on numerous occasions cheered *The Chicago Defender* editor when he rode at the head of the Bud Billiken parades
bowed their heads in sorrow Monday."

More than 250 cars accompanied Abbott's body to Lincoln Cemetery, south of the city, where the honorary pallbearers included a
pantheon from Abbott's past: the former alderman Louis Anderson;
Major Walter Loving, the former military intelligence officer who
had attempted to coerce the editors of the black press during World
War I; Emmett Scott, the respected scholar and government official;
A. Philip Randolph, still doggedly leading the Brotherhood of Sleeping Car Porters; and Henry "Teenan" Jones, now eighty years old, retired and living comfortably in Watseka, Illinois. As a show of thanks
for Abbott's role in promoting the field of aviation, the final honor of
the funeral was performed by two pilots, one man and one woman
from the largely African American National Airmen Association,
who swooped in low to drop, with perfect precision, six American
Beauty roses down over the great man's grave.[36]

"Robert S. Abbott was a man of one idea," wrote Lucius Harper in
his front-page column that week, "which is all that the brain of any
man of action can hold. He was not an idle philosopher, and therefore
believed he had a mission in this world, and that he must early get at
his work, and never rest day or night until that work should be done.

"When he sought to raise the black man to the level of the white
man, he was branded a radical. The radical of today is the conservative of tomorrow and other martyrs take up the work through other
nights and the dumb and stupid world plants its weary feet upon the
slippery sand soaked by the sweat of their brow and moves on.

"Farewell Chief, You have pointed to a star. May it give light to our
weary feet along the pathway to hope as it did to you in your yester-
years of hardships."[37]

• • •

Just a few weeks after Abbott's death, his widow and attorney James Cashin endorsed the plan to have John Sengstacke take over *The Defender* as publisher, issuing public statements of support on the front page of the newspaper. "Every effort will be made to continue this newspaper as a lasting testimonial to my husband," Edna Abbott said. "I am happy that John Sengstacke has consented to continue in the active direction of the Robert S. Abbott Publishing Company."

Sengstacke himself attempted to project both confidence and continuity: "Mr. Abbott was and is my ideal — during the years that I was associated with him he has continually stimulated my heart and my brain for the forward surge of *The Defender.*"[38]

Sengstacke continued to rely on the veterans at the newspaper who had been nearest to Abbott, especially Lucius Harper and Metz Lochard. That summer, he began an editorial-page column under his own byline entitled "Today and Tomorrow," which hewed to topics that echoed the interests and perspectives of the departed editor, especially lynching, the ill effects of segregation, and the economic opportunities available to African Americans. Here, as throughout the paper, Lochard added his own distinct internationalist outlook, with Harper editing the copy to make it flow.[39]

At first, Sengstacke emulated Abbott's independent political course, criticizing President Franklin D. Roosevelt at the end of June for speaking on the segregated campus of the University of Virginia and calling on the president to push for an end to legal segregation as well as for federal legislation against lynching and poll taxes. Skeptical about Roosevelt's posture toward American involvement in the new conflagration in Europe, Sengstacke warned that the government would use the opportunity to crack down on all political dissent, including African Americans' efforts to secure civil rights. Nor was Sengstacke keen on taking sides among the great European powers as they battled over their colonial possessions: though it had strongly opposed the efforts of Italy's fascist leader Benito Mussolini to conquer independent Ethiopia, *The Defender* regarded the rule of other European nations over Africans as equally distasteful. "Will jim crowism and lynching," he asked in one column, "be answered best by dropping bombs and shells on battlefields abroad?"[40]

Nevertheless, as it became increasingly obvious that Nazism was a threat to the entire world, rather than just Europe, Sengstacke made his first major break with Abbott's previous policy by edging toward full support of FDR. In early October 1940, with Roosevelt running for an unprecedented third term in the White House, *The Defender* printed a front-page editorial signed by Sengstacke that now endorsed the president's foreign policy of sending munitions and other supplies to Great Britain. The nation needed Roosevelt's deft touch and experience, the newspaper argued, and at this crucial moment couldn't take a chance on shifting policy. "Certainly Nazism or Fascism is detrimental to the vested interest of the black man," Sengstacke concluded in the editorial.[41]

In a subsequent column, Sengstacke cited a report from a human rights organization which had discovered that the Ku Klux Klan and other homegrown white supremacists were receiving the active support and funding of German agents and that the Nazis had recruited high-ranking military officers as well as executives at the Ford Motor Company and the Hearst newspaper chain, among other corporations. "These groups are not only anti-Negro," Sengstacke wrote, "they are anti-Semitic, anti-Catholic and definite fifth columnists. They are definitely against our democratic form of government."[42]

*The Defender* continued to criticize Roosevelt whenever it felt necessary, as when the administration announced just a few weeks before the election that the military would restrict African American soldiers to segregated units rather than mix them with white troops. Even though Roosevelt promised training for black officers and pilots, Sengstacke derided the idea of "jim crow army units" in his column. But the criticism only went so far: An accompanying editorial registered similar disappointment and then reminded its readers that the Roosevelt administration had hired unprecedented numbers of African Americans and empowered the "black cabinet."

And then there was Eleanor Roosevelt, who had recently resigned from the Daughters of the American Revolution when that organization refused to allow the great vocalist Marian Anderson to sing in their hall. The First Lady then arranged for Anderson to sing at the Lincoln Memorial on the Washington Mall. "It is difficult for us to believe," the editorial explained, "the wife of the President of the United States would be going from place to place making statements that are in direct contradiction to the views held by her husband. We believe that President Roosevelt is singularly free of the deep-rooted racial bias which has characterized nearly all of his predecessors."[43]

The weekend before Election Day, *The Defender* announced what it had been building up to all fall — an enthusiastic endorsement for President Franklin D. Roosevelt. The editorial page expressed general satisfaction with FDR's promises, if not his progress, on race issues, and credited the New Deal with creating social programs that fed people and put them back to work, however unevenly distributed the benefits. Although Roosevelt's Republican opponent Wendell Willkie himself happened to be progressive on race issues, the newspaper argued that he was simply an agent of "Big Business, of public utilities and trusts with their gargantuan thirst for power and money." Besides, looming behind all of the domestic issues was the war raging across Europe, and Roosevelt was the only American leader who was capable of standing on an equal footing with Hitler, Mussolini, Stalin, and Churchill.[44]

The same issue of *The Defender* endorsing FDR carried news of the death from cancer of Robert Vann of *The Pittsburgh Courier.* The rivalry between *The Defender* and *The Courier* had been hard fought at times, but Sengstacke made sure to appear at Vann's funeral to show respect for a man who, like his uncle, had come out of the rural South to build a newspaper as a powerful weapon in the struggle to liberate African Americans.[45]

Vann, an early supporter of President Roosevelt, had lately swung back to the Republicans and given his endorsement to Willkie, making *The Defender*'s support all the more significant to the Democrats. FDR's bid for a third term was controversial, and campaign staff were counting on black votes in northern cities to help deliver a number of key states, including New York, Pennsylvania, Michigan, and Illinois.

FDR indeed defeated Willkie, though by a smaller margin than he had his previous opponents. Still, he had gained among African Americans, especially in Chicago. In the Second, Third, Fourth, and Fifth Wards, where no Democrat had ever won a majority, FDR had captured no less than 52 percent of the black vote, a shift for which *The Defender* endorsement had certainly been responsible. Writing in a postelection column, Sengstacke argued that the African American voters had finally realized that their political debt to the GOP had been paid and that in the future both political parties would have to compete for black support. Black America, he warned, had become "politically conscious and is demanding performance and not promise," such that the results of this election should be interpreted as support for FDR, not necessarily for the Democrats. "Therefore, then, first and last," Sengstacke's column concluded, "it was the man and not the party."[46]

By the beginning of 1941, John Sengstacke felt secure at the helm of *The Defender* and excited by the agenda of the newly reelected Roosevelt administration. He had, after all, been running the newspaper for close to six years now. On the personal front, his wife was expecting their first child, a son who would be named John H. H. Sengstacke III.[47]

Sengstacke was thus insouciant at the end of January when he attended the first meeting of stockholders in the Robert S. Abbott Publishing Company after Abbott's death. Previously, the three members of the board had been Sengstacke, Robert Abbott, and Abbott's wife, Edna, and Sengstacke was expecting a mere formality that would see him and Mrs. Abbott reelected to the board and attorney James Cashin elected to replace Abbott. But Edna Abbott and Cashin had conspired behind his back to dethrone Sengstacke. After getting his approval for their spots on the newspaper's board of directors, Edna and Cashin combined their votes to remove Sengstacke, replacing him with George Dennison, Edna's oldest son from her marriage to Franklin Denison. Sengstacke couldn't be fired outright because he remained the major stockholder, but Edna and Cashin demoted him to vice president, relieved him of all publisher's duties, and slashed his salary from $75 to $35 a week, all moves calibrated to pressure Sengstacke to surrender his stake in the newspaper.[48]

Sengstacke nevertheless continued to come to work every day in his reduced capacity, with little to do other than plot his return to power. Less than a month after this coup, the NNPA had its second annual meeting in Chicago, where John had to appear under his diminished title, his ability to organize and operate severely hampered. This convention was smaller than the last, with only twenty-two attendees, but Sengstacke did score a significant victory when he convinced Robert Vann's widow, Jesse, who had taken over as publisher of *The Pittsburgh Courier,* to serve as the NNPA's treasurer. Sengstacke's own term as president of the group having expired, he was succeeded by William Walker, the publisher of the *Cleveland Call & Post.*[49]

At the end of March, Robert Abbott's eldest sister, Rebecca, filed a suit in probate court which used a novel argument to try to remove his widow from control over his assets, claiming that Edna Abbott was actually white. Although Edna presented herself as black, she had a creamy complexion, blue-gray eyes, and straight, chestnut-colored hair, and was said to have come originally from Winnipeg, Canada. If she *was* proved to be white, her marriage would be invalidated, since it had taken place in Indiana, where interracial unions were prohibited. And if that happened, Abbott's assets would be inherited by his closest relatives, rather than his putative spouse.

It was an odd syllogism for Abbott's family to make, given their own multiracial heritage, and it was soon to be revealed in court to be a flimsy argument. The bizarre court hearing in which Edna tried to prove that she had African ancestry was covered by *The Defender*, now under the direction of a crony she had installed as general manager, in a front-page article that characterized the legal maneuver as a "spite suit." The article went on to blame John Sengstacke for instigating the suit in the first place, and alleged that he had threatened her with legal action unless she kept him at the newspaper's helm. Her key witness was attorney Edward H. Morris, one of Abbott's oldest friends from his first days in Chicago, who had also known Edna since childhood and testified that her parents "were definitely of the Negro race."[50]

The suit alleging Edna was white was dismissed, but the legal maneuvers over Robert Abbott's will continued, attracting widespread coverage in the black press and from *Time* magazine, which focused on the complexion of Robert and his wives: "The late Robert S. Abbott, publisher of the once-powerful Negro *Chicago Defender*, was soot-black. His two wives were white as snow," *Time* wrote in its media column. Opining that *The Defender* had long since passed its prime, *Time* calculated that Nathan McGill's embezzlement as well as the publisher's divorce had drained Abbott's fortune, leaving the callow John Sengstacke unable to handle the sinking ship. "*The Defender* went from bad to worse," *Time*'s column summarized.[51]

* * *

With the Japanese attack on Pearl Harbor on December 7, 1941, *The Defender* was faced yet again with the question of how hard to push for civil rights during wartime and threatened, once again, with suppression by elements within the federal government led by FBI Director J. Edgar Hoover. Later that month, *The Defender* attempted to clarify its position in an editorial that appeared shortly after the United States declared war:

"The Negro press will not blemish its magnificent record of sound patriotism by engaging in subversive advocacy to the impairment of the national will. However, unless and until constitutional guarantees are suspended, the Negro press will continue to use its moral force against the mob in its criminal orgy, against such ultra-violences as lynching, burning at the stake and judicial murder.

"We are for national unity. We are for victory. But, no one must conclude that in opposing clear cut discriminations in civilian life or in the army or the navy, that the Negro press is disloyal. In this opposition is the essence of loyalty and devotion to democracy—and a free press."[52]

Although he lacked the authority to represent *The Defender* officially in December 1941, Sengstacke took it upon himself to reach out to the federal government. Attaching a copy of this editorial to a letter he addressed to Hoover, Sengstacke pledged to cooperate with any inquiry and address any concern the agency had: "We will withhold nothing that may give you a full understanding of the facts and motives which provoked the printing of the article."

Hoover wrote back on January 3 that he appreciated the "sprit" of Sengstacke's letter, but that the offer of transparency would be better directed at Byron Price, director of the Office of Censorship. Sengstacke must have understood this as a brushoff, since the Office of Censorship had authority only over those publications mailed overseas and was intended to prevent news of troop movements, tactics, or similar military information from reaching enemy intelligence services. Any prosecution of a black newspaper for sedition would be investigated by the FBI first and then brought to federal court by the Department of Justice.[53]

Meanwhile, Cashin began to grow restless and annoyed that Mrs. Abbott displayed less interest in the day-to-day operations of the paper, complaining to another black newspaper that she was "too busy getting the brakes fixed on her car or shopping to attend meetings." By the beginning of 1942, the attorney also grew paranoid that the widow might remove him from the board of directors and approached John Sengstacke secretly. Regretfully confessing his prior conniving with Mrs. Abbott, Cashin offered his vote to John at the next stockholders' meeting.

When the fateful day finally came, John arrived with his attorneys as well as his brother Frederick and Metz Lochard. He made sure that everyone else was already in the room before he handed his brother Fred a revolver and ordered him to stand outside the meeting room and not allow anyone else to enter. With Fred, armed and nervous, stationed outside the door, Sengstacke brought Lochard inside and, with Cashin's double cross, reversed the process that had unseated him the previous year. Next, Cashin and Sengstacke removed Mrs. Abbott's son George from the board and replaced him with Lochard.

Immediately proceeding to fire staff Mrs. Abbott had hired, Sengstacke simultaneously summoned police officers to prevent anyone from removing documents from the Indiana Avenue headquarters. The widow attempted to contest all of these actions in court but within a few weeks, a judge had ruled against her and recognized the new board, granting Sengstacke total control over the newspaper's finances.

While Edna Abbott would continue to pursue her case in court, John Sengstacke was back in command at *The Defender*, and this time he used the newspaper to trumpet *his* victory. An article that appeared under the headline "Mrs. Edna R. Abbott Loses Fight to Control *Chicago Defender* Funds" quoted the judge's tribute to the newspaper as "an institution of long and honorable standing, devoted to the interests of the colored citizens of Chicago and the nation, founded upon the sacrifices and struggles of one of Chicago's noble citizens — the late Robert S. Abbott."[54]

# 13

# Victory Through Unity

HAVING RECLAIMED THE helm of *The Defender*, John Seng-stacke understood that his situation as a black publisher in wartime was even more perilous than the one faced by his uncle during World War I. While Hoover and his FBI were building their files, many black newspapers were adopting militant postures based in part on the experience of the black press back in 1918. They had come to see W. E. B. Du Bois's commentary "Close Ranks" during the last world war as a regrettable moment in which the great intellectual had betrayed the movement just as the war had created an opportunity to pressure the federal government on civil rights. This time, the black press was so unified in not wanting to waste this chance that even the NAACP's house organ felt obliged to distance itself from Du Bois's twenty-three-year-old article.

"*The Crisis* would emphasize with all its strength that now is the time not to be silent about the breaches of democracy here in our own land," stated an editorial in the January edition. "If all the people are called to gird and sacrifice for freedom, and the armies to march for freedom, then it must be freedom for everyone, everywhere, not merely for those under the Hitler heel."[1]

*The Pittsburgh Courier* took things even further on January 3, 1942, when it published an exposé that focused on the spectacular performance of one black sailor during the Pearl Harbor attack as evidence that segregation wasted valuable human resources in wartime. After Japanese dive-bombers inflicted fatal wounds on the USS *West Virginia*, a cook named Doris "Dorie" Miller emerged from the galley and, with the ship sinking and much of the crew injured and dead, rescued many fellow sailors, including senior officers, before manning a .50 caliber machine gun and firing at Japanese planes. Saving hundreds of lives, Miller also managed to hit some of the only Japanese planes downed that day.

Despite his obvious courage and aptitude for combat, Miller had been assigned to the mess — the Navy restricted African Americans to noncombat roles and wouldn't allow any black officers, allegedly because of fears of racial conflicts on ships with mixed crews. Now, even in the wake of his moment of valor, the Navy refused to grant Miller official recognition of his heroism. *The Courier* demanded that Miller be awarded the Congressional Medal of Honor, commenting that discrimination in the military was unconscionable "when at the first sign of danger [African American sailors] so dramatically show their willingness to face death in defense of the Stars and Stripes."[2]

Following up on its advocacy for Miller, *The Courier* launched the "Double V" campaign based on a letter from an outraged reader —"the first V for victory over our enemies from without, the second V for victory over our enemies from within."[3]

The Double V targeted the perversity of an American society that fought fascists and Nazis overseas in the name of freedom and justice even as it maintained segregation at home. All across the country, blacks began hanging Double V posters in their windows and hosting like-themed events, while *The Courier* ran photos of black and white notables who supported the effort, including former Republican presidential nominee Wendell Willkie and movie stars Humphrey Bogart and Ingrid Bergman.

FBI Director Hoover, meanwhile, was collecting information against the black press in monthly reports that covered a wide range of ethnic groups designated "enemy" communities within the United States: ethnic Germans, Japanese, and Italians, among many others. Information about African American–owned newspapers was always inserted in the "Communist" section of these reports to suggest some sort of collusion, although Hoover's agents never produced any evidence of an actual connection. Beyond surveillance and data collection, local FBI agents visited *The Courier,* the *Journal and Guide,* and a number of other black newspapers — although not *The Defender* — to express their dissatisfaction with content they deemed damaging to the war effort. Hoover at one point requested an indictment from the Justice Department against the Baltimore-based

*Afro-American* chain, alleging sedition for an article in which several black men interviewed suggested that nonwhites would benefit if Japan won the war, but federal prosecutors ruled that the comments of interview subjects were "mere expressions of individual opinion."[4]

The Post Office Department, too, was monitoring black newspapers. It stopped the Miami-based *New Negro World* from sending one of its weekly editions outside the country for fear that it would be used by the nation's enemies for propaganda purposes. "If my nation cannot outlaw lynching," one of the *World*'s columnists had opined, "if the uniform will not bring me the respect of the people that I serve, if the freedom of America will not protect me as a human being when I cry in the wilderness of ingratitude, then I declare before both GOD and man TO HELL WITH PEARL HARBOR." Postal officials were unanimous in their revulsion to this kind of language and, like the FBI, sent their complaints up the chain of command to the U.S. Department of Justice.

Military intelligence officers were conducting their own review of the black press out of concern that these newspapers were damaging the morale of black troops with their reporting of the conditions on bases in the South. The military collected a dossier of articles they found objectionable in *The Defender, The Courier,* the *Afro-American,* and other papers, and came to their own unfounded conclusion of Communist sponsorship. In the course of its investigation, however, the military inadvertently discovered the power of the black press — its review revealed that fully 75 percent of African American soldiers were subscribers to one or more publications, and that many used the newspaper as a vital link to their families back home. Most challenging to the thesis that the black press was damaging morale among the troops, the report revealed that many of the white officers assigned to segregated units also read *The Defender, The Courier,* and the others, if only to help them better understand their men.[5]

When it came to potential censorship and prosecution for sedition, the key figure was Attorney General Francis Biddle, whose approval was required for any charges brought against a black newspaper. A thin, bald Harvard graduate with a neat mustache, a lineage that went back to the Founding Fathers, and a strong belief in the sanctity of civil liberties, Biddle was just then facing intense pressure from President Roosevelt to do more to stop media outlets considered problematic. Biddle had resisted the forced relocation of Japanese Americans and at first dragged his feet when it came to prosecuting any publication out of a sincere conviction in the right to free speech, especially during wartime. Biddle's procrastination greatly annoyed Roosevelt, who, dropping his usual affability, interrogated, teased, and humiliated his attorney general at staff meetings to try to force him to take action. Finally, at the end of March, Biddle charged 150 people, mostly Nazi sympathizers, with sedition and other offenses, shutting down publications such as *The Galilean,* issued by the Silver Legion of America, *Social Justice,* produced by the Rev. Charles Coughlin, a Catholic priest who blamed the war on an international conspiracy of Jewish bankers.

Not satisfied that Biddle had gone far enough, Roosevelt sent the attorney general clippings of articles from antiadministration organs such as the *Chicago Tribune* and the *New York Daily News,* attaching handwritten notes suggesting that these publications be prosecuted for sedition as well. Then, in May, during a cabinet discussion of the general situation involving African Americans, Roosevelt ordered Biddle and the U.S. postmaster to meet with members of the black press "to see what can be done to prevent their subversive language."[6]

In this tense atmosphere, rumors about the government's intentions filtered out to black newspapers, causing many to fear that Biddle's actions against far-right publications were but a prelude, and that they would be next. The entire black press was alarmed when Westbrook Pegler, one of the most popular white syndicated columnists in the nation, attacked both *The Defender* and *The Courier,* writing, "Negro papers agitate violently and, I think, to the same degree that was alleged against Charles E. Coughlin's weekly, particularly in their appeal to colored soldiers whose loyalty is constantly bedeviled with doubts."

The editorial pages of both newspapers assumed that Pegler's arguments would be used to justify an impending federal prosecution, with *The Courier* writing that the columnist's words were "the buildup to the crackdown." *The Defender,* extrapolating that Pegler must be working with enemies of black newspapers in the U.S. military, took pains to distinguish the black press from the pro-Nazi press, on ideological as well as journalistic grounds. "We do not 'agitate,'" the newspaper protested. "We do not create the issues. We comment upon them and interpret them to our public."

Lucius Harper added his salvo to *The Defender*'s counterattack with a front-page column describing Pegler as "the stooge of some fascist-minded gentlemen, who are working overtime to maintain a dual democracy insofar as the Negro is concerned."[7]

Sengstacke himself was confident that the black press was acting well within the limits of free speech and would be able to resist any federal suppression. Nevertheless, determined to do what he could to avert federal action, he followed up on Hoover's recommendation — whether it was sincere or not — to visit the Office of Censorship, meeting with Director Byron Price on April 3, 1942. The conversation was cordial but just a week later, one of the agency's officials redacted "objectionable" articles from the April 11 edition of *The Defender.* Vendors in Havana and other Caribbean locations complained to Sengstacke that their copies had arrived with little more than the masthead intact, the bulk of the content having been snipped away. This prompted Sengstacke to return to Washington for a second meeting with Price, after which these incidents of censorship ceased.[8]

A few weeks later, Sengstacke got a telephone call from Lucius Bates, publisher of the Little Rock–based *Arkansas State Press,* who feared that federal officials were planning an imminent shutdown of his newspaper. Bates's wife, Daisy, an outspoken critic of segregation in the South, had already received multiple visits from FBI agents, so Sengstacke took the threat seriously, flew to Washington, D.C., and asked Mary McLeod Bethune to help secure him an appointment with Attorney General Biddle.

Contacting Biddle's office, Bethune was initially told by an assistant that the attorney general was available for a meeting. Sengstacke rushed over, only to be kept waiting for two hours before being told that Biddle had left on urgent business.

Sengstacke flew home to Chicago and, undeterred, sent Biddle a telegram stating he was sorry they had not been able to meet and offering to return at a more convenient time. Biddle wired back that he would be pleased to meet with Sengstacke the next time he was in Washington. As soon as he got Biddle's telegram, Sengstacke telephoned the attorney general and said he would be back in the nation's capital the next day. Biddle agreed to see him.

The next morning, Sengstacke was picked up at Washington National Airport by Bethune's assistant, Charles P. Browning, who accompanied him to the Department of Justice. They found Biddle in a conference room at the head of a large table flanked by an aide whose portfolio included relations with the African American community. On the table were copies of *The Defender, The Pittsburgh Courier,* the *Baltimore Afro-American,* and other black newspapers. "Unrest Grows at Army Base," read the headline of an issue of *The Courier,* summarizing the work of an investigative reporter who had snuck into Fort Dix, New Jersey, and chronicled fistfights between white and black units and armed clashes between black troops and white MPs. Similar outbreaks of violence were taking place with regularity on or near a number of southern military bases, as well as in other locations.

Biddle told Sengstacke pointedly that the black press was harming the war effort and threatened to "shut them all up" using sedition laws if black newspapers did not moderate their criticism. The attorney general pointed to a copy of *The Defender* from April of that year, featuring an article about nine black soldiers who were forced to go more than twenty-four hours without eating while their train was stopped in Alabama because of that state's segregation laws. Many of *The Defender*'s articles "came close to being seditious," Biddle told Sengstacke, concluding with the threat that the Department of Justice would continue to monitor the black press "for seditious material."

If Biddle had meant to intimidate Sengstacke, he was unsuccessful. The publisher challenged the very premise of Biddle's argument — that coverage of discrimination against black soldiers or black workers was harming the war effort. Far from lacking patriotism, Sengstacke argued, the black press, in urging African Americans to support the war, was obligated to express its readers' outrage when their contributions were wasted or rebuffed.

Mentioning the threat to the *Arkansas State Press,* Sengstacke told Biddle he obviously hadn't read black newspapers before the war, because they routinely exposed the horrors of segregation and discrimination and had been calling for integration in the military and elsewhere in society for decades. Citing the black press's legacy back through Frederick Douglass and the abolitionists before the Civil War, Sengstacke maintained that the newspapers' mission was as relevant at this pivotal moment as it had ever been.

Then Sengstacke decided to call Biddle's bluff. "You have the power to close us down," he said, staring firmly into the attorney general's eyes. "So if you want to close us, go ahead and attempt it."

Biddle was stunned into silence.

Sengstacke pressed on. "I've been trying to get an appointment to see [U.S. War Secretary Henry] Stimson. I've been trying to get in touch with everybody else. Nobody will talk to us. What do you expect us to publish? We don't want to publish the wrong information. We want to cooperate with the war effort. But if we can't get the information from the heads of the various agencies, we have to do the best we can."

Biddle replied, "Well, I didn't know that."

Sengstacke assured him, "That is correct."

Sengstacke recalled that Biddle's tone abruptly changed at that point in the conversation. "Well, let me see if I can help you in that way," the attorney general said. "What I will do is arrange for you to see some of these people."

Biddle immediately called Secretary of the Navy John Knox and made an appointment for Sengstacke to see him later that month. They continued talking for more than an hour, and by the end of the conversation, Biddle promised that, so long as it did not publish anything more critical than what had already appeared, the black press would be left alone. He finished by expressing his "hope" that the newspapers' coverage would become more positive.

Sengstacke would not guarantee a change in tone. He only reiterated that if black newspapers were able to interview top government officials, he would be "glad" to support the war effort.

Within days of returning home, Sengstacke informed his fellow black publishers of the meeting with Biddle and offered to facilitate greater contact with the Roosevelt administration for them all. The news that they would not be prosecuted for sedition spread rapidly, bringing no small relief.

Sengstacke's next trip to Washington was to meet with Navy Secretary Knox. During their conversation, which included Metz Lochard, who had been promoted to *Defender* editor in chief, Seng-stacke complained about the restrictions against black officers in the Navy, which prompted Knox, the former publisher of *The Chicago Daily News* and an acquaintance of Robert Abbott's, to call in his aide, a young Adlai Stevenson, and instruct him to "work with these people."[9]

Not all of the sessions Sengstacke held with federal officials were as productive as his meetings with Biddle and Knox, however. On June 26, he was back in Washington to talk with postal service officials who were threatening to stop mailing *The Defender* and other black newspapers because they had deemed several articles to be "inflammatory." Sengstacke explained to the postal officials that the mission of the black press was to expose the unjust treatment of African Americans, and then went on to recount his recent meeting with Attorney General Biddle, adding that he would continue to meet with administration officials to determine "just where the line can and should be drawn."

The postal service agents, unlike Biddle, remained unpersuaded that protesting against segregation was acceptable during wartime and recommended that African Americans forestall their campaign for civil rights out of a sense of national responsibility. "Their very reason for existence in addition to the white press is to emphasize and play up discriminations against the negro [*sic*] which are usually played down in the white press," explained a memo about the meeting written by postal officials, before adding, "The benefits of citizenship entail certain duties."[10]

Biddle, for his part, held to his word about blocking the prosecution of black publishers even as he continued to target those who sided with the nation's wartime enemies, an effort that did affect Chicago's African American community. In the summer of 1942, a federal grand jury indicted twenty-eight white supremacists — including some of those writers for extremist newspapers caught in the spring roundup — on federal charges of espionage and sedition. And a little later that year, federal prosecutors brought sedition charges against sixty-three Chicago-based members of the nascent Nation of Islam, as well as five members of the Ethiopian Pacific Movement in New York. Both groups had received propaganda from the Japanese and openly promoted the Japanese concept of the "Asiatic Black Man," a theory that nonwhite peoples had a common ancestor and that, as such, should practice racial solidarity with the Japanese war effort. Unable to prove actual sedition, federal prosecutors instead went after the Nation of Islam members, including their leader, Elijah Muhammad, for lesser crimes such as draft evasion.[11]

Nor did Biddle's laissez-faire policy apply to the military, which continued to express its own doubts about the black press. In July, Sengstacke met with Assistant Secretary of War John J. McCloy, who had been complaining about black newspapers' focus on racial discrimination. As he wrote to an African American official in the U.S. Army, McCloy did not see the connection between the war's aims and black newspapers' campaigns for equal rights: "Frankly, I do not think that the basic issues of this war are involved in the question of whether Colored troops serve in segregated units or in mixed units and I doubt whether you can convince the people of the United States that the basic issues of freedom are involved in such a question."

Sengstacke assured McCloy that greater access for the black press would be the best means to resolve the problem. In a letter thanking him for the meeting, Sengstacke told McCloy that *The Defender* "stands ready to be of every possible assistance in the broad progressive program of the War Department."[12]

The same month he met with McCloy, Sengstacke directed Metz Lochard to begin assembling the newspaper's own version of a "Double V" edition. He wanted to create a special section that would include messages from the nation's highest-ranking figures, beginning with President Roosevelt. Writing to Roosevelt on July 29, he asked for a contribution to the special issue, which would be themed around "inter-racial unity and good will."

White House Press Secretary Stephen Early wrote back on August 4 with a brusque rejection. Early, a Virginian and former reporter for the Associated Press, stated that while the president had frequently issued calls for "interracial good will," he could not provide a special statement for one newspaper. In an administration riven by those who sympathized with the demands of black newspapers as well as others who wanted to silence them, Early would stand with the latter group, remaining a powerful foe of Sengstacke's and the black press throughout the war years.[13]

Sengstacke found a way around Early, however, via the black cabinet. On August 31, he wrote to Secretary of War Henry Stimson complaining about the barriers placed in the path of the black press: "I am beginning to wonder whether the government really wants sincere cooperation or whether there are clandestine forces working against the interest of a section of the Negro Press."[14]

Within a few days of Sengstacke's letter, the African American director of the Office of War Information advised Roosevelt that *The Defender*'s publisher was "very influential" and that the president's contribution to the special edition would be "very useful." This apparently did the trick, because on September 9, Roosevelt sent John Sengstacke a brief personal letter, a facsimile of which appeared on the front page of the special section:

Dear Mr. Sengstacke,

This war will be won by all of us, working and fighting together, and we shall emerge not only victorious but enriched in spirit and understanding by our common effort. In helping to strengthen the sense of unity among our people, you are helping to create the power to crush tyranny and secure freedom for ourselves and all the world.[15]

FDR went even further, contributing a complete essay to the special section Lochard was assembling back in Chicago, which he had dubbed the "Victory Through Unity" edition. Lochard had hired a temporary deputy for this project, Ben Burns, perhaps the first white man to take a post in *The Defender*'s editorial department. A talented editor with a strong work ethic, Burns cheerfully worked long hours with Lochard in Abbott's old office, cutting, pasting, and designing the "Victory Through Unity" edition. In a front-page essay that appeared beneath President Roosevelt's letter, Lochard described the edition as the "biggest venture of its kind ever undertaken by the Negro press" and urged its distribution among black and white Americans around the nation.[16]

The forty-page "Victory Through Unity" insert appeared in *The Defender* on September 26, 1942, with a cover that featured two uniformed men, one black and one white, sounding bugles with an American flag in the background under the headline "Calling America." In addition to the missive from FDR, the special edition contained messages from a legion of politicians, jurists, writers, businesspeople, military officers, foreign dignitaries, and a host of public intellectuals — everyone from science-fiction writer H. G. Wells to socialite and British MP Lady Nancy Astor. Ideas from across the spectrum were given their forum as pro-Soviet Communists argued their case in columns abutting the opinions of conservative Republicans, while W. E. B. Du Bois joined Howard University Professor Alain Locke and others in arguing that African Americans' struggle for equality was connected to Mohandas Gandhi's movement to liberate India from British rule.

One full page was dedicated to a speech written by Frederick Douglass during the Civil War urging African Americans to enlist in the Union army despite lower pay and worse conditions for black troops. "Nothing can be more plain, nothing more certain," Douglass had argued, "than the speediest and best possible way for us to manhood, equal rights and elevation is that we enter the service."

Another page featured an article announcing that black men were now welcome in the Navy. The headline read, "The Navy Needs Men ... Yes, Negro Men."

The "Victory Through Unity" edition was a finely tuned meditation on why African Americans should participate in the war effort, or ultimately, why anyone should participate in any war, when they knew that the ideals they were fighting for were not being upheld in the homeland. In the introductory article Lochard wrote under Sengstacke's byline, he recalled the rapid gains and subsequent disappointment of southern blacks who came to work in northern cities during World War I. In this war, which was even more obviously a struggle of principle, Lochard argued that it only made sense that there would be far greater strides toward equality. "Democracy as the fundamental rule of life for enlightened nations is being put to a fiery test," he wrote. "The sacrifices to which the Negro people and all freedom loving peoples of the world are committed will have been in vain if victory is limited to the defeat of fascism."[17]

But the centerpiece of the "Victory Through Unity" edition was, of course, the essay contributed by President Roosevelt. In "What National Unity Means," FDR warned against "European tricks" that aimed to split Americans along racial lines:

"We must be particularly vigilant against racial discrimination in any of its ugly forms. Hitler will try again to breed mistrust and suspicion between one individual and another, one group and another, one race and another, one government and another.

"We must as a united people keep ablaze on this continent the flames of human liberty, of reason, of democracy and fair play as living things to be preserved for the better world that is to come."[18]

The essays included in the special edition represented the whole spectrum of opinion on black participation in the war effort. Writing in a telegram from Australia, General Douglas MacArthur was simultaneously moving and patronizing, asserting, "Only those like you who were denied personal liberty can fully appreciate its value. Your heroic struggle up to freedom has given you a sense of patriotism, which is one of your finest characteristics."[19]

Robert R. McCormick, the conservative Republican publisher of the *Chicago Tribune,* wrote a stirring argument for the war's greater meaning. Surprisingly, McCormick agreed with those African American intellectuals who saw their cause linked with global liberation movements. Normally a bristly iconoclast who preferred to be called "colonel" after the rank he had achieved in France during the First World War, McCormick's passion for racial equality stemmed from his military service alongside black soldiers.

"Too often, it is said that every tenth one of us is a Negro, that 13 million of 130 million Americans are Negroes," McCormick wrote. "It would be better if we acquired the habit of thinking that there are 130 million of us, inseparably bound to this land, inseparably allied to freedom, inseparably affected by the consequences of victory or defeat, and equally entitled to all that the United States can offer any of us."[20]

Attorney General Biddle contributed a column entitled "Who Is the Common Man?" Under a photo that showed him smiling, a finger posed at his temple, Biddle began with a careful, academic definition of the "Common Man," which included African Americans among those who had a direct stake in an Allied victory. Biddle chastised those who saw the conflict as a "white man's war" but was even harsher toward those who spread racist ideas, arguing that they were effectively supporting the Axis.[21]

As a useful counterpoint to messages from the likes of FDR and Biddle, the "Victory Through Unity" edition included the words of white supremacists, both official and closeted. Printed in its entirety, a letter submitted by newspaper columnist Westbrook Pegler derided *The Defender* as "low grade and utterly unscrupulous . . . perpetrating a grave disservice to the Negro people in particular and the United States in general. You have a great opportunity and great responsibility," Pegler wrote, "and you are abusing both."[22]

Another page featured a quotation from Adolf Hitler's autobiography, *Mein Kampf,* the better to shame those Americans who thought similarly about African Americans: "In each Negro . . . is the latent brute and primitive man who can be tamed neither by centuries of slavery nor by the extreme varnish of civilization. One can therefore understand why, in the Southern States of America, sheer necessity compels the white race to act in an abhorrent and perhaps even cruel manner against Negroes. And, of course, the Negroes who are lynched do not merit any regret."[23]

The article in the "Victory Through Unity" edition that perhaps best reflected the sentiments of black America during wartime was written by Langston Hughes, already a well-known poet and author who had carried the legacy of the Harlem Renaissance into the 1940s. Hughes's essay, entitled "Klan or Gestapo? Why Take Either?" begins with an allegory of the dilemma facing African Americans during the war. One night in the Old South, a grandmother laments to her grandson the poor quality and quantity of their food, to which the grandson replies that their master's pantries are overflowing and suggests that he steal a ham from the smokehouse.

The grandmother angrily rejects her grandson's offer, telling him, "Wouldn't nobody but the Devil steal a ham."

But later that night, the grandmother hears the sound of bare feet on her porch and then sees a juicy ham come flying through the open window.

"It fell ker-plunk in front of the fire as her grandson fled in the dark," Hughes wrote. "The old woman stooped down and picked up the ham.

"'Hallelujah!' she cried, shouting, 'Thank God for this ham — even if the Devil did bring it!'"

Hughes explained his analogy in the context of tangible gains in federal intervention to ban discrimination in the workplace and in transportation. During the lead-up to the war, with American factories gearing up the "arsenals of democracy," white labor unions tried to block black workers from job sites. In response, A. Philip Randolph and other leaders had threatened to lead a massive march on Washington, D.C. Faced with a disruption of the crucial labor force as well as a potential rift between two key constituencies, President Roosevelt responded by issuing an executive order banning discrimination against African Americans at firms producing war materiel.

"That is the way a lot of colored people feel about democratic gains and the war . . . [these] advances are a kind of ham that indirectly the Japanese and the Germans have thrown — by forcing democracy to recognize belatedly some of its own failings in regard to the Negro people."

Hughes conceded that the halfheartedness of the concessions, along with the continued prevalence of legal segregation and extralegal lynching in the South, engendered indifference among many African Americans toward the war effort. Some blacks even celebrated the early victories by the Japanese against the British in Hong Kong and Malaysia. But victory by the Axis, Hughes pointed out, would portend far worse conditions for American blacks.

"Although Alabama is bad, the Axis is worse," Hughes maintained, reasoning that while Nazism, Japanese militarism, and Italian fascism shared a racist ideology with Jim Crow, African Americans retained certain key rights in the United States that would surely be taken away if the Axis won the war. The very existence of the black press in the United States proved his point:

"Negro editors know what democracy is about because they haven't got much of it — and they want it. But we do have in America a freedom of speech denied, for instance, to Jews — and Negroes — in Germany."

Given these realities, the only course of action for African Americans, Hughes argued, was to fight the war in Europe and Japan even as they redoubled their efforts to convince white Americans to abolish segregation.

"Our white fellow citizens must be made to realize that Jim Crow and all it symbolizes — meager educational facilities, discrimination in industries, lynchings — is not decent. It is an anachronism in American life that, especially for the sake of the war effort, must be gotten rid of — and soon.

"After all, this is a war for freedom.

"It is not logical to speak of freedom for Poland and forget Georgia."[24]

The success of the "Victory Through Unity" edition pushed *The Defender*'s weekly count past 250,000, reaching the newspaper's own historic high mark during the first Great Migration. This boost was due, at least in part, to the new relationships Sengstacke was forging in Washington; the Office of War Information, for instance, bought 100,000 copies and distributed them widely among black soldiers. Regular weekly circulation, however, reached 160,000, with more than 60,000 sold in the city, while the newspaper began to receive ad accounts from large white-owned corporations like Pepsi-Cola, Pabst Blue Ribbon, Philip Morris, and Esso, all of which had previously ignored the black press.[25]

Sengstacke immediately reinvested this increasing revenue flow into the editorial department, giving Lochard a budget to hire a slew of new employees, the first of whom was the assiduous Ben Burns, hired as the national editor, certainly the first white man to sit in *that* position. But Burns's appointment was controversial for another reason as well — he was a Communist Party member whose previous journalism experience was with party organs. Born Benjamin Bernstein on Chicago's Jewish West Side, he had joined the Communists as a journalism student at New York University and worked at both *The Daily Worker* and the *People's World* in San Francisco. Back in Chicago with a wife and baby and looking for work, Burns was introduced to Lochard by William Patterson, a Chicago-based attorney who was one of the few black leaders in the American hierarchy of the Communist Party.

Burns's duties at *The Defender* included sifting through letters from over two thousand agent-correspondents, containing news, announcements, and commentaries from communities across the country, and then boiling them down into the state-by-state pages, sections that remained an essential component of the newspaper's national edition. Burns was also responsible for editing the work of several new, national columnists Lochard hired, a roster that included Walter White, the executive director of the NAACP; S. I. Hayakawa, a Japanese American professor who was one of the foremost linguists of the day and later a U.S. senator; and Langston Hughes, whose agreement to write regularly for *The Defender* represented a major coup.[26]

Burns still reported to his superiors in the Communist hierarchy, but he had lost his faith in the dogma and was steadily distancing himself from the party. Less than two years earlier, however, Burns had denounced Hughes as a "turncoat" for renouncing his support of the Soviet Union in an article in the *People's World*. Chagrined that he'd been responsible for such propaganda, he worried that Hughes would confront him about it, but Hughes never did.[27]

Burns devoted hours to reading books and news articles about Black Chicago, creating his own catalog of the political leaders, ministers, intellectuals, artists, and gangsters who filled the newspaper's pages. He appreciated the irony that *The Defender*'s headquarters afforded him: "How strange that I, a non-religious Jew, was entering the Negro world by walking into a one-time Jewish temple," Burns wrote in his memoir.[28]

In his off-hours, Burns was also helping a friend, John H. Johnson, the former DuSable High School valedictorian, who had a vision for a new kind of magazine, a black version of *Reader's Digest*, which would be politically moderate and picture-oriented — *Negro Digest*. In November 1942, the first issue of *Negro Digest* appeared, based on templates Burns borrowed from *The Defender* and containing reprinted articles written by Carl Sandburg, Walter White, and Langston Hughes, among others.[29]

In June 1943, Sengstacke was elected to a new term as president of the NNPA at the group's annual convention in Louisville, Kentucky. This convention was smaller, shorter, and lower-key than the first two NNPA gatherings, but over two days of intensive meetings and lectures, the assembled publishers tackled the various issues confronting them in wartime, which the outgoing president, William O. Walker of the *Cleveland Call & Post*, listed as "drafts, curtailments, priorities and scarcities."

As of January 1943, the War Production Board was authorized to control the allocation of newsprint, and shortly thereafter, a number of black newspapers began to complain of shortages, raising suspicions that they were deliberately being slighted. Several other publications were suffering from the loss of key staff members to conscription, which in at least one case seemed to have been used to silence a critical voice. The NNPA resolved to investigate these issues, register a protest with the Selective Service over discrimination at the local draft boards, and explore the creation of a common bureau in Washington, D.C. "The Negro Press has passed from adolescence to maturity," Walker declared, "and the time has come for us to put aside our childish ways."

If the political situation was challenging, at least the economic reality at most of the newspapers was improving rapidly, as a new generation of African Americans men and women, flush from jobs working in the war-related industries, became new subscribers. Advertisers, even white-owned media corporations, were taking notice as well: the second day of the conference was sponsored by a local white-owned daily newspaper chain with a keynote address from the promotions manager, who proudly informed the black publishers that his publications "[had] made a concerted effort to clean up advertising which reflects prejudice and racial discrimination."[30]

Indeed, several months earlier, *American Salesmanship* magazine, noting the growing economic power of the black consumer, published a "Catalogue of Don'ts" that instructed advertisers, "Don't exaggerate Negro characters with flat noses, thick lips, kinky hair and owl eyes," "Don't constantly name the Negro porter or waiter 'George,'" "Don't picture colored women as buxom, broad-faced, grinning mammies and Aunt Jemimas," and "Don't illustrate an outdoor poster, car-card, advertisement, or any other advertising piece with a Negro eating watermelon, chasing chickens, or shooting craps," among other points.[31]

In late June, just a few weeks after the NNPA convention, a strike at the Packard Motor Car Company in Detroit by white workers protesting the promotion of several blacks erupted into racial street violence. For several days, white mobs attacked blacks unwittingly venturing into their neighborhoods as well as those few black families who had settled in largely white areas, while black mobs destroyed and looted white-owned stores in their neighborhoods, fighting it out with Detroit police as well as white gangs. Some thirty-four people were killed, seventeen of them blacks who died at the hands of police, before U.S. Army troops were deployed to put an end to the fighting.

Louis Martin, whom John Sengstacke had dispatched to Detroit seven years earlier, witnessed much of the violence firsthand, and began to organize the community almost as soon as the troops were in place. Martin had built *The Michigan Chronicle*'s circulation to nearly twenty-five thousand weekly, in part by becoming a strong advocate for increasing the number of African Americans on the police force, an overwhelmingly white and notoriously racist organization that had been infiltrated by the Ku Klux Klan. Now Martin turned up the volume of his speeches and editorials, arguing that the violence could have been stemmed if there had been more African Americans on the force in the first place, and conducting a thorough postriot investigation along with a young attorney working for the NAACP named Thurgood Marshall.[32]

Greatly alarmed by the violence in Detroit, a center for the production of war materiel, the Roosevelt administration immediately reached out to black leaders to try to remedy the situation. On July 16 and 17, 1943, John Sengstacke brought Martin and ten other black publishers to Washington, D.C., for a whirlwind set of meetings with federal officials at which the riots in Detroit and other cities were foremost on the agenda. Including representatives of the *Afro-American* and *The Pittsburgh Courier* as well as the *Atlanta Daily World*, the nation's only African American–owned daily, the delegation met first with Vice President Henry Wallace, a staunch liberal who had been outspoken in his support for civil rights. The publishers rejected the idea that blacks had caused the violence in Detroit, blaming instead "race hatreds," and asked that Wallace use an upcoming speech in Detroit to speak out against lynching and other forms of racial injustice. Wallace impressed the publishers when he agreed, explaining that he saw incidents of racial injustice as "the first steps toward Fascism," according to a report in *The Defender*.[33]

At the War Production Board, the publishers pressed their case for more newsprint, asking for "special consideration" due to the great demand for newspapers from migrants working in vital war-industry factories, among other reasons. Sengstacke had already tried to mitigate the paper shortage by buying excess paper stock from *Chicago Tribune* owner Robert McCormick and redistributing it to the other black papers. But Production Board officials refused to make adjustments, arguing that the black press was the victim of its own success in that the newspapers were increasing their circulation just as paper was becoming a scarce commodity.

The delegation pressed on. In meetings with Army Secretary Mc-Cloy and Navy Secretary Knox, they argued for better treatment of black troops, increased access for their reporters to military commanders, and for more African American employees in their respective press bureaus. Meeting with the director of the Selective Service, the publishers raised the case of the editor of the *Southwest Georgian* newspaper, who was drafted shortly after running an article that claimed local police had been involved in a lynching. After hearing from the NNPA delegation, the Selective Service director quietly stopped any similar incidents from occurring.

The publishers did not divulge the details of their session with Attorney General Biddle, but he greatly impressed them, according to an account by Carter Wesley of the *Houston Informer:* "Naturally, it was off the record," Wesley wrote in the *Informer,* "but this baby talked not only to the point, but to a series of points that were as sharp, frank, clear, concise and unequivocal as anything I've heard yet."[34]

During their off-the-record conversation, Biddle agreed to the publishers' request that he assist them in getting a black reporter named to the White House Press Corps. Biddle promptly followed up with President Roosevelt, suggesting that a reporter from the Associated Negro Press news service be admitted to the corps. The attorney general candidly advised the president that he expected the opposition of Press Secretary Stephen Early, predicting that Early would use the excuse that the White House Press Corps was reserved for daily newspapers and the ANP was a news *service.* Biddle told the president that he felt Early's objection was rooted in nothing but concern about upsetting southern whites.

"[FDR] suggested I take it up with Early," Biddle wrote in his personal notes, "but I rejoined that Steve certainly would be against it. He has in his mind that this might run into unfavorable congressional opinion as they have excluded Negroes from the Press Gallery. I thought that if there was a bonafide daily newspaper he might be represented and the President told me to look into it further."[35]

If Biddle had become something of an advocate for the black press within the administration, he was sometimes on the wrong side of the issues facing black Americans. The month following the publishers' visit, the *New York Post* reported that Biddle had recommended to President Roosevelt that he use his authority to stop the northern migration of African Americans, fearing a future wave of urban violence in cities including Chicago, Baltimore, and Los Angeles. Analyzing what had gone wrong in Detroit, Biddle found that while an earlier arrival of troops surely would have helped, the fundamental issue was that the city's housing supply, police force, and public transportation system were overwhelmed by the influx of migrants. "It would seem pretty clear," Biddle wrote to the president, "that no more Negroes should move into Detroit."

The NAACP, ACLU, A. Philip Randolph, and many others immediately condemned Biddle's idea, and Sengstacke, despite his productive relationship with the attorney general, didn't hesitate to join in. Instead of endeavoring to stop the migration, a front-page editorial in *The Defender* wondered why the attorney general hadn't simply called for the construction of more housing for workers in cities where racial tension was high. Adding his voice to this line of criticism, Sengstacke urged Biddle to hold a conference of all relevant federal, state, and local agencies as well as outside advocacy organizations.[36]

Under this torrent of outrage, Biddle quickly shelved the idea of stopping the migration even as he redoubled his efforts to champion the black press. That summer, the Office of Censorship sporadically blocked several black newspapers from overseas distribution, and in several southern towns, military police seized stocks of *The Defender* and other black newspapers, encouraging nearby townspeople to do the same. Biddle swiftly countermanded the censorship orders, upholding the right of the black press to voice its opinions, and even sent investigators to those southern towns where newspapers were seized to determine if the news vendors' civil rights had been violated.

Biddle protected African American publishers as well from new threats entirely unknown to Sengstacke. In September 1943, the FBI's J. Edgar Hoover issued a new, seven-hundred-page report entitled *Survey of Racial Conditions in the United States,* which focused on the allegedly subversive activities of the black press. Citing numerous alleged acts of Communist infiltration at black newspapers, the report quoted articles that the FBI claimed were harmful to the war effort.

Regarding *The Defender*, the bureau conceded that the Chicago paper had been a strong supporter of the war effort, but made a number of damning allegations nonetheless. The report did not mention Ben Burns by name, although the agency had a detailed file on him as a Communist Party member and was conducting close surveillance of him. The FBI did state, however, that two *Defender* employees had attended party meetings and had even made speeches from the platform. The FBI report also singled out Burns's mentor, William Patterson, who had written a column for *The Defender* in which he took a strong pro-Soviet line, and complained about the paper's reportage on inequality, citing as unacceptable the following sentence from an article on four murdered black soldiers in Arkansas: "In the South, the uniform of the United States has no respect if the wearer is a Negro."

Hoover clearly wanted to prosecute the black newspapers, but Biddle, for the balance of his tenure as attorney general, rebuffed all efforts from the FBI or the Post Office to do so.[37]

In November 1943, a *Defender* editorial entitled "Wanted: Homes" warned that housing conditions in Bronzeville were deteriorating to dangerous levels. Quoting Robert Taylor, a prominent African American architect who had been appointed by Mayor Ed Kelly as the first chairman of the Chicago Housing Authority, the newspaper noted that the African American section of the South Side was denser than Calcutta, with more than 90,000 people per square mile. Such overcrowding, with all its attendant poverty and deprivation, was completely unnecessary, the newspaper asserted, noting that all along the edges of the black neighborhoods, signs were visible advertising apartments for rent, but with the word "restricted" appended immediately afterward.

The migration had slowed slightly during the final years of the Depression, with just 40,000 arriving in the city from 1936 to 1940. But once the wartime economic boom kicked in, black southerners came in ever-larger numbers, so that by 1944, greater Bronzeville contained 337,000 people, an increase of nearly 60,000 in just four years. Representing more than 9 percent of the city's total population, Black

Chicago was continuing to outstrip every other group for its rate of growth, even as the city's overall population reached 3.6 million.[38]

The housing available to the new arrivals had not kept pace, however, leading to stifling congestion, deteriorating conditions, and soaring prices. Back in November 1940, the U.S. Supreme Court had ruled unanimously in favor of the Hansberry family in their effort to break the restrictive covenants in Washington Park, opening up five hundred units to black settlement. But the justices didn't go so far as to invalidate the practice altogether, and homeowners in the neighborhoods just south and east of Bronzeville continued using the covenants aggressively, effectively slowing the community's geographic growth even as more war-industry workers arrived every week.

"In the past," the editorial quipped, "we have had occasion to protest over hold-up rents to ramshackle hovels. Today, however, there are no broken-down shacks to be had at any price. The housing facilities available to Negroes have passed the saturation point."[39]

*The Defender* was still optimistic at that moment that the Chicago Housing Authority, led by Robert Taylor and supported wholeheartedly by Mayor Kelly, would be able to provide some relief by quickly building units on parcels of vacant land on the South Side. The newspaper hoped for certain legal remedies as well: the NAACP was continuing to drive cases challenging restrictive covenants through the appellate courts and found many allies throughout the judiciary; one Cook County judge who steadfastly refused to uphold these racist provisions became a particular hero to the integration activists. Meanwhile, the community continued to nibble away at its borders, as the higher rents blacks were willing to pay continued to lure white property owners. Nevertheless, the covenants, along with other discriminatory practices, succeeded in delaying the community's progress, even as the trains from the South continued to discharge their passengers into a city where the odds of finding a decent place to live got worse every day.[40]

Sengstacke finally achieved a long-sought-after goal on February 5, 1944, when he and twelve other publishers and editors from ten different black-owned publications traveled to the White House to meet with President Roosevelt. They spent thirty-five minutes in the Executive Office, the first time a president had ever met with represen-

tatives of the black press and one of the very few instances in which
a commander in chief met with a large group of African Americans
from any profession. Leading the delegation, Sengstacke presented
each member to FDR, who "shook hands with each of the conferees,"
according to a front-page report in *The Defender,* "acknowledging the
individual introductions with typical Rooseveltian charm and cordiality."

Although the content of the meeting was off the record, the article
did explain that Roosevelt addressed the group for ten minutes before turning to Sengstacke, who read a twenty-one-point statement
of the "Race's war aims and aspirations," a righteous and ambitious
document written by Percival Prattis of *The Pittsburgh Courier* that
opened with a "declaration of unlimited and unsullied allegiance to
the nation and deplored all forms of disunity," but went on to urge the
president to move forward on a broad front of issues, from equal opportunity in employment to equality in public educational facilities,
unrestricted suffrage in national, state, and local elections, and full
government protection of civil rights. It included a demand for full
protection, equal treatment, and opportunity for African Americans
in the military, as well as the extension of Social Security benefits to
black domestic workers and farm workers. The document also included an international goal — the application of the Atlantic Charter
to all colonial and exploited peoples.[41]

One of the attendees, P. Bernard Young of the *Journal and Guide,*
described the interaction in equally glowing terms in a column he
published more than a year later: "It was obvious that this was no
routine audience [President Roosevelt] was giving the Negro group;
he was concentrating his attention on the subject at hand," Young
wrote. "The President explained that each year he had a white association in for a lengthy off-the-record background conference, where
all questions could be asked and any question would be answered. He
invited us to make our visit an annual one too.

"'Come back about this time next year,' he said.

"One of the visiting group spoke up, 'But Mr. President, that will
be February or thereabouts.'

"The President immediately got the point. He laughingly but
meaningfully replied:

"'Go ahead, make your plans. The invitation still holds.'

"February, 1945, would be in his fourth term. Thus every member of the NNPA delegation knew almost a year ahead that the President would stand for a fourth term, something then a top-priority topic of discussion. But it was off-the-record then."

That Roosevelt intended to run for reelection was an open secret, but the publishers were charmed nonetheless. In any case, that the meeting had taken place at all was the most significant accomplishment, in that it changed a presidential meeting with the black press from an aspiration to an expectation that would bind future commanders in chief. Future publishers from the black press would demand their annual appointments at the White House as well.[42]

Nevertheless, these journalists had entered the room determined to push their agenda, Louis Martin later recalled, and had succumbed to Roosevelt's charisma: "Sitting like a grinning white Buddha, Roosevelt wore that broad uplifting smile as we filed before him and shook his hand," Martin wrote. "His touch and presence seemed electric enough to light up the darkest room anywhere, at any time . . . Roosevelt seemed to have anticipated everything we had on our minds as he held forth in high spirits, answering questions before they could be asked.

"We left the White House walking on air with no one quite sure what grievance the president had promised to act upon. Yet there was no doubt in any of our minds, certainly none in mine, that FDR was on our side, understood our complaints, and in due time would try to do something about them."

In one fell swoop, President Roosevelt had significantly strengthened both the NNPA and its founder, John Sengstacke, now acknowledged as the group's leader despite his relative youth. If before this event, Sengstacke had felt that the affiliation of the other publishers — particularly *The Courier* and his other longtime rivals — was tenuous, he now knew that he could move forward with confidence.[43]

Three days after FDR's historic meeting with the NNPA, Harry McAlpin, ostensibly a reporter with the *Atlanta Daily World,* began working in the White House Press Corps. McAlpin had until very shortly before this time been a Washington correspondent for *The Defender,* and his salary at the *Daily World* was still being paid by Sengstacke, albeit secretly, in a ruse carefully choreographed to circumvent Stephen Early's rightly anticipated objection to the presence of a black reporter.

Not that the administration's acquiescence meant that McAlpin would receive anything like a warm reception from his fellow reporters. The day before he attended his first presidential press conference, McAlpin received a call from Paul Wooten, a White House correspondent for *The New Orleans Times-Picayune* and president of the White House Correspondents' Association.

McAlpin arranged a meeting with Wooten, in which he advised his fellow newsman not to enter the Oval Office during the press conference the next day. "'I suggest that when you come down tomorrow,'" McAlpin recalled Wooten saying, "'you sit out in the reception hall. One of us regular correspondents will be glad to tell you what went on in the conference as soon as it is over. And, of course, if you have any question you would like to have asked, if you would let one of us know about it, we'd ask it for you and as soon as the conference is over, we'd let you know what answer the President gave.'"

Wooten continued with a veiled threat. "'Now, the reason I made these suggestions is there is always a large crowd at the conferences . . . It's possible you might step on someone's foot in the rush . . . and there would be a riot right in the White House.'"

Inwardly seething, McAlpin nevertheless restrained himself. After first responding that he was "surprised" by Wooten's comments, McAlpin averred that he would rely on the professionalism of the White House Press Corps. "'I'd be surprised if any of them should start a riot in the White House but if they did it would be one of the biggest stories of the year and I'll be damned if I'd want to miss it. Thanks for the suggestion, but I'll take my chances. I'll be going in to get my own stories and to ask my questions myself.'"

McAlpin did indeed attend his first presidential press conference the next day, and wrote about the experience in an article that appeared in *The Defender* as well as the *Atlanta Daily World* and a number of other black newspapers, neatly leaving out his encounter with Wooten. Indeed, there was more than enough positive news to offset any negative reports: while the reporters waited in the hallway to enter the Oval Office, Steve Early came outside, spotted McAlpin, shook his hand, and chatted with him for a few moments. Early "made

Robert Abbott (second from left) in 1896, with the Hampton Quartet. Abbott traveled to Chicago with the quartet to perform at the 1893 World's Columbian Exposition, where he was inspired by former abolitionist Frederick Douglass and antilynching journalist Ida B. Wells.
*Courtesy of Abbott-Sengstacke Family Papers*

Robert Abbott poses with his newsboys in this undated photo from the 1920s. Abbott's integrity and commitment as a "Race Man," along with his hard-hitting editorials against lynching and segregation in the South, won the support of politicians, businessmen, Pullman porters, artists, and gangsters as well as the general public.
*Courtesy of the Chicago Defender Charities*

*The Defender*'s headquarters, 3435 South Indiana Avenue, 1921. Until that year, the newspaper's offices were located in Abbott's former landlady's apartment.
*Courtesy of Abbott-Sengstacke Family Papers*

Abbott shows guests his pride and joy, a Goss printing press, in November 1927. By this time *The Defender* was established as a national communications vehicle for black America, with a weekly circulation that approached 300,000.
*Courtesy of Abbott-Sengstacke Family Papers*

Robert Abbott's home, 4742 South Parkway, in 1926, the year he purchased it. South Parkway had been the abode of wealthy whites before the turn of the century but had become the African American community's liveliest thoroughfare by this time. *Library of Congress, Prints & Photographs Division, HABS ILL,16-CHIG,97—1*

Robert Abbott and his first wife, Helen, 1927. With blue eyes and a light complexion, Helen Abbott sometimes passed for white, and Robert enjoyed the resulting excitement their appearances together stirred up in this color-conscious era. *Photo courtesy of Abbott-Sengstacke Family Papers*

John Sengstacke and Robert Abbott (bottom row, first and second from right) at the Bud Billiken Parade in August 1934, along with Duke Ellington (top row, fourth from left) and other dignitaries. Sengstacke had graduated from college that spring and began working at *The Defender*, where he discovered that general counsel Nathan McGill (bottom row, second from left) was pilfering funds from the newspaper's coffers. *Courtesy of Abbott-Sengstacke Family Papers*

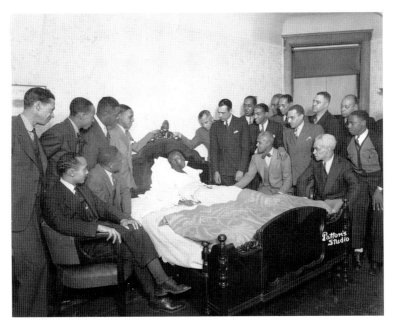

Abbott on his sick bed, surrounded by staff, 1930. Robert Abbott's health declined sharply during the 1930s, the result of a chronic liver condition and associated ailments. *Courtesy of Abbott-Sengstacke Family Papers*

THE NATIONAL

# Negro Printer
### AND PUBLISHER

HEADS MILLION DOLLAR
PUBLISHING AND PRINTING COMPANY

JOHN H. SENGSTACKE
Age 28, General Manager of The R. S. Abbott Publishing Co.

JANUARY, 1940    20c per copy    $2.00 per year

John Sengstacke on the cover of *Negro Printer,* January 1940. As Robert Abbott faded, the members of the black press increasingly looked to Sengstacke for leadership.

*Courtesy of the Chicago Defender Charities*

John Sengstacke, his brother Whittier, and Louis Martin, 1940. Martin began working at *The Defender* shortly after his graduation from the University of Michigan and was soon detailed to manage *The Michigan Chronicle,* a new publication based in Detroit's fast-growing African American community. *Courtesy of the Chicago Defender Charities*

The first conference of the Negro Newspaper Publishers Association, with twenty-six men and two women representing twenty-one black newspapers from around the country, February 29, 1940. Just after John Sengstacke had delivered welcoming remarks, the assembly received word that Robert Abbott had died in his sleep. *Courtesy of the Chicago Defender Charities*

John Sengstacke meets with Ira Lewis, president of *The Pittsburgh Courier, The Defender*'s fiercest competitor, at the first NNPA conference, 1940. Inspired by Abbott's memory, the publishers agreed to meet again in Chicago the following year and named Sengstacke their president. *Courtesy of the Chicago Defender Charities*

John Sengstacke with Eleanor Roosevelt, 1951. Through *The Defender*'s editorial page and his own political efforts, Sengstacke worked closely with Mrs. Roosevelt and other members of FDR's administration to get the first African American reporter assigned to the White House Press Corps and ward off the threat of censorship from the FBI. *Courtesy of Abbott-Sengstacke Family Papers*

Enoch Waters at the typewriter, 1940s. A Hampton classmate of John Sengstacke's, Waters joined the staff in 1935 and stayed at *The Defender* for decades, documenting Bronzeville at its height, the prosperity during the war years, and the civil rights era. *Courtesy of Abbott-Sengstacke Family Papers*

*The Defender* newsroom at 3435 South Indiana Avenue, late 1940s. At the typewriter at center is city editor Audrey Weaver, the first woman editor at any black newspaper and one of many women writers in key positions at the newspaper.
*Courtesy of Abbott-Sengstacke Family Papers*

Former president Harry Truman, Chicago Mayor Richard Daley, and John Sengstacke in the 1956 Bud Billiken Parade. Both Truman and Daley owed much to Sengstacke personally and the African American electorate generally.
*Courtesy of Abbott-Sengstacke Family Papers*

The *Defender*'s new headquarters, 2400 South Michigan Avenue, 1960. By this time *The Defender* was a daily newspaper with unmatched coverage of the emerging civil rights movement.

*Courtesy of the Chicago Defender Charities*

John Sengstacke with President John F. Kennedy in the White House, 1962. Sengstacke played a pivotal role in Kennedy's campaign, providing consistent editorial support through the *Daily Defender* and dispatching Louis Martin to shore up the Democrat's support in the African American electorate.

*Courtesy of Chicago Defender Charities*

Martin Luther King Jr. in the Robert Taylor Homes, July 1965. King came to Chicago to help local activists protesting the city's segregated schools and housing. King's journey through the city was documented by John Sengstacke's middle son, Bobby, a staff photographer for the newspaper in his early twenties. *Photo by Robert Abbott Sengstacke/Getty Images*

The 1966 Billiken Parade featuring boxing champion Muhammad Ali and soul star James Brown. *The Defender* launched the careers of many African American athletes and musicians.

*Photo by Robert Abbott Sengstacke/Getty Images*

Marjorie Stewart Joyner (in glasses) receives an award from Ralph Newman, president of the Chicago Public Library Board, while John and Myrtle Sengstacke look on, 1968. A beautician, civil rights activist, and political player, Joyner was recruited to head the Chicago Defender Charities after Robert Abbott's death, administering the annual Billiken Parade until she was in her nineties. *Courtesy of Chicago Defender Charities*

Chicago Mayor Michael Bilandic (from left), John Sengstacke, State Senate President Cecil Partee, Cook County Commissioner John Stroger, and Cook County Board President George Dunne marching in the 1978 Billiken Parade. The city's Democratic machine was still a mighty political force, but the restive African American community would soon elect Harold Washington, a former machine cog turned independent rebel, as the city's first black mayor. *Courtesy of Chicago Defender Charities*

Frederick Douglass Sengstacke (center) and John Sengstacke meet with officials from the People's Republic of China, 1990. Although he eschewed the limelight, it was Fred who managed the newspaper on a day-to-day basis.

*Courtesy of Chicago Defender Charities*

Publisher Eugene Scott and reporter Beverly Reed with Illinois State Senator Barack Obama in *The Defender*'s editorial boardroom, February 11, 2000, during Obama's failed bid to win the Democratic nomination for the First Congressional District.

*Courtesy of Chicago Defender Charities*

Barack Obama marches down Martin Luther King Drive—once called South Parkway—with Michelle Obama and supporters at the Bud Billiken Parade, 2006. Obama's election culminated more than a century of political strategizing and collective effort from those who staffed *The Defender*.

*Courtesy of Chicago Defender Charities*

me feel I 'belonged' there with his gesture," McAlpin wrote, "and I appreciated it."

It is unclear whether the press secretary had a change of heart about the presence of a black reporter in the White House or was simply acquiescing to a fait accompli. But in the end, whether by accident or intent, Early neglected to introduce McAlpin to the president formally, as tradition dictated. McAlpin, intent on meeting the president in any event, approached Roosevelt, who smiled broadly and extended his hand upward from the desk he sat behind.

"I'm glad to see you McAlpin," FDR said, gripping the reporter's hand firmly, "and very happy to have you here."

It was a simple handshake, accompanying a spare, cordial greeting, but it could not have registered more clearly as a final, irrevocable order from the president of the United States about the right of African Americans to freedom of the press.[44]

# 14

## Santa Claus and a World War

I N JULY 1944, with President Roosevelt's health failing and national elections looming, *The Defender*'s political reporters covering the Democratic National Convention in Chicago focused their
attention on the party's selection of FDR's vice presidential candidate and potential successor. Having dumped Vice President Henry
Wallace as too liberal for white southerners threatening to sabotage
FDR's renomination, the Democrats had settled on U.S. Senator
Harry Truman from Missouri. The selection of the moderate Truman was intended as a compromise, but *The Defender*'s scribes predicted that the African Americans who made up key voting blocs in
northern cities would swing back to the Republicans in support of
nominee Thomas Dewey, the governor of New York.

Dewey had appointed many African Americans to important
positions in his state, White House correspondent Harry McAlpin
noted, and the Republican Party had included a civil rights plank in
its platform that was even stronger than the Democrats'. "Right now,"
McAlpin wrote, "the Republicans are way out in the lead on paper."[1]

In his column, Lucius Harper complained that the African American electorate was a "political orphan" in this contest, with imperfect
candidates in both major parties. One of Dewey's major supporters
was a notorious anti-Semite who had been involved with the German American Bund, a pro-Nazi organization, before the war, a position that Harper said surely meant that he was unfriendly to African
Americans as well. As for Truman, Harper noted that he came from
a "small Missouri town where a black man can't even buy a 'coke' in
a drug store, café or restaurant," and had entered national politics
as the protégé of a corrupt St. Louis political boss. Hoping for a real

alternative, Harper called on Vice President Wallace to form an independent third party.[2]

Recognizing that the crucial African American electorate was at stake, President Roosevelt turned to Black Chicago's new congressman, William Levi Dawson, a tall Georgia native who had served as an officer during the First World War only to lose a foot in a train accident in peacetime. Dawson also happened to be a former Republican alderman who had deftly switched over to the Democrats before running for Congress, and had since established himself as a savvy political boss in the mold of his onetime mentor Ed Wright. Although still the only African American in the U.S. Congress (just for the moment, since Adam Clayton Powell was that same year seeking to represent the district that included Harlem), Dawson was appointed assistant chairman of the Democratic National Committee, the highest rank an African American had ever achieved in the party apparatus.[3]

Hardly thrilled about Truman's selection either, Dawson nevertheless saw him as a moderate alternative to recalcitrant southerners like James F. Byrne, the pro-segregation U.S. senator from South Carolina, who also had been angling for the vice presidency. Still, the grumbling about Truman's selection among the masses prompted Dawson to shift into high gear on behalf of the ticket in early August. Under the headline "FDR Against Army Jim Crow," Dawson gave an exclusive, wide-ranging interview to *The Defender* in which he relayed a pledge from President Roosevelt to desegregate the U.S. Armed Forces "if the war effort was not hindered," as the newspaper paraphrased it. Although FDR's pledge was loaded with caveats, Dawson touted it along with a promise that if Democrats kept their majorities in Congress, the hated poll taxes and other impediments to African American voters in the South would be eliminated. Finally, he did his best to assuage doubts by citing Truman's pro–civil rights votes in the U.S. Senate.[4]

Dawson's careful efforts for the ticket were almost undone in late October, however, when a reporter for the *Chicago Tribune* asked Truman about a rumor that he had been a member of the Ku Klux Klan. Truman denied the charge, calling it a "lie out of the whole cloth," adding that he had fought the Klan during his years as a local elected official in Missouri and alleging that the accusations were "cooked up by Hearst and McCormick," who had positioned their newspapers as decidedly pro-Dewey. "The Klan is repugnant to every policy and every principle I have advocated and struggled for my whole life," Truman wrote in a long telegram he sent to the NAACP.

The vice presidential nominee did not exactly deny the account, however, given by Alabama Governor Chauncey Sparks, of a meeting in which Truman had declared his support for states' rights — a phrase many white southerners both used and heard as a euphemism for segregation — and called himself the "son of an unreconstructed rebel mother." On this issue, Truman protested to the NAACP that his views had been misconstrued, rather than misquoted, and referred to his voting record as proof that he was pro–civil rights, underscoring his support for legislation that would enforce equal employment opportunities, ban lynching, and fund the National Youth Administration. "Especially I believe that on issues affecting fair treatment of Negroes, there is no legislation which has not had my support," Truman told the NAACP. "All I ask is that I be judged on my record."[5]

The Roosevelt/Truman team needn't have worried, as the African American community came out in force for the Democrats on Election Day. *The Defender* published the electoral totals in the black districts of northern cities on the top of the front page: in Chicago's Second and Third Wards, Roosevelt blew past his previous record to garner better than 62 percent — more than fifty-two thousand votes — and scored similarly well in Kansas City, Baltimore, and Philadelphia, all stunning results in places that had once been Republican strongholds. The president won 80 percent of ballots cast in New York, Detroit, and Philadelphia, and even captured majorities in the black communities of upstate Rochester and Buffalo, as well as in the major metro areas of New Jersey. In both Maryland and Pennsylvania, the leaders of the black organizations within the state Democratic parties claimed that their turnout, combined with the efforts of labor unions, had been the decisive factors in winning the state.

Whatever doubts there might be about the future, the Democratic coalition for the moment was intact, held together by FDR's personal magnetism and the nation's need for his leadership through the final months of the bloody world war. John Sengstacke, quoted in *The Defender*'s postelection coverage, saw the campaign as an example of "liberal and progressive forces working together in unison," while

Congressman Dawson, who had won his own race for reelection with a first-ever Democratic majority in the Second Ward, told the newspaper, "Negro Americans of all political parties forgot party lines and came to support President Roosevelt."

Even the few remaining black Republicans had to concede that Roosevelt was irresistible in this race. "You can't beat Santa Claus and a world war," said Perry Howard, a prominent African American attorney and a Republican committeeman in Mississippi.[6]

FDR died just a few months after the inauguration, on April 12, 1945, and while his death was long expected, a wave of grief washed over African American communities across the country. *The Defender* filled the first issue immediately following Roosevelt's death with paeans to his accomplishments for African Americans, noting that common people and high-level officials alike shared in their respect and admiration for the fallen president. The newspaper's Washington correspondent quoted adoring black staff members at the spa in Warm Springs, Georgia, where the president had died, and described townspeople and farmers who lined up along the tracks to salute the funeral train as it steamed to Washington, D.C.

One full page of photographs showed FDR shaking hands with African Americans from a variety of backgrounds: in one shot, he embraced an aged professor at Tuskegee University from the seat of his convertible; in another, he grasped the hand of a uniformed Navy mess man who had been wounded in combat; while yet another showed FDR with the president of the Republic of Liberia, the West African nation founded by freed American slaves, which Roosevelt had visited during his tenure. Roosevelt's vigorous handshake and warm smile conveyed respect and compassion at a time when many whites would have revolted at the prospect of touching a black person, let alone shaking his hand as an equal.

Other photos captured the crowd in Washington that had gathered along the route of FDR's funeral procession, confirming this was a rare moment of national racial solidarity, whites standing shoulder to shoulder with blacks, all of them shedding tears equally for the man who had not only rescued the nation from the Great Depression, but had led them as well to the brink of victory in the Second World War.[7]

At a time when the voices of African American leaders were rare on national radio broadcasts, both Mary McLeod Bethune and John Sengstacke were given time on the Blue Network, the forerunner of the American Broadcasting Company, to express their feelings about the president's passing. Bethune recalled the friendly greeting she received when she visited FDR in the Oval Office early in the administration and praised his vim attitude as much as his considerable accomplishments. "It was not single acts for which we felt so grateful as they were being unfolded," Bethune said. "It was the largeness of his heart, the breadth of his philosophy and the intensity of his determination."[8]

Sengstacke credited FDR with passing legislation and, when it failed, issuing executive orders that guaranteed equal employment opportunities, and for appointing high-level African American officials who "shared in the planning that brought increased school facilities, kept young people in school, gave work experience to out-of-school youth, gave adults a chance to work and helped in the rehabilitation of farm families."[9]

Lucius Harper, among many others, compared Roosevelt with Abraham Lincoln, but he went further than most in his column when he found FDR superior in several respects to the Great Emancipator. Attributing FDR's compassion to his disability, Harper touted Roosevelt's verbal support for integration of the military and in the broader society. "Both [Lincoln and Roosevelt] had wisdom and vision when it came to dealing with it but Roosevelt, by fair comparison, had the greater vision," wrote Harper. As for FDR's political gamesmanship and the fact that the administration had left segregation in the South unchallenged, he glossed over these failings. "In [FDR's] passing," wrote Harper, "the Negro lost one of his greatest friends."[10]

Another *Defender* columnist, who went by the pen name Charley Cherokee, summarized the feelings of many in more vernacular terms: "He's gone, chum, we're on our own. Franklin Roosevelt held us up for 13 years, now we have to stand on our own feet. And y'know, we can do it. We don't have to worry about how Harry Truman or anyone else will act. We don't have to be afraid of anyone or anything."[11]

· · ·

In his first address to the public after Roosevelt's death, Truman pledged that he would continue his predecessor's policies. But the new president alarmed black leaders with some of his first moves, not least his choice of Senator James Byrnes of South Carolina as secretary of state, along with several other white southerners for important cabinet positions. Amid all the tributes in the issue of *The Defender* following FDR's death were a number of articles that, by criticizing Truman, aimed to mobilize African Americans for this new political battle. An editorial entitled "The President Leaves a Legacy" advanced the FDR/Lincoln analogy to worry aloud that Truman would reprise Lincoln's vice president Andrew Johnson, who, no sooner than he took office, attempted to end Reconstruction and restore the former Confederates to power. To ensure that Truman lived up to his promises as well as FDR's legacy, the editorial warned that African Americans, organized labor, and other elements of Roosevelt's coalition would have to stay united as well as vigilant.[12]

Amid all the skepticism in the air over Truman's leadership, White House correspondent Harry McAlpin entered the new president's first press conference a few days later with some trepidation. When his turn finally came, McAlpin opened with a long preamble praising FDR and then asked Truman to "assure 13 million of your fellow Americans who today look hopefully to you." Truman responded by referring McAlpin to his record in the U.S. Senate, as he had done during the presidential campaign. It was not Truman's words that impressed McAlpin, however, so much as the way the new president held his gaze during their exchange. After the conference, as each reporter filed out shaking hands with the new president, Truman hung on to McAlpin for an extended period with a firm grip. "He said he was sure that if I looked up his senate record not only would I find where he stood but that I would be pleased with what I found," McAlpin wrote in his column that week. "He said the Negro had nothing to fear."[13]

Truman continued his friendly if ambiguous relations with the black press throughout that spring, embracing McAlpin at his press conferences and sitting down for an interview with the publisher of *The St. Louis Argus,* the main African American newspaper in his home state. In May, Truman met with the executive committee of

the NNPA, led by John Sengstacke, which included the owners of
*The Pittsburgh Courier,* the *Afro-American,* and all the other major
black newspapers, who came in with a long collective agenda: fair
employment legislation; executive action to enforce voting rights in
the South; and, with the war winding down and black soldiers returning home, the appointment of an African American to a senior position at the Veterans Administration, among other items.

"The publishers reported that the president received their statements with interest and cordiality," wrote Harry McAlpin in his article about the meeting, "but made no express commitments." Mysteriously, Truman also refused to pose for a picture with the publishers.[14]

In the spring of 1945, Frank "Fay" Young, now the dean of African
American sportswriters, was called to cover a press conference held
by Branch Rickey, the bombastic owner of the Brooklyn Dodgers
baseball franchise. Rickey announced that he was launching a new, all-
black team called the Brown Dodgers as part of an entirely new league
for African American players, with which he intended to replace the
two existing Negro Leagues. For the past two years, Rickey said, his
scouts had documented pervasive problems in the operations of the
current black teams: gambling and drunkenness were rife among the
players, while many of the owners were themselves involved in criminal enterprises, the policy rackets in particular. Rickey's agents alleged that even the umpires in the Negro Leagues were compromised,
their calls frequently favoring the home teams. The Brown Dodgers,
by contrast, would benefit from his professional management. In addition, they would be able to play in his Ebbets Field while the white
Dodgers were playing away games. He concluded by expressing his
hope that other white owners would be inspired to show a similar
interest in African American players and fans.

Fay Young was deeply offended by Rickey's characterization of the
Negro Leagues, even as he acknowledged the truth in many of the
charges. Noting that a new antidiscrimination law had been recently
enacted in New York State, Young accused Rickey of merely trying
to appease activists and pointed out that on the single issue black
sportswriters really cared about — the integration of major-league
baseball — the Dodgers owner had evaded a direct answer. "We want

Negroes in the major leagues if they have to crawl to get there but we won't have the major league owners running a segregated league for us," Young wrote. "Rickey is no Abraham Lincoln or Franklin D. Roosevelt, and we won't accept him as the dictator of Negro baseball."[15]

A few months later, Young received new intelligence that Rickey's previous announcement of creating his own black team had been a smokescreen to obscure his true intent. Actually, Rickey had been scouting the Negro Leagues for a black player who could finally break baseball's color barrier, and had settled on a shortstop with the Kansas City Monarchs named Jackie Robinson. Personable, intelligent, and blessed with all-around athletic ability, having lived most of his life in multiracial Pasadena, California, and served as a lieutenant with the U.S. Army during the war, Robinson would surely be able to represent the African American community with dignity, maintaining a sense of calm and cool in the face of what was certain to be a barrage of racist criticism.

To verify the rumors, Young waited until Robinson came to Chicago to play the American Giants in a double-header in Comiskey Park, confronting him during the break between games. Robinson demurred at first, but when pressed, hinted that he was headed to a meeting with the Dodgers owner. Annoyed by the vagueness of this answer, Young admonished the ballplayer in his column, writing that "Robinson will have to learn that he owes something to the public."[16]

At the end of October, Rickey signed Robinson to the Montreal Royals, a minor-league affiliate of the Dodgers, with the explicit understanding that this was a trial run for a major-league team. Now Fay was thrilled, writing an article on the front page that compared Robinson's assignation to the Royals with Joe Louis's defeat of James Braddock in 1937. Even if promotion to the majors was not yet certain, Robinson's selection to the minor leagues, Young noted, was itself progress, as he was the first African American player to make it *this* far.[17]

An editorial published the following week piled on the praise for Rickey, lauding him for defying other baseball officials as well as a few players, including his own outfielder Dixie Walker, a native of Birmingham, Alabama, who vowed the team would refuse to share the field with Robinson. "In some quarters," the editorial explained, "the announcement had the impact of an atomic bomb on a few of the race-prejudiced Southern brothers."[18]

In the fall of 1946, a twenty-eight-year-old recent arrival from the South named Vernon Jarrett walked into *Defender* editor Metz Lochard's office and applied for a job as a reporter. Having dreamed of working at the newspaper ever since performing a monologue as Robert Abbott in his first-grade class in Paris, Tennessee, Jarrett was confident that Lochard would be impressed by his previous experience editing a militant newspaper for his fellow black sailors in the Navy and writing articles for his college publication. Lochard sat at his desk, surrounded by scattered page proofs and newspapers from around the world, and read through Jarrett's samples with interest, but in the end rebuffed the young applicant. Jarrett was persistent, however, trying for over a month before finally landing a position as a general-assignment reporter at $40 a week. "Hell," Jarrett recalled to a biographer some decades later, "I would have paid them to let me work there."[19]

And so this ambitious young man joined *The Defender*'s storied newsroom on South Indiana Avenue, awed to be among "all those famous names in black journalism"—Fay Young, Lucius Harper, Enoch Waters, Dave Kellum, and Albert Barnett. For Jarrett, as for many other young staffers, Harper proved an invaluable resource of context and history while Lochard provided the technical training new reporters invariably needed, cultivating a scholarly approach to journalism based on extensive research and verification. Reporting in Bronzeville in those days was not for the faint of heart. Jarrett was horrified by the random crime scenes he found himself covering, most of all the fires that raged through the overcrowded tenements, each one with a shocking death toll of women and children trapped in the airless warrens in which black Chicagoans were forced to live.[20]

But it was his experiences covering politics on Chicago's South Side that tempered Jarrett's idealism with hard lessons about how things truly worked. In November, he was assigned to report on the general elections in which Republicans swept into majorities in the U.S. House as well as the Senate, all the way down to many local offices in Cook County—everywhere except for Bronzeville, where

U.S. Representative Bill Dawson defeated his Republican rival by nearly ten thousand votes.

Jarrett did not think much of Dawson, whom he considered too moderate in speech and too conciliatory in action. In conversation with his radical friends, he even labeled the congressman an Uncle Tom. Jarrett tried, unsuccessfully as it happened, to conceal his contempt when he interviewed Dawson after the election, but the canny, world-weary pol sensed Jarrett's disapproval and laughed it off. "Just print in your little story that Bill Dawson's machine rolled again," he told Jarrett, shocking the young reporter with his bluntness.

"That's right," Dawson added, "I said machine. Because that's what I've got. And it's the best machine — white or Negro — anywhere in this country."

Dawson then turned the tables on Jarrett and cut to the heart of his query: "What you really want to know is how does old Dawson win without making a lot of loud speeches, isn't it? Well, let me tell you something. The world is full of orators, but it isn't full of organizers. In this Second Ward, we've got organizers. I don't need to make speeches to get the vote out."[21]

If Dawson shocked Jarrett with the realities of Bronzeville politics, the young reporter confronted the truculence on the other side of the color line later that month when he covered a coalition of activists, labor organizers, and city officials as they tried to facilitate a black family's move into a public housing development in an all-white section of the Southwest Side. Previously, Chicago Housing Authority projects for black residents had been built only in black neighborhoods, while those built in white areas had only white tenants. But CHA board chairman Robert Taylor and his executive director, Elizabeth Wood, a white woman with a history as an integration activist, determined that the agency would do something to alleviate the housing shortage for the city's African Americans and decided to make a test case of the Airport Homes, a temporary development of two-story homes for veterans located near Midway Airport.[22]

Jarrett was inside the second-floor apartment designated for an African American veteran and his family when a mob of two hundred white men, women, and children from the neighborhood marched into the development and began to throw stones and mud at the building, chanting racist slogans and calling the whites outside "nigger lovers." City officials responded quickly, sending hundreds of police officers to keep the white mob at bay, and the strong show of force kept the violence from getting out of hand. But there were still many other incidents, as when the police escorted Jarrett back to his car and one protester, shouting, "Maybe Hitler was right," had to be physically prevented from assaulting the reporter.[23]

Mayor Ed Kelly came out strongly against the rioters, support- ing the CHA's policy of providing housing on a nondiscriminatory basis, and vowed to dispatch police to protect black families mov- ing into the developments. The mayor's pledge notwithstanding, the first black family in Airport Homes left soon after the mob attack, prompting The Defender's editorial page to warn that while the riot- ers in Airport Homes were targeting African Americans today, they would surely vent their rage at others if this kind of mob action was allowed to succeed. The newspaper called for concerted action from a united front of progressives and ethnics to block a deterioration of basic rights. "Only a determined stand by the mass of citizens can prevent the present condition from mushrooming until the basic freedoms upon which our country was founded are stolen from the people."[24]

A few weeks later, the CHA tried to move two more black fami- lies into Airport Homes, only to encounter an even larger mob of two thousand whites, who battled police in the streets for two full days. Under the headline "Crossroads for Democracy," The Defender printed a section of photos taken by a courageous staff photogra- pher who covered this incident: at the top was an image of a throng of enraged whites, mainly middle-aged men in hats and overcoats and women in coats and kerchiefs, who were trying to push past a line of policemen. Other photos included an image of white activ- ists offering insouciant smiles as they carried the belongings of one of the black families into the Airport Homes as well as a shot of the two black veterans assigned to live there, both of whom had been awarded for their combat experience in Europe and the Far East, re- spectively.[25]

These families endured the threats for only a few days before, late at night, someone fired several rounds at their homes; both asked CHA officials to move them out the next morning. Discerning a hidden hand stirring up racist passions and inciting "organized terrorism," *The Defender*'s editorial page again sounded the alarm. The crowd had set fire to a four-foot-tall wooden cross much like those used by the Klan, and the editorial worried that this was evidence that the racism that had long been a fact of life in the South was being purposely imported to the North. "It is incredible to see developing before our eyes the full pattern of fascism transplanted from Eastern Europe," the editorial stated, noting clear ideological links between the sentiments of these working-class white Americans and the extreme right-wing movements that had so recently dominated Europe, "with a dash of local color to give it the American smell."[26]

Later that month, the battle over Airport Homes claimed its first political victim when Mayor Ed Kelly announced he would not run for reelection in the elections scheduled for early in 1947. Kelly had built one of the nation's most efficient and reliable political organizations but he had been mortally wounded, career-wise, when he backed the heads of the CHA and deployed police in sizable numbers to stop the white mobs at Airport Homes. Though the mayor won enthusiastic praise from *The Defender* and would have been sure to get a big turnout from black voters if he ran, the city's whites were outraged by his advocacy for integrated housing. Democratic Party bosses conducted telephone surveys of potential voters and found that whites were only moderately upset with Kelly for his perceived ties to organized crime, but were up in arms over the Airport Homes incidents. "The white voters didn't like Kelly," reported Jacob Arvey, one of the party bosses. "They said he had been 'too good to the niggers' what with this public housing business."[27]

Kelly had no choice but to step aside and let Arvey, William Dawson, and the other Democratic Party bosses choose his replacement. But until his last moments in office, the mayor raised concerns about the city's housing crisis, as he did during an interview in the January 25, 1947, issue of *The Defender* after a week in which three separate fires claimed eleven lives and left more than a hundred families homeless in Bronzeville. The city was short at least 137,000 housing units, Kelly told the newspaper, but while there was ample land to build, neither the government nor the private sector would pony up the dollars that were needed.[28]

An editorial from that same week placed blame for the fires on the conditions wrought by the confluence of restrictive covenants, the banking sector's discriminatory practices, and the ever-present threat of white violence. The tone of this editorial, however, was even grimmer than in previous weeks, as it was increasingly clear that there would be no immediate relief from the construction of new public housing. Every elected official understood now that there were large contingents of whites who would take to the streets to prevent African Americans from living next door to them and what was worse, these mobs were supported by the sentiments of the silent majority at the ballot box. "Negro children and women are dying like rats in fires in dilapidated homes unfit for human habitation, homes that are in reality firetraps which should have been condemned long ago by responsible officials," the editorial concluded.

"Something must be done and done quickly if greater tragedies are to be avoided."[29]

"Branch Rickey Sr., president of the Brooklyn Dodgers, is truly on the spot," wrote Fay Young in his weekly sports column the week of March 29, 1947. On one side, Rickey had been hinting for over a year that he was going to make Jackie Robinson the first African American player in major-league baseball and, with just a few days left before the season officially opened, the nation's black sportswriters and pro-integration activists were pressuring him to make it official. But on the other side, Rickey was also being pressured by a gang of his own players, mainly men from the South, who were threatening radical action if an African American joined their team.

Rickey was finally forced to act when Dixie Walker and several other southerners began circulating a petition that protested Robinson's impending move to their team while the Dodgers were playing exhibition games in Central America. The Dodgers' owner flew down to Panama to meet the team, Young reported, and confronted the recalcitrant players individually in a series of meetings in which he threatened them frankly: "If there is any rock of prejudice, then we'll remove the rock."[30]

Backed by a firm, unified stand from the team's manager and coaches, the protests were tamped down. Then, on Thursday, April 10, Robinson was at bat in the sixth inning of an exhibition game with the Royals in Ebbets Field when the Dodgers' press secretary handed reporters a press release announcing that Robinson would indeed play for Brooklyn and break the color barrier in baseball. This event was reported triumphantly in *The Defender* with a strip of photographs of Robinson across the front page and a full page inside.[31]

It was a triumphant moment indeed, but Fay Young, who had fought for the integration of professional sports since his first days at *The Defender* in Mrs. Lee's kitchen, knew that the task was not yet complete. In Jackie Robinson, Branch Rickey had selected an athlete of exemplary character, but now this experiment in desegregation was facing a new test as African American fans, who had been a small percentage of those in the stands until then, came out to support him. In his column, Young tried to ensure that the blacks who came to the ballparks behaved, admonishing the readers of his column that their conduct would play an important role in determining whether Robinson succeeded or not. "The Negro fan can help Robinson," Young wrote. "The Negro fan can ruin him."

With a game between the Dodgers and the Cubs scheduled for several weeks later in Chicago's Wrigley Field, Young was particularly concerned that Bronzeville make a good showing, and warned the "rowdy element" in the community not to drink whiskey or use profane language in the stands. As for those who chose to misbehave, Young warned that Sylvester Washington, a tough African American Chicago police officer better known as "Two Gun Pete," would be patrolling the stands.[32]

Nearly seven years after Robert Abbott's death, his nephew John Sengstacke continued to face multiple challenges to his control over *The Defender*. In the summer of 1947, Sengstacke and attorney James Cashin filed opposing lawsuits, as Cashin charged Sengstacke with incompetence and demanded $20,000 in payment for his services, while Sengstacke asked the court to remove Cashin as executor. The proceedings went on through the fall, and Sengstacke accused Cashin of extending the court case so that he could continue milking the company even as he tried to hire a white journalist as a receiver to oversee the newspaper.

Finally, in late December, Sengstacke and Cashin came to an agreement, canceling the order to hire a receiver as well as the suit to have Cashin removed as executor. A front-page article under the headline "Negro-Owned Always: *Defender* Suits Dropped" underscored that all the parties involved had acted "in a determination that no white person would ever control, and that there would always be a *Chicago Defender* in Negro hands." The article also announced that Sengstacke had bought out all of the stock inherited by Edna Abbott's children when she died some months earlier, which meant that for the first time ever, he was in full command of the newspaper.[33]

No sooner had he solved these long-standing legal issues over *The Defender*'s ownership, however, than Sengstacke had to turn his attention to a resurgence of the newspaper's labor troubles. Thirty members of the typographical union went on strike that winter in a wage dispute, a battle that was also fought in the pages of other newspapers. Sengstacke gave an interview to the *Chicago Tribune* and reprinted his correspondence with the union local's president in *The Defender*, arguing that he had tried to negotiate in good faith, but that the union's expectations that he would pay the same rates as the white-owned dailies were simply unreasonable. Discrimination, after all, prevented the newspaper from securing advertising, getting bank loans, purchasing equipment, and growing circulation. "As a Negro newspaper," he pleaded in a telegram to the union president, "we are circumscribed by all the business limitations imposed on our race."

The strike was part of a citywide protest from the International Typographical Union against the provisions of antiunion legislation then wending its way through the U.S. Congress, but it was also the result of the complicated arrangement that had emerged after Sengstacke's lockout of the entire white printing staff in 1934. After that, *The Defender* hired African Americans who, though technically members of the union, paid at union rates and paying union dues, were not allowed to work at other plants, as their white colleagues were. The printers' loyalty was further divided because many of them had been personally recruited by Sengstacke, and some were even fellow Hamptonites. For a time, only the typographers went on strike, while the stereotypers, engravers, and mailers kept on working through the picketing. The editorial employees, who were members of the Newspaper Guild, also sat out the strike, as did the advertising, circulation, and business departments.

Enoch Waters, who, because of his own time at Hampton, was assigned to serve as a liaison between the printers and the editorial department, recalled that many of the printers "felt that, as *Defender* employees, they were making a contribution to the struggle for civil rights that was crucial to them and their children. However, as union members, they had to walk off their jobs when *The Defender* rejected the contract, even though there was some injustice in requiring the paper to live up to an obligation over which it had no say."

The strike stretched on for months, however, and in time, the other departments walked out to join their colleagues, leaving Sengstacke to scramble to keep producing his newspaper. He turned to the *Tribune*, which, also affected by the strike, had switched to a new technology called photoengraving, which neatly circumvented the typographical process. The *Tribune* agreed to use this new system to help publish *The Defender* as well, and while the first few issues that were produced this way were less than elegant, with a font resembling that of a typewriter, Sengstacke gradually managed to refill his ranks with nonunion printers. The new crew slowly returned the newspaper to its former quality and then surpassed it, expanding the graphics and enhancing the images.[34]

By the beginning of 1948, with the black vote in key northern states deemed essential to his reelection chances, President Truman became a vociferous advocate for African American causes. After appointing a civil rights commission that roamed the country conducting a wide-ranging investigation, the president made a major speech to the U.S. Congress in February, when he issued a ten-point proposal he called an "American charter of human freedom." A far-reaching set of bills that would have brought to an end discrimination against African Americans, Native Americans, Latinos, Asians, Jews, and religious minorities, Truman's charter sought to outlaw lynching, guarantee voting rights, grant statehood to Alaska and Hawaii, allow residents of the District of Columbia to elect their own representatives, and compensate Japanese Americans for their incarceration during the war, among other provisions. The package would have to be passed by both houses of the U.S. Congress, however, and it was unlikely this would happen. Truman also spoke about an issue, the end of segregation in the military as well as the federal government, which he could accomplish by executive fiat. "We cannot be satisfied," the president told Congress, "until all our people have equal opportunities for jobs, for homes, for education, for health and for political expression, and until all people have equal protection under the law."[35]

Truman's words provoked a visceral rage among southern governors, who were meeting just then in Florida. "We have been betrayed by the leadership of the Democratic Party," explained Governor Benjamin T. Laney of Arkansas. These embittered stalwarts began to discuss strategies to stop the party's clear tilt toward civil rights, even countenancing acts of self-sabotage against a Democratic candidate that would cause a loss to a Republican.[36]

Dismissing the southerners' threats, *The Defender's* editorial page praised the president's entire package as "a courageous attack upon racism in America and a noble declaration of principles." Sengstacke deployed the NNPA on Truman's behalf, presenting him with the first-ever John Russwurm citation, named for the very first African American publisher, whose newspaper, *Freedom's Journal,* was printed in New York City from 1827 to 1829. In a ceremony that was broadcast over the NBC radio network to celebrate National Negro Newspaper Week, the president was honored with an award along with Jackie Robinson, Branch Rickey, and Thurgood Marshall, among others.[37]

Not everyone at *The Defender,* however, was so favorably disposed toward Truman: elder statesman W. E. B. Du Bois regularly used his weekly column to assail the president on his foreign and domestic policies in the strongest possible terms, as when he labeled Truman's plan to arm the Greek military against Communists "the most stupid and dangerous proposal ever made by the leader of a great modern nation."

After the "American charter" speech, Du Bois questioned Truman's motives and predicted that the Democrats would reject the president's raft of ideas just as they had Roosevelt's efforts to advance racial justice. Sure, Truman would make some high-profile appointments of African Americans to political jobs, and the black press would get advertising dollars, but the great majority of African Americans, Du Bois argued, would not benefit.

Du Bois used his *Defender* column as well to express his adulation of former vice president Henry Wallace, who was now heading the ticket for the newly created Progressive Party. Extolling Wallace for his outspoken opposition to segregation, Du Bois urged African Americans to support him, even if that meant subtracting crucial support from Truman. In his own proposal for sabotage of the Truman campaign, Du Bois argued that if Truman lost as a result of black support for Wallace, that would only serve to drive home the point that the African American electorate could not be taken for granted. "We can protest," Du Bois asserted, "even if our protests put a reactionary Republican in the White House or a Southern-supported Democrat. At least we can let the country and the nations know that there are people in the United States who are not stupid, who cannot be bought with graft or fooled with lies."[38]

The fact was, Wallace's insurrection was building up steam and beginning to pose a real threat to Truman. *The Defender* covered the Progressives' convention at the Chicago Stadium at which more than two thousand delegates from across the country, including many African Americans, rallied under the slogan "Third Party or Third War." Broadcast coast to coast, Wallace's speech to twenty-two thousand people at the convention immediately attracted droves of new supporters to his fledgling party.[39]

Having begun to imagine that the momentum was shifting to Wallace, Du Bois kept up his harangue of Truman through the spring, criticizing the president for abandoning Jews who were attempting to form their own nation in the British colony of Palestine. Horrified by the atrocities perpetrated by the Nazis during the war, Du Bois wholeheartedly supported the establishment of a state of Israel, and characterized Truman's equivocation as "one act for which President Truman and his advisors can be utterly and finally condemned and refused the support of all decent-thinking people."[40]

That was to be Du Bois's final column in *The Defender*. For while Sengstacke never attempted to exercise control over the content in the newspaper, believing in the autonomy of his editors, he concluded that Du Bois had simply grown too close to the Wallace campaign. It was a far more difficult decision, however, to fire Metz Lochard, who had been Robert Abbott's aide-de-camp and had guided the editorial department in the years that Sengstacke was battling for ownership of *The Defender*. But Lochard, too, had affiliated too closely with the quixotic Wallace campaign and had to go as well; tellingly, immediately after his departure, Lochard took a formal position with the Progressive Party itself. To run the newsroom, Sengstacke brought Louis Martin back to Chicago.[41]

"The United States Supreme Court has made perhaps the greatest contribution to American democracy within its power to make," began a *Defender* editorial on May 15, 1948, celebrating the recent decision to finally invalidate the hated restrictive covenants across the country. After dithering on the issue for years, the justices' 6–0 ruling in the case of *Shelley v. Kraemer*, which stemmed from a house in St. Louis covered by a racist covenant, was unequivocal, declaring that the practice violated the equal protection clause of the Fourteenth Amendment, among other laws. This time, states were specifically enjoined from upholding the covenants, which *The Defender* hoped would open new neighborhoods to black settlement, finally providing relief for the desperately overcrowded conditions within Bronzeville and similar areas across the nation. The decision marked the greatest success yet for the young chief of the NAACP's legal department, Thurgood Marshall, as well as for President Harry Truman, who had dispatched his solicitor general to support Marshall.

"These covenants have been responsible for more human misery, more crime, more disease and violence than any other factor in our society," continued the editorial. "They have been used to build the biggest ghettoes in history. They have been used to pit race against race and to intensify racial and religious prejudice in every quarter."[42]

In Chicago, the ruling canceled restrictions covering forty square miles on the South Side and ten square miles on the North Side, validating the work of the local branch of the NAACP, which had tried to break the covenants by organizing sympathetic real estate agents as well as black families willing to rent or buy in exclusive neighborhoods. The NAACP had successfully placed three thousand African Americans in such homes and then dragged out every ensuing court case, using every possible legal maneuver to contest and delay. Through these tactics, the NAACP lawyers had been able to keep everyone in their home except one family who, sadly, had been evicted just days before the Supreme Court ruling.

"The racial bigots in the field of housing have been completely routed," wrote NAACP attorney Loring B. Moore in a commentary printed by *The Defender.*[43]

On one evening in June 1948, the president traveled to Chicago for a dinner with an exclusive guest list of forty civic and business leaders, including Congressman Bill Dawson, Mayor Martin Kennelly, *Tribune* owner Robert R. McCormick, the prince of Sweden, and John Sengstacke. Although the conversation was off-the-record, an article appeared in the next issue of *The Defender* mentioning the dinner and quoting Sengstacke as having confidence in the president when it came to racial justice: "President Truman is firm on his civil rights stand," stated the article.[44]

By the time of the Democratic National Convention in July, Sengstacke had shifted *The Defender*'s support into high gear. "We March Forward with Truman," read the banner over the masthead on the front page for the issue of the week following the convention. An attached editorial called on Henry Wallace to get out of the race, and criticized the Republicans, represented once again by New York governor Thomas Dewey, for failing to adopt a sufficient civil rights plank. Amid all the accolades, the editorial continued to prod Truman to use his power to desegregate the armed forces, though it concluded that for African Americans, the president was likely their best available option before them. "Negro Americans have but one intelligent choice," the editorial summed up. "A vote for any other candidate is a vote against himself."[45]

Truman's reborn commitment to civil rights only further incensed the white-supremacist wing of the Democratic Party, however, and shortly after the official Democratic convention in Philadelphia, a rival States Rights' Democratic Party held its own convention in Birmingham, nominating U.S. Senator Strom Thurmond of South Carolina for president and Mississippi governor Fielding Wright for vice president. With Confederate flags hanging on the walls, one speaker confided to the audience that the States' Rights Democrats, or "Dixiecrats," as they were commonly known, had little chance of winning, but could scuttle the chances of the mainstream Democrats, which itself would be a better outcome than a Truman victory. "We must prove to the nation that this time," Thurmond said in his acceptance speech, "the South means business."[46]

Truman, however, was resolute, and on July 24 he issued two executive orders ending segregation in the U.S. Armed Forces as well as discrimination in all sections of the federal government. The first order called for the creation of a seven-man presidential advisory committee that was authorized to conduct a top-to-bottom investigation into the "rules, procedures and practices of the armed services." The second order mandated a fair employment practices policy similar to the one FDR had installed over war production–related industries, placing equal-employment officers in every department and overseeing hiring throughout the ranks of the civil service.[47]

In a telegram to Truman reprinted in *The Defender*, Sengstacke described the executive orders as a "mighty blow for freedom" before going on to announce in another article in the same issue that he was forming a fundraising initiative called the National Citizens Committee for the Re-election of President Truman along with Congressman Bill Dawson, Mary McLeod Bethune, and a host of other prominent academics and activists. With so many of the southern state Democratic organizations withholding political contributions from the Democratic National Committee, Sengstacke declared that this was the time to "Put up or shut up," by which he meant that African Americans should compensate for the loss of support on their own. "We will raise ten dollars for every one dollar withheld by the Dixiecrats who are fighting Mr. Truman over the Negro issue," Sengstacke pledged.[48]

It was the first initiative of its type in the African American community, and Sengstacke characterized it in almost religious terms as a "crusade, not a political campaign." Touring the country with Congressman Dawson, he spoke to African American groups wherever he could find them. "We took our message into the South, showing them how the New Deal had given them the great gains they now enjoy," Sengstacke wrote. "We squeezed into the Jim Crow section of a southern-bound train and explained to our people how President Truman's civil rights program meant the end of segregation and discrimination. We talked holding our heads high and walking into any place as free men without fear of embarrassment. Together we planned Jim Crow's funeral."

In Georgia, Dawson and Sengstacke met with a woman whose son had been beaten, burned, and hanged, assuring her that under Truman's next administration, "lynchers will be exposed as the murderers they are and brought to justice."

The duo traveled by train all through the South and the Southwest to California before turning back east to New York City, where they joined the president at a rally in Harlem. Having recruited eighty prominent vice chairmen from states in every region, the committee was garnering donations in small denominations from working-class men and women. Typical of the comments they received were those lines in a letter from one woman living in a Chicago tenement and working as a maid, who contributed five dollars to the campaign. "God is on Mr. Truman's side," she wrote in a letter attached to her bill. "So am I."

But if the president was solidifying his support in the African American community, he was, unfortunately, sinking among other key constituencies. Flanked on the left by Wallace and by Thurmond on the right, Truman was falling behind Dewey in the national polls. Despite his efforts to put a positive face on in public, Sengstacke described these as the "dark and gloomy days" of the campaign.[49]

On Friday, August 13, 1948, the Cleveland Indians played the Chicago White Sox before a record-setting full house of fifty-one thousand people at Comiskey Field, while yet another fifteen thousand frustrated fans stood outside. The big draw for the crowd that night was the debut of the Indians' newest pitcher, Satchel Paige, one of the greatest of all time. Paige had played in the Negro Leagues before moving to the majors, and now, at forty-four years old, was nearing the end of his career. But with a skill that rivaled Babe Ruth's or Lou Gehrig's, Paige pitched a near-perfect game, allowing just five hits in nine innings in which the White Sox were shut out 5–0.[50]

Under the headline "The Ways of White Folks," the newspaper recalled that in the past, major-league team owners had resisted bringing in black players by expressing their fears of driving white fans away and even provoking boycotts. The Defender's editorial page trumpeted the record attendance numbers at Comiskey as proof that integration benefited both blacks and whites. Just as Joe Louis and even Jack Johnson had in their own arenas, Jackie Robinson, Satchel Paige, and their cohort had exposed white fears for their irrationality. "In boxing, baseball, music and in other fields where the masses of white Americans have an opportunity to accept or reject Negroes and show their prejudice plainly," the editorial stated, "our boys and girls have won the greatest acclaim."[51]

Satchel Paige was actually the third black player in the major leagues, after Jackie Robinson and Larry Doby, and the Negro Leagues played on as well. Two days after Paige's debut, Vernon Jarrett accompanied Fay Young to Comiskey Park to see the sixteenth annual East-West Classic all-star game, where the best players from the Kansas City Monarchs, the Birmingham Black Barons, and the Chicago American Giants competed against their fellows from the New York Black Yankees and the Newark Eagles, among others.

In his column, Young covered the game with his usual reverence, detailing the plays and the players with respect for the skill that it took to engage in professional sports under the limitations of a racist society. But Young couldn't help but notice that this East-West Classic was different from its predecessors, with a noticeable lack of enthusiasm in the stands, if not on the field. Just over forty-two thousand fans came to Comiskey that day, leaving nine thousand vacant seats and the scalpers outside selling tickets at face value. Inside the park, the fans' collective mood was riven by politics — when the ballplayers stepped onto the field, they were introduced by some of the remaining Republican elected officials from Bronzeville, prompting a hail of boos from the Democrats in the crowd.[52]

Fay Young had been an advocate for interracial athletics for four decades, but he was fully aware that there was a downside to integration as well. Ever since Jackie Robinson had been hired by the Dodgers, the attendance and therefore the incomes of the individual Negro League teams had dropped precipitously, putting the entire network in jeopardy. The teams' finances had always been precarious, and they were dependent on the black press for publicity, but now the newspapers were losing interest as well, sending their sportswriters to cover Jackie Robinson's training sessions while ignoring the Negro League games. But if the Negro Leagues collapsed entirely, Young warned in his column, then a handful of black ballplayers would have gained at the expense of hundreds of others.[53]

Vernon Jarrett later recalled that Young watched this East-West Classic with tears streaming down his cheeks, saddened by the empty seats both in the stands and in the press box. At one point, Young stood up to salute the ballplayers and insisted that Jarrett do the same. "Just look at them," Young told Jarrett, gesturing at the field. "They're playing their hearts out. And they are doing it for themselves."

The image of Young weeping at the decline of the Negro Leagues was etched into Jarrett's memory as one of the final moments for this race-based institution and, ironically, one of the final moments of his tenure at *The Defender.* For Jarrett, too, would be fired as part of the purge of pro-Wallace staffers, subject to special sanction because he had been working precincts for Dawson's opponents after the workday was over, violating Sengstacke's red line of explicit political work. Having dreamed of working at *The Defender* since he was a child, Jarrett was injured by his firing as well as by the loss of income, but he resumed his journalism career promptly as a reporter with the Associated Negro Press, a wire service for black newspapers founded by a former *Defender* advertising salesman.[54]

In September, with just a few weeks to go before the national election, President Truman announced the appointment of John Sengstacke to the Committee on Equality of Treatment and Opportunity in the Armed Forces, assembled with the specific mandate to achieve "complete integration of all racial and religious minorities" in every branch of the military. Chaired by a former U.S. solicitor general, the seven-member committee included one other African American, Lester Granger, the national secretary of the Urban League, as well as several white businessmen and the president of Oberlin College. As detailed in the executive order, the committee would review all of the military's procedures and make recommendations directly to Truman as well as to the secretaries of the various service branches.[55]

But, of course, only if the president was reelected. Sengstacke's selection underscored just how important the campaign considered the publisher to the black electorate on the South Side of Chicago. The Republicans understood *The Defender*'s significance as well, taking out well-designed full-page ads under the slogan "Dewey Gets Things Done," and quoting speeches by the New York governor in which he pledged to work against racial and religious discrimination. Touting Dewey's passage of legislation banning racial and gender discrimination in employment as well as his construction of housing for veterans in New York, the Republican ads included photographs of black soldiers in uniform and promised that Dewey would work to end segregation in the military. "As far back as 1944," the ads maintained, "Gov. Dewey recognized the harsh conditions imposed upon colored citizens in our armed forces."[56]

The Truman campaign, too, placed full-page ads in *The Defender*: a portrait of the president surrounded by the images of African Americans who had been appointed to high-ranking federal positions, including governor of the Virgin Islands, United States Customs Court judge, the national civil rights commission, and Ralph Bunche as United Nations representative. "THIS IS A STORY ABOUT PROGRESS," read the all-caps headline over these photos. "YOU CAN'T AFFORD TO VOTE AGAINST PROGRESS."[57]

*The Defender*'s editorial page, meanwhile, pitched as strongly for Truman as it did against both Dewey and Wallace. The Republican candidate spoke positively when it came to civil rights, but vaguely, leading *The Defender* to argue that he couldn't be trusted. As for Wallace, several editorials alleged that the Progressive camp had been infiltrated by Communists who had a hidden agenda of sabotaging the Democrats. "No one believes that Mr. Wallace can possibly be elected president in 1948," the editorial reasoned, "and we believe that the votes he will get will only serve to kill off liberal Democrats who can be of practical assistance to us in our fight for first-class citizenship."[58]

Thurmond's insurgency, meanwhile, was proceeding right along with Wallace's, further dividing the Democrats in the run-up to national elections and heightening racial tensions, particularly in the South. In the cities of Atlanta, Birmingham, New Orleans, and Dallas, among others, Republicans activated long-dormant networks to build up the vote count for Dewey, while in the countryside, robed, hooded, torch-wielding Klansmen staged nighttime parades warning blacks not to vote. *The Defender* reported on clashes between blacks and whites as well as between Democrats and Dixiecrats; in many rural places, groups of white men armed with shotguns had stationed themselves near polling places.[59]

Surprisingly, Election Day, November 2, passed without incident and by that evening, the first results trickled in showing an extremely close race nationally between Truman and Dewey. Wallace had proven to be a nonfactor in the race, but Thurmond's Dixiecrats were dominating South Carolina, Alabama, Louisiana, and Mississippi, subtracting from the Democrats' state total and thereby lowering Truman's chance of ultimate success. Illinois and Ohio emerged as the battleground states, where the results would likely indicate who would win the White House, and the first few precincts showed a narrow advantage for Dewey.

The managing editor of the *Chicago Tribune*, up against the deadline for his first edition, had to make a decision about the front-page headline. Dewey's lead was small, but the Republican was widely favored in the polls leading up to the election, and the *Tribune*'s political reporter was confident. Thus the editor approved what would quickly become the most infamous headline in the history of print journalism: "Dewey Defeats Truman."

But as more totals rolled in from the state, Dewey's lead began to shrink, particularly as the massive numbers from Chicago's South Side precincts were registered. It soon became clear that the Democrats would win only with the total dedication of the African American electorate. The final numbers tipped Illinois into Truman's column by just over thirty-three thousand votes, with the president's majority in the black wards coming in at over fifty thousand votes. In Ohio, Truman won by a margin of just over seven thousand, with twelve thousand votes coming from Cleveland's African American community.

By the morning, the news had sunk in — defying all the prognosticators, Harry Truman had won his first election as president, even recapturing for the Democrats both houses of the U.S. Congress. Nor did it go unnoticed just why and how this had happened. Here was the clear confirmation of the national import of black political power, and *The Defender*'s essential role in galvanizing this essential electorate.[60]

"We Told You So!" read the huge cursive script along the top of the issue of *The Defender* produced in the wake of the election. A front-page editorial by John Sengstacke entitled "The People Were Right" elaborated on this theme, boasting that *The Defender* was the first newspaper, black or white, to formally endorse Truman, and claiming that the publisher's travels around the country with Bill Dawson had turned the tide among black voters. Sengstacke continued to cast the contest as an epic battle between those who wanted accelerated progress in the nation and those who wanted to put on the brakes. "When the people spoke, the people snatched victory out of the grave which propaganda had dug for liberalism in America," Sengstacke wrote. "And amid the resounding hallelujahs of the common people, who are hailing President Truman's soul-stirring victory, *The Chicago Defender* pledges to go forward with Truman."[61]

Dawson, the front page bragged, would get his own reward for his work with the campaign; in the new House of Representatives, he was in line to become chairman of the powerful Expenditures Committee, the first African American committee chair in the history of the United States. *The Defender*'s editorial page, reveling in the observation that Henry Wallace's campaign had completely failed to register among African Americans, floated the notion that the new Congress, with its strengthened liberal and labor presence, might finally criminalize lynching and outlaw poll taxes as well as segregation in government jobs, and — who knew? — perhaps even desegregate interstate travel.[62]

Giving every indication that he recognized what the African American community had done for him, Truman reaffirmed his support for racial justice even as he boarded the train from St. Louis back to Washington, D.C. "I meant every word I said about civil rights during the campaign," the president said to reporters before stepping into his train car, moments after posing with a copy of the *Tribune* edition erroneously declaring his defeat.[63]

# 15

# Promises vs. Performance

T HE BATTLE OVER civil rights began even before Truman's inauguration in January 1949, as the Dixiecrats tried to block U.S.
Representative William Dawson's chairmanship of the Expenditures
Committee: one representative resigned rather than serve under
Dawson, while others tried to discard the seniority system altogether
just to prevent an African American from taking that prime spot.
But the House Democratic leadership stood behind Dawson and he
was able to take the post anyway, an advance that *The Defender* celebrated in numerous articles.[1]

Dawson and Sengstacke worked together to make sure African
Americans played a visible role in Truman's inauguration, confronting and cajoling the powerful Washington figures who were organizing the inaugural ball until they secured invitations for more than
a hundred African Americans, an unprecedented number. *The Defender's* coverage of the inauguration reveled in the fact that the black
invitees were able to dance among the white guests at the ball, unhin-
dered. "Although southerners were present and participated in every
event," according to *The Defender's* report, "there was no reported
incident."[2]

In May, at a special ceremony at the White House attended by
newspaper staffers and elected officials, Sengstacke presented Truman with the third annual Robert S. Abbott Award, praising the
president as an "underdog," while Truman, visibly moved when he
received the silver plaque bearing Abbott's image, declared the cause
of civil rights "as old as the Constitution of the United States and just
as new as the Democratic platform of 1948."[3]

But by then, the Dixiecrats had successfully bottled up Truman's entire legislative package with the help of a substantial faction of the Republican Party that was passionately anti–New Deal. To keep civil rights on the agenda, *The Defender* called on the African American community to rally around Truman. "President Truman is a fighter," the editorial maintained, "but he cannot win by fighting alone. We must close ranks and mobilize the political strength of our country."[4]

Sengstacke was also confronting defiance from senior military officers and civilian overseers opposed to the implementation of the president's integration order. Every branch of the armed forces had been directed to create desegregation plans, and both the Air Force and the Navy had acceptable programs in place before the summer. But in the Army, by far the biggest of the services, Sengstacke and the other members of the president's commission found themselves confronting "hide-bound Army officers at the policy-making level," as they were described in a *Defender* report from June 1949, "who argue that it can't be done." Led by the Army's vice chief of staff, these officers ignored the edicts of the committee and instead proposed a series of plans maintaining segregated units, excluded blacks from a wide number of jobs, and capped black troop levels at 10 percent of the total.[5]

Despite a series of meetings throughout the summer, the committee members were unable to wring any concessions from the recalcitrant officers, and in September the Army announced a new plan that called for only one minor change — opening up a few specialized jobs to African Americans, and this only at the discretion of individual commanders. Most egregiously, *The Defender* reported, this new plan included as well a unilateral decision to "dispense with the services of the President's Committee," a move that the secretary of the Army made without consulting with the White House, stating that he would appoint his own board that would set its own timetable for integration of the troops.

President Truman promptly countermanded the Army secretary's extraordinary statement and insisted that the meetings with *his* committee continue until an acceptable plan was devised. But the affair had already spilled out into the public, as administration critics warned that the continuing presence of segregated units overseas was damaging the nation's image. In December, A. Philip Randolph, still the head of the Brotherhood of Sleeping Car Workers and still militant, protested outside the Waldorf Astoria Hotel in New York City while the defense secretary spoke to a lawyers' association inside, demanding an independent investigation into the conditions of black troops overseas.

Under relentless pressure from Sengstacke's committee and pro-integration activists like Randolph, as well as Congress, the Army grudgingly relented on several points at the beginning of 1950, opening up all its professions to African Americans and pledging to place qualified troops in positions without taking race into account. The generals remained obdurate when it came to eliminating a racial quota for African American troop levels, but they did announce that the Army would abolish separate training facilities and barracks, as the Navy and the Air Force had already done. "The Army is trying," summarized a *Defender* editorial page columnist.[6]

In February, Sengstacke brought his wife, Myrtle, to Washington, D.C., for the Jefferson-Jackson Day dinner, an annual fundraiser for the Democratic Party, held at a National Guard armory that served as a showcase for power players and presidential hopefuls. There had been little African American involvement in previous Jefferson-Jackson dinners, but this time, Bill Dawson and John Sengstacke recruited one hundred well-off, politically active African Americans to buy tickets at $100 a plate, and although they were just a tiny contingent in a crowd of five thousand whites, this number represented an unprecedented level of black involvement, their presence only magnified by the performance of Lena Horne at the event, another symbolic "first" that President Truman had orchestrated. Mary McLeod Bethune, who didn't attend the event but had bought a ticket, wrote in her *Defender* column that those who were there didn't care whether the meal was "served in a paper box or on fine china . . . We were there to support the practical aspects of American politics."[7]

As the spring primaries approached, however, *The Defender* began to complain about the Democratic Party bosses, both nationally and locally, and even about President Truman himself, who somehow seemed to have lost his enthusiasm for civil rights. An editorial entitled "Promises vs. Performance" listed grievances that included the replacement of high-level black appointees with whites and leaving some positions open rather than filling them with qualified African Americans. In Chicago, meanwhile, local Democratic officials had failed to build public housing to alleviate the overcrowding that continued to make life in Bronzeville so miserable. If Democrats thought they had the black vote sewn up, *The Defender*'s editorial page begged to differ, quoting the popular Gershwin tune "It Ain't Necessarily So" before warning that the black vote could easily swing back to the Republicans. "The action promised by the Democrats in 1948 caught the imagination of the people," the editorial analyzed. "Now, two years later, we have more promises and few accomplishments."[8]

An early sign of instability in the Truman coalition, the "Promises vs. Performance" editorial caught the attention of the mainstream media, earning coverage in ninety-one daily publications around the country, including *The New York Times,* which saw the article as a break with *The Defender*'s fourteen years of support for the Democrats. Some papers reprinted the editorial in its entirety, while the conservative-leaning *New York World Telegram-Sun* detailed the enthusiasm it generated among those liberal Republicans intent on wooing the black vote.

The editorial, *The Defender* boasted, "had the effect of an A Bomb dropped from peaceful skies." Even weeks after the editorial's initial publication, the newspaper noted with glee that U.S. Representative Jacob Javits, a Republican, had quoted the piece on the House floor, criticizing both the Democrats and his own party for failing to pass equal employment legislation.[9]

Even as *The Defender* was ratcheting up its criticism of the Truman administration, Sengstacke and the other members of the president's military integration commission kept up the pressure on the Army through a series of intensive meetings with the senior staff. In April, the Army announced an end to the quota capping black manpower at 10 percent, which now theoretically opened recruitment to "qualified candidates," in the words of the Army secretary, "without regard to race or color." Nevertheless, *The Defender* analyzed the Army's new policies and determined that the decision of whether or not to include black troops had been left to the "good will" of individual officers. "It is held little likely," the newspaper concluded, "that any large number of commanding officers will move to racially integrate personnel under this voluntary provision."[10]

The following month, the commission issued its final report to President Truman, an eighty-two-page document entitled *Freedom to Serve*, which lauded the Air Force and the Navy for their progress on integration even as it blasted the Army's efforts. The Air Force had launched its integration program by dissolving its all-black fighter squadron and mixing the pilots into white squads, such that by January 1950, less than one year later, fully 74 percent of the Air Force's black soldiers were serving in integrated units, with all of its schools and job-training programs open to all. The Navy, too, had moved from a policy of total segregation to one of total integration, at least at the lower ranks, where basic training, barracks, and training facilities were now mixed. While the number of officers and higher-ranking black sailors was still lacking, the commission was satisfied that Navy ROTC and recruitment would eventually rectify that as well. "Integration of the two races at work, in schools and in living quarters did not present insurmountable difficulties," the report concluded. "As a matter of fact, integration in two of the services brought a decrease in racial friction . . . The enlisted men were far more ready for integration than the officers expected."[11]

The commission used this evidence of progress in the Air Force and the Navy to challenge the Army's main excuses for stalling — that integration would reduce readiness, while open recruitment would lead to a flood of African Americans. In fact, it was segregation that had impinged on military readiness, the commission noted, and the Army officers were merely being obstinate.

President Truman, however, did not go beyond a cursory response to the arrival of *Freedom to Serve.* Praising the commission members for their service, Truman restated his support for the desegregation of the armed forces because, at a time when the battle lines of the Cold War were being drawn, it would set the right example internationally. "The free nations of the world," Truman said, "are counting on our strength to sustain them as they mobilize their energies to resist communist imperialism."

Still, the president expressed general satisfaction with all of the service branches' progress, including the Army's, and did not take up the specific points that the commission had identified as problems. Instead, Truman changed the subject, expressing his hope that the military's putative success on integration would inspire the U.S. Congress to pass a bill that would have guaranteed equal employment. Truman then pronounced the commission's work complete — despite the members' desires to stay on the job — and allowed its mandate to expire.

The Defender registered only mild disappointment with this decision, preferring, for the moment, to concentrate on the inevitability of military integration set into motion by the president's initial order and furthered by the work of its publisher and the other commission members. An editorial entitled "Our Opinion: A Job Well Done" began with this stark assessment: "Those who think you can wave a magic wand and thereby eliminate racial discrimination in American life are, to put it badly, simply nuts." Nevertheless, the editorial continued, "The most stubborn brass hats have now been put on notice and the new orders now in effect are bearing fruit in every branch of the military establishment."[12]

Just one month later, the U.S. Armed Forces were engaged in the Korean War, and The Defender assessed African American involvement in the conflict in a front-page report under the headline "Tan GIs Go into Action." One of the first units to be deployed on the frontline was the all-black Twenty-Fourth Infantry Battalion, originally created in 1869 as one of the "Buffalo Soldier" cavalry units, only this time led by black officers. The newspaper proudly listed as well the names of the two black officers from the Air Force stationed in the Far East and the half-dozen pilots flying in the combat zone. The Navy, meanwhile, told the newspaper that African Americans were represented throughout all of the eighteen ships in the region, including the aircraft carrier USS Valley Forge, taking up spots in communications, weather, gunnery, and aircraft maintenance. As the North Koreans counterattacked in the war's first weeks, The Defender reported that even more African American troops from all three branches of the service were arriving in the region.[13]

In the ensuing months, The Defender began a new editorial campaign for the "outright abolition of all vestiges of Jim Crowism in the military establishment" and for the promotion of an African American general who would be assigned to the staff of the war's supreme commander, General Douglas MacArthur. Claiming a kind of solidarity with East Asians as fellow members of the "colored world," the newspaper averred that the advancement of a black general would counteract the negative propaganda used by the North Koreans and their Communist allies, which presented the United States and its allies as racist imperialists. "The Reds have exploited the abuses of the Negro with consummate skill," the editorial stated. "We must make it clear to the world that our form of democracy is not limited to white folks only . . . At least we can squawk and fight to advance ourselves in this democracy."[14]

In August, *The Defender* dispatched its "ace reporter" Alex Wilson to Korea to join the Twenty-Fourth Infantry and other black units on the frontlines. Dapper and bespectacled, Wilson found himself under fire on his very first morning covering the conflict, while he was drinking coffee with the correspondent of the *Afro-American* chain and was forced to take shelter from incoming artillery shells. This war, Wilson discovered over those next few weeks, was as brutal as any conflict: during Wilson's first battle, he saw the North Koreans using captured South Korean troops, civilians, and children as human shields, sending them to explode minefields and lay their bodies across barbed wire ahead of North Korean troops and tanks. On that day, the American forces succeeded in repelling the ferocious North Korean assault only when aircraft arrived to strafe and bomb the attackers.

Just a few days after witnessing those horrors, Wilson chronicled a days-long battle for a single hill that left all of the Twenty-Fourth's officers either dead or wounded. He was with American troops, too, when they discovered the bodies of twenty comrades who had been captured and killed by North Koreans — each with a single gunshot wound to the head. That grim revelation only spurred the troops on to assault a nearby town, from which they took a barrage of mortar fire before finally closing in.[15]

Amid this carnage, Wilson noted desegregation at work in the Army: soon after he arrived, he encountered a tank unit that had African American enlisted men and even a few sergeants — although no officers — mixed in seamlessly among a majority of whites, including a sizable number of southerners. Granted full access to all the men in the unit, Wilson found a high degree of cohesion and solidarity among the blacks and whites, which impressed him, not least because of how cramped and noisy the tanks' cabins were, as well as permeated with noxious diesel fumes. The colonel commanding the tank squad told Wilson there had been no racial incidents among his men. "We are no longer in the experimental phase when it comes to integration," the colonel said.[16]

The infantry had been far more cautious about creating mixed units, but in September, as the casualties started to mount, twenty-three white men were brought in to fill vacancies in the Twenty-Fourth Infantry Regiment, while eleven black soldiers were assigned to previously all-white units. These assignments created unprecedented situations in which black officers, sergeants and corporals, were placed in command of white troops. Wilson was there to witness the integration and verify that it all took place without incident. For the troops on the frontlines, according to Wilson, the arrival of reinforcements itself was heartening, whether their new comrades were black, white, or Asian. "We might as well face facts," said the general in charge of the infantry division, which included the Twenty-Fourth Regiment. "Integration is working in the Navy and the Air Force, making it clear the same can be true in the Army."[17]

Interviewing the men of the Twenty-Fourth Regiment, Wilson heard many of them long for the Asian women they'd befriended and, in some cases, fallen in love with during their long tours of duty as part of the occupation of Japan following World War II. At first, Wilson took these as little more than wartime romances, but the soldiers insisted that the relationships were serious, displaying photographs of the women and children they had left behind. Fascinated by these cross-cultural connections, Wilson investigated and found that hundreds of men had formally applied to the military for permission to marry their Japanese partners. Realizing that he was witnessing an entirely new chapter in American race relations — and one with details that would play well on the front page — Wilson secured permission from his editors to travel to Japan.

"400 TO WED TOKYO GIRLS: ANXIOUS TO BRING WAR BABIES HOMES," read the banner headline on the front page of *The Defender* on November 4, 1950, the accompanying story detailing

Wilson's visit to the base where the Twenty-Fourth Infantry had been based. He met with some of the women who had already formed households and borne children with the black soldiers, and visited well-kept bungalows and apartments furnished with items ordered out of the Sears, Roebuck and Montgomery Ward catalogs. In a country that had been devastated by the American bombardment before the end of World War II, one in which much of the population hovered near starvation, the African American GIs' relatively high incomes made them attractive spouses. Beyond such mercenary considerations, though, Wilson was impressed by the devotion shown by many of the Japanese women, detecting a level of sentiment and true commitment that went beyond any crass financial motive. "Curly-haired Jean, eight-month-old daughter of Cpl. Haywood Washington of Washington, D.C., and Miss Misako Yamada, won my heart completely," Wilson wrote, "and I'm sure would bring a smile to the lips of the average American."[18]

Wilson's first article received an enthusiastic response, selling out newsstands and prompting *The Defender*'s editors to call for more. The following week, the front-page banner headline read, "WHY TAN YANKS GO FOR JAPANESE GIRLS," with accompanying photos of attractive Japanese women with their African American partners. This installment featured more interviews with black soldiers who praised Japanese women's loyalty and thriftiness as well as critics who disapproved of these relationships, including Ethel Payne, an African American woman from Chicago who was working with the Army Special Services as the manager of a club for black soldiers in Yokohama.[19]

Wilson returned to the front as Chinese forces crossed into North Korea and launched a massive counterattack against the Americans and their allies. But as interest in the Japanese–African American couples had not waned, *The Defender*'s editors turned to Ethel Payne as the source of more articles on this attention-grabbing subject. Thirty-eight years old, Payne was a former employee of the Chicago Public Library who had taken writing courses at Northwestern University and published several freelance articles, including a story in *Abbott's Monthly,* a magazine published by *The Defender* for several years during the Depression. She had gotten to know many of the soldiers before the outbreak of the war and kept a detailed notebook recording her experiences in Japan, which she shared with Wilson when they met at the overseas press club. Impressed with the quality of her observations, Wilson asked if he might bring the notebook with him back to Chicago to see if it could be used by the newspaper's editors. Payne agreed —"foolishly," as she recalled some years later to an interviewer.

*The Defender*'s editors proceeded to edit and rewrite portions of Payne's notebook into a two-part series with her byline, which began appearing on the following week's front-page edition under the banner headline "Army Club Director Playing GIs for Suckers: 'Chocolate Joe' Used, Amused and Abused." In the articles themselves, Payne depicted a much more nuanced relationship, in which the Japanese women were often liberated by their contact with the American soldiers, both in a financial sense and in terms of the rigid societal restrictions that kept many of them in a subservient position. But the obstacles to the success of these interracial relationships, Payne pointed out, were nearly insurmountable on either side of the ocean; current military regulations prohibited marriage between American troops and Japanese women, while the children of these unions had only a nebulous legal status in both Japan and the United States. Moreover, after the troops left for Korea, some of the women were discriminated against by fellow Japanese, and in the worst cases, as when an American soldier was killed in action or simply abandoned his erstwhile spouse, the women were left destitute and their children handed over to orphanages.

"Overnight," Payne wrote, the black soldiers' "carefully nurtured paradise disintegrated into the fragments of a dream which he could remember for many years with nostalgic words, 'Never had it so great.'"[20]

Payne herself was unaware that her notes had been published until Wilson returned to Japan and informed her that the articles had become a sensation in Chicago. But she soon discovered that her writing had also caught the attention of her bosses in the military, who were furious, and Payne was called before the Army high command, who chastised her for damaging morale and threatened to fire her. In the end, the Army simply transferred her to a secretarial position at headquarters, where she was isolated and bored, albeit employed.[21]

• • •

That winter, the NAACP's lead attorney Thurgood Marshall traveled to Korea to investigate what he suspected were the improper courts-martial of dozens of black troops, many of them with the Twenty-Fourth Infantry. Thirty-nine officers and enlisted men had asked for the NAACP's assistance after being accused of cowardice and convicted in battlefield trials where they had little chance to defend themselves. Marshall's request to enter the military zone in Korea was initially rejected, until General Douglas MacArthur, supreme commander of Allied forces, personally intervened.

Once he reached Korea, Marshall discovered that there had been even more trials of African American soldiers than he knew, some sixty in total, with twenty-three convictions on the offense of failure to obey an order on the battlefield. He also found, as he expected, that many of the trials had been conducted quickly, some in as little as fifty minutes, without proper procedures. Only two white soldiers had been similarly charged and convicted during the same time period, and they had received light sentences, while one of the blacks had been sentenced to death and many others to as much as a decade in military prison. Even the Army's senior officers seemed to have noticed some discrimination in these cases, since four of the black soldiers' convictions were overturned on appeal.[22]

At the end of February 1951, after Marshall sent reports of his findings to the NAACP and General MacArthur, he returned to the United States to give a public lecture alongside reporter Alex Wilson, himself just returned from Korea. Before an audience of eleven hundred people at Wendell Phillips High School in Bronzeville, Marshall vowed to continue advocating for the accused troops, and blamed their prosecution on racist elements within the military who sought to denigrate African Americans as unfit for military service.

"Someone is trying to brand Negro fighting men in Korea as cowards," Marshall told the assembly. "They tried it in World War I. They tried it in World War II. And they are trying it in this war."[23]

Having proved his reporting skills and news judgment, Alex Wilson was given a new mission a few months after he returned to Chicago, to head a new newspaper called *The Tri-State Defender*, which would be based in Memphis, strategically located just across the border from Mississippi and Arkansas, within striking distance of Alabama and Louisiana, all states with large African American populations. Both *The Louisville Defender* and *The Michigan Chronicle* were thriving, and on the strength of this John Sengstacke had decided to expand his newspaper empire, adding *The Tri-State Defender* to the roster along with the ailing *New York Age,* a onetime competitor that Sengstacke had purchased in order to preserve its august name.[24]

Ethel Payne, meanwhile, was making her own way home. She met with Thurgood Marshall while he was in Japan, and Marshall had mentioned her in his report on discrimination in the military. Just days after Marshall's return to the United States, Louis Martin, then serving as *The Defender*'s editor in chief, telephoned Payne. Praising her writing ability as well as her knack for piquing the curiosity of the readership, he offered her a position at the newspaper. "Come on home," Martin told Payne. "We've got a job for you."[25]

Payne jumped at the offer, feeling as if she had been liberated after some three years in Japan. On her last day in the country, she got one final glimpse of General MacArthur as he made his daily review before a crowd of admiring onlookers in front of his office at a downtown Tokyo insurance company near the Imperial Palace. Movie camera in hand, Payne looked on as a long black Cadillac pulled up and soldiers in formal uniforms, white gloves, gleaming helmets, and boots took their positions. At precisely 2:31 p.m., all traffic was stopped in the intersection and MacArthur emerged from his office, surrounded by his aides, striding to his vehicle without acknowledging the crowds, behaving very much like an emperor himself, in Payne's estimation, "erect, proud, disdainful of the admiring glances of his subjects and yet fully aware of his role as Destiny's chosen to rule 80,000,000 people."

Flying to San Francisco, Payne then made her way back to Chicago, where she took up her post at *The Defender.* Just a few days after she arrived, President Truman fired MacArthur from his position as supreme commander of Allied Forces in the Far East for blunders in Korea as well as myriad acts of disrespect; Payne's first bylined article recalled the general's daily review under the headline "THE LAST TIME I SAW MACARTHUR." Evaluating his tenure, Payne blamed the general, in particular, for failing to end segregation in the Army, noting that there were no African American soldiers in his honor guard or his senior staff or anywhere in his headquarters. As haughty and dismissive of the press as he was of Truman, she concluded that MacArthur saw no cause to address segregation — or even acknowledge that it was a problem — regardless of how it harmed the overall war effort by leaving black units badly ill equipped and undermanned. "The wanton die-hard attitude of segregation," Payne wrote, "has been a costly and needless waste of lives."[26]

*The Defender* building on South Indiana Avenue was draped in black in February 1952 to mark the death of Lucius Harper, who succumbed to kidney disease at the age of fifty-seven. More than fifteen hundred people attended his funeral in a show of public grief that revealed his broad influence as a journalist. Eulogies were given by Chicago Mayor Martin Kennelly as well as a host of judges, congressmen, businesspeople, and clergy. Among the speakers was a minister who knew Harper back when he was a bellhop at the Chicago Press Club, striving to become a newspaperman.[27]

Harper, who was survived by five children, had devoted his entire professional life to the black press. Serving as pallbearers were his fellow journalists — John Sengstacke, Enoch Waters, Louis Martin, and John H. Johnson, now promoted to the first rank of African American publishers with the tremendous success of *Ebony* magazine, as well as Frank Stanley, the publisher of *The Louisville Defender,* and Claude Barnett, a former *Defender* ad man who ran the Associated Negro Press.[28]

Waters's paean to Harper recalled his colleague as a "walking encyclopedia" with a voracious appetite for news, history, and gossip, who would scour the city for used books and engage friends and strangers alike in wide-ranging conversation, rarely staying in his office unless he was on deadline. Loquacious, ribald, and fun-loving, Harper, he recalled, would "drop dissertation on Biblical philosophy to participate in an office prank in a minute."[29]

Fay Young, in his column that week, praised Harper's generosity, erudition, and kindness, recalling a day shortly before his death when Harper bought shoes for a poor man who had approached him. Now that Harper was gone, Fay was the last of those who had started working with Abbott in Mrs. Lee's apartment. "We spent more time

in the editorial rooms of *The Defender* than we did at home," he recalled. "Sure he pioneered and sacrificed but it was not in vain for he
lived long enough to see some of his efforts bear fruit."[30]

In December 1953, Louis Martin selected Ethel Payne to become *The
Defender*'s new Washington, D.C., correspondent, replacing Venice
Spraggs, who had been the first woman to hold the post but left to
take a better-paying job with the Democratic National Committee. It
was a demanding assignment, but Martin felt that Payne had proven
herself during her months in Chicago as a tenacious reporter who
had the sort of global outlook that would serve her well in the nation's
capital. "Go on down there and do a hell of a job," Martin instructed
Payne, giving her a broad mandate, though hardly an expense account to match.

Payne moved into a small apartment that also served as her office and set out to obey Martin's edict even as she was staggered by
the scope of the job. "I was by myself," she recalled to an interviewer
some years later, "and I knew that was like telling you to cover the
whole world almost, because you had the White House, you had the
Congress, you had the State Department, you had the Defense Department, all those agencies, and you were expected to do something
with all of them."[31]

The political atmosphere in Washington when Payne arrived was
much changed since the days of monolithic Democratic control over
the federal government that had existed under FDR. President Harry
Truman, facing divisions within the Democratic coalition over his
support for civil rights as well as doubts about his competence, had
decided not to run for reelection in 1952, and his successor, Republican Dwight Eisenhower, the former five-star general who had led
Allied forces to victory in World War II, won the presidential election
with just over 20 percent of the African American vote and substantial support from so-called Eisencrats, white southerners dissatisfied
with the Democratic Party's stance on race issues. Having swept to
victory in the U.S. Congress, Republicans also controlled both the
Senate and the House for the first time in decades. Nevertheless,
Eisenhower had been vaguely supportive of civil rights during the
campaign and there was still significant momentum in legislation be-

ing considered by the U.S. Congress as well as desegregation cases proceeding through the federal courts.[32]

Shortly after she arrived in the capital, Payne covered the final arguments in a class-action lawsuit before the U.S. Supreme Court filed by twenty African American public school students from Topeka, Kansas, who were challenging the segregated school system in that state. Segregation was then the law in twenty states, including all of those in the South along with Delaware, Wyoming, New Mexico, and Kansas as well as the District of Columbia. Thurgood Marshall and his legal team from the NAACP sought to use this case, *Brown v. Board of Education of Topeka,* to invalidate segregated schools across the country.

Contending that separating black and white students violated the Constitution's Fourteenth Amendment, the NAACP lawyers asserted that those states that had a dual school system were entirely aware that it was unconstitutional. To prove this latter point, Marshall's team produced specially created charts to show the incremental legislative steps taken by these states to circumvent the law. The NAACP lawyers also compiled data about the inferiority of the public schools designated for blacks, and the damage done to the opportunities and self-esteem of the individual students. For their part, segregationist states challenged the Supreme Court's authority over what they deemed a state issue and even expressed doubt that the 1868 Congress that had passed the Fourteenth Amendment had ever actually meant to prevent segregated schools.

In her coverage of the court, Payne recorded the date and time the arguments before the justices were concluded — 2:37 p.m. Wednesday, December 9. "The fate of segregated public schools is now in the hands of the U.S. Supreme Court," she wrote in the following edition of *The Defender.* "The court must now decide whether to declare Jim Crow unconstitutional or leave it entirely up to the states to settle."[33]

If Payne had in any way felt outclassed in her new assignment in Washington, she was determined and strategic, rapidly building relationships with contacts throughout the branches of government and into the private sector. Martin had secured for Payne an introduction to the White House press secretary, and she began attending Presi-

dent Eisenhower's regular press conferences along with two other African Americans, Alice Dunnigan from the Associated Negro Press
and Louis Lautier from the NNPA.

Payne was too intimidated to ask any questions in her first few
press conferences, but Eisenhower showed himself to be unusually
accessible, holding regular press conferences every week and calling
on many reporters from smaller publications. Finally, in February
1954, she mustered up the courage to ask about an incident in which
the Howard University choir had been turned away from the Republican Party's Lincoln Day Dinner, at which the president was the keynote speaker. Three choirs were asked to perform that evening, but
Howard's, the only African American group, was stopped by D.C. policemen who were apparently incredulous that blacks would be asked
to perform at such an august event.

Asking Payne at first to repeat the question, Eisenhower then requested more background. When Payne finished, the president said
he hadn't heard of the snub, but after a brief, whispered conversation
with his press secretary, allowed that he hoped the choir members
had not been insulted, and apologized if they had been. Not only was
Payne impressed with Ike's courteous response, she felt encouraged
to ask more probing questions in the future.[34]

She began to coordinate with Clarence Mitchell, the director of
the Washington bureau of the NAACP, to formulate her comments,
focusing increasingly on the major civil rights issues of the day. One
week she raised the issue of continued segregation of schools for the
children of soldiers on military bases; the president again responded
that he was not aware of this situation and promised to investigate.
Shortly thereafter, Eisenhower issued an executive order abolishing
the practice.

Feeling positively emboldened by now, Payne took advantage of
the next press conference to ask the president if, while the nation
waited for the high court's verdict on the school system, the administration would sponsor legislation banning segregation in interstate
transportation. While African Americans who could afford their
own Pullman sleepers were now allowed to book them, those who
could not were still relegated, in all of the South and beyond, to Jim
Crow cars and waiting rooms, bathrooms, and ticket facilities. On
bus lines traveling on the new interstate highways, she informed the

president, black passengers were consigned to the seats in the back. Where he had previously indulged Payne, however, Ike hesitated this time, saying that he needed to speak with his cabinet on the issue: "I would have to consult the attorney general," he told Payne, "and see what he says about our authority there."[35]

In the early afternoon of Monday, May 17, 1954, Ethel Payne was called to the U.S. Supreme Court to hear the decision in the school segregation case. Like all of the reporters present at that moment, she was overcome with emotion, stunned by the justices' unanimous decision in favor of the plaintiffs. "The members of the press went completely wacky," she wrote in an article some days later. "I'm so excited I'm like I'm drunk. I'm turning around like one of those spinning tops."[36]

As soon as she heard the decision, Payne called the newsroom in Chicago, but the editorial staff had been tracking a number of civil rights cases at the time and failed, at first, to recognize *Brown*'s importance. That changed, however, as they read the key words in the ruling written by Chief Justice Earl Warren and began to realize their implications: "We conclude that, in the field of public education, the doctrine of 'separate but equal' has no place.

"Separate education facilities are inherently unequal."[37]

This was the ruling that finally overturned the 1896 *Plessy v. Ferguson* decision, which had opened the way for the "separate but equal" public facilities in the first place. When Louis Martin read out these words to the editorial staff, Enoch Waters felt a wave of exaltation wash over those gathered in *The Defender*'s newsroom. The justices' ruling, these journalists began to ascertain, would reverberate into every public institution in the South, even as it curtailed the power of governors and state legislatures. One editor predicted that May 17 would become an African American Independence Day, while another declared that it was "full speed ahead for the drive to achieve equal rights."

The journalists felt a sense of personal pride in the justices' ruling, too, knowing that they had played an essential role in reaching this point. "We weren't members of the regiment of lawyers headed by Thurgood Marshall that had argued the case before the nation's highest court," Waters wrote in his memoir. "On the other hand, we did not look upon ourselves as uninvolved onlookers just reporting what was happening. We felt that our stories and editorials had helped create the climate that made the decision possible."[38]

"Kill Jim Crow," read the banner headline for that week's issue of *The Defender*, printed in a font and size combination that Waters described as "befitting the Return of Christ." Inside, articles quoted the presidents of the nation's leading African American colleges and universities, all of them located in the South, who were ecstatic about the ruling and the prospects for black students in that region. The educators lauded Thurgood Marshall and his legal team and expressed their profound hope that the South would accept integration without protest. Dr. Horace Bond of Lincoln University, the oldest integrated institute of higher learning in the nation, praised the ruling as "a majestic break in the dark clouds with which the face of Man's destiny everywhere has been obscured."[39]

As a useful counterpoint to the optimistic pronouncements from these black educators, *The Defender* printed the words of southern whites who vowed to resist integration at any cost. For instance, James F. Byrnes, the onetime segregationist senator and President Truman's former secretary of state, now South Carolina's governor, threatened to completely eliminate the public school system in his state rather than integrate. "To do that," Byrnes argued, "would be choosing the lesser of two great evils."

The following week's edition of *The Defender*, too, was filled with reactions to the *Brown v. Board of Education* ruling. Celebratory remarks came in from labor unions, Jewish organizations, liberal intellectuals, and from international commentators as far afield as newly independent India, where Prime Minister Jawaharlal Nehru compared the ruling to the ongoing emancipation of the lowest castes in his own country. In the state-controlled media of the Soviet bloc, on the other hand, where segregation was regularly featured in anti-American propaganda, the ruling was completely ignored, *The Defender* noted approvingly.[40]

Meanwhile, back home, *Brown* was eliciting trepidation as much as anticipation. That same issue two weeks after the ruling featured Enoch Waters's interviews with black teachers in the South, most of whom were worried they would lose their jobs in the process of integration. Paid even less than their white counterparts — Waters calculated that a barmaid in Chicago made more in three months than a teacher did annually — African American teachers had just a fraction of the resources with which to educate their students. But at least the segregated public school system employed black teachers; many lacked confidence that they would survive the transition to an integrated one.[41]

*The Defender's* editorial page was certain, however, that the ruling was a decisive step forward for racial equality in the United States: "Neither the atomic bomb nor the hydrogen bomb will ever be as meaningful to our democracy as the unanimous declaration from the Supreme Court that racial segregation violates the spirit and the letter of our Constitution. It is the prelude to the eventual complete emancipation of the Negro in America."[42]

Justice Warren's powerful words, however, specified no particular timeline for change. Deep in the text of the Supreme Court's ruling were additional sentences directing the attorneys for the plaintiffs to submit prospective plans for the desegregation of schools that fall. The U.S. attorney general and the attorneys general of the various segregationist states were all asked to contribute their comments. Thurgood Marshall began consulting with legal delegations from every affected state, as attorneys for the southern states were already arguing that no specific deadline should be imposed and that each state should be allowed to proceed at its own pace, effectively making any integration voluntary.

Eisenhower's solicitor general had supported the NAACP's case and the president had appointed the liberal Earl Warren to lead the Supreme Court, but in this round, the southerners had the support of the Eisenhower administration, whose lawyers now asserted that they were acting to prevent "chaos." Southern white politicians responded with predictable vehemence, even as a few state legislatures actually followed up on Governor Byrnes's threat and actually tried to dissolve their public schools rather than integrate them. U.S. Senator James Eastland from Mississippi, an avowed white supremacist, went so far as to propose a constitutional amendment allowing segregation.

As the weeks went by, Enoch Waters and the other *Defender* staffers realized that the real key to any change in the ruling would be the timetable on which the court had yet to decide. "As momentous as it was," Waters wrote of the ruling, "the May 17, 1954, decision did not conclude the Brown case. Racial segregation in American public schools had been outlawed but the court had not ruled on when the order to desegregate was to be carried out."[43]

While the nation waited for the Supreme Court's direction on implementation, the *Brown* decision did inspire a number of members of Congress to try to move on other antisegregation legislation, which in turn gave Ethel Payne the opportunity to press President Eisenhower on whether his administration would back these efforts. Ike responded that he was reluctant to use legislation to accomplish civil rights goals, telling Payne that he preferred consensus agreements, "progress accomplished through the intelligence of people, and through the cooperation of people, more than law, when we can get it that way."

Payne continued her questioning of Eisenhower, even when it became plain that she was steadily grinding down the president's equanimity. On July 7, 1954, she asked the president again whether his administration would support the desegregation of all interstate transportation facilities, noting that officials in both the Justice Department and the Bureau of the Budget had written approving memoranda. "I would like to know," Payne concluded, "if we can assume we have administration support in getting action on this?"

It was consistent in tone and topic to Payne's prior questions, but this time Eisenhower snapped, becoming noticeably angry and stiffening into a "military posture," even as he raised his voice to answer: "I don't know by what right that you have to have administration support," the president told Payne. "The administration is trying to do what it thinks to be — believes decent and just in this country, and it is not in the effort to support any particular or special groups of any kind."

Ike's acerbic outburst shocked and divided the members of the press corps and, ultimately, the public. Several of Payne's colleagues consoled her after the incident; Ed Folliard of *The Washington Post*, considered the dean of the White House Press Corps, took Payne aside and recalled the time he had angered President Franklin Roosevelt to the point "he almost leaped out of his wheelchair." But many others blamed Payne for annoying the chief executive with questions about topics they saw as irrelevant. A highly critical story on the front page of *The Washington Evening Star* became the dominant narrative of the incident when it was carried by wire services around the country, but Payne also faced an attack from NNPA correspondent Louis Lautier, who, eschewing any sense of racial solidarity, shared widely his opinion that she was pushy, unprofessional, and "out of step."

Even Payne's own mother, a Republican holdout in Chicago, chastised her when she heard about the incident: "I don't think you ought to be down there making the president mad."

Payne's bosses at *The Defender,* on the other hand, were thrilled. Louis Martin and John Sengstacke called after the press conference and teased her, asking, "What are you doing down there, picking on the president?" before adding how pleased they were with the attention she had garnered for the issue of transportation integration.

The first week after the confrontation, Payne's account of the incident was trumpeted on the front page under a defiant banner headline, "*Defender* Query Angers Ike." An accompanying article quoted Payne's question verbatim, demonstrating that it was informed and respectfully phrased, and cited the Justice Department memo approving the desegregation of interstate highways.

The following week, *The Defender*'s front page featured a piece by the ANP's Alice Dunnigan, the first African American woman to be admitted to the White House Press Corps, who had been by Payne's side since she arrived in Washington. Quiet and more formal than Payne, Dunnigan nevertheless supported her colleague's narrative of the breach with Eisenhower, noting that Payne's questions had frequently won policy changes early on, but that the president had lately displayed a "curt manner." Dunnigan also took the opportunity to fire back at Lautier's "inexcusable breach of journalistic ethics," labeling him a sexist who tried but failed to enlist other male reporters in his efforts to harass black women reporters.[44]

An editorial in that same issue, entitled "No Need for Temper," stated that it was the president, rather than Payne, who had been rude, and took issue with Ike's statement that African Americans were a "special group." Segregated travel, after all, was an issue "no less important than questions on Indo China or health care legislation. This paper has no apologies to make for asking the administration to state its position," the editorial asserted.[45]

Indeed, in the weeks after the blowup, *The Defender* continued to push strongly for integrated travel and other civil rights issues, while Payne persisted in attending White House press conferences and posing difficult questions. Just a month later, she asked the president whether he would take action to stop discrimination in federally funded public housing. This time, Ike kept his cool, stating that he "tried as hard as he could" to convince local authorities not to use federal dollars for segregated housing, then made a vague promise to convene an interdepartmental meeting on the subject in the near future.[46]

White House Press Secretary James Hagerty had not forgotten Payne's confrontation with the president, however, and once the midterm elections were over, tried to dislodge her from the press corps. In early 1955, Hagerty brought Payne into a meeting at which he revealed that his office had been conducting an investigation of her finances. It had been discovered, Hagerty said, that Payne had done some outside work for the political action committee of the Congress of Industrial Organizations, a labor union umbrella organization headed by United Automobile Workers leader Walter Reuther, whose leftist beliefs and activities made him a bête noir of the White House. Payne's work for the CIO, Hagerty stated, was a violation of the press corps' protocols that could justify the seizure of her White House credentials. "The CIO PAC is a political organization," Hagerty told Payne, "and I will have to report this to the Standing Committee of Correspondents."

Payne protested that her work for the CIO was temporary and nonpolitical: she had only edited documents for a short time, and ceased working for the organization several months before the election. "I had nothing to do with making policy," Payne said.[47]

Hagerty, though, did not relent, advising Payne that his investigation would continue and that he would inform her of his decision in the near future. Payne immediately rushed to the NAACP's Clarence Mitchell, who began to organize a countereffort. Within a few days, Drew Pearson, a white, Washington-based syndicated columnist who was a fierce critic of Eisenhower, spoke out against the administration's "reign of terror" during a speech at Howard Medical School, listing Hagerty's interrogation of Payne among a number of similar interactions with both blacks and whites; the eminent diplomat Ralph Bunche himself had been subjected to a twelve-hour "interview" before being cleared of charges of subversion. *The Defender* covered Pearson's speech, quoting his contention that the president's staff was trying to "silence the press from asking legitimate but embarrassing questions on racial prejudice."[48]

Just as the storm of controversy over her interactions with the White House was coming to a head, however, Payne found herself headed to the other side of the planet. Early one morning in mid-March, John Sengstacke called her at home and asked, "How would you like to go to Indonesia?"

Payne, half asleep, recalled answering, "Indo *who?*"

"Yes, Indonesia," Sengstacke said. "You know, there's a great conference going to take place there. It's the first conference of darker people of the world. And we thought that you would be the person to go and cover it."

Payne was indeed excited and asked when the conference would take place.

"Well," Sengstacke said, "like yesterday."

Payne stayed in Washington just long enough to get the necessary visas and vaccinations, then, packing two bags with cameras, a portable typewriter, and her personal effects, she returned to Chicago for specific instructions. Sengstacke decided to buy her a round-the-world ticket that allowed her to stop in several countries in Asia and Europe for several more weeks beyond the conference itself. Within days, she was on a flight to San Francisco, the first leg of a multistop journey that would take her to Bandung, a former Dutch resort town on the island of Java.

In a gathering that included the leaders of newly independent nations as well as peoples still colonized by European powers, the conference brought together "the representation of two-thirds of the Earth's population," as Payne described it. Payne was welcomed by the Indonesians she encountered as well as many of the conference attendees, who identified with African Americans and were well informed about the struggle for civil rights in the United States. Where the white reporters from the major American newspapers were often frustrated by a lack of access at the conference, Payne blended in with the delegation from Saudi Arabia and managed to slip into a number of meetings where she was the only journalist.

She moved easily through the social scene as well, hobnobbing with prominent African American writer Richard Wright, who was there to chronicle the event, as well as luminaries like Indira Nehru (later Gandhi), the daughter of Indian Prime Minister Nehru, who would herself become the prime minister some years later.

Payne worked day and night, sending her dispatches back to Chicago through a special air courier. She covered North Africans demanding independence from France as well as a united coalition of South African blacks and Indians protesting against apartheid, but also wrote about the intrigue and drama around the diplomatic duel between Nehru and Chinese Premier Chou En-lai to see who would emerge as the preeminent leader of the nonaligned nations. Disappointed by the relatively weak showing from African nations, she was particularly harsh about the internal struggle of the movement for nationhood in the British colony of Gold Coast, where Kwame Nkrumah was competing for power with various rivals. Reluctantly, she wrote about Congressman Adam Clayton Powell from New York — whom she regarded as a glory hound — presenting the conditions of African Americans, denouncing communism as a possible solution for the race problems in the United States, and confronting Premier Chou about several American pilots who were being held as spies. She wrote far more enthusiastically about the groups of women of Indonesia and other Muslim nations who were fighting against the custom of plural marriage.[49]

On the same front page carrying the news that Ethel Payne was on her way to the Bandung conference, *The Defender* announced that on the morning of the fiftieth anniversary of the newspaper's founding, John Sengstacke would present that year's Robert S. Abbott Award to President Eisenhower in the White House. Explaining that the award was given "to the person or organization which in the preceding year has done most to advance the cause of American democracy," the article touted the symbolism of the date and noted that Eisenhower would join the company of previous awardees Thurgood Marshall, Mary McLeod Bethune, and former Chicago mayor Ed Kelly.[50]

Sengstacke never mentioned it to his biographers or associates but he had clearly orchestrated Payne's absence from Washington just as Eisenhower was to get the Abbott Award. Not that her public conflict with the White House disappeared from the public arena while she was out of town. Just a few days before the award ceremony, columnist Drew Pearson published a detailed account of Payne's tense meeting with Press Secretary Hagerty in his nationally syndicated column. Raising the question of how the administration had learned of Payne's work with the Congress of Industrial Organizations in the first place, Pearson inferred that the White House had procured her tax returns and used the information therein to threaten her press credentials.

While Pearson's column did not run in *The Defender*, the newspaper did print Press Secretary Hagerty's angry response when he was asked about the allegations at a press conference. "I don't normally criticize stories," Hagerty said, "but when any columnist or anyone in the newspaper profession says I am using tax returns, they are either deliberately lying or they are completely uninformed." Hagerty failed, however, to explain how he obtained the reporter's financial information nor did he deny threatening her White House credentials.[51]

Just a few days later, on May 5, with Ethel Payne safely on the other side of the planet, John Sengstacke presented the president with an engraved plaque bearing Abbott's likeness. Eisenhower's coterie in the Oval Office that morning included top staffers and associates as well as Thurgood Marshall, Judge Charles Fahy, the former chairman of the military integration commission, and U.S. Senator Everett McKinley Dirksen from Illinois, a Republican with whom he had a good working relationship. Sengstacke also brought along Roi Ottley, the *Chicago Tribune*'s first African American columnist, who gave Eisenhower a specially bound copy of his book *The Lonely Warrior*, the first comprehensive biography of Robert Abbott.[52]

Bestowing the award, Sengstacke spoke positively but with his usual directness about the doubts that many African Americans had about Ike's leadership: "Mr. President, following the national elections of 1952, a large section of the American population was apprehensive about the future. It was concerned lest there be no continued gains in civil rights, in personal freedom in employability and in human dignity at the instance of the national administration . . . Now, after 28 months in office, you have dispelled those fears."

Sengstacke was vague about what, exactly, Eisenhower had done for civil rights, opting instead to laud the president in general terms "for reinforcing through the noble exercise of your high office the American principle of equality of opportunity and for extending the area of democracy in the United States and the world."

The president, for his part, appeared sincerely moved by the presentation, holding his gaze firmly on Sengstacke until the publisher finished speaking, then smiling and quipping, "I hope I deserve it." Ike spoke with the group for a few minutes and then posed for numerous photographs, in contrast with both FDR and Truman, who had been reluctant to be photographed with groups of African Americans.

"It is my hope that this administration, and succeeding ones, will continue and accelerate the concrete progress that has been made in furthering the dreams of Robert Abbott," Eisenhower wrote in a letter to Sengstacke after the award ceremony, "aspirations that are shared by men of good will everywhere."[53]

A detailed account of the Abbott Award presentation appeared on the same page as Ethel Payne's dispatch from sweltering Bombay, one of the many stops she was making on her meandering path home. "This is the hottest spot I've hit yet," wrote Payne, describing in rich detail streets and alleyways packed with indigent families living in makeshift housing, eking out a living through plantation-style farming and other backbreaking labor.

"The poor are here," she wrote, "and the sight of them toiling in the blazing sun or the endless rows of them sleeping on the roadsides and sidewalks depresses."[54]

# 16

# The *Daily Defender*

ETHEL PAYNE RETURNED to Washington at the end of May, just in time to cover the Supreme Court's final ruling on the implementation of its *Brown* decision. After a full year of arguments in which the NAACP and its allies called for a one-year deadline for implementation of the desegregation order, while southern states, joined by President Eisenhower's attorney general, argued they be allowed to go at their own pace, the justices decided that the main responsibility for implementing the desegregation of schools should be devolved to the federal courts in each region. This decision — issued unanimously, like the first *Brown* ruling — empowered local judges to set their own schedules and required only that the school systems act "with all deliberate speed."

After hearing the verdict, Payne buttonholed Thurgood Marshall in an effort to elicit his thoughts, but Marshall declined to comment, leaving the capital to confer with his board. Payne described the decision as a "poor compromise" between the NAACP's position and the segregationists, noting that the court hewed closely to the line advocated by the attorney general. Progress in the year since the first *Brown* ruling had been decidedly limited, with just five hundred schools serving 250,000 students switched over to an integrated setting. Only Washington, D.C., and Baltimore, along with a few scattered communities in the midwestern and border states, had started desegregating their schools, while in the Deep South, whites had remained obdurate, writing and signing pacts to oppose integration by any and all means. Now, under the new ruling, southern states would have ample opportunity to delay and block school desegregation, while the NAACP would have to engage in further legal action to ensure that integration went forward.[1]

Back in the newsroom in Chicago, Enoch Waters and his colleagues debated the implications of the phrase "with all deliberate speed" before deciding that the court had effectively stalled integration before it had really begun. "We at *The Defender* concluded," Waters wrote in his memoir, "the paradoxical phrase meant, without saying so, that the South could take its own sweet time to begin the transformation required to comply with the May 17th decree."[2]

Gauging the reaction to the ruling, the newspaper's coverage of the *Brown II* decision, as it came to be called, found dismay among the pro–civil rights camp and relief among the segregationists. Among NAACP officials from local chapters around the country, some were confused by the ruling, others frustrated, while a percentage attempted to take solace, at least, in the court's initial decision. But among white southerners, quoted in an article headlined "Dixie Crows Over Mild School Rule," opinions of the Supreme Court's new ruling ranged from elation to concern that *Brown II* merely bought the white South a bit more time.

One of the leaders of the segregationists interpreted the justices' words as a shift in their favor after years in which the momentum seemed to be going against them. "This is the first reasonable thing the court has done in relation to the segregation case," said Robert B. Patterson, executive secretary of the Mississippi Association of Citizens' Councils. "Segregation can have no deadline."[3]

An exasperated *Defender* editorial entitled "The Supreme Court Bows to Dixie" cited the satisfaction expressed by the segregationists as evidence of the faults in the justices' logic, which depended on the white South to move toward integration on its own when it had up to then demonstrated nothing but stubborn resistance.

"However well-meaning the Supreme Court justices may have been," the editorial analogized, "they are now in the position of the cow that gave a full bucket of milk and then promptly kicked it over."[4]

At 2:30 a.m. on Sunday, August 28, 1955, sixty-four-year-old Moses Wright, a tall, wiry cotton farmer, was awakened by someone knocking on the door of his rough, unpainted house set about fifty feet back from a gravel road outside Money, Mississippi.

"Preacher," said a man's voice, using a common nickname for Wright, a minister in the Church of God in Christ. Wright opened the door to find J. W. Milam, a local white man he knew, holding a pistol and a flashlight, as well as two other white men, one of whom introduced himself as Roy Bryant, the owner of a convenience store in town and Milam's half brother. The third man stayed in the shadows on the porch, his hat drawn down to hide his face.

"We want to see the boy from Chicago," said Milam.

Understanding that the men were looking for his fourteen-year-old grand-nephew, Emmett Till, whose mother had sent him to Mississippi for the summer vacation, Wright led the two men through the darkened house — the electricity happened not to be working that night — into a back room where Till was sleeping in a bed with Wright's twelve-year-old son, Simeon. Milam woke up Till and asked him, "Are you that boy from Chicago?"

"Yeah," answered Till.

"Don't say 'yeah' to me or I'll knock the hell out of you," Milam snapped, offended that the boy had not addressed him as "sir," and ordered him to get dressed.

Wright's wife was now awake as well and pleaded with the men not to take Till, offering them money to set aside whatever wrong he might have done, but they ignored her and brought the boy to a car waiting on the road. Wright followed the men in the dark and heard them ask a woman seated inside, "Is this the boy?"

When the woman answered yes, the men took the boy away, beyond Wright's sight.

Within hours, Wright notified the local police and also telephoned Till's mother, Mamie Bradley, in Chicago. That same day, local sheriff's deputies arrested Bryant and Milam on suspicion of kidnapping while Bradley began a frantic effort to coordinate a search for her son, notifying local officials in Chicago as well as *The Defender*, which sent reporter Mattie Smith Colin to sit with the distraught mother through her vigil. Bradley soon ascertained that the kidnapping was related to an incident the previous Wednesday, when her son had gone with a group of friends to the store in Money owned by

Bryant and his twenty-one-year-old wife, Carolyn. Till bought some bubblegum from Carolyn and, on the way out, allegedly let loose a wolf whistle directed at her. A moment later, Mrs. Bryant emerged from the store with a look that frightened the boys.

"She's going to get a pistol," one of them yelled, prompting the boys to run all the way back to Wright's farm, where Till begged his cousins not to tell his uncle about the incident. Over the next few days, the boys tried to put the encounter out of their minds even after they were warned by a neighbor that the Bryants were still upset — right until the night the white men appeared at the house.[5]

The town of Money was located in the Delta, a region rich in cotton with a population that was heavily African American, and where a small group of white families owned virtually all the land and businesses. Well aware of the tense racial dynamic in the region, Mamie Bradley had warned her extroverted son before he left for his summer vacation to be careful not to offend any of the area's whites. "Avoid trouble," she recalled telling him. "If necessary, get on your hands and knees to the white folks to avoid trouble."[6]

On Monday, August 29, Bryant and Milam were formally charged with kidnapping, while insisting they had released Till after determining that he was not, in fact, the one who had insulted Mrs. Bryant. But the following morning, a teenager fishing in the Tallahatchie River saw a pair of feet sticking out of the water and called the local sheriff, H. C. Strider, who arrived soon thereafter and dragged up the body, which, entangled in barbed wire, was attached to the kind of heavy metal fan found in a cotton gin. Although the body was severely swollen from days spent in the water, the sheriff could make out signs of extreme trauma. "We found a bullet hole one inch above his left ear," Strider told the *Chicago Tribune*. "The left side of his face was cut up or smashed up — plumb to the skull."[7]

Moses Wright identified his grand-nephew from a signet ring found on the body inscribed with the letters *L.T.*, for his father, Louis Till, who had died in 1945 while serving in Italy with the U.S. Army.[8]

Local authorities tried to bury Emmett Till in Mississippi, but Mamie Bradley insisted her son be brought back to Chicago. A *Defender* photographer and reporter were there at the Illinois Central Railroad Station when Till's body arrived in a large wooden crate wrapped in soiled paper. Six men from the A. A. Rayner and Sons Funeral Home lifted the body out of the crate and placed it in a waiting hearse while Bradley wept openly at the loss of her only child. Later, at the funeral home, Bradley composed herself enough to inspect the body carefully to verify that it was, indeed, her son and to determine what had been done to him. "I stood a long time looking at that body," Bradley told *The Defender*'s Mattie Smith Colin. Though his face was shattered and his flesh was torn from the barbed wire, she recognized the remnants of his teeth, which she had always encouraged him to care for.[9]

With mortuary reconstruction of Till's face nearly impossible, Bradley made a fateful decision to keep her son's body as it was and have a public, open-casket funeral "so everyone can see what they did to my boy."[10]

The morticians dressed Emmett in a suit and placed him in a special casket with an air-sealed glass case, where he lay in state at the Rayner funeral home on the South Side. Thousands of people lined up outside the building all through that Friday night — almost all of them strangers — to pay their respects. Some fainted at the sight of Till's brutalized body, while most felt rage equal to their horror and sadness. It was a scene that was repeated many times the next day, when the body was brought to nearby Roberts Temple. Here thousands packed the church and tens of thousands clustered along the sidewalk and into the street outside, waiting for their turn to witness the body and listening to the eulogy broadcast over a public-address system. A squad of police officers arrived to keep the restive crowd moving.[11]

Major dailies around the country had more often than not ignored stories of southern atrocities in the past, but Till's disappearance, murder, and funeral remained on their front pages for an entire week. These stories, in turn, generated a wave of public outrage in black neighborhoods and among civil rights leaders. In New York City, NAACP Secretary Roy Wilkins said the Till case revealed just how egregiously Mississippi's elites and the institutions over which they had control — the courts, the church, and the political establishment — abetted a culture of violent racism. "It would appear from this lynching," Wilkins stated, "that the state of Mississippi has decided to maintain white supremacy by murdering children."[12]

Illinois's political leaders were unanimous in calling for federal intervention: Governor Richard Stratton wrote a letter of protest to

Mississippi's governor, and U.S. Senator Paul Douglas pledged to renew efforts to pass antilynching legislation. Chicago's new mayor, Richard J. Daley, sent a telegram to President Eisenhower declaring, in the awkward syntax for which he would become known, "The people of Chicago have been gravely shocked at the brutal murder in the state of Mississippi of Emmett Louis Till, a Chicago teenage youngster."[13]

Printed nearly one week after the funeral, the first issue of *The Defender* to follow the incident devoted multiple pages documenting the entire chain of events, including two pages of photographs depicting the moment Mamie Bradley met her son's body at the Chicago rail station as well as scenes from the funeral. One front-page article included a *Defender* interview with Mississippi Governor Hugh White, who, despite being a staunch segregationist, condemned the slaying and pledged to prosecute those responsible. White refused to call Till's slaying a "lynching"— the term the NAACP was just then using to refer to the political assassinations of two black voting-rights activists in the state earlier that year — but rather than ignore or try to justify the killing as his predecessors had, White called it a "straight out murder," and went on to say, "The people of Mississippi and the governor's office do not condone such an act."[14]

A grand jury — all white and all male — indicted Bryant and Milam on multiple counts, including first-degree murder, charges for which there was a mandatory death sentence in Mississippi if they were found guilty.

The governor's words and the grand jury's actions notwithstanding, an editorial on *The Defender*'s front page entitled "Blood on Their Hands" noted that all five candidates in Mississippi's recent gubernatorial race had supported segregation and the suppression of the black vote. The newspaper called on the Eisenhower administration not only to prosecute Till's murderers in federal court but to put forward legislation that would outlaw lynching once and for all, as well as protect African Americans' voting rights. "There can be no compromise this time," *The Defender* warned. "Your child can be the next victim of the white supremacists."[15]

Even among *The Defender*'s most grizzled veterans, the Emmett Till story elicited a smoldering rage. City editor Charles Davis, for instance, assumed the boy had been killed from the moment the initial report of Till's disappearance was distributed in the newsroom; Davis had covered many similar incidents in the South, after all, and the outcome was always the same. Even he could not help but be moved by the sight of the boy's mutilated corpse. In an era of "constant outrage," as Davis characterized it decades later, the Till story raised the level of indignation to new heights. "This was a youngster who had been a wee bit flirty or disrespectful to a white woman," Davis said in an interview decades after the killing. "There was personal anger, shock. It was just one of the worst lynchings that occurred during that period. The whole mood after World War II was 'We're not taking this anymore.'"[16]

Reflecting that militant outlook, the next edition of *The Defender,* too, was devoted to the Till case, including on one of the interior pages unretouched photographs of the boy's mangled body in its glass casket. Similar pictures appeared in *Jet,* a pocket-sized national magazine published by *Ebony* owner John H. Johnson. There was debate in both newsrooms about the decision, but Mamie Bradley had encouraged the black press to publish the pictures, hoping they would catalyze a mass movement for change.[17]

Readers bought up every available issue of *The Defender* and *Jet* at the newsstands that week, and soon other members of the black press began to reprint the photos of Till's body. Letters poured in to the newspaper now, with readers incensed over Till's killing, some to the point that they demanded armed revolt against the white South. "We must be instructed through your newspaper to fight the white man in the South with bullets," wrote Bronzeville resident Fred Poindexter, espousing a common sentiment.[18]

Noting this hunger for retribution within the community, Louis Martin wrote in his column on the editorial page that the Till murder was the topic of angry discussion in "barbershops, bars, crowded parlors and churches." Martin strongly opposed acts of vengeance against whites, warning that they would be counterproductive and self-defeating, but he worried that another such incident might create an unstoppable response, a "chain reaction in every ghetto and black belt in America."[19]

Bryant and Milam's trial, scheduled to begin the week after *The Defender* and *Jet* published the photos of Till's body, brought more than one hundred reporters from black and white newspapers around the country to Sumner, in Tallahatchie County, the Delta town nearest the point in the river where the corpse had been found. Along with all the Chicago newspapers, *The New York Times, New York Post,* and *New York Daily News* sent reporters, as did the *Afro-American* chain, *The St. Louis Argus,* and *Ebony.*[20]

The *Tribune's* reporter, after several days spent interviewing white planters, described a tense, racially charged environment he described in a story headlined "A Way of Life Going on Trial in Mississippi," which appeared in the paper's Sunday edition the day before the court proceedings began. While the planters were primarily concerned that the publicity generated by the trial would give outsiders a misimpression about life in the state, the reporter saw for himself the absolute power white landowners wielded over their enormous cotton plantations and their impoverished black employees. The sheriff himself was a plantation owner, with 150 acres dedicated to cotton and thirty-five black families living on his property in tenant houses, seven of which had large letters affixed to their roofs spelling out his name, *S-T-R-I-D-E-R.*

"Segregation," the *Tribune's* reporter wrote, "is the cornerstone of this region's society and economy."[21]

*The Defender* was ahead of the pack, having dispatched a team of eight reporters and photographers to the region in the early days of the Till story. Reporter Moses Newson, who interviewed Moses Wright at his house, discovered that the cotton farmer, now living in fear, was planning to leave Mississippi as soon as he'd testified at the trial. Since speaking to the grand jury, Wright and his son had received so many death threats, he dared not sleep at home at night, hiding out instead in neighbors' spare rooms or in the forest, armed with a rifle. His wife and most of his children had already left the state, escaping to Chicago.

Newson himself was terrified whenever a passing car slowed down in front of the house in the course of the interview, but Wright reassured him: "Don't worry. It's all right here."[22]

*The Defender* team was led by Alex Wilson, who from his base in nearby Memphis had built *The Tri-State Defender* into a regional editorial presence, with hard-hitting coverage of the lynchings of voting-rights activists in Mississippi earlier that year. Once he reached

Sumner, Wilson interviewed a number of white townspeople and found them "cordial," though he detected simmering resentment to the scrutiny the trial was attracting from the outside world. Having described Till's murder as "heinous and unnecessary," the owner of a dry goods store on the town's main street, in the next breath expressed anger at the negative image of Mississippi that had emerged in the coverage of the case by the nation's major dailies. "Mississippi is a sovereign state and we have shown we will handle the case," the store owner said. "We don't like meddling from outsiders."[23]

Wilson soon discovered that Mississippi's pernicious racial system applied to journalists as well. At a briefing for reporters before the court proceedings began, Sheriff Strider announced that white reporters would be placed at the front of a section reserved for whites, while black reporters would be consigned to a spot behind the white spectators. When Wilson protested that the black reporters would be unable to hear, the sheriff rebuffed him: "We don't mix down here and don't intend to start now."[24]

Strider made his feelings even more overt once they were inside the courtroom, where he greeted the small contingent of black reporters by saying, "Good morning, niggers."[25]

As the jury-selection process began, it soon became obvious that finding a group of white men who could hear the case would be difficult. Out of the first group of 120 men, most were dismissed when they answered yes to the question posed by the prosecutor, "Would you be moved by any consideration, race or anything else in helping to see that a fair trial be held?"

Of the remnant, three were disqualified for having given money to a relief fund for Bryant and Milam, five were removed for having already formed opinions about the case, one for being related to the defendants, and one for being a family member of one of the defense attorneys.[26]

With the heat and humidity rising to truly unbearable levels in the afternoon, the court recessed that first day without a jury being impaneled. Even when a jury was finally assembled the next day, the atmosphere surrounding the proceedings remained poisonous. *The Defender*'s reporters nevertheless did their best to help the prosecution and the judge, praising both for attempting to mount a fair trial. They also took part in evidence gathering. After prosecutors asked

for a court recess in order to give them time to interview more witnesses, reporter Moses Newson and a group from the NAACP found
two individuals, a man and a woman, who had been on the Milam
farm when Till was brought there, hours after the men claimed they'd
released the boy.[27]

The witnesses were turned over to the prosecutor, who over the
next two days made a compelling case to convict Bryant and Milam,
creating a plausible timeline for Till's kidnapping, beating, and murder that was backed up not only by circumstantial evidence but by
the testimony of multiple witnesses. Repeating the testimony he had
given to the grand jury, Moses Wright pointed out Milam and Bryant as two of the white men who had come to his farm and taken
his nephew on the night in question. Even more damning testimony,
however, came from one of the witnesses discovered by *The Defender*'s reporter, an eighteen-year-old farm hand named Willie Reed,
who told the court he had seen Bryant and Milam bring a young man
onto the farm and heard the sounds of a savage beating as well as the
screaming of a child coming from inside Milam's barn.[28]

Milam and Bryant's team of five defense lawyers — paid by a support fund that was raising money across the state — based their case
on denying that the body found in the Tallahatchie was actually Till's.
Their theory ran that Milam and Bryant had merely beaten the boy to
punish him for insulting Bryant's wife, and that "outsiders" had then
seized on the opportunity, simulating Till's death in order to disgrace
the state of Mississippi. Sheriff Strider lent his own weight to this argument when he told the court that the body he had retrieved from
the river was simply too badly swollen to be properly identified. As for
the ring inscribed with the boy's father's initials, the defense attorneys
suggested that this item was planted by the "outsiders," the better to
achieve their goal of defaming Mississippi and sowing unrest.

To counter this line of reasoning, the prosecution flew Mamie
Bradley to Mississippi to testify at the Sumner proceedings — after
first assuring her of her safety. Neatly dressed and composed, Bradley fought back tears as she recounted the moment the body was returned to Chicago.

"I looked at the face carefully," Bradley told the jury. "That was
my son."

Fifteen feet away at the defendants' table, Bryant stared at Bradley without emotion, while Milam sat in his chair reading letters, simultaneously chewing gum and smoking cigarettes.[29]

When the jury retired to chambers for deliberation on that Friday, the white townspeople who dominated the spectators' benches stayed in their seats, having apparently been informed that a decision would not be long in coming. Nor were they disappointed when, a little over an hour later, the jurors filed back into the courtroom and informed the judge that they had found Milam and Bryant not guilty. Having been sternly warned by the judge to refrain from emotional outbursts when the verdict was returned, white onlookers quietly shook the men's hands in congratulation while the blacks in the courtroom sat stunned. Outside the courtroom, however, the white residents of Sumner erupted into a wild public celebration as soon as word of the verdict filtered out.

The *Chicago Tribune* reporter who was in the courtroom interviewed the jury foreman, a farmer named J. A. Shaw, who said that the panel did not believe the body found in the river was Till's, adding that he was unconvinced by Mamie Bradley's testimony. "If she had tried a little harder," Shaw said, "she might have got out a tear."

Milam and Bryant were not quite free, however, at least not yet. Just after the verdict was pronounced, Sheriff Strider took the men into custody and brought them to neighboring Leflore County, where Moses Wright's home was located and where they still faced kidnapping charges. But kidnapping, unlike murder, was a bondable offense, and the men were soon out of jail after their supporters posted $10,000.[30]

Mamie Bradley was not in the courtroom when the verdict was read. Having guessed what the outcome of the trial would be, she'd left Mississippi and was at a mass rally in Detroit on the day the verdict was announced. But by the next day, she had returned home to Chicago and checked into Provident Hospital for what *The Defender* described as "nervous fatigue." She was not alone. Star witness Willie Reed, having fled to Chicago after his testimony, collapsed after hearing the verdict and was being treated in another South Side hospital. As for Moses Wright, rumors reached Chicago that he was dead, but he turned up in the city as well just a few days after Milam and Bryant were released.[31]

On *The Defender*'s editorial page, Langston Hughes captured the outrage and frustration felt by the entire community when he began that week's column with a blistering poem, the first stanza of which reads,

> *Oh What Sorrow*
> *Oh What Pity*
> *Oh What Pain*
> *That Tears and Blood Should Mix Like Rain*
> *And Terror Come Again*
> *To Mississippi.*[32]

Just a few weeks later, the grand jury in Leflore County refused to indict Milam and Bryant on the kidnapping charge, setting them free once and for all. Because the double jeopardy rule prevented their being tried again for any of these crimes, Mississippi's courts had effectively ensured they got away with Till's murder. Moses Wright was in Seattle on an NAACP-sponsored speaking tour when he received word of the grand jury's decision. "Mississippi hasn't got any law," he summed up.[33]

Nevertheless, the Emmett Till trial, those at *The Defender* realized, marked the end of white America's innocence when it came to the race-related brutality in the South. For generations, the newspaper had fought a grassroots counterpropaganda campaign almost single-handedly when it came to lynchings like Emmett Till's, where an allegation of sexual misconduct was used to justify extreme violence against black men. But this time, the North — and even much of the South — simply did not buy it. An editorial printed on *The Defender*'s front page predicted that those daily newspapers that had previously given the benefit of the doubt to southern institutions would now side at least as often with African Americans demanding their civil rights. "More eloquently than our words ever could do it," the editorial observed, "the grand jury itself has given us a better picture of what is termed 'justice' in Mississippi than we could ever do."[34]

Indeed, the *Chicago Tribune* called on the Eisenhower administration to prosecute the men at the federal level, noting that they could be charged with kidnapping as well as with depriving Emmett Till of his civil rights. "The forms of law may have been observed," a *Tribune* editorial surmised of the trial in Sumner, "but the spirit of justice was absent."[35]

An editorial on the Till slaying in *The Commercial Appeal*—a Memphis paper that, back in 1917, had printed directions to the lynching site of Eli Persons—underscored just how much had changed from one generation to the next. *The Commercial Appeal* was particularly upset by the second grand jury's decision, noting that Bryant and Milam had *admitted* to the kidnapping, and worried that this decision would damage the reputation of all southern courts. "The system has failed in this instance," the editorial concluded, "and a violence has been committed for which the accused, guilty or innocent, will not be called to answer."[36]

The Eisenhower administration remained stubbornly silent, refusing even to issue a message of condolence to Mamie Bradley. Certainly the administration's reticence was, to some extent, due to the president's physical absence: Eisenhower had suffered a heart attack the day after the verdict and did not return to the White House until November 11, two days after the Leflore County grand jury decided not to indict Milam and Bryant. But as thousands of telegrams and letters poured in along with tens of thousands of signatures on petitions, the administration made only the most minor of concessions, allowing an assistant attorney general to describe the episode as "a black mark in the sense that those responsible have not been brought to justice." Neither the Justice Department nor the FBI, however, initiated any effort to erase this "black mark."[37]

On December 2, 1955, to celebrate the newspaper's fiftieth anniversary, John Sengstacke hosted a "Citizens Tribute to *The Chicago Defender*," an evening of speeches and presentations at Chicago's Orchestra Hall for a thousand of the city's political and business leaders, white and black judges, federal officials and attorneys, as well as merchants and service providers. The room was treated to a performance from gospel singer Mahalia Jackson as well as a slide show recounting the entire history of the publication, which focused on Robert Abbott's primary role in catalyzing the Great Migration and building the political and economic foundation for Chicago's African American community. U.S. Representative William Dawson spoke reverently about Abbott, as did keynote speaker Thurgood Marshall. "There is a much needed place for *The Defender* in the next half-century," Marshall said. "The job ahead, as tough as it's going to be, couldn't be as tough as the job that faced Mr. Abbott."

Amid all the reflections on the past, however, the evening culminated with an announcement from John Sengstacke that excited the audience about the newspaper's future: that coming February, as part of a $1 million modernization of its headquarters and its presses, *The Defender* would add a daily edition to serve the still-growing African American community and compete with the city's four other dailies.

"*The Chicago Defender* has grown with Chicago and the expansion taking place today in our city creates new needs which can be met only with the expansion of our facilities and the general press of the city," Sengstacke told the audience. "Over the last half-century, we have become an institution to which citizens of all groups look for an authentic interpretation of the problems and developments on the race relations front. Also we have pioneered in the development of the much-neglected Negro consumer market.

"Although the new daily newspaper will carry forward this tradition, we will not be limited in either our coverage or our circulation by reasons of race or color."[38]

A "Daily Defender" had been the long-standing dream of Sengstacke, among others at the newspaper, and even before the publisher made his announcement to the public, the editorial, printing, advertising, and distribution departments had been busily recalibrating their schedules and resources. There had been only a handful of dailies in the history of the black press, and at that moment there was but one other, the modest *Atlanta Daily World*. Increasing *The Defender*'s frequency would allow the newspaper to cover time-sensitive events like elections and sports, while also facilitating reporters' access to press clubs and other organizations restricted to the employees of dailies. Even though technically the *Daily Defender* would be published only four times per week, Monday through Thursday, with the national edition, dated Saturday, raising frequency to five days a week, this met the minimum qualifications for a "daily" in the bylaws of most newspaper trade organizations of the day.

On the business side, going daily was a gamble, but Sengstacke was trying to stay ahead of a readership whose needs and tastes were only getting more sophisticated. With migrants coming at the rate of 5,000 to 10,000 every month, Chicago's African American population was now more than 650,000 people, nearly 20 percent of the city, a community increasingly self-sufficient and focused on its own struggles as well as what was happening in their ancestral lands below the Mason-Dixon Line. This enormous potential local audience, Sengstacke was wagering, would respond to a newspaper that was able to explore all of these issues on a daily, or near daily, basis.

The most significant factor in *The Defender*'s decision to become a daily, however, was new competition for black audiences from the white-owned media. Until now, the daily newspapers had largely ignored African Americans and their issues, leaving *The Defender* to fight it out only with other members of the black press. But having discovered the "race beat," the white press was beginning to hire black writers, albeit in small numbers, as part of a conscious effort to attract black readers. In their coverage of Emmett Till's disappearance and funeral, and finally the trial of Milam and Bryant, the dailies had demonstrated a distinct advantage, allowing readers to follow the story day by day, while *The Defender* had had to report the news as much as a week late. Nor was it just other newspapers *The Defender* had to worry about; only just beginning to be realized was the burgeoning of news programs on radio and television with their power to deliver news immediately.[39]

In Montgomery, Alabama, just three days after Sengstacke's announcement, Rosa Parks was arrested for refusing to give up her seat on a municipal bus to a white man, violating both state and city segregation laws. After she was convicted and fined fourteen dollars, Parks, a seamstress active with the local branch of the NAACP, decided to try to use her case as a means to challenge the segregation laws. She enlisted the help of E. D. Nixon, a full-time Pullman porter, who not only served as the president of the local chapter of the Brotherhood of Sleeping Car Porters, but was a former NAACP state president, and together they decided to replicate a tactic used successfully by civil rights activists in Baton Rouge, Louisiana, where a bus boycott several years earlier had won several concessions. Working closely with a multidenominational coalition of Montgomery's ministers, Nixon and Parks called a public meeting at which they proposed that the community refuse to ride the buses for a single day to register their disapproval. They won public support for the action, and the protest was renewed by popular acclaim. A committee drew up a list of demands, including the hiring of black drivers and a policy of first-come, first-served seating, and vowed to continue the boycott until black passengers no longer felt "intimidated, embarrassed and coerced."

For its first week, the Montgomery bus boycott was covered only by white and black newspapers in the vicinity of Birmingham, but as it continued into the middle of December, *The Defender* covered it on the front page with an article that featured an interview with Nixon and proclaimed the boycott 90 percent effective. The article included as well a detailed description of a carpool the community had organized to provide alternative transportation to boycott participants. The following week, *The Defender*'s front page carried a report that the protesters had voted to continue the boycott after the bus company rejected their demands, quoting their new spokesperson, the young pastor of Dexter Avenue Baptist Church, Martin Luther King Jr. "We aren't trying to change segregation laws," King said. "But we are trying to peacefully arrange better accommodations for Negroes."[40]

At the end of December, *The Defender* praised the boycott in an article covering a range of protests taking place throughout the South in the wake of the Emmett Till case and other outrages. "In a year of bloody rebellion and new hate campaigns," the newspaper wrote, "there were some encouraging signs in Montgomery, Alabama."[41]

King had been selected by his fellow ministers for his charisma, erudition, and youth; just twenty-seven, he had received his doctorate the previous year. But as the boycott stretched on into its second month, King and his supporters were tested by all of the sinister tactics the white South had at its disposal. At the end of January, King was driving with a friend when he was pulled over by Montgomery police who accused him of speeding. Although exceeding the speed limit was not usually a jailable offense, King was taken to the county lockup and denied the right to post bond. Word of King's arrest spread quickly, however, and within minutes, hundreds of his parishioners and supporters — motivated by the collective memory of what so often happened to outspoken African American men in southern jails — arrived and offered to post bond or otherwise facilitate the pastor's release. The ranking police officers on the scene called the city's mayor, and shortly thereafter decided to release King on his own recognizance.

A second incident occurred on the evening of January 30, when someone threw a firebomb into King's home, leaving the structure badly damaged, though neither King, his wife, Coretta, nor their four-month-old daughter was harmed. A crowd of more than a thousand African Americans gathered outside, as did the city's mayor and a contingent of police in full riot gear, nightsticks at the ready. It was a riot in the making — some said instigated by the authorities — but King calmly told the crowd to disburse. "We have other means to deal with this kind of situation and it will not stop us," King said. "The movement goes on."[42]

The Montgomery bus boycott was back on *The Defender*'s front page at the beginning of February as the mayor, W. A. Gayle, vowed to stop "pussy-footing around" with the boycotters and urged those whites who were giving rides to blacks to cease aiding their cause. He was particularly incensed by the white women who willingly transported the legion of black cooks, maids, and nannies back and forth, a reflection, the newspaper maintained, of the degree to which southern white households depended on black labor. Gayle's administration had proposed various compromises, such as creating all-black buses, but warned that he would not "destroy our social fabric."[43]

On Sunday, February 6, 1956, after months of discussions, plans, revisions, and trial and error, the first edition of the *Daily Defender* was finally ready to roll. John Sengstacke splashed champagne over the sheets of blank newsprint and then lifted up his youngest son, six-year-old Lewis, to press the button starting the massive presses. Within a few minutes, the first copies of the new paper emerged, a twenty-four-page tabloid with large black-and-white photos on the front cover and sports on the back, selling for five cents a copy. It was nearly midnight, far later than had been scheduled, but there was still just enough time to get the newspaper out on the streets for the morning delivery.

A hundred thousand copies were printed and given to a small army of newsboys dressed as town criers, with three-cornered hats, fur-collared leather jackets, and canvas shoulder bags, who now fanned out across Bronzeville and into downtown, ringing bells and shouting, "The Biggest News of 1956." The first copy of the *Daily Defender* was hand-delivered to Mayor Daley in City Hall, who examined the new publication and posed with the two newsboys, brothers Walter and Ross Scott, thirteen and twelve years old, respectively, for a photo on the cover of the *second* issue, which would be printed that evening. "We are proud to welcome a new daily paper to our city," Daley said. "It is a wholesome thing to see more papers going into business here."[44]

In the end, the worst glitch in the daily's launch was that Sengstacke had decided to turn down a number of advertisers rather than cut into the news sections, although the first issue did include full-page messages of congratulations from major corporate entities including Pepsi-Cola and Sara Lee as well as black-owned banks and a few of the white-owned merchants based in Bronzeville. It remained a challenge to get the editorial, advertising, and distribution departments to adjust their routines to the faster pace of a daily, but slowly, this incarnation of the newspaper became a fixture in the community. After the fanfare of the first issue, circulation dropped to just 16,997 daily by the end of the year and then began to steadily climb.[45]

The first issue of the *Daily Defender* included substantial coverage of the ongoing civil rights struggles in the South, with an article about the Montgomery bus boycott that detailed a second bomb attack, this time against the home of civil rights leader E. D. Nixon. Luckily, this bomb fell short of its target, landing on the front lawn, and caused little damage.[46]

On Monday of the following week, the *Daily Defender* included coverage of Martin Luther King's visit to Chicago the day before, when he served as a guest preacher at the South Side's Shiloh Baptist Church. King deeply impressed *The Defender*'s reporter with his sermon "The Knock at Midnight" and with his explanation of nonviolent resistance, which was based on the tactics and philosophy employed by Mohandas Gandhi in India. The reporter noted that King, along with other ministers leading the boycott, had become not only the focus of national adulation but a target of white supremacists, who telephoned the pastor with death threats at the rate of twenty-five per day.

"His message was delivered with the fervor and emotion of an old-time freedom-talking slave preacher and the smoothness of a suave scholar," the reporter recounted.[47]

Based in Montgomery since the start of February, Ethel Payne had discovered an African American community totally galvanized by the boycott and devoted to King as their leader. Packed rallies were held up to five nights every week in churches with an interdenominational roster of ministers — itself a remarkable show of unity among the normally divided black clergy — using all their moral authority to keep the community unified.

"They took turns in the different churches, and each minister would then really pull out all the oratorical stops, to rile the people up to get involved," Payne later recalled to a biographer.

"It became a spiritual thing, a great spiritual experience, and people began to realize that they were involved; every person was involved in a personal way."[48]

Sustaining the boycott required a sophisticated organizing and fundraising operation that Payne detailed in her articles for *The Defender*. The carpool system, for example, deployed some twenty cars to fifty pickup points all over the African American section of town. Most astonishing to Payne was the tacit support of the boycott by many of the city's well-off white women, who collaborated by driving their African American maids, cooks, and nannies back and forth on a daily basis. While not explicitly subscribed to the civil rights cause, these southern white women were certainly acting in defiance of Montgomery's public officials as well as the local pro-segregationist "citizens' councils," though some of this support had less to do with civil rights than a desire to avoid disruption in their household routines.[49]

Payne was particularly impressed with the community's disciplined response when Montgomery's mayor held a convention for citizens' councils from around the state during King's trip to Chicago. As thousands of white supremacists converged on the city's coliseum for a speech by U.S. Senator James Eastland, an arch-segregationist from Mississippi, the boycott organizers imposed their own voluntary curfew to keep African Americans inside their homes and avoid any confrontations.[50]

Returning to Chicago from behind the "color curtain," as she described it, Payne raved about King and the other ministers in Montgomery, praising their resilience in the face of the bombing attacks and other acts of provocation. Where in the past ministers had often been derided for kowtowing to the white power structure, Payne maintained that this new generation was in the vanguard of those fighting for civil rights, a "new, vocal, fearless and forthright Moses who is leading the people out of the wilderness into the promised land," she wrote in the *Daily Defender*. Her advocacy, in turn, made a convert of the editorial page, which printed "A New Hero Emerges in the South," urging local readers to send their dollars to Montgomery.[51]

At the end of February, King and more than ninety other organizers were indicted under state laws that prevented undermining of a business — twenty-four ministers as well as teachers, housewives, merchants, undertakers, and pharmacists were arrested. The *Daily Defender* responded by printing the names of the "Montgomery Heroes" on its front page. Now the white dailies began covering the bus boycott on their front pages as well, focusing their coverage on King as the boycott's highly quotable and photogenic leader while also warning about the potential for violence. In this context, King underscored the need for nonviolent tactics.

"Anything that looks like violence will defeat our purpose," King told the assembly at one rally before his arrest, as covered by *The Defender*. "We are going to prove that nobody can make us ride the buses."[52]

After the arrests of their leaders, the community only became more determined, eschewing the use of cars in a "total walking day" as a show of solidarity. The state of Alabama, however, oblivious both to the unity among the boycotters and King's rapidly growing celebrity, decided to put him on trial ahead of the other protesters, ensuring that the case would become a national sensation. Within days, Thurgood Marshall arrived in town, having volunteered to represent the boycott organizers, even as writers, photographers, and correspondents from every major news media outlet, print and broadcast alike, American as well as international, descended upon Montgomery.[53]

For Payne, this journalistic convergence was a boon, as these reporters were, for the most part, pro–civil rights politically and, on a personal level, friendly to African Americans. Though Payne and the other black reporters stayed in private homes, segregated as the town's hotels and restaurants were, while the white reporters stayed in hotels downtown, they came together on a daily basis at a drugstore lunch counter in the black neighborhood.

"It got to be a real camaraderie," Payne told an interviewer years later.

"That drugstore . . . was a gathering place for us, and we'd all sit there and exchange notes. They would fill us in sometimes about what the white power structure was saying, and, in turn, we'd give them little bits of information that they hadn't yet gotten access to."[54]

Thus, when King's trial began on March 19, the *Daily Defender* was able to compete on a level field with all the white-owned dailies. Indeed, Payne regularly delivered exclusive interviews and nuanced perspectives unavailable in the white press. The newspaper also gleefully charted the attention the white press was showering on Martin Luther King. The cover of one *Defender* during the trial pictured King, dapper in a suit and banded fedora, in the midst of a scrum of white reporters, talking into a microphone being held by NBC reporter Don Goddard as a movie camera on a tripod rolled. "They're Not Boycotting Him," read the headline over the caption.[55]

The trial itself was a by-now-familiar exercise in southern justice, argued before a judge who did his best to make it appear that the outcome was not predetermined by the need to uphold the racial hierarchy. The prosecution cited the organization and funding of the carpool as evidence of the "conspiracy," inferring over defense objections that King and the other boycott leaders had coerced the support of black citizens using threats of violence. The defense, meanwhile, cited a litany of abuses committed by the bus company, presenting one woman who testified that a bus driver called her a "black ape" and another woman who said she was called a "nigger." Defense attorneys called twenty-five witnesses who testified that they'd joined the boycott voluntarily after hearing of Rosa Parks's experience.

"We all did it after that thing happened to Mrs. Parks," said Gladys Moore, as quoted in both the *Tribune* and the *Daily Defender.* "We didn't think she'd been treated justly."[56]

Predictably, King was convicted on the conspiracy charge and ordered to pay a $500 fine and $500 in court costs, a lenient sentence, the judge said, in recognition of the pastor's calming words to the angry crowd that had gathered in the aftermath of the bombing of his home. King refused to pay on principle and immediately filed an appeal, which prompted the judge to convert the penalty to 386 days in jail, suspended pending the outcome of the appeal. Prosecutors agreed to wait for the result of King's appeal before they proceeded with the other cases.

Despite King's conviction, the mood outside the court was positively jubilant. When he emerged from the building, Coretta kissed him passionately on the cheek before the news photographers' cameras as throngs of supporters and media closed in around them. Ethel Payne saw one woman call out, "Long Live the King," and then heard five hundred voices chant the phrase as a salute to their hero.

"They might as well send those buses back to Chicago," another woman exclaimed. "They'll dry rot now."[57]

The *Tribune* had covered the case dutifully, and now that the verdict was in, an editorial entitled "Who Won in Alabama?" questioned the wisdom of bringing the case in the first place, arguing that the prosecution of nonviolent protesters had already backfired in the court of public opinion, strengthening the boycotters' resolve while elevating Martin Luther King into a national figure, a "certified martyr," in the newspaper's description.

"The conviction may be lawful but it will seem unjust to a good many people," the *Tribune* surmised. "It will be harder from now on to pretend that all the Negroes of Alabama are so deficient or backward in moral standards that they must be segregated."[58]

Unfortunately for the *Daily Defender,* the verdict came in on a Thursday just after the deadline for the weekend national edition, so the news didn't appear on its pages until the following Monday. But Ethel Payne scored an exclusive interview with Martin Luther King just a few hours after the verdict was pronounced. Speaking in soaring metaphors laced with biblical references, King told her the bus boycott was a natural and logical reaction to the treatment of African Americans in the city and that it was part of the "worldwide revolt of subjugated peoples." Fully aware of the global attention focused on Montgomery, King pledged that the protest would continue until their goals had been achieved, regardless of the cost.

"Peace can be obnoxious if it is not a true peace without a compromise," King told Payne. "Somehow, I believe that the world will be better for this."[59]

In King, *The Defender*'s editorial page understood, the civil rights movement had discovered the perfect spokesperson, an educated, thoughtful minister who acted out his Christian values. His level-headed behavior only served to confound southern whites, who generally considered themselves devout Christians, while immunizing him against criticism that he was some variety of race agitator or Communist agent in disguise. That King was a southerner, too, was essential to his appeal, for his leadership of the boycott contradicted the notion that African Americans of that region were satisfied with conditions under segregation. Finally, the newspaper praised the strategy of nonviolence, which had the effect of ennobling King and the other leaders of the boycott every time they were attacked.

"Reverend King acts and talks like some sort of prophet, some disciple of Christ walking out of the pages of the Bible," the editorial assessed.

"Now they are discovering the Reverend Martin Luther King is not just another preacher but a profound Christian leader with a grasp of life so tender and devout that his reactions are loaded with sociological dynamite."[60]

On the morning of August 11, 1956, a shiny black Cadillac escorted by a squad of motorcycle policemen, their lights flashing and sirens wailing, rolled through the South Side until they reached the intersection of Pershing Road and South Parkway, where the car stopped, the door opened, and out stepped former president Harry Truman, accompanied by Mayor Richard J. Daley. John Sengstacke greeted the former president and the mayor while the Secret Service kept the cheering crowd back until the three men were able to get into a waiting blue convertible. The marshal of the police marching band then gave the signal, and that year's Bud Billiken Parade was officially underway.

Despite rain-heavy clouds that threatened to burst at any moment, some five hundred thousand people came out to see the former president as well as former heavyweight champion Joe Louis, who rode in a convertible bearing the logo of his milk delivery company, along with the usual caravan of marching bands, dance groups, military units, and floats representing local businesses. Truman himself traversed the entire length of the parade route and then spoke to a huge assembly in front of the reviewing stand in Washington Park before heading back downtown to participate in the Democratic National Convention.[61]

Truman's presence at the parade followed on the close relationship he had enjoyed with Sengstacke during his presidency. For Mayor Daley, this particular Billiken Parade was a chance to demonstrate his support and appreciation for the African American community in general and *The Defender* in particular. As a native son of the South Side's Bridgeport community, with its long history of hostility toward its eastern neighbor Bronzeville, Daley might have seemed an unlikely ally for the African American community. Indeed, during the 1919 race riot, he had been the president of the Hamburg Club, one of the street gangs who attacked African Americans, although Daley steadfastly denied ever having taken part in such violence himself. But in his climb to the executive offices of City Hall, Daley had followed in the path of Mayors Big Bill Thompson and Ed Kelly by building a strong alliance with the African American community. Black votes, in fact, had been critical to his defeat of incumbent mayor Martin Kennelly in the Democratic primary a year earlier and then in the general election against Republican Alderman Robert Merriam.

Daley, too, was personally close to Sengstacke and proud to be pictured in the *Daily Defender* at community events, with NAACP officials as with the city's black aldermen, a bloc that had now grown to five members and was key to his control of the City Council. Daley hadn't deployed any new resources to advance integration in the city, a topic that continued to generate volcanic eruptions of anger from white aldermen as well as their constituents, but at the Trumbull Park public housing development on the far South Side, the mayor had maintained a detail of one hundred police officers who had been there for three years protecting a handful of black tenants from the threats of their white neighbors. The mayor had even appointed Sengstacke and other African American leaders to a special commission charged with devising solutions to the standoff.

Daley's preferred solution was to build high-rise public housing entirely within existing black neighborhoods, thereby increasing the number of units without infringing on white territory. Within his first year in office, he approved the construction of midrise buildings on the edge of the Ida B. Wells development, just a stone's throw from the spot where the mayor had entered the blue convertible with President Truman. On South State Street, meanwhile, Daley greenlighted plans to build multiple clusters of seventeen-story high-rise public housing buildings to replace the old Stroll.[62]

But by the end of the year, *The Defender* editorial page was urging Daley to keep the Chicago Housing Authority free from the real estate brokers and construction moguls who sought to control its $250 million in annual contracts. Although the territory available to black families was expanding bit by bit, one editorial quoted the mayor's own staff to show that the city was "creating slums faster than it was clearing them," while rents remained 25 to 50 percent higher per square foot within the African American neighborhoods.

"These are the same economic forces which precipitated the mass flight of thousands to the suburbs, only to want to reclaim the land they once vacated," the editorial decried.

"They are the ones that herd people into marked-off areas and reshuffle them like decks of cards."[63]

The Montgomery bus boycott continued all through the summer and fall even as white officials kept up the pressure through legal and economic strategies. But on November 13, 1956, as the protest neared its first anniversary, the U.S. Supreme Court affirmed a lower court ruling that the state and city laws segregating the city's public transportation were unconstitutional, invalidating yet another aspect of the Jim Crow system throughout the South. "We agree," wrote the justices, "that the separate but equal doctrine can no longer be safely followed as a correct statement of the law."[64]

With Ethel Payne back on the East Coast, the *Defender* dispatched Enoch Waters to Montgomery. Waters arrived just in time to see the Ku Klux Klan parade through the town as a show of defiance against the court ruling. Eight to ten cars containing robed Klansmen proceeded slowly along Jackson Avenue, the main commercial street in the black district, followed by a number of supporters on foot, their faces bared in accord with a state law prohibiting the wearing of masks. "However, the Negroes along the busy thoroughfare ignored them completely," Waters noted, "and refused to be intimidated."[65]

One month later, on December 21, 1956, the Supreme Court rejected the state of Alabama's final appeal and the city of Montgomery grudgingly prepared to integrate its bus lines. *Tri-State Defender* editor Alex Wilson and photographer Ernest Withers were on hand at a mass rally when the city's black community voted overwhelmingly to return to the buses. "Walking days are over now for the freedom-loving people in the 'Cradle of the Confederacy,'" said the Rev. Ralph Abernathy, Martin Luther King's second-in-command. "We realize this is not a victory for Negroes alone but for democracy."

Organizing the ministers into groups of two and three who would serve as monitors and witnesses on the buses, King himself arranged to ride with a white Methodist minister. Asked by Wilson about the potential for a hostile reception from whites, King said he was "not upset by the resistance which might develop. It is just a part of the overall movement to a new emerging society."[66]

At 6:30 a.m. the next day, Wilson and Withers boarded a bus and found two African American women, neatly dressed and calm, already sitting in one of the front seats, without any of the white passengers seeming to notice or care. Speaking briefly with the driver, Wilson assessed him as "courteous and intelligent."

Wilson and Withers spent the day traveling on a number of different lines, interviewing black passengers and checking in with King and the other boycott leaders, but there were very few incidents of racial animosity to report. One white man struck or shoved a black woman as they were both exiting, but the woman did not confront him, in keeping with the nonviolent tactics of the movement, and the man got into a waiting car and drove off. A few other whites refused to sit next to blacks or even got off the bus rather than ride in an integrated vehicle, and one white man yelled epithets at African Americans on the bus from the safety of a parked car. But he was ignored by the passengers and passersby alike, blacks as well as whites, and drove off when confronted by a reporter. In contrast with these outbursts, Wilson also recorded several moments of racial goodwill, including a white girl riding next to her black nanny as well as an elderly white woman who called out holiday greetings as she got off the bus.

The reality of integrated public transit quickly defeated the doomsday prognostications of the paranoid white supremacists, and Wilson didn't hear of any incidents on the buses the next day or in the following days. One group affiliated with the local citizens' council vowed to create a private, whites-only bus line, but the rest of the South acquiesced quietly to this particular blow to the Jim Crow system.[67]

# 17

# One Vote per Precinct

IN LATE SEPTEMBER 1957, *Defender* writer Alex Wilson traveled to Little Rock, Arkansas, to cover the crisis over the integration of Central High School. Citing the *Brown v. Board of Education* ruling, a federal court had ordered that nine African American students who tried to register at Central High, until then an all-white school, be allowed to attend. But Arkansas Governor Orval Faubus had defied the order, and when Wilson arrived, he saw several hundred heavily armed soldiers from the Arkansas National Guard stationed around the school, blocking the entrance of the "Little Rock Nine," as the black students had been dubbed by the national media.[1]

President Eisenhower declined to take action for the first few weeks school was in session but finally, having grown steadily exasperated with Governor Faubus, he threatened to send in U.S. Army troops to enforce the court order. This last threat forced Faubus to back down, and on Friday, September 20, the governor ordered the guardsmen withdrawn. The following Monday, as the Little Rock Nine prepared yet again to enter Central High, Wilson and three other black journalists — one reporter from the *Afro-American,* another from the *New York Amsterdam News,* and a photographer for the local black paper, the *Arkansas State Press* — decided to drive together in Wilson's car to Central High to record the day's events. A thin cordon of thirty-five police officers, backed up by fifty state troopers, had been assigned to keep order but a mob of some eight hundred angry whites had gathered as well, determined to prevent the black students from entering the school.

When Wilson and his associates stepped out of the car, the mob saw them and charged, either because they thought the black journalists were themselves the Little Rock Nine or because they were simply enraged by the presence of the African Americans. The crowd surrounded the newsmen, taunting them with racial epithets. Then, as the journalists got closer to the school's entrance, two white men blocked their path and said they could not pass. Wilson protested that they were only trying to do their jobs, but the white men refused to move and a policeman on the scene suggested that the journalists go back to their car for their own safety.

Wilson and his colleagues followed the officer's instructions, but no sooner had they tried to retreat than some of the white men in the crowd pushed past the officer, smashing the photographer's equipment and beating the writers for the *Afro-American* and the *New York Amsterdam News* until they ran. Wilson, though, refused to break his stride. The white men kicked, punched, and twice jumped on his back, knocking him to the ground, but he got up without fighting back, even stopping at one point to retrieve his hat, until a contingent of officers interceded and allowed him to reach his car.[2]

While the mob was engaged with the black newsmen, the nine children had arrived together in a station wagon and slipped in through the school's back entrance. Realizing what had happened, the crowd swung back toward the school, determined to rush the police lines, but were repulsed by the policemen swinging their clubs in warning.

Just then, a score of white students came out of the building and two teenage girls inflamed the crowd yet again, shouting, "They're in! They're in! Somebody do something."[3]

The police held their line against a second charge, following which the mob redirected its rage against the white reporters and television cameramen recording the entire incident. The segregationists shoved and threatened one reporter and tried to smash the equipment the newsmen had set up. One police officer, witnessing this scene, threw off his badge and walked away in apparent frustration of having to enforce the court's desegregation order.

As the morning progressed, the ranks of the protesters were swelled by the hundreds of students who left the high school and began chanting racist slogans. Now Little Rock's mayor, who had embraced the school-desegregation order, decided that the black youths were in danger and ordered police to escort them out shortly before noon. But even after having been informed that the African American students had left the premises, the crowd refused to disburse, if anything growing more menacing, and demanding that one of their own be allowed to enter the building and verify the authorities' statement.[4]

Wilson had suffered a severe beating but he continued reporting that day, tracking down the Little Rock Nine for an interview. The youths all said they had been mostly welcomed by Central High's principal, faculty, and the white students during their brief stay at the school. One girl recounted that a white boy passing in the hallway had greeted her with "Hi, black gal, you don't belong here," but then quickly apologized. African American student Ernest Green, who some reports said had been beaten to a bloody pulp, told Wilson that he'd had no trouble at all. "The teachers were pleasant and the white students did not annoy me," Green said. "I am ready to return."[5]

Wilson spent Monday night under police guard at the home of Daisy Bates, editor of Little Rock's African American newspaper, the *Arkansas State Press*. A fearless advocate for civil rights and school integration, Bates had played a highly public role orchestrating the efforts at Central High School, and her home in a white neighborhood of the city had been targeted in the past, with bricks thrown through the window and crosses burned on the lawn, prompting her to install floodlights on the property. That night, however, the two police officers stationed outside Bates's home, having received word that a caravan of twenty-five cars loaded with white supremacists was headed their way, called for reinforcements. Two blocks away, the officers intercepted a number of vehicles loaded with men armed with dynamite, clubs, knives, and bottles. While he was holed up in Bates's home that night, Wilson received word of several skirmishes unfolding in the black neighborhood in what was becoming an increasingly volatile situation throughout the city.[6]

If the black students and their allies had not yet been able to successfully bring into effect the integration of the schools, however, the conduct of the white protesters that day had been thoroughly documented by the national news media and was having a profound impact on national public opinion. All over the country that evening, television viewers were confronted with images of berserk white men beating a dignified Alex Wilson. It was the same on the front pages of the next morning's newspapers, with most of the reports indicating that the black journalists had deliberately planned to distract the crowd to allow the Little Rock Nine to enter.

Now even President Eisenhower, as reticent on civil rights in his second term as he had been in his first, realizing he had no choice, issued an unequivocal statement Monday night that he would use "whatever force may be necessary" to implement the federal court decree.[7]

On Tuesday afternoon, the president ordered a thousand para-troopers from the battle-tested 101st Airborne to be deployed to Arkansas and by that evening, the soldiers were encamped in Central High School's football field, albeit without their unit's African American members, who were being held in reserve at a nearby air force base. Wednesday morning, hundreds of soldiers standing in parade-rest formation, in steel helmets and with bayonets fixed to their carbines, formed a safe zone for two blocks around the school, allowing no protesters. The few segregationists who dared to test them were immediately confronted and told to move on; anyone who resisted was immediately arrested and marched away at gunpoint. One man who tried to grab a soldier's rifle was struck on the head by another soldier's rifle butt, and a fellow protester who got too close was sliced by a bayonet. Only newsmen were allowed near the school but they too were told, "Stay out of the way or you'll get stuck."

At 9:25 a.m., the Little Rock Nine, escorted by editor Daisy Bates, arrived at Central High in a U.S. Army station wagon. Hundreds of their white classmates stayed away from the school to protest but those who remained under military supervision were friendly and the Nine had a full school day that was peaceful, they later told Alex Wilson. Reporters who interviewed white students found that while many retained racist attitudes, some had indeed revised their thinking after experiencing integration firsthand. "I changed my mind on integration after sitting in class with Negroes for the first time in my life," said one "attractive girl student" interviewed in a wire report. "I don't care now if they go to school with us."[8]

Returning to the scene that morning as well, Wilson walked the near-empty streets adjacent Central High School. He saw one elderly white woman on the edge of the soldiers' perimeter praise the president's decision to send in the military, only to be told by a fellow reporter that the same woman on Monday had been yelling, "Keep the niggers out." Adding to the day's surreal quality, Wilson became the subject of interviews from his fellow newsmen in which he corrected the misimpression that the African American journalists had arranged to be decoys and expressed his appreciation for the troops' presence, although he would have hoped that the integration of schools did not require the intervention of the U.S. Army. "It's a relief to be able to perform my duties as a reporter without being attacked by a mob of unmerciful persons," Wilson told the wire services. "Now I can work in peace."[9]

In May 1958, after two years of daily publication of his newspaper, John Sengstacke declared success, albeit with caveats. Writing with characteristic bluntness in the house magazine of the Chicago Newspaper Guild, the trade union for writers, photographers, and commercial employees, Sengstacke said that the *Daily Defender*'s circulation was up to 27,381, while the circulation of the weekly national edition was holding steady. He credited "the great rising middle class of our community" for spending $1 million annually on *The Defender* and its affiliates, making the daily edition's classifieds section a bustling marketplace. But while African Americans themselves had supported the *Daily Defender*, funds from major corporations, Sengstacke complained, had fallen short of expectations. For years, many major advertisers had shunned *The Defender*, claiming that they only purchased space in daily newspapers. But now, some of those same companies suddenly devised new requirements, such as a five-year track record as a daily, and Sengstacke had come to suspect that there were other reasons for their reluctance. "In short," Sengstacke wrote, "we are subject to the same discrimination that victimizes Negroes in general."

Nevertheless, Sengstacke was continuing to implement his ambitious vision for the future, announcing that he had purchased a building to serve as *The Defender*'s new offices as well as a new printing press, "both of which we sorely needed." More than twice as large as in Abbott's day, the staff was bursting out of its confines at 3435 South Indiana Avenue. Relocation, however, would not be quick, Sengstacke warned, for the new building still required some additional equipment as well as substantial renovation.[10]

In the following months, therefore, Sengstacke turned his attention toward raising money for the rehabilitation of the three-story, sixty-three-thousand-foot building, an architectural mixture of art deco and Spanish mission styles with a clock tower in the northeast corner. *The Defender's* new headquarters at 2400 South Michigan Avenue had been built in 1936 as the Illinois Automobile Club, an urban respite for the owners and executives who worked in the surrounding Motor Row district of automobile dealerships, parts stores, and service garages. The building had become vacant as the car dealers followed their clientele to the suburbs but for Sengstacke's growing newspaper empire, the new building was perfectly situated at Bronzeville's northern border and within striking distance of the Loop business district.[11]

Six months later, Sengstacke had amassed the necessary funds to start the interior reconstruction and, with his fifteen-year-old son, Robert, at his side, he held a ceremonial opening of the heavy metal-and-glass doors. The second and third floors were ready six months after that, and on Saturday, March 28, 1959, *The Defender's* staff moved into the executive offices as well as the advertising, accounting, circulation, and personnel departments. This first wave of employees cooed over their new workspaces, which had been stocked with modern furnishings in a technologically up-to-date facility. For the moment, the editorial, composing, and production departments stayed behind at the old building while the swimming pool in the basement of the new building was removed to accommodate the Goss presses and the first-floor smoking lounge retrofitted into a proper newsroom. In the late afternoon, as the first of the staff unpacked their files, Sengstacke made a short speech in which he spoke of the "bright future that lies ahead for all of us," placing the expansion of the newspaper in the context of the ongoing civil rights struggle.[12]

As work on the new building progressed, one of the finishing touches was to etch into the lobby floor one of Robert S. Abbott's aphorisms, characteristically earnest and dedicated: "No greater glory, no greater honor, is the lot of man departing than a feeling possessed deep in his heart that the world is a better place for his having lived."[13]

One *Defender* stalwart who did not accompany the move into the new offices was longtime editor Louis Martin, who had accepted a post with the government of the newly independent state of Nigeria to help build up the media infrastructure there. Martin went overseas with Sengstacke's blessing just as African Americans were beginning to grow excited about the opportunities presenting themselves on the African continent and in other former colonies.[14]

With Martin's departure, Alex Wilson returned to Chicago from Memphis to serve as the *Daily Defender*'s editor in chief, an appointment announced in the newspaper in an article that boasted of the "national and international attention" he had received for his courage during the run-up to the federal intervention in Little Rock. "He refused to run from a jeering, howling mob," the article stated.[15]

On Thursday, February 28, 1960, Sengstacke and his crew of pressmen inspected the last issue of the national edition to be printed at the old building on Indiana Avenue. They stared at the broadsheet intently, smiling for the photographs but with a strong sense of melancholy as well. For nearly four decades, after all, this had been *The Defender*'s home, and Sengstacke allowed himself and his crew just a few moments to reflect before giving the signal to complete the relocation.

Breaking a large hole in the wall of the Indiana building, the moving crews used construction cranes to haul out the Linotype machines one by one. Heavy snowfall hampered the crews' efforts to cart the machines through the streets but after two full days, it was done. Only the old Goss presses were left behind to do piecemeal work and serve as a backup for the inevitable breakdowns of the new, technologically advanced equipment.

By Saturday afternoon, the staff began a truly frantic effort to get the equipment up and running by Sunday night in order to print the Monday edition. Working for twenty-four hours straight to combine the old Linotype machines and several new Teletype devices with the new presses into a single, functional system, they ensured that everything was ready by Sunday afternoon. Monday's *Daily Defender* came off the presses right on schedule and Sengstacke scrutinized it carefully alongside his executives and pressmen before pronouncing it acceptable. Only then, when they knew for sure that the newspaper's record of continuous publication would remain unbroken, did they toast their collective success in earnest, posing for a photo in which the smiles of relief are etched on their faces.[16]

*The Defender's* May 7, 1960, weekly edition marked its fifty-fifth anniversary with a special commemorative section that included an article praising the newspaper's 152 staff members and singling out Alex Wilson for his exemplary leadership of the newsroom. By this time, however, Wilson was frequently out of the office, undergoing extensive medical treatment for a neurological condition that had emerged shortly after he was beaten during the Little Rock incident.[17]

Luckily, Metz Lochard was back in the fold, having given up on running his own publication and made amends with John Sengstacke. Rehired as *The Defender's* chief editorial writer, Lochard now channeled Sengstacke's ideas into print as he had done for Robert Abbott decades earlier. Another staff member who remembered Abbott well was Marjorie Stewart Joyner, the cosmetologist and civil rights crusader, who had taken the role of chairman of the Chicago Defender Charities, which was responsible for producing the annual Billiken Parade.

Indeed, women were playing a heightened role during this era as reporters, production workers, and circulation employees. Jackie Ormes broke a significant gender barrier by becoming America's first black woman cartoonist. City editor Audrey Weaver, prized for her productivity at a daily publication in perpetual need of new material, was one of the only women to lead a daily newsroom. Weaver "turns out copy like an IBM machine," according to a profile of her in *The Defender,* and her work ethic was matched only by her personal courage: she had built her reputation covering white riots against the black tenants of the Trumbull Park public housing development as well as the fierce local battles over school integration.[18]

The most important staff member, however, aside from John Sengstacke, was his younger brother Frederick Douglass Sengstacke, who, holding the title of vice president and production manager, served as an invaluable counterpart to the publisher. Reserved and constant where John was gregarious and bold, Fred had been fully inculcated with the familial mission of liberating African Americans through the vehicle of the black press, but had experienced the world with neither the privilege nor the attention showered on his older brother. Where John was groomed for leadership by Robert Abbott at an early age, Fred was, to the last, grounded, pragmatic, and devoted, both to his older brother and to *The Defender.*

During World War II, Fred had served in the U.S. Army, returning home to finish his college education and raise a family with his high school sweetheart. At the newspaper, he began his tenure with the janitors and worked his way through every department, from the loading dock to classified ads, creating a mental map of every asset, human and mechanical, as well as the flow of every nickel. Where John was a peripatetic whirlwind, traveling frequently to meet with business associates and government officials in Washington, New York, and other destinations, Fred was present every time the presses ran, going home to eat dinner with his family between the afternoon and evening editions.[19]

The brothers frequently described their staff as the "*Defender* Family" and the employees were treated to annual daylong outings at the Sengstackes' summer compound in Yellow Lake, Michigan. As for actual family members who worked at *The Defender,* they were expected to pull their own weight as employees: the Sengstackes' sister Flaurience, whose travels to Europe had been recounted in the pages of *The Defender* two decades earlier, now held a post in production working under her youngest brother, Fred; an aunt was in the accounting department, while a cousin, Isaiah Major, headed the maintenance crew, ensuring the floors, cafeterias, and washrooms were spick-and-span.

Typifying the family work ethic was John's middle son, seventeen-year-old Robert, better known as Bobby, who worked as a yeoman photographer covering a busy circuit of sporting events, political rallies, and crime scenes. Born three years after Robert Abbott's death, Bobby, too, had been reared to believe that working at the newspaper was an obligation and a privilege. Owing to his father's celebrity, however, Bobby grew up in comfort, first in the tony Rosenwald Apartments, then in a mansion in the Kenwood district just south of Hyde Park, a rare bastion of racial, if not economic, integration, and his playmates included the children of other well-off African American parents, drawn from an emerging upper class of educated professionals and successful businesspeople.

Bobby's home life was troubled by his busy parents' frequent absences, however, as well as the erratic behavior of his older brother John Jr., who suffered from violent rages that grew ever more dangerous as he got older. Bobby first discovered photography as an adolescent, using the darkroom as a place to hide from John Jr., but he soon revealed a talent for handling the camera and capturing images of startling effect and even poignancy. Commencing his journalistic career in his early teens by publishing photos of his classmates' parties in the youth section of the paper, he refined his skills by accompanying his father whenever he got the chance.[20]

By inclination, Bobby tended to focus on the community's artists, activists, and street hustlers — the throngs of recent arrivals from the South mingling with the urban sophisticates and the vendors selling everything from freshly slaughtered chickens to folk remedies derived from African traditions. Once he officially joined the newspaper, Bobby saw it as the perfect vantage point from which to photograph the dynamic political and cultural changes taking place in black America. From the civil rights activists to the Black Muslims, he had access to everybody and he kept a camera in his hand to capture every significant moment.[21]

In July 1960, John Sengstacke and reporter Mattie Smith Colin traveled to Los Angeles to cover the Democratic National Convention, interested to see whether the front-runner, U.S. Senator John F. Kennedy from Massachusetts, would be derailed by concerns about the depth of his commitment to civil rights, about his youth, or simply his Catholicism. Skeptical of Kennedy all through the run-up to the convention, *The Defender's* editorial page had criticized his lackluster voting record on civil rights while he was in Congress and his cozy relationship with several Dixiecrat governors. It would not be easy, the newspaper warned in one editorial, to dispel the "anti-Kennedy climate of opinion." As another editorial explicated, "The plain fact remains that even at this late date, Mr. Kennedy is not placing the Negro question in its right perspective."[22]

Shortly after he arrived in Los Angeles, Sengstacke covered an NAACP-sponsored rally timed to coincide with the convention itself, at which seven thousand attendees loudly booed Kennedy as well as U.S. Senator Lyndon Johnson from Texas, who came into the convention with the second-largest number of delegates. Bravely tolerating the harangue, Kennedy was eventually able to deliver a pro–civil rights speech that won a smattering of applause by the end. But so negative was the sentiment that Sengstacke emerged worried African American voters might even defect to the Republican candidate, Vice President Richard Nixon, who had a reputation of being sympathetic to the cause of civil rights. President Eisenhower, after all, had won nearly 40 percent of the black vote in the last election, his personal popularity drawing them back into the Republican fold.

Sengstacke's concerns were only amplified the next day, when the publisher was called to a press conference at the Biltmore Hotel given by former first lady Eleanor Roosevelt, still an influential figure among Democrats. Mrs. Roosevelt, too, expressed her doubts that Kennedy could capture the African American vote, which she deemed crucial to victory in November, "because of the things he has said and done." Instead, she suggested that Kennedy run as the *vice* presidential candidate, ceding the top of the ticket to Adlai Stevenson, the haughty former Illinois governor and two-time loser in the prior presidential contests against Dwight Eisenhower. Stevenson had opted not to run in the primaries this time around, but kept a high profile at the convention anyway, letting his associates know that he hoped the Democrats would call upon him in a draft.[23]

Mrs. Roosevelt's assessment of Kennedy, Smith Colin heard, had inspired more than five hundred people to send pro-Stevenson telegrams to Mayor Richard Daley, widely considered the party's major power broker. Daley brushed off the entreaties from Stevenson's camp, however, and his loyalty ensured Kennedy would get the nomination. But when Lyndon Johnson was placed on the ticket as the vice presidential candidate, liberals and African Americans alike were infuriated. In his acceptance speech, Kennedy did his best to assuage the doubts by lambasting the Eisenhower administration for failing to respond to the civil rights crusaders in the South. "The rights of man," Kennedy proclaimed, "the civil and economic rights essential to the human dignity of all men, are indeed our goal and our first principles."[24]

After the convention, the Kennedy campaign, well aware of its deficiencies with the African American electorate, immediately sought out an operative who could shore up their support in the months remaining before the election. JFK's brother-in-law Sargent Shriver, a Chicago businessman who served as chairman of the city's school board, recruited Louis Martin, who had just returned from his year-long sojourn in Nigeria.

Martin readily accepted a post with the Kennedy team, only to realize that he was facing an uphill challenge in building a grassroots organization that could actually get voters to the polls with just a few months until Election Day.

He began by personally reaching out to every major political personage in black America and by paying off debts of some $50,000 owed to *The Defender, The Michigan Chronicle,* and other newspapers from the Democrats' last presidential campaign. Martin also arranged for Kennedy to meet with U.S. Representative William Dawson, who until that point had been neglected by the campaign. At seventy-four, running for his own tenth term in the House of Representatives, Dawson could deliver two hundred thousand votes on Election Day, Martin argued, and had to be respected.

But the meeting did not go well. A *Defender* reporter approached the congressman just after the meeting with Kennedy and asked whether he would discuss the details of his conversation. "Not if I can help it," Dawson responded.[25]

Clearly there was more work to be done. Remaining on *The Defender*'s official roster as vice president and editorial director, Martin continued to write his column, which he now used to praise Dawson and reach out to civil rights activists as well as church officials in the name of the campaign. He devoted much of his time as well to enlisting Baptist ministers to endorse Kennedy, well aware of the anti-Catholic sentiment among African Americans.[26]

At first, Martin received little support from the campaign manager, JFK's younger brother Bobby, who, preferring to rely on power brokers like Mayor Daley, hadn't planned on building a campaign infrastructure that included a distinct African American component. When Bobby Kennedy finally held a meeting with the campaign's civil rights section in mid-September, he indicated that he had little regard for their efforts thus far, using a tone that was "mocking and acid," Martin told a biographer.[27]

Martin, however, was not about to be intimidated, least of all by someone so callow and inexperienced. Bobby's arrogance, he warned, could cost the campaign the crucial black vote. "If you want it, you can get it," Martin told the younger Kennedy, "but you are going to have to work for it, you are going to have to fight for it, and you are going to have to spend money."[28]

Chastened by the harangue, Bobby Kennedy implemented Martin's recommendations one by one. First, RFK scheduled his own meeting with Congressman Dawson, who shortly thereafter was named vice chairman of the campaign and granted the power to hire a field director. Money, too, began to flow now, especially into the black press, with *The Defender* and other newspapers running full-page ads for Kennedy that showed the candidate shaking hands with a host of black celebrities including singer Nat King Cole, among various politicians and even journalists. Congressman Dawson, not surprisingly, was featured prominently in many of the ads.[29]

The candidate himself stepped up the number of his appearances before African American audiences that month, events that Martin made sure were covered prominently by *The Defender.* When JFK spoke in Washington to the National Bar Association, an African American lawyers' group, and promised that he would appoint several from their number to the federal bench, *The Defender* reprinted his speech and a related photograph on the front page of the national edition.[30]

At this point in the campaign, Richard Nixon was still reaching out to black voters and the same issue of *The Defender* included coverage of the Republican's speech in Portland, Oregon, in which the candidate called for "full equality" and described segregation as an international disgrace. "It is awfully hard to preach the dignity of man abroad," Nixon told his audience, "and to have to explain the prejudices at home in the United States."[31]

But in early October, as the election entered its final phase, Nixon stopped talking about his support for civil rights, concentrating instead on winning the white vote in several southern states. Martin and his team, in turn, tried to exploit Nixon's shift by scheduling a debate between the two candidates in the middle of the month at Howard University, knowing full well that Nixon was unlikely to appear. When Nixon indeed failed to show, Kennedy had the audience to himself. JFK joked with the audience about Nixon's absence and then became serious, declaring that equality under the law was "a matter of national survival as well as a matter of national principle."[32]

Thrilled by Kennedy's words, Howard's students and faculty became all the more enthused when a pregnant Jackie Kennedy appeared onstage next to her husband. The vigorous, progressive couple struck a sharp contrast with the ailing, depleted President Eisenhower, under whom the federal government had acted on integration only when forced by the courts. This excitement, in the wake of the one-sided debate, followed the couple outside as they conducted an impromptu tour of the Howard campus, surrounded by admirers. The enthusiastic crowd overwhelmed the security detail, at one point almost knocking Jackie over, but to Martin, the fact that throngs of bright young African Americans were clamoring to shake his candidate's hand was an unmistakable sign of progress.

Just a few days later, Martin organized a national conference on civil rights in New York to be followed by a massive campaign rally in Harlem. Officially nonpartisan and academic, the gathering was dubbed the National Conference on *Constitutional* Rights to avoid riling southern segregationists, though carefully designed to align the NAACP and myriad other grassroots operations behind the Kennedy campaign. None of it could happen, however, unless Martin was able to reach an arrangement with New York's most important African American politician, the wily and capricious Adam Clayton Powell. In the last presidential election, Congressman Powell, a Democrat, had jumped party lines to endorse President Eisenhower's reelection in exchange for a hefty sum of cash. This time, vacationing on a yacht in the Mediterranean when Martin called, the congressman dispatched an emissary to negotiate. Powell demanded $300,000 at first to participate, but Martin haggled with the emissary until they arrived at the price of $40,000 for ten speeches, payable in installments after each speech.[33]

On October 12, Martin's ostensibly nonpartisan conference at the Park Sheraton in midtown wrapped up and, just as planned, many of the delegates decided to head uptown to the epicenter of Harlem at the intersection of 125th Street and Seventh Avenue for a rally with John Kennedy. Satisfied with his compensation package, Powell had drawn twenty thousand people to the event, and stood at Kennedy's shoulder as the candidate criticized Vice President Nixon for "traveling with a Negro in the North and not in the South"—leaving his African American staff behind when he traveled into Dixie to avoid antagonizing segregationists.[34]

Melding themes that he had refined in a series of speeches to African American audiences, Kennedy pledged to use his power and prestige as president to equalize opportunity in the United States: "I am not satisfied in the area of human rights when a Negro baby born this morning has only half as much chance as a white child to finish high school, only one third chance to finish college and his chances of being a federal judge non-existent," Kennedy said, as recorded by *The Defender*'s Mattie Smith Colin, who covered the conference and the rally.[35]

Alex Wilson died just as the campaign was entering its final weeks, passing while undergoing treatment for the neurological damage he'd suffered at the hands of the white mob three years earlier. Remembered by his colleagues for his award-winning investigative reports and his leadership of the newsroom as well as for the moral courage he'd shown in Little Rock, Wilson, only forty-nine, left behind a wife and two children. His obituary in *The Defender*'s national edition cited his own words about the beating he had suffered: "I was abused — the victim of misguided violence — but I am not bitter."[36]

At the end of October, *The Defender* became the only one of Chicago's daily newspapers to endorse Kennedy, citing the candidate's agenda on school reform, health care, housing, defense jobs, farm subsidies, unemployment assistance, and aid to the war-ravaged Central African nation of Congo as well as his stand on civil rights. In a signed, front-page editorial, John Sengstacke blasted the Eisenhower administration for its failure to embrace the 1954 *Brown* ruling over the past six years, then argued that Kennedy represented a fresh start. "We are inalterably opposed to the notion that all we deserve is a small, carefully-limited blessing of freedom," Sengstacke wrote. "We are tired of oscillating between defiance and appeal, between cynicism and hope."[37]

Martin persuaded many other black newspapers to print similar endorsements — the Baltimore-based *Afro-American* chain, the

*New York Amsterdam News,* the *Journal and Guide,* based in Norfolk, Virginia, the *Los Angeles Sentinel,* and the *Minneapolis Spokesman,* among them. But with just a week to go before the election, the
crowning act of Martin's efforts to enlist African Americans into the
Kennedy campaign came not as the result of his methodical planning, but in a nimble response to an ongoing crisis: earlier that year,
having moved back home to Atlanta from Birmingham, Martin Luther King had joined the sit-ins at segregated lunch counters in that
city. On October 19, during three days of protests, King was arrested
along with seventy-nine students and joined a group who refused to
post bail so as to remain in jail. The national media were all over
the story and, under the glare of the spotlight, Atlanta's conciliatory
mayor, William Hartsfield, after intensive negotiations, agreed not
only to use his influence to have the protesters released but also to
begin integrating public facilities. The students were indeed let go
but at trial on October 25, the county judge unexpectedly sentenced
King to four months of hard labor, noting that the civil rights leader
was on probation for a separate conviction in a traffic case. King was
handcuffed and taken to a state prison in rural Georgia.[38]

Knowing that her husband was under dire threat, Coretta King
called Harris Wofford, one of JFK's senior advisors, and asked for his
help. Wofford happened to be with Louis Martin at the moment of
Coretta's call and the two men reviewed their options: The Kennedys
had no direct authority to intervene, while any public gesture of support for King carried the risk of angering white voters. On the other
hand, the situation was an irresistible opportunity to demonstrate
solidarity with the civil rights cause, so Wofford and Martin decided
to recommend that the candidate make a public gesture of support
to the Kings. Wofford called Sargent Shriver, who was traveling with
the candidate, and Shriver briefed JFK on King's situation before suggesting he reach out to King's wife. JFK paused for just a moment,
then agreed.

"I know this must be very hard for you," Kennedy told Coretta
King, then pregnant with her third child. "I understand you are expecting a baby and I just want to let you know that I was thinking
about you and Dr. King."

"I certainly appreciate your concern," Coretta replied. "I would appreciate anything you could do to help."[39]

Concurrently, Louis Martin sought out Bobby Kennedy, catching him just as he was about to leave the campaign office for the airport. Bobby, outraged by the imposition of a lengthy sentence for King on a mere traffic violation, vowed to take action, but got on the plane without telling Martin what, precisely, he planned to do.

When he arrived in Chicago, Bobby discovered that his brother had already spoken with Coretta King and that the national media were highly interested in the phone call. Concerned over the backlash from southern governors, he chastised Wofford, Shriver, and Martin for "screwing up the whole campaign" and ordered Martin's team to stop issuing any press releases or other statements. But at 1:00 a.m. the next morning, RFK called Martin to announce that he had telephoned the county judge in Georgia to argue that King should be released on bond while his case was appealed. "Louis, I wanted you to know that I told that judge down in Georgia to let King go," Bobby said, in Martin's recollection. "He said he would." As Martin awakened enough to process this news, he quipped that Bobby was now an "honorary brother."[40]

Within hours, the county judge indeed ordered King released on a $2,000 bond — citing "great pressure" from Bobby Kennedy — and Louis Martin got to work publicizing the incident throughout the black community. He made phone calls to essential ward and district leaders and sent telegrams to a long list of political figures throughout the nation, providing them with details of the incident. Understanding that many of the black weeklies would publish just one more issue before Election Day, Martin called all of the editors in his address book to make sure they had whatever information they needed to run a story. Finally, he recounted the entire saga in a leaflet entitled *The Case of Martin Luther King*, two million copies of which were printed and distributed to every black church in Chicago, Detroit, and other major northern cities as well as throughout the rural South. In the leaflet, Louis Martin couldn't resist pointing out that Vice President Nixon had stayed silent during the entire affair, as indeed had President Eisenhower.

Fearing a Republican counterstrike, Martin purposely avoided communications with the white press even as he was blanketing the African American media with information. While King's release was covered by the *Tribune* and other white newspapers in short articles on interior pages, the story dominated the front page of *The Defender*'s national edition, with a three-deck headline and a massive photo of the civil rights leader with his wife and two young children.

Unmentioned in the white press, but featured prominently in *The Defender*, was the announcement that King's father, the Rev. Martin Luther King Sr., pastor of the well-established Ebenezer Baptist Church in Atlanta, had decided to abandon his long-standing support for the Republican Party in favor of the Democratic nominee, taking as many of his legions of parishioners and admirers with him as he could. "Kennedy has the moral courage to stand up for what he knows is right," stated the senior King. "I've got a suitcase of votes, and I'm going to take them to Mr. Kennedy and dump them in his lap."[41]

The front page of the *Daily Defender* edition on November 7, the day before the election, predicted that, with the race between Kennedy and Nixon extremely close, African American voters in Illinois, New York, Pennsylvania, Michigan, California, and Texas would likely determine the outcome. Louis Martin's organizing continued until the last minute as he himself convinced Martin Luther King Jr. to give a radio interview in which King all but endorsed Kennedy. Though reluctant to make a partisan statement, King criticized Eisenhower's leadership on civil rights, not to mention the equivocation of the Nixon campaign, and praised Kennedy as "forthright" when it came to his plans for using presidential power to change the dynamic of race relations.[42]

The timing could not have been more opportune: the *Daily Defender* printed King's comments in the Election Day edition, which was delivered to newsstands and doorstops around the city the very morning readers would be making their way to the voting booth.[43]

Watching the massive turnout in the city precincts throughout the day, Mayor Daley predicted a turnout of over 90 percent and a victory for Kennedy in Illinois by a quarter-million votes. Daley was correct about the turnout in the city — by the time polls closed that evening, more than 1.7 million people had cast ballots, better than 91 percent of registered voters — but as the night wore on, it was clear that enthusiasm in the Republicans' suburban and downstate strongholds was equally strong, bringing Nixon's totals perilously close. Nevertheless, when Nixon's team looked over the returns in Illinois and a few other key states, they concluded that their situation was untenable and decided to concede to Kennedy.[44]

In the next day's edition, *The Defender* claimed that the African American electorate had been decisive for Kennedy, while the white dailies and broadcast media outlets focused on the role of the televised debates between Kennedy and Nixon — debates in which no black journalist had been included on the panel and civil rights had been largely left off the agenda. But as the final election results were tallied over the next few days, it became clear that *The Defender*'s assertion was correct: Kennedy had won Illinois by a mere 8,858 votes, even as Chicago's black-majority wards provided the Democrat with more than 255,000 votes and just 64,000 for Nixon, a ratio in many precincts of more than 80 percent. Congressman Bill Dawson's wards had outperformed their previous, record-setting totals; if they hadn't, Kennedy would have lost not just Illinois but likely the entire electoral college. Indeed, so close was the margin, the editorial page noted, that if black voters had simply voted for Kennedy in the same proportion as they had for Stevenson in 1956, a solid 66 percent, Kennedy would have lost Illinois.[45]

African Americans had provided similar margins of victory in Pennsylvania, South Carolina, and several other states in an election that Kennedy won by just 112,827 ballots nationwide. The chairman of the Republican National Committee, determined to use race to polarize the electorate, conceded that the black vote had put Kennedy over the top, and blamed "the vice president's lack of appeal for black voters."

"We are agreed on that point," stated *The Defender*'s editorial page, "except that we would rather change the preposition and say it was Mr. Nixon's lack of appeal *to* Negro voters which cost him the election."[46]

Louis Martin saw the equation from the other end, recalling the sleepless weeks of the campaign and recounting moves both deliberate and simply fortuitous. The Kennedy brothers' telephone calls to Coretta King and the judge overseeing the case, Martin wrote in his memoirs, were "icing on the cake," but the real challenge had been to organize a massive get-out-the-vote effort. As in any election, the messaging was essential to motivating the voters but the campaign also had to make sure there were legions out there knocking on doors and driving citizens to the polls. "The King calls," Martin wrote, "helped ensure a good turnout in an election that was so close that had we been short one vote per precinct in Illinois, Nixon would have won the election."[47]

With the campaign finally over, Louis Martin formally gave up his title at *The Defender* to work within the Kennedy administration. He had no portfolio at first but was charged with the critical task of overseeing African American political appointees. To that end, after developing a list of hundreds of men and women qualified for a wide range of jobs, he became a zealous advocate for their placement throughout the federal government. Eventually, Martin was named vice chairman of the Democratic National Committee, a position outside the glare of Camelot but that still came with a desk in the West Wing of the White House and responsibility for the Nationalities Division of the party, organizing ethnic and immigrant communities across the United States. It was a job in which Martin could exercise his belief that political activities be fully integrated and he rapidly began building contacts among the leadership of the large Italian and Polish constituencies, among other groups.[48]

Also working at the DNC was Martin's erstwhile protégé Ethel Payne, now a deputy field director with responsibilities for get-out-the-vote efforts targeted at women. Payne had left *The Defender* two years earlier to take a post as a writer for the AFL-CIO but she, like Martin, kept a close relationship with the newspaper and its publisher.[49]

As for John Sengstacke, his support during the campaign earned him unlimited-access privileges at the White House. Sometimes, he boasted, he would just show up and intercept JFK as the president moved between meetings. It was to prove a fruitful relationship, indeed, during the all-too-brief tenure of the Kennedy administration.[50]

# 18

## A Socratic Gadfly

T HE PACE OF the civil rights movement only accelerated in the first months of 1961, even as the Kennedy administration struggled to get its bearings. Inspired by the Montgomery bus boycott and the lunch-counter sit-ins, activists launched new campaigns utilizing nonviolent tactics to expose the persistence of segregation in the South. The widespread media coverage of the protests, meanwhile, brought an additional boon: for the first time, the movement attracted white supporters willing to lay their own lives on the line.

In May, *The Defender* gave extensive coverage to the first teams of racially mixed "freedom riders" from the Congress of Racial Equality, known by the acronym CORE. The plan, defying customs that had persisted despite Supreme Court rulings subsequent to *Brown v. Board of Education* making segregation in interstate transportation illegal, was to send an integrated team of activists on two buses that would journey through the South. The black activists would sit in the front of the bus, some next to white riders to test the reaction of southern authorities.

Departing from Washington, D.C., the riders made it through the first few states without serious incident; one African American student leader, John Lewis, was attacked and beaten by several white men in North Carolina, but local police interceded quickly. Lewis declined to press charges, citing his nonviolent beliefs.[1]

Then, on Mother's Day, as the first bus reached Anniston, Alabama, it was surrounded by a hundred drunken, gun-toting white men who taunted and challenged the riders. The driver behaved courageously, refusing to open the door and trying to drive from the scene, but the mob slashed the tires, and those in automobiles ran the bus off the road outside town. With the bus immobilized, the men picked up rocks and began shattering the windows, finally tossing a firebomb inside. All of those aboard the bus, freedom riders as well as those who just happened to be passengers, now dashed outside, braving the mob's blows until the police arrived. A news photographer captured an image of several of the riders, overcome by smoke, lying dazed on the side of the road watching as their bus transformed into a smoldering heap.

The second bus reached the city of Birmingham successfully, but when five riders, four blacks and one white, attempted to integrate the station's dining room, they were met by a group of white men who punched, kicked, and clubbed them with lead pipes, sending several to area hospitals. The next day, the group of CORE activists boarded flights for New Orleans and from there returned to the North. Unable to complete their journey, they had at least held fast to nonviolent tactics, managing to get the story covered by the national media reporters assigned to the race beat, in addition to the black press.

News about the freedom riders filled the pages of *The Defender*'s daily and national editions that week, using language that echoed Robert Abbott's exhortations to self-defense forty years earlier. The editorial page warned that, were nonviolence to fail, it was possible that blacks would turn to violence to win their freedom. "Unless wiser counsel prevails," seethed the editorial, "there will be bloodshed in more places than Alabama, as a delayed, explosive aftermath."[2]

If anything, the freedom riders were emboldened by the attacks against them; a new team was on the road in Alabama before the end of the week. This group got as far as the Greyhound station in Montgomery, where they were confronted by yet another mob of white men and women. Here the thugs specifically targeted the white riders. The one white male in the group, a college student from Appleton, Wisconsin, was punched and kicked as soon as he got off the bus, while a news reporter and photographer for Time Life, assigned to cover the events at the bus station, were beaten bloody. John Seigenthaler, whom President Kennedy had dispatched to the state several days earlier, was struck in the head and left unconscious in the street after trying to shield the one white woman among the freedom riders from the gang pursuing her.

Incensed by this violence, the Kennedy administration ordered 350 U.S. marshals to Montgomery with orders to facilitate the safe passage of the freedom riders, confronting any hostile gathering as necessary. Wearing steel helmets and armed with handguns as well as clubs, the marshals set up a command center on the roof of the local post office, took up positions around the town's transportation nodes, and began to patrol key city streets. *The Defender* praised the deployment, comparing it to President Eisenhower's use of military units in Little Rock, but Alabama's staunch segregationist governor, John Patterson, was infuriated, describing the marshals as "interlopers" and vowing to have them arrested if they violated any state laws.[3]

That same weekend, *The Defender* learned that Martin Luther King, Ralph Abernathy, and other leaders of the civil rights movement had traveled to Montgomery, their old battleground, with the intent of rallying behind the freedom riders. Concern had grown among these movement leaders, according to one of King's aides, that the riders would "elevate themselves to martyrdom in an unnecessary cause," provoking the segregationists to murderous violence without the real possibility of effecting change. To obviate this possibility, King and the others decided to focus the national spotlight on the campaign and force authorities at every level to impose order on the state.

On Sunday evening, a *Defender* reporter was there when King brought eighteen freedom riders to a downtown church and spoke to a crowd of some fifteen hundred people, while outside two hundred whites armed with clubs and rocks faced off against an equal number of marshals, National Guard troops, and local police. Despite his earlier vow not to extend protection to the protesters, Governor Patterson relented, imposing limited martial law and dispatching state troops as well as law enforcement to work with the marshals. The next night, King and other movement elders met with the students behind the freedom rides, including many newcomers who had recently flocked to this hot spot of race relations. After extensive negotiations, they agreed to collaborate in sending these waves of young people on buses to Mississippi, Florida, and Louisiana before the end of the week.[4]

The first bus left Montgomery for the seven-hour journey to Jackson that Wednesday, only this time, the riders had plenty of company on their journey, with news reporters and National Guardsmen as well as an escort of Alabama state troopers onboard. At the Mississippi border, they were transferred to the custody of law enforcement and militia from that state who proceeded to bring them safely into the city of Jackson. Assembled at that bus station were some two hundred white supremacists who were held back by police. No sooner had the nine black men on the trip tried to enter the whites-only bathroom, however, than the riders were arrested. Officers also arrested the two black women and one white man in this group of riders as well as those who came in on the next bus, charging twenty-five riders in all with inciting a riot.

Though he had withdrawn his force of marshals, Attorney General Bobby Kennedy stayed in contact with state officials in Alabama and Mississippi to make sure the riders were not injured. In addition, he announced that the Justice Department was investigating whether charges could be brought against officials in Birmingham and other parts of Alabama for their failure to uphold the rights of interstate travelers. In the interest of public safety, however, he called on the freedom riders to suspend their protests in Alabama and Mississippi for an unspecified interval, a "cooling-off period," as he described it.[5]

Despite the close relationship between *The Defender* and the Kennedys, the paper responded immediately to this sudden turnaround with an editorial entitled "Ride On, Freedom Riders," which not only rejected the call to suspend the protests but accused the administration of putting political expediency ahead of moral rectitude. The Supreme Court had affirmed African Americans' constitutional right to travel across every region of the country without suffering discrimination, the newspaper pointed out, and the riders were merely exercising that right. Noting the international criticism of the United States for continuing segregation in the South, the editorial attributed Bobby Kennedy's about-face to his brother's upcoming meetings with French president Charles de Gaulle and Soviet premier Nikita Khrushchev. "Just as we were applauding Attorney General Robert F. Kennedy for his forthright stand and definitive action in the Freedom Riders' encounter with the bloodthirsty mobs in Alabama," the editorial began, "he reverses his position and tosses the whole fat into the burning pile of Southern race prejudice."[6]

· · ·

Descending on Jackson that weekend were two busloads of students from around the country, seventeen more freedom riders, two white and fifteen black. Like the others, they were escorted into the city by National Guard troops, their every move recorded by a sizable contingent of news reporters. The riders had planned to go into segregated facilities at every stop along the journey, but local police ensured there were no incidents in these towns, frequently preventing them from disembarking. In Jackson, they did get off the bus to sit at the lunch counters in the terminal, but were immediately arrested. Applauding this new wave of riders, *The Defender* reiterated its criticism of the administration for trying to curtail the protests.

"The new Negro is determined to have his constitutional rights now, and will not surrender those rights to the mob," stated an editorial at the end of May. "So the white folks better get it into their heads that the Sit-in demonstrations and the Freedom Riders are no transient phenomena.

"There can be no cooling off period in matters of human rights."[7]

*The Defender* kept its focus on the freedom riders the following week as several went on trial on the charges of "breaching the peace" in Mississippi. Many of the riders, having been convicted and ordered to pay modest fines, refused and accepted prison sentences instead as a way of extending their protests. Nor did they desist their passive resistance once inside the state's notoriously harsh prison work farms or shackled on its road gangs, even if that meant suffering severe beatings and other tortures.

*The Defender* also charted the extensive coverage of the freedom rides in the white-owned daily newspapers and radio and television networks, noting the growing support for the movement among whites. The student union at Harvard University and the Order of the Elks, for example, announced fundraising drives for the freedom riders, while the Teamsters Union donated $5,000 to CORE.[8]

In June, the first riders to emerge from prison began lecturing to sizable audiences around the country. Martin Luther King traveled to Los Angeles, meanwhile, where, at a fundraising performance for the movement, he shared a stage at a sports arena with Sammy Davis Jr., Mahalia Jackson, Dick Gregory, and Bobby Darin, among other Hollywood celebrities. These activities, in turn, attracted new waves of riders, numbering in the hundreds now, all repeating the same pattern of resistance and ending in the riders' serving sentences on work farms and road gangs in lieu of paying a fine.[9]

Nearly every day, the protests dominated *The Defender*'s front page. "'Freedom Rider' Tells Torture" headlined an interview with a thirty-three-year-old white protester, a native of Austria named Felix Singer, who had fled his homeland and settled in Chicago. Describing the Mississippi State Penitentiary, known as Parchman, as akin to a Nazi concentration camp, Singer said guards responded to his acts of civil disobedience by beating him, dragging him across the ground, stripping him naked, and isolating him. After sixteen days in the prison and a ten-day hunger strike, Singer said he "couldn't take any more" and accepted an offer from CORE to pay a $200 bond for his release. Asked why he signed up with the freedom riders, Singer replied, "The whole thing is as much my business as anyone else's. Segregation is a social cancer that must be cut out by non-violent direct action."[10]

The newspaper's editorial page, too, continued its war of words with the administration, targeting Bobby Kennedy in particular, since the attorney general was now urging the protesters to stop the campaign permanently. True, the attorney general was supporting legal efforts to outlaw, once and for all, segregated facilities in the South, but the editorial argued that while it waited for final rulings from the Interstate Commerce Commission and the Supreme Court, the administration should continue to use marshals or other means to secure the riders' safety. Alleging that Bobby Kennedy was pulling back on his efforts to restrict segregationists because his brother was beholden to certain southern governors, *The Defender* urged the riders to keep up the fight. "To say that the Freedom Riders 'had made their point on travel facilities,' as the attorney general has said, actually amounts to an invitation to surrender," stated an editorial at the end of June.[11]

After all, the newspaper had seen many other presidential administrations feign sympathy for the cause of civil rights even while acquiescing to the demands of southern segregationists. But as the summer progressed, *The Defender* was encouraged when the federal government joined with the NAACP in pursuing a case that would install a permanent injunction against the state from discriminating in all transportation facilities. With the support of the attorney general, this was an "all-out assault on Mississippi's segregation laws," the editorial page proclaimed excitedly. *The Defender* could now foresee the day when integration was imposed and enforced throughout the South. "Old Man Jim Crow" was "pretty feeble" these days, the editorial observed.[12]

All through the end of summer, the freedom riders kept coming, targeting locations throughout the South before finally converging on Jackson. By the middle of August, the number of those arrested in Mississippi on the charge of "breaching the peace" surged past three hundred, with trial dates backed up for several months. Some of the protesters accepted CORE's offer to bail them out but many more stayed to serve sentences in the state's prisons. The riders were by now well represented — attorneys William Kunstler from the American Civil Liberties Union and Carl Richler from CORE traveled from New York to Jackson to challenge the validity of the "breaching the peace" law with the aim of freeing all of them at once.[13]

At the end of September, the Interstate Commerce Commission ruled in favor of a petition filed by the Justice Department prohibiting interstate bus lines from segregating their passengers and even from using stations with segregated facilities. It was a total victory for the freedom riders, one that would be punctuated by signs in all transportation facilities declaring it illegal to discriminate by race, color, creed, or national origin. Easing off its earlier criticism of the administration, *The Defender*'s editorial celebrating the ICC ruling praised Bobby Kennedy for his legal advocacy and noted that the attorney general had filed his case fifteen days after the first freedom ride back in May. Without any reference to Bobby's volte-face when it came to calling for an end to the protests, the newspaper equated his courage to the bravery demonstrated by the riders themselves. "The great lesson to be derived from this development," stated the editorial about the ICC ruling, "is that race prejudice melts away under the pressure of organized public opinion and honest men to enforce the law."[14]

In the summer of 1962, Metz Lochard called his old friend Ben Burns and made him an intriguing offer: "How would you like to take over as the editor in chief of the *Daily Defender*?"

Burns was by then working as a well-paid executive at a public relations firm, having put both his affiliation with the Communist Party and his work in the black press far behind him. Considering public relations the "purgatory of journalism," however, he readily accepted Lochard's offer, even though it meant a significant pay cut. "Here was fresh air to revive my spirits," Burns later wrote in his memoir, "an opportunity to return to the field of black journalism, which had been my first love."[15]

Burns's appointment was announced on the front page of the national edition in an article that touted his prior tenure with *The Defender* as well as his work with *Ebony* and other Johnson publications. Though accompanied by Burns's headshot, the text did not mention that he was the newspaper's first white editor in chief. Indeed, so worried was Sengstacke that this move would provoke a backlash from black readers, the article announced that along with Burns, Lloyd General, an African American journalist who had done a previous stint at the publication, had been hired to oversee the national edition, and that the current managing editor, city editor, and other key staffers were all staying at their posts. Nevertheless, Burns's appointment was noticed by *The Chicago Daily News,* whose columnist praised *The Defender* for "practicing what it preaches — integration."[16]

Burns's second tenure was indeed contentious, however, as he discovered just how much *The Defender* had changed, along with the world around it. Where previously he had been able to get any African American writer to contribute to the newspaper, this new era's black scribes could command far higher rates writing for white publications, rates the Sengstackes were not about to match. In addition, Burns found himself tangling with key staff members, including prized editorial cartoonist Chester Commodore, who quit the paper, vowing not to return until Burns was gone.[17]

One afternoon in mid-August, a clean-cut twenty-nine-year-old named James Meredith appeared in *The Defender*'s lobby and announced he had a "big story." Meredith had been working with lawyers at the NAACP in a yearlong legal battle to become the first African American to enroll at the University of Mississippi, then the bastion of the state's white elite, and expected to begin taking classes there that fall. Burns was skeptical but assigned a reporter, Theresa Fambro, to interview Meredith. "Knowing the Jim Crow policies of

Mississippi," Burns recounted in his memoir, "I did not take seriously the written interview with its high-flow claims and made the mistake of burying it in the back pages of *The Defender*."[18]

Burns discovered how wrong he had been just a few weeks later when the U.S. Supreme Court ordered the University of Mississippi to admit Meredith. The story only got bigger from there, as Alabama's segregationist governor, Ross Barnett, publicly defied the court ruling, prompting the Kennedy administration to dispatch steel-helmeted U.S. marshals to yet another southern state.[19]

This time, however, the marshals proved insufficient to cow state authorities, and Governor Barnett personally blocked Meredith from registering for school four times, risking a violent confrontation with federal forces by assembling hundreds of club-wielding state police in a ring around the school. Only by the end of September, after Bobby Kennedy sent in hundreds more marshals and threatened to prosecute Barnett for contempt of court, did the governor finally withdraw his officers. That evening, however, large groups of students and other enraged whites engaged in running battles with the marshals both on campus and in the nearby town of Oxford, harassing them with sniper fire and Molotov cocktails as well as a torrent of rocks and bottles. After two white rioters were killed, President Kennedy ordered in thousands of U.S. Army paratroopers, who now took full command of the town and arrested more than a hundred people, making a public show of marching the prisoners through the center of town with their hands folded over their heads.[20]

Leading the newspaper through the November midterm elections and into the cold winter months of early 1963, Burns carved out enough time from his management duties to begin authoring a short column in which he opined on political and cultural issues, including the spectacular rise of Cassius Clay, an Olympic-gold-medal-winning heavyweight boxer with a penchant for poetry. But by spring, Burns was exhausted by the relentless publishing schedule and the cash-strapped working conditions at *The Defender*, as well as what he perceived as "the inflamed racial climate of the 1960s" filtering into the newsroom. And so, with a tinge of bitterness, he decided to make his last exit from *The Defender*.[21]

Night editor Arnold Rosenzweig, a self-described "white liberal" a generation younger than Burns, also perceived the heightened tension between blacks and whites, though from a different angle. In a column published in November 1969, after he had worked at the newspaper for almost a year, Rosenzweig bemoaned the way fellow upper-middle-class whites often responded when he told them where he worked. Nor was it just those who worried aloud about an influx of blacks into their neighborhoods; even those who claimed to be sympathetic to the civil rights cause tended to parrot the same canards, Rosenzweig maintained, reflexively employing generalizations about African Americans. "Whether Negroes are all condemned for cooking pork in their back yards or praised for it, you can be sure of one thing," Rosenzweig wrote, "they'll be thought of only in terms of stereotypes and what one Negro does, all Negroes do."[22]

In early August 1963, John Sengstacke announced on the front page of *The Defender* that he had hired a new editor in chief, Chuck Stone, an award-winning thirty-nine-year-old African American journalist. Highly educated, with a bachelor's degree from Wesleyan University and a master's from the University of Chicago, Stone had cut a meteoric path through the black press starting in 1959 with stints at *The New York Age* and *The Pittsburgh Courier* before being named editor of the Washington, D.C., edition of the *Afro-American* chain. He had international experience as well, having served as a representative for the charity organization CARE in India and Egypt; in fact, he turned down a position as a public affairs officer for the United States Agency for International Development (USAID) in the newly independent East African Republic of Tanganyika to take the job at *The Defender.*[23]

Stone's arrival at the newspaper coincided with the moment civil rights organizations in Chicago stepped up their efforts to oust Benjamin Willis, the superintendent of Chicago Public Schools, who, despite massive overcrowding in black schools, had flatly refused any level of integration. Instead of allowing black students to take up the plethora of empty seats in those buildings designated for whites, Willis instituted shifts in the black schools that required some youths to attend class early in the morning and others in the late afternoon. When that obtuse policy failed to alleviate the overcrowd-

ing, the superintendent ordered the deployment of mobile classrooms — cheaply constructed, poorly insulated trailers that activists
promptly labeled "Willis Wagons."

On the twelfth of the month, the local branch of CORE, joined
by comedian Dick Gregory and a contingent of ministers, set up a
picket line in front of several Willis Wagons stationed on the South
Side. It was not long before the protesters were engaged in a full-on
confrontation with city police. More than forty CORE activists were
arrested, many of whom were clubbed, choked, and thrown into the
backs of police vans. A *Defender* reporter and photographer, on the
scene when the arrests were made, witnessed much of this police
abuse directly and the front page of the next day's edition juxtaposed
a photo of Chicago police kicking a prone protester in the groin with
an image of officers using similar tactics in Birmingham, where Martin Luther King had led a months-long boycott that spring. "A short
three months was all it took for police brutality to move north," read
the caption.[24]

*The Defender* had been editorializing for Superintendent Willis's
removal for more than a year, but Stone now took up the cause with
new energy in his column, "A Stone's Throw," rebuking not only Willis but his journalistic apologists at the white-owned dailies as well.
In mid-August, Stone hosted a meeting in the newspaper's headquarters with the local branch of the NAACP as well as student groups,
book clubs, and representatives of the clergy and labor. Though these
various factions differed in their missions and operations, sometimes even clashing outright, they shared one common goal — Willis
had to go. A joint statement from the coalition expressed their collective fury over the damage done to their children's education and
self-esteem and appealed to Mayor Daley to fire the superintendent
forthwith. The mayor, reelected earlier that year with overwhelming
African American support, had thus far managed to avoid taking a
direct stand on Willis's policies, but the coalition noted that African
Americans now made up one-third of the city's population — more
than 923,000 people altogether — and their collective will could not
be ignored. "There is no room for compromise on Dr. Willis' continuing in Chicago," read the statement, quoted on *The Defender*'s
front page. "His administration will continue to hurt the prog-

ress of race relations not only in the school system, but in the city of Chicago."[25]

For Timuel Black Jr., who had come to Chicago as an infant and delivered copies of *The Defender* as a youth, the battle over the Willis Wagons that summer of 1963 meshed with his efforts to build support for the upcoming March on Washington, a mass protest in the nation's capital that had been a longtime dream of civil rights activists. Now a forty-four-year-old high school teacher, Black was in the vanguard of those challenging the Democratic machine, Congressman Bill Dawson, and even Mayor Daley for their failures to address school segregation as well as the community's ever-present housing shortage. He was prominent, too, in the national civil rights movement and it was during a trip to join the protests in Birmingham that past spring that he had been asked by Martin Luther King himself to organize Chicago's contingent in the march.

At first concerned primarily with turnout, Black spent the summer convincing people to travel to Washington, a task in which *The Defender* served as an enthusiastic collaborator. Black wrote a guest column for the newspaper at the beginning of August in which he characterized the march as an extension of the struggle over the city's schools and called upon "all men and women of peace and good will" to join them in the nation's capital. Another article in the same issue stated that the ad hoc committee Black was chairing had reserved a thirty-car train that would leave for Washington the night before the march and return to Chicago the following evening. Organizers hoped that as many as twenty-five hundred people from the city would make the trip.[26]

With the date of departure approaching, concern began to grow about whether the march would remain peaceful, and *The Defender*'s reporters kept checking in with Black, who reassured them that it would be safe and orderly, guided by a cadre of a thousand specially trained activists who would keep things disciplined. Based on the modest excitement so far, he predicted an overall total of one hundred thousand people from across the nation.

The newspaper's editorial page, confidently dismissing the prospect of violence, urged its readers to make the journey. Comparing it to previous mass gatherings in prior decades by war veterans and women's rights activists and even to the biblical march on Jericho, *The Defender* argued that this march would be a unique African American contribution to the long movement for American freedom, a nonviolent demonstration demanding immediate action to dismantle, at long last, the architecture of segregation in the South and beyond.

"Precedent is being established upon this occasion. New history is dawning upon us," read the editorial two days before the march. "We do not look to the past, to what others have done in other situations for other causes. Our plan leads us out of our condition to its own objectives — and we are new history in our own right."[27]

Less than twenty-four hours before they finally set off, *The Defender*'s national editor, Lloyd General, interviewed Timuel Black, finding him exhausted but confident. With every seat on the first train already claimed, Black had to add a second, which quickly sold out too, while hundreds of others were traveling by plane or in additional vehicles organized by the committee; Black had no idea how many more were going on their own.[28]

At 3:00 p.m. on Tuesday, August 27, General and two *Defender* photographers joined the thousands of blacks and whites packing into Chicago's Grand Central Station and boarded one of the two "Freedom Trains" bound for Washington. The mood was positively jubilant, General wrote. All through the night, musicians who had brought their instruments led their fellow travelers in civil rights anthems; only a few enervated activists overcame their excitement to sleep a little. They were all bleary-eyed but still exuberant when they arrived in Washington just before 9:00 a.m. local time and emerged into a cloudless day underneath a blazing sun that would see the temperature rise into the nineties. "For many it had been a tiring all-night journey," General observed, "but they left the train filling the air with songs of freedom."[29]

Joining the masses arriving at D.C.'s Union Station, General made his way to the nearby Washington Monument, where he saw hundreds of buses parking and disgorging their passengers. At 10:00 a.m., the march formally began, with elected officials, entertainers, and labor union leaders mixing in with the masses as they slowly advanced to the Lincoln Memorial, each person in the enormous crush of people restricted to taking tiny steps. General could see there were far more assembled than the organizers' original estimate of one hundred thousand; and yet there was no tension at all, with the marchers accommodating each other happily, singing all the way.

General accompanied the Illinois delegation as they found their state's designated spot in front of the memorial and proceeded to cheer the arrival of each group from the various states and territories. The crowd was positively abuzz when the "Celebrity Delegation"—among them black and white Hollywood stars including Harry Belafonte and Lena Horne as well as Marlon Brando and Charlton Heston—took up their spots on the grand steps of the memorial near the speakers' platform. In the VIP section, General could see John Sengstacke, who had been in Washington for several days in advance of the march, as well as Louis Martin in a coterie of African American leaders from political and business circles.[30]

Flying in to Washington on the morning of the march, editor in chief Chuck Stone, too, realized upon his arrival that the number of marchers on the Mall far exceeded the organizers' expectations. Stone marveled at how peacefully the multiracial crowd moved and interacted, noting that the only incidents at the event were a few lost children and several individuals fainting from the heat. Hard-edged as he was, Stone found himself truly moved by the sight of marchers of every age group, racial background, and economic level, Jews and Christians of all denominations, removing their shoes and dipping their bare feet in the pool that spanned the vast distance between the Washington Monument and the Lincoln Memorial. Indeed, when he saw a woman with her leg immobilized in an iron cast laboring through the intense heat, clearly suffering through every step but determined to walk under her own power all the way, he was moved to tears. "She became my symbol of the Negro Revolution," Stone wrote in his column. "She knew why she was there. Those of you who stayed home should get down on your knees and thank God for letting her fight your freedom battle."[31]

All through the morning and into the afternoon, Stone listened as the long succession of speakers took their turn demanding and imploring the U.S. Congress to pass meaningful civil rights legislation that would put an end to legal segregation once and for all. He found it particularly poignant that W. E. B. Du Bois had died just a few days earlier at age ninety-five, and thought it thoroughly appropriate that A. Philip Randolph, at seventy-four still the leader of the Brotherhood of Sleeping Car Porters, spoke first; the march, after all, had been Randolph's dream for decades now. Stone was particularly impressed by John Lewis, the fearless young leader of the first crew of freedom riders, who critiqued both Republicans and Democrats for failing to put an end to legal segregation and necessitating the massive rally in the first place.

The speeches and songs continued into midafternoon, by which point some in the crowd were overcome by the heat and quite a few others broke from their delegations to stand in the shade of the trees lining the Mall. Several delegations left early to catch their trains, frightened by rumors of an impending rail strike that might have stranded them in the nation's capital. By the time Martin Luther King stepped to the podium to close the march, it was, unfortunately, too late to transmit either text or photographs to Chicago, but *The Defender* staffers who heard him utter those immortal words, "I have a dream today," knew immediately that they were experiencing something of great significance. "Rarely has history witnessed a more moving, dramatic or eloquent moment," proclaimed an editorial introduction to the text of King's speech printed in the weekend edition, "than the hour when Martin Luther King, Jr., delivered his brilliant address on the steps of the Lincoln Memorial with the brooding countenance of the Great Emancipator looking down on the 300,000 people assembled."[32]

From his perch on the steps of the Lincoln Memorial, Louis Martin looked out into the crowd as King spoke and felt a surge of conflicting emotions, elation and pride as well as relief and gratitude. Many within the Kennedy administration had worried the march would explode into violence, which would have certainly derailed the civil rights agenda, but Martin had been its champion, cajoling government officials and labor unions to get involved. Now that it was over and had been disaster-free, Martin brought King and nine other leaders back to the White House for a meeting.

President Kennedy, having watched the march on television and concluded that it presented the civil rights movement in an overwhelmingly positive light, was beaming when he came into the Cabinet Room where the activists were waiting. Kennedy spoke with the group for over an hour, praising King for his speech and promising to take steps to advance the cause with new legislation and regulations.[33]

Lloyd General rode back home onboard the Freedom Train that evening, interviewing his fellow passengers as they steamed north. Some were optimistic that the march would spark immediate action in the U.S. Congress, while others simply savored the experience of participating in the special day. Fully 30 percent of Chicago's delegation was made up of whites, he noted proudly, a ratio that, indeed, reflected the march's overall composition. "They were a little too tired to dance in the aisles," General wrote of the return journey in the weekend edition of *The Defender,* "but they sang freedom songs with the sure knowledge that what they had done expanded the cause of freedom."

Rolling in to Grand Central Station two hours ahead of schedule, the train was met by a crowd of people who welcomed the marchers as returning heroes. "We couldn't be there in body, but our spirits were with you," read one sign that could be seen by the passengers as they pulled into the gate.[34]

As soon as the passengers disembarked, a host of reporters gathered around Timuel Black, asking him about the march and its impact. He was elated with the city's turnout, Black told the throngs of journalists, estimating that some three thousand people from Chicago alone had participated in the march. But the racial harmony on display in Washington would not last, he warned, if real change was not delivered soon. "We could never again put on this type of demonstration with so much success," Black told the reporters, "and if another demonstration becomes necessary, it will take on a different character.

"The rest is up to the American people."[35]

In the wake of the triumph of the March on Washington, the activists fighting to remove Chicago Schools superintendent Willis stepped up their efforts, finding in *The Defender* a reliable ally. In early September, columnist Lillian Calhoun conducted an investigation of eight white elementary schools on the edge of the black community and found empty classrooms as well as empty desks in all of them. Using data provided by the Urban League, Calhoun calculated classroom sizes and found that where the average number of pupils in many schools was just in the teens or low twenties, classrooms in black schools were well over forty students per class.[36]

On the strength of this investigation, the newspaper pressed Mayor Daley to fire Willis, in response to which the mayor insisted that he would allow the Board of Education to make its decisions completely independently. "I think that education should transcend the political arena," Daley told *The Defender*'s reporter.[37]

For the moment, the newspaper did not challenge the mayor directly on this line of defense, no matter how unconvincing it was for Daley, who exacted control over every minute aspect of city government, to claim a hands-off policy when it came to schools. Nevertheless, Chuck Stone kept up his critique of Willis, comparing the superintendent's actions to block even the most modest effort at integration with the bombing several days earlier that had killed four girls at an Alabama church.

"I see little difference between the bomb thrown at the 16th Street Baptist Church in Birmingham Sunday," Stone wrote, "and the bomb of race hatred fired by 5,000 noisy all-white demonstrators protesting the most minute racial integration in all-white Bogan High School. Unless [Willis] does go, I predict one of the worst racial blood baths this city has ever seen."[38]

Such language came across as biased and threatening to the other daily newspapers, which promptly criticized Stone in their columns and editorials. Stone, however, fought back, arguing that the white-owned newspapers were every bit as biased, citing as a prime example *The Chicago Daily News*'s coverage of the Sixteenth Street Baptist Church bombing. While generally liberal on race issues — Stone described it as his "second favorite Chicago newspaper"— *The Daily News* had placed the headline for the girls' murder, "New Bombing in Birmingham," at the bottom of the front page, below a headline for an investigation of a local black labor organization. "See the bias?" Stone asked. "Lives will go on in the wake of violence and more violence, but there's the old, steady, reliable Daily News working its lil' ol' heart out to show to the public that here's a group of Negroes that 'just ain't right.'"

Moreover, if *The Defender* was strident in its opposition to Willis, Stone averred, it was justified, because the schools' superintendent had become a "common enemy" for the entire African American community. No publication could legitimately claim to speak for *all* blacks, but the fact was that every African American, regardless of their political outlook, economic status, religious affiliation, or complexion, experienced racial discrimination personally and every African American could agree that it had to stop.

"We are a watchdog," Stone wrote, "and to many bigots in Chicago, an irritation, a Socratic gadfly, a pain in the neck or even a 'black hysterical voice,' but we proudly accept this role at this critical juncture in American history and will jealously cling to it until we can become 'just another daily newspaper.'"[39]

It seemed for a moment at the beginning of October that the schools crisis would be resolved when Superintendent Willis, finally responding to the unified outrage of African Americans, offered to resign. But after several days of debate — with Mayor Daley still refusing to intervene publicly — the school board voted to reappoint Willis to another term at his job.

With the black population seething, activists announced a one-day student boycott of the schools and a concurrent march on the Board of Education's downtown offices. The local branches of the NAACP, CORE, the Student Nonviolent Coordinating Committee, and many other groups set aside their usual bickering to agree on a comprehensive list of demands that began with Willis's immediate removal.

For the next several days, the organizers based themselves at the building on South Parkway housing the old Appomattox Club, Robert Abbott's social lodge, still operating if no longer as influential, and conducted an intense campaign distributing fliers, posters, stickers, and other material. *The Defender* covered the preparations extensively and then, on the eve of protest day, gave its editorial endorsement to the boycott, arguing that Willis's dictatorial style and obdurate refusal to desegregate the schools necessitated a radical response. "The Freedom Day Protest March," the editorial declared, "is more than a demonstration against Superintendent Willis and his gutless, feeble Board of Education . . . It is manifest resentment against the lily white, anti-Freedom, anti-Negro forces that insist on extending the perimeter of race prejudice."[40]

On the morning of the boycott, Tuesday, October 22, the streets leading to the city's major schools throughout black neighborhoods on the South and West Sides, usually ringing with the cacophonous sounds of excited young people, were starkly quiet. As the bells sounded to empty classrooms and hallways, it was clear that the protest had received nearly universal support — virtually the entire African American student body stayed away, more than 224,770 youths, according to a complete, school-by-school tally printed in *The Defender*, nearly 50,000 high school students and 175,000 elementary school students. Of the 5,000 students at DuSable High School on the South Side, for example, 4,050 stayed away, as did 3,140 of the 3,200 pupils at Jenner Elementary School on the North Side near the Cabrini-Green public housing development. Instead of studying their regular curriculum, many of these children spent the day in "freedom schools" hastily convened in church basements, community centers, and other neighborhood facilities, where activists and ministers taught lessons in African American history, among other topics.

Many older students, meanwhile, joined the twenty thousand protesters who assembled at the school board headquarters downtown. Most remarkably, the march included several machine aldermen and other elected officials, who had thus far stayed silent on whether Willis should stay or go. So strong was the support for the boycott that these politicians, who feared *not* being there, obtained a special pass from Mayor Daley and Congressman Dawson to attend. "We are tired of bigotry and racism in Chicago's schools," the Rev. W. N. Daniel, head of the local branch of the NAACP, told the gathering. "We are tired of being tired."[41]

The boycott did not succeed in forcing Willis's resignation, however, and even provoked a strong reaction from the city's white-owned dailies. Particularly hostile to the boycott was the *Chicago Tribune*, which called for government intervention to stop future protests and claimed that the civil rights organizations' constant pressure on the school system had exhausted the city's patience with their "reign of chaos." Demanding that the community forgo protesting and register their opinion through the courts or the ballot box instead, the

*Tribune* even questioned the fundamental argument that segregated schools provided an inferior education to African Americans. "Negroes are still a minority in Chicago," the *Tribune* editorialized. "A minority cannot enforce its will on the majority, under our system of government."[42]

Fighting back vigorously against the *Tribune*'s diatribes, *The Defender* printed an investigative story using figures wrested from the school district to show that African American youths were, in fact, the bare majority in the city's public elementary schools with 50.9 percent of the total number of students, even as an increasing share of white parents sent their children to Catholic schools or fled to the suburbs. In his column, editor Chuck Stone cited the dailies' commentary as evidence that the protests were, in fact, working. Before the boycott, the city's civil rights groups had simply been ignored by the school board as well as by Mayor Daley and even by black politicians. Now, however, these groups had "the supporting power of the Negro masses," Stone wrote.

"The entire Negro-white power relationship of Chicago has changed," he observed. "Naturally, the *Chicago Tribune, American,* the *Sun-Times* and the Willis forces and the downright nasty bigots of Chicago are going to oppose more demonstrations. Demonstrations unify people. Demonstrations nourish power in the community. Demonstrations impart a greater equality in the bargaining process."[43]

In the early afternoon of Friday, November 22, John Sengstacke called Chuck Stone and told him, in a voice so low as to be barely understood, "Chuck, you'd better get ready to put out a special tomorrow," and then conveyed the news that President John Kennedy had been assassinated in Dallas.

Feeling the president's murder on a visceral level, Stone immediately broke down in tears. He had covered the White House, after all, not only at *The Defender* but in his previous job as editor of the Washington edition of the *Afro-American.* Stone had to set aside his heartbreak for the moment, however, as the assassination had taken place on a Friday, after the national edition had already been printed and was due to be shipped out. *The Defender*'s staff was in a bind, but working at lightning speed, Stone and his team were able to switch out the front pages, filling them with coverage of the assassination and its aftermath written by Lloyd General, who was in Dallas, as well as local reactions and retrospective photographs of the president. Unfortunately, there wasn't sufficient time to revise the editorial page, which included an analytical piece about the upcoming 1964 elections predicting that JFK would face Republican Barry Goldwater in his reelection bid.[44]

Still emotional when he gave an official statement to a *Defender* reporter, John Sengstacke captured the sentiment of many African Americans when he compared the killing of President Kennedy to that of Abraham Lincoln a century earlier. And if *The Defender* had been critical of the Kennedy administration lately because of what it perceived as a watering-down of the civil rights bill, Sengstacke now focused on the full arc of the president's relationship with African Americans, his appointments of judges and other federal officials, and, above all, the staunch determination he showed during multiple federal confrontations with southern governors.[45]

Nell Brown, a barmaid from the South Side interviewed by *The Defender*, agreed that Kennedy had sincerely supported the cause of black liberation, and was sure that was the reason the president had been targeted. "He spoke up for us," Brown said of Kennedy. "It wouldn't have happened if he hadn't tried to do the right thing by us."[46]

Indeed, many found it significant that Kennedy was murdered in the South, suspecting that Lee Harvey Oswald had received assistance from white supremacists; even if there wasn't a direct link, they blamed the region's culture of intolerance for abetting the assassination. Edwin Griffin, a printing salesperson, summarized the sentiments of many when he told the newspaper, "The president's assassination and the bombing of the four innocent little girls in Alabama show just what type of people Negroes have been trying to protect themselves from for over 100 years."[47]

The front page of the next issue, on Monday, November 25, was dominated by a full-color photograph of a smiling President Kennedy. For several weeks, John Sengstacke wrote in a message to readers, the staff had planned to run, for the first time, a color image on *The Defender*'s front page to demonstrate the capabilities of the new printing press. Given the developments of the past week, the staff had decided to replace the photograph they'd intended to run with a portrait of the late president, purchased from the *Milwaukee Journal*. The interior of the issue was filled with black-and-white photographs from *The Defender*'s archives of JFK's life as well as his funeral, while a grief-filled editorial was entitled "We've Lost a Friend."

"He was crucified," lamented the editorial, "because, like Lincoln, he believed in the equality of men, in justice and right. He died for us — for all of us — a martyr to the cause of civil rights and world peace."[48]

As his editorial protests against Benjamin Willis continued into the winter without success, Chuck Stone began to hold Mayor Daley personally accountable. In December, he wrote in his column that the schools' superintendent seemed to have a "fantastic and mesmerizing hold" over the mayor as well as the Chicago Board of Education itself, and warned that, if Daley did not act, there would be consequences at the polls.

Pointing out that Daley would not have been reelected if the tally in the seven predominantly black wards had delivered just twenty thousand fewer votes, Stone asserted that Willis's tenure had become a make-or-break issue with the African American electorate. Daley was popular, Stone admitted, and it was unlikely blacks would return to the Republican Party any time soon, but frustration over this issue, he predicted, could dampen enthusiasm for President Lyndon Johnson's election campaign.[49]

In February, a second boycott drew a smaller, if still substantial, number: 172,350 students participated, with picket lines established at schools all over the city. This time, Daley came out openly against the boycott and demanded that all of his machine operatives, too, make clear their opposition, including the six black aldermen who counted on the mayor's support, dubbed the "Silent Six" by activists. Afterward, Daley threatened as well to prosecute "outsiders" who blocked young people from entering schools, including the sole independent black alderman, Charles Chew, who had participated in the protests. "What do they prove?" the mayor asked of the boycotts. "I don't think that anything that keeps children out of school could be considered successful."[50]

With Willis now publicly protected by the mayor, *The Defender* turned up the heat against the superintendent. When Willis alleged that the students who participated in the boycott were responsible for an increased number of assaults in the public schools, the newspaper ran an investigative story that found he had manipulated the numbers to support the accusation. In his front-page column commenting on the story, Chuck Stone compared the school superintendent to Joseph Goebbels, placing a headshot of Willis next to an image of Adolf Hitler's propaganda minister. "Both were masters in distorting facts to meet their selfish purposes," Stone wrote, "Goebbels the practitioner of the 'Big Lie,' Willis the skillful juggler of the statistic."[51]

Just a few weeks later, Stone urged his readers to continue organizing against Willis, while recognizing that it was Mayor Daley who wielded the real power over the school system. "Daley is the key," Stone wrote. "He is the ultimate and final decision-maker for Chicago, his phony, Buddha-like posture of non-involvement notwithstanding . . . Sure, let's keep on picketing, demonstrating and sitting in and make it as hot politically for Daley as we can."[52]

During the April 1964 Democratic primaries, *The Defender*'s editorial page refused to endorse U.S. Representative William Dawson, who had remained obdurately silent on Willis's tenure, or his opponent, A. A. "Sammy" Rayner, a funeral home owner backed by comedian Dick Gregory and other influential figures in the movement. But when the election results came in, it was clear that the activists had not been able to translate the widespread support for the school boycott into votes: Dawson won reelection with more than 45,737 ballots to Rayner's 20,577.

In his postelection column, Stone tried to put a positive spin on these results, arguing that Dawson's victory had been narrower than before and that the "luster of invincibility had been wiped off." Nevertheless, he had to admit that the Democratic machine continued to control not only the flow of political money but also the vast network of precinct workers. It would take a far more sophisticated operation to be truly viable in electoral politics. "Enthusiasm," Stone conceded, "is no substitute for organization."[53]

At the end of June, Stone gave the keynote address at the twenty-fourth annual convention of the recently renamed National (substituted for "Negro") Newspaper Publishers Association in San Francisco, where he presented a frank assessment of the state of the black press in a rapidly changing media landscape. The once-mighty *Pittsburgh Courier* and the *Afro-American* chain, among other black publications, had lost circulation and prestige due to the seismic shifts in the African American population, beginning with a mass migration from rural areas of the country; 60 percent of blacks now lived in cities. A new generation of young people had grown up within these teeming urban communities, and while some were choosing to commit fully to the freedom struggle, others opted to take advantage of the opportunities offered through integration.

This was a different readership, with different expectations from their newspapers, and Stone argued that the black press would have to make major changes to ensure that it remained a vital and relevant force. The black press was "too dull and too angry," he complained, urging more African American newspapers to become dailies and proposing that they combine their efforts and speak collectively on the major issues of the day, amplifying their collective voice through shared editorials and news pieces. Black newspapers had to be improved if they were to survive — from their design to their reporting methods, to their public reputation. "Finally," he told the assembled publishers, "the Negro press must find the soul of the Negro community and reflect it in its news pages."[54]

Stone was leading the way by aligning *The Defender* with Chicago's social justice activists in the battle against Superintendent Willis and Mayor Daley. But this explicit political posture did not sit well with John Sengstacke, who increasingly saw Stone as too volatile and vindictive to lead the newspaper. Sengstacke might have vested his editors with autonomy, while he himself used the editorial page to criticize politicians, even close allies, but he had always maintained a pragmatic posture. More than fifteen years earlier, Sengstacke fired Metz Lochard for siding too openly with Henry Wallace over President Harry Truman. Now here was another editor insisting that the newspaper tether itself to another quixotic campaign.

Sengstacke articulated his differences with Stone to a biographer just a few years later: "Once you blast an individual, as Stone always wanted to do, you ought to be able to follow through to some reasonable conclusion. Otherwise, you've shot your wad and received no results."[55]

Sengstacke and Stone had numerous confrontations, including one blowup in the newsroom in which the publisher tore up a story Stone had written. Stone protested that the story — on housing discrimination in Mayor Daley's neighborhood of Bridgeport — adhered to the standards he had learned at the Medill School of Journalism. "I don't care what you learned in school," replied an infuriated Sengstacke. "I wrote the book on *The Defender*."[56]

The tension grew more palpable into the fall and finally, in early October, Sengstacke made the decision to fire his editor. Stone left embittered, convinced that Sengstacke intended for the newspaper to be a cog in Mayor Daley's machine. Not a few civil rights activists were of similar mind, and the day after Stone's firing, protesters carrying signs demanding his reinstatement set up a picket line in front of 2400 South Michigan and marched in a circle until nightfall.[57]

The activists were unsuccessful in persuading Sengstacke to rehire Stone, although the next day's edition of *The Defender* did include photos of the protesters under the tongue-in-cheek headline "Always on Top of the News." Letters praising Stone and lambasting Sengstacke for firing him were printed in subsequent issues of the newspaper as well, including a missive from Carole Anderson, a musician who had written several arts reviews for the paper. "I wonder what kind of man you are Mr. Sengstacke, sitting behind the desk of a newspaper office afraid of truth and controversy," wrote Anderson. "Didn't anyone ever teach you how to hold up your head and be proud?[58]

Sengstacke recognized that Stone had a point when it came to the systemic issues facing the black press as it tried to compete with both the white-owned dailies and the burgeoning broadcast media. And so, the day after Stone was fired, Sengstacke announced that *The Defender* would start printing an "owl" edition to provide the latest news to readers as they made their way home from work every evening.[59]

Sengstacke also decided after Stone's departure to tilt the newspaper's content more heavily toward African American issues. When he originally launched the daily, Sengstacke had theorized that by broadening the newspaper's scope, he might attract new audiences, even white readers. But neither the white readers nor the white advertisers had materialized, and Sengstacke now ordered that 90 percent of the space in each issue be devoted to articles about African

Americans in Chicago and across the nation, rather than the fifty-fifty split between community and general news with which he had previously been working. Sengstacke had come to understand that his core readers "want to know what's happening in the Negro community — an area that the metropolitan press does not really cover, is not really concerned about, and can't do as good a job as we can."[60]

# 19

# A Prayer for Chicago

CONTRARY TO THE fears and accusations by Stone and his supporters, *The Defender* kept up its coverage of the continuing protests against Schools' Superintendent Benjamin Willis through the winter of 1964 and into the spring of 1965. The editorial page, too, persisted in demanding Willis's ouster and, after the superintendent was reappointed in May, called for the resignation of the entire school board, which it now described as "contemptuous of the wishes of the people of the community."[1]

In early June, the newspaper gave front-page treatment to a protest march led by Al Raby, a public school teacher turned full-time convener for the Coordinating Council of Community Organizations, which had been formed to focus the anti-Willis movement and had sponsored the previous school boycotts. Leading hundreds of activists through downtown to City Hall during the evening rush, Raby orchestrated a traffic-blocking sit-in at one of the Loop's major intersections, at which point police swooped in, arresting fifty-three men, women, and children, all of whom were gently handcuffed and placed into waiting paddy wagons.

Mayor Daley, alarmed at the public disruption, asked area ministers to arrange for a meeting with civil rights leaders, indicating to *The Defender* that he might be willing to negotiate their demands. After further acts of civil disobedience at Raby's trial a few days later, Daley attended a meeting between the school board and the activists at which the mayor urged the CCCO to practice "cooperation, not conflict," while the protesters insisted on Willis's immediate removal as a precondition for any serious talks.[2]

The fight against Willis was now a community-wide effort. Thirty-nine black business leaders, including John Sengstacke, took out a full-page ad appealing for the school board to "reconsider its decision to retain" the superintendent. Then, on July 7, Martin Luther King appeared with Raby at a press conference in Chicago, declaring that he would bring his civil rights crusade to the North for the first time, joining the battle to oust Willis and equalize educational opportunity in the city. Speaking at the Palmer House Hotel, King, now internationally renowned, having won the Nobel Peace Prize as well as led the marches in Selma that spring, said he would return with his staff later that month for three busy days of tours, marches, street corner rallies, and church meetings, all geared to support the collective efforts of local organizations and galvanize the "forces of good will."

Asked by *Defender* editors if his tactics would change in Chicago, the civil rights leader said they would: "In the North," King told them, "laws appear just on their face but are unconstitutionally applied . . . Civil disobedience is used in the North to the overall alive-ness of unjust situations. It is a weapon whereby we dramatize the evils of segregation and discrimination both North and the South."[3]

King arrived as planned on the evening of Friday, July 23, holding a press conference in which he made it clear that his objectives were far broader than simply removing Willis. Labeling Chicago "one of the nation's most segregated cities," he argued that now that the freedom struggle had set in motion the effort to end legal and political segregation in the South, its next phase, logically, would be to tear down the structures of economic discrimination in the North. "When a man cannot get a good job and good wages," King asserted, "he is a slave. When he cannot get good, substantial housing, he is a slave. When a man cannot get integrated education, he is a slave. Before I'll be a slave, I'll be buried in my grave. We are eternally through with racial segregation."

The next day, King began a tour of the city with an interfaith breakfast at a Baptist church before proceeding to the Altgeld Gardens public housing development, a community of low-rise cottages on the far South Side proximate to steel mills and other lakefront industries, where, greeted by the president of the resident council, he spoke to more than a thousand residents from the back of a flatbed truck. Next, he went to another public housing development, the

Robert Taylor Homes, whose high-rise buildings were infamous for poverty, depredation, and horrendous acts of violence.

Bobby Sengstacke joined *The Defender*'s team of reporters and photographers covering King's visit and snapped crisp images of the civil rights leader arriving with a squad of police officers to protect him as the crowd pressed in. But the residents gathered in the development's courtyard, though enthusiastic, were peaceful, and King was escorted to a dais prepared for him by a leader of that community's resident council. Standing in the manmade canyon formed by the high-rises around them, he preached the gospel of nonviolence to thousands of residents and others who, when he was finished, burst into ecstatic applause.

From the Robert Taylor Homes, King traveled east into Kenwood to meet with Timuel Black and other local leaders on his way to spend the afternoon in the African American communities on the West Side, where a rapidly growing population of 250,000, mostly recent migrants from the South, lived under even worse conditions than on the South Side — higher levels of poverty, overcrowding, and discrimination further stressed by a corrupt political structure dominated by white organized crime. Accompanied by a small entourage, King stopped at several West Side locations that afternoon, speaking on street corners and in vacant lots as people came out of crowded tenements to watch him from the wooden back porches and the rooftops, joining in singing the freedom songs that echoed through the streets. At every stop, King urged his rapt listeners to come out to the march from Grant Park to City Hall he was organizing for that coming Monday.

"Men, women and children of all ages, whites, black, popsicles, collars, habits, babes-in-arms, candy bares, craned necks, camp stools, fans and the look of bright-eyed wonder and anticipation lighting the faces of young and old alike were only a few of the ingredients blended into a rousing West Side street rally to greet and hear Dr. Martin Luther King," wrote *The Defender*'s reporter, capturing the diverse group that coalesced around the civil rights icon.[4]

But on Monday afternoon, King came down with a fever and sore throat and was being treated in his hotel room even as the throngs began to arrive in Grant Park. The organizers delayed the proceedings for over an hour while he rallied his strength, and by the time he finally emerged, there were thirty thousand people gathered, nearly three times the number expected, about one-quarter of whom were white, an unprecedented level of diversity in the city. At last they began to march, fourteen abreast, through the streets of the Loop in a line stretching for several blocks, while a cordon of hundreds of police officers lining the route redirected the rush-hour traffic. Unlike some of the previous marches, this one did not include any acts of civil disobedience; there were no arrests as the protesters made their way to the western entrance of City Hall along LaSalle Street, where they stopped and gathered until the entire block was packed with people.

King, visibly exhausted, paused for a short rest under the shade of an umbrella before turning to address the marchers. Once he actually began speaking, however, he displayed no lack of energy. The crowd roared when he equated segregation in Chicago and the South, declaring that African Americans in the city endured "educational and cultural shackles that are as binding as those of a Georgia chain gang."

The city might once have been a refuge for millions but African Americans now were trying to free themselves from the "manacles of the ghetto," of which discrimination in the schools was the paramount issue. "Negroes have continued to flee from behind the Cotton Curtain but now they find that after years of indifference and exploitation, Chicago has not turned out to be the new Jerusalem," King said. "We march here today because we believe that Chicago, her citizens and her social structure are in dire need of redemption and reform."[5]

From City Hall, a number of the marchers broke off to cross the nearby Chicago River and protest outside the distinctive Marina Towers, home of Charles Swibel, a highly successful real estate mogul serving as the head of the Chicago Housing Authority, who had become the civil rights groups' second-most-hated city official after Benjamin Willis. Unsurprisingly, neither Swibel nor Willis made any public response to King's march. Mayor Daley, meanwhile, was conveniently out of town — in Detroit, at a convention of fellow mayors. A small contingent of the Chicago protesters chased Daley down in that city, and the mayor was queried by a *Defender* reporter inside the hall for his reaction to the protest. Responding with a terse "No comment," he then ducked out through a side entrance.[6]

Nevertheless, *The Defender* editorial page understood that the overwhelming success of King's protest represented only the beginning of a major challenge to the mayor and predicted a collision between "Irresistible Forces" and "Immovable Objects." The lead editorial, written the day after the march and entitled "Your Move, Mr. Mayor," stated that the local movement, having accumulated only more power in the course of King's short visit, would surely continue pressuring City Hall to dump Willis once and for all. "His worst enemy never has accused the mayor of Chicago of being short on political savvy," the editorial concluded. "And it is unthinkable, after Monday, that he can miss the tall, bold handwriting plainly on the wall."[7]

In December 1965, *The Defender* announced the introduction of an exclusive column in the newspaper's weekend edition to be authored by Martin Luther King. In "My Dream," the civil rights leader would write frankly about the struggle for civil rights as well as on other issues of the day, especially his controversial opposition to the American military involvement in Vietnam.[8]

In his first column, King criticized U.S. Attorney General Nicholas Katzenbach for failing to intervene in the murders of two civil rights workers in Alabama. The following week, in a piece entitled "The Myth of the Promised Land," King made it clear that Chicago was still very much on his mind. Reprising the theme of his speech in front of City Hall the previous summer, King argued that the North had disappointed African Americans with its own brand of segregation, which, even if enshrined simply in custom rather than law, was every bit as damaging as Jim Crow. If the problems he had seen firsthand during his tour of Chicago and other northern cities were not addressed, King warned, violence would surely result, just as it had the previous summer in the deadly street battles in Watts, an African American section of Los Angeles. "As the South has slowly, reluctantly begun to turn and face her destiny, the rigidities of Northern discrimination and segregation have stiffened," King wrote in mid-December 1965. "The ghetto has become more intensified than dispersed. Explosive racial tensions in these metropolitan areas have produced riots."[9]

Just a few days later, *The Defender* discovered just how serious King was about planting the civil rights movement in the city. On January 5, reporter Betty Washington got the scoop that he had flown into O'Hare Airport and was meeting in secret at a nearby hotel with Al Raby, Timuel Black and other civil rights leaders, both local and national figures. Although King refused to comment while the meeting was underway, Washington did manage to interview one of his aides and learned that he had agreed to spend an extended period of time in Chicago working on a variety of fronts, ranging from "political education" to jobs and the housing crisis. This was far more than just an anti-Willis effort: fifteen staff members from King's Southern Christian Leadership Conference, including a charismatic young minister named Jesse Jackson, had already stationed themselves in Chicago and were organizing workshops on the West Side and the Near North Side near the Cabrini-Green public housing development, establishing contacts with students, teachers, gang members, and even Latinos and poor whites.[10]

Betty Washington was there two days later when King, finally emerging from the conference, announced that, as part of a phased campaign to "bring about the unconditional surrender of the forces dedicated to the creation and maintenance of slums and ultimately to make slums a moral and financial liability upon the whole community," he would rent an apartment in the West Side neighborhood of Lawndale.[11]

While the actual unit where King would live had not yet been chosen, he pledged to spend two to three days every week in the apartment during the winter months while the activist groups geared up for a mass mobilization during the spring and summer. The campaign would incorporate public protests and economic boycotts as well as explicitly political actions. At the same time, King made it clear he was willing to work with Mayor Daley and even Superintendent Willis, if the opportunity presented itself. "We're going all out to end an evil system," King said, "and not get bogged down with an individual."[12]

Betty Washington stayed on the story for the next few weeks while King's emissaries sought a suitable apartment. Attractive and well educated with a degree from DePaul University, the twenty-eight-year-old Washington, married with four children, had joined *The Defender*'s staff a year earlier. Like most fledgling reporters, she began her tenure covering murders and other crimes but had quickly graduated to writing about housing and politics as well as civil rights, traveling to Selma, Alabama, in 1965 to write about the marches there. Bob Black, the photographer who typically partnered with her on assignment, recalled in an interview that Washington was "totally committed, passionate about her work and how to use it to help the black community."[13]

Back in Chicago during those heady days of King's residency, Washington would get a tip that a march or other event was happening, and then dash down to the photo lab in *The Defender* building's subbasement to find Bob Black before setting off. For Black (no relation to Timuel), working with Washington was the highlight of what was already a dream job. Also in his midtwenties, he had grown up on the South Side with *The Defender* as his family's mainstay news source. As an intern for the newspaper just after his graduation from Englewood High School, Black had the chance to photograph major news figures; one highlight was his photo-essay on the Little Rock Nine's visit to John Sengstacke's Yellow Lake compound.[14]

Bob Black bonded with fellow photographer Bobby Sengstacke during his internship at *The Defender,* and when a staff position opened up in 1965, Bobby recommended him for the position. The pay was low and as one of two staff photographers, he had to juggle multiple assignments each day, only to return to working conditions in *The Defender*'s subbasement that were decidedly Spartan. But the newspaper afforded him unbeatable access to national African American figures and issues, so whenever Betty Washington knocked on his door, Black came running.[15]

In an article published in mid-January, Washington revealed that the organization King and others had founded in Montgomery, the Southern Christian Leadership Conference, had successfully rented an apartment for King under the name of one of its staffers, several landlords having balked at the prospect of the civil rights leader as their tenant. The activists tried to keep the exact location secret but the building's owner inevitably discovered who would be moving in and dispatched a team of plasterers, painters, carpenters, and electricians to perform extensive renovations in his four-room, third-floor walkup apartment as well as throughout the building. With just three days before King's arrival, the workers replaced the stove and refrigerator, changed floorboards, plumbing and electrical fixtures, the toilet, and even the doorknobs in King's apartment, and then repaired radiators in the building's other apartments while the landlord insisted to Washington that he would have performed the same service for any new tenant.

"It Wasn't the Plan," read the tongue-in-cheek headline over Washington's story, "but Dr. King Shows How to 'Cure' a Slum Building."[16]

On the afternoon of Wednesday, January 26, Betty Washington and Bob Black stationed themselves outside the apartment amid hundreds of neighborhood residents who crowded around King's car when it arrived. People cheered from the balconies and windows up and down the block as King and his wife, Coretta, made their way slowly through the throng, then paused before entering the building at 1550 South Hamlin Avenue to speak with Washington, succinctly stating his motive for coming to the city: "I can learn more about the situation by being here with those who live and suffer here."[17]

Washington and Black hung around that evening while the Kings welcomed groups of their new neighbors, including many curious children. In the evening, six members of the Vice Lords street gang stopped by the apartment, engaging King in deep conversation over the movement's strategy and philosophy.

The Kings began the next day at the Chicago Police Department headquarters, meeting at length with the top police commanders to discuss the movement's plans for the city. Reporters were not allowed to cover the conversation but a spokesperson told Washington afterward that it had been perfectly friendly. For his part, King pledged to obviate any violence, although he warned that the movement would use tactical demonstrations of civil disobedience that could result in mass arrests, even his own, vowing, "I will go to jail again and again."

On Thursday afternoon, King walked through Lawndale and the adjacent community of Garfield Park with aides and reporters in tow, along with the six Vice Lords who had engaged him in conversation the previous night. Despite the zero-degree weather, Washington saw people stop on the street and open the windows of their homes when they saw the civil rights leader. Even the "down and outs" stretched out their arms to shake King's hand and offer their support. One older gentleman walking with a cane on the icy sidewalk nearly fell when he saw King and was caught by one of the activists. "Great God almighty," the man declared, "I didn't ever think this day would come."

In Garfield Park, a neighborhood where violent confrontations between police and youths had taken place the previous summer, King gave an impromptu speech before six hundred people at the First Church of the Brethren. Garfield Park's riots had not been nearly so deadly as those in Watts but King said that he found striking similarities in the two communities and urged the residents of the West Side to organize themselves to eliminate slums. That evening, he lectured at the University of Chicago, part of his effort to balance the requests for his presence from the South Side factions of the freedom movement. Then, after sleeping one more night in the apartment on South Hamlin, he left Chicago for voter-registration events in Birmingham and appointments in New York City over the weekend, promising to return for several days the following week and every week for the foreseeable future.[18]

*The Defender* continued covering Martin Luther King's every move as he and his allies implemented their plan to make Chicago their northern base. The following week, King proceeded directly to a South Side church, where a rally of civil rights activists had been called to inaugurate a new organization, the Kenwood Oakland Community Organization, created by his twenty-four-year-old protégé Jesse Jackson, newly ordained as a Baptist minister. Declaring that KOCO would begin its efforts by intervening in the neighborhood's schools, Jackson came equipped with an armful of statistics that compared health, employment, and education levels in Kenwood with other Chicago communities, including Mayor Daley's home neighborhood of Bridgeport.[19]

Back on the West Side the week after that, Betty Washington joined Martin and Coretta King and their associates on a tour of a nearby six-flat building at the invitation of its tenants, who had been living without heat, hot water, and electricity for months. Interviewing mothers who stayed awake all night to protect their children from the giant rats prowling the shadows, Washington documented the extreme neglect she saw, as in one third-floor unit that was the home of Mrs. Louise Mitchell and her ten children: "Her apartment, like all of the others, showed no signs of having been painted," Washington wrote. "Walls and ceilings were caked with dirt and grease, and boards and bottles were being used to barricade holes in the wood-work."[20]

King listened to each of the tenants and then asked them whether they had considered a rent strike, just one of the tactics he was planning on deploying in his Chicago crusade. In a column appearing in the same issue of *The Defender* as Washington's article, King argued that even as the walls of segregation were coming down in the South, conditions in the North were deteriorating unforgivingly, such that the continuing flow of migrants who had pushed Chicago's African American population beyond one million people were now finding only cold hardship and disappointment. They needed to be mobilized to fight for their rights.

"Why Chicago?" he wrote. "We do not hold that Chicago is alone among cities with a slum problem, but certainly, we know that slum conditions here are the prototype of those chiefly responsible for the Northern urban racial problem."[21]

But if King was determined to make Chicago a "prototype" for the freedom movement's northern expansion, Mayor Daley was equally determined to avoid becoming a target. An autocrat who presided over an administration that perpetuated segregation in schools and housing, Daley was, nevertheless, no white supremacist and would not be baited into responding the way that southern authorities had. The mayor had the entire city apparatus at his disposal, after all, and was fully capable of creating the impression that whatever problem identified by the civil rights leader was already well in hand.

Thus, even as King was conducting his inspection of that building on the West Side, Mayor Daley held his own press conference to announce, in the tortured, yet demotic language that was his trademark, that he was "deploying the full power of resources of the city to be used in an unlimited way to erase slum blight."

Flanked by his buildings commissioner and the county welfare director, the mayor announced that the city was withholding rent from 331 subsidized apartments in twenty different privately owned buildings on the South and West Sides for code violations, and threatened to take legal action against the owners if they did not ameliorate the problems within ten days. In addition to these steps, Daley said the city would deploy fifty new housing inspectors, use the Chicago

Housing Authority to purchase private structures, and pursue class-action suits for tenants in slum buildings. Overall, the mayor pledged his administration to "the elimination of slums by 1967," just coincidentally the year of the next mayoral election.

Asked by *The Defender*'s City Hall reporter whether King's arrival had inspired the city's sudden zeal, Daley demurred, asserting that the city had always been serious about slums but that several recently passed laws had empowered his agencies to go even further. Nevertheless, the county's public aid director, Raymond Hilliard, very publicly requested a meeting with King and offered to coordinate his staff's work with the SCLC.

King may have had the mayor beat when it came to eloquence, but Daley was fighting a war of attrition, a conflict he could win so long as he avoided any major blows. In the next day's *Daily Defender*, Betty Washington's narrative of King's work on the West Side shared the front page with coverage of the mayor's press conference, the latter actually receiving the bold type because it contained numbers and obvious drama: "Daley, Hilliard Crack Down: 331 Slum Flat Rent Cut-Offs."[22]

King drew crowds wherever he went on the West Side and Washington was there to record every step. During another stroll with Al Raby, the civil rights leader stopped at one dilapidated structure, a worn-out tenement that had been converted from a six-flat to a twelve-flat. King also visited a pool hall and Marshall High School, where hundreds of students came outside to sing freedom songs. "I need not remind you that things are not right in Chicago," King told the students. "I need not remind you that things are not right at Marshall." Delighted to hear that the movement needed their participation, the students called him "Martin Luther Cool."[23]

At the end of February, Betty Washington and Bob Black were summoned back to that same twelve-flat building to hear an announcement about a new tactic the civil rights workers were trying. Taking a fresh approach to "creative social planning," King said they were placing the building in a "receivership" in which they — instead of the landlord — would collect the tenants' rents, using the funds to pay for renovation of the building. "We are not dealing with the legality," King told Washington, "but with the morality of the situation."[24]

Bob Black shot pictures of King and Al Raby in work clothes alongside a white Catholic priest and others helping the tenants clean and upgrade the building. Washington, meanwhile, tracked down the building's owner in his suburban home, but where she expected to find a ruthless slumlord, she met instead an eighty-one-year-old man ill with a respiratory ailment. J. B. Bender claimed that the building had been a money pit for some time, and said he was willing, even happy, to turn the property over to King and the activists. The city administration offered no resistance to King's takeover, either; in fact, the city's corporate counsel Timothy O'Hare expressed real satisfaction at seeing the building rehabilitated.

Confronted with such acquiescence from his intended foes, King conceded that the conditions in low-income neighborhoods could not be blamed on any single entity or individual. "Rather, the slum seems to be a victim of a historic conspiracy involving real estate codes, mortgage practices, federal, state and local housing authorities," King told Washington, "and finally going back to the harsh reality that our government has long neglected our cities and has suffered the influence of Southern and rural power blocs in Congress."[25]

Washington decided to test King's analysis for herself, convincing one of the families in the six-flat to let her move in with them for several days and write a series about her observations for *The Defender.* Both R. V. and Rosie Townes were Mississippi natives who had come to Chicago in their late teens. R. V. had worked as a punch press operator at the same factory almost since his arrival in Chicago, but with seven children, several of whom were disabled, the family was stuck with the dilapidated, overpriced hovels available in West Side neighborhoods like Lawndale and Garfield Park.

Despite the confluence of economic and social forces trapping the Townes in a world of limited opportunities, King's presence, at least temporarily, had improved their circumstances. Until recently, Rosie Townes got up at 6:30 a.m. every day to chase away the large rats that gathered in her kitchen at night; King's inspection of the building prompted a city rodent-control team to move in and block the holes in the structure's walls.

It was only a temporary measure, however. "You can still hear them scratching inside the walls," Washington wrote of the rats, "looking for a thin spot where they'll eventually nibble and make another entrance."[26]

King spent the winter and spring months forging alliances in Chicago and building up the movement's local assets. In February, he visited Nation of Islam leader Elijah Muhammad's stylish mansion in the Kenwood neighborhood. Speaking with a *Defender* reporter afterward, King delineated the sharp philosophical differences with the enigmatic Muhammad's black separatist variant of Islam, then added, "there now appear to be some areas, slums and areas other than slums, in which our movements can cooperate."[27]

Certainly King steered clear of discussing the assassination of Malcolm X, Muhammad's onetime protégé, who had been shot down only a year earlier at a public event in Harlem and whose accused murderers, themselves members of the Nation, were even then on trial.

In March, pulling out all the stops to try to build the local movement, King brought in celebrities Sidney Poitier, Harry Belafonte, and Mahalia Jackson for a show called the Chicago Freedom Festival to raise funds as well as awareness among fifteen thousand fans. Mayor Daley remained a wily and elusive adversary, praising King publicly while his close ally, the Rev. Joseph Jackson, the current pastor of Olivet Baptist Church, blasted away at the civil rights leader in print and in the pulpit. Daley and King finally met at the end of March and though the four-hour exchange was deemed off the record, *The Defender* interviewed some of those who had been present and they described a decidedly tense scene. King came in with Al Raby, and after they'd listened to detailed presentations from Daley's various department heads, Raby stood up and began to complain about the number of precinct captains on the West Side who did not live in their particular wards. Daley cut Raby off in midsentence. "I will be glad to discuss politics with you or with any appropriate people at an appropriate time and place," the mayor said. "This isn't it."

Now King got up and spoke, extemporaneously, for the next twenty minutes, describing his impressions of the city and his certainty that the rising level of frustration in the community had the potential to become a disaster in the streets. "Let the civil rights movement show gains," King said bluntly at one point, "or we'll face violence." He urged the mayor to develop a serious response to the movement, warning that he had given similar advice the previous year to the mayor of Los Angeles but had been ignored, the result being the racial explosion in Watts.[28]

The meeting ended without resolution, and as winter gave way to spring, the civil rights movement only intensified its attacks on Chicago's establishment. In April, Betty Washington reported on Jesse Jackson's new initiative, Operation Breadbasket, a targeted boycott program that organized teams of ministers to confront owners of soft drink, milk, bread, and soup companies who had not hired sufficient numbers of African Americans. The presence of Jackson and the ministers carrying signs in front of a business was usually enough to win some jobs, if not even to get one or two African Americans on the companies' boards of directors.[29]

King, meanwhile, continued to use his *Defender* column to fire verbal salvos at the mayor and other establishment political figures. In "A Prayer for Chicago," which appeared in the middle of April, King, writing in the style of a Sunday sermon, recounted the trials and tribulations faced by the civil rights crusaders as they sojourned through the South, and posited Chicago, with its endemic issues in schools, housing, and employment, as "the gate of a new understanding of the dimensions and depth of our struggle with racial injustice in this country. We pause therefore to pray earnestly and fervently for Chicago, a beautiful city, set so impressively by the majestic waters of Lake Michigan, which now finds itself in the throes of a momentous social revolution . . . May the leadership of Chicago rise to the lofty heights of statesmanship. Help them to substitute courage for caution and the socially relevant for the politically expedient."[30]

Mayor Daley also used *The Defender* to convey his sentiments about King, albeit indirectly. The very issue of the national edition carrying King's "Prayer for Chicago" featured a small item on the front page, a leaked account describing a putatively closed meeting in which, before the top rank of his political organization, the Central Committee of the Cook County Democratic Party, Daley lambasted King as an arrogant interloper. All of his machine operatives were there, precinct captains, committeemen, and lower-ranking elected officials including all of William Dawson's crew and the "Silent Six" aldermen. "We have no need to apologize to the civil rights leaders who have come to Chicago to tell us what to do," the mayor said. "We'll match our integrity against their independence. We have our critics but they are the people who are jealous of the things we have managed to get done."[31]

At the beginning of May, *The Defender* reported on the boldest effort yet by the civil rights forces, an outreach campaign to the city's street gangs. The Rev. James Bevel, who shared leadership of the Southern Christian Leadership Conference with Martin Luther King, brought four hundred gang members to a church in the Woodlawn neighborhood on the South Side to enlist them into the movement. Vowing "we're going to shut down Chicago," Bevel showed them a documentary film about the Watts riot the previous summer and discussed in detail the philosophy and tactics of nonviolence.

When gang members fought each other over territory, Bevel argued, they were essentially "killing each other over white folks' houses" while failing to address the root causes of the community's problems. Bevel also ruled out armed confrontation with the police, explaining that this strategy would only result in large numbers of African American deaths, as it had in Watts. "A man who throws rocks at a man with a machine gun is not only violent," Bevel told the gang members, "but a fool." Nonviolence, on the other hand, had proven effective, promoting legislative change on the national level and dislodging explicitly racist, violent public officials.[32]

For Chicago, Bevel proposed a concerted campaign of civil disobedience, taking actions such as shutting down the Dan Ryan Expressway by having protesters lie across the pavement. With a view to building on the gang members' feelings of racial solidarity and redirecting their energies to a political purpose, the minister said he wanted three thousand courageous teenagers to become full-fledged participants in the struggle. They had to break the law, Bevel told the assembly — which included many young men who had already been incarcerated for various criminal acts — only this time in the name of social justice. "You have to be ready to go to jail and stay there."[33]

An editorial in *The Defender* noted that the work with street gangs alarmed many African American leaders, who felt that Bevel and the other SCLC activists were attempting to teach tactics and ideology to teenage criminals with little inclination to advance the movement.

Still, after reporting extensively on the issue, describing several meetings in which the gang members had shown a sense of civic responsibility and restraint, the newspaper gave the initiative its endorsement.

"Responsible Negro leaders felt that the King people were trifling with the chance of setting off bloody riots," the editorial explained, before adding, "The big question hangs on the gangs themselves. If the members can remember that they are taking on a man-sized project, and they can remember the vital need for self-discipline — instead of resorting to the switch knife, then they will have gained great stature and Chicago will owe them a debt."[34]

Just then, the hated Chicago Public Schools superintendent Benjamin Willis abruptly resigned his post. Though he had a contract for two and a half more years and had previously told reporters he might resign in December on his sixty-fifth birthday, he now announced he was leaving in order to protect "those in whom I am deeply interested." The strong suggestion was that Willis had cut a deal with Mayor Daley, trading the job security of his cronies for a politically expedient exit.[35]

Either way, Black Chicago's leaders were ecstatic. The head of the local branch of the Urban League told *The Defender* he was considering going to the center of the Loop and "dancing across State and Madison, even at the risk of confinement to an institution."[36]

Leaving his post early did not compensate for Willis's deplorable record when it came to integrating the city's public schools, stated *The Defender*'s editorial page; still, he had shown at least "a spark of decency we did not believe was in him."[37]

A victory for the civil rights forces, Willis's sudden exit also deprived them of their most hated enemy just as they were gearing up for a summer of protests. It was no accident that in the June Democratic primary, Raby's effort to field an antimachine slate failed completely; even William Dawson, nearing his eightieth birthday and ailing, easily trounced several opponents in the primary elections to win a nomination for a twelfth term.[38]

Martin Luther King, meanwhile, announced the postponement of a major rally and march on City Hall planned for the end of the month so that he could travel to Mississippi, where James Meredith had been shot and wounded during a solo march across the South.

In keeping with the nonviolent philosophy of mass reaction to an act of aggression, King and other civil rights figures descended on the state to complete Meredith's march. "The cowardly attempt on the life of James Meredith has created a national emergency which has focused our immediate energies on Mississippi," King told Chicago civil rights leaders in explaining that the rally would be delayed.[39]

Certainly King's decision to decamp to Mississippi made sense, given the movement's philosophy. But those who understood that only a sustained, focused mass movement could defeat Mayor Daley were alarmed by what seemed to be a series of critical missteps from the civil rights movement. When John Sengstacke spoke at the convention of the American Society of Newspaper Editors in Montreal that month, he praised King for avoiding the extremes of communism and black nationalism, for his advocacy for open housing, and even for the SCLC's work with the gangs. Nevertheless, Sengstacke criticized King for failing to propose a practical program to defuse the "powder keg" of tensions that threatened to erupt into street violence at any moment. "His overall ideology is beyond debate so far as the Negro masses are concerned," Sengstacke said of King. "But some do believe that his formulation of the means to bring about social change is too broad and disjointed to accomplish the desired ends. Dr. King is a superb crusader . . . But he is not an organizer. Seldom is a crusader an organizer; seldom is an organizer a crusader."[40]

The dispatches sent back by the reporter covering the Meredith March for *The Defender* depicted a frightening and dangerous scene, with both whites and blacks demonstrating an increasing propensity toward bloodshed. In the small town of Philadelphia, where three civil rights workers had been murdered two years earlier, fistfights broke out in several instances between marchers and white onlookers, while several television crews were attacked and had their equipment destroyed. King himself was pelted with firecrackers and taunted by white men as local police and Mississippi state troopers stood by, more menacing than protective.

Tensions continued to mount after an evening rally at which the new leader of the Student Nonviolent Coordinating Committee, Stokely Carmichael, a Caribbean-born, Harlem-reared veteran of the movement at just twenty-four, declared that after being arrested twenty-seven times and beaten numerous times, he would no longer submit himself to such violence and vowed to fight back if he was attacked again. He articulated this new attitude, in a spontaneous bit of phrase making, as "black power," which immediately caught on with the crowd.

By the time the Meredith March reached its terminus in Jackson, Carmichael was in the front rank alongside Martin Luther King and many of those behind them chanted "black power" as often as "freedom."[41]

King, plainly disturbed by the term, tried to stop Carmichael and the mass of marchers from using it. "Black power," to King, connoted separatism that was anathema to the whole spirit of the civil rights movement. But the protesters in Jackson, their ranks swollen by black residents of the city who had never been trained in the techniques of nonviolence, proceeded to tear up lawns in white areas of town and snatch Confederate flags from the hands of white onlookers, chanting "Black Power" as they passed. Noting all of this, *The Defender* chronicled the march's deterioration into acrimony as the ideological split between King and Carmichael became pronounced, and disputes over finances further divided these erstwhile allies.[42]

Shortly afterward, another civil rights group, CORE, formally adopted black power as its creed, setting aside nonviolence entirely and declaring that members would henceforth practice militant self-defense. Though black power was still being defined, *The Defender* discerned here a vital new concept, a logical response to the numerous acts of terror against civil rights activists in the South that had gone completely unpunished by either state or federal law enforcement. Although one editorial criticized Carmichael's stated desire to exclude whites entirely from the movement and another tried to delineate the differences between black power and the racial separatism preached by the Nation of Islam, the newspaper warned those leaders who insisted on adhering to nonviolence that they risked losing relevance among the masses. "The voices of those who once preached the use of the other cheek," asserted the lead editorial of the July 2 national edition, "are losing their sonority. Their logic is one of despair which no longer suits the awakening black masses. Power, black power, has become the battle cry of the Black Revolution."[43]

King, of course, was not easily sidelined or deterred from the path of nonviolence, and at the beginning of July, while in New York City to receive a $100,000 donation for the SCLC from the nation of Sweden, he took the opportunity to deconstruct "black power." The term, he argued, suggested black supremacy, which was philosophically incompatible with a movement that aimed to foster equal rights for all, and he registered his disapproval of the plans from CORE and SNCC to teach "defensive violence," arguing that "the line of demarcation is thin" between self-defense and initiating violence. "I think we've been aggressive all along — non-violently," King said. "I think it's possible to be militantly non-violent."[44]

King's immediate challenge on returning to Chicago was to generate turnout for the protest delayed by his work on the Meredith March. Betty Washington wrote in *The Defender* that the local civil rights groups were hoping to attract a hundred thousand people to a rally at Soldier Field, a lakefront stadium normally utilized for football games, for the afternoon of Sunday, July 10. The plan was to march three miles from Soldier Field to the entrance of City Hall and then to have King leave a six-page document with fourteen collective demands at Mayor Daley's office, echoing his namesake's nailing of his theses to the church door. To ensure that this march was multiracial and interreligious, King's emissaries fanned out across the metropolitan region trying to enlist all of those they had engaged during the past months.[45]

On Freedom Sunday, as it had been dubbed, the temperature soared to ninety-eight degrees under cloudless skies as thousands of people made their way to Soldier Field, rabbis and priests, gang members and college students, white labor leaders shoulder to shoulder with Puerto Rican activists. When they arrived, the marchers were entertained by singers Peter Yarrow, of Peter, Paul and Mary fame, and Oscar Brown Jr., following which they heard rousing speeches by Al Raby, the president of the United Packinghouse Workers, and the president of the Spanish American Foundation, among others. Many faith leaders were represented and the city's most powerful prelate, Archbishop John Cody, having been pressured by Mayor Daley not to appear in person, issued a strongly worded message of support both for King and for the goals of the rally.

*Defender* photographer Bob Black shot an image of one section of the stands full of cheering throngs, which ran on the next day's front page. In fact, there had been many seats left vacant in the stadium, with just thirty thousand people turning out, roughly the same number who had come out the previous summer to Grant Park. King had made every effort to make the rally a success, even sharing the stage with Floyd McKissick, the new head of CORE who had explicitly rejected nonviolence, but his enervation was evident as he spoke to the crowd, rejecting gradualism as well as separatism even as he defended nonviolence as a still-relevant tactic: "We are here today because we are tired," King said. "We are tired of being seared in the flames of withering injustice. We are tired of paying more for less. We are tired of living in rat-infested slums and in the Chicago Housing Authority's cement reservations. We are tired of being lynched in Mississippi and lynched spiritually and economically in the North."[46]

The day after the march, Mayor Daley met with King and Raby to discuss the fourteen points, but the two sides soon emerged to separately express their frustration to Betty Washington and the other reporters who had assembled outside. King complained the mayor refused to commit to specific timetables or develop new initiatives, demanding that the city adopt a policy of open housing. King also charged that city workers were being ordered not to participate in the movement and alleged that the mayor was co-opting certain African American allies with the "sophisticated granting of minor concessions."

Asked if there would be future meetings with the mayor, the normally imperturbable King, visibly frustrated, told Washington that "the time for meeting is over" and vowed to begin the next phase of his program, which would include large-scale demonstrations of civil disobedience. "There will be marches," he promised, "and there will be mass jailing."

Daley retorted, in his own comments, that King's plans were vague and his expectations unrealistic, adding that slum conditions existed in the civil rights leader's hometown of Atlanta just as they did in Chicago. The mayor insisted that the city was already doing much of what was being asked, citing his departments' stepped-up rodent-control efforts and building inspections. Flustered in his conversation with reporters, Daley dismissed all of King's dire prognostications as well as the threat of a major black defection during the next mayoral election. "They have a right to demonstrate," Daley said of King and the civil rights protesters. "They have a right to picket, but they have no right to violate the laws. This will not be tolerated in the city of Chicago as long as I am mayor."[47]

The very next day, as a heat wave continued to roast the city, a confrontation between Chicago police and African American residents of the Near West Side erupted into mass violence. The trouble began along a section of Roosevelt Road near the ABLA public housing development when officers shut off a fire hydrant that had been opened by residents seeking relief from the heat. A crowd gathered around the hydrant, arguing with the police, noting that most of the municipal swimming pools nearby were off-limits for blacks and asserting that the opening of hydrants was tolerated on white blocks.

At first, activists tried to lead the crowd in freedom songs, but when more police arrived, people began pelting them with bricks, bottles, rocks, and other projectiles as hundreds of youths from the surrounding neighborhood rushed to the scene, engaging in running battles with police. The Liberty Shopping Mall at the southeast end of the development was wrecked and looted, and a paddy wagon was destroyed by a gasoline bomb. More than thirty squad cars descended on the area, chasing groups of young people through the trash-strewn streets as officers on foot used their clubs and revolvers, showing little restraint.

*The Defender* sent two reporters, Betty Washington and Donald Mosby, to cover the melee along with two photographers, Bob Black and John Gunn, who arrived to find a scene simultaneously terrifying and carnivalesque, with children playing in the streams shooting out of the reopened hydrants even as projectiles flew over their heads and police grappled with gang members. Black captured images of an older man who said he had been beaten bloody by police and of a dazed child in diapers with a bloody mouth and missing teeth, injured in the crossfire between police and residents.

Alerted to the violence, Martin Luther King set up a command post inside the Shiloh Baptist Church at the edge of the community, where, with Al Raby at his side, he gathered some seven hundred people, mostly young gang members, and tried to convince them to remain off the streets while he preached about nonviolence and the need for the police department to create a civilian review board, one of the demands that Mayor Daley had rejected. When some of the youths said their comrades had been arrested and that they feared for their safety in custody, King went to the local police station and won the release of seven young men, bringing them back with him into the stifling church.

As King continued to call for calm, a woman in the crowd began to yell out accusations of police brutality, while a man called for a march on the station to free forty more "brothers" who were supposedly under arrest there. Hundreds left the church despite King's exhortations to remain, some to join the fracas and others to go back to their homes. As for those who remained, King led them through what became an all-night prayer session.

In the end, the toll from that first night was twenty-three arrests and ten injured, including three policemen. An outraged King immediately claimed that the violence was a consequence of the mayor's intransigence. "I want to make it quite clear that you bet I condemn any violence," King told Washington, "but it is the refusal of persons in power to deal with conditions on the West Side that caused this outbreak. All our demands fell on deaf ears."

The next day, *The Defender* news team was back in the neighborhood when a new round of combat between police and area residents ignited after officers once again tried to shut down opened fire hydrants, this time at Roosevelt Road and Loomis Avenue, the key intersection in the ABLA development. Bob Black captured images of police in helmets being pelted with bricks and other items hurled from sixteen-story high-rises, and of bloodied neighborhood residents who had been wounded by debris as well as by police clubs.

Reporter Donald Mosby, a veteran police reporter, phoned the newsroom in tears to report that he had seen three police officers set upon one black youth, leaving him in a battered heap on the ground. Just ten minutes later, Mosby himself was struck when he tried to intervene in another beating, an officer knocking him to the ground with a nightstick and then raising it to strike again, stopping only after Mosby identified himself as a journalist. He saw police beat more civilians, including one young woman who was held down as an officer punched her in the abdomen. He witnessed another officer fire his pistol over the heads of the crowd, with the effect of increasing the tension rather than dispelling it. Police shot an eighteen-year-old man twice, and a three-year-old boy was injured when he was hit accidentally by a squad car moving in reverse.

As daylight waned and the police officers' mood darkened, Mosby began to fear for his own safety. Noticing officers who had been on the line for some hours point him out to newly arriving reinforcements, he expressed his concerns about being targeted to a police chaplain onsite. "Stay by my side," the chaplain told Mosby, validating his fear.

*The Defender* team saw several police officers seriously injured when they were hit by flying bricks. The area youths worked out a routine where a line of teenage girls hurled rocks at the police and then retreated, whereupon the officers who chased them were confronted by teenage boys who shouted, "Brutality! Don't touch those girls!"

On this second day of rioting, Martin Luther King engaged in mediations with smaller groups throughout the West Side, having ascertained that his presence in front of large groups would be neither safe nor effective, but other civil rights activists were out in the streets doing whatever they could to prevent more unnecessary bloodshed. Comedian Dick Gregory traveled through the neighborhood with an African American policeman at his side, urging residents to stay calm.

Betty Washington was stunned that so much mayhem had occurred over such a trivial issue — whether the youths could open fire hydrants. "None of this makes any sense," she said to the exhausted, aggravated policemen she encountered. "What running fire hydrant is worth a man's life?"

Returning to the newsroom, she could barely conceal her despair and disappointment as she described the scenes of wanton destruction and brutality she had witnessed: "It was as meaningless and dangerous as anything that happened in Watts," she wrote in the next *Daily Defender*, "with the imminent possibility that lives would be lost for no apparent meaning."[48]

The carnage only intensified on Thursday night as rioting spread farther west to Lawndale and Garfield Park, and even northeast to the Henry Horner Homes public housing development, within striking distance of the Loop. The major roadways running through the African American sections of the West Side streets were closed, but *The Defender* news team went back into the cordoned-off area, where Betty Washington wrote that the police became the targets of "guerilla-type warfare" as snipers fired from the rooftops — one captain was shot in the back and six other officers were injured in the course of the day.

The angry youths patrolling the streets were no longer talking about swimming pools, Washington noted. Now they yelled, "Get whitey out," "It's war time," and "Black Power" as they hurled Molotov cocktails to set buildings aflame or charged back and forth with police. The civil rights workers and ministers were still walking the pavement as well, trying to convince young people to go home or to wait out the violence in a church, while others tried to document the widespread accounts of police brutality that enraged community members anew. These concerned activists coordinated their efforts with WVON, the "Voice of the Negro," the independent radio station whose deejays broadcast a continuous message to "cool it."[49]

On Friday morning, Mayor Daley called on the governor to deploy three thousand National Guard troops armed with rifles and fixed bayonets to augment the worn-out police force. Ironically, one of those called to put on his uniform was Bob Black, who, having joined the Guard to avoid being sent to Vietnam, had been assigned to a signal unit as a photographer. Offered a sidearm by his commanding officer before he headed out onto the same streets he had been traversing for *The Defender* the past few days, Black said, "My camera is all I need."

But now that he had reappeared on the West Side in uniform, area residents eyed him suspiciously as he captured their images. "I am here to document this for you," Black insisted, only partially assuaging them.[50]

Nevertheless, the arrival of thousands of battle-ready soldiers quelled the violence, except for a few scattered incidents on the West Side and an outbreak of looting and arson on businesses and stores near the Robert Taylor Homes on the South Side. The death toll had been low, with just two fatalities, although hundreds had been injured and at least three hundred arrested during the three-day conflagration, which left many factories and businesses destroyed by fire.

Roosevelt Road, a thriving strip of stores and workplaces before the riot, was now strewn with charred debris.[51]

After at first minimizing the extent of the riot, Mayor Daley subtly blamed Martin Luther King during a press conference Thursday, alleging to reporters that SCLC activists' work with gang members had encouraged the violence. King charged into City Hall after reading Daley's comments and demanded to see the mayor. When the two finally met, the mayor was conciliatory and friendly, however, embracing King's ideas and announcing immediately afterward that the city would install spray nozzles on fire hydrants, provide police protection for black children who wanted to swim in heretofore-segregated public pools, build additional swimming pools in the black sections of the West Side, and create a citizens' board for the police department, albeit one with *advisory* power rather than real authority over uniformed officers. "Most civil rights spokesmen agreed the concessions were minor, but meaningful," wrote *The Defender*'s City Hall reporter.[52]

A front-page editorial entitled "Let's Face Facts," however, assessed the riot as "a dismal failure of Mayor Daley and his administration" and placed the onus on the police for allowing events to spin out of control. The mayor had ignored the tensions building up on the West Side, as had the Chicago Real Estate Board and others who had the power to break down the economic and social barriers that kept blacks confined to the ghettos. *The Defender* also called out the *Sun-Times*, which used its editorial page to ascribe the violence to mysterious outsiders, and scoffed at the *Tribune*'s obtuse recommendation to somehow revive the ancient Greek practice of sending the rioters into exile. As for suggestions that Martin Luther King had somehow played a catalyzing role in the destruction, the editorial called these charges ludicrous. Whatever criticism *The Defender* and others had for King, the idea that he had done anything to contribute to the rioting was "as dishonest as it was insulting. It is an affront to the intelligence of the Negro people to suggest that they could be swayed against a man as devoted to civil rights as Dr. King."

Rather than try to assign fault to the civil rights movement, *The Defender* urged the mayor and other principals of the "white power structure" to examine the root causes of the violence, particularly the lack of political representation, since the West Side continued to be run by a tightly knit crew of white politicians with deep ties to the organized crime syndicate. "Riots are always symptomatic of untended social tumors that fester beneath the surface," the editorial summed up. "The corrective is not to be found in the policeman's billy, or in the hysterical outbursts of dishonest politicians looking for a scapegoat or through the misguided utterances of a misinformed metropolitan press."[53]

# 20

# A Dark Hour in the Life of America

O N THE EVENING of Sunday, July 31, 1966, photographer Bob Black and reporter Donald Mosby joined five hundred black and white activists for a march through two of the remaining all-white neighborhoods on the South Side, Chicago Lawn and Gage Park, to a Methodist church whose pastor had invited them. These protests were a new tactic of the movement's drive for open housing, to directly target those communities that discriminated against African Americans. Led by James Bevel and Al Raby, the activists met at a Baptist church in the African American area just east of these neighborhoods and then drove to the parking lot of Marquette Park, an expanse of woods and playing fields with a large lagoon.

From there they proceeded on foot, but as soon as they left the park and neared the neighborhood boundary, they were confronted by hundreds of white people of every age, yelling out obscene taunts and throwing bricks, bottles, and other projectiles. "I wish I was an Alabama trooper," some chanted, "then I could kill a nigger single-handedly."

Bob Black was frightened. "I saw the hatred," he recalled many years later. "It was coming out of their bodies."[1]

At first, the whites formed a gauntlet on both sides of the march-ers, turning on the fire hydrants and lawn sprinklers to soak them. Swallowing their terror as well as their pride, the marchers, whose numbers included veteran activists, white sympathizers, and street gang members, just kept going. Even one woman who was hit with a rock refused to leave the line. But just a few blocks into the protest-ers' route, the whites blocked their path with a car and a "human wall," as reporter Donald Mosby described it. The small contingent of police officers assigned to the march did little to intervene, swinging their clubs at only the most belligerent of the white counterprotesters. Indeed, Mosby saw officers arrest several young white men and bundle them into a waiting police van only to drive them around the corner and release them.[2]

Forced to turn back, the marchers discovered when they returned to the Marquette Park parking lot that their cars had been damaged; more than thirty had their windows smashed, six were turned over, and one had been pushed into the lagoon. But the human toll from the march was even more severe, with twenty-two people injured, among them Jesse Jackson and several police officers.[3]

Martin Luther King, in Atlanta when the marches took place, issued a statement decrying the lack of adequate police protection and vowing to lead the civil rights forces back through Gage Park when he returned to Chicago that weekend. Meanwhile, at another protest in Belmont Cragin, a North Side neighborhood with a large Polish and Italian population, the marchers were met by more than a thousand whites yelling out "White Power" as well as "Polish Power" and other racist phrases. Some white youths spat at the police officers arrayed in full riot gear, while one middle-aged woman in the crowd, confronting a white Catholic priest among the marchers, screamed at him, "You're making me give up my religion."[4]

All through the week, the activists kept up the pressure by holding protests at real estate offices and in other white neighborhoods. After King's complaint, the police superintendent dispatched hundreds of additional officers, and most of the marches were able to proceed unimpeded. But on Friday, August 5, as King led his promised march in Gage Park, thousands of hostile whites came out and engaged police in an all-out battle that lasted for hours. King himself was hit in the head by a stone; momentarily stunned, he was not seriously injured, however. Once safely back in Black Chicago, King described the sentiment that had been directed against the marchers: "I think the people in Mississippi should come to Chicago to learn how to hate," he told reporters sarcastically.[5]

Nevertheless, the civil rights workers pressed on, staging multiple marches in different neighborhoods on the same day, a strategy designed to tax police resources to their limits. City officials responded by requesting a court injunction to limit the number of protests that could be conducted at any given time. Police had to contend with the reaction the protests had produced from the extreme right, with both the Ku Klux Klan and the American Nazi Party sending emissaries to the Gage Park area to recruit and incite. A Nazi spokesperson said her group was organizing a "White Guard" that would conduct armed patrols of the neighborhood. "This organization is for self-defense," explained Nazi spokesperson Ericka Himmler. "We are not out to attack anyone but to defend ourselves, our families and our neighborhood."[6]

Still the civil rights groups intensified their campaign, holding a prayer vigil outside the headquarters of the Chicago Board of Real Estate and announcing plans to march into Cicero, an all-white, working-class suburb just west of the city. Having once served as the base of operations for Al Capone's criminal syndicate, Cicero retained a notorious reputation for violence and racism. Just that year, one young black man had been beaten to death when he stayed in the area into the evening hours after a job interview, and many still recalled the riot that had occurred back in 1951 after a single African American family tried to move into the area; then, five thousand area whites came out to battle police and National Guard troops.

Since Cicero was an independent suburb, marching there would be the responsibility of the Cook County Sheriff's Office and the Illinois State Police, both of which were smaller forces less equipped to handle large-scale protests than the Chicago Police Department. The sheriff had already requested that the governor activate the Illinois National Guard in the event of a protest.[7]

The prospect of a violent march in Cicero was enough to finally bring the Chicago Real Estate Board, the representatives of the business community, top clergymen, labor leaders, Mayor Daley, and other key players to the negotiating table for a "summit conference." Held downtown at the historic St. James Presbyterian Cathedral, the meeting began with the city's human relations commissioner calling on the civil rights groups to immediately suspend the marches and thereby "avoid turning these communities into battlegrounds for extremist and racist elements who are now flocking to those neighborhoods to foment more trouble."

The president of the real estate board, for his part, asked for the protesters to stop testing whether real estate offices discriminated, describing this tactic as "unwarranted harassment." The brokers he represented were only implementing the prejudices of their customers, he maintained, while the protests were actually further antagonizing whites, making them less likely to accept black neighbors.

Unimpressed, King and the other civil rights leaders reiterated their demands that the real estate board as well as the mortgage lenders' associations adopt open housing policies, to be backed up by new legislation at the city as well as the state level. They insisted on other policy changes, too, including a total moratorium on "any more high-rise housing projects in Negro ghetto or high-density areas." Al Raby once again raised the specter of marching through Cicero, warning that the brutality of fifteen years earlier could be reprised.[8]

This first meeting ended after eight hours without a resolution but with a commitment to reconvene at the end of the following week. The civil rights forces, intent on increasing their leverage with a show of force before the next summit, announced that they would send protesters to a hundred real estate offices in ten different white neighborhoods throughout the city.

Mayor Daley made a move before the next confab as well, declaring in a televised speech that while the protesters had a constitutional right to demonstrate, he was deeply concerned about "what the marches are doing to our police department, our community and our neighborhood," and was therefore asking a Cook County judge to set limits on the protests. Naming Martin Luther King, Jesse Jackson, and Al Raby, as well as other leaders, the judge — an elected Democrat who depended on the mayor's support — compliantly issued an order restricting the movement to one march with five hundred people per day. The order also required that the civil rights activists give police twenty-four hours' notice before launching a march.[9]

A *Defender* editorial entitled "Invitation to Disorder" blasted Daley's legal maneuver as a blatantly unconstitutional "sneak play" that threatened to derail the negotiations with King and his coalition. Better than trying to reign in the civil rights activists, the newspaper urged the mayor to focus on taking on the large real estate interests flouting the nondiscrimination laws already on the books as well as the "Mississippi-minded white people" using violence against King and his protesters. "This indicates that Daley is not really interested in settling the racial conflict via the conference table," the editorial continued. "He seems more intent on imposing his will and having the Negro people and their leaders goose-stepping to his tune."[10]

Despite driving rain, the movement held three marches on Sunday, August 21, circumventing Mayor Daley's court injunction by locating only one inside city limits, in the far South Side neighborhood of South Deering. *Defender* reporters Donald Mosby and Arnold Rosenzweig joined Martin Luther King and several hundred protesters as they trekked through this hostile territory populated mainly by the families of steelworkers, stopping at several real estate offices to pray while fifteen hundred whites threw rocks and fruit and yelled out racist slogans. This time, a cordon of hundreds of police officers in riot gear kept the white counterprotesters far enough away to prevent any injury.[11]

The same day, the Chicago Police Department had to contend as well with a rally of Nazis, Klansmen, and states' rights advocates in Marquette Park, where Martin Luther King had been struck by a stone a few days earlier. After hearing speeches from Nazi leader George Lincoln Rockwell and other demagogues, roaming bands of infuriated white men took to the park and surrounding area. One group descended on a station wagon in which a black woman and a white man were riding together, smashing the car's windows before police could stop them. Officers in flying-wedge formation subdued the Nazis and arrested many, including one diminutive Klan "ambassador" wearing a vest made of a Confederate flag who spoke from the shoulders of a massive young follower.

As for the two suburban marches that day, the protesters who came to the integrated suburb of Chicago Heights met no resistance, but in the Italian/Polish suburb of Evergreen Park, just across the border from the city's South Side, not even a combined force of 140 state troopers and suburban police officers proved capable of keeping the raging mob of whites, numbering in the thousands, far enough away to prevent injury to James Bevel and his contingent. Some twenty to thirty of these protesters, injured by flying objects, marched with blood streaming down their faces.[12]

On Monday, Jesse Jackson told *The Defender* that the freedom movement would hold two "actions" the following day, a return march to South Deering and a prayer vigil at a North Side real estate office.

With only one of these events technically a "march," Jackson believed he was in the clear when it came to the judge's restriction. The next night, when the protesters were met with still more angry mobs, police mobilized a massive presence to ensure that the violence was kept to a minimum, while undercover officers who had infiltrated the marchers advised their superiors about their routes and tactics. In South Deering, the two hundred protesters were completely enveloped by five hundred police officers while a dozen squadrols led the way. On Wednesday, a similar number of protesters were shielded by an equally large group of police as they held brief prayer services in front of real estate offices in the far Southwest Side neighborhood of West Elsdon.

As the protesters geared up for the march to Cicero scheduled for that Sunday, panicky county and state officials called up state troopers from all over the state, leaving some southern Illinois counties entirely bereft of law enforcement, while Cicero's city attorney sent a telegram to Illinois's governor requesting a mobilization of National Guard troops as well, warning, "The possibility of danger and destruction to human life and property has become a certainty."[13]

With everyone predicting a bloodbath in Cicero, the second summit on Friday was moved from the cathedral's stuffy confines to the elegant appointments of the Palmer House Hotel in the Loop, and this time, the conversation moved briskly toward an agreement. What emerged was a ten-point document in which the real estate brokers and mortgage bankers caved, agreeing to adopt aggressive open housing policies and practices to be monitored by city, state, and federal housing agencies. In exchange, the movement agreed to suspend their protest campaign and cancel the march in Cicero that Sunday.[14]

*The Defender* editorial page was positively inspired by the settlement, not so much by its particular promises, which would need to be carefully watched, than for what it demonstrated about the constructive power of public protest. All the meetings and conferences and traditional downtown marches through the spring and early summer had been ineffective, as had the violent outburst on the West Side in the heat of July, but the sustained, disciplined display of nonviolent courage in the August marches had forced the power structure to make a public compromise. "The demonstrations, so loudly denounced by City Hall and most of the press, have proved their justification beyond the shadow of the doubt," observed the main editorial about settlement. Nevertheless, the newspaper warned the mayor and those around him that this agreement would assuage the community only if it were actually implemented.[15]

Not every activist agreed to the moratorium, and a few organizations did stage a small, bloody march in Cicero several weeks later, declaring "open war on Dr. Martin Luther King" for allegedly abandoning Chicago in what they saw as an ongoing fight. Indeed, the settlement did mark an end to Martin Luther King's day-to-day involvement in the city; while he continued to fly in to Chicago to speak to civil rights rallies, he gave up his apartment on the West Side, increasingly deferring to Jesse Jackson, who was establishing himself as the movement's Chicago representative on local issues. It was left to Jackson to respond to King's critics in an interview with Betty Washington for *The Defender*. "I can't believe that anyone in his right mind would think that Dr. King is keeping him from being free," Jackson said. "And anyone who sees no accomplishments toward the solution to his problems here in Chicago is blind."[16]

During his tumultuous, yearlong focus on Chicago, Martin Luther King met with John Sengstacke just once, after the settlement with the mayor and the real estate board, when he was already on his way out of town, literally. They had known each other since early 1965, when Sengstacke brought his sons Bobby and Louis to the protest march in Selma, Alabama, and Sengstacke, feeling snubbed by King until this point, bluntly scolded the civil rights leader. "I told Martin I knew why he hadn't talked to me," he recalled to a biographer just a few years later. "Because people told him I was part of the establishment. But maybe I could have showed him how to get Daley's goat."[17]

Regardless of any personal conflict between Sengstacke and King, *The Defender* and the movement had benefited each other greatly. The newspaper had provided detailed, unbiased coverage of the protests, while the editorial page had consistently dispelled the mayor's excuses and obfuscations; the community responded by buying more papers, driving circulation up to nearly fifty thousand daily. Establishment-friendly or not, *The Defender* was in tune with this muscular, edgy moment in black America. In addition to the standard cavalcade of floats, marching bands, and elected officials, the Billiken Parade's headliners that August were heavyweight boxing champion Muhammad Ali and the "Godfather of Soul," James Brown, both men known for their outspokenness and pride.[18]

In October, Sengstacke announced he had purchased *The Pittsburgh Courier*, which had declined to the point that it would have simply disappeared altogether without his intervention. With a portfolio that included other black newspapers he had acquired in New York, New Orleans, Florida, and Georgia, as well as *The Michigan Chronicle*, *The Tri-State Defender*, and *The Louisville Defender*, Sengstacke now published and delivered some four hundred thousand newspapers every week. *The Defender* alone had a staff of 150, with $2 million in annual sales, while *The Michigan Chronicle* brought in an additional $1 million each year.[19]

In December 1966, John Sengstacke asked Ethel Payne to serve as *The Defender*'s correspondent in Vietnam. Payne's byline had not appeared in the newspaper since 1963, but she was working at the Democratic National Committee several tiers below Louis Martin, who was serving President Johnson in the same capacity as he had President Kennedy. Payne flew back to Chicago with Martin and sat down with Sengstacke to discuss the assignment. "We think it would be a unique thing to have a woman cover the war," Sengstacke said, according to Payne's recollection. There was great danger, she knew, in serving as a war correspondent — especially the first African American woman war correspondent — but feeling that the assignment would be "a gamble and an adventure," she readily accepted.[20]

Even as her plane flew into Saigon's airport a few days before Christmas 1966, Payne was struck by the contrast between the bucolic sight of rice farmers working their fields with water buffalo in a "sea of emerald green" and the massive military presence, punctuated by the sounds of artillery fire. The airport "bristles with arms and the implements of combat," she wrote in her first dispatch back to Chicago, "tanks and helicopters, gun carriages, camouflaged emplacements, barbed wire. No peace on Earth here or good will towards men; but the deadly business of kill, kill, kill."[21]

With a broad assignment to document the lives of the black troops in Vietnam over a tour of several weeks, Payne had access to every sector and rank, traversing the entire theater of war. She spent a few nights on an aircraft carrier, joined wounded soldiers for a Christmas Day performance headlined by comedian Bob Hope, visited the frontlines, and interviewed General William Westmoreland, the supreme commander in Vietnam, as well as hundreds of black soldiers and sailors. To reach one village in the hills outside the coastal city of Da Nang, where African American troops were engaged in development projects, Payne endured a terrifying ride in a jeep guarded by three U.S. Marines, two of them white and one black, who constantly scanned the thick foliage for Vietcong guerrillas intent on ambush.

When they finally arrived, Payne was deeply impressed by the compassion and dedication of the integrated unit of ten marines who were building sanitation and health care facilities and teaching villagers how to resist the Vietcong. There were signs, however, that the enterprise was going against the tide: many of the adults, she noted, refused to have their picture taken, fearing retaliation from the guerrillas, and the troops slept cradling their rifles. One nineteen-year-old from Memphis, Lance Corporal Lorenzo Forest — whom Payne dubbed an "Ambassador in Khaki" — described the development work in this village and many others as the most important factor in the war's outcome. "If you can't win these people over," he told Payne, "you can forget about the war."[22]

During nine weeks in Vietnam, Payne observed that while the lower ranks of the military were now completely integrated, African Americans made up a disproportionate share of the troops from every branch of the Armed Services, both because they volunteered at higher levels and because the draft then in place selected them in greater numbers. The number of black officers, too, was increasing rapidly, with many earning combat promotions, although there were none on General Westmoreland's staff, just as there had been none on General MacArthur's. Among the combat troops, support staff, and fighter pilots she spoke with, Payne found unanimous reverence for Martin Luther King and overwhelming support for the civil rights protests — but also strong support for the war, which they regarded as an effort to liberate the Vietnamese people from the tyranny of communism. Although King himself had spoken against the war and opposition was growing in the general population, these soldiers were still convinced of the American mission. "I'm all for the civil rights demonstrations," said Specialist Carl Wheatly, a twenty-three-year-old from Chicago, in a representative comment, "because it's just as important to clean house at home as it is to be fighting the Communists over here. I wish I were there to take part in them."[23]

Many of the men Payne interviewed expressed the same hope that had always motivated African American soldiers, that the service they were providing to their country would guarantee their equal status when they returned home. "We shouldn't have to go back and accept second-class citizenship like our forefathers did in World War II," said Private First Class Ernest Lavender, a native of Atlanta. "I don't believe we will either."[24]

Leaving Vietnam, Payne traveled back to the United States via Japan, a nation she found completely transformed since her tour of duty there two decades earlier. New highways and skyscrapers had altered the landscape of Tokyo, with the Ginza District, for instance, remolded from a warren of ramshackle stalls into a boulevard of glamorous department stores and luxury boutiques. Where back in 1947 Payne had written about Japanese women struggling against the constraints of a highly traditional society, she now found a new generation steeped in the emerging global youth culture, wearing miniskirts, driving Hondas, and practicing free love. Not unlike the youth of America who were protesting the Vietnam War, the young Japanese Payne met in the streets voiced a passionate, homegrown antinuclear pacifism born of their own past, a cause for which many youths were entirely willing to defy their hierarchal culture and protest publicly.

For the mixed-race children of the African American soldiers who had been stationed in Japan, however, the situation had not improved; they were still regarded as outcasts. Payne tracked down a woman who had run an orphanage for these children; she concluded sadly that many would be best off emigrating to Brazil or other South American countries where they would face less discrimination.[25]

Returning to the United States, Payne began to regret that she had not used her time in Vietnam to more thoroughly gather evidence of the war's "immorality," as she described it to a biographer some years later. Not that her assessment of the troops' attitudes was anything but accurate — morale among the military remained high, at that moment — but public opinion among African Americans at home was turning against the war, largely due to the opposition of Martin Luther King. In the middle of April, a team of *Defender* reporters surveyed several hundred African Americans at shopping plazas on the South and West Sides and found that King's antiwar comments were the major factor in shifting a majority against the war, despite the pro-war stands of the leaders of the Urban League, NAACP, and other mainstream organizations. Many of those surveyed also ascribed their change of heart on the war to the execution of the draft, which they felt made it more likely that young African Americans would go to war than young white men.[26]

Payne resumed writing regularly for *The Defender*, sending dispatches from Washington, D.C., that made full use of her contacts within the Johnson administration, the U.S. Congress, and the capital's international media circles, a network that had only grown during her years at the Democratic National Committee. From this unique vantage point, she documented the rapid gains being made toward racial equality, but also the powerful forces threatening to rend the civil rights movement in the summer of 1967.

In early June, when Thurgood Marshall was nominated to become the first African American on the U.S. Supreme Court, Payne was able to get the behind-the-scenes picture from Louis Martin, who had played a key role guiding Marshall's path from the NAACP to the nation's highest court. Martin clued Payne in as to the subterfuge the president had employed to keep the nomination secret until the last possible moment in order to prevent his enemies from scheming against it.

Having made his decision about the appointment, Johnson ordered Martin to sneak Marshall into the White House. Martin arranged for Marshall to arrive disguised as a tourist so that he wouldn't be seen by the press, and then, after Martin and another African American aide, Clifford Alexander, had crept into the Oval Office through a side entrance, Johnson called the chief justice of the Supreme Court and key congressional leaders to tell them of his decision. Immediately following those calls, Johnson stepped outside into the Rose Garden to announce Marshall's nomination. The White House Press Corps, on hand for the announcement, had not been alerted beforehand as to the subject of the president's address.

With Marshall's ascension to the high court, Martin felt he had reached the pinnacle of his long career. "Well boys, this is it," he exclaimed to Payne and the other members of his inner circle after President Johnson's press conference. "There's nowhere else to go but heaven."[27]

The nomination won immediate and full-throated praise from most of the leaders of the civil rights movement, especially Martin Luther King, who commended Johnson, in comments that were printed on *The Defender*'s front page, for taking "a momentous step toward a color-blind society."[28]

The fact that the great-grandson of slaves was headed to the U.S. Supreme Court held a special significance for the newspaper, removing yet another demand from "*The Defender*'s Platform for America," which Robert Abbott had first printed in 1922. Only one year earlier, John Sengstacke had removed item number 3, the appointment of an African American to the president's cabinet, when President Johnson named Robert Weaver as secretary of housing and urban development, and substituted in a new plank "the appointment of a Negro to the U.S. Supreme Court." And now this condition had been satisfied as well. *The Defender*'s editorial page described Marshall's nomination as "a great moment in the evolutionary history of this nation and in the annals of the Negro people."[29]

On the same day that Marshall's nomination was announced, Ethel Payne covered King's speech at the annual black tie awards banquet of the Capital Press Club, an organization founded by African American journalists as an alternative to the National Press Club when that group refused to admit blacks. Even among this friendly group, King's stance on Vietnam was controversial, and the membership, Payne discovered, had fiercely debated whether he should even be invited given his opposition to the war. And though King was introduced as the "Conscience of America," Payne wrote, the crowd was visibly skeptical as he began to speak on his three declared topics, racism, economics, and war.

Only when King conceded that the civil rights movement was "moving from one phase of the revolution to another" did their ears prick up. The era of bus boycotts and protest marches was over, King told the assembled editors, publishers, and reporters, but while it might appear that the movement was losing steam, he could assure them the campaign for full equality was continuing. "We won a few gains at bargain rates," King said. "It didn't cost America anything to open up restaurants and hotels and to break the color line in public transportation. The real cost lies ahead. Jobs are costlier and harder. The eradication of slums has become more complex."[30]

By now, the cadence and power of King's voice had focused the audience's full attention. The white backlash to his efforts would intensify, he predicted, because the civil rights movement was demanding that the nation spend billions of taxpayer dollars to alleviate poverty and desegregate the nation's schools. Then, with the crowd still riveted, he turned to Vietnam, taking to task the editorial pages of many black newspapers, including *The Defender*'s, which had criticized King for wasting energy on his opposition to the war when the civil rights movement was still unfinished.

"To those who say, 'Why don't you stick to civil rights and leave the peace issue alone?' I say, 'I refuse to be limited or segregated in my moral concern.' I know that my position is neither popular nor safe but I stand up against the war in Vietnam because I love America."[31]

Payne marveled at how this once-tepid crowd rose to its feet for a standing ovation, moved by King's moral courage to respect his views, even if he had not brought them to suddenly oppose the war themselves.[32]

One week later, Payne followed King to Cleveland to cover a luncheon meeting of the National Newspaper Publishers Association, where he used his speech to the principals of the black press as an opportunity to vent his frustration with black power organizations. King reprised his opposition to the war in Vietnam in this speech, as well as his insistence that the nation invest the necessary taxpayer funds to aid the impoverished at home, noting that one tenth the number of dollars being used to kill every enemy soldier was being spent on every beneficiary of President Johnson's War on Poverty. And before the 150 African American journalists in the audience, he displayed anger when he spoke of self-proclaimed revolutionaries who incited the masses without considering the consequences. "When I urge people to march in non-violent peaceful protest for their rights," King said, "I make sure that I am at the head of the line, leading them, and not skulking behind."[33]

King had harsh words for the mainstream media as well, which tended to cover the civil rights movement as an ongoing popularity contest between the tribunes of black power and the apostles of non-violent integration. In commenting on the bias of daily newspapers, however, King made sure to emphasize that he was not criticizing the black press. "I'm talking about the white-owned press," he clarified.[34]

Sengstacke, for his part, used terms very similar to King's to describe the black power set when he spoke before the NNPA in Cleveland a few days later. Without naming Stokely Carmichael or any of his colleagues, Sengstacke urged his fellow publishers to avoid excessive coverage of demagogues and provocateurs in the interest of selling newspapers. Black newspapers should set a positive example and play their part in obviating a return to the mayhem that had erupted in northern cities over the past two years. *The Defender*, for example, was running a "Keep a Cool Summer" campaign featuring in-house ads, posters, and contests for its readers. "We have to strive to make the Negro press a positive force for good in the big cities instead of just a sensational rag," Sengstacke said. "We've got to keep from cramming our news columns with inflammatory statements from so-called Negro leaders who aren't leaders at all. When the chips are down, they are powerless to stop a riot or influence ghetto thinking."[35]

King may have reaffirmed his bond with the black press, but Ethel Payne saw his efforts at this juncture as part of a strategy to recapture the leadership of the movement from Stokely Carmichael and the other black power radicals. The SCLC's finances, she learned, always precarious, were now thoroughly drained as its membership had aged out of the struggle and new cadres were signing up with Carmichael and his ilk instead. While King had opposed the Vietnam War on moral grounds since the earliest days of large-scale American involvement there, Carmichael had successfully taken credit for it by associating the phrase "black power" with the equally memorable "Hell, no, we won't go."

In Payne's analysis, King could not afford to be outflanked on Vietnam, even if it meant sacrificing the relationship with President Johnson, for whom the war was an existential issue in the upcoming election. Gone was the open invitation to the White House King had previously enjoyed, according to Payne's White House sources, as he grew more outspoken on Vietnam in the early summer of 1967.[36]

• • •

On Thursday, July 14, after several days of confrontation between young black men and the city's police force, the streets of Newark, New Jersey, erupted into open warfare. More than 250 officers wielding shotguns, automatic assault rifles, and pistols tried to stop a mob of thousands in the city's Central Ward from looting stores, destroying cars, and setting fires, only to be repelled by the sheer number of enraged youths throwing firebombs, rocks, and bottles from the street corners and rooftops. New Jersey's governor called out the National Guard but even the presence of heavily armed troops was not enough to stop the fighting; dozens of snipers, firing from carefully concealed nests in the alleys and multistory buildings of the neighborhoods, held out for days against the combined forces of police and National Guard troops.

*The Defender* edition published the Monday after that weekend of turmoil in Newark included a series of stark photographs on the front page as well as inside: a black man shot to death for allegedly violating a policeman's order; stores and businesses with their windows broken out and their interiors reduced to charred holes; streets littered with debris; soldiers bearing rifles with fixed bayonets arresting young men accused of looting. The toll in Newark was twenty-seven dead, twenty-five blacks and two whites, a policeman and a fireman. Many hundreds had been injured, among them fifty policemen. The rioting in the city incited youths in African American communities in surrounding towns as well, resulting in looting and shooting that in one case prompted the New Jersey National Guard to set up roadblocks around an entire neighborhood.[37]

A *Defender* editorial about the upheaval in Newark and its environs blamed long simmering resentments common to every African American community: the failure to integrate schools, residential segregation, a higher chance of being drafted for service in Vietnam, and a new factor, growing unemployment and with it, increasing economic frustration, even as the rest of the country was enjoying a flush jobs market. Conscious of being relegated to second-class citizenship, a new generation of young black men felt only resentment and animus when it came to the institutions of the world around them, sentiments amplified when Congress cut back on social programs to fund antiriot measures. "The accumulation of painful grievances has deepened the sense of frustration and despair among Negroes who feel no moral compunction to restrain their emotion when provoked by unbearable incidents or when the struggle for daily existence offers no alternative to violence," the editorial averred. "This is the stark reality of the volcanic situation which will be quieted only when America and Americans learn the value of social justice."[38]

Detroit's streets ignited that same weekend, beginning five days of destruction deadlier even than the Watts riots two years earlier. At least forty-three people, all African American, were killed, nearly all shot by police and guardsmen, while more than a thousand were injured. Seventeen hundred stores were looted, among them those displaying signs clearly indicating they were African American–owned, while more than a thousand arsons left five thousand homeless. The snipers in this riot targeted police, firemen, and even guardsmen, and though they failed to kill anyone, four state troopers, seventeen soldiers, and fifty Detroit policemen were wounded.[39]

That same week, racial violence spread to ten smaller cities throughout the North as well as Birmingham in the South, adding to what had already been a bloody summer. Rioting had already struck Minneapolis, New York City, Rochester, Buffalo, Hartford, Connecticut, and New Brunswick, New Jersey, so that by the end of that month, thirty-seven municipalities had experienced such urban disruptions.[40]

Amid these scenes of carnage and chaos, a somber President Johnson went on television to plead with the young rioters to go home and reassure the public that federal troops could be deployed to help states reimpose law and order. "Pillage and looting and arson have nothing to do with civil rights," Johnson told the nation.[41]

Although widespread violence had yet to break out in Chicago, *The Defender* was in panic mode, claiming that it had discovered evidence of mysterious "hate-peddlers" who were paying $1,000 to young black men to launch arson attacks or lootings. Alleging that an unidentified conspiracy was actually orchestrating racial confrontation to derail the civil rights movement, the newspaper urged young people not to be "used as tools to stop the wheels of progress."[42]

*The Defender* may have been alarmed to the point of paranoia, but Stokely Carmichael, in Cuba as part of a world tour at that moment, greeted the news of the destruction in America's cities with enthusiasm. For him, reports of organized sniper squads and other military-like activity among the rioters were indications that the urban core of the United States was in the early stages of an all-out revolution. "In Newark, we applied war tactics of the guerillas," Carmichael said in an interview published in *The Defender.* "We are preparing groups of urban guerillas for our protection in the cities. This fight is not going to be a simple street meeting. It is going to be a fight to the death."[43]

Martin Luther King, back on Chicago's West Side as Detroit and the other cities went up in flames, laid the blame for the violence at the feet of Congress. Interviewed by Betty Washington at a jobs program on the West Side funded by President Johnson's Great Society, King insisted that people in the ghettos were well aware that even as federal legislators recently cut back on housing, jobs, and development programs, they were spending $35 billion a year on the war in Vietnam. "They have declared a war on poverty, yet only financed a skirmish," King said. "People in the slums are dying spiritually even as they have been killing each other in the streets."[44]

With *The Defender* pushing its "Keep a Cool Summer" campaign, and ministers and civil rights workers intensifying their outreach, Chicago managed to avoid a deadly racial confrontation that summer. City officials did their part as well, opening schools and recreational facilities to keep the community's young busy. Even so, *Defender* reporter Donald Mosby found that the police force was on high alert all over the South and West Sides, responding in force to the slightest sign of unrest. When a few dozen angry men gathered along a stretch of West Madison Street lined with shops and offices, officers arrested thirteen people but showed uncharacteristic restraint in doing so, adhering to strict orders to avoid using racial slurs or otherwise antagonize African American neighborhood residents. "Every working police officer has been told that any unnecessary abuse of a citizen might flare into trouble," a spokesperson for the police department's human relations section told Mosby. "We increase the chances of avoiding trouble if we don't start something ourselves."[45]

The concerted efforts of black leaders and civic officials, coupled with the absence of incidents of police brutality, proved an effective firewall against the riots' spread to Chicago, at least that summer, allowing *The Defender* to adopt a calmer stance itself in its editorials. The newspaper now dismissed reports of conspiracies behind the violence as "inept analysis and incompetent deductions," blaming the urban eruptions elsewhere on "a long history of abject poverty and unrelieved segregation." Republicans and their allies in the U.S. Congress who were using the riots as a reason to cut back even further on federal programs were engaged in perverse logic, one editorial continued, completely ignoring the value of such programs in alleviating racial tension. Surely things would have been that much worse without the president's antipoverty initiatives, just as their absence would only serve the interest of those who wanted to harness the violence for truly revolutionary purposes.

"Should Congress succeed in destroying the poverty program," the editorial concluded, "that would be the kind of impetus the Black Power movement needs to give it national sweep, unchallenged respectability and fanatical discipleship. It would feed the wrath of the militant advocates of racial isolation and make the recent riots look like a Fourth of July picnic."[46]

Only one year earlier, *The Defender*'s editorial page had welcomed Stokely Carmichael and his brand of black power as a reinvigorating force; now, however, it turned sharply against his incendiary language and agenda in the weeks following the riots. Carmichael himself had reached Hanoi, where he pledged the support of black America to the North Vietnamese, and now the newspaper labeled his calls for racial separatism an ideological dead-end, "self-imposed Apartheid" that would "never be accepted by the black masses which have struggled too long for recognition and integration as an essential denominator in the equation of American citizenship."[47]

In mid-August, Ethel Payne traveled to Atlanta to cover the tenth-anniversary convention of the Southern Christian Leadership Conference, whose aptly chosen theme was "Where do we go from here?" For Martin Luther King, who had founded the organization during the movement's nascence in Montgomery, the answer lay in a massive campaign of civil disobedience, including sit-ins in Washington, D.C., that would shut down the capital and pressure Congress to pass laws that would guarantee full employment, as well as a nationwide expansion of Operation Breadbasket, with its targeted boycotts of discriminatory private businesses.

Writing in *The Defender*, Payne described these initiatives as a major recalibration of SCLC's tactics, designed to direct the ener-

gies of a new generation that had come through the flames of Newark, Detroit, and other cities. The recent riots had exposed the huge
ideological rift between the middle-aged members of SCLC and the
"suspicious hostile, ghetto youth, the 15 to 25 year olds who give vent
to their rage by smashing store windows and hurling Molotov cocktails. To them, it seems that non-violence is Whitey's way of keeping
things quiet in order to keep exploiting black people. Dr. King knows
he is in a race against time to defuse the ticking bombs of impatience
in the big cities."[48]

Over several days of meetings, King succeeded in convincing the
SCLC to adopt a strongly worded resolution criticizing President
Johnson for intensifying the war in Vietnam and vowing to make the
1968 general election a referendum on the war "to vote into oblivion
those who cannot detach themselves from militarism."

Another resolution committed SCLC to hosting "African American unity conferences" around the country that would build racial
pride by focusing on black cultural contributions and encouraging
black entrepreneurship and other forms of black control in their
neighborhoods. Payne saw this resolution, modeled on a precept
that had emerged at a recent meeting of black power organizations
in Newark, as a departure from SCLC's previously firm integrationist
stand.

At a press conference after these resolutions were passed, an angry King returned to the subject of Vietnam, telling reporters that
he would instruct SCLC branches throughout the United States to
work for the defeat of any congressional or presidential candidate
who supported the war. When Payne pressed him on whether that
included President Johnson, King at first refused to be drawn out.
She persisted, however, asking if the two men would meet, and King
responded that he and Johnson had nothing to discuss, adding that
he would be open to endorsing a rival candidate, even a Republican like Michigan Governor George Romney or New York Governor Nelson Rockefeller, if he ran on a peace platform. Clearly, Payne
concluded, King's relationship with Johnson had been damaged seriously, perhaps permanently.[49]

But if rejection of President Johnson was supposed to be a sacrifice
that would allow King to reclaim the crown of the civil rights movement, a subsequent *Defender* editorial professed itself unconvinced.

The editors had come to agree that it was obscene to spend funds on Vietnam while they were badly needed at home, and likewise concurred that the antiriot measures being debated in Congress would do little to address the root causes of the violence. But after Newark and Detroit, the editorial averred, nonviolence had lost its magic when it came to holding back the vengeful impulses of youths in the community, and any mass demonstration, no matter how peaceful its original intent, might easily devolve into bloodshed, which was, in turn, certain to provoke a swift, brutal response from the power structure. "Marches and demonstrations have lost their appeal," the editorial asserted. "If this be a mere technique for preventing Negro leadership from falling into the hands of the advocates of Black Power, it will defeat its own purpose because the apostles of black Apartheid would thrive in an environment in which civil disobedience is the order of the day."[50]

Nevertheless, King plowed ahead with his call for mass protests in Washington, intensifying his critique of President Johnson and the Vietnam War, as Payne had predicted. At the end of August, he returned to Chicago to deliver the keynote address at the National Conference for New Politics, a gathering of leftist and militant organizations dedicated to ousting Johnson in favor of a president who would pull U.S. troops out of Southeast Asia. But forging unity out of these disparate groups proved an impossible challenge, as the conference's plenary sessions were derailed by raucous, impassioned debates in which some black power activists refused to speak to their white colleagues and advised African Americans to arm themselves for the coming confrontation.

To this radical audience, King was a suspiciously mainstream figure, too close to the establishment by half, despite his many contributions to the movement and steadfast opposition to the war. Nor, when he rose to address those assembled at the old Chicago Coliseum, did King shy away from their skepticism, accepting the blame for his share of the younger generation's disappointment even as he faulted President Johnson for failing to deliver the promise of the social programs he had launched under the labels of the "Great Society" and the "War on Poverty."

"For nearly 12 years," King said, "I have traveled this country and held out radiant promises of progress for Negroes. I preached about my dream and I lectured about the not-too-distant future when there would be freedom and equality. My promise of a better life for Negroes has simply not materialized and there is no evidence that Johnson's Great Society will ever get off the ground."[51]

In Cincinnati the next month, King excoriated Johnson before two thousand delegates to the Progressive National Baptist Convention, a confab for the nation's powerful African American churches from this denomination. Urging them to become the first Baptist organization to join publicly with the broad coalition of faith groups opposed to the war, King argued that American intervention in Vietnam had alienated the United States internationally while harming African Americans domestically. "The promise of the Great Society is being shot down on the battlefields of Vietnam," King told the conventioneers. "We are losing two wars — the righteous War on Poverty and the unjust war in Vietnam."[52]

At the end of October, King was to report to an Alabama prison to serve a five-day sentence for a case that dated back to 1964. The civil rights leader had appealed his conviction for violating a court order blocking a march in that state, but the Supreme Court — just a few days before Thurgood Marshall was to be formally sworn in as the newest associate justice — upheld the lower court rulings, effectively requiring King and several of his colleagues to fly back to Alabama for the short prison stay.

The incarceration interrupted King as he planned another mass gathering event in Washington, D.C., to pressure the U.S. Congress to pump billions of new federal dollars into a large-scale jobs program and the nation's school system. On the day he flew from his home in Atlanta to Birmingham, King dressed down in blue jeans rolled up at the cuff, an open-collared shirt, and a cardigan sweater, telling Payne, among other reporters, that he hoped the short stay in prison would give him the time to meditate on new solutions to the endemic racial and economic issues confronting the nation. "I am disturbed that four years after the heroic efforts of thousands of young people and adults in Birmingham, our country finds itself in a moral stalemate where the rights of Negroes are concerned. All the signs of our time indicate that this is a dark hour in the life of America."[53]

# 21

# The Last Remains of Nonviolence

O N  T H E  E V E N I N G  of Thursday, April 4, 1968, women's editor Theresa Fambro Hooks was relaxing in *The Defender*'s basement cafeteria, the editorial team having just finished work on the "Big Weekend Edition" when she heard someone running through the building call out "Dr. King's Been Shot." She ran upstairs to find the staff clustering around the Teletype machine, where the brief, incoming reports provided no hint as to whether or not the civil rights leader, in Memphis to support a garbage collectors' strike, had been seriously wounded. Regardless, Hooks and her colleagues knew immediately that they would need to rewrite the front page and other sections, a complicated and time-consuming process, not unlike unraveling a carpet and then reweaving it, so they headed off to dinner to fortify themselves for the long night ahead.

They gathered at Batt's, a restaurant specializing in eastern European Jewish delicacies, located on the ground floor of the same hotel two blocks away, on the northeast corner of Michigan and Cermak Avenues, that had served as Al Capone's headquarters during Mayor Big Bill Thompson's third term. Usually, Batt's was where *The Defender* staffers went to celebrate finishing the weekend paper, but on this night, the group, including Betty Washington, Theresa Fambro Hooks, Donald Mosby, and Arnold Rosenzweig, ordered their meals and ate mostly in silence.

They had almost finished eating when their waitress came back to the table and quietly gave them the bad news. "He's dead."

Returning to *The Defender* building, the devastated reporters and editors got to work, diving into their editorial duties with energy and purpose that served to distract them from their grief: monitoring the wire, calling local leaders to get their responses, and combing through the archives to assemble background pieces. John Sengstacke, phoning into the newsroom from Detroit, delegated the assembly of this historic edition to Fred Sengstacke and Tom Picou, Myrtle's nephew, who had recently been hired as executive editor. In the composing room, the day manager and the night manager had both come in and were busy tearing out pages and columns to make space, while the Linotype operators and pressman waited patiently for their turn. Everyone worked diligently to re-create the newspaper, though occasionally, a staffer would slip away from their task to be alone and shed a few tears.[1]

From their wire sources and the incoming broadcast reports, they learned that King had been standing on the balcony of his hotel room, just about to head off to dinner, when he was hit in the neck by a single bullet and knocked onto his back. Rushed into the emergency room of a nearby hospital, he was pronounced dead at exactly 7:00 p.m. His driver, Solomon Jones, told reporters that after hearing the gunshot, he had seen a white man with his face partially concealed creep away from the scene. From the angle of the man's position relative to the balcony, Jones realized that King must have been looking directly at his killer when he was shot. Police were reportedly pursuing a suspect described as a white man driving a late-model car.[2]

The response to King's death from around the nation, collected by *Defender* staffers, ranged from shock and outrage to despair. All of King's erstwhile foes in Chicago quickly made public statements of tribute. Mayor Daley, among them, praised King as a "dedicated and courageous American who commanded the respect of the people of the world." Jeff Fort, a charismatic leader of the Blackstone Rangers street gang who had once eyed King suspiciously, now pledged his members to nonviolence while a spokesperson for the Nation of Islam said briefly but sincerely, "We're sorry about it."[3]

President Lyndon B. Johnson, who just four days earlier had announced that he would not run for reelection and would instead spend the remainder of his time in office working to achieve peace in Vietnam, went on national television and radio to plead for calm. "I ask every citizen to stay away from the violence that struck Dr. King," said the president. "We can achieve nothing by violence. It is only by joining together and working together that we can continue to move toward full equality for all people. I pray that his family can find comfort in the memory of all that he tried to do for the land that he loved."

Louis Martin, reached at his desk in Washington, was despondent. Not only had the civil rights movement lost its brightest star, but the timing of the assassination would surely scuttle Johnson's efforts to end the war in Vietnam. Martin saw tragic irony in that King's own death would likely derail what would have been his greatest victory. "This is what the land needed the least," he said, "as we were on the threshold perhaps of international peace negotiations and a new day."[4]

Jesse Jackson, who was with King in Memphis, spoke tearfully to reporters about the scene of the murder but vowed, along with the rest of the leadership of the SCLC and the affiliated civil rights groups, to continue his mentor's work. Their first major task would be to implement King's plan to bring thousands of activists to Washington, D.C., that month for a "Poor Peoples March." One of King's colleagues, the Rev. Fred Shuttlesworth, tried to reassure the public that they would continue to adhere to nonviolence, promising that "not one hair on the head of one white man shall be harmed by us."[5]

But on the streets of Washington, D.C., hundreds of young black men had an entirely different reaction to King's assassination. Hundreds came out to the headquarters of the SCLC on Fourteenth and U Streets, growing angrier as they discussed the news. At one point, Stokely Carmichael, back in the country after his sojourn abroad, attempted to channel the compounding rage into a protest march but he was ignored as the mob began to loot, torch, and destroy businesses.[6]

While their colleagues wrote up reports from around the country, Donald Mosby and Betty Washington went out into the streets of Chicago, where they discerned a molten rage shifting just below the surface calm. Mosby checked in with his police sources and heard of a few scattered incidents of broken windows at a few businesses near the Robert Taylor Homes development while Washington, attending a memorial service for King at a large Baptist Church on South Parkway, observed black power activists shouting down elder ministers calling for prayer and a restrained reaction to this assassination with their own chants of "Damn the honkies" and "No honkies by Sunday." At one point, a young man in an African tunic commandeered the microphone and issued an ominous prognostication: "Martin Luther King warned that there was going to be violence this summer and there *is* going to be violence this summer."

When a popular West Side activist named Russell Meek entered the church, he was greeted with calls of "Black Power." Interviewed later by Washington, he cited a long list of acts of terror committed by white racists against both activists and innocent African Americans alike, going back to Emmett Till, before making his own tribute to King that was at once eloquent and menacing: "Dear dead brother, in your resting place also rests the last remains of nonviolence."[7]

Betty Washington rushed back to the newsroom and quickly wrote up her account of this scene and sent it down to the composing room. By midnight, they had finished revising the newspaper. Just then, John Sengstacke strode into the newsroom, having grabbed the first available flight back from Detroit. The weekend edition was all but finished by this point and *The Defender* staffers could have all gone home, but they didn't. Theresa Hooks recalled the emotion of those hours four decades later in a commemorative article: "We had done all we could do. We had worked as a team. We had put into print the death of our beloved leader, a husband and a father. We knew then that the world would never be the same. It was over, but we could not leave. We sat around until dawn, but the words spoken were minimal and infrequent. We comforted each other as best as we could. But it was all for naught! The King Was Dead! Long Live The King!"[8]

The first night after King's assassination passed without an eruption of violence but the anger in the community was only building. That next morning, Friday, April 5, the tens of thousands of students who came into their high schools on the South and West sides talked only of King's slaying and how they should respond. More than a thousand students of Forrestville High School in Bronzeville held an assembly at which they pledged not to "create any disturbances" and voted unanimously to petition the school board to change their school's name to "Martin Luther King Jr. High School." But at Hyde Park High School, one of the city's few integrated schools, black students roamed the hallways searching for white students and beat any they found. Meanwhile, at all-black Marshall High School and the surrounding grade schools on the West Side, four thousand students poured out of their buildings and marched in the direction of Madison Avenue, where they joined with crowds of adults in an orgy of looting and arson.

The destruction in this riot took place in multiple sections of the city, especially on or near the commercial strips of the West Side along Madison Street all the way to Roosevelt Road as well as in the Cabrini-Green public housing development, where snipers in the towers took aim at police and firefighters alike, and in Englewood on the South Side. Mayor Daley immediately called for reinforcements from the Illinois National Guard, who by Sunday night had restored a semblance of order.

The toll from this three-day outburst of mayhem included eleven dead, some shot by police and guardsmen while others were caught in the crossfire or burned in the flames. More than a thousand fires had been set, leaving hundreds of families homeless, while twenty-nine hundred black people had been arrested, mostly boys and girls under the age of eighteen. Power was cut in some areas and parts of the West Side resembled "war-torn Europe," as *The Defender* described it underneath photographs of smoldering piles of bricks patrolled by soldiers in gas masks brandishing rifles with fixed bayonets.[9]

Some days after the violence was over, Mayor Daley, still scrambling to explain how such large swaths of his city had devolved so quickly into anarchy, complained during a press conference that he had been ignored by the city's police superintendent when he issued an order to "shoot to kill" anyone with a Molotov cocktail or firebomb in their hand and to "shoot looters to detain them."

The reporters in the room were shocked that the mayor had advocated the use of deadly force against rioters but Daley, seemingly oblivious to their dismay, added in defense of his policy, "A looter is a burglar."[10]

Daley's "shoot to kill" order became national news and the resulting outrage was immediate, universal, and vociferous. Leaders of the city's civil rights groups maintained that contrary to Daley's wild statement, it was only the police superintendent's sober decision to ignore the "shoot to kill" order that had kept the violence from being even worse. Interviewed by Betty Washington, Jesse Jackson blamed the mayor for having "supplied the fuel that fed the local insurrection."[11]

Even more remarkable than the criticism from the civil rights activists, celebrities, and the city's few independent elected officials, however, was the public disappointment expressed by prominent ministers, previously Daley's stalwart allies, and by African American lawyers' groups, many of whom depended on the good will of machine-appointed judges and machine-affiliated corporate clients. Even those black politicians who were full-fledged members of the Daley machine were forced to register their discontent and promise that the mayor would back down.[12]

Describing Daley's "shoot to kill" order as "inhumanly harsh," *The Defender's* editorial page quoted the U.S. attorney general, among others, to bolster the argument that more aggression from the police would only have provoked more violence and bloodshed in Chicago as everywhere else there had been rioting. "Let's get it straight once and for all," the editorial continued, "until the people of the slums are brought into the mainstream of American society, there'll continue to be violent eruptions as an expression of their anger against unrelieved poverty and oppression."[13]

But Mayor Daley took only the most minimal steps to address the housing and police brutality issues that had so infuriated Black Chicago. In June, the mayor asked the City Council to impose new nondiscrimination rules on Chicago Realtors and regulate the police's "stop and frisk" procedures but these bills together went only just far enough to bring the city's laws into compliance with recent Supreme Court decisions. Ever the crafty politician, Daley urged as well one cosmetic change as part of the same package that would help create the appearance of progress, renaming the historic boulevard that had been Robert Abbott's home, South Parkway, as Martin Luther King Drive.[14]

Bob Black photographed the destruction following the assassination of Dr. King, but not for *The Defender*. A few months earlier, he had been hired by the *Chicago Sun-Times*, becoming the first African American in that newspaper's photo department at a time when the dailies had begun hiring African American journalists for both pragmatic as well as ideological reasons. The riots of 1967 and 1968 had finally forced the dailies to recognize that they needed African American staff to navigate the community as much as they needed black perspectives in the meetings of their editorial boards and front-page committees.[15]

Betty Washington would be the next to go. In July, she typed in one of her last stories, about a protest against the Chicago Housing Authority led by a young resident of the Harold Ickes development named Bobby Rush. Wearing a dashiki and dark sunglasses, Rush held a press conference to announce the formation of a citywide organization to represent the interests of public housing tenants and eventually take control of management of the developments. The city's population of public housing tenants had grown to 140,000 in high- and low-rise developments across the city, 90 percent of them black, and those residents had no voice in deciding how the Chicago Housing Authority was directed, Rush complained. Washington quoted Rush's appraisal of CHA as "a paternalistic, racist institution which oppresses black residents living in public housing."[16]

At the beginning of August, Betty Washington accepted an offer to become the second African American at *The Chicago Daily News*, the first black woman. She was one of many veterans of the black press making their way to the white-owned dailies that year. A few months after she arrived, *The Daily News* also hired Lutrelle Palmer, a former reporter for *The Defender* and editor of *The Tri-State Defender* who had become an outspoken and respected radical voice in the city. Then the *Chicago Tribune*, trying not to fall too far behind its competitors, hired former *Defender* reporter Vernon Jarrett on a trial basis to write one column a week. Jarrett was only too happy to seize this opportunity to get back into print, as he had been working at a variety of other endeavors, none of them allowing him an outlet for his views. Doing his best to impress his bosses there by attracting a new readership, Jarrett was soon writing several columns a week.[17]

The next time Bob Black appeared in *The Defender*, it was as the subject of coverage of the infamous Democratic National Convention held in Chicago's downtown at the end of August. After the police made a national spectacle of their brutal treatment of the yippies and other mostly white antiwar protesters outside the parks, *The Defender* printed a front-page editorial decrying officers' "thug-like behavior" toward the journalists covering the protests, among whom was Bob Black for the *Sun-Times* along with three other African American journalists, a photographer for the *Chicago American* as well as a cameraman and a reporter for NBC News. The presence of even this tiny contingent of black journalists represented significant progress into the ranks of these mainstream media institutions, as perhaps did the fact that they were treated with equal — rather than exceptional — viciousness by the Chicago Police Department's club-swinging officers.[18]

The success of these individual black journalists, however, presented Sengstacke with a new concern. *The Defender* could never hope to compete with the salaries offered by the white dailies, let alone the broadcast news outlets. For now, the opportunities in the mainstream were limited and many black journalists still preferred to write for their own community but Sengstacke could see that finding and keeping talented people would become a major issue in the near future. Privately, he began to complain that he was running a "training ground" for the white-owned media.[19]

One far more welcome staff change was the return of Louis Martin in January 1969 after an eight-year absence. Martin had worked assiduously until the very last moment to try to rally African Americans and other groups behind the candidacy of the eventual Democratic nominee, Vice President Hubert Humphrey, and he could have stayed on in Washington as a high-ranking member of the Democratic opposition even after Republican President Richard M. Nixon's narrow victory, but he decided instead to come back to Chicago and take up the position of executive editor at *The Defender.* In an article announcing his return, Martin portrayed it as the resumption of his career in journalism, which had simply been interrupted by a brief sojourn in the corridors of power. The reality, of course, was that Martin, transformed by his experience working closely with two presidents, was now a Washington power player. Martin's boss, Democratic National Chairman Lawrence O'Brien, showered him with accolades when he left, hinting that his time at *The Defender* was likely to be a temporary exile. "In heading the Minorities Division of the DNC, you served and spoke for a vital constituency," O'Brien wrote Martin in a formal letter. "We needed you over these last eight years. We still do."[20]

*The Defender's* front page on Monday, November 17, 1969, carried the long-expected, yet-hugely significant news that Congressman

William Dawson would retire at the end of this term, his fourteenth in the U.S. House of Representatives. Tight-lipped to the last, Dawson, eighty-three and ailing, made this official announcement not at a press conference but in a weekend conversation with his old friend John Sengstacke, who was then authorized to inform the public through the newspaper. The article about Dawson's retirement described his service under six presidents as well as his longtime chairmanship of the powerful Government Operations Committee, and included as well the congressman's own modest statement thanking the voters for their support. "My record speaks for itself and I am proud of having had the opportunity to make my contribution to the well-being of my fellow citizens," Dawson wrote. "We have come a long way together and we have walked together in the best tradition of American democracy."[21]

Having begun his political career as the protégé of Oscar De Priest and Ed Wright, he had ended it as the African American standard-bearer of the Chicago machine, respected as well as reviled by a community that had grown far too politically sophisticated and diverse to be controlled by a single boss with an army of patronage workers, fueled by dollars handed under the table by bootleggers, pimps, club owners, and gamblers. Whether in the Congress or in City Hall, Dawson had seen his role as maximizing the power of a minority by leveraging their electoral unity to bargain with the power structure. In this formula, it was pointless to engage in "loud speeches" and get into ideological disputes with fellow legislators whose vote might be needed for some crucial moment. Shrewd and pragmatic, Dawson exchanged his discretion for the behind-the-scenes power that yielded jobs and dollars, the real lifeblood of politicians in Chicago as everywhere else.

There would be no battle for succession, nor was there any chance of an independent taking Dawson's congressional seat. His designated successor was Alderman Ralph Metcalfe, a former track star who had won a gold medal in the 1936 Berlin Olympics along with Jesse Owens and gone on to become a loyal cog in the Daley machine. Nevertheless, Dawson's exit was one more sign that the long partnership between black voters and the city's Democratic Machine was crumbling. Though still hemmed in by white resistance, Black Chicago was now 1.4 million men, women, and children, more than one-third of the city's population, a network of communities that was still expanding geographically on the South and West Sides even as whites were abandoning the city at a rapid clip. New generations had been reared on the expectations of the civil rights movement and the rhetoric of black power, and were coming of age wanting far more than a few low-level government jobs. Lacking a national spokesperson of the same caliber as Martin Luther King or a sympathetic occupant of the White House, these veterans of protest marches and street battles with police focused their efforts close to home, on the city that had become their home, setting their sights on City Hall itself.

For Sengstacke, adapting to the realities of this new era meant accommodating new voices in *The Defender* while maintaining a professional understanding with white-owned advertisers, distributors, and printers as well as politicians. Just a few days after Dawson revealed his impending retirement, Sengstacke printed an announcement in *The Defender* that Jesse Jackson would begin writing a new column for the newspaper. Though he was increasingly seen as a mainstream figure, Jackson was still described as a "militant," especially in the white press, and his column, according to Sengstacke's description in the announcement, was designed to help translate the younger, radical voices for the newspaper's older, more conservative readership. "Though the exclusive column is as yet unnamed," Sengstacke stated, "I do know that Rev. Jackson will pass on to *Daily Defender* readers his vital insight into the black revolution both here and across the changing face of America."

Jackson ultimately decided to call his column "Country Preacher on the Case," and in it he mixed intense criticism of City Hall with advocacy for his own agenda as well as that of other civil rights groups. For the moment, Sengstacke could incorporate Jackson's voice into his newspaper without fear of damaging his personal relationship with Mayor Daley but in the coming months and years, it would become increasingly difficult to steer *The Defender* between the mayor's increasingly erratic policy on one side and the community's rapidly expanding aspirations on the other.[22]

The front page of *The Defender*'s Big Weekend Edition dated December 6, 1969, carried multiple stories about an early-morning raid on a West Side apartment that left two members of the Black Panther Party dead and four others injured. The police account of the incident held that a team of officers under the command of Cook County state's attorney office had gone to the apartment to conduct a search for weapons only to become engaged in a prolonged shootout in which both Fred Hampton, the Panthers' twenty-one-year-old local chairman, and Mark Clark, a twenty-two-year-old from Peoria, were killed.

But just a few hours after the raid, Bobby Rush, who had moved on from organizing public housing residents and was now the Panthers' deputy minister of defense, asked a *Defender* reporter named Faith Christmas to come out to the West Side apartment. A chain-smoking former teacher who had interviewed Fred Hampton the previous summer, Christmas was part of a group of trusted journalists Rush now summoned for an impromptu press conference on the apartment building's rickety steps in which he called the police account of the incident a "dirty lie."[23]

With the temperature hovering at twenty degrees Fahrenheit, Rush told the shivering reporters and cameramen that Hampton, Clark, and the others had been sleeping when officers burst into the apartment, their guns blazing. Rush had arrived that morning at the apartment, which served as a collective living space for the Panthers, to find his comrades missing and the unit ransacked, riddled with bullets, and splattered with blood.

Then Rush invited the journalists inside. Despite being a crime scene, the apartment was still oddly unguarded and he showed them evidence directly contradicting the police narrative. He showed them two large holes in the front door and a pool of blood on the floor of the living room which he said were caused by the shotgun blasts that killed Mark Clark as he sat in a chair in front of the door on security duty. Then he brought the reporters to the back of the apartment, past another pool of blood that stretched from the kitchen back into a small bedroom, the door to which was riddled with bullet holes. Inside, amid the broken glass, shredded clothing, and torn copies of the Panthers' newspaper, he pointed to a mattress soaked with blood where he said Hampton had been sleeping with his pregnant girlfriend when the police attacked, noting that all the bullet holes were inside the room, rather than out in the hallway, which suggested that Hampton had not even had the chance to shoot at the officers. Hampton was a rising star, who had been targeted as part of a broad-based campaign directed by President Richard Nixon to extinguish militant African American leadership, Rush alleged. "Black people better get it through their heads that this isn't just a terrorist act against the Panthers," Rush said. "It's directed at us but it means that every black person better get himself together and arm himself against the pigs."[24]

The impromptu press conference and tour were covered by a number of local television stations as well as newspapers and that afternoon, Cook County State's Attorney Ed Hanrahan responded with his own hastily assembled press conference. An ambitious prosecutor with deep ties to Mayor Daley, Hanrahan stood before a table laden with handguns, rifles, and ammunition he said had been seized from the apartment, including a shotgun that had been stolen from a police vehicle that spring, and pledged to charge the Panthers who survived the assault with crimes ranging from weapons violations to attempted murder. The incident "emphasizes the extreme viciousness of the Black Panther Party," Hanrahan insisted.[25]

The officer in charge of the assault, Sergeant Daniel Groth, told reporters he and his fourteen-man team had arrived at the apartment at 4:30 a.m. and stationed themselves at both the front and rear doors of the apartment. Groth said they had announced they were police before entering but that a woman, presumably Hampton's pregnant girlfriend, fired a blast from a shotgun at the first officer through the door, prompting his comrades to rush in and respond with three separate fusillades from their shotguns, revolvers, and a .45 machine gun. The ten-minute shootout with the Panthers was so ferocious, Groth said, that they had to call for backup from the Chicago Police Department, which sent fifty heavily armed officers.[26]

Public skepticism grew with each recitation of the police account, but the state's attorney redoubled his office's efforts on the very next morning after the deadly confrontation with the Panthers, sending investigators to search Rush's apartment on the South Side. Rush was not there when the officers came into his home, but the officers did discover an unregistered gun, on the basis of which they secured a warrant for Rush's arrest later that day.

On Saturday morning, Faith Christmas was called to a large theater on the corner of Seventy-Ninth and South Halsted Streets, where Rush had agreed to turn himself in to police at a large public ceremony hosted by Jesse Jackson. When Christmas arrived, she found an overflow crowd of thousands filling the theater's seats and aisles, listening with rapt attention as Jackson questioned the police account of the Panthers' raid and demanded that the police department hire more African American officers. Fred Hampton's brother Bill urged the crowd to be peaceful but unified and to throw Ed Hanrahan out of office in the next election.

The crowd cheered when Rush came onto the stage in the Panthers' uniform of black sunglasses, black beret, and black leather jacket. Jackson embraced him before turning him over to the custody of two African American police commanders on the stage, one of whom promised to the crowd that Rush would be treated fairly. On his way out, Rush made a positively apocalyptic prediction about the future of the struggle: "Black people will be free or we will level the Earth in our attempts to be free," Rush told the audience, prompting enthusiastic applause and shouts of approval.[27]

Following this dramatic sendoff, as a final step to ensure his safety, Rush was escorted to the police station by an attorney for the ACLU and Renault Robinson, a black policeman who had recently founded the Afro American Police League, an activist group that had earned the ire of the police hierarchy. But when they got to the police station, Rush was merely asked to pay a $1,500 bond on the gun charge before being released.

That same afternoon, Rush attended a rally at a West Side church with thousands of African Americans as well as several hundred whites and Latinos, a radical crowd that responded to his exhortations against "the pig power structure" with shouts of "All Power to the People" and "Right On." Faith Christmas arrived in time to see Rush speak tearfully about his comrade, nineteen-year-old Ronald Satchel, who had been wounded during the raid that killed Hampton and Clark and was still in the hospital. Satchel, a medical student, had been leading the effort to open a free medical clinic as part of the Panthers' program of providing alternative services.[28]

Until that point, the Panthers had been a fringe element within the community, a local offshoot of a loose national organization that fused revolutionary and black nationalist ideas but had few resources with which to implement their grand schemes. Under Hampton's leadership, they had successfully held several free breakfast events for children in the West Side's poorer districts and were soliciting for volunteer medical staff as well as equipment and financial donations to open the health clinic. During an interview with Faith Christmas over the summer, Hampton had expressed disdain for the federal government's negligence as well as the all-too-abstract efforts of mainstream civil rights activists, whom he described as "apathetic blacks," naming Jesse Jackson specifically. Even the NASA space program, in Hampton's estimation, was an example of misplaced priorities at a time when many in the United States still needed basic services and infrastructure: "While the buffoons are busy going to the moon, we're down here on Earth giving free food and medical services to oppressed people," he explained to Christmas.[29]

Even before the raid on the West Side apartment, the Panthers had been involved in several armed confrontations with Chicago police. In October, a large squad of officers invaded the Panthers' West Side headquarters after they claimed someone shot at them from that building, although all charges were dropped shortly thereafter. Then, in early November, a nineteen-year-old Panther named Spurgeon T. Winters fatally shot two officers on the South Side before being killed himself; a twenty-year-old Panther also involved in the gunfight was wounded and arrested on the scene.

Hampton himself had no record of violence, however. His worst offense had taken place the previous summer, when he "liberated" an ice cream truck in his hometown by frightening away the driver and distributing the contents to neighborhood children. Convicted of felony robbery for this act and sentenced to two to five years in prison, he was free on an appeal bond at the time he was slain.[30]

*The Defender*'s writers and photographers documented the unfolding legal and political situation from multiple angles. In one column, longtime crime reporter Donald Mosby questioned the state's attorney's direct involvement in the deadly Panthers raid, noting that as the county prosecutor, Hanrahan had an ethical responsibility to allow the police department to conduct investigations and gather evidence. A second columnist opined that Hanrahan's direction of this fiasco had, in a single stroke, turned him from a rising star into a real liability and predicted a major defection of black voters from the entire Democratic ticket in the next election — a major threat for the entire Daley machine, which had recently suffered some losses on the county level to Republicans. Several of *The Defender*'s writers also noted that Hampton's killing coincided with the ongoing trial of Bobby Seale, a West Coast Panther who had come to the city to participate in the antiwar protests around the 1968 Democratic National Convention and ended up one of the "Chicago 8" accused of conspiracy to cause a riot.[31]

An editorial headlined "Was It Murder?" articulated the central issues that had arisen for many African Americans in the wake of the Panther raids. Not only *The Defender*'s reporters but many white journalists from other news outlets who had toured the West Side apartment emerged with serious doubts about the police account of the raid, doubts that were only exacerbated by Hanrahan's subsequent less than reassuring remarks. And if indeed the Panthers had been deliberately targeted, that only led to additional concerns; FBI Director J. Edgar Hoover had infiltrated their ranks and had already announced that his agency was investigating the group for subversive activity. Given the potential for conspiracy and cover-up, the editorial demanded a full and transparent investigation into the case, overseen by African American elected officials:

"Are blacks to be murdered for what they believe or what they say? Is the slaying of leaders of the Black Panthers across the nation a part of a national conspiracy to destroy their organization? These and similar questions are being asked in the black community of Chicago even by those who have little or no sympathy for the Panther Party. At issue in their minds is the question of fundamental human rights in our democracy."[32]

Jesse Jackson played a prominent role in organizing the various activities dedicated to Hampton's remembrance and devoted a two-part series of his "Country Preacher on the Case" column to the young Panther leader, painting him as a Christ-like figure who, like Martin Luther King and many others, had been martyred for the civil rights crusade. Omitting, of course, Hampton's harsh criticism of Jackson himself, along with other established civil rights leaders, the column recounted Hampton's upbringing in the suburbs and the process of his political awakening, and urged his readers to register to vote so they could defeat Ed Hanrahan in the next election. Even if the

Panthers showed little interest in electoral politics, Jackson argued, casting ballots would ensure Hampton's sacrifice was not in vain. "If we do our duty," Jackson wrote, "the dynamic essence of Fred, his emancipated and soaring spirit will continue to live, will continue to flow freely into our lives and throughout the land. Thus, we will have transformed Fred's crucifixion into a resurrection."[33]

With just a few weeks before retirement, Congressman Dawson, like the rest of the Silent Six, stayed characteristically quiet on the Panthers raid, but a contingent of African American state legislators, openly breaking ranks, disparaged the police's narrative of the raid. Visiting the West Side apartment for himself, Illinois Representative Harold Washington found that the state's attorney's explanations simply did not jibe with the physical facts. Already known as a maverick among the machine loyalists, Representative Washington told *The Defender*'s reporter that the Panthers' treatment correlated with the general behavior of police toward black men in the city and called for a series of investigations by elected officials as well as independent researchers.[34]

Washington and the other state legislators invited the entire contingent of the nation's African American congressmen to Chicago for a fact-finding hearing. There were now seven members of the U.S. House of Representatives from Ohio, Michigan, California, and Missouri and Illinois, of course, as well as two from New York. Five of the seven accepted — Dawson, maddeningly, was one of the two who did not — and just a few days later, the congressmen came into town with Ethel Payne to cover the hearing. They heard testimony about the particulars surrounding the Panthers case as well as the general circumstances in Black Chicago from Bobby Rush, Jesse Jackson, and the heads of the local NAACP, Urban League, and other civil rights groups along with a host of activists and political aspirants.

The congressmen had invited Mayor Daley and State's Attorney Hanrahan to speak, but neither showed, designating Alderman Ralph Metcalfe instead to speak for the machine. Metcalfe, questioned intensely about the assault on the Panthers' apartment, was also asked whether the mayor's "shoot to kill" order from the previous year was still in effect. The alderman assured the congressmen that this policy had already been moderated.[35]

Even for Louis Martin, unflappable after nearly a decade in Washington that included multiple assassinations of beloved national leaders, Hampton's death landed a dispiriting blow. Most African Americans, he wrote after Hampton's funeral, were convinced the incident at the West Side apartment had been nothing less than "cold-blooded murder." The incident would surely have political reverberations for a generation, he predicted, particularly incensed by the state's attorney's ill-considered decision to target a group like the Panthers — who already harbored deep suspicions about the government — with what appeared to be an actual covert conspiracy. "The police are apparently hell-bent on proving the Panther thesis," Martin wrote, "that the cops really are pigs, that they really are the mortal enemies of the black and the poor, and that genocide is around the corner. Perhaps Oscar Wilde had a point when he suggested that there is no greater sin than stupidity."

Martin felt Hampton's loss personally. Although the two had met just once the previous summer for two hours, Martin was as impressed by Hampton's raw intellectual energy as by his dedication to fighting racism. For Martin as for many others, Hampton's killing piqued his fears that the community's promise was being snuffed out along with the lives of many of its most committed young leaders. "After stripping away the over-worked rhetoric of his movement, it seemed clear that here was a bright, eager and angry youth still reaching for new knowledge," Martin wrote. "Like so many youngsters today, the cruelty of racism, the vicious abuse of the lives and liberties of the black and the poor at every turn, every day, had already seared his soul."[36]

The summer of 1970, the Jackson 5's song "ABC" sold more than one million copies in its first two weeks, displacing the Beatles' "Let It Be" in the number one spot on the pop charts. Suddenly, the Jackson 5 were selling out major shows before audiences in the tens of thousands. In October, *Defender* fine arts editor Earl Calloway conducted a telephone interview with ten-year-old Michael Jackson and his brothers in their new home in Los Angeles.

What the boys described in their conversation with Calloway was not the thrill of stardom or the perks it provided but a packed schedule of private school, household chores, rehearsals, and performances, with time for only an occasional trip to the beach. Young

Michael, in particular, surprised Calloway by recalling nostalgically the venues on the South Side of Chicago and in their hometown of Gary. "I remember singing around the Capitol, the Guys and Dolls, the Regal and at other community programs in Gary and Chicago," Michael said, adding that he was looking forward to their upcoming performances in the Midwest. "I will be glad to see Chicago again."[37]

If the boys felt comfortable speaking with Calloway, it was because they had known him for several years already since the very beginning of their career. He had been the first journalist to write about the Jackson 5 just before their first serious gig in June 1968, a "benefit gospel show and movie" at a South Side theater with twenty-five hundred seats. That was just a few weeks after they had been signed to Detroit's Motown Records and over the following months, Calloway tracked the Jackson 5 as they wrote and rehearsed new songs and performed at other venues. At the end of 1969, they released "I Want You Back," which worked its way into the top ten of *The Defender*'s "Soul Sounds."[38]

*The Defender* had been a launching pad for generations of entertainers, and during his seven years as fine arts editor, Earl Calloway had enhanced the newspaper's role in this area, serving as a talent scout and coach as well as a critic. New acts, in particular, benefited from his open mind and gentle writing style, in which guidance was always preferred over ridicule. An accomplished lyric tenor himself, Calloway was a distant relative of the famous Cab Calloway, whose recognizable hairstyle he adopted.

Calloway's passion for helping his fellow artists was only matched by his dedication to *The Defender*. Indeed, working for the newspaper was actually a childhood dream come true. Born in Birmingham in 1926, he had begun selling *The Defender* when he was ten years old as a way to augment the family's income. During the Depression, the three cents' profit he earned from every newspaper made a real difference in what food the family ate, while old copies of the newspaper were used for wallpaper in his home. "Sometimes, even at night, when you were going to bed, by the lamp, you could read what was going on in the paper," Calloway recalled as he sat at his desk at *The Defender* surrounded by the press releases, letters, photographs, books, tapes, and albums sent in by hundreds of stars and aspirants alike. It never ceased to amaze him that now he was writing the very sort of articles he had once read on his walls by lamplight.[39]

Robert McClory started working at *The Defender* as a reporter in June 1971, becoming the latest white man to join the staff but the first to have been a Catholic priest. McClory had served fourteen years as a priest, much of it at a church at St. Sabina, a massive, yellow-brick Gothic structure in a South Side neighborhood undergoing racial change. Located on Seventy-Eighth Street just east of Ashland Avenue, then the latest dividing line between white and black Chicago, St. Sabina was exclusively white when McClory arrived in 1964 and exclusively black when he left six years later, a reflection of the transformation throughout the surrounding neighborhood.

In 1970, after falling in love with a nun who worked at the parish school, McClory decided to resign from the priesthood, get married, and start his life anew. Suddenly, at the age of thirty-nine, with a master's degree in theology, he was faced with the challenge of finding employment. He had always been fascinated by journalism and took a fast-track course at Northwestern University's Medill School of Journalism, where a friend referred him to *The Defender,* which just then had an opening for a reporter.[40]

Though he had virtually no experience as a journalist, McClory convinced executive editor Tommy Picou to give him the position as a general assignment reporter, earning the modest sum of $150 per week, which was still a large increase from the $75 per month he received as a priest, though his housing was no longer covered, of course. Working under the direction of Louis Martin and a brilliant managing editor named Leroy Martin (no relation to Louis), McClory quickly proved himself an able reporter, first by handling stories of people who walked into the newspaper, and then hitting the streets as he began to accumulate his own sources and contacts. Filling the newspaper's daily pages required constant hustle but McClory thrived in this environment, even coming in on Fridays, usually a day off for a newspaper printed Sunday to Thursday, to write additional feature stories, which he enjoyed most of all. "I was a crazed chipmunk," he quipped. "I would be at City Hall in the morning and go cover a fire in the afternoon."[41]

Among McClory's first sources was Harold Washington, the insurgent state representative, who proved invaluable on the workings of the Illinois General Assembly, among many other topics, political or otherwise. McClory could call Washington with almost any question and look forward to a fifteen-minute lecture, complete with relevant quotations from William Shakespeare. A graduate of DuSable High School, Roosevelt University, and Northwestern University's School of Law, Washington had been inducted into the Daley machine by his father, a popular precinct captain, and understood the way the city's politics worked from the inside out. Unlike his more reticent colleagues, however, Washington was unafraid to reveal secrets or criticize those higher up in the hierarchy.

Moved by the guidance and support he received from his colleagues and superiors alike at the newspaper, McClory took it as a sign that the noble dream of racial integration had not yet been vanquished. When he went out into the community, he was almost always warmly received, especially when he announced he was a reporter for *The Defender.*

On one occasion, he entered a black-owned business and asked the staff member if he could conduct an interview. The staff member agreed but asked him to wait a moment while he went into the back. When the staff member returned, he had a coworker alongside and said, "Look, we got them working for *us* now."[42]

# 22

# Victories Are Contagious

T HE NEXT PHASE of the black revolt against Mayor Daley was led by the most unlikely of champions, U.S. Representative Ralph Metcalfe. As expected, Metcalfe had been rewarded for his loyalty to the machine with a promotion from the City Council to William Dawson's old congressional seat. But in the spring of 1972, disgusted by a never-ending stream of police assaults on blacks, Metcalfe began to publicly criticize not only the superintendent but also the mayor.

At the end of April, Metcalfe stormed into police headquarters accompanied by prominent ministers as well as *Tribune* columnist Vernon Jarrett and demanded that the department undergo a series of reforms to stem "the increasing rise of police misconduct toward the decent black people of this city."[1]

Metcalfe and his entourage met with the superintendent behind closed doors for an hour, discussing the Chicago Police Department's general reputation for brutality, the tiny proportion of black officers relative to the community's share of the population, and a number of recent incidents that had taken place around traffic stops. After the private conversation, Metcalfe insisted on holding a press conference with the superintendent standing uncomfortably by his side. Angrily listing African American grievances, he then set a one-month deadline to begin implementing changes as *The Defender* documented these commitments.

When the superintendent appeared to momentarily equivocate, an annoyed Metcalfe emphasized that he was referring to "the tactics of stopping motorists, men and women of distinction being abused and cursed. "In one case, a woman was kicked and suffered complete harassment and violation of her civil rights. That's what I'm talking about."[2]

Metcalfe's insurrection was soon joined by other members of the black establishment, including John Sengstacke. After the congressman's public showdown with the superintendent, Mayor Daley organized a meeting on police conduct and invited Sengstacke as well as many other community leaders. But when the publisher discovered that Metcalfe had not been invited, he turned down Daley's invitation and urged his colleagues to likewise reject "this attempt to divide black people." Instead, Sengstacke hosted Metcalfe and nearly forty others in *The Defender*'s boardroom, where they drafted a telegram to the mayor reiterating the demands to reform the police department and expressing their collective frustration over the superintendent's failure to move ahead.

Vernon Jarrett, present at this meeting, saw it as the birth of a new civil rights movement that would have long-lasting consequences, a momentous event on par with the 1955 Montgomery bus boycott. This gathering, he noted, had brought together different camps, including many who had been enemies before they entered that room. But there they sat under a huge portrait of Robert Abbott, the paragon of the struggle from the first half of the twentieth century, solemnly forging a common agenda under a united banner: "Like Metcalfe, many of the speakers had been identified as 'appeasers' and spokesmen for the mayor on racial issues," Jarrett wrote in his *Tribune* column. "One could gather that many of these men, like Metcalfe, were expressing a hunger they had kept alive in their bosoms for many years — the desire to place loyalty to their cause, to their race, over loyalty to one man and one party."[3]

During his years with the Daley machine, Metcalfe had learned to keep a distance from community organizations and media institutions, *The Defender* in particular. But now that he was liberated, Metcalfe traveled all over the South and West Sides meeting with church groups, civil rights activists as well as more traditional groups, with the newspaper's reporters covering every stride. Metcalfe was rushing to build an independent political operation that could withstand the mayor's inevitable retribution. That next Saturday morning, he was the special guest at the regular meeting of Jesse Jackson's new organization, Operation PUSH, which, just a few weeks earlier, would have been hostile territory. Now Jackson introduced Metcalfe as "our favorite son who happened to be caught in a bind" to the cheers of two thousand people who filled Shiloh Baptist Church on the South Side.

When Metcalfe spoke, he did not hesitate to charge Mayor Daley with ignoring and disrespecting the black community for failing to respond to their demands. "It is not only Ralph Metcalfe on the spot today," he explained, "because every black man is on the spot because the big question being asked downtown is how long will the black community keep up the fight."

To this, he added a quip that he had repeated any number of times during his conversion tour. When people inevitably asked him, "What took you so long?" Metcalfe invariably replied, "It's never too late to be black."[4]

In July, *The Defender* sent Ethel Payne, Louis Martin, and Bobby Sengstacke to cover the raucous Democratic National Convention in Miami, where the battle between Black Chicago and the Daley machine spilled over into an extraordinary scene on national television. Taking advantage of a party rule change that required more diversity in state delegations, Jesse Jackson and an independent white Jewish alderman named William Singer had succeeded in unseating Daley and his slate of fifty-eight "regular" Democrats in favor of an alternate, mostly African American group.

Bobby Sengstacke captured the image of the incredible moment on the convention floor when Jackson, in a thick Afro and African-print shirt, was handed the microphone to speak for Illinois while the mayor and his crew, mostly white men in tailored suits, stood by him looking stunned and infuriated.[5]

In his column about the convention, Louis Martin charted not only the battles between Jackson and Daley but also those among the various black factions — nationalists versus integrationists, and radicals versus those who were more inclined to accommodate. Jackson, in Martin's estimation, was actually a moderate figure because he supported U.S. Senator George McGovern of Minnesota, the leading candidate, over African American congresswoman Shirley Chisholm of New York, who was running her own upstart bid for the nomination, the first African American to try for the presidency. Indeed, the fact that black leaders found themselves on different sides was a sure sign of the maturity of the African American political class and a necessary step along the road to real democracy.

"The clashing views of some black delegates should not be permitted to hide the broader picture," Martin wrote. "For the first time, you could see Black Power break out into the mainstream of American politics, making a major impact on a major American political party. For the first time, black citizens share freely in the exercise of true political power."[6]

A *Defender* editorial concurred, noting the 472 African Americans among the 3,016 delegates at this convention, some 15 percent of the total, more than double their share of delegates in 1968. The noise and disorder were only the joyous sounds of a generational transition within the Democratic Party as well as within Black America. "The Old Guard goes after crumbs from the table of the white folks in power," the editorial summed up. "The new leadership goes after its proportionate share of the loaf."[7]

In early October, John Sengstacke joined a twenty-two-person delegation from the American Society of Newspaper Editors on a trip to China in the wake of President Nixon's visit earlier that year. Sengstacke and the other high-ranking journalists spent several weeks in the country touring schools and hospitals as well as the nation's most important newspaper, *The People's Daily,* and meeting with an array of government officials, including Premier Chou En-lai.[8]

During John's absence, the printers union representatives confronted his brother Frederick, threatening to strike unless they received higher wages, among other concessions. When John learned about the union's demands upon his return to Chicago, he was enraged by the printers' disloyalty and summarily fired them all. With the cost of newsprint low, he farmed out all the newspaper's printing work to the *Southtown Economist,* a white-owned newspaper based on the city's Southwest Side. The massive machines in the basement suddenly fell silent. For the first time since 1921, *The Defender* was again printed by someone else.[9]

With the November 1972 election fast approaching, the newspaper's staff continued to focus on the ongoing insurgency against the Daley machine. For U.S. Representative Ralph Metcalfe, Jesse Jackson, and others who were seeking to build the power of the black electorate, this contest represented more than a collection of individual races; Cook County State's Attorney Ed Hanrahan was also seeking reelection, despite the smoldering resentment against him over the raid on the Panthers three years earlier. Hanrahan's reelection was an irresistible test of the community's unity and independence.

Bob McClory spent the months leading up to the election covering the political maneuvers between Metcalfe and his insurgents, on one side, and Mayor Daley and his machine, on the other. Metcalfe was up for reelection to his congressional seat but faced no significant challenge. At the end of August, McClory interviewed those black aldermen and committeemen in the mayor's camp and found that they were still willing to support Hanrahan, fearing the mayor's wrath more than they did the public's. Only Harold Washington, who had emerged as one of Metcalfe's lieutenants, would not back Hanrahan, though neither would he work actively to defeat him, putatively out of respect for party unity. "I'm a member of the Democratic organization," Washington told McClory, "but on this point, I won't go along."[10]

In early October, Metcalfe revealed that the mayor had initiated the machine's protocols for betrayal, just as might have been expected, deploying building inspectors to his ward office, where they cited him for a minor infraction. His personal detail of police officers suddenly disappeared as well. More painfully, five of Metcalfe's patronage appointments in various departments were fired summarily while the chieftains of the Park District, Chicago Housing Authority, and other job banks were instructed to refuse any applications from those affiliated with the congressman. "[The mayor] apparently feels that I must be totally loyal to him even if it goes against the best interests of the people of Chicago," Metcalfe told *The Defender*. "Someone is trying to play a game and that someone is Daley."[11]

Demonstrating precisely where it stood, the newspaper gave a full-throated endorsement to Metcalfe just a few days after he spoke out against the mayor under the headline "A True Leader." Though the endorsement was officially for Metcalfe's reelection to a second term in the U.S. House of Representatives, it focused exclusively on his work within the city, praising the congressman's campaign against police brutality in particular. "Ralph Metcalfe is the kind of leader this community has been waiting for," the editorial extolled, "a fighting Representative who is not afraid to raise his voice and carry the battle to the lion's den. The City Hall powerful forces know now that Metcalfe means business in the fight for decency and fair play in the police department."[12]

If neither *The Defender* nor Metcalfe had focused on State's Attorney Hanrahan until that point, this was about to change. At the end of October, just a few days before the election, a Cook County judge found the prosecutor and twelve of his officers not guilty of conspiring to obstruct justice around the Panther raid. After hearing fourteen weeks of testimony from a special prosecutor, the judge ruled that there was not enough evidence to validate the charges. Amid shock and outrage from the Panthers' supporters around the world, the judge conceded from the bench that it was a "damned if you do, damned if you don't case . . . replete with speculation and conjecture and inference."[13]

Moments after the ruling was issued, Robert McClory was summoned to a City Hall press conference, where a smiling, unusually ebullient Mayor Daley emerged to praise the judge for his legal fortitude and issue his own opinion that the trial had established the truth about the Panther raid once and for all. Lauding the state's attorney's record against gangs, the mayor confidently predicted that Hanrahan would win reelection with the usual overwhelming African American turnout for the Democratic Party. "Black people are no different from anyone else," Daley observed. "They want the streets kept safe for their wives and mothers."[14]

The mayor's analysis notwithstanding, Metcalfe and *The Defender* recognized that the upcoming election was now regrettably their last chance to hold Hanrahan accountable for the deaths of Fred Hampton and Mark Clark. Indeed, if Hanrahan were to win, he might even become a contender to succeed the aging Mayor Daley. Metcalfe decided there was no choice, when it came to this key race, but to try to split the ticket and work against his own party. Assembling those members of his ward organizations who had joined his rebellion, he merged those forces with the organizers at Jesse Jackson's Operation PUSH. Together, they launched a voter education campaign that would teach people how to cast their vote for the Republican candidate, a liberal white attorney named Bernard Carey. Even among those who had been going to the polls for decades, there were many who had never bothered to examine the Republican section of the ballot and there were still others whose votes had always been cast for them.[15]

*The Defender* went all out to support the ticket-splitting effort with a front page editorial that labeled the verdict exonerating Hanrahan a "Miscarriage of Justice" and accused the local judicial system of having staged the court proceeding to create the appearance of equity without any real possibility of an actual conviction. Citing the judge's own blunt admission of the forces influencing his decision, the newspaper flatly demanded that the community vote en masse against Hanrahan: "A black voter who fails to vote on this issue," proclaimed the editorial, "is a traitor to the black cause."[16]

On Election Day, both *The Defender* and Operation PUSH served as informal fraud monitors and each received a large volume of telephone complaints. Jesse Jackson said that he had received more than seven hundred calls of irregularities by 10:00 a.m., including reports of more than fifty broken voting machines as well as locked vote keys and judges who arbitrarily removed some voters from the rolls. Pledging to forward every incident to the federal prosecutors, Jackson told the newspaper he was concerned how many voters were affected by breakdowns of equipment as well as intimidation at the actual poling site.[17]

By early evening, the returns for the presidential race had begun to show a landslide for Nixon, as expected, but on the local level, it soon became clear that Hanrahan was indeed facing a serious African American insurgency, no matter how many voters were being suppressed. By 11:00 p.m., with nearly 90 percent of the ballots counted, most of the city's media had concluded Hanrahan had lost, though the state's attorney himself refused to concede and, abandoning his supporters in the hall they had rented for the occasion, went to bed.[18]

The next day, Bob McClory analyzed the election results and determined that out of the city's thirteen largely African American wards, the Republican Carey had won majorities in ten, some by ratios of better than two to one and a few by three to one, all in wards that skewed overwhelmingly Democratic at the top of the ballot. Hanrahan was able to eke out narrow wins in the remaining three black wards, McClory found, two of them outside Metcalfe's congressional district on the West Side. Combined, the African American community had generated a margin of nearly sixty thousand votes for Carey — almost exactly the number by which he had won.[19]

Labeling Metcalfe and Jackson "Giant Killers," *The Defender* added hopefully that this victory would mark the end of the era in which party bosses decided on the community's leaders. Metcalfe himself was cautious about declaring an end to the Daley machine, but Jackson predicted to a *Defender* reporter that this electoral success would fuel the aspirations of those who were planning the next phase of black political empowerment. "Victories," Jackson mused, "are contagious. When you win one, you think you can win again."[20]

In the summer of 1973, John Sengstacke asked Ethel Payne to move back to Chicago to become *The Defender's* associate editor, a position in which she would not only direct the entire news operation but also oversee all of the reporters on a day-to-day basis. Payne was reluctant: she loved Washington and this was an exciting moment to be a journalist in the capital, with the Watergate scandal just beginning to unfold. But Sengstacke promised to let her continue traveling and doing freelance work, including contributing to *Spectrum*, a nationally televised news-analysis program airing on CBS. He even rented her a luxurious apartment with a view of Lake Michigan, all to entice her back.

Payne finally agreed and received an effusive, personal welcome when she arrived: Sengstacke personally helped her set up her office and Doc Lochard, still guiding the newspaper's editorial voice some four decades after Robert Abbott first recruited him, arrived with a bouquet of flowers and bottles of spirits. Nevertheless, she confessed her longing for D.C. in her column, "So This Is Washington," which she had renamed to "From Where I Sit." Certainly Chicago had more than its share of stories with national import but just at the moment Payne arrived, the biggest issues were the trial of a corrupt police sergeant and the rising price of food, local matters that were far afield from the Supreme Court cases, presidential politics, and international intrigue she had covered back in Washington. "The pursuit of power on the banks of the Potomac produces more plots and characters than Shakespeare ever dreamed of," Payne wrote in *The Defender* with a literary sigh. "But it's nice to be back and even nicer to be wanted."[21]

In its June 1974 edition, *Black Enterprise* magazine, featuring a list of the top one hundred African American–owned businesses in the nation, ranked *The Defender* group as twenty-fourth, with $7.6 million in annual sales and 184 employees. And within Chicago, where eighteen of the businesses on *Black Enterprise*'s list were located, *The Defender* placed fifth. The John H. Johnson Publishing Company, with $27.8 million in sales and 245 employees, was the number one black business in the city and number two in the entire country, and the local black economy continued to be vibrant, with a cosmetics firm, sausage maker, mortgage lender, and auto dealerships, in addition to the publishing companies, with combined gross earnings of $133.5 million in 1973, an increase of 51.8 percent over the previous year. Nevertheless, none of those on *Black Enterprise*'s list anywhere in the country even made it into the top one thousand companies ranked by *Forbes* magazine.[22]

Elected chairman of the board of trustees of Provident Hospital in early June 1974, John Sengstacke took the lead on a last-ditch campaign to save one of the few institutions in Black Chicago even older than *The Defender*. The hospital had moved into its current building on East Fifty-First Street in 1932 and the two-hundred-bed facility was so worn out and perennially overcrowded that the federal government had threatened decertification. Several years earlier, Provident had lost its nursing school, once a key institution for African American women medical professionals, and the remaining medical staff was exhausted by financial mismanagement and lax medical standards.[23]

It would not be enough simply to bring Provident up to code; the hospital would have to be expanded and modernized to become a viable institution. Sengstacke had already served on the hospital's board for more than one year, and in that capacity had met repeatedly with Mayor Daley and his key aides until they agreed to donate a parcel of city-owned property immediately next door. Now Sengstacke committed to raising $50 million for a complete rehabilitation of the old building and the construction of a new, five-hundred-bed facility that would make Provident a teaching institution again.[24]

After accepting the chairmanship of Provident's board, Sengstacke relinquished day-to-day control of *The Defender* to his brother Fred and oversight of the newsroom to Louis Martin and Ethel Payne while he set off to implement his vision for the hospital. The price tag for the new Provident was daunting but Sengstacke was a tenacious fundraiser, squeezing the city's African American business leaders as well as the city's more progressive white Brahmins, and the top executives of utility companies, banks, and financial companies. In his first two weeks as chair, he netted one-half million dollars. Next, he turned his attention to the Illinois legislature, from whom he shortly secured a $14.6 million grant by assembling a singular coalition of the Chicago machine Democrats who ran the state house of representatives and the suburban Republicans controlling the state senate.

Sengstacke's role as chairman was not only fundraising, however. He engineered the departure of Provident's executive director and other key employees, dissolved the development department, and fired the African American–owned architectural firm that had been drawing up the plans for the expansion project. When the fired architects complained that they were the only local African American firm capable of designing a hospital, Sengstacke shot back that he would gladly consider bids from white-owned companies, regardless of any criticism this engendered. "We are looking for qualified people who can do the job well," Sengstacke said, "no matter whether they are blue, green, black, white or anything else."[25]

In May 1975, *The Defender* passed its seventieth anniversary, and marked the occasion by publishing a special issue filled with photos and essays tracing the newspaper's history through decades of segregation and migration, war, prosperity, depression, and protest. The editorial page lamented that the accomplishments of Robert Abbott and his cohort were already being forgotten and reminded *The Defender*'s readers that the battles for free speech which they fought and won were the prerequisite for all of the subsequent successes in civil rights. "What was thought to be an impossible dream 70 years ago has taken on the flesh and blood of living reality today," the editorial declared. "Stinging like a gadfly, the conscience of America, Abbott succeeded in awakening the nation to its moral responsibility to a world that is still spilling blood in the struggle for freedom, justice and equality for all mankind."[26]

On another page in the commemorative issue, Bob McClory wrote a profile of the newspaper's sixty-four staff members detailing the responsibilities and tenure of the reporters and editors as well as those who distributed *The Defender* and sold its ads. Several generations of the Abbott-Sengstacke clan were still on the job, from John and Fred's older sisters Ethel and Flaurience, both of whom were themselves nearing seventy, still at their posts in the cashier's booth, to John's middle son, Bobby, who, having established himself as a world-class photographer, continued to shoot for *The Defender* regularly while recruiting other prominent visual artists to contribute their work to the newspaper.

Veterans Ethel Payne, Louis Martin, and Metz Lochard guided the newsroom, while longtime city editor Audrey Weaver, fine arts editor Earl Calloway, and women's editor Theresa Fambro Hooks cranked out columns and features. *The Defender,* McClory boasted, "was racially integrated before the downtown dailies had ever heard of the word 'integration.'" Indeed, at that particular moment there were two white staff members in the editorial department, McClory and Joy Darrow, the grandniece of famed defense attorney Clarence Darrow, herself a relentless investigator and champion of the underdog.[27]

The commemorative issue was packed with more than thirty pages of congratulatory ads in addition to the usual complement of coupons and circulars from supermarkets, furniture and drug stores. The city's African American–owned businesses were well represented among these ads, as were Chicago's white-owned banks, car dealers, insurance companies, and media outlets, including all of the local television stations and the *Chicago Tribune.* But in addition to these, the issue also included full-page notices from national corporate brand names that had generally ignored the black press, including Chevrolet, Zenith, United Airlines, American Airlines, and McDonald's.[28]

*The Defender*'s seventieth anniversary was recognized, too, by the Washington, D.C.–based Society of Professional Journalists, which presented the newspaper with a plaque marking the 2400 S.

Michigan Avenue headquarters as a "Historic Site in Journalism," the only African American newspaper to receive this honorific. William Small, the news director for CBS and the president of Sigma Epsilon Chi, the national fraternity for journalists affiliated with SPJ, came to Chicago to dedicate the plaque, praising both Abbott and Sengstacke for making *The Defender* the "founder and outstanding black representative of modern black journalism."[29]

Interviewed by United Press International about this milestone, John Sengstacke expressed continuing dissatisfaction, however, both with the state of the black press and the economic progress of black America in general. Sengstacke was frank about his own travails and successes, and took pride in his efforts to crack open the national advertising market for black newspapers, noting that *The Defender* now received 75 percent of its revenue from advertising and the balance from circulation, a reverse of the proportions in Abbott's day.

Nevertheless, he complained that black-owned businesses were still in a state of "tokenism," in which he and a small group of other high-profile African American businessmen were accorded honors and board memberships as "window-dressing" to demonstrate concern for the African American community while the overall financial situation remained dire. "Politically, we have made a lot of progress," Sengstacke told UPI, "but economically we are the low man on the totem pole. It probably won't come during my lifetime but I hope we will graduate from tokenism to become full-fledged members of the American scene."[30]

John Sengstacke was still devoting most of his time to the effort to save Provident Hospital even as the task grew ever more challenging. More than a year had passed since he assumed the chairmanship of the hospital's board, but construction had not yet begun and the projected cost had already ballooned to more than $90 million. Now opponents to the plan began to emerge as well, both within the community and among whites who thought the hospital too expensive for the South Side.[31]

Focused on the hospital, Sengstacke spent long periods of time away from *The Defender*, and from his family as well, which was reeling from tragedy. He and his wife, Myrtle, had divorced the previous year after more than three decades of marriage and in May 1976, his

oldest son, John Jr., thirty-five, who had changed his last name to
"Subor," died during a confrontation at a downstate truck stop after a
long battle with mental illness.[32]

Sengstacke mourned his son's death privately, maintaining his
role as the public face of the effort to save Provident throughout that
summer even as the hospital's fiscal crisis grew more severe. Scaling
down the entire project to cut $30 million from the cost, he then
enlisted Jesse Jackson, along with the Democratic governor as well
as his Republican challenger in the then-ongoing political campaign
to rescue the hospital. Only when President Gerald Ford instructed
the U.S. Department of Health, Education and Welfare to provide
a package of financial assistance, however, was the immediate cash
crunch finally alleviated.

These steps represented only a temporary solution, but for the
moment, he had succeeded in propping up yet another of Black Chicago's aging institutions. Like his own newspaper, Provident was
straining to adapt to a community getting only poorer and needier,
abandoned by government agencies as by those resourceful enough
to leave the neighborhood for newly opened suburbs. Gone was the
forced conviviality of Robert Abbott's day, replaced now by relentless, remorseless class stratification, and the newspaper would have
to redouble its efforts to make sure those who had been left behind
weren't forgotten.[33]

Mayor Daley suffered a fatal stroke on December 20, 1976, setting
off a scramble for power among those with an interest in keeping his
machine chugging along as well as those who sought to dismantle it.
After decades in which Daley dominated not only the city and county
but the Illinois Democratic Party as well, Black Chicago's political
class sensed that this might be the moment to elect a black mayor,
particularly if whites continued to fight among themselves while
they managed to unify the African American electorate. Math was
their greatest ally: now 1.5 million people strong, Black Chicago, if
its constituents could coalesce behind a single candidate for the all-
important Democratic primary scheduled for March 1977, would be
an unstoppable electoral force.[34]

In early January, Sengstacke joined Jesse Jackson and forty other
businessmen and political figures at a meeting hosted by John H.

Johnson at *Ebony/Jet*'s downtown headquarters. This ad hoc committee met behind closed doors for several intense weeks in a parallel process to a second group formed by grassroots activists. Both groups arrived at the same candidate, U.S. Representative Ralph Metcalfe; the congressman, however, had decided to make amends with the remnants of the machine now that Daley was gone, and declined to run.

The committees' next choice was Harold Washington, who had just been elected to the state senate. However, Washington set several preconditions, telling a young *Tribune* reporter named David Axelrod that he needed to see $400,000 pledged to his campaign fund before he would agree to throw his hat into the ring. This potential candidate had a serious liability, moreover, in that he had been convicted for failing to file several annual tax returns in 1971 and had served a month in jail. It was a conviction that *The Defender*'s political columnists suspected had been manufactured simply to damage Washington — rarely was anyone prosecuted for failing to file returns, and a jail sentence was almost unheard of — but in the eyes of the general public, a felony record was a serious vulnerability, perhaps even fatal politically.[35]

Washington never got the money he was promised but decided to run anyway, quickly assembling his own organization of several hundred young people and committed activists, including the Independent Voters of Illinois, a group of mostly white progressives. Vernon Jarrett remained a stalwart supporter as well, using his *Tribune* column to tout Washington as the first viable contender for the mayoralty put forward by Black Chicago. "Maybe the real question is," wrote Jarrett, "did the heralded Daley Machine in Chicago die last December with the passing of Mayor Daley?"[36]

The results of the mayoral primary indicated that the answer to Jarrett's question was "no." Interim mayor Michael Bilandic, the favored candidate for many of Mayor Daley's former cronies, won the Democratic nomination with 51 percent of the vote, while Alderman Roman Pucinski, who drew most of his support from the Polish American community on the city's Northwest Side, came in second with 32 percent. Harold Washington was third with 11 percent, just seventy-three thousand ballots.

The results were disappointing but Washington was unrepentant and determined to challenge the machine in the future. Even weeks after the election, Washington was still taking on the establishment in the city's Democratic Party, describing them as racist to their core. "I'm going to run against the Machine," Washington told Jarrett. "I'm going to unfold it. I'm going to pull the cover off of it. I am going to do everything I can conceivably do to awaken black folks inside the media and out as to what's happening in this town."[37]

John Sengstacke emerged from the campaign season with nothing like Washington's optimism or determination. Interviewed in May 1977 for an Associated Press series, "The Ten Most Powerful People in Illinois," he described a fractured political landscape in which Mayor Bilandic, unable to wield the same kind of power Mayor Daley had, would have to negotiate not only with the Republican governor but also rival power centers within his own party. Nor had the Washington campaign changed Sengstacke's assessment about the state of Black Chicago or black America. "There's a big gap yet between white and black leaders," Sengstacke told his interviewer. "They want a nice black to serve on the board and not cause any trouble so they can show everyone they're concerned about the black community. He may not even be knowledgeable."[38]

There was not a single black Chicagoan Sengstacke felt deserved to be rated among "Illinois' most powerful," not even himself, and in any case, he was in no way interested in such public recognition. Asked if he thought he would make the list, Sengstacke answered, "I hope not. I'd really like for people to leave me alone for a while. I've already got too much to do. After 40 years, I've been involved in too many things. It's not that I'm not interested. I'm just a little tired." Instead, Sengstacke was quoted in the AP article without being officially named to the list.

As for whether he saw a young black leader on the way up in Illinois, Sengstacke responded, "I don't see him yet. There may be one out there that I'm not aware of yet, but I don't see him."[39]

Louis Martin resigned from Sengstacke Enterprises in January 1978 and returned to Washington, D.C., as an aide to U.S. Senator Adlai Stevenson III for what was supposed to be a temporary sojourn on the way to a comfortable retirement. Within a few months of Martin's return to the capital, however, he was recruited by President Jimmy

Carter to a post with duties similar to those he'd held during the Kennedy and Johnson administrations. As he always had when the White House called, Martin accepted.[40]

Just a few months after Martin's departure, the newsroom lost another of its senior staffers when John Sengstacke fired Ethel Payne in a dispute over her freelance work. Payne had never really settled back in Chicago or embraced the city's news culture, but Sengstacke had allowed her to travel frequently for short-term gigs in Washington, New York, and other locales around the world. When she agreed to an appointment reviewing resumés for the United States International Aid agency, however, a stint that would require her to be in the nation's capital for three months, the publisher had finally had enough. Accusing her of disloyalty to the newspaper, Payne recalled to her biographer, Sengstacke "curtly told me we could no longer be associated."[41]

Payne held no grudge, both out of gratitude for Sengstacke's role in launching her journalism career and because she had come to understand by now that *The Defender*'s publisher could be capricious; she charitably described him as a "brooder." Besides, Sengstacke's decision to cut her loose freed her to pursue her own work. She began writing a column for several other black newspapers and was awarded a Ford Foundation grant to conduct an eighteen-month assessment of the nation's black colleges. After that, she planned on moving back to her beloved Washington, where she would resume writing her column and making regular appearances on television and radio.[42]

There would be one more departure that year: having lined up freelance projects that could keep him going for the foreseeable future, Bob McClory, too, stopped working full-time at *The Defender* at the end of 1978. McClory continued to play a role in the newspaper, however, writing two to three editorials every week to augment those produced by Metz Lochard, who had been greatly weakened and nearly silenced by throat cancer, though he remained as cogent as ever.[43]

As the 1970s drew to a close, *The Defender*'s clout was waning. Circulation of the daily edition had fallen below twenty thousand, leading major advertisers including Marshall Field's to cancel their large-scale ad buys. At least as damaging, with the national and local branches of the civil rights movement somnolent, the content on the front page drifted inevitably into the eddies of crime news even as the general print quality dropped. Rushed and sloppy copy editing, mislabeled jumps, and even the occasional misspelled headline all conspired to further erode the newspaper's reputation. The commensurate loss in revenue made 1981 the first year in which Sengstacke Enterprises' total sales would not qualify the organization for *Black Enterprise* magazine's "Top 100" list.[44]

John Sengstacke's political clout was eroding as well, while a new breed of Democrat took over in Chicago's City Hall and the White House. In April 1980, Jane Byrne, who had been elected Chicago's first woman mayor with strong support from the African American community one year earlier, offered Sengstacke a spot on the Chicago Public Library Board. This would normally have been considered a prestigious appointment, but Byrne had also offered a board slot to Charles Swibel, whose long reign as chairman of the Chicago Housing Authority was infamous for perpetuating the segregation of the city's African Americans. Sengstacke turned the mayor down, making the excuse to a *Tribune* reporter that he was simply too busy. But another potential black nominee who also rejected the offer ridiculed the mayor's choice, saying that Swibel "knows nothing about books and has no interest in academia, to my knowledge."[45]

Just a few months after that fiasco, in the summer of 1980, Sengstacke and the whole black press were snubbed by President Jimmy Carter's White House. Scheduled as keynote speaker at the NNPA's fortieth annual convention, held in Chicago to celebrate *The Defender's* seventy-fifth anniversary, the president canceled at the last minute to go to Venice and meet with the heads of western Europe's national governments. Sengstacke tried to arrange for Vice President Mondale — or another member of the administration — to stand in for Carter but couldn't get his phone call returned, not even when Louis Martin exerted his influence.

Infuriated, *The Defender* publisher ended up delivering the keynote himself and used his time at the podium to lambaste the president for focusing on international issues at a time of domestic crisis. The black press may have been diminished from its height but the conference still drew 130 men and women representing black newspapers around the country and Sengstacke urged his fellow black journalists to exercise their collective power in the upcoming presidential elections at the end of that year.

Interviewed by Vernon Jarrett after his speech, Sengstacke surmised that President Carter was taking the black vote for granted and warned that *The Defender* and other black publishers might well throw their support behind independent John Anderson or even the likely Republican nominee, Ronald Reagan. "With unemployment getting worse and worse for black people who are trying to survive in a period of depression plus inflation," Sengstacke told Jarrett, "I can't understand why the president of the United States would schedule his trip to Europe at this moment."

At sixty-nine, Sengstacke was exhausted by the decades of relentless challenges and bereft of the longtime relationships that had helped him in the past, but determined to restore *The Defender* to a sustainable financial condition before it was too late. In a conversation with Larry Muhammad, an incisive former *Defender* editor who was drafting his biography, Sengstacke said he was focused on ensuring that the newspaper, like Provident Hospital, survive as African American–founded institutions that serve the people and provide living examples of achievement and independence. "John Sengstacke is not important," he told Muhammad. "*The Defender* is important, as long as I can keep it a viable institution. If it fails, so does John Sengstacke."[46]

After successful careers in both the federal government and banking, Chinta Strausberg joined *The Defender*'s staff in January 1981 as a volunteer reporter. Although she had some experience as a radio talk show producer and writer, Strausberg, diminutive and fine-featured with a formal manner, didn't immediately strike John Sengstacke as someone who could function effectively as a *Defender* reporter. But she soon proved herself with unmatched dedication and indefatigability, tracking down public officials and neighborhood activists all day and then working on her stories all night. Thus it was that after five months on the job in an unofficial capacity, John Sengstacke finally agreed to put Strausberg on the payroll.[47]

Strausberg gravitated to political stories, spending time watching the aldermen in the City Council as well as checking in at key venues in the community, including Jesse Jackson's Saturday morning gatherings at Operation PUSH headquarters. Jackson, who had by this time trimmed his afro and exchanged his dashikis for three-piece suits, was spending most of his time leading national boycotts against major corporations he accused of discriminating against African Americans — the latest being Anheuser Busch, the nation's largest beer brewer. But the Saturday-morning sessions at PUSH remained the best place to gauge the community's mood, and week by week, Strausberg charted the increasing frustration with Mayor Jane Byrne, who continued to snub the African American community while favoring the worst elements of the old Daley machine.

By the fall of 1982, it was clear to the city's politicos that Byrne was vulnerable in the next mayoral election scheduled for the following spring. The *Tribune* quoted insiders who said that Richard M. Daley, the son of the longtime mayor, who was then serving in his first term as Cook County state's attorney, would run against Byrne in the Democratic primary. But in *The Defender,* there were reports of a grassroots process to select an African American consensus candidate. Ralph Metcalfe had died suddenly in 1978 and Harold Washington was now the U.S. representative of the First Congressional District. Many had come to admire Washington for his eloquent speeches against President Ronald Reagan's policies on the floor of the House of Representatives, while among activists, Washington's courageous stand in the aftermath of the Panthers raid as well as his failed 1977 mayoral bid amounted to stamps of legitimacy. The real question was whether Washington would run at all and risk exposing himself to another humiliating defeat.[48]

In early November 1982, Jesse Jackson gave Strausberg the scoop: Harold Washington had agreed to run as a candidate in the all-important Democratic primary for mayor on February 22, a decision he would announce at a press conference the next day at a hotel in Hyde Park. Citing data from the election just a few days earlier, Jackson noted that the number of registered African American voters in the city had risen to 600,000, one-third of whom had signed up in just the last few months, and there were still 150,000 and 200,000 more who could be registered. These numbers might not be able to carry a

black candidate to victory on their own but this time, the white electorate would be split between Daley and Byrne, giving Washington a
fighting chance.[49]

Strausberg attended the press conference the next day when
Washington, as promised, formally announced his bid for mayor,
setting out an ambitious reform agenda of ending patronage in employment, curbing crime, reducing poverty and unemployment, and
improving the schools. Vowing to "open the secret files in City Hall,"
Washington alleged that Mayor Jane Byrne's alignment with the
most corrupt elements of the machine had driven up the cost of Chicago's city services while also rendering them inefficient. "The 'City
That Works' doesn't work anymore," Washington quipped, riffing on
a slogan that the first Mayor Daley had coined during the height of
his popularity.[50]

The following week, *The Defender* collaborated with a local
black-owned radio station to conduct a poll of several hundred voters, white and black, in which they detected weakening support for
Byrne. A little over 40 percent of those surveyed thought she was
doing a good job, but only 9 percent of blacks intended to vote for
her. Washington himself received just 40 percent of the black community's support, while Daley actually received a higher share of African American support, almost certainly owing to his father's lingering aura.

But in the streets, Washington was drawing large, enthusiastic
crowds wherever he appeared, even on the first days on the campaign
trail. A thousand people filled Bethel AME church on Forty-Fourth
Street and Michigan Avenue, where he took a more militant tone
than in his initial declaration. In this election, he announced to those
in the packed pews, African Americans "don't have to make any excuses or apologies."[51]

In January, Byrne and Daley pummeled each other with ads on
television while Washington's grassroots campaign "bounced from
one obstacle to another," in the words of the *Tribune*'s David Axelrod,
now promoted to political columnist. Totally nonplussed by Washington's organization thus far, Axelrod noted that it had taken the
candidate more than a month from the date of his announcement to
hire a manager and open a headquarters, and he still lacked the kind
of money to go on television. When Washington finally did settle on

a campaign manager, he chose Al Raby, Martin Luther King's former aide-de-camp, who had never run a citywide electoral effort before. The rest of Washington's campaign staff was equally inexperienced and Axelrod noted that they had only arranged a few events outside of the African American community where he might expand his base. Nor had they assembled fundraisers that could get their candidate on the airwaves, Axelrod complained.

Axelrod took Washington to task as well for visiting Cook County Jail on Christmas Day, dismissing the congressman's insistence that his annual pilgrimage to visit with jailhouse prisoners would enhance his reputation with black voters. Instead, Axelrod pointed out, the television coverage simply reminded viewers of Washington's brief incarceration for failing to file tax returns. "It is hard to believe that the jail episode will help Washington among black voters any more than it will with whites," observed Axelrod.[52]

The community was mobilizing for Washington without waiting for his campaign staff to get their act together. The Urban League, as just one example, was registering new voters at the city's black-owned banks and McDonald's franchises, found *Defender* investigative reporter Juanita Bratcher. Usually, the conservative owners of these businesses kept a wide berth of any political activity, particularly any effort aimed at the machine — for they all depended in varying proportions on city government — but Washington's drive for mayor had somehow inspired them all, whether he had deep coffers or a smooth operation or not.

James Compton, the leader of the Urban League's local branch, couldn't formally endorse a candidate because of the rules governing nonprofits but explained that "The Black McDonald's Association believes that Blacks should be registered to vote and that they have the political strength to make a difference in the city."[53]

Seeking to inspire confidence, Washington's campaign opened multiple offices on the South and West Sides as well as downtown and on the North Side near African American pockets and the large gay and lesbian neighborhoods along the lakefront. Recognizing belatedly that it was crucial to expand their constituency to the Latino community, they also invited the president of the League of United Latin American Citizens to speak at Operation PUSH after his group, the oldest Latino organization in the city, endorsed Washington.[54]

Even now, though, Washington continued to flout the established practices of professional politicians. In the face of continuing questions about blights in his record, he persisted in offering full transparency, holding a press conference at which he listed his flaws and errors and provided full documentation to interested reporters. "Everyone has skeletons," Washington told Chinta Strausberg. "The only difference is that you may now look at mine." In addition to his conviction and imprisonment for failing to file tax returns, Washington admitted that his law license had been suspended for five months in 1976 after he failed to do any work on behalf of a couple who paid him to represent them on a parking ticket. He also provided reporters with financial statements dating back to 1964, promising to make the most recent documents available as soon as they were complete.[55]

While Washington strove to convince voters of his plausibility, former *Defender* reporter Lu Palmer and a group of like-minded activists policed the community on the campaign's behalf. Gathering under the banner of the Task Force for Black Political Empowerment, they picketed outside the Palmer House Hotel, where a group of 150 black ministers had gathered to endorse Rich Daley. The protesters charged Daley with buying the ministers' support and quipped that the same meeting could not have been held in Bridgeport, where blacks were generally unwelcome.

When Strausberg interviewed the ministers, she found them at once recalcitrant and defensive. The clerics' leader vowed to stand by Daley despite receiving death threats, while others expressed skepticism as to whether Washington had a realistic chance at victory. Yet another predicted that a Washington victory would only cause corporations to abandon Chicago "and the city would go to pot."

As for Daley's qualifications, the Rev. Richard Posey, pastor of a large, well-established Baptist Church in the middle of the Robert Taylor Homes public housing development, spoke of the young man's pedigree as a sufficient resumé. "Daley is the most logical candidate," Posey told Strausberg. "Besides, he has been in politics all his life and he knows city government."[56]

The candidates agreed to four televised debates, the first of which was held on January 18 at the First Chicago Center in the Loop. Mostly civil, this exchange yielded none of the candidates an outright victory, though Washington's display of wit and intellect alongside both the sitting mayor and the son of the last mayor convinced many African Americans that he might actually win the race and successfully administer the city. Conducting a number of "man on the street" interviews after the debate, Strausberg found a surge of confidence in Washington among African Americans. "I like the way he handled himself," went one typical comment from a passerby Strausberg encountered on the South Side.[57]

The second debate, sponsored by an African American radio station, focused on the city's surging crime rate. Washington went on the offensive now, accusing Byrne's administration of deliberately failing to properly investigate incidents of police brutality, citing statistics from the department's own Office of Professional Standards. Byrne's and Washington's supporters in the debate's audience clashed as well, shouting at each other from across the room.[58]

Strausberg and the *Tribune*'s David Axelrod were panelists in the third debate, in which Byrne focused her rebuttal on Washington, whose support the polls showed was growing along with the voter-registration numbers in the African American community. Daley's performance in the debates, meanwhile, was judged lackluster as he struggled to summon articulate sentences, managing to mangle even his own clearly rehearsed catch phrases. Not surprisingly, his poll numbers were falling, even as the crucial black electorate rallied to Washington's banner.[59]

By the end of the month, with just three weeks left before the primary election, *The Defender* detected real momentum behind Washington. On one day, the front page featured an endorsement event with three hundred ministers, five incumbent aldermen, and four aldermanic candidates. Farther back in the same issue, Strausberg wrote about Lu Palmer and his activists heckling Mayor Byrne at the opening of her Third Ward office at Forty-Seventh and King Drive, which happened to be kitty-cornered from the Washington campaign office in which the Task Force was based.[60]

So intense had the passion for Washington become that anyone who supported another candidate risked public rebuke and even ostracism from their neighbors, peers, and even family members. Two days after *The Defender* printed an article announcing that a group of resident leaders from fourteen different public housing developments had endorsed Byrne, those leaders were forced to backtrack, claiming their lives were being threatened. Several of the resident leaders called the newspaper's offices and confessed that Byrne's campaign team had threatened to oust them from positions or cut them off from the modicum of patronage to which they were entitled if they didn't endorse the mayor.[61]

On the first Sunday in February, the newspaper sent reporter Ken Green, a sharp-eyed recent college graduate who had spent most of his childhood in Robert Taylor Homes, to cover Washington's most ambitious event yet, a rally at the University of Illinois Pavilion, a large facility usually used for rock concerts and sports games. Raby and the other Washington campaign staffers weren't sure until the last minute whether people would actually come, but in the end, more than fifteen thousand descended on the facility, overflowing its capacity. Green recorded a carnivalesque atmosphere, complete with vendors selling T-shirts, buttons, and other paraphernalia to raise money for the campaign, while onstage with Washington were fellow members of the Congressional Black Caucus from around the country, as well as U.S. Senator Alan Cranston from California and musician Curtis Mayfield, who had grown up in the Cabrini-Green development.[62]

Even the *Tribune's* Axelrod was impressed by the enthusiastic turnout at this rally, though he continued to doubt Washington's chances on Election Day. In a column entitled "No Matter What, Washington Wins," Axelrod reiterated his critique of the campaign's organization even while expressing skepticism about who would actually turn out to vote on the day. Still, as one of the few white reporters who had developed sources within the community, he could hardly help but notice that registration was up significantly in many black wards, even exceeding numbers in many white areas.

Axelrod remarked on a phrase that Washington repeated often on the trail, "It's our turn," arguing that whites should not interpret this as a threat of racial revenge so much as a matter of inclusivity. After all, he pointed out, in the police department, Chicago Housing Authority, public school system, and every other agency controlled by City Hall, African Americans weren't hired in numbers even close to their actual proportion of the city's population, he pointed out. "The truth is," Axelrod wrote, "Blacks have been excluded from key positions of power for years. They have been shut out even though they have been among the most loyal supporters of the Democratic Machine ... Washington is running to redress some of these inequities and grievances. What is wrong with that? When this city and others have erupted in violence in the past, the standard plea to inner-city residents was to work for change 'through the system.'

"Now they are."[63]

Axelrod's respectful take notwithstanding, the *Tribune* endorsed Rich Daley along with the *Sun-Times*. Only *The Defender* went for Washington, prefacing its endorsement with an indictment of Jane Byrne's leadership. "Watch Jane run. Mayor Jane Byrne is running again. Our question is: Who runs Jane Byrne?" began the editorial on the front page of the weekend edition dated February 12, 1983. "We don't know for sure but we have a damn good idea."

Both Harold Washington and Rich Daley, the editorial explained, had met with the editorial board, while Byrne had not. Nevertheless, even Byrne's absence did not doom her with *The Defender* as much as the conduct of her emissaries, who, the editorial alleged, offered a substantial sum of cash in exchange for the newspaper's endorsement. Perhaps it was true, as a recent Urban League study claimed, that *The Defender* was now less influential among African Americans than the white-owned dailies, but that did not mean that its integrity was for sale. "We have never claimed that *The Defender* has power in the black community," the editorial stated. "We do claim that *The Defender* does its homework and knows what's going on in Chicago — both black and white. Some months ago, those who run Jane Byrne wanted to compromise *The Defender* for its editorial support. During our 77 years of existence, *The Defender*'s endorsement has never been for sale and it is not for sale now."

Rich Daley was a "nice fellow," the editorial continued, but could offer little from his record as state's attorney to show that he had been a champion of the common man, let alone Black Chicago. *The Defender* was endorsing Washington because he was the best-qualified candidate with an agenda that would benefit the entire city. Addressing the concerns of conservative blacks, the editorial admitted that perhaps the city's major corporations were not on Washington's side now but averred they would come along once he proved that he could run the city not only competently, but without the corruption and favoritism characterizing Byrne's reign. "We endorse and recommend you vote for Washington not because he is Black (he is Black) but we are convinced he can bring this City of Chicago together," the editorial summed up. "In spite of his gray record with the IRS, etc., he is much more of a man than some politicians we know who should be in jail.

"They just haven't been caught yet."

The implicit accusation against Byrne and her campaign prompted a media dust-up in those heated final days before the primaries, fueled partially by the mayor's curious denial that her emissaries had solicited *The Defender's* endorsement at all. A white columnist with the *Tribune* demanded that *The Defender* reveal who had made the offer on Byrne's behalf, but *The Defender* refused, instead printing another front-page editorial repeating both the charges and their endorsement for Washington, citing his dignified performance during the debates and his clean record in the state legislature as well as the House of Representatives. "If Jane Byrne does not know what her bosses are doing," the editorial jibed, "she ought to know now."[64]

*The Defender* editions during the final days just before the primaries mirrored the intensity of the moment not only in their coverage, but in the numerous full-page ads purchased by all three campaigns and their affiliates. The articles focused in particular on the last-minute preparations and rallies among Washington's grassroots supporters, including the training of election monitors and the prepositioning of attorneys as well as a final weekend session at Operation PUSH at which Jesse Jackson brought in Rosa Parks as a guest star.[65]

As for the full-page ads, a few featured second-tier African American leaders endorsing Byrne or Daley but the overwhelming majority were pro-Washington, touting his credentials and character from every angle. One full-page from the Black Business Coalition to Elect Harold Washington phrased its message with language that captured the hope and anxiety felt by many: "Harold Washington must win," read the copy. "We cannot afford to let this opportunity slip by."[66]

On Election Day, Bobby Sengstacke captured an image of Washington casting his own ballot in the polling place at the base of the Hyde Park high-rise where he lived and then followed the candidate as he walked key precincts on the North Side. *The Defender's* reporters and photographers spent the day in the streets frantically documenting reports from Jesse Jackson and other monitors of potential fraud, including names that mysteriously disappeared from registration lists and menacing characters who lurked about polling sites, pressuring voters to choose Byrne. The Chicago police made a dozen arrests, slightly more than the usual number for an election, but the local U.S. attorney took the calls coming in to his office seriously and obtained permission to assign federal marshals to guard the ballots once they had been collected.

When a fire stalled a southbound CTA train line exactly at rush hour, threatening to delay thousands of black voters from reaching their home neighborhoods before the polls closed at 7:00 p.m., the Washington campaign went into panic mode. Al Raby, preparing to dash to the county courthouse to file an injunction to allow the commuters to cast their ballots, told *The Defender* he suspected that the blaze had a political origin. "Given the creative nature of vote-stealing in Chicago," Raby said, "we wouldn't be surprised if it had been set."

As evening descended, thousands of Washington supporters streamed into the hall at the McCormick Inn, a hotel along the south lakefront adjoining the McCormick Place Convention Center, just a short hike away from the *Defender* building. Assigned to cover the rally for the newspaper was Henry Locke, a heavyset, gregarious native of Buffalo, New York, who specialized in police and crime stories. The crowd was expectant rather than aggressive, however, and shortly before midnight, they received their first bit of good news when Rich Daley conceded.

Now it was a race between Byrne and Washington. Byrne's spokesmen, initially confident, claimed their lakefront totals would put them over the top, but a short while after Daley's concession, the mayor told her supporters gathered in a downtown hotel to go to bed, saying that the race was too close to call and, "We'll see in the morning."[67]

The throng at the McCormick Inn stayed on, however, watching the results come in precinct by precinct, becoming ever more buoyant as the results kept adding to their margin. At *The Defender*'s press deadline, with 97 percent of the precincts counted, Washington was ahead by just over twenty thousand votes on the strength of an unprecedented black turnout and Locke reported back to the newspaper that people had begun to chant, "We have won."

Victory had not been confirmed yet, however, and as the clock neared 2:00 a.m., the chant changed to "We Want Harold, We Want Harold." Finally, Washington emerged in a corner of the room, slightly rumpled but beaming, and made his way to the stage, where he asked the cheering crowd, "You want Harold?" He paused for a moment, then answered, "You got him."

It was a cathartic experience, and many began to sing "We Shall Overcome," while others cried silently to themselves. Every class and sector was well represented, with well-heeled lawyers standing side by side with street-corner activists, church pastors next to single mothers who lived in public housing. Washington spoke in magnanimous, conciliatory terms: "Our lifelong commitment is to heal the city. We will lead willingly those people who want to see positive change. And to those who oppose us, we open our arms and offer you an opportunity to join our movement. Our campaign will reach out to build, to heal, to bring together to make Chicago a first-class city with open doors to everyone, regardless of race, creed, color or handicap."[68]

When the final vote count was tabulated, Washington had won with 36 percent of the vote, 419,296 votes, to Byrne's 33 percent with 386,456 votes and Daley's 29 percent with 343,506 votes. The turnout for this primary election after an unprecedented surge in registration was 80 percent. In the historic Third Ward, where the registration rolls had risen from 20,403 voters in 1979 to 32,530, Washington received 16,656 ballots to 2,517 for Byrne and just 638 for Daley. The figures in the white wards had been just as lopsided, with Washington garnering only tiny amounts as Byrne and Daley battled for the majority. But in the end, it was black turnout, rather than a multiethnic coalition, that had equaled victory.[69]

There was still a general election to contest two months away, but Washington was not particularly worried. Not since Big Bill Thompson had a Republican won the mayoralty, and the GOP nominee this year, Bernard Epton, got a grand total of eleven thousand votes in his primary. Epton, moreover, was an awkward standard-bearer for the Republicans; liberal and Jewish, he had served alongside Washington as a state representative from Hyde Park with a strong pro–civil rights and antipoverty voting record.

The racial tension was palpable in the city in the days just after the primary; Washington was subjected to death threats by phone and mail, requiring the twenty-four-hour presence of uniformed Chicago Police officers outside the campaign headquarters downtown. But Epton told *The Defender* he did not want the votes of "racist Democrats who cross over," and said he would meet with Washington to find ways to prevent the campaign from degenerating into something ugly. "I have no desire to win a vote because an opponent is Black and I am white," Epton elaborated. "A bigot is a bigot and I want no part of it."[70]

As for Washington, he was brimming with confidence as he sat down for an extended interview with *The Defender*'s Henry Locke, predicting that he would beat Epton by a three to one margin. Washington was already planning to begin his mayoral reign with a mandate to end patronage in Chicago's city government. Even though he now enjoyed the attention of Democratic luminaries including U.S. Senator Edward Kennedy and former vice president Walter Mondale, both of whom supported Daley during the primary, Washington said he would not alter his grassroots strategy. He was sticking with the community and its institutions, *The Defender* included. "I never would have won the primary contest without the support of *The Defender*, the most respected black newspaper in America," Washington told Locke. "I can't thank John Sengstacke enough for that support and I'm looking forward to it in the General Election."[71]

Despite Washington's sanguine predictions in the days after the primary, what was officially a contest of Democrats and Republicans very quickly became a racial battle as white aldermen, committeemen, and precinct captains who had been lifelong Democrats suddenly declared they were for the Republican Epton, while African American machine figures sided with Washington. Chinta Strausberg interviewed Alderman Aloysius Majerczyk, who said he was supporting Epton because he had already concluded that the constituents of his Twelfth Ward on the Southwest Side, a diverse mixture of people of Polish, Lithuanian, German, Irish, and Mexican heritage, "will not be fairly represented in Washington's administration."[72]

On the other hand, Strausberg covered a press conference to endorse Washington held by Aldermen Robert Shaw and William Carrothers, two black machine stalwarts who had backed Byrne in the primary. Both had been challenged by Washington allies in the primary and failed to win an outright majority of the votes in their wards, meaning that they would face runoffs on the same date as the mayoral election. Carrothers, a gruff character who represented an impoverished West Side ward, stayed silent through the press conference while Shaw, a crude pragmatist, did not even try to hide his reasons for switching. "I am adhering to the wishes of the people," he told Strausberg.[73]

Analyzing the changing contours of the campaign, *The Defender*'s editorial page saw danger. Epton's admirable statements notwithstanding, race had been an issue in every city where a black mayor had been elected, in Birmingham, Los Angeles, Detroit, and Atlanta, and Chicago would be no different, the newspaper predicted. "In this city where segregation is a baptismal font in which nearly all whites dip their fingers," the editorial augured, "a mayoral contest in which a Black candidate is opposed by a white candidate — there is no way to keep race out of the contest."[74]

The following week, *The Defender* reported that racist literature targeting Washington was being posted on bulletin boards in police stations around the city. Several black officers at these stations had seen the fliers and brought them to the newspaper — crude cartoons imagining a new coat of arms for the city festooned with stereotypical imagery, watermelons, large lips, and malt liquor, all of which reflected "the new ethnic order." The cartoon's caption made it clear, moreover, that this was no random racist statement but rather a piece of political propaganda: "Remember: the other candidate had never been Dis-Bare; never jailed; never accused of losing clients' money."

Police superintendent Richard Brzeczek denied any involvement in the distribution of the fliers, although he had a history of tension with the Washington campaign. During the primary campaign, Brzeczek had publicly expressed his doubts about Washington's leadership, prompting the candidate to announce his intention to fire the superintendent once elected. Republican candidate Epton denied as well that his campaign had anything to do with the fliers, though he defended the general conduct and intentions of the police department.[75]

Throughout March, *The Defender* reported on the behind-the-scenes moves from white Democrats to undermine Washington. Strausberg discovered that the commissioner of the city's Department of Neighborhoods, having devoted much of his time to supporting Byrne during the primary, was now working for Epton. She also documented police officers in a number of districts who freely spent their shifts using office supplies to invite their colleagues, family, and friends to fundraisers.[76]

With Election Day fast approaching, Epton himself became meaner in his critique, harping on Washington's past issues with the IRS during their single televised debate and adopting for his campaign the ominous tag line "Before It's Too Late." Although the Republican continued to eschew making racist statements himself, *The Defender's* editorial page lamented that its predictions about Epton's campaign had come to pass: "90% of the financial and volunteer support offered to [Epton] is presented by disgruntled racists who would do anything to prevent a Black mayor from running Chicago," stated an editorial from March 23. "Without his consent, his candidacy has been seized by the worst elements in Chicago politics. He is increasingly viewed as the Great White Hope."[77]

*The Defender's* Henry Locke witnessed the level of white fear and anger over Washington's candidacy firsthand when he accompanied the congressman and former vice president Walter Mondale as they attempted to visit a Catholic church on the Northwest Side for Palm Sunday service several weeks before the election. Mondale, a future presidential hopeful, was making amends for having supported Rich Daley during the primary and made an appointment for him and Washington to meet with the pastor and parishioners of St. Pascal's. But when they arrived, they were confronted by 175 aggressive protesters carrying signs with pro-Epton messages as well as pro-life slogans — Washington was also an outspoken defender of abortion rights — whose jeering and threats were sufficiently meaningful to prompt them to leave.[78]

Election Day was cool with a light rain, weather that reflected the mood, somber and potentially stormy. If people had been giddy and expectant at the polling places on the day of the primary, this time they were dead serious, and the lines even longer. In the evening, Henry Locke, Chinta Strausberg, and a few other *Defender* staffers joined the anxious, hopeful masses who yet again filled the hall of the McCormick Inn. As the news broadcasts showed a massive turnout in black precincts and wards across the South and West Sides, the crowd's expectation morphed first into relief and then outright jubilance, and shortly before midnight, they once more began to chant, "We Want Ha-rold, We Want Ha-rold."[79]

Finally, at 1:00 a.m., Washington made his entrance and the hall erupted — he had won the election, though by nothing like the overwhelming margin he had originally predicted. Washington had received just 51.4 percent of the vote, 656,727 ballots to 617,159 for Epton, a difference of less than 40,000. Washington did receive an impressive majority of the votes cast in the Latino community, but the support from whites could only be seen as disappointing, 12 percent overall, low even in the supposedly liberal lakefront wards. Yet again, Black Chicago won the election largely on its own, this time with an even larger turnout of 85 percent. Victory had only been possible because of near-unanimous turnout in places like the Third Ward, where Washington received 16,656 votes in the primary and now garnered 24,472, as compared with just 178 for Epton.[80]

Despite the racial divide so starkly evident in the voting results, the mayor-elect issued a conciliatory statement promising, "We will unify and rebuild a troubled but still vibrant city."[81]

But the headline on *The Defender*'s front page on the day after the election, April 13, 1983, was not so sanguine, expressing the enervation felt by many in the community: "Washington Wins, Dirtiest Election Is Over — Amen."

It was not a moment to celebrate. Rather, the newspaper urged Washington in another front-page editorial to immediately begin the process of assiduously producing "order out of chaos." The new mayor would at least have some support from several new aldermen who had benefited from his endorsement, including former Black Panther Bobby Rush, freshly elected to represent the Second Ward. But Mayor Washington would have to contend with a majority in the Chicago City Council that was made up of recalcitrant white aldermen, all of whom had been reelected in their own wards. The newspaper observed, moreover, that Washington's campaign staff "did not measure up to the standards we must have to keep Chicago the greatest city in the country" and stated flatly that his administration would have to do better. "Please, Harold, do your homework and make sound decisions based upon adequate information rather than decisions based on ego trippers."[82]

Still, for all the disillusionment, this was the high point for the African American struggle for political empowerment, the culmination of nearly a century of work by those who first arrived in the city for the 1893 World's Fair, commemorated by *Ebony* magazine as a moment of equal significance to the 1963 March on Washington and Joe Louis's victory over Max Schmeling in 1936. Washington's victory had even prompted both *Ebony* and *The Defender* to muse about a black candidate in the 1984 presidential elections, a conversation that would soon embolden Jesse Jackson. Washington's victory would also bring a recent college graduate named Barack Obama to Chicago with dreams of working for the administration. When he couldn't find a spot in City Hall, Obama found a position as a community organizer on the far South Side.[83]

*The Defender,* for its part, signaled that it would continue to play a critical role as a "Socratic gadfly" to Mayor Washington, just as it had to every previous mayor. For while the *Tribune, Sun-Times,* network television and radio stations had already decided that Washington was simply trying to replace a white apparatus with an inferior black one, *The Defender* understood that Washington was a different kind of leader: his mission really was to create a new kind of city government, one that transcended race to foster an equitable, diverse urban environment. In that spirit, when the mayor was right, he could count on the newspaper's support, and when he was wrong, he could be likewise certain that *The Defender* would hold him accountable.

With the election of Mayor Washington, Chicago had reasserted its role as a mighty garrison of those engaged in the ongoing struggle for racial justice. Meanwhile, in the nation's capital, President Ronald Reagan and his re-energized Republican Party were moving to unbridle market forces and dismantle the welfare state, an agenda they justified with racially coded language that made the "Chicago welfare queen" the nation's new bête noir.

It was long past the time when any one newspaper, television, or radio station could claim to speak for an entire people and *The*

*Defender* was struggling to hold on to its remaining readers, rather than expanding its audience. Nevertheless, *The Defender* continued to punch far above its weight, a resolute voice of conscience in a city rife with hatred, fear, and greed, and in a nation that was not nearly done expiating its original sin.

# 23

# Stick Around for a While

IN THE FALL of 1985, I arrived in Chicago to matriculate at the college of the University of Chicago in the South Side neighborhood of Hyde Park. I had visited the university just once before, on a cold, rainy weekend the previous spring, and was charmed by the school's Gothic structures shimmering on either side of the Midway as well as by the dour, disheveled, brilliant students I met on campus. This was the rigorous academic environment I was seeking, with the added benefit of being located in the middle of a big city. Throughout my high school years in Brighton, a comfortable, largely Jewish suburb of Rochester, New York, I longed for the excitement, diversity, and authenticity of a large metropolis, and Chicago fit the bill. Not quite as daunting as New York, it seemed the perfect portal through which to transition to an urban lifestyle.

As new students, however, we were treated to a lecture even before classes began from several well-armed officers of the university's three-hundred-strong police force, who warned us explicitly that the school occupied only a section of Hyde Park, an integrated, middle-class outpost surrounded by dangerous, poor, all-black neighborhoods. My own experiences on infrequent forays to the Loop or the North Side on public transportation tended to validate the officers' proscriptions, as I witnessed the numerous dilapidated, burned-out hulks and weed-strewn vacant lots, careful to evade the occasional would-be mugger or aggressive street gang.

I had other experiences of Black Chicago that were less offputting, of course. I feasted on the delicious fried food served through a Plexiglas turnstile at Harold's Chicken and spent late nights listening to Magic Slim and the Teardrops play the blues at the old Checkerboard

Lounge on Forty-Third Street. Although very few of my fellow students were black and none had grown up on the South Side, I worked alongside African Americans at my student jobs and befriended my neighbors when I rented an off-campus apartment.

Chicago's history was not covered in the courses I took for my major in English literature or for my minor concentration in South Asian civilization, nor was the city a topic in any of the core classes in physics, biology, sociology, and the humanities that were required for graduation. I was vaguely aware that Harold Washington was the city's first African American mayor but had no context in which to appreciate the significance of that accomplishment. I had heard that the city was called "Beirut by the Lake" for the political combat between Mayor Washington and a majority of the City Council, and knew that there was a racial dimension to their battles. But without any historical understanding, it seemed just another contest of atavistic tribal loyalties that would be shed as people evolved.

Fully immersed in my studies during my sophomore year, I failed to vote in either the primary or the general election of 1987 in which Washington was reelected, and though I was alarmed by the divisiveness of the campaign, I didn't know precisely whom to blame. Some months later, when Washington died suddenly of a heart attack at his desk, I was equally mystified by the outpouring of grief from Black Chicago. Why were people so upset over the death of a mere politician? I wondered.

I graduated two years later with a BA in English literature and moved to Wicker Park, a neighborhood on the city's Northwest Side just at the beginning stages of gentrification, with a trickle of white artists and young professionals infiltrating an area that was still mostly Puerto Rican and Polish. I dreamed of writing novels but needed to support myself in the interim, so I obtained a certification as a substitute teacher to work in the city's public school system while I sent out resumés for jobs at magazines specializing in literary criticism and fiction.

On a particular afternoon in the late fall of 1990, after over a year of stringing together teaching gigs and not finding writing jobs, I was sitting with a friend at a neighborhood Polish diner when I ran into Gordon Mayer, a fellow white, Jewish University of Chicago graduate who told me that he had been working as a copyeditor at *The Chicago*

*Defender,* a daily newspaper based on the South Side, but would soon be leaving to work for the UPI press service. I hadn't heard of *The Chicago Defender,* I told him, but the prospect of working at a newspaper sounded exciting and I convinced Gordon to recommend me as his replacement.

Gordon must have mentioned during our conversation that *The Defender* was an African American–owned newspaper, but I didn't really understand how, exactly, that was significant. On the day of my interview, I boarded the El train into the Loop and then took the bus south through a district of mostly derelict apartment buildings, factories, warehouses, and offices before getting out at the corner of Twenty-Fourth Street and Michigan Avenue. I paused outside the building, which, too, looked as if it was part of a bygone era: The words *Chicago Defender* were inscribed in a cursive font reminiscent of the 1950s, some of the windows were cracked, and on a rectangular tower jutting out of the building, two large clocks indicated two different times, both wrong.

Only when I was being led through the newsroom and saw that almost everyone there was black did it begin to dawn on me what *The Defender* was. Sitting down in the office of the city editor, Alberta Leak, I asked her, "Do white people work here?" It was an awkward way to begin a job interview, I realize in retrospect, although I meant it respectfully; that is to say, I did not want to waste her time if there was no way I could get the job because I happened not to be black. Luckily for me, Alberta laughed heartily. "Sure they do," she said. "*The Defender* has always had white employees."

Barely five feet tall, with a moon-shaped face, bright oval eyes, and a broad smile framed by loose strands of hair falling from her bun, Alberta sketched out the history of the newspaper, emphasizing *The Defender*'s influential role in both national politics and the civil rights movement. As for the job itself, the newspaper was published five times a week, Monday through Friday, she explained, which meant that the newsroom staff had to work Sunday through Thursday. The copyeditor's daily hours were from 8:30 a.m. to 7:00 p.m., with a two-hour lunch, and the pay was $18,000 a year.

It sounded like a dream job. Feeling comfortable with the way the interview was going, I decided I had nothing to lose by putting my whole story out there. I told Alberta about my family's experiences in concentration camps during the Holocaust as well as my dreams of becoming a writer, and talked about backpacking through Alaska and India, all in the hope that she would overlook the fact that my degree from the University of Chicago was in English lit, rather than journalism.

When I finished my spiel, Alberta told me about her own background. She had been a civil rights activist in her youth, then had married the son of the Rev. A. R. Leak, founder of the A. R. Leak and Sons Funeral Home, a highly profitable enterprise that commanded great respect in the community.

"Black people weren't allowed to own a lot of businesses in the old days," she explained. "But we could always have our own funeral homes and churches, because white folks didn't want to be buried with us and didn't want to sit next to us in their pews on Sunday morning. So preachers and funeral home owners, those are just about the only old-money folks we've got today."

At the end of the interview, Alberta led me out of her office to an empty desk in the corner of the newsroom, where she handed me a ten-page journalism test and wished me luck. The test included sections on editing, headline writing, current events, and story writing, and I applied myself diligently. But a half hour into it, I realized that the sweat rolling off my brow and the accumulating mucus in my throat were something more than nerves. Probably the flu, I thought.

Sniffling and shivering now, I glanced up to see another candidate for the job walk toward Alberta's office. He was white, too, slightly taller and thicker than me, with perfectly parted straight blond hair and wearing a tailored navy blue suit. Through Alberta's office window, I noticed him pulling out a neat sheaf of papers from a case that bore the Northwestern University logo. Unlike the University of Chicago, Northwestern offered an undergraduate degree in journalism, a program that included internships with prestigious publications, and I presumed that he must be showing Alberta clips of actual articles he'd written and published. Soon enough, Mr. Northwestern was sitting at the desk next to mine, taking his own test, which he managed to finish before I did, without glancing in my direction once.

I completed the test in a haze and stumbled out of the building feeling woozy. In the days that followed, the flulike symptoms revealed themselves to be the viral infection mononucleosis, leaving me unable to get out of bed for weeks. While I considered giving up on my urban sojourn and moving back to Rochester, I continued to call Alberta once a week, after forcing myself to get out of bed and drinking several mugs of piping hot tea to clear my throat. Each time, she told me they hadn't made a decision about the copyeditor's job and that I should call back the following week.

After six weeks of this routine, when I had thoroughly given up and was calling just for a sense of closure, Alberta told me I was hired. Dumbfounded, I happily accepted and came into work that Sunday charged with excitement, though only 75 percent recovered from the mononucleosis, and soon found myself overwhelmed, both physically and intellectually. The newsroom's sole copyeditor, I was equipped with an antiquated computer that lacked the capacity to check spelling or grammar and used a complicated coding system for all its commands.

Every morning, I would receive hand-drawn pages from the entertainment, features, and lifestyle editors with six-digit numbers corresponding to the stories I was supposed to edit. With open copies of a dictionary, thesaurus, and *The Associated Press Stylebook* at my side, I did my best to make every article readable, journalistically defensible, and appropriate in terms of length. I was never instructed in the tenets of "black journalism"—like most newspapers, *The Defender* followed AP style, imposing just a few of its own variations, capitalizing the word "Black" when it referred to people of African heritage, for instance. Without any education in the mechanics of journalism, I operated from a theoretical understanding that news writing should present multiple sides of an issue without bias and allow the readers to make up their own minds. That simplistic approach was sufficient, especially since in daily practice, my work was consumed by the challenge of making sure no misspellings or grammatical mistakes made it into print.

*The Defender* had by that point acquired such a reputation for typos and misspellings that longtime readers had taken it upon themselves to score the paper. I would often pick up my phone line to hear an older lady announce that she had been a loyal reader for decades, then proceed to chew me out for allowing this many mistakes to make it into print, embarrassing all African Americans with my carelessness and inattention. I could only apologize humbly and pledge to do better.

I had to finish the back pages before noon and then deliver them to the production department in the basement, where the articles were printed out in long strips, cut and pasted alongside ads and photos on a mockup of the paper while we waited for the news deadlines in the evening. I had about two hours of downtime, during which I would drive over to Chinatown nearby to buy some barbecued pork buns, and then return to eat them in the cafeteria. Sometimes I would check out the old printing press, silent but still glistening with old oil, or explore the ruined warehouses and car lots in the empty streets nearby. By late afternoon, the action would finally pick back up, and between 6:30 and 7:00 p.m. I would send the final pages down to production. Shortly thereafter, the whole package of cardboard pages was handed to a messenger, who carried it to *The Defender*'s contract printer on the Southwest Side. By 6:00 a.m. the next morning, some twenty-five thousand copies in bound, bulk bundles were loaded onto vans and delivered to newsstands across the metro area.

The other staff members were generally tolerant and friendly in those first few months, though my lack of grounding in African American culture sometimes led to awkward moments, as on the morning when I loudly asked the newsroom what "chitterlings" were. I made the mistake of pronouncing the word phonetically, prompting an eruption of laughter in the newsroom before someone kindly explained to me that "chitlins," as they were properly called, were spicy, cooked pork intestines, considered a culinary delicacy.

One day after I had been at *The Defender* for some months, Alberta Leak revealed that I had been her first choice for copyeditor, but she had had to engage in subterfuge to hire me. Her dilemma was that I had done well on the grammar sections of the journalism test but performed dismally on the journalism parts, while my blond competitor from Northwestern had done well on the whole exam. After considering the matter for several weeks, she was suddenly struck by inspiration: she disassembled both exams to create one high-performing candidate from the two tests, then put my name on the fused document and brought it up to her bosses.

I asked her why she had done that. "I just knew you *was* different," she laughed, emphasizing the word "was" for ironic effect. "I thought you would stick around for a while."

The first articles I opened every day usually began with the word "trickdog," a nonsense word Chinta Strausberg had invented for this purpose, followed by a string of expletives — these were stories she had written overnight and submitted via the phone lines through an early-model laptop computer. Sending text digitally was still a new and unproven technology in those days, and Chinta, invariably proper in her in-person speech and behavior, added the four-letter words to make sure none of her writing was cut off at the beginning and end. Nevertheless, I had to be vigilant in making sure none of the curse words found their way into print.

I was awed by the sheer volume of Chinta's output — at least five stories every day, on topics that ranged from local to international affairs. It was largely through her writing that I was familiarized with the pantheon of politicians, businesspeople, ministers, activists, and scholars as well as the community organizations, civic institutions, churches, and government agencies who mattered in Black Chicago.

As the weeks ticked by, I got to know the newsroom staffers around me through their writing as well as our interactions. Editorial Page Editor Walter Lowe was as infallibly kind, calm, and wise as his pages were grammatically clean, properly proportioned, and correctly coded. For each edition of the paper, Walter wrote an incisive and reasonable main editorial and also curated the letters to the editor as well as commentaries. Yet somehow this man always had time to peer patiently at me through his thick, plastic-framed glasses and respond to my endless queries about journalistic protocol, the city's history, and the myriad personages filling the pages of *The Defender.*

Behind me at a desk piled high with shaky stacks of press releases, movie stills, and wire story printouts sat fine arts editor Earl Calloway. Dressed in vintage three-piece suits and prone to break out into song, Earl interviewed a steady stream of celebrities and aspirants at his desk, all of whom he treated with the same respect and encouragement. One afternoon, for instance, he introduced me to a "talented young comedian," a slender man with a wry smile named Chris Rock who had just started performing on *Saturday Night Live.*

Another day, I picked up a call meant for Earl only to hear a mellifluous, high-pitched voice identify himself as Michael Jackson and say that he wanted to make sure Earl was coming to his latest concert in Chicago. Skeptical that the King of Pop was making a personal phone call to a Chicago newspaper writer, I yelled out, "Hey Earl, some guy pretending to be Michael Jackson is on the phone for you."

Stunned to learn that this was, in fact, Michael Jackson, I was better prepared a few months later when I picked up another call intended for Earl from Michael's sister Janet Jackson, who asked me to make sure Earl knew that his tickets were at the "will call" window, "as usual."

The features desk was manned by two editors from different generations: Soft-spoken, kind, and polite, Mattie Smith Colin cast an elegant figure in the newsroom in her furs and jewels; her articles on fashion, food, literature, and culture were crisply written and meticulously self-edited. Proud of having worked for the newspaper for many years, she never bragged about her work as a "hard news" reporter, though she had covered the return of Emmett Till's body to Chicago, among many other stories. Smith Colin's much younger colleague Natalie Pardo had been reared in Hyde Park by highly educated Haitian immigrant parents and brought a modern, worldly sensibility to her pages.

The only section I wasn't responsible for copyediting was sports — a good thing, too, since I have never been a fan of professional athletics — but I was seriously impressed with its editors, Ken Green, who had been a fresh college graduate during Harold Washington's 1983 campaign for mayor and was now a grizzled veteran, and Larry Gross, a slovenly yet brilliant writer and sports historian.

The newsroom's most respected figure, however, was neither a reporter nor an editor. Dr. Marjorie Stewart Joyner was already ninety-four years old when I started at the newspaper, but still came to work most days, driven to 2400 South Michigan in a Chicago Police squad car by a uniformed officer who escorted her to her desk in the corner and then unpacked her lunch. As chairman of the Chicago Defender Charities, she continued to organize the Billiken parades, which required months of preparation and promotion, much of which she accomplished by telephone from her desk. She might have taken one of the executive offices on the building's upper floors but Dr. Joyner preferred to stay in the newsroom with all the young faces. She would occasionally engage us with questions about our work, smiling benevolently and recounting her own experiences as lessons to learn from.

Within a few months, I had mastered copyediting to the point where I could meet my deadlines easily and there were far fewer errors in the paper — and far fewer calls from aggravated readers. Still, I sometimes regretted that as an editor, my best work appeared under someone else's byline, so I decided to try writing for the newspaper, beginning with a few short news pieces, book reviews, and commentaries. At the *Tribune,* say, or the *Sun-Times,* new reporters often had to struggle to get their articles in print but at *The Defender,* filling the pages of the daily issues was a perennial challenge and once it became known that I could write fairly competently, I began to receive assignments.

At the end of May 1991, Walter Lowe asked me to write an obituary for Ethel Payne, who had died alone in her Washington apartment at the age of seventy-nine. Walter gave me a large folder filled with biographical information, lists of awards, and copies of Payne's articles, which I now read through, learning with a certain amount of awe about her work in military social services during the occupation of Japan and the beginning of her work at *The Defender,* her confrontation with President Eisenhower, the trip to the Bandung Conference, and her coverage of the war in Vietnam, among her many adventures and accomplishments. While I was still in the midst of this folder, I glanced up and saw Walter smiling at me. John Sengstacke wanted to be quoted in the story as well, he told me.

I nervously followed Walter upstairs to the executive offices on the second floor and was ushered inside, where Sengstacke was sitting impatiently behind a large desk. Dressed smartly in a tailored shirt with the sleeves folded neatly onto his forearms, improbably lithe for his eighty years, he sat back in his leather chair, an extralong lit cigarette dangling from his lip, and told me to write down that Payne had added greatly to the newspaper's credibility. "Ethel was a good friend," he began. "She was an excellent reporter for *The Defender* covering the White House and traveling the world for us."

This was my first peek into *The Defender*'s illustrious history. Just a few weeks later, I was assigned to cover an editorial board meeting with Mayor Richard M. Daley, who had finally been elected mayor in the wake of Harold Washington's untimely demise. I considered this assignment a great privilege and came to the office early that morning wearing my best khakis and my only tie, then joined Walter Lowe and several others in the lobby when it was time to greet the mayor, who arrived just on time with an entourage of burly plainclothes policemen and several aides.

Mr. Sengstacke kept us waiting for several minutes and then descended the staircase quickly. Without pausing, he pinched Daley's elbow and wordlessly guided him back out the front door, waving at the bodyguards to remain in the lobby. I stared at the door wondering what I should do, but after a few minutes, with Mr. Sengstacke and the mayor still outside and the entourage settled into the easy chairs in the lobby, I decided to go back to my desk.

Confused as to what had transpired, I looked out the window to Twenty-Fourth Street below and saw Mr. Sengstacke gesturing forcefully at the broken sidewalk and shattered curb outside the building, while Mayor Daley stood nodding thoughtfully. The mayor never came back into the building for the editorial board meeting. He finished examining the sidewalk, collected his entourage from the lobby, and got back into his waiting limousine.

When I arrived in the morning, a crew from the city's Streets and Sanitation Department was already hard at work repairing the sidewalk.

As the second Saturday in August approached, the entire *Defender* staff shifted gears and prepared for the Billiken Parade. Dr. Joyner was busier than ever, talking on the telephone, coordinating her small army of volunteers and paid staff, and deciding on the all-important order of the politicians, floats, and marchers. The editorial department was also busy producing extra feature articles, historical pieces, and photo-essays to fill out the ad-packed Billiken weekend parade edition.

Parade day that year was gloriously hot and sunny, and I arrived at the reviewing stand in Washington Park a little after 10:00 a.m., just in time to see John Sengstacke seated in the back of a yellow convertible alongside Mayor Daley as the crowds lining the route cheered and applauded. Behind them, the long convoy of floats representing politicians and black-owned businesses and corporations inched

along, followed by the marchers, dancers, and groups of smiling tod-
dlers, simply thrilled to be walking along Martin Luther King Drive.

After a few hours in the reviewing stand, I decided to walk along
the route myself, strolling down the boulevard and back into Washington Park, where vendors were selling barbecue, hot dogs, and African curios. The entire community was out—young and old, wealthy
and indigent, teenage boys in baggy jeans scoping teenage girls in
miniskirts and perfectly sculptured hairdos, dapper gentlemen in
matching shorts, shirts, and hats elbow to elbow with church ladies
in elegant, modest dresses. I marveled at the southern drawls mixing
with crisp northern enunciation, Caribbean English, Haitian Creole,
and continental African languages. Amid this ingathering of the African Diaspora, I occasionally caught sight of Dr. Joyner zooming up
and down the parade route in a golf cart, inspecting the volunteers
and making sure that any crises were being resolved appropriately.

I kept writing more and more, squeezing in as many reporting assignments as I could between my copyediting duties. At the end of
July 1992, I even got to try my hand at national politics when I covered a press conference from the new Democratic nominee for president, a little-known Arkansas governor named Bill Clinton. Luckily
for me, the event had been scheduled out in La Grange, a suburb at
the southwestern edge of Cook County, and none of the other reporters wanted to go, so I quickly finished up my pages and jumped into
the dusty Volkswagen Scirocco belonging to *Defender* chief photographer Walter S. Mitchell III.

We arrived late after a long, hot drive, in the course of which we
had to ask for directions several times, but Clinton was, characteristically, even later yet, so we had plenty of time to kibitz with the other
journalists gathered around a sumptuous buffet in the campaign's
media tent on the lawn of La Grange Memorial Hospital. With his
week-old beard and tan, multipocketed vest, Mitchell fit right in with
the other photographers, but he was also very popular with the reporters, television cameramen, and even the on-air personalities. I
took note of *The New York Times* reporter writing careful notes in a
college-lined spiral notebook and the network television guys with
perfectly coiffed hair and suit jackets over jeans and sneakers.

Reflecting the Democrats' newfound dedication to women's issues, the event was sponsored by Y-Me, the breast cancer survivors' support group, and on the stage with Clinton was Carol Moseley Braun, a black woman and minor Cook County official who had swiped the Democratic nomination from incumbent Alan Dixon in a wave of voter outrage over Dixon's support for the ultraconservative Supreme Court nominee Clarence Thomas. Actually a loyal functionary in the new machine being built by the new Mayor Daley, Moseley Braun had nonetheless managed to tap into a restive African American electorate as well as suburban women, both key constituencies for Clinton's bid for the White House. "You look beautiful," Moseley Braun told the crowd, ignoring a small but noisy group of antiabortion protesters. "You're going to put this country back on track."

In his remarks, Bill Clinton focused on his pledge to reform the health care system, arguing that the problems with the high cost of care were "at the core of our national discontent."

He listed his other campaign promises as well, installing more controls over the financial sector to prevent another savings and loan crisis, reducing the size of the military, free trade that would "bring Mexicans up without bringing Americans down," and creating programs to move people "from welfare to work."[1]

That fall, I finally left the copyediting desk altogether and took over the police beat, a position that came with no increase in salary but with the prestigious title of "investigative reporter." Now I spent the first half of my day at *The Defender*'s designated desk in the smoke-filled press room at police headquarters, where I collected information on homicides, assaults, robberies, rapes, and other serious crimes. My job was to pick four or five incidents for the "Police Roundup" appearing on page 4 of every issue and then focus on one particularly interesting crime as a main story.

Chicago, in those years, was reeling from the recent introduction of crack cocaine, which drove ferocious competition among African American and Latino gangs for control of high-traffic street corners and public housing buildings where they could sell it. In neighborhoods where factory jobs had evaporated, leaving behind hundreds of thousands of suddenly impoverished families, the infusion of crack created an attendant scene of desperate addicts who preyed on each other and, in turn, became prey for the multiple serial killers lurking in the city's abandoned buildings and alleys.

Overall, the city suffered more than a thousand murders each year, and a siege mentality had set in within the overwhelmingly white police force. Most of the officers I dealt with were suspicious of reporters and particularly hostile to *The Defender,* which they resented for what they saw as its excessive focus on cases of police brutality. As a white guy working for *The Defender,* moreover, I was subject to an extra dollop of skepticism, even if my city-issued press pass compelled them to cooperate to some extent. But eventually I was able to develop productive relationships with a select number of sergeants in the various violent crimes units around the city. Photographer Walter Mitchell, too, proved an invaluable mentor, teaching me what details to record at a crime scene and how to talk to the grieving relatives of crime victims.

On the morning of October 13, just a few weeks into my tenure, I arrived at police headquarters a little late and read the following typed report at the top of that day's log:

> 1000 Plan I Homicide 18th District     502 W. Oak St. (CHA)
> Dantrel Davis, M/B/7, of same address, pronounced DOA at Children's Mem. Hospital from gsw to the head. Vict. was w/his mother in front of the building when sniper fired a shot from one of the buildings, striking the vict.
> CHA Police Crime Lab Med Exam A6 VC

Translating the police shorthand, I learned that a seven-year-old African American boy named Dantrell (correctly spelled with two *l*'s) Davis, had been shot by a sniper in front of his public housing building. "CHA" stood for Chicago Housing Authority, and from the address, I knew that the shooting had taken place in Cabrini-Green, the city's most infamous housing project. The code "Plan I Homicide" indicated that this was a big deal. I called the sergeant at the Area 6 Violent Crimes Unit, who confirmed that, indeed, the little boy had been hit while crossing the street from the high-rise where he lived to his elementary school.

"The kid was just standing there with his mother, waiting for the final school bell to ring," Sergeant Frank Kajari told me, "when shots rang out from a nearby building and he got hit with a single gunshot to the head." The gunman had apparently fired multiple times with a high-powered rifle from a nearby high-rise, perhaps aiming at a group of teenagers standing somewhat within the same field of fire as the elementary school kids.

That day, I spoke with two teachers who had been standing in the kill zone trying to get students into the school when the little boy was hit. Without hesitation, they stayed on the scene, braving additional sniper fire as they tried to stanch his bleeding. "I kept telling [Dantrell's mother] that he would be OK," recounted one teacher. "But then I saw a lot of blood pouring out of his head onto the street."

"An awful lot of blood," added the other.[2]

I only dared make a short foray into one of the high-rises that day, stepping through a doorway that had no door into a dark lobby smelling of urine, garbage, and moldy concrete. Though the space was empty at that moment, I could see plenty of evidence of the grim reality of this place: Artless graffiti, mostly scribbled names followed by the letters "RIP," covered the visible portions of the walls from the floor up, while many of the doors of the mailboxes had clearly been pried open and others showed thick soot streaks from where they had been burned.

In my short time on the beat, I had already seen several children murdered with little public response and didn't expect this case to be any different. Two other children had been killed in Cabrini-Green earlier that year and nothing had been done to make the development a safer place. But I hadn't taken into account the fact that we were just one month away from a national election. A few days after the murder, Chinta covered a rally in Chicago's downtown Loop in which Bill Clinton, now riding high in the polls, criticized incumbent president George H. W. Bush for failing to sign a crime bill that would have added police officers to the streets of big cities. Cabrini-Green stood just a few blocks west of the conspicuous wealth and tourist attractions of the Gold Coast, a contrast that Clinton used as a metaphor for the bifurcated opportunities of the Reagan/Bush era. "We have an obligation to the children who cry themselves to sleep because our streets are dangerous," Clinton said. "We owe it to Dantrell Davis."[3]

The day after Clinton's rally, the managing editor called me at home and told me to go straight to Cabrini-Green instead of police headquarters. When I arrived, I was shocked to see that a great expeditionary force had occupied the development. Hundreds of Chicago police officers and city workers were flanked by sheriff's deputies and teams of federal agents from the FBI, Drug Enforcement Agency, and Bureau of Alcohol, Tobacco and Firearms as well as CHA's own police force. Sleek-looking armor-plated mobile command trailers had been planted in the vacant lots while a state police helicopter whirred overhead. A unit of television trucks, from local stations as well as national networks, had set up operations near the police command.

Heavily armed officers moved from building to building, establishing a perimeter and then searching everyone coming in and out, frisking men and women, going through purses and shopping bags, and even looking in infants' diapers. Once the buildings were secure, crews of city workers cut down trees and installed new, supposedly bulletproof entrance/exit turnstiles as tow trucks chained, jacked, and hauled away numerous burnt-out car chassis. Gang markings were erased with specially designed graffiti blasters and CHA officials roamed about with clipboards looking for squatters to evict.

This "sweep" was ostensibly intended to rid Cabrini-Green of the gangs once and for all. But the sniper who shot Dantrell Davis had already confessed to the crime, and the great fanfare preceding this police action, including a televised press conference from Mayor Daley, had provided the gangs with plenty of time in which to move or hide their guns, drugs, and personnel.

On the second day of the sweep, I joined a half-dozen television cameramen and reporters accompanying an "inspection team." Our team consisted of two men, one white police officer from the city force and one black officer from CHA's own three-hundred-person police force as well as a black woman CHA inspector bearing a clipboard. Reporters in tow, this team went door to door through an entire high-rise searching for guns, drugs, illegal tenants, or anything else. In almost every case, the information on the CHA official's clipboard was incorrect. Apartments that were supposed to be occupied showed signs of being vacant for an extended period of time, while in other units that were supposed to be empty we found families cooking lunch.

In a few units where residents did not answer the door, the officers simply kicked them in, guns drawn. But at apartment 305, the door was opened promptly by Katrina Harden, a trim, fashionably dressed young woman with perfectly straightened hair who listened for a moment to the inspector's garbled explanation as to why a gaggle of reporters was standing there and then announced, guardedly but without shame, "Y'all can come in."

I followed the others into the living room. The floor was covered with a plush, sky-blue carpet and crisp, white curtains billowed over the windows as furnishings and curios floated tastefully in the corners or against the walls, producing the effect of a placid lake. An indignant toddler, rustling gently in his immaculate white diaper, gazed at the noisy group of reporters scribbling in their notebooks or aiming their giant lenses at him. Watching the reporters move through her home, his mother set her jaw in a firm but cooperative pose. "It's about time they did this," she said. "Some nights, you have to lie on the floor to hide from the bullets."[4]

As the sweep operation entered into its second week, Chinta covered a major announcement from Chicago's African American gangs at a community organization on the edge of Cabrini-Green. Flanked by a coalition of storefront ministers, Black Muslims, Hebrew Israelites, and civil rights activists including Lu Palmer, a coalition of representatives of the major gangs held a press conference to declare a citywide truce, explaining that they had sent orders down to the street level to immediately stop the violence. "We have all made mistakes, being men," said Al-Jami Mustafa, King of the Cobra Nation. "But today, we are asking you to have the will to forgive as men and give us this opportunity to correct our mistakes as men for the benefit of the future as a nation of people."[5]

Mayor Daley and police officials immediately dismissed the truce, complaining that the gangs were merely trying to get the police out of Cabrini-Green. I myself was skeptical, particularly when, on the first day after the truce, I found three gang-related shootings on the police log, and I reported them in a special box on the front page. But on the following mornings, I did notice that the number of intergang shootings on the South and West Sides had decreased markedly.

The police, on the other hand, proved less than their word and did not maintain a presence in the community. On November 2, the day before the national election, the sweep force decamped from Cabrini-Green. In just a few hours, all the uniformed officers and federal agents with their trucks and helicopters were gone, and with them, all the television cameras and newspaper reporters.[6]

Our own attention in the newsroom turned as well to the national election and then to the formation of Bill Clinton's administration, the first Democratic administration in twelve years. But in January 1993, I approached managing editor Michael Brown and asked him to formally include CHA issues in my portfolio. Michael looked at me carefully after I posed this question, narrowing his eyes behind his thick glasses and stroking his thick goatee. Corpulent, intense, and quick-witted, Michael had a PhD from the University of Chicago under his belt and a sophisticated understanding of *The Defender*'s role in the community. "OK," he said at last, extending his index finger in my direction. "But I want to see residents quoted in every story. Not deep in the story either. In the lede. That means your story begins with 'Mrs. Jones said . . .' not 'CHA officials said . . .'"

A sizable percentage of the newspaper's daily copies were sold in the developments, Michael continued, and my articles would be read carefully by residents. If I made any mistakes, they would be sure to let me know even before he did.

In June 1993, I wrote about a sixteen-year-old resident of the ABLA Homes public housing development who saved nine of his younger siblings and cousins from a fire in their apartment. Waking to the sound of an alarm and a room full of smoke, Greg Wilson had kept calm, waking the sleeping children around him and organizing their escape through the window when firefighters arrived. Wilson's courage was all the more remarkable because he had been shot earlier that year during a fight with rival gang members and left partially paralyzed so that he used a wheelchair.

The day this story ran, Dr. Joyner asked me to come to her desk, where she told me that she had been deeply moved by the article and asked for Wilson's contact information. One week after that, she asked me to come along with her to a youth club near ABLA. Inside, dozens of neighborhood children were assembled to see her present Wilson with an award and a $500 check. Wilson, sitting in a wheelchair, his baseball cap turned respectfully backward, sat next to Dr. Joyner in her wheelchair, focused along with the youths in the audience. "Any time anybody saves a life," she told them, her voice quaking but strong, "they are a hero."[7]

Soon after this event, Dr. Joyner's health began to fail. Her appearances at the office became less frequent and, for the first time in decades, she even missed that summer's Billiken Parade. Finally, the following December, just after her ninety-eighth birthday, the newsroom received the inevitable, yet deeply sad, news of her passing.[8]

In early July 1993, the newsroom was abuzz over Nelson Mandela's visit to Chicago as part of his tour of the United States on the eve of the first race-inclusive elections in South Africa. Mandela had been released from prison just two years earlier and this trip through the United States was a fundraising tour for the African National Congress, which was transforming itself from an underground revolutionary group into a modern political party.

I backed up Chinta during Mandela's whirlwind, two-day tour of the city, beginning with a raucous public event at Operation PUSH where an overflow of thousands of people spilled onto the steps and the lawn listening to the proceedings from giant speakers erected in the grass. In a tone more grave than celebratory, Mandela briefly described his African National Congress as the only party capable of leading South Africa and avoiding violence before Jesse Jackson took the microphone and began the fundraising drive in earnest. One by one, Jackson called out individuals he recognized in the crowd and demanded that they write a large check, exhorting them to give more if he deemed their donation insufficient. Spotting Bobby Sengstacke standing in the aisles snapping pictures of Mandela with a telephoto lens, Jackson forced him to empty his wallet into a basket being passed through the pews.[9]

Later that same day, Mayor Daley and the city's corporate leaders hosted Mandela at the enclosed winter garden on the top floor of the new Harold Washington Library in the Loop, where the South African leader smiled warmly as he donned a Chicago Cubs hat and jacket, but gave precisely the same message he had at Operation PUSH in the same serious tone.

"We expect you to join with the democratic forces in the fight against tyranny and racism," Mandela told the well-heeled audience sipping cocktails. "We are not concerned with color. We are concerned with ideas."[10]

Amid all the excitement surrounding Mandela's visit, however, John Sengstacke was furious. The South African leader had completely neglected the black press during his U.S. tour, even though *The Defender* had covered the antiapartheid struggle and the African National Congress since the very beginning, even when the white-owned media insisted on describing Mandela and his cohort as terrorists — when they didn't simply ignore South Africa altogether. In a front-page editorial entitled "Wake Up Mandela," Sengstacke chastised Mandela for ignoring *The Defender* and the rest of the NNPA, an unacceptable oversight that he said raised questions about the competence of the whole ANC. As always, Sengstacke was taking the lead for the black press, upholding its honor even as its influence was waning along with that of his own publication.[11]

Bobby Sengstacke took over as managing editor in the fall of 1993 with the aim of injecting creative energy into the newsroom and remaking *The Defender*'s front page with photos and features. Bobby strongly resembled his father in appearance as well as demeanor, though he was taller and more casual, favoring a neatly pressed photographer's vest over the tailored suit jacket his father wore. Where his father was aloof, moreover, Bobby was gregarious; his office positively hummed — and sometimes roared — with conversation and laughter from an ever-changing crew of visiting journalists, photographers, and artists as well as businessmen, community activists, clergymen, and hustlers. At rousing meetings with the reporters and editors, he talked of restoring *The Defender*'s glory and making it a real competitor for the *Sun-Times* and the *Tribune*.

In October, Bobby recruited me to work with him on a special series on artists and musicians that he conceived as a showcase of the newspaper's deep connections within the community. We began in the Valley, a neighborhood just south of Provident Hospital named for a slight depression in the city's topography. Though it looked just like many of the battered sections of the South Side, Bobby knew that this tiny quadrant had produced a disproportionate number of artists and musicians. As we walked the streets together, Bobby saw only jewels among the ruins. Pointing at one burned-out hulk of a church, he talked about a music program in the basement where an esteemed teacher from the early years of jazz taught a new generation. Passing a rather forbidding alley strewn with garbage and debris, Bobby pointed out the fading outline of a mural and recalled that this had been the "Universal Alley," a cultural gathering spot and the original site of an annual jazz concert called the "Valley Fest."

In the series "Tales from the Valley" and the other projects on which I worked with Bobby, we focused on artists who had been ignored by the mainstream, the noble souls whose treasures remained hidden in the community's tattered corners. In one ramshackle apartment building, we found Daniel Polk, a disabled elderly artist known as the Sandman, who created elaborate crowns from found objects. For decades before his health had failed him, Polk had physically swept the streets of the Valley to try to maintain the neighborhood's spirit, so he saw his crowns as a symbolic way for him to continue maintaining the community. "I wanted them to be streets of hope instead of streets of dope," Polk told me, craning his neck toward the window from the hospital bed he had set up in his living room. "In my mind, I have never stopped cleaning these streets."[12]

*The Defender* often seemed to me like it was the last redoubt of tolerance and integration in an era of ascendant conservatism. To be sure, the newspaper sometimes made embarrassing missteps, as when it responded to racist statements from the prime minister of Japan by printing messages about "Japanese Americans who control America with the Green Dollar," which, in turn, prompted a vigorous protest from the Japanese American Service League.

But at a time when homophobia and paranoia over AIDS were rife both inside and outside the African American community, I was assigned to write features about the Kupona Network, one of the few organizations in the community with members who were openly gay and HIV positive. My interview with Bill McGill, a Kupona activist who had been living with AIDS for several years, was printed on the front page with a portrait photo under the headline "Profile of Courage."[13]

In February 1994, Michael Brown added one more item to my portfolio, the Nation of Islam. It was sure to be a contentious appointment, given just how much the Nation's leader, Louis Farrakhan, was under fire for anti-Semitic and anti-white remarks he had made recently. Still, I was dispatched as *The Defender*'s reporter to Savior's Day, the Black Muslims' annual gathering at the University of Illinois Pavilion. Inside, once I passed through a metal detector and pat down from the Nation's taciturn security detail, I found an enthusiastic mass of fifteen thousand riveted to the speeches and appearances from Farrakhan and his guests, including black nationalist icon Kwame Ture, formerly Stokely Carmichael.

Farrakhan spoke spontaneously for hours, interspersing a stream of black nationalist ideas with stories of the wisdom of Elijah Muhammad as well as his own idiosyncratic interpretations of Islam, Christianity, American race relations, numerology, and other topics. At the crescendo, Farrakhan held aloft a copy of a recent edition of *Time* magazine with his own scowling visage on its cover under the headline "Ministry of Rage," and fumed about an overarching conspiracy of Jewish media tycoons who were trying to destroy him. "This is not a ministry of rage," Farrakhan insisted. "This is a ministry of love and divine truth."[14]

After my story ran, Michael Brown certainly did receive a number of telephone calls from several midlevel Nation representatives who questioned his decision to send a "white boy" to cover "the Minister," as they referred to Farrakhan. But Michael stood by me, arguing that the reporter wasn't important if the reportage was accurate, and not long after, he got another call, this time from Leonard Muhammad, Farrakhan's son-in-law and chief of staff, who said that I had quoted Farrakhan correctly and described the event just as it happened, "even better," Muhammad had said, "than some of the so-called black reporters who work for the white newspapers."

And so I was allowed to stay on the Nation of Islam beat. That spring, Farrakhan came to *The Defender* for an editorial board meeting in which he made an overture to "that secular community that really forms Jewish opinion," offering to meet with representatives to hash out differences in the interest of rebuilding the partnership that had existed between African Americans and Jews during the civil rights crusades.[15]

A few weeks after that, we were visited by Abraham Foxman, the executive director of the Anti-Defamation League of B'nai B'rith, the Jewish organization taking the lead in demanding Farrakhan's political isolation and disqualification from government contracts. Sitting in the board room under Robert Abbott's portrait, Foxman declared that Farrakhan was "not our enemy" and reciprocated the offer to meet.[16]

Ultimately, nothing came of these tentative steps toward a rapprochement as the ADL's board balked at its leader's overtures just as reflexively as Farrakhan's inner circle. There was just too much bitterness between these two organizations, and perhaps between the two communities, to make peace at that moment. The truth was that Farrakhan was just then gaining influence within black America, and his anti-Semitism only strengthened his image as a defiant iconoclast, in some quarters. But at least *The Defender* had done its best to bring them together and, by keeping me on the Nation beat, continued to make a silent statement about exactly where it stood on the issue of racial separatism versus integration.

In March 1994, I drove to the Little Village neighborhood on the city's Southwest Side to cover a march organized by a local branch of Public Allies, part of President Clinton's youth public service initiative. The march had been billed as an effort in multiracial solidarity, a rare enough event in those days that the press release caught the editor's attention. I arrived in Little Village, a solidly Mexican American neighborhood just west of the sprawling Cook County Jail complex where the street signs were all in Spanish, to find this march exactly as advertised: marching shoulder to shoulder were Latinos, African Americans, and white college types. Mayor Daley was there as well, striding forward alongside this veritable rainbow of youth, an enthusiastic grin on his face.

Intrigued, I made my way to the head of the march and introduced myself to Public Allies' local executive director, the tall, beautiful, and brilliant Michelle Obama. Interviewing her briefly as we walked, I asked her about Public Allies' connections to the Clinton and Daley administrations. At the end of our conversation, Michelle smiled and asked me, "Have you ever met my husband, Barack?"

I hadn't — he was then a former organizer and part-time law school professor finishing his memoir — but recognizing "Barack" as a common Israeli name, from the Hebrew word meaning "lightning," I concluded that Michelle's husband must be Jewish.[17]

I had taken Michael Brown's mandate on the public housing beat seriously, focusing my coverage on residents' lives, both their travails and their accomplishments under these adverse circumstances. There was no shortage of topics: I found families in Cabrini-Green who endured wintertime floods that left icy water ankle-deep in their apartments for days, describing children doing their homework by lamplight while they wore rubber boots that splashed beneath the kitchen table.

I got to know the resident leaders, too, almost always older women with a knack for street-level politics, some of them highly adept at collaborating with the CHA, while others fought ongoing campaigns against the agency in the streets and in court. I also established a wide network of CHA employees, press spokespersons, police officers, youth workers, building managers, and warehouse employees, many of them residents themselves contending with an absurd lack of resources for the myriad problems they confronted daily.

Although nominally under mayoral control, the agency was run by Chairman Vince Lane independently of the Daley administration with a budget that was allocated directly from the federal government. Charismatic and brilliant, Lane had a background in urban development and spoke of transforming public housing by demolishing the high-rises and replacing them with scattered site housing throughout the city. He was also African American, which made him threatening to Mayor Daley, a tension that was heightened by persistent rumors that Lane wanted to run for office, though he steadfastly denied that, as any true political player would.

When President Clinton announced that he would visit Robert Taylor Homes in June 1994, I made sure that my credentials were in order and, early that morning, joined the presidential press pool to watch Clinton jog along the city's lakefront before being bundled into a caravan and driven into the heart of the development. When we entered the lobby of one of the Robert Taylor high-rises, I noticed that it had been thoroughly swept and cleaned so that it smelled more like bleach than urine. The ubiquitous graffiti had been painted over and the mailboxes had been repaired as well.

The Secret Service agents and presidential staff were hypervigilant as we left our vehicles, although the national press corps was nonchalant, seemingly bored by yet another locale on the presidential route. Many were looking forward to attending a World Cup game at Soldier Field that afternoon.

The president, joined now by First Lady Hillary Clinton, toured a dingy CHA police substation in the building, moving through a series of dimly lit chambers until he reached the evidence room, where he examined a table laden with seized weapons, AK-47 assault rifles and Tec-9 pistols among them. Then he paused, glancing in the direction of the assembled reporters, to indicate that he would take questions. I paused for a moment, then jumped at the opportunity, asking President Clinton if he supported the warrantless sweeps of public housing buildings as a solution to the endemic violence that terrorized residents in their own homes, homes that were federally funded and supervised.

President Clinton, lean and lawyerly in person, focused his eyes on mine for a moment and then surprised me by saying that he supported the sweeps. Remarkably well versed on the legal limitations of this police tactic, the president compared them to going through a metal detector at the airport.

"There are children here," Clinton said. "There are working people. There are mothers and fathers. They deserve a chance to live in safety."

My question momentarily sparked some interest from the other reporters, who asked the president if this approach risked trampling the civil liberties of American citizens. But Clinton held firm, arguing that the sweeps were consistent with the approach of the crime bill he was just then driving through the U.S. Congress. If passed, this legislation would pay municipalities to hire a hundred thousand police officers across the nation while also delivering a small pool of dollars for recreational programs such as midnight basketball.[18]

Walter Lowe's editorial in the next edition of *The Defender* didn't focus on the sweeps or the crime bill, however. What he wanted to know was, if the CHA was able to muster the resources to spruce up the Robert Taylor Homes for the president's visit, then why was the agency unable to maintain conditions on other days?

"We are in total sympathy with the residents' complaints," Walter wrote, "and wonder what is so terribly wrong with the system that it can make such needed changes for the president's visit but can't do so for the residents of Robert Taylor Homes."[19]

"Ninety years ago, Mr. Robert Sengstacke Abbott published the first edition of *The Chicago Defender*," began a front-page editorial in *The Defender*'s May 6, 1995, weekend edition. "Sitting at the kitchen table of a Chicago rooming house, he pounded out that edition's first stories on a battered typewriter. Although he was a lawyer by training, he knew he could accomplish a lot more with a newspaper than in a courtroom to right the wrongs committed against Black America.

"It turns out he was right. The pages of this newspaper have heralded the successes and lamented the failures of Black America," the editorial summed up. "But the hard work lies ahead of us, not behind us."[20]

Consumed with my own work in those days, I barely noticed that *The Defender* had reached this important milestone. The ninetieth edition was filled with photos and articles tracing the newspaper's history, many of which I had seen before. From reading the newspaper every day for four years, I knew a little bit about Robert Abbott and his role in the Great Migration as well as the accomplishments of Ida B. Wells-Barnett, Oscar De Priest, Jesse Binga, and their cohort.

But Chicago these days had little resemblance to a Promised Land. Gone were the industrial jobs that had once been so abundant, while crime and poverty were on the increase in just about every black neighborhood. Though the data was not yet in, the editorial sensed something that we felt viscerally whenever we looked at block after block of empty storefronts, abandoned buildings, and empty lots. After nine straight decades of growth, Chicago's African American community was shrinking as thousands slipped away from the city, some for the suburbs and others for cities in other parts of the country, including Atlanta and other southern urban centers. The city's black population would dip only slightly in the years I was at *The Defender* but the reverse exodus kicked into high gear during the next decade, as Black Chicago lost 20 percent of its population.[21]

A scout for the multitudes who escaped Jim Crow during the Great Migration, *The Defender* was now a rear guard as their descendants increasingly abandoned Chicago for someplace better.

At the end of May 1995, I dashed to the Loop to cover a press conference from HUD Secretary Henry Cisneros, who announced that his agency was taking direct control of the Chicago Housing Authority. Tall, aquiline, and serene, Cisneros, a former mayor of San Antonio, Texas, allowed that for the foreseeable future, the CHA would be run by HUD officials dispatched from Washington, D.C. The takeover, he insisted, was not directed at Vince Lane, who, like his entire board, had resigned voluntarily, nor was the CHA chairman under any criminal investigation, for the moment. Cisneros even asserted that the agency would move to expedite Lane's vision for CHA by demolishing buildings at the Cabrini-Green and Henry Horner developments in the near term.

Bobby Rush, now the U.S. representative from the historic First District, charged that Mayor Daley had engineered the takeover to remove Lane as a potential rival, but regarded HUD as a neutral party and therefore did not protest its installation at CHA. "HUD will not allow policies to be dictated by the mayor," Rush said when he emerged from a meeting with Cisneros. "[Daley] is just concerned with the contracts and the jobs — he's not concerned with the residents."[22]

The following month, the mayor's minions were dispatched to take over the Chicago Public Schools, an even larger, equally independent public agency that was still packed with many appointees from the days of Harold Washington's administration. Promising "accountability" from teachers, principals, and employees, Daley convinced the state legislature to grant him the power to appoint a new board as well as new top staff members, and then promptly installed his former chief of staff as chairman and his former budget director as CEO of the school system. "Business as usual is over," the mayor declared. "The bureaucrats who stand in the way of change will be removed and their power dissolved."

If the CHA and the public schools continued to serve the African American population in the city, the mayor made sure that they would never again serve as points of resistance to his rule. The political movement that had offered so much hope to Black Chicago seemed to have died with Harold Washington, while this new Mayor Daley was rapidly coming to dominate city politics as his father had done, co-opting whatever elements of the black community he was unable to neutralize.[23]

That summer, *The Defender*'s front page was dominated by the trial of a South Side congressman that would have far-reaching consequences for the city and ultimately the nation. Accused of the statutory rape of a sixteen-year-old campaign worker, U.S. Representative Mel Reynolds, a well-spoken former Rhodes Scholar, vehemently denied the charge and took the case to trial, claiming that he was the victim of an extortion scheme. But when prosecutors gave the girl immunity from prosecution, she reluctantly testified that they had, in fact, had intercourse, prompting the salacious headline quoting the witness on the front page, "We had sex."[24]

Reynolds, found guilty, was sentenced to five years in prison, and that fall, once he was formally pried from office, the congressional seat for Illinois Second District, a heavily Democratic, African American area stretching into the first ring of suburbs south of the city limits, was declared vacant. A special election was scheduled with the all-important party primary on November 28 and general balloting just two weeks later.

The three leading candidates were all prominent black Democrats: Emil Jones, the leader of the Democratic minority in the state senate, an ally of Mayor Daley's; Alice Palmer, a fellow state senator who had the support of activists and intellectuals, women's groups, and white progressives in Hyde Park, South Shore, and its environs; and Jesse Jackson Jr., the thirty-year-old son of the Operation PUSH leader.

Despite the formidable competition, Palmer began her campaign confidently by declaring that she was all-in the congressional race, even going so far as to name a successor for her state senate seat, an attorney named Barack Obama. Chinta Strausberg profiled Obama in the middle of September in an article entitled "Harvard Lawyer Eyes Palmer Seat," describing his upbringing in Hawaii as well as his background as a neighborhood organizer and as the first black president of the *Harvard Law Review.* "My entire adult life has been devoted to community service," Obama, then thirty-four, told Strausberg, pledging to create jobs and promote ownership among African Americans.[25]

On November 28, Jesse Jackson Jr. won an outright majority of the votes in the Democratic primary, having assembled an impressive field operation and sophisticated media team, while Palmer came in a distant third. Some of her supporters argued she should cancel her endorsement of Obama and run for reelection to her state senate seat, pointing out that the Democratic primary for state offices would not be held until the following March and there was still time for her to get the necessary signatures.

Palmer was reluctant to go back on her word, but her die-hard supporters turned to *The Defender* to express their concern that the inexperienced Obama would lose to a Daley crony. "We have asked her to reconsider not running because we don't think Obama can win," Robert Starks, a college professor who had been part of Lu Palmer's Task Force during the Harold Washington campaign, told Chinta. "He hasn't been in town long enough. Nobody knows who he is."[26]

Obama, however, refused to bow out, protesting that he had already recruited volunteers, raised money, and rented a campaign office. He had acquired real momentum, moreover, by gathering three thousand signatures on his nominating petitions, far beyond the required six hundred signatures, and insisted that he could not stop now. "I've made a commitment to a great number of volunteers," Obama said, "people who've gone out on cold days and circulated petitions, raised funds on my behalf."[27]

Palmer's forces decided to get her on the ballot anyway and scrambled to collect the needed number of signatures before the deadline. They submitted paperwork with 1,580 signatures, but Obama then decided to challenge Palmer's petitions—a tactic that had been developed by the Chicago machine to disqualify pesky independents and other would-be challengers. By removing signatures from those who weren't registered to vote, Obama drove Palmer's number below the minimum required, and she capitulated. Obama, for his part, was gracious in victory. "I got involved in this race based on Alice's original endorsement," he told Strausberg, "and I continue to respect her and she has made contributions in the community."[28]

Obama ended up running unopposed in the Democratic primary

and faced only token opposition from the Republican in the general election that November. Nevertheless, he deployed seventy-five volunteers to get out the vote. Clearly thinking already about offices beyond the Illinois State Senate, *The Defender* was, for the moment, his major vehicle for communicating with the public. "It's important to let people know who I am and about my agenda," Obama told Strausberg on the day before the primary.[29]

# 24

# The Roar of the El Train

I LEFT *THE DEFENDER* in late July 1996 to take a job as the founding publisher of an independent magazine that would be written both for and by public housing tenants, a position that had a mandate from the resident leadership as well as funding from the federal officials in charge of the CHA. Paying nearly double what I had been making at *The Defender,* the job would allow me to work with the many residents I had met during my tenure on the public housing beat who were amateur writers, poets, and photographers. I was excited to document what life was really like in the "projects," contradicting any number of stereotypes in the process.

Though I felt very much that I was continuing in *The Defender*'s mission, it was with a heavy heart that I departed 2400 South Michigan Avenue for the last time as an employee. The newspaper had changed the way I saw Chicago, the United States, and the world, taught me about journalism, and afforded me unparalleled access to the political and cultural figures of my day. It had filled in so many of the blanks in American history left by the textbooks of my youth and showed me how things really work. Truthfully, I didn't want to leave, but I knew John Sengstacke's health was failing and I worried that without him, the newspaper would not be able to survive.

One sunny Saturday in late May 1997, Walter Lowe was sitting at his desk in *The Defender* newsroom when he saw John Sengstacke come in. Somewhat in awe of Sengstacke, even after having worked for him for so many years, Lowe noticed that the publisher looked ill. When he asked him how he was doing, Sengstacke replied, "Not too well."

Saturday wasn't a regular workday, and they sat alone in the newsroom for some time, just talking. Sensing he might not get another chance to express his appreciation, Lowe, who had grown up with *The Defender* in his household in Gary, Indiana, thanked Sengstacke on behalf of all those who struggled for brotherhood and justice.

"As long as God knows," Sengstacke replied before agreeing to let Lowe drive him home.[1]

John Sengstacke died just a few days later, on the afternoon of May 28, 1997, at the age of eighty-four. He was honored with a dignified ceremony at a Congregationalist church on the South Side attended by more than two hundred people, nearly all of them prominent political leaders and cultural figures if they were not family members. His brother Frederick, son Bobby, and eldest granddaughter, Myiti, all spoke, and tributes were read out from President Clinton and Mayor Daley, among others. Jesse Jackson, his namesake congressman's son, and Vernon Jarrett were among those who provided their remembrances to the assembly. John H. Johnson spoke about Sengstacke warmly. "I feel very indebted to John Sengstacke," Johnson said. "John Sengstacke reached out and gave me support and introduced me to very distinguished people. He always believed in reaching out and never felt threatened by anybody else. I truly believe John Sengstacke was one of America's most influential leaders, white or black."[2]

Appropriately, commemorations ran in newspapers around the country, black as well as white. The *Tribune* editorial page saluted him under the headline "Epitaph for a Newsman," listing among his major accomplishments the transformation of *The Defender* into a daily newspaper and the integration of the U.S. Armed Forces. Brent Staples, an African American member of *The New York Times*'s editorial board, dubbed him the "Charles Foster Kane of the Negro press," whose discretion and modesty made it possible for him to wield greater influence behind the scenes, maintaining the newspaper's credibility as he cultivated relations with presidents, members of Congress, and mayors.[3]

Sam Logan, his longtime editor at *The Michigan Chronicle*, recalled Sengstacke's partnership with Louis Martin and his role in building community newspapers around the country, quoting his favorite aphorisms: "If we take care of our community first, the community will take care of us."[4]

The most moving paeans came from *The Defender*'s colleagues, and sometime rivals, in the black press, from the *Los Angeles Sentinel,* the *New York Amsterdam News,* and publications from all points in between. The ranks of the black press were greatly diminished from its heyday, and mainstream media frequently predicted its complete demise — as they had for decades — but there were still two hundred members of the NNPA, and its current president remembered John Sengstacke as the group's founder and guiding star. Dorothy Leavell, the publisher of the *Crusader,* a community newspaper in Chicago and in Gary, Indiana, had been elected NNPA president that year, and she knew Sengstacke as both a generous mentor and a ruthless competitor: "John Sengstacke was a pioneer, a publisher, and a person of great persuasive power," Leavell wrote in her official statement published by many NNPA member publications. "His power was not bestowed upon him by being a puppet for the rich or by profiting from the status quo. The source of his power came from his lifelong dedication to lifting up others. Though he had access to presidents and politicians, to clergy and captains of industry, John Sengstacke's concerns were always for his community, for the common man and woman, and for the children. As a newspaper publisher, and as president of the National Newspaper Publishers Association, the organization that he helped bring into existence and nurtured into influence with his careful guidance, I owe much to him.

"We all owe much to him."[5]

John's younger brother Frederick stepped easily into the role of *The Defender*'s publisher, and in the short term, the rhythm in the newsroom continued uninterrupted. Fred Sengstacke had effectively managed the organization's finances for decades, after all, and was well versed in every aspect of the operation. At the Bud Billiken Parade later that summer, it was Fred who sat in the blue convertible next to Mayor Daley, but otherwise, Eugene Scott continued to run the newspaper as general manager, Chinta Strausberg kept covering politics, and Earl Calloway kept writing about music and cinema.

Nevertheless, change was inevitable, catalyzed by a looming $3 million estate tax payment that was due to the IRS. In a complicated arrangement designed to shield *The Defender* from an even greater tax burden, John Sengstacke's will instructed his executors to give his remaining son, Bobby, shares representing 9 percent of the newspaper company and to place shares representing 70 percent of the company into a trust for his grandchildren, with the intent of selling *The Defender* and its remaining affiliates, *The Michigan Chronicle*, *The Tri-State Defender*, and *The Pittsburgh Courier*. Sengstacke's will further specified that bankers from Northern Trust, a Chicago-based financial firm, would oversee the process. When Northern Trust analyzed the newspaper group's finances, however, it found that only *The Michigan Chronicle* was profitable; it was actually subsidizing *The Defender*. Overall, the company was generating revenues of about $9 million but losing $1 million annually, a difference that John had made up with debt and periodic infusions from his own funds.[6]

Bobby's eldest daughter, Myiti, intelligent, serious, and, at twenty-five, energetic, was troubled by the plan to sell the newspaper and suspicious of Northern Trust's management. On his deathbed, Sengstacke had told Myiti that he wished the newspaper chain to stay in the family's hands; she was determined to make that happen. By March 1998, the whole matter was in Cook County Circuit Court as Myiti and her brothers argued that Northern Trust should be removed while they searched for an investor who might help the family retain *The Defender* and fulfill their grandfather's final edict.[7]

In 2000 Fred formally turned the publisher's title and responsibilities over to Eugene Scott while continuing to oversee the newspapers as chairman of the board of Sengstacke Enterprises. As a former high-ranking U.S. Army officer who had served in Vietnam, Scott was a product of military integration, one of the major goals for which Robert Abbott and John Sengstacke had worked so assiduously. Scott was also a family member, a nephew of their sister Flaurience's husband; he had spent his high school years living at Flaurience's house in Chicago.

Scott had served at *The Defender* since 1991, just after he retired from the military at the rank of colonel, and Flaurience asked him to come back to Chicago to "help my brother," as she phrased it. At the time, Scott was being recruited for high-paying jobs at major defense contractors, but remembering Flaurience's kindness during his adolescence, he dutifully accepted her request.

As publisher, Scott knew full well the difficulty of the task before him. Circulation of *The Defender*'s daily edition had dropped below twenty thousand and resources were being pinched commensurately, further stretching the staff's dedication and abilities, but he did everything he could to maintain the newspaper's credibility and influence. Circulation and ad revenue stabilized, and content improved. Scott was even able to attract Vernon Jarrett back to the newspaper. Jarrett was seventy-nine and had recently accepted a buyout from the *Sun-Times*, where he had taken his column in 1983 and ultimately became a member of the editorial board, but he took up writing for *The Defender* again with the same zeal he had always shown for the black press, recounting his experiences as a cub reporter covering Bill Dawson under the guidance of Metz Lochard as well as his years writing about Harold Washington, his friend and hero.[8]

Despite John Sengstacke's modesty, his family and friends continued to pursue recognition for his accomplishments, and in 2001 President Clinton, in one of his last acts in office, awarded Sengstacke a posthumous Presidential Citizens Medal as "a lifetime crusader for equal opportunity for African Americans [who] used the power of the press to bring our nation closer to its ideals."[9]

In late 2002 a deal to sell *The Defender* was finally sealed with a company called Real Times, which included Tommy Picou, Myrtle Sengstacke's nephew and *The Defender*'s onetime executive editor, as one of its principals. The new owners agreed to pay the newspaper's tax bill and keep both Bobby and Myiti in prominent roles at the newspaper. They also promised to revitalize *The Defender* by boosting circulation with a younger, upwardly mobile readership. Colonel Scott was relieved of his duty as publisher and replaced by a Real Times executive, while Picou announced plans to add sections covering hip-hop culture and to eventually reopen the Washington bureau.[10]

Vernon Jarrett used his column to congratulate Real Times and declare his support for its efforts, urging readers to buy subscriptions, contribute their opinions, and do all they could to make the new *Defender* "an indispensable arm of our national human rights movement."[11]

One month later, Jarrett wrote about the continued need for the black press, explaining that African American writers for mainstream corporate media were constrained by the need to reach a broad audience. "Regardless of how many fine Black writers they hire," Jarrett summed up, "there is not enough space in their publications to fit our needs. In a word, we need a media devoted largely to Black issues that can be viewed and solved by dedicated Black thinkers who can view our problems in the context of a world dominated by whites."[12]

It soon became clear that Real Times did not have the resources to revitalize *The Defender* either, however. Shortly after taking over in January 2003, Picou sold the company's largest remaining asset, the building at 2400 South Michigan Avenue, for $1.4 million. The buyers, a father and son who were Ukrainian immigrants suspected by the federal government of involvement in organized crime, agreed to let *The Defender* stay in the building as a tenant for the time being.[13]

Picou brought in a succession of new editors, but none stayed long and circulation began to dwindle again. The newsroom remained one of the few lively spots in the building, even as other parts of the building were steadily abandoned to the dust. The boardroom, the site of so many editorial board meetings with political aspirants, was rarely visited now.

In March 2004, as the community rallied around Barack Obama's campaign for the Democratic nomination for Illinois's U.S. Senate seat, Vernon Jarrett underwent surgery for esophageal cancer. Hoping to inspire any last-minute voters, he wrote a column about submitting an absentee ballot from his hospital bed. In the column, entitled "This Is the Odyssey of One Man's Vote for Barack Obama for the U.S. Senate," Jarrett paid Obama the highest compliment possible by comparing him favorably with Mayor Harold Washington. "Ever since my friend Harold's death," Jarrett wrote, "I've heard thousands of Black people raise the question, 'When will we find another Harold Washington?' Well, I am here to tell you that you have another Harold Washington in Obama. Only he's younger, brighter and equally committed."[14]

This was the last column Jarrett would ever write. He lived long enough to see Obama capture the nomination, but surgery failed to stop the spread of his cancer and by the end of May, Jarrett was dead.

His homegoing ceremony was held, appropriately, at Operation PUSH headquarters, with Jesse Jackson officiating. State Senator Obama attended, along with a host of other elected officials, journalists, and community leaders, some of whom had been the targets of Jarrett's acid pen. "Vernon sought to interpret his time, act and advocate," Jackson said in his eulogy. "He defied the expectation of Jim

Crow and other birds, buzzards, hawks, and vultures. He knew that strong minds can break strong chains."[15]

Soon after Jarrett's death, Chinta Strausberg accepted a long-standing offer for a position as a spokesperson for Illinois's lieutenant governor. Her departure after twenty-three years prompted several prominent aldermen to hold a special session in the City Council, where they paid tribute to her reportage as well as her role as a standard-bearer for *The Defender*. Interviewed by other members of the press, Strausberg refused to criticize the new management, though she told the prominent media columnist Michael Miner that the lieutenant governor had been asking her for an entire year to take a position in his office, which paid several times what she had been earning. "I guess I was having a very bad day and I said yes," she told Miner. "The newspaper, *The Defender*, has been my first love. It's been my life, and I'll miss it. I worked seven days a week. I took no vacation. I don't take lunch or breaks. I work at my desk. I live it, I love it, but like a divorce, it's time to say good-bye."[16]

Roland Martin, a thirty-five-year-old journalist from Texas, arrived at *The Defender* just after Strausberg's departure. Bombastic and opinionated, Martin tried to revive *The Defender* with the force of his personality, but had to contend with the same budgetary limitations as his predecessors. In his first few months, he lost or laid off most of the staff and was soon nearly alone in the newsroom, filling the newspaper with articles from the Associated Press and the wire service produced by students at Northwestern University's journalism school.

Martin led the newspaper through its centennial, a rocky period in which he was forced to drop the Tuesday edition as a cost-saving measure, though he was able to launch the newspaper's first website and publish a few issues of glossy magazines designed to attract younger readers. That summer, Martin gave extensive coverage to John H. Johnson's death, crediting him as one of the founders of the black press and chastising talk show host Oprah Winfrey for not attending the funeral.[17]

The following spring, Martin made a radical change to *The Defender*'s masthead, removing Robert Abbott's Sphinx and installing a new motto: "Honest. Balanced. Truthful. Unapologetically Black." Shortly thereafter *The Defender* was forced to vacate its longtime headquarters, as 2400 South Michigan was sold to a politically connected real estate firm associated with Mayor Daley's son and nephew. With the surrounding neighborhood showing the first signs of gentrification, the new owners wanted to transform the building into condominiums as soon as possible. *The Defender* moved to rented space in a posh high-rise across the street from the Art Institute in the Loop. Martin saw the move as a means to enhance the newspaper's profile and make a bid for a more upscale readership.[18]

After the staff had vacated the old building, Bobby Sengstacke decided to take one last look around. Wandering the halls nostalgically, he moved through the newsroom and the advertising department, strangely silent after so many decades of bustle. When he reached *The Defender*'s library on the third floor, Bobby noticed a pile of papers and decided to take a closer look. In the pile he discovered letters and memoranda written by his great-uncle, father, and other *Defender* executives, including correspondence with dozens of national figures. As he scanned the back offices and the drawers, he found yet more stacks of abandoned documents, photographs, letters, financial records, and even a few reels of film. Additional items had been stuffed into cabinets in the newsroom, subbasement vaults, and even in the dumpsters out in the alley.

Bobby decided in that moment that he had to save whatever he could. Working alone and late into the night, he packed the files into the back of his SUV, making several trips back and forth to his loft apartment nearby on Prairie Avenue. Not even this spacious apartment was able to accommodate the collection, and eventually Bobby hauled much of the trove to a storage loft in a warehouse on the city's Northwest Side, raw space without heat or air-conditioning. For the next few months, Bobby considered what to do with the collection, whether he should sell the items piece by piece or donate the lot to a public institution.[19]

At *The Defender*, meanwhile, Roland Martin departed at the beginning of 2007, to be replaced ultimately by Lou Ransom, a veteran of the black press who had served as editor of the *New Pittsburgh Courier* for a number of years. Martin's masthead motto was quietly dropped as well, and the following year, when Real Times announced *The Defender* would be cut to once a week, the newspaper

was redubbed simply "America's Best Black Weekly." After more than
a century, *The Defender* had returned nearly to its point of origin as
the first among many small African American community newspapers.[20]

Bobby Sengstacke entertained numerous offers for his archives
from various scholars and institutions, including the Smithsonian
in Washington, D.C., but he was ultimately convinced by Jacqueline
Goldsby, an African American professor at the University of Chicago,
and Michael Flug, a librarian and archivist at the Chicago Public Library whom he'd known for many years. Bobby took Goldsby into
the loft and showed her the disorganized piles of treasures throughout the room, stacked right up to the ceiling in some spots. Opening
the first cardboard box at hand, Goldsby saw a stack of photographs,
and gasped when she realized that these were candid shots of Booker
T. Washington playing with his grandchildren. She gasped again, this
time with trepidation, when she realized that these precious photographs and papers were protected from the elements only by bare
brick walls pocked with cracked windows. Knowing that the collection was vulnerable to any number of disasters, Goldsby moved with
urgency.

    She and Flug worked with a small cadre of fellow African Ameri-
can professors at the University of Chicago to assemble a team of
graduate students and archivists who would evaluate, categorize,
and catalog the items in the loft. They worked three days a week for
two years and produced eighty-three boxes — an archive larger than
that of the Hearst, Pulitzer, or Ochs families — which they deposited
at the Carter G. Woodson branch of the Chicago Public Library on
Ninety-Fifth Street. The Woodson's quotidian appearance and pot-
holed parking lot belie the magnificence of its contents, specifically
the Vivian G. Harsh Collection, an unrivaled assemblage of essential African American historical documents that had been painstakingly assembled by several generations of librarians, where the
Abbott-Sengstacke Family Papers collection would become the crown
jewels.[21]

    On May 26, 2009, *The New York Times* printed an article about
the archives, praising Bobby first for saving this vital historic material
and then for making the collection available to the public when he

might have sold the items off for a small fortune. Summarizing *The Defender*'s history in a few paragraphs, the article also included several photos, one of an ill-looking Robert Abbott and a youthful John Sengstacke together at the 1934 Bud Billiken Parade, and another of Sengstacke riding in a convertible with former president Harry Truman and the first Mayor Daley during the 1956 parade.

The next day, I attended a press event announcing the Abbott-Sengstacke Family Papers. Bobby was the guest of honor, basking in the attention as he stood in the library's sunny atrium surrounded by a crowd of family and colleagues, scholars, elected officials, and other luminaries. Just as library officials prepared to begin the formal remarks, Mayor Richard M. Daley arrived, surrounded by an entourage of bodyguards and aides. He was stockier than when I had first seen him in 1992 and his hair was noticeably thinner, but he seemed more relaxed as well, confident to the point of ebullience. After more than two decades in office, Daley had surpassed his father's tenure and seemed to be sure of endless reelection, should he wish it.

The mayor strode up to the lectern and read a few prepared comments about *The Defender*'s role in the Great Migration, claiming that the newspaper helped to make Chicago a "center of tolerance." His press secretary then opened the floor to any reporters present who might have questions "on this topic."

I raised my hand and asked about the Daley family's relationship with the Sengstackes. Unhesitatingly, the mayor fondly recalled the decades of collaboration between John Sengstacke and his father: "My dad, [Congressman] Bill Dawson, and John Sengstacke — they were the trifecta of business and politics in Chicago. They did unbelievable things behind closed doors. No one would believe what they were able to accomplish."

While Bobby Sengstacke was preserving the legacy of his family's work building *The Defender*, the newspaper itself was stabilizing after many years of turmoil. Just over a month after the event at the library, *The Defender*'s owners held a neighborhood party to celebrate its return to Bronzeville. I attended the grand opening of the new office, a refurbished funeral home on Martin Luther King Drive, and found the newspaper's employees, supporters, and community members all thrilled to be back on the South Side. Rent in the Michigan Avenue office tower had eaten up more revenue than the entire newspaper brought in every year, and the newspaper's few remaining advertisers and longtime contributors had all complained about the added expense of traveling downtown.

Hundreds of people came out to welcome *The Defender's* homecoming. They toured the new newsroom, modern and well equipped, if compact, then went down the street to a church whose sanctuary had been rented out for a party in honor of the newspaper. When I walked in, Mayor Daley was already at the microphone, flanked on the stage by executives from Real Times. The mayor repeated many of the same sentiments about *The Defender* he had expressed during the dedication of the Abbott-Sengstacke Family Papers, though this time, he made no mention of the "trifecta" of the Boss, the Man, and John Sengstacke. Even Daley seemed to sense that this was yet another incarnation of *The Defender*, one that, like its predecessors, necessarily focused on the present rather than the past. So what if it was no longer a daily? Calculating that the tiny circulation and limited frequency had never really reflected the respect the name "Defender" actually commanded, the mayor knew it was advantageous to retain an association. Even as the era in which news was packaged in bundles of paper and ink was drawing to a close, and many seemingly better-established publications had already gone into oblivion or were headed in that direction, *The Defender*, having defied the predictions of its imminent demise since its inception, was persisting into this new, digital age.

A little later that summer, on Wednesday, July 1, 2009, Frederick Douglass Sengstacke died at the age of ninety. His funeral was held at a nondenominational mortuary home just a few blocks away from *The Defender's* new headquarters on King Drive. As full of joy as grief, this event was a celebration of a life well lived, made evident in the host of children, grandchildren, and great-grandchildren present, as well as nieces and nephews, cousins, and more-distant family members. Also present were dozens of former employees of *The Defender*, men and women who had worked at the paper for only short periods as well as those who had been there for decades — reporters, photographers, and editors as well as printers, production and advertising staff, janitors, and distributors — all of whom had worked with the man we called "Mr. Fred," to distinguish him from his brother.

Mr. Fred having been the last physical connection to Robert Abbott and the world that had created *The Defender* in the first place, his death, for me, brought into stark relief just how much had changed, and just how much had not. Among the crowd at the funeral were many with PhDs and other advanced degrees they had acquired, without incident, from integrated universities around the country. Likewise, many of the Sengstacke family members and former *Defender* staffers held important jobs in integrated institutions, corporations, and government agencies, all of which would have been impossible in Robert Abbott's lifespan. Most impressively, perhaps, Barack Obama was president of the United States, commander in chief of the U.S. Armed Forces, culminating a project that had begun with Abbott, Ida B. Wells, Ed Wright, and Oscar De Priest, and then continued through John Sengstacke and Bill Dawson, and into the next generation of journalists, politicians, and activists.

But for the young people in my journalism classes on the South and West Sides, "American Race Prejudice," just as Abbott had known it, seemed far from being destroyed; like their forefathers, they were born into a world with segregated schools, violent streets, and brutal police, a world in which their futures were circumscribed by a political class that was as venal as it was cynical. Many of their families had been moved out of public housing high-rises built by the first Mayor Daley only to be demolished by his son, while the mixed-income communities that were promised to replace the buildings never materialized. Much of South State Street, so vibrant in Abbott's day, was now vacant, a vast field of overgrown weeds in the middle of the city, with only a few chips of concrete foundation peeking out from the dirt to indicate that humans had lived there.

Working at *The Defender* allowed me to see the truth about America, that "race" is a pernicious lie that permeates our laws and customs, revived in each generation by entrenched interests that threaten to undermine the entire national enterprise, just as it is challenged in each generation by a courageous few who believe that this nation can truly become a bastion of justice and equality. And now that I know the truth, I am compelled to try to correct our mutual story. That is the mission to which Robert Abbott committed himself when he first pressed his fingers against the keys of a battered typewriter, inspired by the sounds of the people in the street below and the roar of the El train on the next block.

# Acknowledgments

THIS BOOK WOULD not have been possible without the support and encouragement of my wife, Kimiyo, and my son, Kobo; they were my inspiration from start to finish. I also would like to thank my in-laws, Sadako and Ken Naka; my brothers, Gabi and Dani, their spouses, Nira and Diane, as well as my cousins Julie and Dan Horton, all of whom contributed in myriad ways that went well beyond familial duty.

Eugene Scott, publisher of *The Defender* when I was a reporter there, was an invaluable source about the newspaper and its management. As this book evolved from concept to completion, Colonel Scott and his wife, Beverly Reed Scott, also a former *Defender* scribe, read multiple drafts, made crucial corrections, and allowed me to use photos from the collection of the Chicago Defender Charities.

Robert A. "Bobby" Sengstacke spent innumerable days with me sharing stories about the newspaper, explaining the significance of various artifacts, and opening his personal network to me. A world-class photographer, Bobby also contributed some of his iconic images from his own collection to the photos section. Bobby's eldest daughter, Myiti Sengstacke Rice, author of her own book about *The Defender*, was likewise generous in sharing her formative experiences at the newspaper.

Dr. Marc Sengstacke and Helena Sengstacke Haley were essential to my understanding of the role played by their father, Frederick Douglass Sengstacke, very much the equal partner to his older brother John Sengstacke. Joselyn DePasaglyne, Robert Abbott's grandniece, revealed what it was like to grow up in a family where the sense of duty began in childhood.

I was overwhelmed by the generosity of former staffers at *The De-fender*, those from my own era as well as from other times, whose recollections helped me to reconstruct both the newsroom and the city we covered: Charles Davis, Walter Lowe, Chinta Strausberg, Ken Green, Ingrid Bridges, Juanita Bratcher, Ron Childs, Don Terry, Gordon Mayer, Alberta Leak, Natalie Pardo, Audarshia Townsend, Laticia Greggs, Scott Burnham, Robert McClory, Michael Brown, Heather F. G. Flamme, Henry Locke, Stan West, Art Sims, Dobie Holland, Glenn Reedus, Kathy Chaney, Mema Ayi, Theresa Fambro Hooks, Ron Carter, LaRissa Lynch, Scott Noblitt, Lucille Younger, Annah Mitchell, Bill Clark, Tim Jackson, Bob Black, Walter S. Mitch-ell III, Martha Brock-Leftridge, Keith Kysel, Worsom Robinson, the Great Jeff Davis, Lynelle Hemphill, Zerlene Colasso, Betty Fulcron, and Kevin Turnbull. A few deceased former *Defender*-ites also should be recognized for their contributions: Larry Gross, Earl Calloway, Reg Patrick, and Hank Martin.

I was likewise humbled by the positive responses and support I re-ceived from scholars, many of whom had spent decades researching *The Defender*'s role in historical events: Timuel Black; Christopher Reed at Roosevelt University; James R. Grossman at the American Historical Association; Patrick Washburn at Ohio University; Adam Green and Jacqueline Stewart at the University of Chicago; Mary Petillo at Northwestern University; Christopher Manning at Loyola University; Juliet E. K. Walker at the University of Texas — Austin; Paula Giddings at Smith College; and William G. Jordan at Phillips Exeter Academy. Jacqueline Goldsby, now at Yale, played an impor-tant role while she was at the University of Chicago working with Bobby Sengstacke to rescue and organize the Abbott-Sengstacke Family Papers. The archives are managed by the amazing staff of the Vivian Harsh Collection at the Chicago Public Library's Carter G. Woodson Regional Library: Robert Miller, curator, Michael Flug, Cynthia Fife-Townsel, Denise English, and Beverly Cook, who was an invaluable ally in navigating this amazing treasure trove. Dr. Dick Dart of the Marshfield Clinic helped me understand Bright's disease, the liver ailment that ultimately killed Robert Abbott.

My fellow writers counseled me through the book-creation pro-cess, served as my advocates when needed, and kept me from going down too many rabbit holes: Alex Kotlowitz, Rick Perlstein, Jonathan Eig, Jonathan Alter, Ben Austen, Jake Austen, Yuval Taylor, Jamie Kalven, Cameron McWhirter, David Maraniss, Tom Glynn, Tem Horwitz, David Isay, Dale Hoiberg, Jim Merinner, Natalie Y. Moore, Kari Lydersen, Chris Hayes, Carol Felsenthal, Salim Muwakkil, Rich Cahan, Elizabeth Taylor, Robert K. Elder, Nathan Thompson, and Kevin Young. My friends served as sounding boards, gave me shots of mental adrenaline just when I needed it, and provided invaluable perspective: Eric Hudson, Stelios Valavanis, Francine Washington, Sandra Young, Jonathan Rothstein, Sunil Garg, Quintana Woodridge, Crystal Carvajal, Mary C. Piemonte, Dave Lundy, Mark Hallett, Chris Robling, Micah Maidenberg, Jesse Ruiz, Yuri Lane, Rachel Haverlock, Kay Berkson, James Litke, Lee Bey, Rachel Feit, Lee Greenhouse, Rob Novak, Rob Moore, Rick White, Admir Kusuran, Jacqueline Thompson, Steve Edwards, Frank Nava, Cass Miller, Shemika Swann-Thompson, and Barbara Holt. My best friend, the eminent scholar Nathaniel Deutsch, guided me through the book-writing process with great wisdom and sense. Without Kristen Harol, who believed in this book from the moment I conceived of it, I would never have met my most excellent agent, Rob McQuilkin, who believed in me and in this book long before we had an actual proposal, gave shape to the narrative during the years while I wrote, and stuck by me right down to the last invaluable line edit.

Last, but by no means least, I am filled with gratitude for the team at Houghton Mifflin Harcourt, for George Hodgman for believing in this book in the first place, and for Nicole Angeloro for courageously stepping in and getting me to the finish line.

# Notes

PREFACE: DELPHI ON THE PRAIRIE

1. "Black Chicago" refers both to Chicago's African American community and the region of the city that had a rapidly expanding black population and dynamic borders on the South Side and eventually West Side. Terms referring to particular eras in Black Chicago's history include the "Dearborn Street corridor" during the eighteenth century, and "Bronzeville," which denoted the South Side from 1930 to 1950. "Black Chicago" is also used as a substitute for "Black Belt," which was sometimes used derogatorily by whites.

2. Video of Robert Jordan of WLS-TV in Chicago interviewing Illinois State Senator Barack Obama, August 14, 2004.

3. David Mendell, "Billiken Crowd Jeers Keyes, Cheers Obama; Dissent Heats Up When GOP Senate Hopeful Makes Appearance at South Side Parade," *Chicago Tribune* (hereafter, *CT*), August 15, 2004; see also Karen E. Pride, "More Than 1 Million Attend 75th Annual Billiken Parade," *The Chicago Defender* (hereafter, *CD*), August 16, 2004, p. 3.

4. Beverly A. Reed, "Barack Obama Promises Vision, Leadership in 1st Congressional Seat," *CD*, February 12, 2000, p. 3.

5. Author interviews with Eugene Scott and Beverly Reed, June 9, 2010, and February 4, 2011.

6. Reed interview, and Reed, "Barack Obama Promises Vision, Leadership in 1st Congressional Seat," *CD*, February 12, 2000, p. 3.

7. Bill Clark, "Rush Touts His Record in Reelection Bid," *CD*, February 14, 2000, p. 3.

8. "Our Endorsements," *CD*, March 18, 2000, p. 1.

9. Chinta Strausberg, "Rush, Obama and Trotter Return to Teamwork," *CD*, March 27, 2000, p. 5.

10. Chinta Strausberg, "Obama to Challenge Sen. Fitzgerald," *CD*, January 22, 2003, p. 5.

11. Chinta Strausberg, "Jesse's Plea to Black Voters: Take Your Souls to the Polls on Dignity Day," *CD*, March 15, 2004, p. 3.

12. David Mendell, "Obama Routs Democratic Foes; Ryan Tops Crowded GOP

Field; Hynes, Hull Fall Far Short Across State," *CT*, March 17, 2004, p. 1.

13. *Paper Trail: 100 Years of* The Chicago Defender. DVD. Directed by Barbara E. Allen. Chicago: WTTW/Chicago, 2005.

14. Author interviews with Reed and Scott.

## 1. A DEFENDER OF HIS RACE

1. Christopher Robert Reed, *All the World Is Here!: The Black Presence at White City* (Bloomington: Indiana University Press, 2000), p. 174.

2. Philip Dray, *Capitol Men: The Epic Story of Reconstruction Through the Lives of the First Black Congressmen* (Boston: Houghton Mifflin, 2008), pp. 300–302, 333–34; Lawrence Goldstone, *Inherently Unequal: The Betrayal of Civil Rights by the Supreme Court, 1865–1903* (New York: Walker and Company, 2011), p. 151.

3. Ibid.

4. William S. McFeely, *Frederick Douglass* (New York: W. W. Norton, 1991), pp. 370–71; Arna Bontemps and Jack Conroy, *Anyplace But Here* (New York: Hill and Wang, 1966), p. 103; "Appeal of Douglass," *Chicago Daily Tribune,* August 26, 1893, p. 3.

5. Reed, *"All the World Is Here!,"* p. 194; "Appeal of Douglass," *Chicago Daily Tribune,* August 26, 1893, p. 3.

6. "Appeal of Douglass," *Chicago Daily Tribune,* August 26, 1893, p. 3.

7. Roi Ottley, *The Lonely Warrior: The Life and Times of Robert S. Abbott* (Chicago: Henry Regnery, 1955), pp. 6, 74.

8. Abbott and his biographers differ slightly on his date of birth, but family documents found in his personal papers indicate he was born in November 1869, a date that aligns with his father's death as described in other records as well. Abbott-Sengstacke Family Papers, Boxes 22-1 and 22-2, Vivian G. Harsh Research Collection of Afro-American History and Literature, Chicago Public Library (hereafter, AS Papers).

9. Ottley, *The Lonely Warrior,* pp. 19–20.

10. Ibid., pp. 17–20; Flora Abbott Sengstacke unfinished autobiography, Box 1, Folder 1, AS Papers.

11. Box 1, Folder 1, AS Papers.

12. Ibid.; Ottley, *The Lonely Warrior,* pp. 24–27.

13. Ottley, *The Lonely Warrior,* pp. 24–27.

14. Box 1, Folder 1, AS Papers.

15. Robert S. Abbott, "Quest for Equality, an Autobiography: First Installment," *CD,* March 16, 1940, p. 1; Ottley, *The Lonely Warrior,* pp. 28–34.

16. Abbott, "Quest for Equality, an Autobiography: Second Installment," *CD,* March 23, 1940, p. 1; author interview with University of Chicago professor Ralph Austen, January 1, 2013.

17. "Days When Georgia Cadets Were Supreme in Savannah Recalled by Old Timers," *CD,* April 7, 1934, p. 10.

18. Abbott, "Quest for Equality, an Autobiography: Third Installment," *CD,* March 30, 1940, p. 5.

19. Ottley, *The Lonely Warrior*, pp. 35–36.
20. Letter from John Abbott to Samuel Chapman Armstrong, June 6, 1888, Box 10, Folder 7, AS Papers.
21. Abbott, "Quest for Equality, an Autobiography: Third Installment," *CD*, March 30, 1940, p. 5. See also "Samuel Chapman Armstrong," Hampton University website, http://www.hamptonu.edu/about/armstrong.cfm.
22. Ottley, *The Lonely Warrior*, p. 71; M. W. Farrow, "Art and the Home: Art and the Present-Day Negro," *CD*, April 18, 1925, p. 8.
23. Reed, *"All the World Is Here!,"* p. 99.
24. Ibid., pp. 17, 99; Donald L. Miller, *City of the Century: The Epic of Chicago and the Making of America* (New York: Simon and Schuster, 1996), pp. 488–505.
25. Reed, *"All the World Is Here!,"* p. 115; Miller, *City of the Century*, pp. 488–505.
26. Ottley, *The Lonely Warrior*, p. 71; Farrow, "Art and the Home: Art and the Present-Day Negro," *CD*, April 18, 1925, p. 8; Reed, *"All The World Is Here!,"* pp. 70, 186.
27. A. N. Fields, "Intimate Glimpses of Early Chicago: Louis B. Anderson and John R. Marshall Come to Windy City and Join Colony of Early Settlers," *CD*, December 3, 1932, p. 11; Bontemps and Conroy, *Anyplace But Here*, p. 103; Christopher Robert Reed, *Black Chicago's First Century* (Columbia: University of Missouri Press, 2005), p. 329.
28. St. Clair Drake and Horace R. Cayton, *Black Metropolis: A Study of Negro Life in a Northern City* (Chicago: University of Chicago Press, 1993), p. 33; Allan H. Spear, *Black Chicago: The Making of a Negro Ghetto, 1890–1920* (Chicago: University of Chicago Press, 1967), pp. 56–57; Reed, *"All the World Is Here!,"* pp. 48–50.
29. "Rope 'Round His Neck: Maddened Workmen Attempt to Lynch William Broda," *CT*, April 18, 1893, p. 1.
30. Reed, *"All the World Is Here!,"* pp. 125–26, 141, 179–86.
31. Ibid.
32. Paula J. Giddings, *Ida, a Sword Among Lions: Ida B. Wells and the Campaign Against Lynching* (New York: Amistad/HarperCollins, 2008), p. 208; A. N. Fields, "Colorful History of Early Chicago: Mrs. Mary Graham Barnett, Attorney's Wife, Is First of Race to Graduate from University of Michigan; W. R. Cowan in Control of Big Estate," *CD*, December 31, 1932, p. 11.
33. Giddings, *Ida*, 230–41.
34. Ida B. Wells, ed., *The Reason Why the Colored American Is Not in the Columbian Exposition* (Chicago: privately printed, 1893); Giddings, *Ida*, 230–41.
35. Ottley, *The Lonely Warrior*, p. 74.
36. McFeely, *Frederick Douglass*, 381–82.
37. Reed, *"All the World Is Here!,"* pp. 47, 48, 129–30, 190; *Life*, July–December 1901, p. 364; *Booker T. Washington's Speech at the Cotton States Exhibition* (Atlanta: privately printed, 1895).
38. Giddings, *Ida*, pp. 353–56.
39. Ottley, *The Lonely Warrior*, p. 74.
40. Robert S. Abbott, "Quest for Equality: an Autobiography, Installment VI," *CD*, April 20, 1940, p. 5.

41. Deton J. Brooks Jr., "From Buffalo Bill's Aide to Mayor's Floor Leader: Council Floor Leader," *CD*, February 27, 1943, p. 13.
42. "The First Negro Colonel," *New York Times*, June 22, 1898; Reed, *Black Chicago's First Century*, pp. 428–32.
43. Spear, *Black Chicago*, pp. 12–21.
44. Ottley, *The Lonely Warrior*, p. 78; Metz T. P. Lochard, "Robert S. Abbott — Race Leader," *Phylon* 8, no. 2 (1947, 2nd Qtr.), pp. 124–32; Robert S. Abbott, "A Recapitulation of 25 Years Work: Editor Robt. S. Abbott's Story of Early Struggles and Success of the World's Greatest Weekly/Twentieth Century Moses," *CD*, May 3, 1930, p. A1; A. N. Fields, "Noted Lawmakers of Early Chicago: Edward H. Morris, Major J. C. Buckner and John J. Jones Were Stanch Champions of the Race," *CD*, February 25, 1933, p. 10.
45. "31st and State Streets," *CD*, February 12, 1910, p. 1; Fay Young, "People Who Helped Abbott Make *Defender* Great," *CD*, August 13, 1955, p. 3A.
46. Young, "People Who Helped Abbott Make *Defender* Great," *CD*, April 13, 1955, p. 3A; Robert S. Abbott to John H. Sengstacke, typed four-page letter dated April 17, 1934, Robert Abbott Super Series, Box 8, Folder 33, AS Papers.
47. Albert G. Barnett, "Chicago: What the City Was Like at Birth of *Defender*," *CD*, August 13, 1955, p. 10A; Robert S. Abbott, "Quest for Equality: An Autobiography, Installment VII," *CD*, April 27, 1940, p. 5.
48. Young, "People Who Helped Abbott Make *Defender* Great"; Abbott to Sengstacke, April 17, 1934, AS Papers.
49. Letter to H. B. Frissell, Hampton Institute, August 25, 1904, Robert Abbott Super Series, Box 6, Folder 21, AS Papers; Ottley, *The Lonely Warrior*, pp. 78–80.
50. Barnett, "Chicago: What the City Was Like at Birth of *Defender*," *CD*, August 13, 1955, p. 10A; Ottley, *The Lonely Warrior*, pp. 86–87.
51. Ottley, *The Lonely Warrior*, pp. 88–90.

## 2. IF YOU SEE IT IN *THE DEFENDER*, IT'S SO

1. Harper Barnes, *Never Been a Time* (New York: Walker and Company, 2008), pp. 46–49.
2. Lochard, "Robert S. Abbott — Race Leader," p. 126; *The Atlanta Georgian and News* (hereafter, *AGN*), September 25, 1906, p. 3; U.S. Census Bureau, "United States: Race and Hispanic Origin, 1790–1990."
3. Young, "People Who Helped Abbott Make *Defender* Great," *CD*, August 13, 1955, p. 3A; Fay Young, "The Week," *CD*, May 3, 1930, p. 13; Fay Young, "Through the Years Past Present Future," *CD*, May 9, 1942, p. 19; Ottley, *The Lonely Warrior*, pp. 93–95, 113, 115–16, 118.
4. "*Defender* Once Could Have Been Bought for a Song," *CD*, June 7, 1930, p. 5.
5. Robert S. Abbott, "*Defender* Had No Easy Time in Its Youth," *CD*, June 7, 1930, p. 22.
6. Ibid.; Photo Standalone 1, *CD*, February 19, 1910, p. 4; "Col. John R. Marshall Not Bothered," *CD*, April 8, 1911, p. 1; "Col. Marshall Returns from Norfolk," *CD*, December 14, 1912, p. 6.
7. All from *CD*: A. N. Fields, "Chicagoans Make Political History: E. H.

Wright, Peer of Politicians, Rises to Power, but Is Dethroned as He Deserts Thompson for Lundin," January 14, 1933, p. 9; A. N. Fields, "Chicago's Early History Presents Brilliant Features: Writer Chronicles Events of Other Days; Social and Political Life Told," November 12, 1932, p. 10; "Chicago Police Gives Colored Man Up to Lynchers," August 27, 1910, p. 2; "Do You Want a Colored Alderman?" January 29, 1910, p. 1. See also Lloyd Wendt and Herman Kogan, *Big Bill of Chicago* (Evanston: Northwestern University Press, 2005), p. 38.

8. "*Defender* Once Could Have Been Bought for a Song," *CD,* June 7, 1930, p. 5; Ottley, *The Lonely Warrior,* pp. 100–102.

9. "*Defender* Once Could Have Been Bought for a Song," *CD,* June 7, 1930, p. 5; Ottley, *The Lonely Warrior,* pp. 100–102.

10. From *CD:* Juli Jones Jr., "Teenan Jones 'Spills the Beans' on Boxers of Today and the Past," March 24, 1923, p. 10; Henry Teenan Jones, "Reminiscenses from an Old-Timer's Scrap Book," February 18, 1933, p. 8.

11. From *CD:* "Teenan Jones Is Seasick," August 29, 1914, p. 4; Installments of Henry Teenan Jones, "Reminiscenses from an Old-Timer's Scrap Book," March 18, 1933, p. 11; May 6, 1933, p. 11; July 1, 1933, p. 11; July 8, 1933, p. 11; June 24, 1933, p. 10; A. N. Fields, "Fred Douglass at 1893 World's Fair: Dedicates Famous Haitian Building on Exposition Grounds in Speech of Matchless Oratory," July 1, 1933, p. 11; Fay Young, "People Who Helped Abbott Make *Defender* Great," August 13, 1955, p. 3A.

12. From *CD:* Editorial Article 2, February 5, 1910, p. 2; "Does Drinking Pay?" September 11, 1915, p. 8; "Chicago's Nite Life — of Former Years: Crimson! Tragic!" November 13, 1948, p. 22. Mary E. Stovall, "The *Chicago Defender* in the Progressive Era," *Illinois Historical Journal* 83, no. 3 (Autumn 1990), pp. 159–72; Spear, *Black Chicago,* p. 77; Ottley, *The Lonely Warrior,* pp. 97–99.

13. Fay Young, "People Who Helped Abbott Make *Defender* Great," *CD,* August 13, 1955, p. 3A; Ottley, *The Lonely Warrior,* p. 118; Juliet E. K. Walker, "The Promised Land, *The Chicago Defender* and the Black Press in Illinois, 1862–1970," in *The Black Press in the Middle West,* edited by Henry Lewis Suggs (Westport, CT: Greenwood Press, 1996), pp. 24–25.

14. Walker, "The Promised Land," pp. 24–25. From *CD:* Masthead 1, January 1, 1910, p. 1; Masthead 2, January 1, 1910, p. 2; Masthead 1, June 1, 1912, p. 1; "A Man Who Was Master of His Profession and Refused to Be Called One of Us Until He Could Work Scientifically," October 16, 1915, p. 4; "325 Negro Men and Women Lynched and Shot for Fun," January 1, 1910, p. 1; "100 Negroes Murdered Weekly in United States by White Americans," March 19, 1910, p. 1; "Texas Has Bloody Spree, 2,000 Persons Attend Confession False," June 1, 1912, p. 1; W. Allison Sweeney, "Fifty Years of Frenzied Hatred," August 14, 1915, p. 1; Ottley, *The Lonely Warrior,* pp. 107–10; Spear, *Black Chicago,* pp. 47–48.

15. Giddings, *Ida,* pp. 470–72, 482–87; "Bethel Literary and Historical Club Doing Great Work," *CD,* January 1, 1910, p. 1.

16. "Jack Johnson Sheds Tears," *CD,* January 1, 1910, p. 1.

17. "Gladiators of Ring in Greatest Fight of Century," *AGN,* July 4, 1910, p. 1. From *CT:* "Battle to Be Bitter Test," January 2, 1910, p. C2; Harvey T. Woodruff, "Jeffries Signs for World Tour," February 1, 1910, p. 14; "Black

Tells Why He'll Win," February 27, 1910, p. C2; HEK, "In the Wake of the News: A Policy on Jack Johnson, March 26, 1910, p. 14; Walter H. Eckersall, "Jack Wires Jeff His Best Wishes," April 16, 1910, p. 8; "Jack Johnson Takes Stump," March 27, 1910, p. 1; "Johnson Weighs 220 Pounds Now," May 11, 1910, p. 15.

18. L. N. Hoggatt, "He Will Have Them All to Beat," *CD,* February 5, 1910, p. 1; *"Defender* Leads in Number of Big Departments," April 17, 1915, p. 5.

19. "Jack Johnson Heavy Weight Champion of the World, Praises *The Defender,"* *CD,* February 19, 1910, p. 1.

20. "Jack Johnson Takes Stump," *CT,* March 27, 1910, p. 1; "Mr. Jack Johnson Is Mighty Busy," *CT,* April 1, 1910, p. 14; "White Jury Good to Jack Johnson," *CT,* April 5, 1910, p. 14; "Jack Johnson 32 Years Old," *CD,* April 9, 1910, p. 4.

21. "Rich Pullman Car Clerk Stuns Judge," *CD,* March 26, 1910, p. 1.

22. All from *CD:* "Plea of the Pullman Porters," December 31, 1910, p. 1; John R. Winston, "Sparks from the Rail," June 1, 1912, p. 2; "Pullman Porter Beaten Up by a Half Drunken Passenger," December 20, 1913, p. 2; "Porter Uses Fists," March 7, 1914, p. 6; "Railroad Men Great Help to *Chicago Defender,"* February 13, 1915, p. 2; Jack [pseud.], "Railroad Rumblings," October 23, 1915, p. 8; Ottley, *The Lonely Warrior,* pp. 102, 115.

23. John R. Winston, "The Railroads: In the Railroad Center," *CD,* July 23, 1910, p. 4.

24. Ottley, *The Lonely Warrior,* pp. 91–93.

25. "Railroad Men Great Help to *Chicago Defender,"* February 13, 1915, p. 2.

26. "James J Corbett: Tradition Factor in the Big Fight," *CT,* July 1, 1910, p. 13; "Fans to Welcome Champion," *CT,* July 6, 1910, p. 11; "Gladiators of Ring in Greatest Fight of Century," *AGN,* July 4, 1910, p. 1.

27. Ottley, *The Lonely Warrior,* pp. 111–13.

28. John L. Sullivan, "Jack Johnson, and Tools Which Brought Him World's Pugilistic Victory," *CT,* July 5, 1910, p. 25; Associated Press, "Jeffries Blames Age for Downfall," *CT,* July 5, 1910, p. 23; James J. Corbett, "Jeff a Hulk, Says Corbett," *CT,* July 5, 1910, p. 24; "How the Georgian's Friends Received the News Monday," *AGN,* July 5, 1910, p. 1.

29. "Eleven Killed in Many Race Riots," *CT,* July 5, 1910, p. 1.

30. "Cities Prohibit Fight Pictures," *CT,* July 6, 1910, p. 1.

31. W. M. Pickens, "Talladega College Professor Speaks on Reno Fight," *CD,* July 30, 1910, p. 1.

32. "Fans to Welcome Champion," *CT,* July 6, 1910, p. 11; "Cheering Throng Greets Johnson," *CT,* July 8, 1910, p. 13.

33. All from *CD:* A. N. Fields, "Chicagoans Make Political History: E. H. Wright, Peer of Politicians, Rises to Power, but Is Dethroned as He Deserts Thompson for Lundin," January 14, 1933, p. 9; A. N. Fields, "Chicago's Early History Presents Brilliant Features: Writer Chronicles Events of Other Days; Social and Political Life Told," November 12, 1932, p. 10; "Chicago Police Gives Colored Man Up to Lynchers," August 27, 1910, p. 2; F. H. Hamilton, "Steve Green Liberated," September 24, 1910, p. 1. See also Giddings, *Ida,* pp. 495–96.

34. Sylvester Russell, "Musical and Dramatic: A Quarterly Review, Negro Yiddish Theaters and Other Notes," *CD,* April 9, 1910, p. 4.

35. From *CD:* Julius N. Avendorph, "Mr. Avendorph Explains His Attitude as to the 'Rambler' Column," May 7, 1910, p. 6; Julius N. Avendorph, "Why Not Dress in Keeping with the Occasion or Not at All," December 3, 1910, p. 2; Julius Avendorph, "Do We as a Race Progress with the Times?" January 28, 1911, p. 1; "Julius Avendorph, Society Editor, Returns from Western Trip," October 23, 1920, p. 2; "Julius Avendorph Promoted," January 22, 1921, p. 2; Julius N. Avendorph, "Chicago Social Life in Years Past as Compared with Today," October 22, 1921, p. 3; "All Chicago Mourns the Death of Julius Avendorph," May 12, 1923, p. 5.

36. Larry Tye, *Rising from the Rails* (New York: Henry Holt, 2004), pp. 76, 81–82, 93–95, 135; Spear, *Black Chicago,* p. 130; Drake and Cayton, *Black Metropolis,* pp. 235–38; James Grossman, *Land of Hope: Chicago Black Southerners and the Great Migration* (Chicago: University of Chicago Press, 1989), pp. 74, 78; "The Porter and His Worth to the Pullman Company," *CD,* December 26, 1914, p. 1; "Pullman Company Has Heart-to-Heart Talk with Porters," *CD,* August 15, 1914, p. 1.

37. From *CD,* Fay Young: "People Who Helped Abbott Make *Defender* Great"; "The Week," May 3, 1930, p. 13; "Through the Years Past Present Future," May 9, 1942, p. 19. Ottley, *The Lonely Warrior,* pp. 93–95, 113, 115–16, 118.

38. All from *CD:* The Rambler, "Rambling About Chicago," March 4, 1910, p. 1; "Negro Hater Playwright in New Scandalous Producing," March 18, 1911, p. 1; "A Gentle Spring Song," April 8, 1911, p. 1.

## 3. GETTING THE SOUTH TOLD

1. "Southern White Gentleman Rapes Colored Lady; Is Killed by Husband," *CD,* November 4, 1911, p. 1.

2. "Rope About Neck Negro Escapes," *The Atlanta Constitution* (hereafter, *AC*), October 29, 1911, p. C4; "Escapes from a Mob Bent Upon Lynching," *AGN,* October 30, 1911, p. 7; "Negroes in Conspiracy to Murder a Merchant," *AGN,* November 4, 1911, p. 7.

3. "White in Jail at Washington," *AC,* November 26, 1911, p. 4.

4. "Editor Abbott Calls Roll of Those Who Aided *Defender:* Roll of Honor," *CD,* May 31, 1930, p. 10.

5. All from *CD:* A. N. Fields, "Chicagoans Make Political History: E. H. Wright, Peer of Politicians, Rises to Power, but Is Dethroned as He Deserts Thompson for Lundin," January 14, 1933, p. 9; A. N. Fields, "Chicago's Early History Presents Brilliant Features: Writer Chronicles Events of Other Days; Social and Political Life Told," November 12, 1932, p. 10; "Chicago Police Gives Colored Man Up to Lynchers," August 27, 1910, p. 2.

6. "Negro Editor to Be Released," *AC,* November 30, 1911, p. A2; "Negro Editor Arrested by Washington Officer," *AGN,* November 25, 1911, p. 3; Mark Robert Schneider, *We Return Fighting: The Civil Rights Movement in the Jazz Age* (Boston: Northeastern University Press, 2002), p. 359.

7. "Wilkes County Negro Convicted of Murder," *AGN,* November 18, 1911, p. 3; "About to Be Executed, Negro Makes Escape," *AGN,* November 29, 1911, p. 7; "Cheats Gallows in Nick of Time," *AC,* November 29, 1911, p. 1.

8. From *AGN:* "Negro Is Recaptured by Glascock Co. Man," December 4, 1911, p. 2; "Celebrate Thanksgiving by Hunting a Negro," December 11, 1911.

9. From *AC*: "Second Sentence of Same Slayer to Be Made Today," December 5, 1911, p. 1; "Medical College Gets Body of Negro Killer," December 8, 1911, p. 5; "Tries to Cheat Gibbet of Slayer of His Brother," December 6, 1911, p. 1; "Victim's Brother Shoots Walker," *AGN*, December 5, 1911, p. 1.

10. *Crisis*, January 1912, p. 101, column 2; William G. Jordan, *Black Newspapers and America's War for Democracy, 1914–1920* (Chapel Hill: University of North Carolina Press, 2001), pp. 28–29.

11. "Tried to Bulldoze, Not Prosecute *The Chicago Defender*," *CD*, January 6, 1912, p. 5.

12. "Negro Editor Is Fined for Libelous Article," *AC*, March 7, 1912, p. 5.

13. *CD* masthead, June 1, 1912; "Obituary TB Hollenshead," *AC*, June 10, 1912, p. 2.

14. J. Hockley Smiley, "Jack Johnson Opens the Cafe de Champion," *CD*, July 13, 1912, p. 1.

15. "Jack Johnson's Wife, Ill Kills Self," *CD*, September 14, 1912, p. 1.

16. "Jack Johnson's Wife Self-Shot," *CT*, September 12, 1912, p. 1; "Johnson Denies Beating Up Wife," *CT*, September 13, 1912, p. 10.

17. "Jail Girl to Foil Pugilist Johnson," *CT*, October 18, 1912, p. 3; "Pugilist Johnson Hanged in Effigy," *CT*, October 20, 1912, p. 3; "Condemns J. Johnson's Acts," *CT*, October 21, 1912, p. 3.

18. From *CD:* "Daily Newspapers Try to Incite Riot," October 26, 1912, p. 1; "L'accuse," October 26, 1912, p. 2; Henry Teenan Jones, "Reminiscences from an Old-Timer's Scrap Book," May 13, 1933, p. 10.

19. From *CD:* "Important Conference on the Negro," August 17, 1912, p. 8; "Jane Addams' Bold Stand," August 17, 1912, p. 8; "Woodrow Wilson Praises Work of Bishop Walters," November 9, 1912, p. 1; Barnes, *Never Been a Time*, p. 79. Woodrow Wilson, "The Reconstruction of the Southern States," *The Atlantic Monthly*, January 1901, pp. 1–15; Jordan, *Black Newspapers*, pp. 10–14, 75; Goldstone, *Inherently Unequal*, pp. 70–75.

20. "Champion Jack Johnson Is Sentenced to Year in Prison," *CD*, June 7, 1913, p. 1.

21. M. A. Majors, "Jack Johnson Is Crucified for His Race," *CD*, July 5, 1913, p. 1; "Canada to Let Johnson Sail," *CT*, June 28, 1913, p. 2.

22. "Jack Johnson to Return October 1st," *CD*, July 12, 1913, p. 1.

23. From *CD:* Display ad 13, August 30, 1913, p. 7; Editorial Article 4, September 20, 1913, p. 4.

24. Ralph W. Tyler, "One Year Under President Wilson and the Democratic Party," *CD*, March 7, 1914, p. 7.

25. See *CD*, March 7, 1914, for the first Hearst-style masthead.

26. From *CD:* "Y.M.C.A. Receives $10,000 from Pullman Co," May 3, 1913, p. 2; "The Pullman Employees," August 15, 1914, p. 8; "Pullman Company Has Heart-to-Heart Talk with Porters," August 15, 1914, p. 1.

27. "Pay for Shining Shoes Is Not a Tip Says Porter," *CD*, August 29, 1914, p. 1.

28. From *CD*, August 15, 1914, p. 8: "War Pro Tem"; "Where We Stand." Jordan, *Black Newspapers*, pp. 37–39.

29. From *CD:* "The Wilson-Trotter Interview," November 21, 1914, p. 8; "Wil-

liam Monroe Trotter's Address to the President," November 21, 1914, p. 7.

30. "Government Should Stop Daily Lynchings," *CD*, January 23, 1915, p. 1.

31. From *CD*: "Race Men Show Mettle; Use Guns on Assailants," January 2, 1915, p. 1; "Wolves in Sheep's Clothing," March 6, 1915, p. 8.

32. From *CD*: "*Chicago Defender* Rapidly Forging to the Front," January 30, 1915, p. 2; "Railroad Men Great Help to *Chicago Defender*," February 13, 1915, p. 2; AS Papers, Box 11, Folder 1, includes receipt dated July 22, 1915, from Western Newspaper Union, paid August 2, 1915, for $243.27, for composition, makeup, ad time, and mailing list for 14,100 copies; Walker, "The Promised Land," p. 25.

33. "Alpha Suffrage Club," *CD*, November 7, 1914, p. 3; Wendt and Kogan, *Big Bill*, p. 42; Giddings, *Ida*, p. 527; Harold F. Gosnell, *Negro Politicians: The Rise of Negro Politicians in Chicago* (Chicago: University of Chicago Press, 1935), p. 50.

34. Drake and Cayton, *Black Metropolis*, pp. 361–65; "Fear Aldermen of Poor Caliber Will Win Seats," *CD*, February 21, 1915, p. 6.

35. From *CD*: Captain John L Fry, "Louis B. Anderson Logical Man for Alderman," January 23, 1915, p. 1; Editorial Cartoon 1, January 30, 1915, p. 8; John P. Sneed, "Another Ward Leader Declares for Anderson," February 13, 1915, p. 4; "A Good Husband Should Make a Good Alderman," February 13, 1915, p. 1; "Our Aldermanic Candidate," February 13, 1915, p. 8; "De Priest Is Winner," February 27, 1915, p. 1; "For Alderman, Oscar De Priest," February 27, 1915, p. 4; "Oscar De Priest," February 27, 1915, p. 2; "Louis B Anderson," February 27, 1915, p. 2.

36. Wendt and Kogan, *Big Bill*, pp. 103–4; "Results of the Mayoralty Primaries," *CT*, February 24, 1915, p. 1.

37. Article 1, *CD*, March 27, 1915, p. 2; "Vote for De Priest," *CD*, April 3, 1915, p. 8.

38. *Birth of a Nation*, D. W. Griffith Productions, 1915.

39. Jordan, *Black Newspapers*, pp. 48–58; Arnie Bernstein, *Hollywood on Lake Michigan: 100 Years of Chicago and the Movies* (Chicago: Lake Claremont Press, 1998), pp. 50–51; Giddings, *Ida*, p. 527.

40. All from *CD*: Editorial Cartoon 1, April 8, 1911, p. 1; Special to *The Chicago Defender*, "Clansman Is Kicked Out of New York," March 27, 1915, p. 1; Special to *The Chicago Defender*, "Birth of a Nation Arouses Ire of Miss Jane Addams," March 20, 1915, p. 1.

41. Special to *The Chicago Defender*, "Boston Race Leaders Fight Birth of a Nation," *CD*, April 24, 1915, p. 4.

42. Jackson J. Stovall, "Can Willard Return the Pugilistic Scepter to the Caucasian Race?" *CD*, April 3, 1915, p. 7; "Johnson in Fine Form," *CD*, April 3, 1915, p. 1.

43. William H. Rocop, "Right to Jaw Gives Kansan Title Victory," *CT*, April 6, 1915, p. 11; Herbert Swope, "Johnson Knockout Dramatic Climax to Battle," *CT*, April 6, 1915, p. 13.

44. "Jess Willard Is Not Considered Real Champion," *CD*, April 24, 1915, p. 7.

45. From *CD*: Special to *The Chicago Defender*, January 2, 1915, p. 3; "Aftermath," April 17, 1915, p. 8; Henry "Teenan" Jones, "Reminiscences from an Old-Timer's Scrap Book," May 13, 1933, p. 10.

46. From *CD:* Frank Young, "Through the Years Past Present Future," May 9, 1942, p. 19; *"Defender* Leads in Number of Big Departments," April 17, 1915, p. 5; May 1, 1915, p. 7; Russ J. Cowans, "'Fay' Young, Former Sports Editor, Dies," November 2, 1957, p. 1.

47. "Thompson Carries City by 139,489," *CT,* April 7, 1915, p. 1.

48. "Thompson Inaugurated," *CD,* May 1, 1915, p. 1.

49. From *CD:* Article 1, March 27, 1915, p. 2.; "Thompson Inaugurated," *CD,* May 1, 1915, p. 1; "A Friend in the Mayor's Chair," May 1, 1915, p. 8; Wendt and Kogan, *Big Bill,* p. 168.

50. From *CD:* "Mayor Wm. Hale Thompson Signing First City Ordinance," May 8, 1915, p. 4; "History Making Week for Afro-Americans," May 22, 1915, p. 1; "Mayor Thompson Bars 'Birth of Nation' from Chicago," May 22, 1915, p. 2; "Killing a Film," May 22, 1915, p. 8.

51. Gosnell, *Negro Politicians,* p. 51; "Remembering Friends," *CD,* August 7, 1915, p. 8.

52. From *CD:* Special to the *The Chicago Defender,* "Will Robert T. Lincoln Be the Second Emancipator," May 8, 1915, p. 1; "Editorial," May 8, 1915, p. 8; "Pullman Porter's Pay," May 15, 1915, p. 8; "Pullman Company Believe Porters Receive High Enough Pay," August 21, 1915, p. 1; "Pullman Co. Puts Leven in Porters' Wages," January 1, 1916, p. 2; Ottley, *The Lonely Warrior,* p. 138.

53. Kitty Kelly, "Emotion Rocked Crowd Watches Birth of Nation," *CT,* June 6, 1915, p. A1.

54. From *CD,* Mrs. K. J. Bills, "Facts About Birth of a Nation Play at the Colonial," September 11, 1915, p. 3; "Clubs and Societies: The Alpha Suffrage Club," August 23, 1913, p. 2.

55. From *CD:* Z. Withers, "Psychology of Lynch-Law," September 11, 1915, p. 8; "Editor's Mail: Long Live Mr. Sweeney," August 21, 1915, p. 8; Advertisement: *"Pullman Porters' Review;* Big Issue Is Now Ready," April 27, 1918, p. 12; Z. Withers, "Prayer Proves Efficacious," November 6, 1915, p. 5.

56. Kenneth T. Jackson, *The Ku Klux Klan in the City, 1915–1930* (New York: Oxford University Press, 1967), pp. 3–4.

57. Fon Holly, "The Empty Chair," *CD,* October 16, 1915, p. 8.

58. *"Chicago Defender* Rapidly Forging to the Front," *CD,* January 30, 1915, p. 2; *"Chicago Defender's* Greatest Number," *CD,* September 25, 1915, p. 9. AS Papers, Robert S. Abbott Super Series, Box 11, Folder 1, includes receipt dated July 22, 1915, from Western Newspaper Union, paid August 2, 1915, for $243.27 for composition, makeup, ad time, and mailing list for 14,100 copies; Walker, "The Promised Land," p. 25.

## 4. THE GREAT NORTHERN DRIVE

1. From *CD:* "World Weeps for Washington," *CD,* November 20, 1915, p. 1; "The News Came to *The Defender* Office," *CD,* November 20, 1915, p. 4; Ottley, *The Lonely Warrior,* pp. 121–22.

2. "Washington and Du Bois," *CD,* February 27, 1915, p. 3.

3. "Cementing Factions," *CD,* January 9, 1915, p. 8; AS Papers, Robert S. Abbott Super Series, Box 11, Folder 1: from a fold-up eight-panel brochure from

1926 entitled "A Bit About Chicago — Where to Go What to See How to Get There"; Ottley, *The Lonely Warrior*, pp. 1, 58, 96, 125–26; Spear, *Black Chicago*, pp. 81, 167; Reed, *Black Chicago's First Century*, p. 442; Giddings, *Ida*, pp. 433–61.

4. "Southland, Farmers," *CD*, April 3, 1915, p. 8.

5. Emmett J. Scott, *Negro Migration During the War* (New York: Oxford University Press, 1920), p. 51; Grossman, *Land of Hope*, pp. 197–98.

6. "Opportunities North-South," *CD*, October 2, 1915, p. 8.

7. From *CD:* "Making Good Employees," July 31, 1915, p. 8; "Peonage Slave System Starts After Flood," September 25, 1915, p. 1; "Victims Without Food," March 4, 1916, p. 1; "Diversified Crops," August 19, 1916, p. 12; W. J. Latham, "Migration," August 26, 1916, p. 12; "Expose Arkansas Peonage System," November 1, 1919, p. 1. Scott, *Negro Migration*, p. 22; Walker, "The Promised Land," p. 26.

8. From *CD:* "Peonage Slave System Starts After Flood," September 25, 1915, p. 1; "Victims Without Food," March 4, 1916, p. 1; "Diversified Crops," August 19, 1916, p. 12; "Expose Arkansas Peonage System," November 1, 1919, p. 1.; Scott, *Negro Migration*, p. 22.

9. "The Labor Question," *CD*, January 15, 1916, p. 10; Scott, *Negro Migration*, p. 52.

10. "Race Labor Leaving," *CD*, February 5, 1916, p. 1.

11. From *CD:* Editorial Article 1, April 22, 1916, p. 8; "Occupying the White House," April 22, 1916, p. 8; A. P. Holly, "Haiti Captured by United States Government," October 30, 1915, p. 1.

12. Henry Walker, "Southern White Gentlemen Burn Race Boy at Stake," *CD*, May 20, 1916, p. 1.

13. From *CD:* Editorial Cartoon 2, July 22, 1916, p. 13; "Southerners Plan to Stop Exodus," August 12, 1916, p. 3.

14. "Our Industrial Opportunity," *CD*, August 12, 1916, p. 12.

15. "The Exodus," *CD*, September 2, 1916, p. 1.

16. Fon Holly, "The Desertion," *CD*, September 2, 1916, p. 12.

17. From *CD:* "Farewell, Dixie Land," October 7, 1916, p. 12; "A Second Emancipation," October 28, 1916, p. 12.

18. *Chicago Defender* News Service, "Police Make Wholesale Arrests; Emigration Worries South," *CD*, November 11, 1916, p. 2.

19. From *CD:* M. Ward, "Bound for the Promised Land," November 11, 1916, p. 12; "Bound for the Promised Land," December 23, 1916, p. 1; "Getting the South Told," November 25, 1916, p. 12.

20. From *CD:* "Bound for the Promised Land," December 23, 1916, p. 1; "A Letter from Dixie Land," November 4, 1916, p. 12.

21. "Getting the South Told," *CD*, November 25, 1916, p. 12.

22. The Scrutinizer, "Somebody Lied," *CD*, October 7, 1916, p. 3.

23. "Northern Invasion Starts," *CD*, January 20, 1917, p. 1.

24. "Freezing to Death in the South," *CD*, February 24, 1917, p. 1.

25. AS Papers, Robert S. Abbott Super Series, Box 1: draft article by L. C. Harper; Enoch B. Waters, *American Diary* (Chicago: Path Press, 1987), pp. 125–27, 147–49.

26. Lucius Clinton Harper, "Dustin' Off the News," *CD*, May 14 1949, p. 1;

Robert S. Abbott Super Series, Box 1: draft article by L. C. Harper; Waters, *American Diary*, pp. 125–27.

27. From *CD:* "Hattiesburgers Arrive," March 10, 1917, p. 7; "Northern Drive to Start," February 10, 1917, p. 3.
28. "One North — Two Schools — One South," *CD*, April 7, 1917, p. 8.
29. "Down in Georgia," *CD*, April 7, 1917, p. 2.
30. "White Soldiers Fail to Salute Officers of 'Eighth,'" *CD*, August 12, 1916, p. 2.
31. "Jim Crow Training Camps — No!," *CD*, April 7, 1917, p. 10; Jordan, *Black Newspapers*, pp. 78–79.
32. Theodore Kornweibel Jr., *Investigate Everything* (Bloomington: Indiana University Press, 2002), pp. 120–21.
33. Junius B. Wood, "City to Keep Negro Out of Black Belt," *The Chicago Daily News*, April 21, 1917, p. 6.
34. From *CD:* "Playing to the Gallery," May 19, 1917, p. 2; "Berry Crop Hurt by Exodus to Northland," May 19, 1917, p. 3; *Chicago Defender* News Service, "Arrest White Man for Enticing Men North," May 19, 1917, p. 6.
35. From *CD:* "Determined to Go North," March 24, 1917, p. 10; "Emigration Worries," March 24, 1917, p. 1.
36. Foreword to Scott, *Negro Migration.*
37. Scott, *Negro Migration*, pp. 30–33.
38. Ibid., p. 65.
39. Ibid., pp. 38, 45.
40. Ibid., p. 68.
41. Ibid., pp. 3, 129, 106.
42. Ibid., pp. 47, 92, 167–68.
43. "Reading Poetry Causes Arrest," *CD*, June 2, 1917, p. 9.
44. Ottley, *The Lonely Warrior*, p. 146; Grossman, *Land of Hope*, p. 44.
45. A Staff Correspondent, "Horrible Memphis Lynching Astounds Civilized World," *CD*, May 26, 1917, p. 1.
46. Ibid.
47. "Black Man, Stay South!," *CT*, May 30, 1917, p. 6; "The Proper Kind of Fruit Will Entice Him to Stay Home," *CT*, May 30, 1917, p. 6; Spear, *Black Chicago*, p. 146.
48. "Resents Press Attack on Race," *CD*, June 9, 1917, p. 10.

### 5. THE GREATEST DISTURBING ELEMENT

1. "Troops Quell Illinois Riots," *CD*, July 7, 1917, p. 1; Barnes, *Never Been a Time*, pp. 112–36.
2. Giddings, *Ida*, pp. 559–66.
3. "The Shame of Illinois," *CT*, July 4, 1917, p. 6.
4. Editorial Cartoon 1, *CT*, July 4, 1917, p. 1; Henry M. Hyde, "Half a Million Darkies from Dixie Swarm the North to Better Themselves," *CT*, July 8, 1917, p. 8.
5. Giddings, *Ida*, p. 561; Barnes, *Never Been a Time*, pp. 176–81.
6. From *CD:* "East St. Louis Aftermath," July 28, 1917, p. 12; "Thousands March in Silent Protest," August 4, 1917, p. 1.

7. From *CD:* "Protest to President Wilson Against Riots and Lynchings," August 11, 1917, p. 1; "Thousands March in Silent Protest," August 4, 1917, p. 1; Barnes, *Never Been a Time,* pp. 187–91.

8. "Read This, Then Laugh," *CD,* September 15, 1917, p. 1; "Negro Paper Doing Great Damage," *Athens Daily Banner,* September 7, 1917, p. 4.

9. Scott, *Negro Migration,* pp. 104–6; Spear, *Black Chicago,* p. 149.

10. From *CD:* "Boudoir Caps and Kitchen Apron," May 8, 1915, p. 5; "Overstepping the Bounds," August 4, 1917, p. 12; "Things That Should Be Considered," October 20, 1917, p. 12; William M. Tuttle, *Race Riot: Chicago in the Red Summer of 1919* (New York: Atheneum/Macmillan, 1970), p. 100; Grossman, *Land of Hope,* p. 139.

11. William S. Braddan, *Under Fire with the 370th Infantry (8th I R G.) AEF "Lest You Forget"* (Chicago: privately printed, 1927), pp. 19–25; Giddings, *Ida,* p. 61; "A Mother's Son," *CD,* June 24, 1916, p. 1; Tye, *Rising from the Rails,* p. 106; ad for *Pullman Porters' Review, CD,* April 27, 1918, p. 6; Emmett J. Scott, *The American Negro in the World War* ([Tuskegee, AL?]: privately printed, 1919), p. 54.

12. "Good Luck Farewell to Eighth Regiment Boys Best Wishes," *CD,* October 20, 1917, p. 7.

13. "Address of Emmett J. Scott," *CD,* October 20, 1917, p. 12.

14. Walker, "The Promised Land," p. 25; "Notice to Agents and Correspondents," *CD,* March 23, 1918, p. 3; Ottley, *The Lonely Warrior,* pp. 190–91; "The Hand That Rocks the Cradle," *CD,* March 16, 1918, p. 10; Grossman, *Land of Hope,* p. 79.

15. Ottley, *The Lonely Warrior,* pp. 95, 219, 222.

16. Ibid., 40–41; Masthead, *CD,* March 23, 1918.

17. "Readjustment of Labor," *CD,* March 23, 1918, p. 16.

18. Ibid.

19. A. N. Fields, "Chicago People Pay Homage to Emmett Scott," *CD,* p. 6; Spear, *Black Chicago,* pp. 72–73.

20. Roger D. Cunningham, "The Loving Touch," *Army History,* Summer 2007, pp. 3–17; "Major Loving Here," August 26, 1916, p. 10; Kornweibel, *Investigate Everything,* pp. 231–237; Giddings, *Ida,* p. 577.

21. Kornweibel, *Investigate Everything,* pp. 121–25, 232–34, 244–45; Cunningham, "The Loving Touch," pp. 16–17.

22. Kornweibel, *Investigate Everything,* p. 124; Jordan, *Black Newspapers,* p. 121; Cunningham, "The Loving Touch," pp. 16–17.

23. AS Papers, Box 7, Folder 15: correspondence with Major W. H. Loving; Kornweibel, *Investigate Everything,* pp. 124–25; Ottley, *The Lonely Warrior,* pp. 55–158.

24. "Southern Stunts Surpass Hun: Man Bound to Railroad Track as Fast Train Approaches," *CD,* June 8, 1918, p. 1.

25. Jordan, *Black Newspapers,* pp. 119–22; Kornweibel, *Investigate Everything,* pp. 126–28.

26. From *CD:* "Where the Blame Lies," June 8, 1918, p. 16; Robert S. Abbott, "Loeb's New Propaganda," August 17, 1918, p. 16.

27. Jordan, *Black Newspapers,* pp. 119–22; Kornweibel, *Investigate Everything,* pp. 122–24.

28. "Editor Abbott, with Uncovered Head," *CD,* June 22, 1918, p. 2; Jordan, *Black Newspapers,* pp. 122–23; Cunningham, "The Loving Touch," p. 17.

29. From *CD:* "Editor R. S. Abbott Dined at the Famous Libya," June 22, 1918, p. 3; *"Defender* New York Office Reaches Year of Existence," March 1, 1919, p. 4.

30. From *CD:* "Newspaper Men and Leaders in Important Conference," July 6, 1918, p. 4; "Where the Color Line Begins to Fade," June 29, 1918, p. 1; "Educators' and Editors' Conference," July 6, 1918, p. 4. Jordan, *Black Newspapers,* pp. 122–26.

31. Masthead, *CD,* August 17, 1918; Jordan, *Black Newspapers,* pp. 123–25.

32. Jordan, *Black Newspapers,* pp. 122–26; "Newspaper Men and Leaders in Important Conference," *CD,* July 6, 1918, p. 4.

33. Jordan, *Black Newspapers,* p. 123; Cunningham, "The Loving Touch," p. 18; Kornweibel, *Investigate Everything,* pp. 258–61.

34. *Crisis,* July 1918, p. 111; Giddings, *Ida,* pp. 580–81; Jordan, *Black Newspapers,* pp. 111–15.

35. "Du Bois Editorial Causes Big Stir," *CD,* July 20, 1918, p. 1.

36. Kornweibel, *Investigate Everything,* pp. 144–45; Cunningham, "The Loving Touch," p. 17.

37. A. N. Fields, "Woodrow Wilson," *CD,* August 3, 1918, p. 1; Jordan, *Black Newspapers,* pp. 127–28.

38. "Editors' Conference Yields Big Results," *CD,* August 3, 1918, p. 1.

39. Ibid.; "Our President Has Spoken," *CD,* August 3, 1918, p. 16.

40. From *CD:* "Pres. Wilson Asks Mississippi Voters to Oust Vardaman," August 17, 1918, p. 1; "Senator Vardaman Banished from U.S. Senate by Voters," August 24, 1918, p. 1.

## 6. THE BONDS OF AFFECTIONS

1. "Eighth Regiment in Thick of Fighting," *CD,* July 20, 1918, p. 1.

2. From *CD:* Sgt. E. A. Tooke, "Chicago Hears from Eighth Regiment," August 10, 1918, p. 1; "Eighth Regiment Soldiers Gassed by Germans," August 17, 1918, p. 1; "African Troupers Battle Angry Yanks," May 3, 1919, p. 1. Scott, *The American Negro in the World War,* p. 228; Braddan, *Under Fire with the 370th Infantry* p. 64.

3. A. N. Fields, "Glorious Record of Regiment Told," *CD,* February 22, 1919, p. 3; Braddan, *Under Fire with the 370th Infantry,* pp. 65–68; Scott, *The American Negro in the World War,* pp. 215–16.

4. Braddan, *Under Fire with the 370th Infantry,* pp. 65–68.

5. "Chicago Officer Writes Mother Amid Shell Fire," *CD,* August 24, 1918, p. 2.

6. "Editor Abbott Becomes Benedict," *CD,* September 21, 1918, p. 11.

7. Ibid.; Ottley, *The Lonely Warrior,* pp. 219–22.

8. Ottley, *The Lonely Warrior,* pp. 311–16.

9. From *CD:* "New Yorkers Will Honor Col. Denison," September 21, 1918, p. 1; Cary B. Lewis, "Col. Franklin A. Denison, 370th Infantry, in Chicago for a Few Hours," September 28, 1918, p. 11.

10. Scott, *The American Negro in the World War,* pp. 219–24; Braddan, *Under Fire with the 370th Infantry,* pp. 87–88.

11. Scott, *The American Negro in the World War,* p. 230; A. N. Fields, "Glorious Record of Regiment Told," *CD,* February 22, 1919, p. 3; Cary B. Lewis, "History of the Old Eighth Regiment," *CD,* February 22, 1919, p. 2.

12. Braddan, *Under Fire with the 370th Infantry,* pp. 94–96; Scott, *The American Negro in the World War,* pp. 226–27.

13. Robert E. Butler, "Throngs Greet Eighth," *CD,* February 22, 1919, p. 1; "Camera's Story of How Chicago Showered Affection on Her Famous 'Black Devils,'" *CT,* February 18, 1919, p. 3; Scott, *The American Negro in the World War,* pp. 226–27; "Mayor Appears as Gladiator for Oppressed Race," *CT,* February 17, 1919, p. 7; Gosnell, *Negro Politicians,* pp. 46–47.

14. "Welcome, Eighth!," *CD,* February 22, 1919, p. 24.

15. "Camera's Story of How Chicago Showered Affection on Her Famous 'Black Devils,'" *CT,* February 18, 1919, p. 3.

16. From *CT:* "Aldermanic Primary Vote by Wards," February 26, 1919, p. 4; "Mayoralty Primaries," February 26, 1919, p. 1; "Mayor Ahead in All Wards Except Five," February 26, 1919, p. 1; Arthur M. Evans, "It's Thompson by 17,600!," April 2, 1919, p. 1; Gosnell, *Negro Politicians,* p. 43; Wendt and Kogan, *Big Bill,* p. 170.

17. "Thompson Re-Elected: Second Ward Vote Decided the Political Battle," *CD,* April 5, 1919, p. 1.

18. Tuttle, *Race Riot,* pp. 157–59.

19. "Whites Place Bomb on Housetop," *CD,* May 31, 1919, p. 1; "Bomb Throwers Are Still Active," *CD,* May 24, 1919, p. 19.

20. From *CD:* "Home of White Real Estate Dealer Bombed," June 21, 1919, p. 16; Nahum Daniel Brascher, "Bedlam of Bombs," June 21, 1919, p. 20. Tuttle, *Race Riot,* pp. 157–59.

21. "Ragan's Colts Start Riot," *CD,* June 28, 1919, p. 1; Bontemps and Conroy, *Anyplace But Here,* pp. 175–78.

22. Michael Royko, *Boss* (New York: Penguin Books, 1988), pp. 36–38; Tuttle, *Race Riot,* 237–38; Bontemps and Conroy, *Anyplace But Here,* pp. 175–78.

23. From *CD:* "Home of White Real Estate Dealer Bombed," June 21, 1919, p. 16; Nahum Daniel Brascher, "Bedlam of Bombs," June 21, 1919, p. 20. Tuttle, *Race Riot,* pp. 157–59.

24. "Booze, Its Use and Abuse," *CD,* July 5, 1919, p. 20; "Some Cry, Some Weep in Barleycorn Passing," *CD,* July 5, 1919, p. 15; "Dry Lid Bangs Down on City as Police Act," *CT,* July 2, 1919, p. 1.

25. Tuttle, *Race Riot,* pp. 239–41.

26. From *CD:* "Beach Opens in Full Bloom," July 5, 1919, p. 17; "Editorial Article 2," July 5, 1919, p. 20. Tuttle, *Race Riot,* p. 3.

27. "Police Work to Keep Lynching a Secret," *CD,* July 5, 1919, p. 2; "Renew Capital Riot; 2 Die," *CT,* July 23, 1919, p. 1; "Flees Southern Mob; Now Kansas Merchant," *CD,* September 27, 1919, p. 1; Cameron McWhirter, *Red Summer* (New York: Henry Holt, 2011), pp. 84–95.

28. "Civilians Battle 10th Cavalry," *CD,* July 12, 1919, p. 1.

29. From *CD:* Leslie Rogers, "Birds of a Feather," July 12, 1919, p. 20; "Ruffianism in the Parks," July 12, 1919, p. 20.

30. Carl Sandburg, *The Chicago Race Riots July 1919* (New York: Harcourt, Brace and Howe, 1919), pp. 3–4; McWhirter, *Red Summer,* p. 126.

31. Sandburg, *The Chicago Race Riots,* pp. 51–52; "This Week's Issue 201,125 Read by One Million," *CD,* June 21, 1919, p. 1.

32. Sandburg, *The Chicago Race Riots,* pp. 5–7, 51–52; Emmett J. Scott, *Negro Migration During the War* (New York: Oxford University Press, 1920), p. 102.

33. Sandburg, *The Chicago Race Riots,* pp. 2, 7, 48.

34. Ibid., pp. 64–65; Scott, *Negro Migration During the War,* p. 51; Grossman, *Land of Hope,* pp. 197–98.

35. Sandburg, *The Chicago Race Riots,* pp. 13–16.

36. Ibid., pp. 13–16, 38–41.

37. "Renew Capital Riot; 2 Die," *CT,* July 23, 1919, p. 1.

38. Ibid.; Tuttle, *Race Riot,* pp. 29–30; McWhirter, *Red Summer,* pp. 101–4.

39. "Renew Capital Riot; 2 Die," *CT,* Jul 23, 1919, p. 1; McWhirter, *Red Summer,* pp. 96–115; Tuttle, *Race Riot,* pp. 29–30; Sandburg, *The Chicago Race Riots,* pp. 55–57.

40. Sandburg, *The Chicago Race Riots,* pp. 4, 56; Tuttle, *Race Riot,* pp. 5–8, 26; McWhirter, *Red Summer,* pp. 98–99.

41. "Report Two Killed, Fifty Hurt, in Race Riots," *CT,* July 28, 1919, p. 1; Tuttle, *Race Riot,* pp. 5–8.

42. "Report Two Killed, Fifty Hurt, in Race Riots," *CT,* July 28, 1919, p. 1.

43. "I.W.W. and Race Prejudice," *CT,* July 28, 1919, p. 6.

44. From *CD:* Lucius C. Harper, "Showered with Bullets," August 2, 1919, p. 1; "Riot Sweeps Chicago," August 2, 1919, p. 1; "List of Slain in Four Days' Rioting," August 2, 1919, p. 1. "List of Slain in Day's Rioting," *CT,* July 29, 1919, p. 1.

45. Lucius C. Harper, "Showered with Bullets," *CD,* August 2, 1919, p. 1.

46. From *CD:* Lucius C. Harper, "Showered with Bullets," August 2, 1919, p. 1; "Riot Sweeps Chicago," August 2, 1919, p. 1; "List of Slain in Four Days' Rioting," August 2, 1919, p. 1; "List of Slain in Day's Rioting," *CT,* July 29, 1919, p. 1.

47. Tuttle, *Race Riot,* pp. 29–30, 34; "List of Slain in Day's Rioting," *CT,* July 29, 1919, p. 1.

48. "Strike Is On; Cars Stop! 20 Slain in Race Riots," *CT,* July 29, 1919, p. 1; "'Death for Rioters,' Court Says," *CD,* August 9, 1919, p. 1.

49. "Strike Is On; Cars Stop! 20 Slain in Race Riots," *CT,* July 29, 1919, p. 1.

50. Tuttle, *Race Riot,* pp. 43–46.

51. "Riots Spread, Then Wane," *CT,* July 30, 1919, p. 1.

52. Ibid.; Tuttle, *Race Riot,* pp. 43–46.

53. Tuttle, *Race Riot,* p. 57; Ottley, *The Lonely Warrior,* pp. 182–84; "Negro Business Men Act to Curtail Lawlessness," *CT,* July 30, 1919, p. 2.

54. Tuttle, *Race Riot,* pp. 54–55. From *CT:* "Torch Rioters Give Firemen Continuous Job," July 31, 1919, p. 2; "Negroes Call on Mayor, Lowden, to Stop Riots," July 31, 1919, p. 3.

55. "Negroes Call on Mayor, Lowden, to Stop Riots," *CT,* July 31, 1919, p. 3.

56. Ibid.

57. Ibid.

58. From *CT:* "Mayor's Call for Troops to Stop Riot," July 31, 1919, p. 1; "Troops Act; Halt Rioting," July 31, 1919, p. 1; "5 Regiments Begin Patrol of Riot Areas," July 31, 1919, p. 1.

59. From *CT*: "Regain Order at Once," July 31, 1919, p. 6; John T. McCutcheon, "The Answer," July 31, 1919, p. 1.
60. "Voice of the People: A Sedative for Race Prejudice," *CT*, July 31, 1919, p. 6.
61. Ibid.
62. "Troops Act; Halt Rioting," *CT*, July 31, 1919, p. 1; "5 Regiments Begin Patrol of Riot Areas," *CT*, July 31, 1919, p. 1.
63. "Rioting Calms, but Problems Are Unsolved," *CT*, August 1, 1919, p. 1.

## 7. REAPING THE WHIRLWIND

1. "Attention Agents and Subscribers," *CD*, August 9, 1919, p. 1; Ottley, *The Lonely Warrior*, pp. 189–92.
2. *CD*, August 2, 1919, p. 1.
3. "Reaping the Whirlwind," *CD*, August 2, 1919, p. 16.
4. Tuttle, *Race Riot*, pp. 60–62; "Troops Freed; Chicago Men at Home To-night," *CT*, August 9, 1919, p. 3."'Death for Rioters,' Court Says," *CD*, August 9, 1919, p. 1. AS Papers, Box 18, Folder 4: RSA clippings; "Lowden Names Body to Solve Race Problems," *CT*, August 21, 1919, p. 1; "Seeking the Cause," *CD*, August 9, 1919, p. 20.
5. "Attention Agents and Subscribers," *CD*, August 9, 1919, p. 1.
6. "Lowden Names Body to Solve Race Problems," *CT*, August 21, 1919, p. 1; Ottley, *The Lonely Warrior*, p. 186; Chicago Commission on Race Relations, *The Negro in Chicago: A Study of Race Relations and a Riot* (Chicago: University of Chicago Press, 1922), pp. xv–xxii; Tuttle, *Race Riot*, pp. 109–111, 258; AS Papers, Box 18, Folder 4: RSA clippings.
7. Author interviews with Dr. Timuel Black, July 25, August 5, and August 6, 2010; Drake and Cayton, *Black Metropolis*, pp. 349–51.
8. Timuel Black interviews.
9. A. W. Lester, "Marcus Garvey," *CD*, April 4, 1925, p. 1; Kornweibel, *Seeing Red: Federal Campaigns Against Black Militancy, 1919–1925* (Bloomington: Indiana University Press, 1998), pp. 46–47; Bontemps and Conroy, *Anyplace But Here*, pp. 197–202; Ottley, *The Lonely Warrior*, pp. 212–17.
10. A. W. Lester, "Marcus Garvey," *CD*, April 4, 1925, p. 1; Bontemps and Conroy, *Anyplace But Here*, pp. 191–93; Ottley, *The Lonely Warrior*, pp. 212–17.
11. Giddings, *Ida*, pp. 584–86; A. W. Lester, "Marcus Garvey," *CD*, April 4, 1925, p. 1.
12. "Organization Says Black Star Line Will Be Launched," *CD*, June 28, 1919, p. 5; Bontemps and Conroy, *Anyplace But Here*, pp. 197–202.
13. From *CD*: "Seeing Ourselves," June 8, 1918, p. 16; "Weekly Comment," September 6, 1919, p. 4; "District Attorney Swan Now Handling Garvey Case," September 6, 1919, p. 4.
14. "Editors in Highway Argument," *CD*, June 21, 1919, p. 4; Bontemps and Conroy, *Anyplace But Here*, pp. 202–3; "Scheme to Oust Juvenile Court Judge Exposed," *CT*, October 1, 1919, p. 10; *Broad Axe*, October 11, 1919, p. 1.
15. "Brundage 'Sinks' Black Star Line," *CD*, October 4, 1919, p. 1; Bontemps and Conroy, *Anyplace But Here*, pp. 202–3; Kornweibel, *Seeing Red*, pp. 46–47; "Scheme to Oust Juvenile Court Judge Exposed," *CT*, October 1, 1919, p. 10; *Broad Axe*, October 11, 1919, p. 1.

16. Ottley, *The Lonely Warrior*, pp. 212–17; Bontemps and Conroy, *Anyplace But Here*, pp. 191–206.

17. From *CD:* "Self Appointed Spokesmen," November 1, 1919, p. 20; "*Chicago Defender* Retains Counsel in Two Libel Suits," November 1, 1919, p. 4.

18. "Brundage 'Sinks' Black Star Line," *CD*, October 4, 1919, p. 1; Bontemps and Conroy, *Anyplace But Here*, pp. 202–3; Kornweibel, *Seeing Red*, pp. 46–47; "Scheme to Oust Juvenile Court Judge Exposed," *CT*, October 1, 1919, p. 10.

19. Ottley, *The Lonely Warrior*, pp. 216–18; Bontemps and Conroy, *Anyplace But Here*, pp. 201–3.

20. AS Papers, Box 22-1; Robert S. Abbott, "Riding the Hog Train," *CD*, February 28, 1920, p. 2.

21. Ibid.

22. Ibid.

23. AS Papers, Boxes 22-1, 22-3.

24. Robert S. Abbott, "Riding the Hog Train," *CD*, February 28, 1920, p. 2.

25. "Equal Accommodations," *CD*, February 28, 1920, p. 20.

26. AS Papers, Box 18-28.

27. "Mr. and Mrs. Abbott Arrive," *CD*, June 5, 1920, p. 13.

28. Ibid.

29. "Seeks $200,000 Damages; Gets Only Six Cents," *CD*, June 19, 1920, p. 1; Bontemps and Conroy, *Anyplace But Here*, pp. 192–94, 198–204.

30. Bontemps and Conroy, *Anyplace But Here*, pp. 192–94.

31. From *CD:* Leslie Rogers, "Will He Let It In?," October 30, 1920, p. 12; "Political Preferences," October 30, 1920, p. 12; "Advice with a Kick in It," October 30, 1920, p. 12.

32. Ibid.; "Julius Avendorph, Society Editor, Returns from Western Trip," *CD*, October 23, 1920, p. 2.

33. "Republicans Sweep the Country," *CD*, November 6, 1920, p. 1; Gosnell, *Negro Politicians*, pp. 157–60.

34. "Lynched Man Who Wanted to Vote," *CD*, November 6, 1920, p. 1.

35. Lucius C. Harper, "Dustin' Off the News," *CD*, October 25, 1947, p. 1.

36. From *CD:* David W. Kellum, "Bud Tells History of Billiken Club," May 3, 1930, p. 2; Lucius C. Harper, "Dustin' Off the News," October 25, 1947, p. 1; Ottley, *The Lonely Warrior*, pp. 351–54; Dorothy Jean Ray, "Billiken Lore," *Alaska Journal*, Winter 1974.

37. From *CD:* Robert Watkins, "Chicago Defender Jr.," April 2, 1921, p. 5; David W. Kellum, "Bud Tells History of Billiken Club," May 3, 1930, p. 2; Lucius C. Harper, "Dustin' Off the News," October 25, 1947, p. 1; Ottley, *The Lonely Warrior*, pp. 351–54.

38. From *CD*, Robert Watkins: "Chicago Defender Jr.," April 9, 1921, p. 5; "Chicago Defender Jr.," May 7, 1921, p. 8.

39. "Formal Opening," *CD*, April 30, 1921, p. 1; "5,000 Inspect *Defender*'s New Plant 'Welcome Day,'" *CD*, May 14, 1921, p. 4; Ottley, *The Lonely Warrior*, pp. 193–98; Frederick G. Detweiler, *The Negro Press in the United States* (Chicago: University of Chicago Press, 1922), pp. 65–66.

40. Ibid.; Waters, *American Diary*, p. 126; Ben Burns, *Nitty Gritty: A White Editor in Black Journalism* (Jackson: University Press of Mississippi, 1986), pp. 3–5.

41. Ibid.; AS Papers, Box 11, Folder 1; Walker, "The Promised Land," pp. 34–35.
42. Ibid.; Ottley, *The Lonely Warrior*, p. 198.
43. Ibid.
44. Ibid.; Abbott Sengstacke Family Archives, Box 11-1; Walker, "The Promised Land," pp. 34–35.
45. Ibid.; Ottley, p. 198.

## 8. BOMBING BINGA

1. "Bomb Rips Front Porch from Jesse Binga's Dwelling," *CD*, September 3, 1921, p. 3; "Binga's Guard Tries Gun Play After Bombing," *CT*, August 26, 1921, p. 13; "Fourth Bomb for Negro's Home in White Section," *CT*, February 7, 1920, p. 1.
2. Ibid.; Frank "Fay" Young, "Binga Put Personal Pride Before Depositors' Savings; Wrecked Bank," *Baltimore Afro-American*, June 17, 1933, p. 9.
3. From *CD*: "Bombing Binga," September 3, 1921, p. 16; "Binga Sounds Key-Note for Race Progress," December 17, 1921, p. 2; "Binga Gives Points upon Which Race Must Build," June 10, 1922, p. 4.
4. "Aviatrix Must Sign Away Life to Learn Trade," *CD*, October 8, 1921, p. 2; "Writer Recalls Memory of the Late Bessie Coleman," *CD*, January 26, 1929, p. 7.
5. E. B. Jourdain Jr., "Bessie Coleman, Aviatrix, Killed," *CD*, May 8, 1926, p. 1; "Miss Bessie Coleman Among the First to Clamp on 'Flu' Lid," *CD*, November 2, 1921, p. 12; Ottley, *The Lonely Warrior*, pp. 257–58.
6. From *CD*: "Aviatrix Must Sign Away Life to Learn Trade," October 8, 1921, p. 2; "Bessie Coleman Leaves New York for France," February 25, 1922, p. 2; "Writer Recalls Memory of the Late Bessie Coleman," January 26, 1929, p. 7.
7. From *CD*: "Fraud Charged to Garvey," January 21, 1922, p. 1; "Charge Garvey Hurts," January 28, 1922, p. 2; "This and That and t'Other," March 25, 1922, p. 12; "Rum Made Ship Shake the Shimmy," April 8, 1922, p. 8. Bontemps and Conroy, *Anyplace But Here*, p. 201; Spear, *Black Chicago*, pp. 210–14.
8. Roscoe Simmons, "The Week," *CD*, July 8, 1922, p. 13; "Garvey Has Wrong Idea as Uplifter," *CD*, July 22, 1922, p. 1.
9. "Imperial Wizard Has Conference with Mr. Garvey," *CD*, July 8, 1922, p. 2.
10. From *CD*: "New Exodus of Laborers from South," June 24, 1922, p. 1; "Klan Gobbles Up Los Angeles Cops One by One," April 22, 1922, p. 1; "Colorado Law Has Teeth to Gnaw Ku Klux," April 8, 1922, p. 2; "Up-State New Yorkers Battle Ku Klux Klan," January 28, 1922, p. 9; Jackson, *The Ku Klux Klan in the City*, pp. 10–12, 30–36.
11. From *CD*: "Garvey a Crook or Liar, Charges Editor Randolph," August 26, 1922, p. 8; "Marcus Garvey's Move Is Scored by Dean Pickens," July 29, 1922, p. 8; "Garvey Has Wrong Idea as Uplifter," July 22, 1922, p. 1; Roscoe Simmons, "The Week," July 8, 1922, p. 13.
12. From *CD*: "Garvey's Clan in Attempt to Stop Street Meetings," August 12, 1922, p. 2; "Garvey a Crook or Liar, Charges Editor Randolph," August 26, 1922, p. 8; "Garvey Dubs Dr. Emmett Scott a Knight, Report," August 26, 1922, p. 1.
13. From *CD*: "Philip Randolph Stamps Garvey Little Half-Wit," August 12, 1922,

p. 3; "Garvey's Clan in Attempt to Stop Street Meetings," August 12, 1922, p. 2; "Garvey a Crook or Liar, Charges Editor Randolph," August 26, 1922, p. 8.

14. From *CD*: "Owens Demands That Americans Deport Garvey," September 2, 1922, p. 2; "Editor of *Messenger* Analyzes Planks in *Defender* Platform," September 2, 1922, p. 14; Walker, "The Promised Land," p. 36.

15. Jackson, *The Ku Klux Klan in the City*, pp. 96–97.

16. "Chief Upsets Ku Klux Klan Parade Plans," *CD*, September 18, 1921, p. 1; "Two Societies Press Attack on Ku Klux Klan," *CT*, September 16, 1921, p. 16; Jackson, *The Ku Klux Klan in the City*, pp. 93–97.

17. "Nation-Wide War on Ku Klux Klan Is Launched Here," *CD*, August 19, 1922, p. 3.

18. "Class of 4,650 Takes Oath of Ku Klux Klan," *CT*, August 20, 1922, p. 1; Jackson, *The Ku Klux Klan in the City*, pp. 97–98.

19. "Members of Race 'Pass' and Join the Ku Kluxers," *CD*, August 26, 1922, p. 3; Jackson, *The Ku Klux Klan in the City*, pp. 101–2.

20. From *CD*: "Harding Tables Anti-Lynch Bill," September 2, 1922, p. 1; "American Unity League," September 2, 1922, p. 12; "Ku Klux Made Possible by Bigotry and Cowardice of American White Man," September 2, 1922, p. 1; "Desecrating the Church," September 9, 1922, p. 12.

21. "Klansmen in Chicago to Be Exposed," *CD*, September 16, 1922, p. 2; Jackson, *The Ku Klux Klan in the City*, pp. 102–5.

22. Ibid.; "Tolerance," *CD*, October 7, 1922, p. 12.

23. From *CD*: "Bessie Gets Away; Does Her Stuff," September 9, 1922, p. 3; "Rain Halts the Initial Flight of Miss Bessie," September 2, 1922, p. 9; "Bessie to Fly Over Gotham," August 26, 1922, p. 1; "Bessie Coleman Leaves New York for France," February 25, 1922, p. 2; "Go Up in Aeroplane," September 9, 1922, p. 9. "Negress Pilots Airplane," *New York Times*, September 4, 1922; Walker, "The Promised Land," *CD*, p. 36; Ottley, *The Lonely Warrior*, pp. 257–58.

24. "Bessie Coleman Makes Initial Aerial Flight," *CD*, October 21, 1922, p. 3; Ottley, *The Lonely Warrior*, pp. 257–58.

25. "Bessie Coleman Makes Initial Aerial Flight," October 21, 1922, p. 3.

26. From *CD*: "The Defender Junior," December 2, 1922, p. 14; Lucius C. Harper, "Dustin' Off the News," October 25, 1947, p. 1; David W. Kellum, "Bud Tells History of Billiken Club," May 3, 1930, p. 2. Ottley, *The Lonely Warrior*, pp. 351–52.

27. From *CD*: Willard Motley, "The Defender Junior," March 3, 1923, p. 14; Lucius C. Harper, "Dustin' Off the News," October 25, 1947, p. 1; Willard Motley, "First Bud Billiken Tells About Himself After 15 Years," *CD*, January 20, 1940, p. 19.

28. Willard Motley, "Captain Zeno Is Rival of Joseph of Bible Times," *CD*, November 10, 1923, p. 19; Ottley, *The Lonely Warrior*, pp. 351–52.

29. Ralph Elliot, "Bessie Coleman Says Good Will Come from Hurt," *CD*, March 10, 1923, p. 3.

30. Ibid.

31. From *CD*: "Resolves for 1923," January 6, 1923, p. 2; "Firemen in Klan Order Are Caught," January 13, 1923, p. 3. Jackson, *The Ku Klux Klan in the City*, pp. 107–9.

32. Roscoe Simmons, "The Week," *CD*, February 24, 1923, p. 13; Wendt and

Kogan, *Big Bill*, pp. 206–7; Gosnell, *Negro Politicians*, pp. 26–27, 43–44, 176–77.

33. "Louis B. Anderson Returned to Lead City Council," *CD*, March 3, 1923, p. 1; Oscar Hewitt, "Voters Kick Lundinism Out of Council," *CT*, February 28, 1923, p. 1.

34. From *CD*: "Chicago's Next Mayor," March 17, 1923, p. 12; "The Onlooker," March 24, 1923, p. 12; Roscoe Simmons, "The Week," March 31, 1923, p. 13. Jackson, *The Ku Klux Klan in the City*, pp. 110–12.

35. "A House Divided Against itself," *CD*, March 31, 1923, p. 12; "Dever Wins Mayoralty, 'Ghosts' Defeat Lueder," *CD*, April 7, 1923, p. 1; Parke Brown, "Lueder Charges 'Dirty Politics' Spikes Canard," *CT*, March 17, 1923, p. 5; Gosnell, *Negro Politicians*, pp. 26–27, 43–44, 176–77; Jackson, *The Ku Klux Klan in the City*, pp. 110–12.

36. Parke Brown, "Lueder Charges 'Dirty Politics' Spikes Canard," *CT*, March 17, 1923, p. 5; "Fight for Mayor Hot, with Lueder Taking the Lead," *CD*, March 24, 1923, p. 3; Gosnell, *Negro Politicians*, pp. 26–27, 43–44, 176–77; Jackson, *The Ku Klux Klan in the City*, pp. 110–12.

37. "Lawyers Clash over Oath as Fireman's Klan Trial Opens," *CT*, March 17, 1923, p. 3; "Firemen in Klan Order Are Caught," *CD*, January 13, 1923, p. 3; Roscoe Simmons, "The Week," *CD*, March 24, 1923, p. 13; Jackson, *The Ku Klux Klan in the City*, pp. 109–10.

38. "Dever Wins Mayoralty, 'Ghosts' Defeat Lueder," *CD*, April 7, 1923, p. 1; Gosnell, *Negro Politicians*, pp. 26–27, 43–44, 176–77; Jackson, *The Ku Klux Klan in the City*, pp. 210–12.

39. Robert S. Abbott, "My Trip Through South America," *CD*, August 4, 1923, p. 1; Robert S. Abbott, "My Trip Through South America," *CD*, August 11, 1923, p: 13; Ottley, *The Lonely Warrior*, pp. 228–36.

40. From *CD* by Robert S. Abbott, "My Trip Through South America," August 4, 1923, p. 1; October 6, 1923, p. 13; August 11, 1923, p. 13.

41. From *CD* by Robert S. Abbott, "My Trip Through South America," August 18, 1923, p. 13; September 1, 1923, p. 13; September 8, 1923, p. 13.

42. From *CD* by Robert S. Abbott, "My Trip Through South America," September 22, 1923, p. 2; September 15, 1923, p. 13.

43. Robert S. Abbott, "My Trip Through South America," *CD*, September 29, 1923, p. 13.

44. From *CD* by Robert S. Abbott, "My Trip Through South America," October 6, 1923, p. 13; October 13, 1923, p. 13.

45. Robert S. Abbott, "My Trip Through South America," *CD*, October 20, 1923, p. 2.

46. "All Chicago Mourns the Death of Julius Avendorph," *CD*, May 12, 1923, p. 5.

47. From *CD*: Julius N. Avendorph, "Mr. Avendorph Explains His Attitude as to the 'Rambler' Column," May 7, 1910, p. 6; Julius N. Avendorph, "Why Not Dress in Keeping with the Occasion or Not at All," December 3, 1910, p. 2; Julius Avendorph, "Do We as a Race Progress with the Times?," January 28, 1911, p. 1; "Julius Avendorph, Society Editor, Returns from Western Trip," October 23, 1920, p. 2; "Julius Avendorph Promoted," January 22, 1921, p. 2; Julius N. Avendorph, "Chicago Social Life in Years Past as Compared with

Today," October 22, 1921, p. 3; "All Chicago Mourns the Death of Julius Avendorph," May 12, 1923, p. 5.

48. "Mr. Abbott Returns to Home Town," *CD*, May 26, 1923, p. 1.
49. Ibid.
50. Ibid.

### 9. CHICAGO VINDICATED

1. T. M. Charles, "Marcus Garvey in Serious Mood as Trial Starts," *CD*, May 26, 1923, p. 13; Bontemps and Conroy, *Anyplace But Here*, p. 203; Kornweibel, *Seeing Red*, pp. 127–31.
2. "Fanatic Sentenced for Death Threat at Garvey Trial," *CD*, June 2, 1923, p. 1.
3. From *CD*: "Court Tightens Grip on Garvey in Fund Probe," June 9, 1923, p. 1; "Style Garvey 'Clown' in Court Room; Case Goes to Jury Soon," June 16, 1923, p. 1.
4. From *CD*: "Garvey Guilty," June 23, 1923, p. 1; "Garvey Changes Front in Face of Prison Door," June 30, 1923, p. 10; "Garvey Blames 'Color War' for Failure of His Plans," July 7, 1923, p. 1; "Garvey Spends Birthday with Prison Guests," August 18, 1923, p. 3. Ottley, *The Lonely Warrior*, pp. 247–55; Bontemps and Conroy, *Anyplace But Here*, p. 203; Kornweibel, *Seeing Red*, pp. 127–131.
5. Ottley, *The Lonely Warrior*, pp. 247–55; AS Papers, Box 8, Folder 21.
6. "Garvey to Prison," *CD*, February 7, 1925, p. 1.
7. From *CD*: "No. 19,359," February 21, 1925, p. 4; "Very Latest News," March 28, 1925, p. 1; A. W. Lester, "Marcus Garvey," April 4, 1925, p. 1.
8. "No. 19,359," February 21, 1925, p. 4. Bontemps and Conroy, *Anyplace But Here*, pp. 203–4.
9. "Father and Son Banquet Addressed by Publisher," *CD*, March 7, 1925, p. 3; George S. Nettie, "My Scrap Book of Doers," *CD*, March 14, 1925, p. 4.
10. "McGill Appointed State's Attorney," *CD*, May 2, 1925, p. 2; "A. L. Jackson Made *Chicago Defender*'s General Manager," *CD*, May 2, 1925, p. 2; Ottley, *The Lonely Warrior*, pp. 247–55.
11. Ottley, *The Lonely Warrior*, pp. 247–55.
12. Tye, *Rising from the Rails*, pp. 127–34.
13. "Sleeping Car Porters Hold Mass Meeting," *CD*, September 26, 1925, p. 3.
14. "Good-by, 'George,'" *CD*, September 19, 1925, p. 1.
15. Evangeline Roberts, "Chicago Pays Parting Tribute to 'Brave Bessie' Coleman," *CD*, May 15, 1926, p. 2.
16. Ibid.; E. B. Jourdain Jr., "Bessie Coleman, Aviatrix, Killed," *CD*, May 8, 1926, p. 1.
17. Ibid.
18. Ibid.
19. "*Defender* Editor's New Home," *CD*, July 31, 1926, p. 8; Ottley, *The Lonely Warrior*, pp. 227, 255.
20. Ottley, *The Lonely Warrior*, p. 255.
21. "Pullman Prosperity Has Helped Race," *CD*, July 31, 1926, p. 8; Tye, *Rising from the Rails*, pp. 141–43.

22. "Pullman Prosperity Has Helped Race," "Mays Charges Randolph with Misrepresenting Pullman Case," *CD*, March 27, 1926, p. 2; "Pullman Porter Agitators Still Bungling, Says Mays," *CD*, March 6, 1926, p. 4; Andrew Buni, *Robert L. Vann* of The Pittsburgh Courier (Pittsburgh: University of Pittsburgh Press, 1974), pp. 161–71; Ottley, *The Lonely Warrior*, pp. 260–64.

23. Tye, *Rising from the Rails*, pp. 141–43; Buni, *Robert L. Vann*, pp. 161–71; Ottley, *The Lonely Warrior*, pp. 260–64.

24. Vernon Jarrett, "Lesson in American History," *CT*, March 5, 1982, p. 1; John H. Johnson, *Succeeding Against the Odds* (New York: Amistad Press, 1989), p. 47.

25. Author interviews with Dr. Timuel Black, July 25, August 5, and August 6, 2010.

26. "We're for Thompson," *CD*, February 5, 1927, p. 1.

27. A. N. Fields, "Chicagoans Make Political History," *CD*, January 14, 1933, p. 9; Wendt and Kogan, *Big Bill*, pp. 249–50, 256–58; Gosnell, *Negro Politicians*, pp. 160–61.

28. Gosnell, *Negro Politicians*, pp. 57, 122–23, 130–33; Drake and Cayton, *Black Metropolis*, pp. 350–51.

29. Gosnell, *Negro Politicians*, pp. 57, 122–23, 130–33; Wendt and Kogan, *Big Bill*, pp. 241–45, 250.

30. Arthur Evans, "Crime Capital Is in Chicago, Says Litsinger," *CT*, February 15, 1927, p. 1; Arthur Evans, "Thompson Victor by 180,000," *CT*, February 23, 1927, p. 1; "Dever and Thompson," *CT*, February 23, 1927, p. 10; "Thompson Is Given City's Biggest Vote," *CD*, February 26, 1927, p. 1; Wendt and Kogan, *Big Bill*, pp. 241–45, 250.

31. Wendt and Kogan, *Big Bill*, pp. 254–57; "Thompson Calls Halt on 'Cossack' Police Raids," *CD*, March 19, 1927, p. 1.

32. "Colored Voters Tell Why They Bask Thompson," *CT*, March 26, 1927, p. 5; Gosnell, *Negro Politicians*, pp. 41, 54; Wendt and Kogan, *Big Bill*, pp. 254–57, 268–70.

33. Arthur Evans, "Thompson Victor by 83,072," *CT*, April 6, 1927, p. 1; Philip Kinsley, "Crowds Roar for Big Bill After Victory," *CT*, April 6, 1927, p. 1; Wendt and Kogan, *Big Bill*, pp. 271–73.

34. "Thompson, *Defender*'s Candidate, Now Chicago's Mayor," *CD*, April 9, 1927, p. 1; "Chicago Vindicated." *CD*, April 9, 1927, p. 12; Gosnell, *Negro Politicians*, pp. 57, 122–23, 130–33, 160–61.

35. Wendt and Kogan, *Big Bill*, p. 274.

36. "The Pullman Porters' Case," *CD*, August 20, 1927, p. 1; "U.S. Mediation Board Drops Pullman Porters' Wrangle," *CD*, August 20, 1927, p. 1; Tye, *Rising from the Rails*, pp. 144–48; Buni, *Robert L. Vann*, pp. 161–65.

37. Tye, *Rising from the Rails*, pp. 144–48; Buni, *Robert L. Vann*, pp. 161–65; Ottley, *The Lonely Warrior*, pp. 260–66.

38. "The Pullman Porters' Organization," *CD*, November 19, 1927, p. 1; Ottley, *The Lonely Warrior*, pp. 260–66.

39. A. Philip Randolph, "Porters' Union Renews Fight Against Pullman Company," *CD*, November 19, 1927, p. 1.

40. Tye, *Rising from the Rails*, pp. 144–48; Buni, *Robert L. Vann*, pp. 161–65; Ottley, *The Lonely Warrior*, pp. 260–66.

41. "Time to Free Marcus Garvey," *CD*, November 19, 1927, p. 1.

42. "Marcus Garvey Free," *CD*, December 3, 1927, p. 1.

43. "Garvey Sails with Pledge to Fight on," *CD*, December 10, 1927, p. 1.

44. "All America Mourns for M. B. Madden," *CD*, May 5, 1928, p. 1; "Editor Abbott Calls Roll of Those Who Aided *Defender*," *CD*, May 31, 1930, p. 10; Gosnell, *Negro Politicians*, pp. 77–78.

45. From *CD:* "De Priest Nominated for Congress," May 5, 1928, p. 1; "Nominated for Congress," May 5, 1928, p. 4; "See Fulfillment of White's Prophecy," May 12, 1928, p. 5; "Colored Men in Congress," May 12, 1928, p. 1; Evangeline Roberts, "Major Lynch Tells of Days in Congress," May 12, 1928, p. 5. Gosnell, *Negro Politicians*, pp. 79–81.

46. From *CD:* "See Fulfillment of White's Prophecy," May 12, 1928, p. 5; "Colored Men in Congress," May 12, 1928, p. 1.

47. "*Defender* Platform for America," *CD*, May 24, 1930, p. 14; "*Defender* Platform," *CD*, August 11, 1928, p. 1.

48. "Who Won the Rebel War?" *CD*, August 11, 1928, p. 1.

## 10. THE BURDENS OF THE FUTURE

1. "What We Want," *CD*, October 20, 1928, p. 1; "Senator Moses Raises Racial Issue in Political Speech," *CD*, October 20, 1928, p. 1; Gosnell, *Negro Politicians*, pp. 79–80.

2. "Some More Facts," *CD*, October 27, 1928, p. 1; Nancy J. Weiss, *Farewell to the Party of Lincoln: Black Politics in the Age of FDR* (Princeton, NJ: Princeton University Press, 1983), pp. 6–9.

3. From *CD:* "Indict Jackson and De Priest," October 6, 1928, p. 1; Roscoe Holloway, "Hoover Landslide Grows," November 10, 1928, p. 1; "Election of De Priest in Doubt," November 10, 1928, p. 1. Gosnell, *Negro Politicians*, pp. 182–83.

4. "Congressman Tells Plans for Future," *CD*, November 24, 1928, p. 2; Gosnell, *Negro Politicians*, pp. 183–84.

5. A. N. Fields, "Edward N. Wright Dies," *CD*, August 9, 1930, p. 1.

6. Robert S. Abbott, "My Trip Abroad," *CD*, November 9, 1929, p. 1.

7. Ibid., January 18, 1930, p. 1.

8. From *CD:* "Spreads Hate in Paris by Bribe Route," August 24, 1929, p. 1; Robert S. Abbott, "My Trip Abroad," November 9, 1929, p. 1; Robert S. Abbott, "My Trip Abroad," November 16, 1929, p. 1; Robert S. Abbott, "My Trip Abroad," November 23, 1929, p. 1.

9. Robert S. Abbott, "My Trip Abroad," *CD*, November 30, 1929, p. 1.

10. Robert S. Abbott, "My Trip Abroad," *CD*, December 7, 1929, p. 1; Ottley, *The Lonely Warrior*, pp. 275–76.

11. Robert S. Abbott, "My Trip Abroad," *CD*, December 21, 1929, p. 1; Ottley, *The Lonely Warrior*, pp. 359–62.

12. Robert S. Abbott, "My Trip Abroad," *CD*, November 9, 1929, p. 1; Robert S. Abbott, "My Trip Abroad," *CD*, December 21, 1929, p. 1.

13. From *CD:* Robert S. Abbott, "My Trip Abroad," January 4, 1930, p. 1; Robert S. Abbott, "My Trip Abroad," January 11, 1930, p. 1; Robert S. Abbott, "My Trip Abroad," January 18, 1930, p. 1; Ivan H. Browning, "Across the Pond,"

October 5, 1929, p. 7; Ivan H. Browning, "Ivan H. Browning Explains Spreading of Prejudice; Is Host to the R. S. Abbotts," September 14, 1929, p. 6; "The Abbotts Return Home from Europe," October 26, 1929, p. 3. Ottley, *The Lonely Warrior*, pp. 278–82.

14. Robert S. Abbott, "My Trip Abroad," *CD*, January 25, 1930, p. 1.
15. Ibid., January 18, 1930, p. 1.
16. "The Abbotts Return Home from Europe," *CD*, October 26, 1929, p. 3.
17. AS Papers, Box 6, Folder 36, Correspondence.
18. AS Papers, Boxes 22-6, 22-3, 22-1.
19. From *CD*: "*Defender* Newsboys Win Bicycles, Prizes," February 22, 1930, p. 1; "4,500 Kiddies Attend Bud's Regal Party," February 22, 1930, A3; "They Just Had the Time of Their Lives," February 22, 1930, p. A3.
20. "4,500 Kiddies Attend Bud's Regal Party," *CD*, February 22, 1930, p. A3.
21. Ottley, *The Lonely Warrior*, pp. 352–53.
22. "Hold Your Jobs," *CD*, December 7, 1929, p. 1.
23. "330,000 Without Work," *CD*, March 22, 1930, p. 13; Drake and Cayton, *Black Metropolis*, pp. 82–84.
24. Walker, "The Promised Land," pp. 40–41.
25. Drake and Cayton, *Black Metropolis*, pp. 8–10; Grossman, *Land of Hope*, p. 3.
26. From *CD*: "Banker Binga in Jail Hospital," March 14, 1931, p. 2; "3 Chicago Banks Closed," August 9, 1930, p. 1; "Court Asks for Accounting of Jesse Binga's Property," November 15, 1930, p. 13. Drake and Cayton, *Black Metropolis*, pp. 465–66.
27. "3 Chicago Banks Closed," *CD*, August 9, 1930, p. 1; Frank "Fay" Young, "Binga Put Personal Pride Before Depositors' Savings; Wrecked Bank," *Baltimore Afro-American*, June 17, 1933, p. 9.
28. From *CD*: "3 Chicago Banks Closed," August 9, 1930, p. 1; "Court Asks for Accounting of Jesse Binga's Property," November 15, 1930, p. 13; "Binga Bank Had Only 2 Accounts of Over $10,000," October 31, 1931, p. 3. Drake and Cayton, *Black Metropolis*, pp. 465–66.
29. "'Black Belts' Cause Chicago's Bank Failures," *CD*, August 23, 1930, p. 13.
30. "Binga's Wife Sues, Charging Incompetency," *CD*, October 11, 1930, p. 1; "Banker Binga in Jail Hospital," *CD*, March 14, 1931, p. 2; Ottley, *The Lonely Warrior*, p. 299.
31. Wendt and Kogan, *Big Bill*, pp. 314–33.
32. "South Side Voters Give Mayor Thompson Big Plurality," *CD*, February 28, 1931, p. 1; "Stir Caused in New Orleans When Mayor Dines with De Priest," *CD*, March 7, 1931, p. 13.
33. "Democratic Landslide Beats Thompson," *CD*, April 11, 1931, p. 1; Wendt and Kogan, *Big Bill*, pp. 314–33.
34. "Thompson Defeated Himself," *CD*, April 11, 1931, p. 14.
35. Gosnell, *Negro Politicians*, pp. 132–34.
36. Ottley, *The Lonely Warrior*, pp. 306–9.
37. From *CD*: "Amos 'n' Andy to Cheer Billikens at Picnic," August 15, 1931, p. 16; Nahum Daniel Brascher, "35,000 Cheer Amos 'n' Andy at Bud's Picnic," August 22, 1931, p. 16; Albert G. Barnett, "A Few Sidelights on Bud's Big Jubilee," August 22, 1931, p. 16; "A Message to Youth," August 22, 1931, p. 1.

38. "Bishop Walls Deplores Amos 'n' Andy Chats," *CD*, May 3, 1930, p. 7; Buni, *Robert L. Vann*, pp. 227–30.

39. Yuval Taylor and Jake Austen, *Darkest America* (New York: W. W. Norton, 2012), pp. 143–46; "Miller and Lyles Booked by Columbia to Counter 'Amos 'n' Andy' on National Chain," *CD*, July 18, 1931, p. 5.

40. Tutt W. Salem, "Timely Topics," *CD*, August 29, 1931, p. 5.

41. AS Papers, Box 8, Folder 33.

42. Ibid.

43. Ibid.

11. WE'LL TAKE THE SEA

1. "Wife Sues R. S. Abbott," *CD*, June 4, 1932, p. 1; Ottley, *The Lonely Warrior*, pp. 316–22.

2. From *CD*: "Has Setback," June 25, 1932, p. 2; "Editor in Reply to Suit of Mrs. Abbott," August 20, 1932, p. 1. "Bury Mother of Editor in Savannah, Ga.," October 1, 1932, p. 1. Ottley, *The Lonely Warrior*, pp. 316–22.

3. "Failures of Hoover," *CD*, June 4, 1932, p. 1; Henry Brown, "Editorial Cartoon: If This Is the Ship . . . ," *CD*, June 4, 1932, p. 1

4. "Democrats Adopt *Defender's* Platform," *CD*, July 9, 1932, p. 13.

5. "Roosevelt Grants *Defender* an Interview," *CD*, July 9, 1932, p. 1.

6. Ibid.; Walker, "The Promised Land," p. 39.

7. "Will Democracy Yield?," *CD*, July 9, 1932, p. 14.

8. From *CD*: "Attention, Mr. Garner," September 4, 1932, p. 14; "Governor Roosevelt on Haiti," September 10, 1932, p. 14. Weiss, *Farewell to the Party of Lincoln*, pp. 12–15; Buni, *Robert L. Vann*, pp. 174–202.

9. From *CD*: "De Priest Says South Wants Garner in President's Chair," September 17, 1932, p. 3; "De Priest Begins Speaking Tour to Aid Hoover," September 24, 1932, p. 13; "Southern Democrats Hate to Admit That Race Vote Is Wanted," October 1, 1932, p. 3.

10. "Hoover Renews G.O.P. Pledge to Race," *CD*, October 8, 1932, p. 1.

11. "Hoover or Roosevelt, Which?" *CD*, October 22, 1932, p. 14; "Expose Roosevelt as Rabid Jim Crower," *CD*, October 15, 1932, p. 1.

12. From *CD*: "The People Have Spoken," November 12, 1932, p. 14; "New Political Map of the United States," November 12, 1932, p. 3; "Republican Party Swamped by Anti-Hoover Vote," November 12, 1932, p. 1.

13. "De Priest in Close Fight for Congress," *CD*, November 12, 1932, p. 1; "Race Candidates Hold Their Own in Big Election Storm," *CD*, November 19, 1932, p. 2; Weiss, *Farewell to the Party of Lincoln*, pp. 13–33.

14. AS Papers, Box 11, Folder 2.

15. From *CD* by Roberta G. Thomas and Flaurience L. Sengstacke: "Thrills That Come Once in a Lifetime Greet Travelers Through Romantic Italy," December 10, 1932, p. 8; "America Welcomes Travelers at End of World Trip," April 15 1933, p. 11; "Italy and Switzerland Still Hold Spotlight as Young Travelers See Europe," December 17, 1932, p. 11.

16. From *CD* by Roberta G. Thomas and Flaurience L. Sengstacke: "Tourists Get Real Thrills on Rhine," December 31, 1932, p. 11; "American Express Is Aid to Tourists," December 24 1932, p. 11.

17. From *CD* by Roberta G. Thomas and Flaurience L. Sengstacke: "Tourists Get Real Thrills on Rhine," December 31, 1932, p. 11; "Bremen Holidays Prove Delightful," January 7, 1933, p. 10; "American Express Is Aid to Tourists," December 24, 1932, p. 11.

18. A. N. Fields, "Nominate Nathan K. McGill for Circuit Court Bench," *CD*, April 22, 1933, p. 1.

19. "Mrs. Ida Lee McGill Is Granted Divorce," *CD*, April 22, 1933, p. 13.

20. "The Press: Black McLean," *Time*, June 26 1933.

21. Ottley, *The Lonely Warrior*, pp. 316–22; Buni, *Robert L. Vann*, p. 379.

22. AS Papers, Box 1, Folder 21; "Divorce Ends Abbott Case," *CD*, July 1, 1933, p. 1.

23. AS Papers, Box 1, Folder 21.

24. "Divorce Ends Abbott Case," *CD*, July 1, 1933, p. 1.

25. AS Papers, Box 8, Folder 33.

26. Ibid.

27. Ibid.

28. "Mrs. Robert S. Abbott Now 'at Home' with Husband," *CD*, September 1, 1934, p. 1; "Milestones," *Time*, August 20, 1934.

29. George M. Daniels, "John Sengstacke III: America's Black Press Lord," manuscript, AS Papers, Box 22, Folder 8, and Box 11, Folder 3; Ottley, *The Lonely Warrior*, pp. 333–36.

30. From *CD:* "Mourned," October 27, 1934, p. 2; "Death Claims Rev. H. A. Sengstacke," October 20, 1934, p. 1.

31. AS Papers, Box 22, Folder 8; Ottley, *The Lonely Warrior*, pp. 301–4.

32. AS Papers, Box 22, Folder 8; "*Defender* Linotype Operators Swear They Are Best in Race Journalism," *CD*, November 16, 1935, p. 10.

33. AS Papers, Box 11, Folder 3; Drake and Cayton, *Black Metropolis*, pp. 84–85.

34. From *CD:* "Pick 'Miss Bronze America' and Bronzeville Mayor on Sept. 22," September 22, 1934, p. 21; "Bronzeville Elects 'Mayor,'" October 6, 1934, p. 20. Drake and Cayton, *Black Metropolis*, p. 383; Waters, *American Diary*, 69–71.

35. Drake and Cayton, *Black Metropolis*, pp. 379–83.

36. From *CD:* Cleveland C. Allen, "De Priest Flays NRA in New York Address," January 13, 1934, p. 1; "De Priest Jolts Congress!," March 31, 1934, p. 10.

37. From *CD:* Parker Brown, "Democrats May Give De Priest Negro as Rival," May 16, 1934, p. 10; "Democrats Select Mitchell to Run Against De Priest," August 11, 1934, p. 1; Arthur Evans, "Campaign at Heated Climax," November 4, 1934, p. 1; Stanley Armstrong, "Demand Halt in New Deal Waste," November 4, 1934, p. 2.

38. A. N. Fields, "Democrats Win Country by Landslide," *CD*, November 10, 1934, p. 1.

39. Waters, *American Diary*, pp. 110–11.

40. Ibid., pp. 112, 125–33, 140–42; Ottley, *The Lonely Warrior*, pp. 336–37; Kenan Heise, "'Doc' Lochard; 50 Years as Editor at *Defender*," *CD*, February 3, 1984, p. 1.

41. Waters, *American Diary*, pp. 147–53.

42. Ibid., pp. 144–46.

43. Ibid., pp. 68–72.

44. Alex Poinsett, *Walking with Presidents: Louis Martin and the Rise of Black Political Power* (Lanham, MD: Rowan & Littlefield, 1997), pp. 1–9.

45. "Universal Unrest Among Black People Revealed at National Congress Here," *CD*, February 22, 1936, p. 1; Poinsett, *Walking with Presidents*, pp. 12–13.

46. From *CD*: "The Bahai Faith — What Is It?" May 6, 1933, p. 10; Robert S. Abbott, "Baha'ism Called the Religion That Will Rescue Humanity," December 15, 1934, p. 11; Robert S. Abbott, "New Book Sets Forth Growth of Baha'i in 40 Countries," February 15, 1936, p. 5; Monroe Ioas and Mark Perry, "A Door to the Masses Part 1," *The Michigan Chronicle*, October 10, 1995, p. 1; Ottley, *The Lonely Warrior*, pp. 13–15.

47. From *CD*: Robert S. Abbott, "Baha'ism Called the Religion That Will Rescue Humanity," December 15, 1934, p. 11; Robert S. Abbott, "New Book Sets Forth Growth of Baha'i in 40 Countries," February 15, 1936, p. 5; Monroe Ioas, "The Bahai Faith — What Is It?" May 6, 1933, p. 10. Mark Perry, "Robert S. Abbott and *The Chicago Defender:* A Door to the Masses," *The Michigan Chronicle*, October 10, 1995, p. 1-A; Ottley, *The Lonely Warrior*, pp. 13–15.

48. From *CD*: Robert S. Abbott, "Baha'ism Called the Religion That Will Rescue Humanity," December 15, 1934, p. 11; Robert S. Abbott, "New Book Sets Forth Growth of Baha'i in 40 Countries," February 15, 1936, p. 5; Monroe Ioas, "The Bahai Faith — What Is It?," May 6, 1933, p. 10. Mark Perry, "Robert S. Abbott and *The Chicago Defender:* A Door to the Masses," *The Michigan Chronicle*, October 10, 1995, p. 1-A; Ottley, *The Lonely Warrior*, pp. 13–15.

49. Author interview with Marc and Helena Sengstacke, February 23, 2012; author interviews with Eugene Scott, February 4 and 7, 2010; Ottley, *The Lonely Warrior*, pp. 357–59; B. V. J. Sensgtacke, "Georgia State News," *CD*, January 4, 1936, p. 21.

50. Author interviews with Marc and Helena Sengstacke, February 23, 2012; AS Papers, Box 7, Folder 45; Bill and Lori Granger, *Lords of the Last Machine: The Story of Politics in Chicago* (New York: Random House, 1987), pp. 20–21.

51. Johnson, *Succeeding Against the Odds*, pp. 61–82; "Class of 206 Is First to Graduate from Recently-Named DuSable High School," *CD*, June 20, 1936, p. 20.

52. Poinsett, *Walking with Presidents*, pp. 10–13.

53. Walker, "The Promised Land," p. 40; Buni, *Robert L. Vann*, pp. 282–83; Daniels, "John Sengstacke III: America's Black Press Lord," AS Papers, Box 22, Folder 8, pp. 17–18.

### 12. FAREWELL CHIEF

1. From *CD* by Robert S. Abbott: "Roosevelt in Role of Jekyll and Hyde with Rich and Poor," September 5, 1936, p. 1; "Roosevelt's Job Program Reveals Horror Stories When Facts Are Exposed," September 26, 1936, p. 1; "Roosevelt, with Congress Under His Thumb, Fails to Push Anti-Lynch Bill," October 10, 1936, p. 1; "Sharecroppers Plight Sad Story of Misery Under Roosevelt Rule," September 19, 1936, p. 1.

2. A. N. Fields, "Mitchell Beats De Priest as Nation Reelects Roosevelt," *CD*, November 7, 1936, p. 1.

3. Ottley, *The Lonely Warrior*, pp. 359–62. From *CD: "Defender* Staff Writer Back from Tour of World; To Write Series of Articles," October 31, 1936, p. 1; "Around the World with Flaurience Sengstacke," August 7, 1937, p. 5.

4. From *CD:* "Mary McLeod Bethune Is *Chicago Defender* Guest," July 6, 1935, p. 7; "Mrs. Bethune Ends 1st Year with NYA," July 3, 1937, p. 4. Weiss, *Farewell to the Party of Lincoln*, pp. 130–56.

5. William Pickens, "The Story of Mary McLeod Bethune Bares South's Educational 'Equality,'" *CD*, November 26, 1921, p. 3.

6. "Mary McLeod Bethune Is *Chicago Defender* Guest," *CD*, July 6, 1935, p. 7.

7. "Mrs. Bethune Ends 1st Year with NYA," *CD*, July 3, 1937, p. 4.

8. "Dr. Robert Weaver Gets High Post in New Deal," *CD*, October 27, 1934, p. 1.

9. From *CD:* Jeanette Carter, "National Conference on Youth Closes," January 16, 1937, p. 4; Kelly Miller, "Weekly Forum Views and Reviews," February 6, 1937, p. 16. Weiss, *Farewell to the Party of Lincoln*, p. 136.

10. From *CD:* "Dr. Bethune Leads On!," February 13, 1937, p. 16; "Seek to Keep Mrs. Bethune in Washington," February 27, 1937, p. 10.

11. From *CD:* Al Monroe, "3 Win N.Y. Golden Gloves," March 17, 1934, p. 1; "Joe Louis Is Ring Champ," April 14, 1934, p. 16; Russell J. Cowan, "Solid South Decides Joe Louis Must Be Somebody," April 13, 1935, p. 17.

12. "Joe Louis Gets Hoarse from Speaking — 6 Words," *CD*, July 20, 1935, p. 15.

13. From *CD:* James J. Gentry, "A New Champ Is Born, 'Flesh Celebs' Witness Great Show," June 26, 1937, p. 7; "Billikens See Fight," June 26, 1937, p. 12; "Thousands Dance to Goodman's Music," June 26, 1937, p. 11; "Additional Fight Sidelights," June 26, 1937, p. 3; Al Monroe, Sports Editor, "Terrific Right K.O.'s. Braddock," June 26 1937, p. 1. "South Side Goes Wild as Louis Wins," *CT*, June 23, 1937, p. 19; Arch Ward, "Louis Wins Title Knockout," *CT*, June 23, 1937, p. 1; Lane French, "Louis Calls Braddock Toughest Opponent," CT, June 23, 1937, p. 19; Jay Jackson, "Editorial Cartoon — The Voice of Experience," *CD*, June 26, 1937, p. 15.

14. "Joe's Old Home Town Whoops It Up for Champion," *CT*, June 23, 1937, p. 21.

15. Al Monroe, "Terrific Right K.O.'s. Braddock," *CD*, June 26 1937, p. 1; "South Side Goes Wild as Louis Wins," *CT*, June 23, 1937, p. 19; Arch Ward, "Louis Wins Title Knockout," *CT*, June 23, 1937, p. 1; Lane French, "Louis Calls Braddock Toughest Opponent," *CT*, June 23, 1937, p. 19.

16. Lane French, "Louis Calls Braddock Toughest Opponent," *CT*, June 23, 1937, p. 19.

17. "A Subversive Covenant," *CD*, July 10, 1937, p. 16.

18. Hirsch, *Making of the Second Ghetto*, pp. 29–31; Drake and Cayton, *Black Metropolis*, pp. 179–190; Spear, *Black Chicago*, p. 221.

19. "University of Chicago and the Black Belt," *CD*, July 24, 1937, p. 16.

20. From *CD:* "Building Ghettoes," October 2, 1937, p. 16; "Judge Gives Hansberrys New Chance," October 30, 1937, p. 6.

21. "Railroad Discrimination Case Settled Out of Court," *CD*, August 20, 1938, p. 2.

22. From *CD:* "Irresistible Charm," December 19, 1931, p. 15; "Attend NYA Conference," March 28, 1936, p. 20; "Mme. Joyner Is Campaign Director," May 22, 1937, p. 4; "Mme. Joyner Warns of New Act Covering Beauty Ads," November 26, 1938, p. 7.

23. From *CD:* "What the People Say," June 4, 1938, p. 16; "Duke Ellington, George Cohan, and Other Greats Visit Joe Louis' Camp," June 18, 1938, p. 9; Al Monroe, "Joe and Max Hard at Work for Big Scrap," June 11, 1938, p. 1; "Joe Louis Starts Drill for Schmeling Bout," June 4, 1938, p. 10; James M. Reid, "Reid Cites Qualities of Louis Which Have Inspired Race Youth," June 25, 1938, p. 7.

24. Al Monroe, "Louis Beats Schmeling," *CD*, June 25, 1938, p. 1.

25. Arch Ward, "Louis Whips Max: 1 Round!" *CT*, June 23, 1938, p. 1.

26. Marcia Winn, "Colored Folks March and Yell 'Ah Told You So,'" *CT*, June 23, 1938, p. 19; "Joy, Tragedy in Wake of Joe's Victory," *CD*, July 2, 1938, p. 6.

27. From *CD:* "Invite Joe Louis to Billiken Picnic," July 2, 1938, p. 12; Frank A. Young, "Joe to Rest; No Fight This Year," July 9, 1938, p. 1; "Thousands Give Joe Louis Reception, 'Fit for A King,'" August 19, 1939, p. 11.

28. From *CD:* "Thousands Give Joe Louis Reception, 'Fit for a King,'" August 19, 1939, p. 11; "250,000 Hail Joe Louis at Billiken Picnic," August 19, 1939, p. 1.

29. From *CD:* "Why We Can't Hate 'Reds,'" January 14, 1933, p. 14; "Injustice, Not Reds, Causes Race Riots, Says R. S. Abbott," April 20, 1935, p. 9; "Cultural Progress Is Retarded by 'Black Belts,'" March 30, 1935, p. 16. Ottley, *The Lonely Warrior*, 349–52; Walker, "The Promised Land," p. 39.

30. Daniels, "John Sengstacke III: America's Black Press Lord," pp. 17–18, AS Papers, Box 22, Folder 8. From *CD:* "Trust to Run Negro Paper Left by Abbott," March 8, 1940, p. 6; "Workman Hurt When Trapped by Steel Pile," February 4, 1942, p. 20; "Cashin Scored on Handling of Abbott Estate," June 27, 1947, p. 16. "Mrs. Abbott Ousted from Presidency," *Afro-American*, February 7, 1942, p. 9.

31. Waters, *American Diary*, pp. 153–54; Kenan Heise, "Myrtle P. Sengstacke of Newspaper Group," *CT*, August 23, 1990, p. 10; Earl Calloway, "Myrtle Picou Sengstacke Transformed Society in Chicago; Was Responsible for Marian Anderson's Triumph," *CD*, February 21, 2004, p. 19.

32. Roi Ottley, "Chicago Negro Paper's Editor Achieves Fame," *CT*, June 18, 1955, p. 8.

33. Untitled, unpublished biography of John Sengstacke by Lawrence Muhammad, 1982, AS Papers, Box 22, Folder 21, Galley 4; Patrick Washburn interview with John Sengstacke, April 21, 1983. From *CD:* "Publishers Favor Forming News Service," March 9, 1940, p. 4; "Publishers Slate 3-Day Meet in Chicago," March 2, 1940, p. 7.

34. From *CD*, March 9, 1940, David H. Orro, "Thousands Mourn at Bier of Editor Abbott," p. 1; "Leaders in All Walks of Life at Final Rites," p. 8; "Hundreds Express Grief at Editor Abbott's Death," p. 8; David W. Kellum, "Nation's Leaders Pay Respect to Publisher," p. 9; "Police, Firemen Form Honor Guard for Editor," p. 9; "Fliers Drop Flowers on Editor's Grave," p. 1; "Robert S. Abbott Dies After Long Illness," p. 9; Nahum Daniel Brascher, "A Little Light Along the Way," p. 15. From *CD:* "Southernaires in Radio Tribute to Robert S. Abbott," March 23, 1940, p. 20; "Teenan Jones, Pioneer Chicagoan, Dies at 85," April 20, 1946, p. 7.

35. From *CD:* "Abbott Boy Scouts Write Chicagoan," December 23, 1939: p. 2; "Boy Scouts Mourn Editor's Death," March 16, 1940, p. 8. AS Papers, Box 1, Folder 1.

36. From *CD*, March 9, 1940: David H. Orro, "Thousands Mourn at Bier of Editor Abbott," p. 1; "Leaders in All Walks of Life at Final Rites," p. 8; "Hundreds Express Grief at Editor Abbott's Death," p. 8; David W. Kellum, "Nation's Leaders Pay Respect to Publisher," p. 9; "Police, Firemen Form Honor Guard for Editor," p. 9; "Fliers Drop Flowers on Editor's Grave," p. 1; "Robert S. Abbott Dies After Long Illness," p. 9; Nahum Daniel Brascher, "A Little Light Along the Way," p. 15. From *CD:* "Southernaires in Radio Tribute to Robert S. Abbott," March 23, 1940, p. 20; "Teenan Jones, Pioneer Chicagoan, Dies at 85," April 20, 1946, p. 7.

37. Lucius C. Harper, "Dustin' Off the News," *CD,* March 9, 1940, p. 1.

38. "File Will of Editor Abbott for Probate," *CD,* March 16, 1940, p. 1.

39. From *CD* by John Sengstacke, "Today and Tomorrow": June 8, 1940, p. 14; June 29, 1940, p. 14.

40. John Sengstacke, "Today and Tomorrow," *CD,* June 22, 1940, p. 14.

41. John Sengstacke, "*Defender* Endorses Roosevelt's Foreign Policy," *CD,* October 12, 1940, p. 1.

42. John Sengstacke, "The Way of All Things," *CD,* October 19, 1940, p. 14.

43. From *CD:* "National Defense," October 26, 1940, p. 14; John Sengstacke, "The Way of All Things," October 26, 1940, p. 14. Weiss, *Farewell to the Party of Lincoln,* pp. 274–79.

44. "President Roosevelt and Mr. Wilkie," *CD,* November 2, 1940, p. 14.

45. From *CD:* "Robert L Vann," November 9, 1940, p. 14; "Hold Rites for Vann, Courier Editor," November 2, 1940, p. 1. Weiss, *Farewell to the Party of Lincoln,* pp. 282–83; Buni, pp. 318–23.

46. From *CD:* "The Man of the Hour," November 16, 1940, p. 14; John Sengstacke, "The Way of All Things," November 30, 1940, p. 14.

47. From *CD:* "Baby Boy Is Born to the Sengstackes," February 15, 1941, p. 1; "Friends Enjoy Afternoon Shower," December 7, 1940, p. 17; "Mrs. Edna R. Abbott Loses Fight to Control *Chicago Defender* Funds," March 7, 1942, p. 2; "Court Petition Names Sengstacke Principal Owner of Abbott Stock," March 7, 1942, p. 1. "Mrs. Abbott Ousted from Presidency," *Afro-American,* February 7, 1942, p. 1; Daniels, "John Sengstacke III: America's Black Press Lord," pp. 17–18, AS Papers, Box 22, Folder 8.

48. From *CD:* "Mrs. Edna R. Abbott Loses Fight to Control *Chicago Defender* Funds," March 7, 1942, p. 2; "Court Petition Names Sengstacke Principal Owner of Abbott Stock," March 7, 1942, p. 1. "Mrs. Abbott Ousted from Presidency," *Afro-American,* February 7, 1942, p. 9; Daniels, "John Sengstacke III: America's Black Press Lord," pp. 17–18, AS Papers, Box 22, Folder 8.

49. "Walker Named Head of Publishers' Group," *CD,* March 8, 1941, p. 4; Daniels, "John Sengstacke III: America's Black Press Lord," pp. 17–18, AS Papers, Box 22, Folder 8.

50. From *CD:* "Mrs. Edna R. Abbott Loses Fight to Control *Chicago Defender* Funds," March 7, 1942, p. 2; "Court Petition Names Sengstacke Principal Owner of Abbott Stock," March 7, 1942, p. 1. "Mrs. Abbott Ousted from Presidency," *Afro-American,* February 7, 1942, p. 1; Daniels, "John Sengstacke III: America's Black Press Lord," pp. 17–18, AS Papers, Box 22 Folder 8.

51. "The Press," *Time,* March 24, 1941.

52. "Freedom of Negro Press," *CD*, December 20, 1941, p. 1.

53. Patrick S. Washburn, *A Question of Sedition* (New York: Oxford University Press, 1986), pp. 63–65.

54. From *CD:* "Mrs. Edna R. Abbott Loses Fight to Control *Chicago Defender* Funds," March 7, 1942, p. 2; "Court Petition Names Sengstacke Principal Owner of Abbott Stock," March 7, 1942, p. 1. "Mrs. Abbott Ousted from Presidency," *Afro-American*, February 7, 1942, p. 1; Daniels, "John Sengstacke III: America's Black Press Lord," pp. 17–18, AS Papers, Box 22, Folder 8.

## 13. VICTORY THROUGH UNITY

1. Washburn, *A Question of Sedition*, pp. 52–53; Patrick Washburn interview with John Sengstacke, April 21, 1983.

2. Washburn, *A Question of Sedition*, pp. 53–54.

3. Ibid.

4. Ibid., pp. 62–63.

5. Ibid., pp. 55–56.

6. Ibid., pp. 78–81.

7. From *CD:* "Westbrook Pegler," May 23, 1942, p. 14; Lucius C. Harper, "Who Is Westbrook Pegler?," May 16 1942, p. 1; Washburn, *A Question of Sedition*, pp. 85–86; "The Press: Negro Publishers," *Time*, June 15, 1942.

8. Washburn, *A Question of Sedition*, pp. 108–10; Patrick Washburn interview with John Sengstacke, April 21, 1983.

9. Washburn interview with Sengstacke; Washburn, *A Question of Sedition*, pp. 87–94; Burns, *Nitty Gritty*, p. 22.

10. Washburn interview with Sengstacke; Washburn, *A Question of Sedition*, pp. 118–34.

11. Washburn, *A Question of Sedition*, pp. 171–73.

12. Ibid., pp. 117–18.

13. Ibid., pp. 133–35.

14. Ibid., pp. 134–35; Washburn interview with Sengstacke.

15. Washburn, *A Question of Sedition*, p. 134; "From President Roosevelt," *CD*, September 26, 1942, p. 3; Burns, *Nitty Gritty*, pp. 5–8.

16. John Sengstacke, "A Dedication," *CD*, September 26, 1942, p. 1; Burns, *Nitty Gritty*, pp. 5–8.

17. *The Chicago Defender*, "Victory Through Unity" edition, September 26, 1942. Franklin D. Roosevelt, "What National Unity Means," *CD*, September 26, 1942. Douglas MacArthur, "From Overseas," *CD*, September 26, 1942. Robert R. McCormick, "Thirteen Million Black Americans: A Bulwark of Our Country's Might," *CD*, September 26, 1942.

18. Francis Biddle, "Who Is the Common Man," *CD*, September 26, 1942.

19. "Westbrook Pegler Sends Us a Mash Note," *CD*, September 26, 1942.

20. *CD*, September 26, 1942.

21. Langston Hughes, "Klan or Gestapo? Why Take Either," *CD*, September 26, 1942.

22. Washburn, *A Question of Sedition*, p. 133; Walker, "The Promised Land," p. 44; Washburn interview with Sengstacke.

23. Burns, *Nitty Gritty*, pp. 1–15.

24. Ibid., pp. 15–16.

25. Ibid., pp. 10–11.

26. Ibid., pp. 27–43; Johnson, *Succeeding Against the Odds*, pp. 113–24.

27. "Publishers Parley Elects Sengstacke New President," *CD*, June 19, 1943, p. 1.

28. Armistead S. Pride and Clint C. Wilson II, *A History of the Black Press* (Washington, DC: Howard University Press, 1997), pp. 240–42.

29. From *CD:* "Army to Keep Troops in Detroit Until August," July 17, 1943, p. 3; "Detroit Seeks to Return to Normalcy After Riot," July 3, 1943, p. 7. Poinsett, *Walking with Presidents*, pp. 30–33.

30. "Publishers Lobby Sees Federal Chiefs; Demand Full Race Role in War Effort," *CD*, July 24, 1943, p. 3; Pride and Wilson, *A History of the Black Press*, pp. 191–92.

31. Washburn interview with Sengstacke; Washburn, *A Question of Sedition*, pp. 161–64; "Publishers Lobby Sees Federal Chiefs; Demand Full Race Role in War Effort," *CD*, July 24, 1943, p. 3; Pride and Wilson, *A History of the Black Press*, pp. 191–92.

32. Patrick Washburn, *The African American Newspaper: Voice of Freedom* (Evanston, IL: Northwestern University Press, 2006), pp. 173–75; Washburn, *A Question of Sedition*, pp. 197–99.

33. From *CD:* "FDR Told to Halt Negro Migration to War Plants," August 14, 1943, p. 1; Valoris B. Washington, "FDR Urged to Junk Biddle Scheme Banning Migration," August 21, 1943, p. 1; Valoris B. Washington, "Text of Biddle Letter Proposing Ban of Dixie Negro Migration into North," August 21, 1943, p. 2.

34. Washburn, *A Question of Sedition*, pp. 183–84.

35. Drake and Cayton, *Black Metropolis*, pp. 8–9, 184–186; Hirsch, *Making of the Second Ghetto*, pp. 16–23, 30–31; "Wanted: Homes," *CD*, November 27, 1943, p. 14.

36. From *CD:* "The Hansberry Case," November 30, 1940, p. 14; Carl Hansberry, "Realtor Tells His Role in Covenant Case," November 23, 1940, p. 9; "Text of Hansberry Decision," November 23, 1940, p. 9; Enoch Waters, "Hansberry Decree Opens 500 New Homes to Race," November 23, 1940, p. 1. Drake and Cayton, *Black Metropolis*, pp. 8–9, 184–86; Hirsch, *Making of the Second Ghetto*, pp. 16–23, 30–31.

37. Drake and Cayton, *Black Metropolis*, pp. 8–9, 184–86; Hirsch, *Making of the Second Ghetto*, pp. 16–23, 30–31; "Wanted: Homes," *CD*, November 27, 1943, p. 14.

38. From *CD:* "Newspaper Publishers Visit Roosevelt," February 12, 1944, p. 5; "End Jim Crow, FDR Tells Union," February 12, 1944, p. 1. Pride and Wilson, *A History of the Black Press*, pp. 191–92; Washburn, *A Question of Sedition*, pp. 198–200.

39. Washburn interview with John Sengstacke.

40. Ibid.; Poinsett, *Walking with Presidents*, pp. 42–45.

41. Poinsett, *Walking with Presidents*, pp. 42–45; Washburn, *The African American Newspaper*, pp. 172–78; McAlpin, "Un-Covering Washington," *CD*, March 4, 1944, p. 13.

42. Ibid.; Washburn interview with John Sengstacke.

43. Ibid.; Poinsett, *Walking with Presidents,* pp. 42–45.

44. Ibid.; Washburn, *The African American Newspaper,* pp. 127–28; McAlpin, "Un-Covering Washington," *CD,* March 4, 1944, p. 13.

## 14. SANTA CLAUS AND A WORLD WAR

1. From *CD:* McAlpin, "Un-Covering Washington," March 4, 1944; "Everybody Goes When the Wagon Comes," July 29, 1944, p. 10; Venice T. Spraggs, "Negro Vote at Stake in Wallace's Defeat," August 5, 1944, p. 3.

2. Lucius C. Harper, "Dustin' Off the News," *CD,* August 5, 1944, p. 1.

3. Christopher Manning, *William L. Dawson and the Limits of Black Electoral Leadership* (De Kalb: Northern Illinois University, 2009), pp. 94–99; "Truman Election Pledges on Negro Issue Recalled," *CD,* April 21, 1945, p. 1.

4. Richard Durham, "FDR Against Army Jim Crow — Dawson," *CD,* August 19, 1944, p. 1; Manning, *William L. Dawson,* pp. 94–99.

5. From *CD:* "Truman Attacks Klan; Denies Hearst Charge," November 4, 1944, p. 1; "Truman Not Klansman, Newspaper Files Show," November 4, 1944, p. 10; Richard Durham, "Truman Stand on Negro Told to *Defender* Scribe," April 21, 1945, p. 1.

6. From *CD:* Fred Atwater, "Roosevelt Sweeps Negro Vote by Record Margin," November 18, 1944, p. 1; "How Negro Vote Went for Roosevelt in Big Cities," November 18, 1944, p. 1.

7. From *CD,* April 21, 1945: "Taverns Close Doors to Mourn President," p. 17; "Memorable Scenes Tell FDR's Friendship for Negro," p. 3; "Carry on FDR Ideals — Truman," p. 1; Venice T. Spraggs, "Negro America Joins in D.C. Homage to FDR," p. 2; Venice T. Spraggs, "D.C. Notables Pay Their Last Tribute to President," p. 11.

8. "Mrs. Bethune, Publisher Sengstacke in Nationwide Radio Tribute to FDR," *CD,* April 21, 1945, p. 3

9. Ibid.

10. Lucius C. Harper, "Dustin' Off the News," *CD,* April 21, 1945, p. 1.

11. Charley Cherokee, "National Grapevine," *CD,* April 21, 1945, p. 11.

12. From *CD:* "Carry on FDR Ideals — Truman," April 21, 1945, p. 1; "The President Leaves a Legacy," April 21, 1945, p. 12; "Truman Election Pledges on Negro Issue Recalled," April 21, 1945, p. 1.

13. Harry McAlpin, "Truman Stands by Pro-Negro Senate Record," *CD,* April 28, 1945, p. 1.

14. From *CD:* Harry McAlpin, "Publishers, Walter White See President Truman," June 2, 1945, p. 1; "Truman Meets with Publisher," May 5, 1945, p. 5; "Truman Told His Record on Negro Found Excellent," May 12 1945, p. 4. Pride and Wilson, *A History of the Black Press,* p. 192.

15. From *CD:* Frank Young, "Through the Years," May 26, 1945, p. 7; Lucius C. Harper, "Dustin' Off the News," September 27, 1947, p. 1. Jonathan Eig, *Opening Day* (New York: Simon and Schuster, 2007), pp. 20–26.

16. Frank Young, "Through the Years," *CD,* September 1, 1945, p. 7; Eig, *Opening Day,* pp. 20–26.

17. Frank Young, "Dixie Sports Scribes Differ on Robinson," *CD,* November 3, 1945, p. 1.

18. "Hats Off to Branch Rickey," *CD*, November 10, 1945, p. 14.

19. Florence Hamlish Levinsohn, "Where Vernon Jarrett Is Coming From," *Chicago Reader*, March 24, 1988; Vernon Jarrett, "At Last, a Tribute to 'Doc' Lochard," *CT*, May 14, 1976, p. 1.

20. Langston Hughes, "Here to Yonder," *CD*, December 14, 1946, p. 14; Burns, *Nitty Gritty*, p 48.

21. Vernon Jarrett, "William L. Dawson: A Look at 'the Man,'" *CT*, November 15, 1970, p. 1; "Chicago Voters Take Strong Stand for Liberal Candidates," *CD*, November 16, 1946, p. 1.

22. From *CD*: Vernon Jarrett, "Mob Lays Siege to Negro, White Vets in Housing Project," November 23, 1946, p. 1; "Housing Projects Give 85 Vets Chicago Homes," December 28, 1946, p. 5; Levinsohn, "Where Vernon Jarrett Is Coming From," *Chicago Reader*, March 24, 1988; Jarrett, "At Last, a Tribute to 'Doc' Lochard," *CT*, May 14, 1976, p. 1; Bradford Hunt, *Blueprint for Disaster: The Unraveling of Chicago Public Housing* (Chicago: University of Chicago Press, 2009), pp. 79–81.

23. Jarrett, "Mob Lays Siege to Negro, White Vets in Housing Project," November 23, 1946, p. 1; Jarrett, "At Last, a Tribute to 'Doc' Lochard," *CT*, May 14, 1976, p. 1; Levinsohn, "Where Vernon Jarrett Is Coming From," *Chicago Reader*, March 24, 1988.

24. From *CD:* "Mayor Assures Vet Protection," November 30, 1946, p. 5; "Airport Homes," November 30, 1946, p. 14.

25. "Crossroads for Democracy," *CD*, December 14, 1946, p. 13; Hirsch, *Making of the Second Ghetto*, pp. 88–89.

26. From *CD:* "It Happens in Chicago," December 14, 1946, p. 14; "Crossroads for Democracy," December 14, 1946, p. 13.

27. Bill and Lori Granger, *Lords of the Last Machine*, pp. 126–27; Adam Cohen and Elizabeth Taylor, *American Pharaoh: Mayor Richard Daley; His Battle for Chicago and the Nation* (Boston: Little, Brown and Company, 2000), pp. 78–81; Royko, *Boss*, pp. 54–56.

28. "State Authorized Slum Clearance 'Drop in Bucket,'" *CD*, January 25, 1947, p. 13.

29. "Our Mounting Fire Tragedies," *CD*, January 25, 1947, p. 14.

30. From *CD* by Frank Young: "Through the Years," March 22, 1947, p. 11; "Through the Years," March 29, 1947, p. 19; "Rickey Lauds Jackie Robinson," June 29, 1946, p. 1. "Baseball Fans Puzzled Over Robinson's Status," January 25, 1947, p. 1. Eig, *Opening Day*, pp. 40–47, 59–60.

31. From *CD:* "Jackie Robinson's Life Story in Pictures," April 19, 1947, p. 12; "Jackie Robinson Opens the Door . . . Makes History," April 19, 1947, p. 1; "Robinson Plays Flawless Ball with Brooklyn Dodgers Club," April 19, 1947, p. 19.

32. From *CD:* Frank Young, "Through the Years," April 19, 1947, p. 19; Frank Young, "Through the Years," May 17, 1947, p. 20; "Robinson Plays Flawless Ball with Brooklyn Dodgers Club," April 19, 1947, p. 19. Eig, *Opening Day*, pp. 51–54.

33. From *CD:* "Judge Denies Cashin Claim," July 5, 1947, p. 1; "A Lie, Nailed!," December 6, 1947, p. 1; "'No Receiver' Says Judge," December 6, 1947, p. 1; "Negro-Owned Always: *Defender* Suits Dropped," December 27, 1947, p. 1.

From *CT:* "WM. H. Stuart Named Receiver of Negro Paper," July 1, 1947,
p. 8; "Cashin Scored on Handling of Abbott Estate," June 27, 1947, p. 16.

34. From *CD:* John Sengstacke, "This Is Our Case," December 13, 1947, p. 5; "It's
15 Cents Now and Worth It," October 16, 1948, p. 1; *The Defender* Bomb-
ing," July 30, 1949, p. 6. From *CT:* "Printers on Strike at *Chicago Defender,*
Negro Weekly Paper," December 7, 1947, p. 4. Daniels, "John Sengstacke III:
America's Black Press Lord," pp. 32–33, AS Papers, Box 22, Folder 8; Waters,
*American Diary,* pp. 154–56.

35. From *CD:* Lucius C. Harper, "Dustin' Off the News," February 14, 1948, p. 1;
"Pres. Truman Hails Civil Rights Report," November 8, 1947, p. 1; "'Damn
Democracy! — South to Truman," February 14, 1948, p. 1. "Special Message
to the Congress on Civil Rights," February 2, 1948, Public Papers of the
President, Harry S. Truman Presidential Library.

36. From *CD:* "'Damn Democracy! — South to Truman," February 14, 1948, p. 1;
"'No Retreat!' Truman's Answer to Governors," February 21, 1948, p. 1.

37. "Negro Publishers Award Truman First John Russwurm Citation," *CD,*
March 27, 1948, p. 14.

38. W. E. B. Du Bois, "The Winds of Time," *CD,* March 20, 1948, p. 15; February
7, 1948, p. 15; January 3, 1948, p. 13; April 19, 1947, p. 15.

39. "Third Party or Third War; Ill. Slogan for Wallace," *CD,* April 17, 1948, p. 5.

40. W. E. B. Du Bois, "The Winds of Time," *CD,* May 15, 1948, p. 15.

41. Levinsohn, "Where Vernon Jarrett Is Coming From," *Chicago Reader,*
March 24, 1988; Waters, *American Diary,* p. 159; Poinsett, *Walking with
Presidents,* pp. 50–51; Robert Howard, "Top Leftists Spark Rally for Wal-
lace," *CT,* July 20, 1948, p. 1.

42. From *CD:* Venice Spraggs, "Kill Restrictive Covenants!," May 8, 1948,
p. 1; "Let Freedom Ring," May 15, 1948, p. 14. Hirsch, *Making of the Second
Ghetto,* pp. 30–31.

43. From *CD:* "Illinois Restrictive Covenant Decision Paves Way for Appeal,"
December 6, 1947, p. 1; Loring B. Moore, "Court Can't Block Sales to Negroes," May 15, 1948, p. 1.

44. "John Sengstacke Greets President," *CD,* June 12, 1948, p. 1.

45. From *CD:* "We March FORWARD — with Truman," July 24, 1948, p. 1;
Venice Spraggs, "Dem Convention Finds Negroes in Key Roles," *CD,* July 24,
1948, p. 1.

46. "Southerners Secede Again," *CD,* July 24, 1948, p. 1.

47. From *CD:* "We March FORWARD — with Truman," July 24, 1948, p. 1;
"President Truman Wipes Out Segregation in Armed Forces," July 31, 1948,
p. 1.

48. From *CD:* Louis Martin, "Million Dollar Truman Fund," August 7, 1948,
p. 1; John H. Sengstacke, "Let's Put Up or Shut Up," August 7, 1948, p. 1.

49. John Sengstacke, "The People Were Right," *CD,* November 13, 1948, p. 1;
Manning, *William L. Dawson,* pp. 109–13.

50. From *CD:* Morgan Holsey, "Scalpers and Politics Mar East-West Game,"
August 28, 1948, p. 10. A. S. Young, "Paige Is Baseball's Greatest Drawing
Card," August 28, 1948, p. 11. "West Defeats East, 3–0, Before 42,099 Fans,"
August 28, 1948, p. 10. Vernon Jarrett, "Blacks Find Success Among Their
Peers," *CT,* October 18, 1970, p. 1.

51. "The Ways of White Folks," *CD*, August 28, 1948, p. 14.

52. From *CD*: Morgan Holsey, "Scalpers and Politics Mar East-West Game," August 28, 1948, p. 10; A. S. Young, "Paige Is Baseball's Greatest Drawing Card," August 28, 1948, p. 11; "West Defeats East, 3–0, Before 42,099 Fans," August 28, 1948, p. 10; Vernon Jarrett, "Blacks Find Success Among Their Peers," *CT*, October 18, 1970, p. 1.

53. Frank Young, "Through the Years," *CD*, June 12, 1948, p. 11.

54. Jarrett, "Blacks Find Success Among Their Peers," *CT*, October 18, 1970, p. 1.; Levinsohn, "Where Vernon Jarrett Is Coming From," *Chicago Reader*, March 24, 1988.

55. "Names Sengstacke, Granger to Military Board," *CD*, September 25, 1948, p. 1.

56. "Display Ad — Now Is the Time to Help Yourself," *CD*, October 16, 1948, p. 10.

57. "Display Ad — This Is the Story of Progress," *CD*, October 9, 1948, p. 6.

58. "Mr. Wallace and Company," *CD*, September 25, 1948, p. 14.

59. From *CD*: "Voters Terrorized in South," October 30, 1948, p. 1; "Photo Standalone — The Ridiculous Ku Klux Klan," November 13, 1948, p. 4.

60. From *CT*: Tim Jones, "Dewey Defeats Truman: Well, Everybody Makes Mistakes," September 9, 2012; Arthur S. Henning, "Farms, Cities Give Truman a Heavy Vote," November 3, 1948, p. 1; "Bulletins on Elections," November 3, 1948, p. 1; Arthur Evans, "Early Dewey Lead Narrow; Douglas, Stevenson Win," November 3, 1948, p. 1; "Bulletins on Elections," November 3, 1948, p. 1.

61. John Sengstacke, "The People Were Right," *CD*, November 13, 1948, p. 1.

62. From *CD*: "Our Opinions — The Winner and Still the Champion," November 13, 1948, p. 6; "A Lot of People Have a Lot to Say about Truman's Victory," November 13, 1948, p. 3; "Action on FEPC, Civil Rights," November 13, 1948, p. 1; "The Wallace Bust," November 13, 1948, p. 6.

63. From *CD*: "The New Congress," November 13, 1948, p. 6; "Dawson Slated for Key Chairmanship in Congress," November 13, 1948, p. 1.

## 15. PROMISES VS. PERFORMANCE

1. From *CD*: Venice Spraggs, "William (Bill) Dawson's Rise — Democracy on the March," January 8, 1949, p. 13; "Dawson's New Post," December 25, 1948, p. 6. Manning, *William L. Dawson*, pp. 119–22.

2. "Integration Feature of Inaugural," *CD*, January 22, 1949, p. 5.

3. "Truman Given Abbott Award," *CD*, May 21, 1949, p. 1.

4. From *CD*: "Mr. Truman Responds," June 4, 1949, p. 6; Venice Spraggs, "HST Renews Pledge on Civil Rights," June 4, 1949, p. 1.

5. From *CD*: Venice Spraggs, "Report Navy Integration Plan Ready," June 11, 1949, p. 1; Venice Spraggs, "Gives Army 3rd Chance to End Jim Crow," June 25, 1949, p. 1.

6. From *CD*: Venice Spraggs, "Military Order Shakes Color Bar," October 8, 1949, p. 1; Venice Spraggs, "Expect New Race Policy for Army," January 14, 1950, p. 1; "Mix Units in U.S. Army," January 21, 1950, p. 1; "Truman Lauds Military Equality Report," May 27, 1950, p. 1; "Picket Defense Chief," De-

cember 31, 1949, p. 1; "Army's Trying," January 21, 1950, p. 6; "Army Throws Out Another Racial Bar," April 8, 1950, p. 1.

7. From *CD:* Mary McLeod Bethune, "Jefferson-Jackson $100 Plate Dinner Proves We Are Learning to Pay Our Way," March 11, 1950, p. 6; "We're Rising," February 4, 1950, p. 6; "All This and Dinner, Too," February 25, 1950, p. 1; "Dems Flock to Dine with HST at $100 Plate," February 18, 1950, p. 1.

8. From *CD:* "National Grapevine," March 11, 1950, p. 6; "Our Opinions," March 11, 1950, p. 6; "Await Truman Action on D.C. Court Post," March 4, 1950, p. 1; "No Offense to Dawson Meant, Say Democrats," March 4, 1950, p. 1; "Press Senate for 'Teeth' in FEPC," March 4, 1950, p. 1.

9. From *CD:* "*Defender* Is Quoted on House Floor," April 1, 1950, p. 1; "Dems Study Editorial in *Defender*," March 25, 1950, p. 1; "The Republicans State Their Case," February 18, 1950, p. 6.

10. "Army Throws Out Another Racial Bar," *CD*, April 8, 1950, p. 1.

11. "Report Reviews Progress Made in Race Relations in Armed Forces," *CD*, May 27, 1950, p. 5.

12. From *CD:* Willard Townsend, "Harry Truman to Congress: Armed Forces Are Solving Racial Bias," July 22, 1950, p. 7; "Our Opinions," June 3, 1950, p. 6; "Photo Standalone — The President's Committee," June 3, 1950, p. 1; "Truman Lauds Military Equality Report," May 27, 1950, p. 1.

13. From *CD:* "Tan GIs Go into Action!," July 8, 1950, p. 1; "More Negro Troops into Korean War," July 15, 1950, p. 1.

14. From *CD:* "A Negro General," July 22, 1950, p. 6; "*Defender* Drive for Negro General Gains Widespread Support, Interest," July 22, 1950, p. 1; "How About That General?," August 26, 1950, p. 6.

15. From *CD:* "*Defender* Ace Joins Yanks Piling into Korea," August 12, 1950, p. 1; L. Alex Wilson, "Shell Fire Perils *Defender* Ace," August 19, 1950, p. 1; L. Alex Wilson, "Fresh Troops, Planes Help 24th Overcome Red Gains," September 9, 1950, p. 1; L. Alex Wilson, "Tan GIs Find 20 Slain Buddies During Advance," September 30, 1950, p. 1.

16. L. Alex Wilson, "Along the Korean War Front," *CD*, September 2, 1950, p. 4.

17. From *CD* by L. Alex Wilson: "2-Way Integration of Negro, White Soldiers Praised by Army General," September 16, 1950, p. 1; "Integration Is Forced to Test by War in Korea," February 3, 1951, p. 1; "Tells How Jim Crow Was Broken in a Regiment of the Second Division," February 17, 1951, p. 2.

18. From *CD:* L. Alex Wilson, "400 to Wed Tokyo Girls," November 4, 1950, p. 1; Ethel Payne, "Says Japanese Girls Playing GIs for Suckers," November 25, 1950, p. 12; Currie, "Interviews with Ethel Payne."

19. L. Alex Wilson, "Why Tan Yanks Go for Japanese Girls," *CD*, November 11, 1950, p. 1; Currie, "Interviews with Ethel Payne."

20. From *CD:* L. Alex Wilson, "400 to Wed Tokyo Girls," November 4, 1950, p. 1; L. Alex Wilson, "Quick Victory Fades as China Reds Attack," November 11, 1950, p. 1; Ethel Payne, "Says Japanese Girls Playing GIs for Suckers," November 25, 1950, p. 12; Ethel Payne, "Says Japanese Girls Playing GIs for Suckers, pt. 1," November 18, 1950, p. 1; Currie, "Interviews with Ethel Payne."

21. Currie, "Interviews with Ethel Payne."

22. From *CD:* Venice T. Spraggs, "American Legion Probes Gilbert Case," November 4, 1950, p. 1; "MacArthur Opens the Door," January 6, 1951, p. 6; "Thurgood Marshall Arrives in Japan," January 20, 1951, p. 1; "Marshall Ends Preliminary Probe in Japan," February 3, 1951, p. 1; Walter White, "Thurgood Marshall's Trip to Japan Bears Fruit Already," February 3, 1951, p. 7; "Marshall Says Korea Army Trials Unfair," February 24, 1951, p. 2.

23. Lutrelle Palmer, "NAACP's Marshall, *Defender* War Newsman Cite GIs' Plight in Korea," *CD*, March 10, 1951, p. 4.

24. Hank Klibanoff, "L. Alex Wilson," in *Profiles in Journalistic Courage*, edited by Robert Giles and Robert W. Snyder (New Brunswick, CT: Transaction Publishers, 2001), pp. 67–79; "Ike Award Kicks Off *Defender* Anniversary," *CD*, May 7, 1955, p. 1.

25. Currie, "Interviews with Ethel Payne."

26. Ethel Payne, "The Last Time I Saw MacArthur," *CD*, April 28, 1951, p. 1; Currie, "Interviews with Ethel Payne."

27. From *CD*, February 23, 1952: John H. Sengstacke, "Our Opinions," p. 10; Enoch P. Waters, "Lucius C. Harper — Portrait of an All-Around Man," p. 12; Frank 'Fay' Young, "Lucius Clinton Harper," p. 17; Marion B. Campfield, "Mostly about WOMEN," p. 6; "Strolling with the BILLIKENS," p. 1; "1,500 Jam Final Rites for Harper," p. 1. "Lucius Harper, Exec Editor of *Chicago Defender*, Dies," *Jet*, February 21, 1952.

28. "1,500 Jam Final Rites for Harper," *CD*, February 23, 1952, p. 1.

29. Waters, "Lucius C. Harper — Portrait of an All-Around Man," *CD*, February 23, 1952, p. 12.

30. Young, "Lucius Clinton Harper," *CD*, February 23, 1952, p. 17.

31. Currie, "Interviews with Ethel Payne"; Waters, *American Diary*, pp. 405–7; Poinsett, *Walking with Presidents*, p. 52; author interview with Charles Davis, August 8, 2010.

32. Ethel Payne, "The Donkey Packs a Wallop," *CD*, May 15, 1954, p. 1; David A. Nichols, *A Matter of Justice: Eisenhower and the Beginning of the Civil Rights Revolution* (New York: Simon and Schuster, 2007), pp. 17–18, 22.

33. By Ethel Payne from *CD:* "NAACP in Fast Move on Trial Eve," December 12, 1953, p. 1; "School Decision Expected by June," December 19, 1953, p. 1.

34. From *CD:* "Have You Met Miss Payne?," March 30, 1974, p. 4; "Ike Sorry for GOP Blunder," February 20, 1954, p. 1; "GOP Centennial Huddle," April 17, 1954, p. 2.

35. Currie, "Interviews with Ethel Payne"; Waters, *American Diary*, pp. 405–7; Poinsett, *Walking with Presidents*, p. 52; author interview with Davis.

36. Ethel Payne, "Ethel Meets Boy Made Immortal by U.S. Supreme Court Decision," *CD*, May 29, 1954, p. 4.

37. By Ethel Payne from *CD:* "History of School Cases Covers Five Years," May 22, 1954, p. 21; "Educators Comment on Schools Decision," May 22, 1954, p. 5.

38. Waters, *American Diary*, pp. 405–25.

39. From *CD*, May 29, 1954: "Dixie Clerics Have Mixed Emotions Over Decision," p. 7; "Southern Comment on Decision," p. 5; "North Applauds School Decision," p. 4.

40. From *CD*, May 22, 1954: "History of School Cases Covers Five Years," p. 21;

"Educators Comment on Schools Decision," p. 5; "Dixie Clerics Have Mixed Emotions Over Decision," p. 7; "Southern Comment on Decision," p. 5; "North Applauds School Decision," p. 4.

41. From *CD*, May 29, 1954: Enoch Waters, "How Decision Affects Teachers in the South," p. 1; "Dixie Clerics Have Mixed Emotions Over Decision," p. 7; "Southern Comment on Decision," p. 5; "North Applauds School Decision," p. 4.

42. "Our Opinions," *CD*, May 29, 1954, p. 11.

43. Waters, *American Diary*, pp. 407–8; "Our Opinions," *CD*, June 5, 1954, p. 11; "500 Schools Desegregated Year After Court Ruling," *CD*, May 14, 1955, p. 4.

44. From *CD*: Alice A. Dunnigan, "Why Press Query Fired Ike's Ire," July 24, 1954, p. 1; "*Defender* Query Angers Ike," July 17, 1954, p. 1. Currie, "Interviews with Ethel Payne"; Robert Frederick Burk, *The Eisenhower Administration and Black Civil Rights* (Knoxville: University of Tennessee Press, 1984), p. 146.

45. "No Need for Temper," *CD*, July 24, 1954, p. 11.

46. From *CD*: "Ike Hits Bias in Public Housing," August 14, 1954, p. 1; "Ask Ike to Back Traval Bias Ban," August 14, 1954, p. 3; "Ask Ike for Federal School Aid," July 31, 1954, p. 5; "Asks Passage of Jim Crow Travel Ban," July 24, 1954, p. 1.

47. "Reporter, Race Leaders Intimidated, Says Pearson," *CD*, March 26, 1955, p. 1; Drew Pearson, "Bicket Sees News Influencing," *Michigan Daily*, April 27, 1955, p. 4; Currie, "Interviews with Ethel Payne."

48. "Hagerty Denies Probing Payne," May 7, 1955, *CD*, p. 1.

49. From *CD*: "Payne to Cover Afro-Asia Meet for *Defender*," April 16, 1955, p. 1; Ethel Payne, "Payne Reports from Asia," April 23, 1955, p. 1; "National Grapevine," April 30, 1955, p. 2; Ethel Payne, "Africa-Asia Conference Rocked by Freedom Fever," April 30, 1955, p. 12; Ethel Payne, "Afro-Asian Parley Blasts S. Africa's Racial Policies," April 30, 1955, p. 1; "Powell Seeks to Free Fliers," May 7, 1955, p. 12; Ethel L. Payne, "Indonesian Chief Called Most Eloquent Asiatic," May 7, 1955, p. 12; "Dutch Blend," May 7, 1955, p. 2; Louis Martin, "Dope 'n' Data," May 14 1955, p. 5; Ethel Payne, "African Nations Play Minor Role at Bandung," May 15, 1955, p. 12; "Ethel Payne Back and Glad of It," May 28 1955, p. 2. Currie, "Interviews with Ethel Payne."

50. From *CD*, April 16, 1955: "Payne to Cover Afro-Asia Meet for *Defender*," p. 1; "President to Get 9th Abbott Award," p. 1. From *CT*: Clarence Page, "The Other Chicago," June 8, 1997.

51. From *CD*: "Reporter, Race Leaders Intimidated Says Pearson," March 26, 1955, p. 1; Drew Pearson, "Bicket Sees News Influencing," *Michigan Daily*, April 27, 1955, p. 4; "Ike Award Kicks Off *Defender* Anniversary," May 7, 1955, p. 1. Currie, "Interviews with Ethel Payne."

52. From *CD*: "Distinguished Party with Sengstacke at White House," May 14, 1955, p. 1; "Sengstacke Lauds Ike on Rights," May 14, 1955, p. 3; Louis Martin, "Dope 'n' Data," May 21, 1955, p. 7; Ethel Payne, "Ike Award Kicks Off *Defender* Anniversary," May 7, 1955, p. 1.

53. From *CD*: "Distinguished Party with Sengstacke at White House," May 14, 1955, p. 1; "Sengstacke Lauds Ike on Rights," May 14, 1955, p. 3; Louis Martin,

"Dope 'n' Data," May 21, 1955, p. 7; Ethel Payne, "Ike Award Kicks Off *Defender* Anniversary," May 7, 1955, p. 1.

54. Ethel Payne, "Bombay to Ethel Is Heat, People and Kindly Doctor," *CD*, May 14 1955, p. 1.


16. THE *DAILY DEFENDER*

1. From *CD:* Ethel Payne, "Decree Labeled a Compromise," June 11, 1955, p. 1; "National Grapevine," June 11, 1955, p. 2.
2. "500 Schools Desegregated Year After Court Ruling," *CD*, May 14, 1955, p. 4; Waters, *American Diary*, pp. 405–9.
3. From *CD*, June 11, 1955, p. 1: "Dixie Crows Over Mild School Rule"; "U.S. Supreme Court Directive Analyzed."
4. "Supreme Court Bows to Dixie," *CD*, June 11, 1955, p. 9.
5. From *CD:* "'Murder,' White Says; Promises Prosecution," September 10, 1955, p. 1; Mattie Smith Colin and Robert Elliott, "Grieving Mother Meets Body of Lynched Son," September 10, 1955, p. 5; E. J. Mays, "Till Case Trial Opens Sept. 19," September 17, 1955, p. 1; Robert H. Denley, "Kinsman Recalls Tragic Night on Eve of Trial," September 24, 1955, p. 2.
6. "Our Opinions," *CD*, September 17, 1955, p. 9.
7. "Find Kidnaped Chicago Boy's Body in River," *CT*, September 1, 1955, p. 1; Albert Barnett, "Till's Murderers Didn't Know That a Drowned Body Floats to the Surface," *CD*, September 17, 1955, p. 9; John Barrow, "Here's a Picture of Emmett Till Painted by Those Who Knew Him," *CD*, October 1, 1955, p. 4.
8. From *CD:* Mattie Smith Colin, "Slain Boy's Mother Lauds *The Defender*," September 17, 1955, p. 1; Barrow, "Here's a Picture of Emmett Till Painted by Those Who Knew Him," October 1, 1955, p. 4; Mattie Smith Colin, "Mother's Tears Greet Son Who Died a Martyr," September 10, 1955, p. 1; Smith Colin and Elliott, "Grieving Mother Meets Body of Lynched Son," September 10, 1955, p. 5.
9. Smith Colin and Elliott, "Grieving Mother Meets Body of Lynched Son," September 10, 1955, p. 5.
10. Barrow, "Here's a Picture of Emmett Till Painted by Those Who Knew Him," October 1, 1955, p. 4.
11. "2,500 at Rites Here for Boy, 14, Slain in South," *CT*, September 4, 1955, p. 2; From *CD:* Smith Colin, "Mother's Tears Greet Son Who Died a Martyr," September 10, 1955, p. 1; Robert Elliott, "Thousands at Rites for Till," September 10, 1955, p. 1.
12. "2,500 at Rites Here for Boy, 14, Slain in South," *CT*; "Ask Ike to Act in Dixie Death of Chicago Boy," *CT*, September 2, 1955, p. 2; L. Alex Wilson, "Lynching in Mississippi," *CD*, May 21, 1955, p. 1; "Protest Mississippi Shame," *CD*, September 10, 1955, p. 1.
13. "Ask Ike to Act in Dixie Death of Chicago Boy," *CT*, September 2, 1955, p. 2.
14. "'Murder,' White Says; Promises Prosecution," *CD*, September 10, 1955, p. 1.
15. "Blood on Their Hands," *CD*, September 10, 1955, p. 1.
16. Author interview with Charles Davis, August 8, 2010; Karen E. Pride, "Former *Chicago Defender* Editor Remembers Till Case," *CD*, August 26, 2005, p. 3.

17. From *CD*, September 17, 1955: Barnett, "Till's Murderers Didn't Know That a Drowned Body Floats to the Surface," p. 9; E. J. Mays, "Till Case Trial Opens Sept. 19," p. 1. Johnson, *Succeeding Against the Odds*, pp. 239–41.

18. From *CD:* "Enter *Defender* as Till Evidence," October 1, 1955, p. 3; "Readers Flood *Defender* with Letters About Till," September 24, 1955, p. 3.

19. Louis Martin, "Dope and Data," *CD*, September 17, 1955, p. 9.

20. Klibanoff, "L. Alex Wilson," pp. 67–79.

21. Paul Holmes, "A Way of Life Going on Trial in Till Case," *CT*, September 18, 1955, p. 1.

22. From *CD:* "Urges Husband to Leave Dixie," September 17, 1955, p. 1; Robert H. Denley, "Kinsman Recalls Tragic Night on Eve of Trial," September 24, 1955, p. 2; Moses J. Newson, "Death Threat to Till's Uncle," September 17, 1955, p. 1; Moses Newson, "Emmett's Kin Hang on in Miss. to Harvest Crop," September 17, 1955, p. 1. Klibanoff, "L. Alex Wilson," pp. 67–79.

23. From *CD:* L. Alex Wilson, "Sumner Unhappy Over Trial," September 24, 1955, p. 1; "Eight Men Covering Trial in Mississippi for *Defender* Readers," September 24, 1955, p. 1.

24. L. Alex Wilson, "Jim Crow Press at Till Trial; Frisk Newsmen," *CD*, September 24, 1955, p. 1; Klibanoff, "L. Alex Wilson," pp. 67–79.

25. Klibanoff, "L. Alex Wilson," pp. 67–79.

26. L. Alex Wilson, "Jim Crow Press at Till Trial; Frisk Newsmen," *CD*, September 24, 1955, p. 1.

27. "*Defender* Writer in Witness Hunt," *CD*, October 1, 1955, p. 1.

28. From *CD:* "Ready for Till's Mom to Testify," September 24, 1955, p. 1; Mattie Smith Colin, "Till's Mom, Diggs Both Disappointed," October 1, 1955, p. 1; James L. Kilgallen, "Mrs. Bradley Sheds Tears on Stand," October 1, 1955, p. 1.

29. Paul Holmes, "Open Defense Fight in Till Slaying Trial," *CT*, September 23, 1955, p. 1; Paul Holmes, "Acquit Two in Till Slaying," *CT*, September 24, 1955, p. 1; Kilgallen, "Mrs. Bradley Sheds Tears on Stand," October 1, 1955, p. 1.

30. Paul Holmes, "Acquit Two in Till Slaying," *CT*, September 24, 1955, p. 1; "Bryant, Milam Freed, Face New Kidnap Rap," *CD*, October 1, 1955, p. 1; "Jurors Refuse to Indict 2 as Till Kidnapers," *CT*, November 10, 1955, p. 2.

31. Holmes, "Acquit Two in Till Slaying," *CT*, September 24, 1955, p. 1. From *CD:* "Till's Mother, Reed Collapse," October 8, 1955, p. 1; "Moses Wright in Chicago," October 8, 1955, p. 1; "Weigh Kidnap Charges Against Milam, Bryant," November 12, 1955, p. 1.

32. Langston Hughes, "Langston Hughes Wonders Why No Lynching Probes," *CD*, October 1, 1955, p. 4; "Jurors Refuse to Indict 2 as Till Kidnapers," *CT*, November 10, 1955, p. 2.

33. "Jurors Refuse to Indict 2 as Till Kidnapers," *CT*, November 10, 1955, p. 2.

34. From *CD:* "They Did It for Us," November 19, 1955, p. 1; "NAACP Asks FBI: Clarify Policy," November 19, 1955, p. 3.

35. "Justice for Illinois Citizens," *CT*, November 13, 1955, p. 20.

36. "Governors Row Over Probe," *CD*, November 19, 1955, p. 1.

37. "President's Illness Jars Politicos," *CD*, October 8, 1955, p. 1; "U.S. Aid Calls Till Slaying a 'Black Mark,'" *CT*, November 21, 1955, p. 1; "Courts and Crime," *CD*, November 19, 1955, p. 5; "Our Opinions: Eisenhower's Health

and Future," *CD*, October 8, 1955, p. 9; "NAACP Asks FBI: Clarify Policy," *CD*, November 19, 1955, p. 3; Nichols, *A Matter of Justice*, pp. 116–18.

38. From *CD:* "Sengstacke Statement on *Defender*," December 10, 1955, p. 1; "Bare $1,000,000 Expansion Plan," December 10, 1955, p. 1; "*Chicago Defender*, Negro Weekly, to Become Daily," *CT*, December 3, 1955, p. 14.

39. "Negro Influx Is Estimated at 5,000–10,000 Monthly," *CT*, October 22, 1955, p. 12; Hirsch, *Making of the Second Ghetto*, pp. 6–9; Pride and Wilson, *A History of the Black Press*, pp. 228–29; Waters, *American Diary*, pp. 413–17; Walker, "The Promised Land," p. 45.

40. From *CD:* "Boycott Over Bus Bias in Montgomery 90% Effective," December 17, 1955, p. 1; "Vote to Continue Ala. Bus Boycott," December 24, 1955, p. 1.

41. From *CD:* "Civil Rights Front," December 31, 1955, p. 2; Ethel Payne, "The South at the Crossroads," May 7, 1956, p. 8.

42. Payne, "The South at the Crossroads," *CD*, May 7, 1956, p. 8.

43. "Bus Boycott Scores Hit; Montgomery 'Gets Tough,'" *CD*, February 4, 1956, p. 1.

44. From *CD:* "Thank You, Chicago," February 7, 1956, p. 11; "Birth and Delivery of a Daily," February 7, 1956, p. 5. Pride and Wilson, *A History of the Black Press*, pp. 228–29; Waters, *American Diary*, pp. 413–17; Walker, "The Promised Land," p. 45.

45. "*Daily Defender* Hit by Serious Paper Shortage," *CD*, February 6, 1956, p. 1; Pride and Wilson, *A History of the Black Press*, pp. 228–29.

46. From *CD:* "Violence Flares in Bus Boycott," February 6, 1956, p. 5; "Owners of Montgomery Bus Line Won't Talk," February 8, 1956, p. 7.

47. From *CD:* George Daniels, "Leader of Montgomery Bus Boycott in City," February 13, 1956, p. 3; Lee Blackwell, "Off the Record," February 14, 1956, p. 10.

48. Currie, "Interviews with Ethel Payne." From *CD:* Payne, "The South at the Crossroads," May 7, 1956, p. 8; "Photo Standalone 15 — Keep the Bus Boycott Rolling," February 14, 1956, p. 13.

49. Payne, "The South at the Crossroads," *CD*, May 7, 1956, p. 8.

50. Ethel Payne, "Strikers Set Up Their Own Curfew," *CD*, February 14, 1956, p. 18.

51. From *CD*, February 15, 1956: Ethel Payne, "The South's New Hero," p. 8; "A New Hero Emerges in the South," p. 11.

52. "Race Talks Urged by Adlai," *CT*, February 28, 1956, p. 1. From *CD:* "Prepare for Boycott Trials," March 3, 1956, p. 1; "Here Are Names of Montgomery Heroes," March 3, 1956, p. 1.

53. "Prepare for Boycott Trials," *CD*, March 3, 1956, p. 1; Klibanoff, "L. Alex Wilson," pp. 67–79; Currie, "Interviews with Ethel Payne."

54. Currie, "Interviews with Ethel Payne."

55. "Photo Standalone 1 — They're Not Boycotting Him," *CD*, March 21, 1956, p. 1.

56. "Negroes' Fund for Auto Rides Told at Trial," *CT*, March 20, 1956, p. 5; "Tell Threats for Not Aiding in Bus Boycott," *CT*, March 21, 1956, p. 1; "Negroes Testify to Mistreatment of Bus Riders," *CT*, March 21, 1956, p. 7; Ethel Payne, "Fanatic Throws Boycott Trial into Uproar; Jailed," *CD*, March 21, 1956,

p. 1; "Picture Highlights of Boycott Trial," *CD*, March 22, 1956, p. 5; Robert H. Denley, "Bare Boycotters' Ire; Ike Talks," *CD*, March 22 1956, p. 1.

57. "Negro Pastor Convicted in Bus Boycott," *CT*, March 23, 1956, p. 1; Ethel Payne, "The South at the Crossroads," *CD*, May 7, 1956, p. 8; Ethel Payne, "The South at the Crossroads," *CD*, May 10, 1956, p. 8.

58. "Who Won in Alabama?," *CT*, March 26, 1956, p. 22.

59. Ethel Payne, "Rev. King's Own Story of Montgomery Boycott," *CD*, March 26, 1956, p. 4.

60. "The Reverend Martin Luther King," *CD*, March 26, 1956, p. 11.

61. Al Monroe, "So They Say," *CD*, July 25, 1956, p. 19; "Expect HST in Billiken Big Parade," *CD*, August 9, 1956, p. 3; Ethel Payne, "Truman, Gloria Thrilled by Parade, Each Other," *CD*, August 13, 1956, p. 4; "Truman Leads Bud Billiken Day Marchers," *CT*, August 12, 1956, p. 2; "Billiken Photos," *CD*, August 13, 1956, p. 18; Lee Blackwell, "Off the Record," *CD*, August 13, 1956, p. 10; Lloyd L. General, "500,000 Watch Billikens Parade," August 18, 1956, p. 1; Albert Barnett, "Gloria Lockerman, Harry Truman Share Honors in Billiken Parade," *CD*, August 25, 1956, p. 9.

62. From *CD:* "Open Trumbull Park Riot Probe," July 16, 1955, p. 5; "War or Peace at Trumbull Park? Top Cop, Housing Boss Don't Agree," May 5, 1956, p. 3; "Negroes Gain New Jobs in Midwest Elections," April 16, 1955, p. 1; "1,000 Honor Negroes in Government at Banquet," June 25, 1955, p. 3; "Receive Bids for Stateway Construction," April 12, 1956, p. 5; Albert Barnett, "Chicago Holds Top Position in Low Rent Pubic Housing," April 7, 1956, p. 9. Hirsch, *Making of the Second Ghetto*, pp. 256–58; Cohen and Taylor, *American Pharaoh*, pp. 183–87; Royko, *Boss*, pp. 86–106.

63. From *CD:* "Outlook for Housing," November 29, 1956, p. 11; "Want Negro as Housing Chief," December 5, 1956, p. 4; "What's the Answer to Housing?," December 17, 1956, p. 11.

64. From *CD:* "U.S. Upholds Bus Integration," November 14, 1956, p. 1; "Legal End to Travel Bias," November 20, 1956, p. 9.

65. From *CD:* Enoch Waters, "Klan Parades in Montgomery," November 15, 1956, p. 1; "South Denounces New Bus Ruling," November 15, 1956, p. 3; Enoch Waters, "Klan Parades in Montgomery," November 24, 1956, p. 1.

66. From *CD:* L. Alex Wilson, "*Defender* Writer Tells of Ride with History," December 24, 1956, p. 1; "Montgomery Stunned by New U.S. Bus Decision," December 18, 1956, p. 1; L. Alex Wilson, "'All Serene,' Bus Passengers Say," December 24, 1956, p. 8; "Ala. Whites Map Bus Boycott Plan," December 24, 1956, p. 4; "Montgomery Boycotters Usher in New Era of Democracy for South," December 26, 1956, p. 10.

67. From *CD:* L. Alex Wilson, "*Defender* Writer Tells of Ride with History," December 24, 1956, p. 1; "Montgomery Stunned by New U.S. Bus Decision," December 18, 1956, p. 1; L. Alex Wilson, "'All Serene,' Bus Passengers Say," December 24, 1956, p. 8; "Ala. Whites Map Bus Boycott Plan," December 24, 1956, p. 4; "Montgomery Boycotters Usher in New Era of Democracy for South," December 26, 1956, p. 10. Gene Roberts and Hank Klibanoff, *The Race Beat* (New York: Alfred A. Knopf, 2007), pp. 141–42.

## 17. ONE VOTE PER PRECINCT

1. Klibanoff, "L. Alex Wilson," pp. 67–76; Nichols, *A Matter of Justice*, pp. 169–87.

2. From *CD*: L. Alex Wilson, "Ruse Helps Get 9 into School," September 24, 1957, p. 8; "Mob Violence in Little Rock," September 24, 1957, p. 7; "'Now I Can Work in Peace,' Says Wilson," September 26, 1957, p. 11; "Ike to Use Troops If Needed," September 24, 1957, p. 1. Nichols, *A Matter of Justice*, pp. 189–91; Klibanoff, "L. Alex Wilson," pp. 67–76.

3. William Theis, "Scenes of Wild Disorder Mark School Integration," *CD*, September 24, 1957, p. 4; Nichols, *A Matter of Justice*, pp. 189–91; Klibanoff, "L. Alex Wilson," pp. 67–76.

4. From *CD*: William Theis, "Scenes of Wild Disorder Mark School Integration," September 24, 1957, p. 4; "Ike to Use Troops If Needed," September 24, 1957, p. 1.

5. L. Alex Wilson, "Students Tell Experiences Inside Central High School," *CD*, September 24, 1957, p. 5.

6. From *CD*: William Theis, "Scenes of Wild Disorder Mark School Integration," September 24, 1957, p. 4; L. Alex Wilson, "Wilson Marooned in Bates' Home by 25 Cars of Hoods," September 25, 1957, p. 4.

7. From *CD*: Robert E. Clark, "Ike Takes Steps to Summon Troops," September 24, 1957, p. 2; "Ike to Use Troops if Needed," September 24, 1957, p. 1. Nichols, *A Matter of Justice*, pp. 188–99.

8. From *CD*: "Troops Arrive, School Today," September 25, 1957, p. 1; "Ike's Steel Ring Grips Little Rock," September 26, 1957, p. 25; Bob Considine, "1,500 Man Unit to Join Troops," September 26, 1957, p. 24; "Troops Teach the Lesson at Little Rock School," September 26, 1957, p. 14; "Troops Demonstrate How to Handle Rabble Rousers," September 26, 1957, p. 10; Bob Considine, "9:25 A.M., Thurs., Sept. 25, 1957," September 26, 1957, p. 8; L. Alex Wilson, "Mrs. Bates Thankful for Troops," September 26, 1957, p. 7.

9. From *CD*: "'Now I Can Work in Peace,' Says Wilson," September 26, 1957, p. 11; L. Alex Wilson, "Wilson Revisits Scene of Attack: Finds Peace, Quiet," September 26, 1957, p. 5; L. Alex Wilson, "Faubus Gave Ike Chance to Warn South on Civil Rights Compliance," October 5, 1957, p. 1. Klibanoff, "L. Alex Wilson," pp. 67–76.

10. John Sengstacke, "New Daily Meets Challenge," *CD*, May 10, 1958, p. 11.

11. From *CD*: "*Defender*, 3, Continues Its Expansion; Hires 2 Execs," February 9, 1959, p. 2; "*Defender* Moving to New Building," April 4, 1959, p. 2; "After 38 Years, *Defender* Moves," April 11, 1959, p. 9; "Photo of John and Bobby Sengstacke," November 3, 1958, p. 3; "*Defender* Papers Still Expanding," February 28, 1959, p. 4.

12. From *CD*: "Photo of John and Bobby Sengstacke," November 3, 1958, p. 3; "*Defender*, 3, Continues Its Expansion; Hires 2 Execs," February 9, 1959, p. 2; "*Defender* Papers Still Expanding," February 28, 1959, p. 4; "After 38 Years, *Defender* Moves," April 11, 1959, p. 9; "*Defender* Moving to New Building," April 4, 1959, p. 2; "New *Defender* Press Rolls," February 29, 1960, p. 2.

13. Myiti Sengstacke-Rice, *The Chicago Defender* (Charleston, SC: Arcadia Publishing, 2012), pp. 84–85.

14. From *CD:* Louis Martin, "Dope and Data," February 28, 1959, p. 10; Ethel Payne, "Ghana Born!," March 6, 1957, p. 4; "Alex Wilson New Editor of *Defender*," February 28, 1959, p. 1.

15. From CD: "Alex Wilson New Editor of *Defender*," February 28, 1959, p. 1; "L. Alex Wilson, *Defender* Editor-in-Chief, Dies," October 12, 1960, p. 1; "L. Alex Wilson Was Devoted Journalist," October 29, 1960, p. 21. Klibanoff, "L. Alex Wilson," pp. 67–76.

16. From CD: "*Defender* History . . . from the Old to the New," February 29, 1960, p. 1; "*Defender* Editorial Staff to Move into New Office," February 3, 1960, p. 2; "New *Defender* Press Rolling!," March 5, 1960, p. 2; "New *Defender* Press Rolls," February 29, 1960, p. 2; Baker E. Morten, "Come Along on a Tour of New *Defender* Plant," May 7, 1960, p. 3; "When *Defender* Family Works, It Works; When It Plays — It Eats, Too," September 1, 1956, p. 11; "Photo Page: Americans Are Guests of Cuban Government," January 23, 1960, p. 12.

17. From *CD:* "L. Alex Wilson Was Devoted Journalist," October 29, 1960, p. 21; Alvin C. Adams, "Combined Efforts of 152 Produce *Defender*," May 7, 1960, p. 1. Author interview with Charles Davis, August 18, 2010.

18. From *CD:* Audrey Weaver, "Shades of Dixie Terror Seen at Chicago Project," November 5, 1955, p. 2; "Our Audrey Weaver a Rare City Editor," December 22, 1956, p. 4; "Combined Efforts of 152 Produce *Defender*," May 7, 1960, p. 3.

19. Author interviews with Marc and Helena Sengstacke, February 23, 2012; author interviews with Eugene Scott, February 4 and 7, 2010.

20. From *CD:* "At Bobby Sengstacke's Birthday Party," June 8, 1946, p. 20; "When *Defender* Family Works, It Works; When It Plays — It Eats, Too," September 1, 1956, p. 11; "Photo Page: Americans Are Guests of Cuban Government," January 23, 1960, p. 12.

21. From *CD:* Baker E. Morten, "5,000 Hear Muhammad," February 29, 1960, p. 3; "Nation of Islam Convention," February 28, 1966, p. 3; Faith C. Christmas, "Black Muslims: A Force for Change," May 27, 1972, p. 4.

22. From *CD:* "Kennedy and the Southern Bloc," July 4, 1960, p. 10; "Kennedy's Racial Stand," June 28, 1960, p. 1; John H. Sengstacke, "Jack Gets Boos at NAACP Rally," July 12, 1960, p. 2.

23. From *CD:* "Negroes 'Boo' Kennedy at Los Angeles," July 11, 1960, p. 1; "Kennedy Gives Truman 'Hell,'" July 5, 1960, p. 1; "Daley to Back Kennedy in L.A," July 11, 1960, p. 1; Mattie Smith Colin, "Move for Adlai Grows; Kennedy Loses Votes," July 14, 1960, p. 2; John H. Sengstacke, "Fears Jack Can't Carry Negro Vote," July 23, 1960, p. 12.

24. Mattie Smith Colin, "Kennedy Says Rights Are Basic," *CD,* July 18, 1960, p. 4.

25. "Dawson Meets with Kennedy," *CD,* August 18, 1960, p. 1; Poinsett, *Walking with Presidents,* pp. 68–74.

26. From *CD:* Louis Martin, "Dope and Data," August 27, 1960, p. 10; Louis Martin, "Baptist Leader Taylor Backs Kennedy Ticket," October 20, 1960, p. 4.

27. Poinsett, *Walking with Presidents,* pp. 76–80.

28. Ibid.

29. "Dawson Selects Hill for Post," *CD,* October 1, 1960, 3.

30. Mattie Smith Colin, "Jack Repeats Rights Stand," *CD*, October 22, 1960, p. 2.

31. "Nixon Calls for Full Equality," *CD*, September 24, 1960, p. 3.

32. "Kennedy, Wife Visit Howard," *CD*, October 15, 1960, p. 1.

33. Poinsett, *Walking with Presidents*, pp. 79–80.

34. Mattie Smith Colin, "Jack Repeats Rights Stand," *CD*, October 22, 1960, p. 2; Poinsett, *Walking with Presidents*, pp. 76–78.

35. Smith Colin, "Jack Repeats Rights Stand," *CD*, October 22, 1960, p. 2.

36. "L. Alex Wilson Dies; Editor of *Defender*," CT, October 12, 1960, p. 1. From *CD:* "L. Alex Wilson, *Defender* Editor-in-Chief, Dies," October 12, 1960, p. 1; "L. Alex Wilson Was Devoted Journalist," October 29, 1960, p. 21.

37. John H. Sengstacke, "Kennedy Is Our Choice," *CD*, October 29, 1960, p. 1.

38. Poinsett, *Walking with Presidents*, pp. 80–85. From *CD:* Alan B. Gillion, "Atlanta Mayor to Seek Integration," October 29, 1960, p. 1; "Persecution of Dr. King," October 31, 1960, p. 10.

39. Poinsett, *Walking with Presidents*, pp. 80–85. From *CD:* "Hail Jack's Role in King Case," October 31, 1960, p. 2; "Rev. King Free on Bond," November 5, 1960, p. 1.

40. Poinsett, *Walking with Presidents*, pp. 80–85.

41. "King Freed on Bond After Phone Call from Sen. Kennedy," *CT*, October 28, 1960, p. 7; "Hail Jack's Role in King Case," *CD*, October 31, 1960, p. 2.

42. From *CD:* "Rev. King Free on Bond," November 5, 1960, p. 1; "Tomorrow — Day of Decision," November 7, 1960, p. 14.

43. "King Lauds Jack on Race Issue," *CD*, November 8, 1960, p. 2; Poinsett, *Walking with Presidents*, pp. 84–85.

44. "See Negro Vote as the Key in Election," *CD*, November 7, 1960, p. 1; "Daley Predicts Demo Sweep in City, State," November 8, 1960, p. 1; George Tagge, "Kerner and Douglas Easy Victors," *CT*, November 9, 1960, p. 1; Walter Trohan, "Nixon Says He Concedes Poll Defeat," *CT*, November 9, 1960, p. 1; Joseph Hearst, "Kennedy Wins Presidency," *CT*, November 9, 1960, p. 1; "1,767,891 Vote in Presidential Election Here," *CD*, November 9, 1960, p. 3; Cohen and Taylor, *American Pharaoh*, pp. 263–70.

45. From *CD:* "The People Have Spoken," November 12, 1960, p. 10; "*Daily Defender* Wins with Senator Kennedy," November 9, 1960, p. 3.

46. From *CD:* "Admit Negro Vote for Jack Whipped Nixon," November 10, 1960, p. 1; "Why Kennedy Won?," December 1, 1960, p. 14; "A 'Squeaker' in Illinois," November 10, 1960, p. 4. Cohen and Taylor, *American Pharaoh*, pp. 263–70.

47. Poinsett, *Walking with Presidents*, pp. 80–85.

48. Ibid., pp. 87–92; "Ex-*Defender* Writer Begins Political Job," *CD*, May 7, 1962, p. 3; Currie, "Interviews with Ethel Payne"; Muhammad biography of John Sengstacke, 1982, AS Papers, Box 22, Folder 21.

49. Poinsett, *Walking with Presidents*, pp. 87–92; "Ex-*Defender* Writer Begins Political Job," *CD*, May 7, 1962, p. 3; Currie, "Interviews with Ethel Payne."

50. Muhammad biography of John Sengstacke, AS Papers, Box 22, Folder 21.

## 18. A SOCRATIC GADFLY

1. From *CD:* "Dogs Are Treated Better, 'Freedom Rider' Charges," May 17, 1961, p. 2; "The Frame Remains," May 18, 1961, p. 13; Roberts and Klibanoff, *The Race Beat,* pp. 242–54.

2. From *CD:* "FBI Probes Bus Riots in Alabama," May 16, 1961, p. 1; "Alabama Hoodlums," May 17, 1961, p. 11; "U.S. Sends Armed Posse to Quell Alabama Violence," May 20, 1961, p. 1; Roberts and Klibanoff, *The Race Beat,* pp. 242–54.

3. From *CD:* "Governor Defies U.S. in Alabama," May 22, 1961, p. 1; "Kennedy Order Recalls Chaos in Little Rock," May 22, 1961, p. 2.

4. From *CD:* Samuel Hoskins, "'Freedom Riders' Vow to Continue," May 24, 1961, p. 1; "Martial Law Rules in Montgomery Racial Clash," May 23, 1961, p. 2; "Wild Beasts at Large," May 23, 1961, p. 11.

5. From *CD:* "Kennedy Confident of Miss. Mob Control," May 25, 1961, p. 11; "Jail 25 Freedom Riders in Miss," May 25, 1961, p. 1. "Photo — Rocky Road to Freedom," May 25, 1961, p. 1.

6. "Ride On, Freedom Riders," *CD,* May 29, 1961, p. 11.

7. From *CD:* Samuel Hoskins, "'Freedom Riders' Hit Miss. Around the Clock," May 31, 1961, p. 4; "Freedom Riders — Mob Rule," May 31, 1961, p. 11.

8. From *CD:* Hoskins, "'Freedom Riders' Hit Miss. Around the Clock," May 31, 1961, p. 11; "19 More 'Freedom Riders' Balk at $200 Fines, Join Others on Chain Gang," June 1, 1961, p. 3; "Voting Rights Next: King," June 17, 1961, p. 11.

9. From *CD:* "Voting Rights Next: King," June 17, 1961, p. 11. "Tearful Crowd Hears 'Freedom Riders' Detail Mistreatment; Vow More Effort," June 8, 1961, p. 6.

10. Kenneth C. Field, "'Freedom Rider' Tells Torture," *CD,* June 24, 1961, p. 1.

11. From *CD:* "Bob Again Asks Riders to Cool It," June 15, 1961, p. 3; "We Must Press Onward," June 26, 1961, p. 11.

12. "Mississippi and the Law," *CD,* July 19, 1961, p. 11.

13. From *CD:* "10 from Chicago Face Mississippi 'Rider' Trials," August 14, 1961, p. 1; Adolph Slaughter, "'Freedom Riders' Bare Beatings in New Orleans," August 19, 1961, p. 3.

14. "A Major Victory," *CD,* September 26, 1961, p. 11.

15. Burns, *Nitty Gritty,* pp. 210–16.

16. "Ben Burns New Editor-in-Chief of *The Defender*; Other Changes Announced," *CD,* July 28, 1962, p. 1; Burns, *Nitty Gritty,* pp. 210–16.

17. Burns, *Nitty Gritty,* pp. 210–16; Chester Commodore, "Editorial Cartoon — Civil Rights," *CD,* August 28, 1963, p. 11.

18. Burns, *Nitty Gritty,* pp. 210–16.

19. Theresa Fambro, "Tells Why He Wants to Go to U. of Mississippi," *CD,* August 27, 1962, p. 4; Burns, *Nitty Gritty,* pp. 210–16.

20. "Miss. U. Bars Negro Again," *CT,* September 27, 1962, p. 1; "Mississippi Surrenders!," *CD,* October 1, 1962, p. 1; "Meredith Enrolls After Riot," *CD,* October 2, 1962, p. 1; "Troops Clamp Grip on Oxford," *CT,* October 2, 1962, p. 1.

21. Burns, *Nitty Gritty,* pp. 210–16; Ben Burns, "Cassius Clay Still Writing Poetry," *CD,* January 2, 1963, p. 13.

22. Arnold Rosenzweig, "'White Liberal' Discusses Role in Predominantly Negro Institution," *CD*, November 2, 1963, p. 4.

23. From *CD:* Charles S. Stone, "The People Speak," March 20, 1963, p. 12; "C. Sumner Stone *Defender*'s New Editor-in-Chief," August 7, 1963, p. 1.

24. From *CD:* "Birmingham," August 14, 1963, p. 1; "This Is Chicago in the Summer of 1963," August 14, 1963, p. 3; Ted Coleman, "Rap Cop Brutality at Protest Site," August 13, 1963, p. 2.

25. From *CD:* Charles S. Stone, "A Stone's Throw," August 24, 1963, p. 1; Dave Potter, "'Willis, Scram!' SAY 50,000," August 24, 1963, p. 1.

26. From *CD:* "Expect 2500 from Chicago on 'March,'" August 7, 1963, p. 4; "'Jobs, Freedom' Cry of Marchers on Washington," August 15, 1963, p. 4; "Photo Standalone — Washington, Here We Come," August 24, 1963, p. 2; Lloyd General, "'I Rode the Freedom Train,'" August 31, 1963, p. 1; Steve Bogira and Mick Dumke, "Fifty Years Later, Participants in the March on Washington Still Hoping for Justice," *Chicago Reader*, August 21, 2013.

27. From *CD:* "7 Liberal Demos Revolt, Assail Daley, Dawson Rule," February 19, 1963, p. 1; Timuel Black, "Confetti," August 8, 1963, p. 13; "March on Washington," August 26, 1963, p. 11; "March on Washington Wed. with Your *Daily Defender*," August 27, 1963, p. 3.

28. From *CD:* Lloyd General, "A Whole Nation Will Hold Its Breath While 250,000 March," August 27, 1963, p. 3; Lloyd General, "2500 Jam Station En Route to March," August 28, 1963, p. 1; "March on Washington Wed. with Your *Daily Defender*," August 27, 1963, p. 3; Lloyd General, "'I Rode the Freedom Train,'" August 31, 1963, p. 1.

29. From *CD:* "Photo — Boarding the Freedom Train," August 28, 1963, p. 1; Lloyd General, "2500 Jam Station En Route to March," August 28, 1963, p. 1; Lloyd General, "'Freedom Day' Will Live Forever; Engraved on History's Page," August 29, 1963, p. 2.

30. From *CD:* "March on Washington Wed. with Your *Daily Defender*," August 27, 1963, p. 3; Lloyd General, "'Freedom Day' Will Live Forever; Engraved on History's Page," August 29, 1963, p. 2.

31. Charles S. Stone, "A Stone's Throw," *CD*, August 31, 1963, p. 1.

32. From *CD:* "King's Entire Aug. 28 Speech," September 7, 1963, p. 1; "Rev. Martin Luther King's Speech Was History Talking," August 31, 1963, p. 4.

33. "March Advanced Mankind: JFK," *CD*, August 29, 1963, p. 2.

34. Lloyd General, "'I Rode the Freedom Train,'" *CD*, August 31, 1963, p. 1.

35. Ibid.

36. Lillian S. Calhoun, "15 Empty White Classrooms Found in Chicago by *Defender*," *CD*, September 7, 1963, p. 1.

37. From *CD:* Ted Coleman, "Mayor on Willis: Still 'Hands Off,'" September 7, 1963, p. 1; Ross Sherwood, "The Human Relations Beat," August 31, 1963, p. 5. Cohen and Taylor, *American Pharaoh*, pp. 326–28.

38. From *CD:* Chuck Stone, "A Stone's Throw," September 18, 1963, p. 4; "Willis Favors Bogan Parents over Negroes," September 16, 1963, p. 1.

39. Chuck Stone, "A Stone's Throw," *CD*, September 28, 1963, p. 1.

40. From *CD:* Lillian S. Calhoun, "Willis Stays! 'No School' Day Tues., Oct. 22," October 17, 1963, p. 1; "Angry Rights Leaders Denounce Willis Deal,"October 17, 1963, p. 3; "Bias Wins as Willis and Board Kiss and Make

Up," October 17, 1963, p. 3; "Freedom Day March," October 22, 1963, p. 11; "It's Freedom Day! Expect Thousands to Participate," October 22, 1963, p. 1.

41. From *CD:* UPI telephoto, "20,000 at Rally Call on Willis to Resign," October 23, 1963, p. 1; "Chicago's Finest Hour," October 23, 1963, p. 1; photos by Tony Rhoden, "School-by-School Story of Boycott," October 23, 1963, p. 4; "School Boycott Success; 224,770 Pupils Absent," October 23, 1963, p. 1; "Photo — 'Twas a Great Day for Chicago," October 24, 1963, p. 12.

42. From *CT:* "Civil Commotion — To What Purpose?," October 24, 1963, p. 20; "Who's Being Shortchanged?," October 27, 1963, p. 18; "The School Boycott," October 22, 1963, p. 14.

43. From *CD:* Charles S. Stone, "A Stone's Throw," November 11, 1963, p. 1; Charles S. Stone, "A Stone's Throw," October 28, 1963, p. 4; "Negroes Now Ahead in Grade School Pupils," October 24, 1963, p. 2.

44. From *CD:* "In the Life of a President," November 23, 1963, p. 3; "As a Friend of Africans," November 23, 1963, p. 4; "The 1964 Election," November 23, 1963, p. 8; Lloyd L. General, "JFK 4th to Be Killed in Office," November 23, 1963, p. 1; Chuck Stone, "A Stone's Throw," *CD,* November 25, 1963, p. 1.

45. From *CD:* Ernestine Cofield, "Kennedy's Assassination Worst Tragedy since Lincoln's Death, Says Sengstacke," November 23, 1963, p. 2; "The Kennedy Retreat," October 23, 1963, p. 1, "We've Lost a Friend," November 25, 1963, p. 15.

46. "Nation Pays Last Respects to a Great President," *CD,* November 25, 1963, p. 1.

47. Ted Coleman, "Kennedy, Like Lincoln, Killed: A Dear, Dear Friend Is Dead," *CD,* November 23, 1963, p. 1.

48. From *CD:* "We've Lost a Friend," November 25, 1963, p. 15; "Nation Pays Last Respects to a Great President," November 25, 1963, p. 1; John H. Sengstacke, "A Memo from the Publisher," November 25, 1963, p. 2.

49. From *CD,* Charles S. Stone, "A Stone's Throw": December 19, 1963, p. 1; January 16, 1964, p. 4; February 25, 1964, p. 2.

50. From *CD:* "Boycott a Flop, Declares Daley," February 27, 1964, p. 4; Ted Coleman, "Daley Threatens Negro Parents, Backs Bigots," February 26, 1964, p. 4; Peggy Robinson, "2 Big Upsets: Boycott Wins! Clay Does, Too!," February 26, 1964, p. 1.

51. From *CD:* Lillian S. Calhoun, "Willis Juggles Figures, Slanders City's Negroes," March 14, 1964, p. 1; Charles S. Stone, "A Stone's Throw," March 14, 1964, p. 1.

52. Charles S. Stone, "A Stone's Throw," *CD,* April 2, 1964, p. 2.

53. From *CD:* C. C. J. Nugent, "Where Was the Revolt During Recent Primary," May 2, 1964, p. 9; "Gregory Told by FBI: 'We'll Probe All Vote Frauds,'" April 14, 1964, p. 1; "A Weird Primary," April 14, 1964, p. 11; Charles S. Stone, "A Stone's Throw," April 16, 1964, p. 1.

54. Charles S. Stone, "A Stone's Throw," *CD,* June 30, 1964, p. 4; Charles S. Stone, preface to *Tell It like It Is* (New York: Trident Press, 1967).

55. Muhammad biography of John Sengstacke, AS Papers, Box 22, Folder 21.

56. "Daley's Neighborhood Under 'Martial Law,' Mayor Denounces Mob," *CD,* October 7, 1964, p. 2.

57. From *CD:* Charles M. Jenkins Jr., "The People Speak," April 16, 1964, p. 17; "*Defender* Announces 10 Staff Appointments," September 19, 1964, p. 3.

58. From *CD:* "Always on Top of the News," October 13, 1964, p. 12; Carole L. Anderson, "Chicago's Bob McCord on Way Up in New York City's Ballet Co," August 15, 1964, p. 4; Carole L. Anderson, "The People Speak," October 15, 1964, p. 17.

59. From *CD:* "*Defender* Adding New Owl Edition Oct. 26," October 13, 1964, p. 1; "Here I Am, Your Owl," October 26, 1964, p. 1.

60. Daniels, "John Sengstacke III: America's Black Press Lord," p. 26, AS Papers, Box 22, Folder 8.

### 19. A PRAYER FOR CHICAGO

1. From *CD:* "Let Willis Go," May 18, 1965, p. 13; "A New School Board," May 31, 1965, p. 13.

2. From *CD:* "Present Demands to Daley," June 16, 1965, p. 1; "Board, Daley, Raby Meet," June 30, 1965, p. 1. Taylor Branch, *At Canaan's Edge,* pp. 235–43.

3. From *CD:* Brenetta Howell, "King Joins Willis Ouster," July 8, 1965, p. 1; "Board to Meet," July 8, 1965, p. 1; "Raby Expresses His 'Shock' as Daley Cold Shoulders King," July 19, 1965, p. 2.

4. From *CD:* "King Shakes Up Chicago," July 24, 1965, p. 1; "City Braces for Mass Rally," July 26, 1965, p. 1; "Dr. Martin Luther King Spotlights Civil Rights Movement Here," July 26, 1965, p. 14. Branch, *At Canaan's Edge,* pp. 262–66.

5. From *CD:* "King, Ailing, Leads 30,000 Marchers in 'Greatest Demonstration Ever Seen,'" July 27, 1965, p. 14; "Chicago No Promised Land, Says King," July 27, 1965, p. 3; Betty Washington, "After the March Was Over," July 28, 1965, p. 4; "King Lauds Massive Turnout," July 27, 1965, p. 1. Branch, *At Canaan's Edge,* pp. 262–66.

6. "Daley Target of Mass Picketing in Detroit," *CD,* July 27, 1965, p. 4.

7. From *CD:* "Irresistible Force," July 27, 1965, p. 13; "Your Move, Mr. Mayor," July 28, 1965, p. 15.

8. "Dr. King's Column Set to Begin," *CD,* December 8, 1965, p. 3.

9. From *CD:* "'My Dream' — Dr. King's New Column Is Coming," *CD,* December 6, 1965, p. 1; "King to Tell Viet Stand in Column," December 9, 1965, p. 3; Martin Luther King, "Great Expectations," December 11, 1965, p. 1; Martin Luther King, "My Dream," December 18, 1965, p. 10.

10. From *CD:* Betty Washington, "Dr. King Travels in Secret to Chicago," January 6, 1966, p. 1; "Dr. King Launches Attack on Chicago School Setup," February 5, 1966, p. 2; Betty Washington, "Dr. King Will Occupy Chicago Slum Flat in New Rights Drive," January 8, 1966, p. 1. Branch, *At Canaan's Edge,* pp. 407–9; Cohen and Taylor, *American Pharaoh,* pp. 352–56.

11. Betty Washington, "King Urges U.S. Work Plan for 'Jobs, Jobs, Jobs,'" *CD,* January 10, 1966, p. 10.

12. Ibid.

13. From *CD:* Betty Washington, "Exclusive from Selma: 'My Night in Hell,'" March 13, 1965, p. 1; Betty Washington, "March to End at Ala. Capital,"

March 25, 1965, p. 1; "New Editorial Dept. Titles Given," November 4, 1967, p. 3. Author interview with Bob Black, May 13, 2011.

14. From *CD:* "When *Defender* Family Works, It Works; When It Plays — It Eats, Too," September 1, 1956, p. 11; "'Little Rock 9' Frolic at Sengstacke Farm to End 'Perfect' Chi Visit," June 14, 1958, p. 13. Author interview with Bob Black, May 13, 2011.

15. Betty Washington, "Dr. Martin L. King Sets Move to Westside Slum," *CD*, January 22, 1966, p. 1; author interview with Bob Black, May 13, 2011.

16. From *CD:* Betty Washington, "Dr. King Shows How to 'Cure' a Slum Building," January 24, 1966, p. 1; Betty Washington, "Dr. Martin L. King Sets Move to Westside Slum," January 22, 1966, p. 1.

17. "King and Wife Move into Slum," *CD*, January 27, 1966, p. 1; Branch, *At Canaan's Edge*, pp. 407–9, 427–29.

18. Betty Washington, "Dr. King Meets with Top Cops; Map Plan to Prevent Violence," *CD*, January 29, 1966, p. 1; Branch, *At Canaan's Edge*, pp. 427–29; Kenan Heise, "Obituary Journalist Betty Washington Worked at *Defender, Sun-Times*," *CT*, January 11, 1994; author interview with Bob Black, May 13, 2011.

19. "Dr. King Launches Attack on Chicago School Setup," *CD*, February 5, 1966, p. 2.

20. Betty Washington, "Rev. Abernathy to Move in Next to Dr. King's Flat," *CD*, February 12, 1966, p. 1.

21. Martin Luther King, "My Dream," *CD*, February 12, 1966, p. 10.

22. From *CD:* Bill Van Alstine, "331 Slum Flat Rent Cut-Offs," February 12, 1966, p. 1; "Where Rents Are to Be Withheld," February 12, 1966, p. 3. Branch, *At Canaan's Edge*, pp. 443–45; Cohen and Taylor, *American Pharaoh*, pp. 358–66.

23. From *CD* by Betty Washington: "Clergy, King Map Chicago Boycotts," February 5, 1966, p. 1; "King and Raby Tour the Slums, Meet the Folks," February 19, 1966, p. 1.

24. Betty Washington, photos by Bob Black, "King Group's Novel Plan to Repair Slum," *CD*, February 24, 1966, p. 1.

25. Ibid.

26. From *CD*, Betty Washington: "Every Morning, a War on Rats," March 15, 1966, p. 1; "How Ghetto Families Are Penalized," March 17, 1966, p. 4; "What's It Like in Westside Flat?," March 14, 1966, p. 1.

27. From *CD:* "Malcolm X Assassins Get Life Sentences," April 16, 1966, p. 1; "King, Muslims Join Forces in War on Slums," February 26, 1966, p. 1; "13,000 Thrilled at Jam-Packed Chicago Freedom Festival," March 14, 1966, p. 14. Branch, *At Canaan's Edge*, pp. 440–41.

28. From *CD:* Betty Washington, "Rev. Jackson Differs with Comedian," November 17, 1965, p. 3; "King Won't Attend Meet with Mayor," March 16, 1966, p. 3; "What King Said in Meet with Daley," March 28, 1966, p. 1; "Jackson, SCLC Rights Concept Split Is Widening," July 2, 1966, p. 37. Cohen and Taylor, *American Pharaoh*, pp. 371–72; Branch *At Canaan's Edge*, pp. 440–54.

29. From *CD*, Betty Washington: "Businesses Ignore 'Breadbasket' Demands,"

March 28, 1966, p. 4; "'Breadbasket' Launches Chicago Boycott," April 11, 1966, p. 7; "Breadbasket Boycott Talk Produces 44 Negro Jobs," April 16, 1966, p. 1.

30. Martin Luther King, "My Dream," *CD*, April 16, 1966, p. 10.

31. "Daley, Aides Have Word for King: 'Go!'" *CD*, April 16, 1966, p. 1.

32. Donald Mosby and Arnold Rosenzweig, "3,000 Teens Will 'Close Chicago,' Bevel Says," *CD*, May 11, 1966, p. 1.

33. Ibid.

34. "King and the Gangs," *CD*, June 15, 1966, p. 15.

35. From *CD*: "Yes, but WHO Put the OK on Redmond?," May 12, 1966, p. 1; "Leaders React to Ben's Going," May 24, 1966, p. 3; "Willis Quitting His School Post Ahead of Time," May 24, 1966, p. 1.

36. "Leaders React to Ben's Going," *CD*, May 24, 1966, p. 3.

37. "Willis' Resignation," *CD*, May 25, 1966, p. 15.

38. From *CD*: "Dr. Martin Luther King Urges Chicagoans to Register — and Vote," May 14, 1966, p. 1; "Few Surprises in Quiet Primary Voting," June 15, 1966, p. 5.

39. From *CD*: "King Postpones June 26 Rally at City Hall," June 13, 1966, p. 4; "Meredith Marchers Clash with Mississippi Whites," June 22, 1966, p. 1.

40. John Sengstacke, "Black Revolt Is Unfinished Job of 1863," *CD*, June 25, 1966, p. 5.

41. From *CD*: "Meredith Marchers Clash with Mississippi Whites," June 22, 1966, p. 1; "10,000 Wind Up Thunderous Meredith March," June 27, 1966, p. 1; "Consolidation of Power," July 16, 1966, p. 10. Branch, *At Canaan's Edge*, pp. 481–94.

42. From *CD*: "10,000 Wind Up Thunderous Meredith March"; Andrew Reese, "Meredith March Chiefs Huddle on What Next Move Should Be," June 28, 1966, p. 1; Al Kuettner, "Rights Groups Scrap over Ideology," June 30, 1966, p. 16; Stanley S. Scott, "CORE Adopts New Resolution; End Non-Violence," July 5, 1966, p. 6. Branch, *At Canaan's Edge*, pp. 481–94.

43. From *CD*: "Racial Solidarity," June 30, 1966, p. 21; "Black Power," July 2, 1966, p. 10.

44. "'Black Power' Decried," *CD*, July 7, 1966, p. 5.

45. From *CD*: Betty Washington, "100,000 Expected at Freedom Rally," July 2, 1966, p. 37; "CIC Backs, Urges Other Support of Sunday's Big 'Freedom Rally,'" July 9, 1966, p. 16; "'Cooling' That Long, Hot Summer Forecast," July 9, 1966, p. 5; "Rally Drawing Many City Segments," July 2, 1966, p. 2.

46. From *CD*: "30,000 Hear Dr. King at Soldier Field Rally," July 11, 1966, p. 3; photo by Bob Black, "Thousands Join Dr. King's Rally at Soldier Field," July 11, 1966, p. 1; "Here's What Dr. King Told Vast Thousands," July 11, 1966, p. 1. Branch, *At Canaan's Edge*, pp. 501–6; Cohen and Taylor, *American Pharaoh*, pp. 381–84.

47. Betty Washington, "King, Daley Lock Horns on 'Open City,'" *CD*, July 12, 1966, p. 1; Branch, *At Canaan's Edge*, pp. 501–6; Cohen and Taylor, *American Pharaoh*, pp. 381–84.

48. From *CD*: "Westside Taverns Closed," July 14, 1966, p. 3; Betty Washington and Donald Mosby, "300 Police Put Down Raging Westside Riot," July 14, 1966, p. 1; photos by Bob Black, "Anatomy of a Bloody, Savage Westside

Riot," July 16, 1966, p. 21; Betty Washington, "Westside Riots Parallel Earlier Outbreaks," July 18 1966, p. 4; Betty Washington, "Police Get 12-Hour Duty in Westside Uproar," July 16, 1966, p. 1; Betty Washington, "Westside Riots Parallel Earlier Outbreaks," July 18, 1966, p. 4. Cohen and Taylor, *American Pharaoh*, pp. 387–91; Branch, *At Canaan's Edge*, pp. 501–5.

49. From *CD:* Betty Washington, "Police Get 12-Hour Duty in Westside Uproar," July 16, 1966, p. 1; "Westside Riots Parallel Earlier Outbreaks," July 18, 1966, p. 4; "Leaders Voice Ideas on Riots," July 18, 1966, p. 3. Cohen and Taylor, *American Pharaoh*, pp. 387–91; Branch, *At Canaan's Edge*, pp. 501–5.

50. "Here Was the Riot Scene as Westside Cooled Again," *CD*, July 18, 1966, p. 6; author interview with Bob Black, May 13, 2011.

51. From *CD:* "Here Was the Riot Scene as Westside Cooled Again," July 18, 1966, p. 6; Donald Mosby and Arnold Rosenzweig, "Shooting and Fire Mar Calm in Riot Area," July 19, 1966, p. 1.

52. Bill Van Alstine, "Violence Moves to Southside; Stores Hit," *CD*, July 18, 1966, p. 1.

53. "An Editorial: Let's Face Facts," *CD*, July 18, 1966, p. 1.

## 20. A DARK HOUR IN THE LIFE OF AMERICA

1. From *CD:* Donald Mosby, "Gage Park's Whites Stone Marchers," August 1, 1966, p. 1; Donald Mosby, "Don't Hesitate; Let People Go!," August 4, 1966, p. 16; "Demonstrators Cancel Their 3rd Gage Park March," August 2, 1966, p. 1; "Leaders Take Housing Drive to New Area," August 3, 1966, p. 1; "Youths Protect Marchers," August 2, 1966, p. 4. Author interview with Bob Black, May 13, 2011; Branch, *At Canaan's Edge*, pp. 505–511; Cohen and Taylor, *American Pharaoh*, pp. 392–99.

2. Donald Mosby, "Gage Park's Whites Stone Marchers," *CD*, August 1, 1966, p. 1.

3. From *CD:* Donald Mosby, "Don't Hesitate; Let People Go!," August 4, 1966, p. 16; "Demonstrators Cancel Their 3rd Gage Park March," August 2, 1966, p. 1; "Leaders Take Housing Drive to New Area," August 3, 1966, p. 1; "Youths Protect Marchers," August 2, 1966, p. 4. Author interview with Bob Black, May 13, 2011; Branch, *At Canaan's Edge*, pp. 505–11; Cohen and Taylor, *American Pharaoh*, pp. 392–99.

4. "King Vows New Gage Park March," *CD*, August 4, 1966, p. 1.

5. From *CD:* "Meanwhile, March Goes Peacefully," August 8, 1966, p. 3; "Nazis Organize 'White Guard' in Gage Park," August 8, 1966, p. 1; "Wilson Admits Too Few Cops Sent to Gage Park," August 3, 1966, p. 3. Branch, *At Canaan's Edge*, pp. 506–11; Cohen and Taylor, *American Pharaoh*, pp. 394–96.

6. From *CD:* "Nazis Organize 'White Guard' in Gage Park," August 8, 1966, p. 1; "SCLC Meeting in Mississippi," August 9, 1966, p. 4; Thelma Hunt, "Confetti," August 10, 1966, p. 12; "Politicians Meet King, Raby; Agree to Civil Rights Demands," August 6, 1966, p. 1.

7. From *CD:* Photos by Bob Black, "Marchers Say Prayer," August 11, 1966, p. 1; "Chicago Marchers Visit the Loop," August 11, 1966, p. 3; "Racial Unrest Boils in a Witch's Cauldron," August 11, 1966, p. 1; "Cicero Action Sought," August 22, 1966, p. 4.

8. From *CD:* "Stop Fighting Open Housing, Realtors Told," August 18, 1966, p. 3; "Summit Meet Hears Realty Demands, 'No March' Plea," August 18, 1966, p. 1; "Renewed Cicero Riot Forecast by Al Raby," August 18, 1966, p. 4; Bill Van Alstine, "City's Freedom Movement Set for Realty War's Hottest Week," August 20, 1966, p. 1.

9. From *CD:* "Chicago Marchers Visit the Loop," August 11, 1966, p. 3; Bill Van Alstine, "City's Freedom Movement Set for Realty War's Hottest Week," August 20, 1966, p. 1; Donald Mosby and Arnold Rosenzweig, "2 Marches Greeted by Bricks, Jeers," August 22, 1966, p. 3.

10. From *CD:* "Invitation to Disorder," August 23, 1966, p. 13; Bill Van Alstine, "City's Freedom Movement Set for Realty War's Hottest Week," August 20, 1966, p. 1.

11. Donald Mosby and Arnold Rosenzweig, "2 Marches Greeted by Bricks, Jeers," *CD*, August 22, 1966, p. 3.

12. "Nazis, KKK Stage Screaming Riot," *CD*, August 22, 1966, p. 1.

13. From *CD:* "Cicero Action Sought," August 22, 1966, p. 4; "New March in South Deering Set for Today," August 23, 1966, p. 3; "Kerner Ponders Calling Guard into Cicero," August 24, 1966, p. 1; "Cops Squelch S. Deering Violence," August 24, 1966, p. 3; "O.W. Tells Why Crime Is Up 25%," August 24, 1966, p. 1; "200 Marchers Demonstrate in West Elsdon," August 25, 1966, p. 3; Donald Mosby, "Undercover Cops Invade Rights Groups," August 27, 1966, p. 1.

14. "King, Realty Forces Reach Agreement," *CD*, August 27, 1966, p. 1.

15. From *CD:* "Half a Loaf, Not Enough," August 27, 1966, p. 10; "The Settlement," August 30, 1966, p. 13; "White Power," September 3, 1966, p. 10.

16. From *CD:* Arnold Rosenzweig, "Gangway, Gage Park! King Is House Hunting!," August 27, 1966, p. 1; "WSO Plans to 'Mobilize' March into Cicero Sunday," August 29, 1966, p. 3; Betty Washington, "Dr. King to Address Rights Rally," August 31, 1966, p. 4; "Rally Tonight on Urban Renewal Battle," September 22, 1966, p. 4; Betty Washington, "Southsiders Call for 'War' on King," September 7, 1966, p. 3; "Robert Lucas: He's Where the 'Action' Is," September 7, 1966, p. 6; "King May Move Home Base Here Permanently," September 12, 1966, p. 8.

17. Muhammad biography of John Sengstacke, AS Papers, Box 22, Folder 21; Daniels, "John Sengstacke III: America's Black Press Lord," AS Papers, pp. 17–18; Betty Washington, "March to End at Ala. Capital," March 25, 1965, p. 1.

18. Muhammad biography of John Sengstacke, AS Papers, Box 22, Folder 21; Walker, "The Promised Land," p. 11; Bob Black and John Gunn, "Billiken Photos," *CD*, August 15, 1966, p. 1; Poinsett, *Walking with Presidents*, pp. 157–63.

19. "Sengstacke Buys Courier Papers," *CD*, October 25, 1966, p. 4; Walker, "The Promised Land," p. 11; Washburn, *The African American Newspaper*, pp. 187–89; biography written for the *National Cyclopedia of American Biography*, submitted April 15, 1966, AS Papers, Box 22, Folder 17; Daniels, "John Sengstacke III: America's Black Press Lord," AS Papers, pp. 17–18.

20. Kathleen Currie, "Interviews with Ethel Payne"; *"Daily Defender* to Have Its

Own 'Man' in Viet Nam," *CD*, December 17, 1966, p. 1; Wolseley, *The Black Press*, p. 259; Walker, "The Promised Land," p. 18.

21. From *CD*, Ethel Payne: "First Impressions in Viet Nam," January 3, 1967, p. 4; "Two Views of the Conflict in Vietnam," January 23, 1967, p. 1. Currie, "Interviews with Ethel Payne."

22. From *CD*, Ethel Payne: "Just Reminiscing," December 27, 1975, p. 4; "How the Press Works in Viet Nam," January 4, 1967, p. 1. Currie, "Interviews with Ethel Payne."

23. From *CD*, Ethel Payne: "GIs Tell How They Stand on the Viet War," April 11, 1967, p. 1; "Negro Air Fighters Think About Home," February 28, 1967, p. 6.

24. Ibid.

25. Ethel Payne, "'Brown Babies' Still Facing Japanese Scorn," *CD*, March 28, 1967, p. 4.

26. Sam Washington, "Negro Opinion on Viet Is Shifting," *CD*, April 22, 1967, p. 1; Currie, "Interviews with Ethel Payne."

27. Ethel Payne, "Marshall Appointment an LBJ Drama," *CD*, June 15, 1967, p. 1.

28. Sam Washington, "Marshall's High Court Nomination Hailed," *CD*, June 14, 1967, p. 1.

29. From *CD*: "Justice Marshall," June 15, 1967, p. 19; "Well! New Platform for *Defender!*," January 22, 1966, p. 1; Walker, "The Promised Land," pp. 47–49.

30. From *CD*, Ethel Payne: "Howard Still Seethes with Unrest," May 20, 1967, p. 2; "Civil Rights Commission Has Woes," May 24, 1967, p. 5; "So This Is Washington," June 21, 1967, p. 2; "King Still Holds Sway as U.S. 'Conscience,'" June 14, 1967, p. 2. Currie, "Interviews with Ethel Payne."

31. Ethel Payne, "King Still Holds Sway as U.S. 'Conscience,'" *CD*, June 14, 1967, p. 2.

32. Ibid.

33. From *CD*: "Negro Publishers' Parley to Hear Dr. King, Wilkins," June 17, 1967, p. 2; Ethel Payne, "Angry King Assails Rights 'Extremists,'" June 24, 1967, p. 1; "Sengstacke Papers Top Awards List," June 24, 1967, p. 1.

34. Ibid.

35. From *CD*: Ethel Payne, "Publishers Vow to Face Challenges," June 29, 1967, p. 10; "City Council Backs 'Keep Cool' Drive," June 24, 1967, p. 1; "Reader's 'Cool Summer' Idea: Organize the Ghetto," June 24, 1967, p. 3.

36. Ethel Payne, "What's Behind LBJ-King Rift," *CD*, August 26, 1967, p. 1; Poinsett, *Walking with Presidents*, pp. 162–64.

37. From *CD*: "Four Shot, 50 Injured in Newark's Night of Rioting," July 15, 1967, p. 3; "Newark Leaders Struggle to Halt Rioting," July 17, 1967, p. 1; "Newark Blows Its Cool," July 17, 1967, p. 14; "Guards Seal Off Jersey Riot Area," July 18, 1967, p. 1; "Newark Racial Unrest Fades," July 20, 1967, p. 7.

38. "Racial Justice," *CD*, July 24, 1967, p. 13.

39. From *CD*: "Citizens Look on in Sadness," July 27, 1967, p. 3; "Looting, Burning Rampant in Detroit," July 24, 1967, p. 2; "Riot Deaths," August 26, 1967, p. 11; "Detroit Riot Is History's Most Damaging," July 27, 1967, p. 1.

40. From *CD*: "Looting, Burning Rampant in Detroit," July 24, 1967, p. 2; "Of 11 Towns, Only Chicago Keeps Cool," July 25 1967, p. 3.

41. "Our President Speaks," *CD*, July 25, 1967, p. 1.

42. Ibid.; Ethel Payne, "Behind Scenes as LBJ Takes Riot Action," *CD*, July 29, 1967, p. 3; Branch, *At Canaan's Edge*, pp. 629–34.

43. From *CD*: "Citizens Look on in Sadness," July 27, 1967, p. 3; "Looting, Burning Rampant in Detroit," July 24, 1967, p. 2; "Riot Deaths," August 26, 1967, p. 11; "Detroit Riot Is History's Most Damaging," July 27, 1967, p. 1.

44. Betty Washington, "King Assails Congress for 'Inviting' Violence," *CD*, July 27, 1967, p. 2.

45. From *CD*: "Keep a Cool Summer," July 15, 1967, p. 1; "School System Aiding Cool Summer Cause," July 24, 1967, p. 4; "Of 11 Towns, Only Chicago Keeps Cool," July 25, 1967, p. 3; Donald Mosby, "Police Take Fast Action on Violence Threat Here," July 27, 1967, p. 2; "Keep a Cool Summer," July 15, 1967, p. 1.

46. From *CD*: "Too Little, Too Late," August 1, 1967, p. 13; "Wake Up America!," August 8, 1967, p. 13.

47. From *CD*: "The New Orientation," August 26, 1967, p. 11; "Stokely Calls for N. Viet Support," August 31, 1967, p. 3.

48. Ethel Payne, "Civil Disobedience Without Riots," *CD*, August 19, 1967, p. 1; Branch, *At Canaan's Edge*, pp. 634–37.

49. Ethel Payne, "The 'Inhuman' War in Viet Is SCLC's Battleground," *CD*, August 21, 1967, p. 12; Branch, *At Canaan's Edge*, pp. 634–37.

50. "Civil Disobedience," *CD*, August 22, 1967, p. 13.

51. From *CD*: "King Re-States Refusal to Bid for Presidency," August 30, 1967, p. 8; Raymond McCann, "LBJ Deferred Negro Dreams: Dr. King," September 2, 1967, p. 1; Sam Washington, "Militants Could Disrupt New Politics Convention," September 2, 1967, p. 1; "New Politics Confab Left Its Mark on Loop Hotel," September 9, 1967, p. 2; Raymond McCann, "Whites Bow to Black Demands," September 5, 1967, p. 1; "The New Party," September 5, 1967, p. 13; Raymond McCann, "Violence Threatened as Rap Brown Enters Politics Parley," September 5, 1967, p. 3; Raymond McCann, "New Politics Parley Rejects Presidential Bid," September 6, 1967, p. 10. Branch, *At Canaan's Edge*, pp. 637–40.

52. "King Calls Vietnam War 'Evil, Unjust,'" *CD*, September 11, 1967, p. 8.

53. From *CD*: Ethel Payne, "King Wants Congress to Act on Ghettos," October 25, 1967, p. 8; "King Warns of 'Dark Hour in U.S.'" October 31, 1967, p. 4; "Dr. King 'Most Influential' Civil Leader: Survey Study," November 7, 1967, p. 9.

## 21. THE LAST REMAINS OF NONVIOLENCE

1. Sam Washington, "*Daily Defender* Staff Reacts Fast to News," *CD*, April 8, 1968, p. 25; Joan Giangrasse Kates, "Nathan 'Nate' Batt, 1917–2011," *CT*, January 25, 2011; Theresa Fambro Hook, "April 4, 1968: A Day of Infamy at *The Defender*," *CD*, April 4, 2012.

2. "King Murdered," *CD*, April 6, 1968, p. 1.

3. From *CD*: "Local Leaders React Tearfully, Nostalgically," April 6, 1968, p. 22; Sam Washington "1,000 Rangers Make Promise to Pull for Peace in Area," April 8, 1968, p. 10.

4. From *CD*: "President Johnson," April 3, 1968, p. 15; "Common Reaction of Nation Leaders: We're Deeply Saddened," April 6, 1968, p. 22.

5. From *CD:* "Dr. King and Memphis," April 2, 1968, p. 13; "Jesse Jackson, King Aides Vow to Carry on," April 6, 1968: p. 22. Branch, *At Canaan's Edge,* pp. 755–60.

6. "Dr. King's Murder Sparks Black Youths in D.C.," *CD,* April 6, 1968, p. 2.

7. From *CD:* Betty Washington, "Uproar at First Memorial Rites for King," April 6, 1968, p. 22; "Slaying Could Heat Up Summer, Westside Militant Meek Warns," April 6, 1968, p. 22.

8. Washington, "*Daily Defender* Staff Reacts Fast to News," *CD,* April 8, 1968, p. 25; Kates, "Nathan 'Nate' Batt, 1917–2011," *CD,* January 25, 2011; Hook, "April 4, 1968: A Day of Infamy at *The Defender,*" *CD,* April 4, 2012.

9. From *CD:* Donald Mosby, "Despite Guard, Cops, Federal Troops More Looting Hits Ghetto," April 8, 1968, p. 1; John L. Taylor, "7 Minutes of Hell in Westside Riot," April 8, 1968, p. 14; "Student Reactions Mixed Over King's Death," April 8, 1968, p. 16. Cohen and Taylor, *American Pharaoh,* pp. 453–57.

10. "'Kill Rioters' Daley Ordered," *CD,* April 16, 1968, p. 3; Cohen and Taylor, *American Pharaoh,* pp. 453–57.

11. From *CD:* Betty Washington, "Rights Leaders, Clergy Call Mayor to Task on 'Shoot to Kill' Stand," April 16, 1968, p. 1; Dave Potter, "Rights Figures Blast Daley on 'Shoot Looters' Order," April 16, 1968, p. 3.

12. From *CD:* Donald Mosby, "Black Cops, Lawyers 'Shocked' by 'Shoot to Kill' Statement," April 16, 1968, p. 3; Dave Potter, "Daley Gets Bad Review from Sammy Davis," April 17, 1968, p. 1; Dave Potter and Bob Hunter, "Black Office Holders Rap Daley's Shoot, Kill Edict," April 18, 1968, p. 3; Bob Hunter, "Mayor's 'Shoot' Order Still Under Council Attack," April 24, 1968, p. 5; "Black Clerics See Daley on 'Shoot Order,'" May 4, 1968, p. 1.

13. "Wrong Prescription," *CD,* April 20, 1968, p. 1.

14. "Daley Renames Street, OKs Housing, Frisk Laws," *CD,* June 20, 1968, p. 5.

15. Author interview with Bob Black, May 13, 2011.

16. From *CD* by Betty Washington: "RFK Slaying Brings Anti-Black Hysteria," June 8, 1968, p. 1; "Call CHA 'Paternalistic, Racist' Institution," July 25, 1968, p. 1.

17. Barbara A. Sizemore, "From Our Readers," *CD,* January 29, 1972, p. 6; Florence Hamlish Levinsohn, "Where Vernon Jarrett Is Coming From," *Chicago Reader,* March 24, 1988; Kenan Heise, "Obituary: Journalist Betty Washington Worked at *Defender, Sun-Times,*" *CT,* January 11, 1994; author interview with Bob Black, May 13, 2011.

18. From *CD:* "Police Brutality," August 28, 1968, p. 1; Sheryl Fitzgerald, "Black Newsmen Bore Brunt of Cops' Attack," August 28, 1968, p. 3. Author interview with Bob Black, May 13, 2011.

19. Washburn, *The African American Newspaper,* pp. 192–94; Muhammad biography of John Sengstacke, AS Papers, Box 22, Folder 21.

20. From *CD:* Ethel Payne, "D.C. in Last Minute Rush to Aid HHH," November 2, 1968, p. 8; "Martin Rejoins Sengstacke Publications," December 21, 1968, p. 36; Currie, "Interviews with Ethel Payne."

21. John Sengstacke, "Dawson Will Not Run!," *CD,* November 17, 1969, p. 1; AS Papers, Box 22, Folder 21; Manning, *William L. Dawson,* pp. 161–63.

22. From *CD:* "Joins *Daily Defender*," November 17, 1969, p. 3; Jesse Jackson, "'Country Preacher' on the Case," December 6, 1969, p. 1.

23. Faith Christmas, "'It Was Murder,' Rush," *CD*, December 6, 1969, p. 1.

24. "*Daily Defender* Cameraman at Death Scene," *CD*, December 6, 1969, p. 40.

25. Donald Mosby, "Panthers Vicious: Hanrahan," *CD*, December 6, 1969, p. 1.

26. John Vasilopulos, "Police Tell Their Version of Fred Hampton Slaying," *CD*, December 6, 1969, p. 1; Ronald Koziol and Edward Lee, "Attempted Murder Charge Eyed in Panthers Gun Fight," *CT*, December 5, 1969, p. 3.

27. Faith Christmas, "Bobby Rush Surrenders Before 5,000," *CD*, December 8, 1969, p. 2.

28. Faith Christmas, "Hampton's Brother Tells Audience, 'Maintain Peace,'" *CD*, December 8, 1969, p. 3.

29. From *CD:* Donald Mosby and Joseph L. Turner, "$6,000 Lost in Shoot-Out," August 2, 1969, p. 1; Faith Christmas, "Panther Chief Fred Hampton Tells Party's Goals," August 23, 1969, p. 1.

30. From *CD:* Donald Mosby, "Hampton Gets OK to Travel," November 6, 1969, p. 2; "Carmichael vs. Cleaver," August 4, 1969, p. 13; "Black Panthers Stand for What?," August 16, 1969, p. 6; Faith Christmas, "Panther Chief Fred Hampton Tells Party's Goals," August 23, 1969, p. 1; Donald Mosby, "Now Comes Bobby Seale!," November 4, 1969, p. 5; John D. Vasilopulos and Julius J. Blakeny, "Ask U.S. Probe of Shootout," November 15, 1969, p. 1; Faith Christmas, "Rush Disputes Police Details of Killings," December 13, 1969, p. 1; Donald Mosby, "Black Panther Indicted! He Killed 2 Cops: Jury," December 23, 1969, p. 1.

31. From *CD:* Pierre Guilmant, "See Hanrahan a Political Liability," December 8, 1969, p. 2; Donald Mosby, "Who Polices Hanrahan?," December 8, 1969, p. 2.

32. From *CD:* "U.S. Probing Panthers," August 7, 1969, p. 19; "Was It Murder?," December 8, 1969, p. 13; "Will They Tell the Truth?," December 23, 1969, p. 13.

33. From *CD:* "Fred Hampton Rites: An Epitaph to a Revolutionary," December 11, 1969, p. 1; Jesse Jackson, "Country Preacher on the Case," December 13, 1969, p. 1; Jesse Jackson, "Country Preacher on the Case," December 15, 1969, p. 2.

34. From *CD:* "Reps Set Probe Here," December 11, 1969, p. 1; Toni Anthony, "Hampton Probe Demands Mount," December 13, 1969, p. 1.

35. Ethel Payne, "Emotions Flare at Hearing," *CD*, December 22, 1969, p. 1.

36. Louis Martin, "Hampton Tragedy Raises Questions for All America," *CD*, December 13, 1969, p. 3.

37. From *CD:* "Sharp Jackson Five Is Alive Beating Beatles," June 6, 1970, p. 15; "Joe Absent, but They Still Came," August 15, 1970, p. 1; "The Jackson 5 Return Home for Two Concerts," September 30, 1970, p. 17; Earl Calloway, "The Jackson Five Offers Advice to Ease Nation's Drug Problem," October 17, 1970, p. 20.

38. From *CD:* "Benefit Show to Help Finance New Youth Center," June 1, 1968, p. 5; "Display Ad 30," April 12 1969, p. 16; "*Daily Defender*'s Top Twenty," December 23, 1969 (Daily Edition), p. 11.

39. *Paper Trail: 100 Years of* The Chicago Defender. DVD. Directed by Barbara E. Allen. Chicago: WTTW/Chicago, 2005.
40. Author interview with Robert McClory, May 9, 2011.
41. Ibid.; Gary Rivlin, *Fire on the Prairie: Chicago's Harold Washington and the Politics of Race* (New York: Henry Holt, 1992), pp. 42–47.
42. Author interview with Robert McClory, May 9, 2011.

## 22. VICTORIES ARE CONTAGIOUS

1. Tony Griggs, "Conlisk Considers 6 Demands," *CD*, April 25, 1972, p. 1.
2. Lucille Younger, "Death Prompted New Police Order," *CD*, May 1, 1972, p. 1.
3. Lucille Younger, "Press Daley on Police Racism," *CD*, May 2, 1972, p. 1; Vernon Jarrett, "Blacks Determined About Police Reform," *CT,* May 3, 1972, p. 18.
4. From *CD:* "Metcalfe PUSH Speaker," May 4, 1972, p. 6; Faith Christmas, "Metcalfe: Unity Victory Key," May 8, 1972, p. 1.
5. From *CD:* Robert McClory, "Jesse Pushes for Truce in Democratic Squabble," July 6, 1972, p. 1; "Our Pros in Miami," July 8, 1972, p. 1; Ethel Payne, "Some Win, Some Lose at Dems Convention," July 15, 1972, p. 36; Faith Christmas, "See Daley Outwitting Rebels," July 13, 1972, p. 4.
6. From *CD:* Louis Martin, "Minorities Help Democrats Find Soul," July 15, 1972, p. 3; Ethel Payne, "Attack 'Dump McGovern' Plot," July 11, 1972, p. 1; Joe Ellis, "Politicians Here Mixed on Ouster," July 12, 1972, p. 3; Robert McClory, "Jesse Pushes for Truce in Democratic Squabble," July 6, 1972, p. 1.
7. From *CD:* Robert McClory, "Blacks 'Deluge at' Dems' Convention," July 10, 1972, p. 5; "Road to Black Power," July 12, 1972, p. 13.
8. From *CD:* "Sengstacke to Report on China," October 9, 1972, p. 4; "Black Medics in China," October 17, 1972, p. 13; "Sengstacke Talks to Medics in China," October 17, 1972, p. 2; "Editors Complete Trip," October 23, 1972, p. 2.
9. AS Papers, Box 22, Folder 21.
10. Robert McClory, "Black Politicians for Hanrahan," *CD*, August 22, 1972, p. 4.
11. "Metcalfe Blasts Daley 'Scheme,'" *CD*, October 2, 1972, p. 1.
12. "Metcalfe a True Leader," *CD*, October 9, 1972, p. 15.
13. "Judge Rules for Hanrahan," *CD*, October 26, 1972, p. 2.
14. Robert McClory, "Blacks Favor Hanrahan," *CD*, October 26, 1972, p. 1.
15. From *CD:* James M. Stephens, "Push Split Ticket to Beat Hanrahan," October 28, 1972, p. 1; "Judge Rules for Hanrahan," October 26, 1972, p. 2.
16. "Miscarriage of Justice," *CD*, October 28, 1972, p. 1.
17. Michael L. Culbert, "Evidence Compiled by PUSH," *CD*, November 8, 1972, p. 8.
18. From *CD:* "Metcalfe, Collins in Victories," November 8, 1972, p. 1; Robert McClory, "How Blacks Upset Hanrahan," November 9, 1972, p. 1.
19. From *CD:* "Carey Leads Hanrahan," November 8, 1972, p. 1; Robert McClory, "How Blacks Upset Hanrahan," November 9, 1972, p. 1; Robert McClory, "Blacks Hold Key in Tight Races," November 7, 1972, p. 1.

20. From *CD:* "Machine Defeated by Nixon," November 8, 1972, p. 3; "Walker Wins, Experts Claim," November 8, 1972, p. 1; Robert McClory, "Walker: Machine Dying," November 9, 1972, p. 1; James M. Stephens, "Leaders Laud Split Vote Swing," November 9, 1972, p. 4; "Metcalfe Tops Reps Here," November 9, 1972, p. 7.

21. Ethel Payne, "A Shift in Scenery," *CD,* August 11, 1973, p. 8; Currie, "Interviews with Ethel Payne."

22. "Chicago's Top Black-Owned Businesses," *CT,* July 21, 1974, p. 1.

23. From *CD:* "It's 80th Year for Provident," January 23, 1971, p. 1; "Pick John Sengstacke," June 3, 1974, p. 4; Betty Washington, "A New Provident Needed," January 4, 1968, p. 4. AS Papers, Box 22, Folder 21.

24. From *CD:* "Sengstacke, Ogilvie to Hospital Bd.," May 24, 1973, p. 5; Ted Watson, "Provident Remodeling Plans Roll," November 17, 1973, p. 2; "Provident Expansion," April 17, 1974, p. 6; Robert McClory, "Link Provident, County Hospital," April 25, 1974, p. 1. Edward Schreiber, "Daley Promises Metcalfe," *CT,* December 21, 1973, p. 6; AS Papers, Box 22, Folder 21.

25. From *CD:* "Provident Exec Gets Key Medical Post," November 9, 1974, p. 5; "New Head for Provident," November 14, 1974, p. 4; Sidmel Estes, "'Growing Pains' Stall Provident Project," December 21, 1974, p. 25.

26. "Abbott and History," *CD,* May 5, 1975, p. 15.

27. Robert McClory, "*Defender*ites: Colorful and Hardy," *CD,* May 5, 1975, p. 5; Robert McClory, "Angel of Mercy," *Chicago Reader,* September 12, 1996.

28. *CD,* May 5, 1975.

29. Lynette Miller, "*Defender* Named Historic Site in Journalism," *CT,* May 6, 1975, p. 1; "Journalist Society Honors *Defender,*" *CT,* April 16, 1975, p. 1; John Taylor, "He Nearly Declined the Job," *CD,* May 5, 1975, p. 1.

30. Taylor, "He Nearly Declined the Job," *CD,* May 5, 1975, p. 1.

31. From *CD:* J. I. Adkins, "Leaders Back Provident in New Center Plan," July 31, 1975, p. 1; "No Second-Class Provident," October 4, 1975, p. 1; "State Okays New Provident," November 3, 1975, p. 1.

32. "*Defender* Publisher's Son Kills Self with Pistol," *CT,* May 19, 1976, p. 1.

33. From *CT:* James Pearre, "Provident Settles for 340-Bed Unit," July 15, 1976, p. 3; "Provident's Need for Aid Told," August 14, 1976, p. 1; George Estep, "HEW Seeking to Aid Provident," September 29, 1976, p. 1; Vernon Jarrett, "Provident's Fate Is in Others' Hands," December 15, 1976, p. 1; "$14.8 Million for New Hospital," January 5, 1977, p. 1.

34. From *CT:* David Axelrod, "Debate Over Adding New People," January 3, 1977, p. 3; Vernon Jarrett, "Who Should Select a Black Candidate?," January 9, 1977, p. 1.

35. Neil Mehler and David Axelrod, "Blacks Favor Mayor Bid by Washington," *CT,* January 20, 1977, p. 10; Rivlin, *Fire on the Prairie,* pp. 54–55.

36. From *CT:* David Axelrod, "Loses Promised Support," January 22, 1977, p. 1; Vernon Jarrett, "Ralph Metcalfe Takes His Stand," January 23, 1977, p. 1; Vernon Jarrett, "Machine's Bubble Will Burst in April," February 27, 1977, p. 1; Vernon Jarrett, "Black 'Leaders' Fear a Black Vote," March 25, 1977, p. 1; Vernon Jarrett, "The Ballot Box Is the Road to Power," April 6, 1977, p. 1.

37. From *CT:* F. R. Ciccone, "Bilandic Wins," April 20, 1977, p. 1; Vernon Jarrett, "For Washington, the Party's Over," May 11, 1977, p. 1.

38. Vernon Jarrett, "Blacks Not Plugged into Power List," *CT*, July 20, 1977, p. 1.

39. Ibid.

40. Poinsett, *Walking with Presidents*, pp. 173–201.

41. Currie, "Interviews with Ethel Payne."

42. Ibid.

43. Author interview with Robert McClory, May 9, 2011.

44. Muhammad biography of John Sengstacke, AS Papers, Box 22, Folder 21.

45. "CHA Chairman Accepts Post on Library Board, Draws Fire," *CT*, April 15, 1980, p. 3.

46. From *CT*: Vernon Jarrett, "*Daily Defender* Has a Birthday," May 2, 1980, p. 1; Vernon Jarrett, "Black Publisher Blasts Carter," June 25, 1980, p. 1.

47. *The Chinta Strausberg Story*, documentary video, PCC Studio, 2012; "Proclaiming a Victory," *CD*, January 11, 1983, p. 1.

48. Rivlin, *Fire on the Prairie*, pp. 97–98.

49. Chinta Strausberg, "Expect Washington to Say 'Yes' Wed," *CD*, November 9, 1982, p. 3.

50. Chinta Strausberg, "It's Official: Washington in Mayoral Race," *CD*, November 11, 1982, p. 1.

51. From *CD*, November 16, 1983: "Mayor Byrne Slips Among Voters," p. 1; "Washington Gets Thunderous Applause," p. 5.

52. David Axelrod, "Politics," *CT*, January 16, 1983, p. 1; Rivlin, *Fire on the Prairie*, p. 124.

53. Juanita Bratcher, "McDonald's to Assist in Voter Registration Drive," *CD*, January 10, 1983, p. 5.

54. From *CD*: "Congressman Washington Opens 6 Campaign Offices," p. 5; Chinta Strausberg, "Hispanic Leader Urges Coalition," January 10, 1983, p. 1.

55. Chinta Strausberg, "Washington Bares His Financial Skeletons," *CD*, January 12, 1983, p. 3.

56. From *CD*: Chinta Strausberg, "Coalition Tells 'Political Targets,'" January 11, 1983, p. 1; "Protest Ministers' Support of Richie Daley," January 13, 1983, p. 1; Chinta Strausberg, "Clerics: A Black Can't Win," *CD*, January 13, 1983, p. 3. Rivlin, *Fire on the Prairie*, pp. 136–38.

57. Chinta Strausberg, "Candidates Meet in First Debate," *CD*, January 19, 1983, p. 1.

58. "Crime Is the Subject," *CD*, January 24, 1983, p. 1.

59. Henry Locke, "*Defender* Reporter to Quiz Mayoral Candidates," *CD*, January 26, 1983, p. 5.

60. Chinta Strausberg, "Pickets Greet Mayor at Southside Opening," *CD*, January 31, 1983, p. 1.

61. From *CD*: "CHA Group Endorses Byrne," February 15, 1983, p. 5; Henry Locke, "CHA Leaders Deny Byrne Endorsement," February 17, 1983, p. 1.

62. Ken Green, "15,000 at Rally for Washington," *CD*, February 7, 1983, p. 3.

63. From *CT*: David Axelrod and Thom Shanker, "Washington Raises $200,000 at Fete," January 22, 1983, p. 5; David Axelrod, "Politics," February 13, 1983, p. 1.

64. From *CD*: "Our Endorsement," February 12, 1983, p. 1; "Watch Jane Run: An Editorial," *CD*, February 17, 1983, p. 1. Rivlin, *Fire on the Prairie*, p. 169.

65. From *CD*: "Washington: We Talk Language of Struggle," February 17, 1983,

p. 10; photos by George Murphy, "For Washington," February 21, 1983, p. 1; Henry Locke, "Lawyers Vow to Prevent Voter Fraud on Tuesday," February 21, 1983, p. 3.

66. From *CD:* Full-page ad from the Harold Washington for Mayor Campaign, February 16, 1983, p. 10; three-quarter-page ad from Richard M. Daley for Mayor Campaign, February 17, 1983, p. 9; full-page ad from Jane Byrne for Mayor Campaign, February 21, 1983, p. 7; full-page ad from Black Business Council, February 21, 1983, p. 14.

67. "Race for City Hall," *CD*, February 22, 1983, p 1; Rivlin, *Fire on the Prairie*, pp. 158–60.

68. Henry Locke, "Washington Faces One Major Hurdle," *CD*, February 24, 1983, p. 25.

69. From *CD:* "Race for City Hall," February 22, 1983, p 1; Henry Locke, "Washington Set for Next Step," February 24, 1983, p. 3; Juanita Bratcher, "Washington Beats Byrne 5–1 in Many Majority Black Wards," February 24, 1983, p. 10.

70. Pierre Guilmant, "Epton Hits White Democrat Turncoats," *CD*, February 24, 1983, p. 1.

71. Locke, "Washington: Healing Chicago Is My Goal," *CD*, February 28, 1983, p. 1

72. Chinta Strausberg, "12th Ward Alderman Bolts," *CD*, March 1, 1983, p. 3.

73. Chinta Strausberg, "Shaw, Carrothers Endorse Washington," *CD*, March 2, 1983, p. 3.

74. "Is Race the Issue?," *CD*, March 2, 1983, p. 1.

75. "Despite Brzeczek's Denial, Racial Propaganda Continues," *CD*, March 7, 1983, p. 1.

76. Chinta Strausberg, "City Equipment Used for Epton," *CD*, March 22, 1983, p. 3.

77. "Racist Support," *CD*, March 9, 1983, p. 9; Rivlin, *Fire on the Prairie*, pp. 176–91.

78. Henry Locke, "Picket Harold, Fritz," *CD*, March 28, 1983, p. 1; Henry Locke, "Bernadin Rips Jeering Whites," *CD*, March 29, 1983, p. 1.

79. From *CD*, April 13, 1983: Henry Locke, "Washington Wins, Dirtiest Election Is Over — Amen," p. 1; Henry Locke, "Throngs Jam Victory Site," p. 5; Chinta Strausberg, "I Won't Push Anybody Around," p. 5.

80. From *CD*, April 14, 1983: "Washington Received Largest Black Plurality," p. 3; Charles Davis, "Will Washington Meet the Challenge?," p. 5.

81. Locke, "Washington Wins, Dirtiest Election Is Over — Amen," April 13, 1983, p. 1.

82. From *CD:* Locke, "Washington Wins, Dirtiest Election Is Over — Amen," April 13, 1983, p. 1. "Editorial," March 14, 1983.

83. Rivlin, *Fire on the Prairie*, p. 198; Barack Obama, *Dreams from My Father* (New York: Three Rivers Press, 1995), pp. 146–48.

## 23. STICK AROUND FOR A WHILE

1. Ethan Michaeli, "Clinton Promises Health Care to All," *CD*, July 29, 1992, p. 1.

2. Ethan Michaeli, "Boy, 7, Gunned-Down," *CD*, October 14, 1992, p. 1.

3. Chinta Strausberg, "Clinton, Gore Draw Thousands," *CD*, October 21, 1992, p. 1.

4. Ethan Michaeli, "2nd Sweep Breaks Gangs' Backs," *CD*, October 22, 1992, p. 1.

5. From *CD* by Chinta Strausberg: "We Will Stop the Killing," October 26, 1992, p. 1; "Street Leaders March on City Hall," November 24, 1992, p. 1.

6. Ethan Michaeli, "CHA Violence Like Vietnam," *CD*, November 3, 1992, p. 1.

7. From *CD*, Ethan Michaeli: "Disabled Hero Modest About Feat," June 28, 1993, p. 1; "Hero Earns Billiken Award," July 8, 1993, p. 1.

8. Earl Calloway, "Dr. Joyner Dies at 98," *CD*, December 29, 1994, p. 1.

9. Chinta Strausberg, "Welcome, Mandela," *CD*, July 7, 1993, p. 1.

10. Ethan Michaeli, "Mandela Stresses Need for Funds for Democracy," *CD*, July 8, 1993, p. 5.

11. "Wake Up, Mandela," *CD*, July 12, 1993, p. 1.

12. From *CD*, Ethan Michaeli: "Tales from the Valley: An Artist's Story," October 4, 1993, p. 5; "Stories from the Valley (Part II)," October 11, 1993, p. 5; "Bringing Life Back to the Valley," October 18, 1993, p. 5; photos by Bobby Sengstacke, "Turning Wordly Elements into Images," November 10, 1993, p. 1.

13. Ethan Michaeli, "Profile of Courage," *CD*, September 15, 1993, p. 5.

14. Ethan Michaeli, "Farrakhan Hits Critics," *CD*, February 28, 1994, p. 1.

15. Walter Lee Lowe, "Farrakhan: Rebuild Community Bridges," *CD*, April 23, 1994, p. 1.

16. From *CD*, Ethan Michaeli: "ADL: Farrakhan 'Not Our Enemy,'" April 30, 1994, p. 1; "Farrakhan Proposes ADL Meeting," May 4, 1994, p. 1.

17. Ethan Michaeli, "Young People March for Their Communities," *CD*, March 28, 1994, p. 3.

18. Ethan Michaeli, "Clinton Touts Sweeps, Crime Bill as CHA Cure," *CD*, June 20, 1994, 3.

19. "The Chicago Housing Authority's Hypocrisy at Robert Taylor Homes," *CD*, June 20, 1994, p. 11.

20. "90 Years of Service," *CD*, May 6, 1995, p. 1.

21. William Mullen and Vikki Ortiz-Healy, "Chicago's Population Drops 200,000," *CT*, February 15, 2011.

22. Ethan Michaeli, "HUD Takes Over," *CD*, May 31, 1995, p. 1.

23. Vladimire Herard, "'New Era' at CPS," *CD*, July 1, 1995, p. 1.

24. Vladimire Herard, "We Had Sex," *CD*, August 8, 1995, p. 1.

25. Chinta Strausberg, "Harvard Lawyer Eyes Palmer Seat," *CD*, September 19, 1995, p 3.

26. Chinta Strausberg, "Draft Palmer Campaign Launched," *CD*, December 5, 1995, p. 4.

27. Chinta Strausberg, "Palmer Challenger Says He Won't Step Aside in Race," *CD*, December 21, 1995, p. 3.

28. Chinta Strausberg, "Palmer Throws in the Towel," *CD*, January 18, 1996, p. 3.

29. Chinta Strausberg, "Several Candidates Run Unopposed," *CD*, March 18, 1996, p. 19.

### 24. THE ROAR OF THE EL TRAIN

1. Author interview with Walter Lowe, January 23, 2011.
2. Jerry Thomas, "Who's Who Remembers Trailblazing Publisher of *Defender*," *CT*, June 8, 1997.
3. "Epitaph for a Newsman," *CT*, May 31, 1997; Brent Staples, "The Lives They Lived: John H. Sengstacke; Citizen Sengstacke," *New York Times Magazine*, January 4, 1998.
4. "John H. Sengstacke — the End of a Generation," *The Michigan Chronicle*, June 4, 1997, p. 6.
5. Dorothy Leavell, "Statement from Dorothy R. Leavell on the Passing of John Sengstacke," *The Michigan Chronicle*, June 11, 1997, p. 7.
6. Jeff Borden, "An Uncertain *Defender*," *Crain's Chicago Business*, August 25, 1997; "Death Tax Claims Storied Tabloid," *Editor and Publisher*, January 3, 2000.
7. John Cook, "*The Defender* Staggers," *CT*, February 5, 2002; "New *Defender* Owners Aim to Modernize," *Editor and Publisher*, January 29, 2003.
8. From *CD:* Bill Clark, "Eugene Scott Named New Publisher of *The Chicago Defender*," April 10, 2000, p. 1; Vernon Jarrett, "Emmett Till's Mom Speaks Again," October 15, 2003, p. 2; Vernon Jarrett, "Don't Weep Long: When Black Unity Gets Lost," May 29, 2004, p. 3.
9. White House, "President Clinton Awards the Presidential Citizens Medals," press release, January 8, 2001.
10. Kathy Bergen, "*Defender* Parties Work Out Differences," *CT*, May 2, 2002; "New *Defender* Owners Aim to Modernize," *Editor and Publisher*, January 29, 2003.
11. Vernon Jarrett, "New *Defender* Needs 'New' You," *CD*, February 1, 2003, p. 5.
12. Vernon Jarrett, "Black Press Still Vital Today," *CD*, March 12, 2003, p. 4.
13. Kathy Bergen, "*Defender* Parties Work Out Differences," *CT*, May 2, 2002; Michael Miner, "*Defender* Prepares Its New Offense," *Chicago Reader*, January 23, 2003; Tim Novak, "The $413,000 Flip," *Chicago Sun-Times*, May 29, 2008; Frank Kalman, "Restaurateur Faces Foreclosure on Former *Defender* Building," *Crain's Chicago Business*, August 15, 2011.
14. Vernon Jarrett, "This Is the Odyssey of One Man's Vote for Barack Obama for U.S. Senate," *CD*, March 15, 2004, p. 2.
15. Chinta Strausberg, "Hundreds Say Farewell to Vernon," *CD*, June 1, 2004, p. 2; Yvonne Shinhoster Lamb, "Vernon Jarrett, 84; Journalist, Crusader," *Washington Post*, May 25, 2004, p. B7.
16. Michael Miner, "News Bites," *Chicago Reader*, April 29, 2004; Rob Kaiser, "*Defender* Tries to Regroup," *CT*, June 19, 2004.
17. Johnathon E. Briggs and Rob Kaiser, "Martin on a Mission to Wake Up *Defender*," *CT*, September 26, 2004; Mark Fitzgerald, "The Revival of the Black Press in America," *Editor and Publisher*, November 26, 2004; Mark Fitzgerald and Jennifer Saba, "Who Ever Said a 'Daily' Has to Appear Every Day?," *Editor and Publisher*, October 1, 2006; Mark Fitzgerald, "'Chicago Defender': It's 'Unapologetically Black' No More," *Editor and Publisher*, January 18, 2007.

18. Fitzgerald, "*'Chicago Defender'*: It's 'Unapologetically Black' No More," *Editor and Publisher,* January 18, 2007; Lolly Bowean, "*Chicago Defender* Goes Back to Bronzeville," *CT,* May 27, 2009.

19. Dirk Johnson, "Historical Trove, Freed from Storage, Gets a Home," *New York Times,* May 27, 2009; "Collecting Chicago's Forgotten Black History," *CT,* December 15, 2010.

20. Fitzgerald, "*'Chicago Defender'*: It's 'Unapologetically Black' No More," *Editor and Publisher,* January 18, 2007; Bowean, "*Chicago Defender* Goes Back to Bronzeville," *CT,* May 27, 2009.

21. Dirk Johnson, "Historical Trove, Freed from Storage, Gets a Home," *New York Times,* May 26, 2009; "Collecting Chicago's Forgotten Black History," *CT,* December 15, 2010.

# Sources

Barnes, Harper. *Never Been a Time*. New York: Walker and Company, 2008.

Bernstein, Arnie. *Hollywood on Lake Michigan: 100 Years of Chicago and the Movies*. Chicago: Lake Claremont Press, 1998.

Black, Timuel D., Jr. *Bridges of Memory: Chicago's First Wave of Black Migration, an Oral History*. Chicago: Northwestern University Press, 2003.

Blackmon, Douglas A. *Slavery by Another Name*. New York: Doubleday, 2008.

Bontemps, Arna, and Jack Conroy. *Anyplace But Here*. Columbia: University of Missouri Press, 1963.

Boyle, Kevin. *Arc of Justice: A Saga of Race, Civil Rights, and Murder in the Jazz Age*. New York: Henry Holt and Company, 2006.

Branch, Taylor. *At Canaan's Edge: America in the King Years, 1965–68*. New York: Simon and Schuster, 2006.

———. *Parting the Waters: America in the King Years, 1954–63*. New York: Simon and Schuster, 1988.

———. *Pillar of Fire: America in the King Years, 1963–65*. New York: Simon and Schuster, 1999.

Buni, Andrew. *Robert L. Vann of* The Pittsburgh Courier. Pittsburgh: University of Pittsburgh Press, 1974.

Burns, Ben. *Nitty Gritty: A White Editor in Black Journalism*. Jackson: University Press of Mississippi, 1986.

Chicago Commission on Race Relations. *The Negro in Chicago: A Study of Race Relations and a Riot*. Chicago: University of Chicago Press, 1922.

Cohen, Adam, and Elizabeth Taylor. *American Pharaoh: Mayor Richard J. Daley; His Battle for Chicago and the Nation*. Boston: Little, Brown and Company, 2000.

DeSantis, Christopher C., ed. *Langston Hughes and* The Chicago Defender: *Essays on Race, Politics, and Culture, 1942–1962*. Chicago: University of Illinois Press, 1995.

Detweiler, Frederick G. *The Negro Press in the United States*. Chicago: University of Chicago Press, 1922.

Drake, St. Clair, and Horace R. Cayton. *Black Metropolis: A Study of Negro Life in a Northern City*. Chicago: University of Chicago Press, 1993.

Dray, Philip. *Capitol Men: The Epic Story of Reconstruction Through the Lives of the First Black Congressmen*. Boston: Houghton Mifflin, 2008.

Eig, Jonathan. *Opening Day*. New York: Simon and Schuster, 2007.

Finkle, Lee. *Forum for Protest: The Black Press During World War 2.* Cranbury, NJ: Associated University Presses, 1975.

Fredrickson, George M. *Racism: A Short History.* Princeton, NJ: Princeton University Press, 2002.

Giddings, Paula J. *Ida, A Sword Among Lions: Ida B. Wells and the Campaign Against Lynching.* New York: Amistad/Harper Collins, 2008.

Goldstone, Lawrence. *Inherently Unequal: The Betrayal of Civil Rights by the Supreme Court, 1865–1903.* New York: Walker and Company, 2011.

Gosnell, Harold F. *Negro Politicians: The Rise of Negro Politicians in Chicago.* Chicago: University of Chicago Press, 1935.

Granger, Bill, and Lori Granger. *Lords of the Last Machine: The Story of Politics in Chicago.* New York: Random House, 1987.

Green, Adam. *Selling the Race: Culture, Community and Black Chicago, 1940–1955.* Chicago: University of Chicago Press, 2007.

Grimshaw, William J. *Bitter Fruit: Black Politics and the Chicago Machine, 1931–1991.* Chicago: University of Chicago Press, 1992.

Grossman, James R. *Land of Hope: Chicago, Black Southerners, and the Great Migration.* Chicago: University of Chicago Press, 1989.

Henri, Florette. *Black Migration: Movement North, 1900–1920.* Garden City, NY: Anchor Press/Doubleday, 1975.

Hirsch, Arnold R. *Making of the Second Ghetto: Race & Housing in Chicago, 1940–1960.* Cambridge: Cambridge University Press, 1983.

Hughes, Langston. *Big Sea.* New York: Alfred A. Knopf, 1940.

Hunt, D. Bradford. *Blueprint for Disaster: The Unraveling of Chicago Public Housing.* Chicago: University of Chicago Press, 2009.

Jackson, Kenneth T. *The Ku Klux Klan in the City, 1915–1930.* New York: Oxford University Press, 1967.

Johnson, John H. *Succeeding Against the Odds.* New York: Amistad Press, 1989.

Jordan, William G. *Black Newspapers and America's War for Democracy, 1914–1920.* Chapel Hill: University of North Carolina Press, 2001.

Kornweibel, Theodore, Jr. *Investigate Everything.* Bloomington: Indiana University Press, 2002.

———. *Seeing Red: Federal Campaigns Against Black Militancy, 1919–1925.* Bloomington: Indiana University Press, 1998.

Kotlowitz, Alex. *Never a City So Real.* New York: Crown Journeys, 2004.

Lemann, Nicholas. *The Promised Land: The Great Black Migration and How It Changed America.* New York: Vintage Books, 1992.

———. *Redemption: The Last Battle for the Civil War.* New York: Farrar, Strauss and Giroux, 2006.

Loewen, James W. *Sundown Towns: A Hidden Dimension of American Racism.* New York: Touchstone Books, 2000.

Manning, Christopher. *William L. Dawson and the Limits of Black Electoral Leadership.* De Kalb: Northern Illinois University, 2009.

McClory, Robert. *Radical Disciple: Father Pfleger, St. Sabina Church, and the Fight for Social Justice.* Chicago: Chicago Review Press, 2010.

McFeely, William S. *Frederick Douglass.* New York: W. W. Norton and Company, 1991.

McWhirter, Cameron. *Red Summer.* New York: Henry Holt and Company, 2011.

Merriner, James. *Grafters and Goo Goos: Corruption and Reform in Chicago, 1833–2003.* Carbondale: Southern Illinois University Press, 2004.

Miller, Donald L. *City of the Century: The Epic of Chicago and the Making of America.* New York: Simon and Schuster, 1996.

Moore, Natalie Y., and Lance Williams. *The Almighty Black P. Stone Nation: The Rise, Fall, and Resurgence of an American Gang.* Chicago: Lawrence Hill Book, 2010.

Nichols, David A. *A Matter of Justice: Eisenhower and the Beginning of the Civil Rights Revolution.* New York: Simon and Schuster, 2003.

Ottley, Roi. *The Lonely Warrior: The Life and Times of Robert S. Abbott.* Chicago: Henry Regnery Company, 1955.

Perlstein, Rick. *Nixonland: The Rise of a President and the Fracturing of America.* New York: Scribner, 2008.

Poinsett, Alex. *Walking with Presidents: Louis Martin and the Rise of Black Political Power.* Lanham, MD: Madison Books, 1997.

Pride, Armistead S., and Clint C. Wilson. *A History of the Black Press.* Washington, DC: Howard University Press, 1997.

Rakove, Milton L. *Don't Make No Waves . . . Don't Back No Losers: An Insider's Analysis of the Daley Machine.* Bloomington: Indiana University Press, 1975.

Rampersad, Arnold. *The Life of Langston Hughes.* Vol. 1, *I, Too, Sing America: 1902–1941.* New York: Oxford University Press, 1986.

———. *The Life of Langston Hughes.* Vol. 2, *I Dream a World: 1941–1967.* New York: Oxford University Press, 1988.

Reed, Christopher Robert. *All the World Is Here!: The Black Presence at White City.* Bloomington: Indiana University Press, 2000.

———. *Black Chicago's First Century.* Columbia: University of Missouri Press, 2005.

Rivlin, Gary. *Fire on the Prairie: Chicago's Harold Washington and the Politics of Race.* New York: Henry Holt and Company, 1992.

Roberts, Gene, and Hank Klibanoff. *The Race Beat.* New York: Alfred A. Knopf, 2007.

Royko, Mike. *Boss: Richard J. Daley of Chicago.* New York: Penguin Books USA, 1988.

Sandburg, Carl. *The Chicago Race Riots, July 1919.* New York: Harcourt, Brace and Howe, 1919.

Satter, Beryl. *Family Properties: How the Struggle Over Race and Real Estate Transformed Chicago and Urban America.* New York: Metropolitan Books/Henry Holt and Company, 2009.

Scott, Emmett J. *Negro Migration During the War.* New York: Oxford University Press, 1920.

Sengstacke-Rice, Myiti. *Chicago Defender.* Charleston, SC: Arcadia Publishing, 2012.

Spear, Allan H. *Black Chicago: The Making of a Negro Ghetto, 1890–1920.* Chicago: University of Chicago Press, 1967.

Stange, Maren. *Bronzeville: Black Chicago in Pictures, 1941–1943.* New York: New Press, 2003.

Stone, Charles S. *Tell It like It Is.* New York: Trident Publishing, 1968.

Suggs, Henry Lewis, ed. *The Black Press in the Middle West, 1865–1985.* Westport, CT: Greenwood Press, 1996.

Sugrue, Thomas J. *Sweet Land of Liberty: The Forgotten Struggle for Civil Rights in the North.* New York: Random House, 2009.

Taylor, Yuval, and Jake Austen. *Darkest America: Black Minstrelsy from Slavery to Hip Hop*. New York: W. W. Norton and Company, 2012.

Thompson, Nathan. *Kings: The True Story of Chicago's Policy Kings and Numbers Racketeers; An Informal History*. Chicago: Bronzeville Press, 2006.

Travis, Dempsey. *An Autobiography of Black Chicago*. Chicago: Urban Research Institute, 1981.

Tuttle, William M., Jr. *Race Riot: Chicago in the Red Summer of 1919*. New York: Atheneum/Macmillan, 1970.

Tye, Larry. *Rising from the Rails*. New York: Henry Holt, 2004.

Washburn, Patrick S. *The African American Newspaper: Voice of Freedom*. Evanston, IL: Northwestern University Press, 2006.

——. *A Question of Sedition*. New York: Oxford University Press, 1986.

Waters, Enoch B. *American Diary*. Chicago: Path Press, 1987.

Weiss, Nancy J. *Farewell to the Party of Lincoln: Black Politics in the Age of FDR*. Princeton, NJ: Princeton University Press, 1983.

Wendt, Lloyd, and Herman Kogan. *Big Bill of Chicago*. Evanston, IL: Northwestern University Press, 2005.

Wilkerson, Isabel. *The Warmth of Other Suns: The Epic Story of America's Great Migration*. New York: Vintage Books, 2011.

Wolseley, Ronald E. *The Black Press, USA*. Ames: Iowa State Press, 1990.

# Index